THE OFFICIAL®
2014
PRICE GUIDE TO WORLD COINS

SEVENTEENTH EDITION

Marc Hudgeons, N.L.G., Tom Hudgeons, Jr. and Tom Hudgeons, Sr.

HOUSE OF COLLECTIBLES

RANDOM HOUSE REFERENCE • NEW YORK

House of Collectibles and colophon are registered trademarks of Random House, Inc.

RANDOM HOUSE is a registered trademark of Random House, Inc.

Please address inquiries about electronic licensing of any products for use on a network, in software, or on CD-ROM to the Subsidiary Rights Department, Random House Audio Publishing Group, fax 212-572-6003.

This book is available for special discounts for bulk purchases for sales promotions or premiums. Special editions, including personalized covers, excerpts of existing books, and corporate imprints, can be created in large quantities for special needs. For more information, write to Random House, Inc., Special Markets/Premium Sales, 1745 Broadway, MD 3-1, New York, NY 10019 or e-mail specialmarkets@randomhouse.com

Visit the Random House Web site:
www.randomhouse.com

ISBN: 978-0-375-72366-7

ISSN: 1094-1207

Printed in the United States of America

10 9 8 7 6 5 4 3 2 1

Seventeenth Edition: June 2013

CONTENTS

OFFICIAL BOARD OF CONTRIBUTORS

We would like to thank the following contributors for sharing their professional expertise and experiences in the field of World Coins with our readers.

- **Tom Bilotta,** President of Carlisle Development Corporation in Carlisle, Massachusetts, for his article "Numismatic Inventory Software" as well as the coin listing information from Carlisle's Collector's Assistant Software.
- **Tom Culhane**, owner of the Elusive Spondulix in Union, New Jersey, for his pricing information on Philippine coinage. Tom has devoted his professional career to numismatics with over 20 years experience as a full-time coin dealer.
- **Arnoldo Efron** of the **Monetary Research Institute**, Houston, Texas, for the "International Rates of Exchange Table" from their quarterly manual "MRI Bankers' Guide To Foreign Currency," currently in its 77th year of publication.
- **Bret Evans**, Managing Editor and Associate Publisher of the **Canadian Coin News** in St. Catharines, Ontario, Canada, for information for the section "Publication—Canadian Coin News."
- **The Gold and Silver Institute**, Washington, DC, for the information on International World Mints.
- **Dr. Lawrence J. Lee**, Numismatic Curator in Lincoln, Nebraska for his "Introduction and Market Review." Former director and curator Edward C. Rochette Museum of Money, American Numismatic Association, Colorado Springs, Colorado. Former curator Byron Reed Collection of Coins and Manuscripts, Western Heritage Museum, Omaha, Nebraska.
- **Numismatic Network Canada**, for information from their website for the sections "Numismatic Network Canada—Coin Clubs, Canadian Coin Organizations, Publication—Canadian Coin News."
- **The Royal Canadian Mint**, Ottawa, Canada, for information and photographs on the Royal Canadian Mint and the Canadian coin releases.
- **Michael White** of the **Department of the Treasury, United States Mint**, Washington, DC, for the section "World Coins Minted by US Mints 1876–1980."

COLLECTING WORLD COINS

By Dr. Lawrence J. Lee

What does a French duke from the 14th century have to do with your kitchen cupboards and what do either have to do with that pile of "foreign" coins on the table in front of you?

If you are somewhat confused, yet still strangely attracted to the bewildering variety of world coins, this book is for you. *The Official 2014 Price Guide to World Coins* is basically your personal museum guide to this planet's gigantic cross section of world coins. There are a lot of kings and rulers, a lot of nations and republics and a lot of denominations to keep track of, to say nothing of bullion values, conditions, mintages, and rarities. If you couldn't tell the players without a program before, you most assuredly now can with this year's edition.

The urge to collect goes back into man's earliest history and seems to be part of our genetic makeup. There is archeological evidence that Neanderthal man (or woman!) collected certain rocks and stones just because they were 'pretty,' not because they served any real purpose. As soon as written documents separated history from pre-history, we have records of individuals and groups gathering unusual or rare items together and keeping them separate from more profane objects. Coins likewise serve as one of mankind's oldest collectibles, dating back over 2,000 years, when some early Greek and Roman collectors collected, what else? Greek and Roman coins. As with your own collection, these classical coins were clearly set aside for the personal pleasure of their owner and out of admiration for the coin's artwork, not because of their monetary value.

One early world coin collector was Duke Jean de Berry (b. 1340), the third son of King Jean of France. As royalty, the Duke had plenty of free time and, for a while at least, plenty of money. This made him the perfect collector and he set about his task with the same burning passion known to most unfocused collectors to this day: that is, he collected everything in sight. His vast collection was known for being one of the first to include works of art but it also contained perfumes from around the world, insects trapped in amber, shells, manuscripts, silverware, pottery, fossils, and of course, "ancient medals" (coins). De Berry and subsequent collectors through the Middle Ages and Renaissance kept their "curiosities" in specially designed wooden cupboards or "cabinets." These cabinets of curiosities in turn became the basis for many of the national museums in Europe and Asia. The word "cabinet" continues in the English vocabulary as the kitchen cupboard—I just wish my own cabinet of curiosities was full of world coins or even insects in amber, instead of mismatched dishes.

What I and the *Blackbook* editors would like to suggest is that you create your own "cabinet of curiosity," your own collection of world coins to serve as your own personal museum. It is not only easy, it is also a great deal of fun as well, as you must surely know by now. Holding an English copper halfpenny from, say the 1700s or a silver mohar from Nepal—no matter the coin or its age or value—the true thrill for the collector is knowing that once, long ago in a far-away land, this very object that you now hold was held by someone you will never meet and can only begin to imagine. That is the lure of collecting coins: tiny bits of history that you can hold in your hand.

Just as with an actual museum, you should develop a collection philosophy; don't just be an accumulator and grab everything is sight including multiples of the same coin type. Sooner or later your eyes will outspend your wallet. Instead, plan ahead to locate the type of coins you want to select for your museum. Your collection policy might be as broad as "a coin from every country" (much harder than it sounds) to something more general and open-ended (coins with animals) or even a closed collection set that can be completed given enough time and money: say die varieties of the 1859 Canadian Victorian penny. The great thing about your museum is that you are the one who gets to set your own collection policy.

Something else you can do, again like a museum, is to have more than one collection going at once. You might have a date run of British three-pence, another collection that is type coins from Central America and still another group of coins given to you by relatives or brought home from vacation. Again, it doesn't matter what you collect as long as you are somewhat systematic about it: museum records are very important as they determine ownership and provenance. Ideally you should mark on the coin holder when, where, and for how much you bought the coin, so you can later track the details of how that coin was added (or *accessioned,* in museum parlance) to your collection. Many collectors also develop their own coding system, so they can tell at a glance of their private code how much they paid for a coin without other people knowing.

You will also need to strongly consider how you store the coins in your collection. Some packaging material and coin flips contain harmful chemicals, such as polyvinyl chloride (PVC), which can rapidly degrade a coin. It is not always the best idea to leave coins in their original holders. You should check both sides of every coin in your collection periodically to make sure they are not corroding due to exposure to air, moisture or other contaminants. The best coin holders are made of non-reactive material like Mylar. As a rule of thumb, most soft plastic holders are bad, hard plastic holders are usually inert and will thus not damage a coin.

Although it is not necessary or always practical to display your collection, most museums do have a small portion of their collection on exhibit. You could do this formally by developing a themed coin exhibit for local coin shows where there is usually a section reserved for such displays. These can be as basic as typed labels inside flat-top display cases all the way to elaborate shadow-boxes and dioramas. You can also develop private exhibit space in your home or office to display particular treasures you might wish to share or admire privately in a more formal museum-like setting. And if you have a really grand collection, call me: I have developed secret coin displays within private houses for the wealthy collector on multiple occasions: literally the old room-behind-the-bookcase trick!

Of course like any museum you will have to think about collection security. How (if you do not have your own hidden room) do you keep your coins safe and secure yet easily accessible? For security reasons, every coin should ideally have its own storage location, even if that location is in a 2 x 2 holder in a binder full of other coins. If you are computerizing your coin collection, make sure to leave a database field for storage location; that way you don't have to remember where every one of your coins are, you can let the computer remember for you. It is also much easier to tell if a coin is missing if it has a specific place it is supposed to be.

One final museum insight: don't call your coins from other countries "foreign" coins and don't let anyone else get away with calling them that either. They are "world" coins, not "foreign" coins. Every coin is foreign outside its country of origin. In Mexico or Canada, for instance, it is the American coins that are foreign!

And as a matter of historical fact, coins from many different countries were legal tender in the United States until 1857, including for payment of American taxes. This included Spanish, British, French, Dutch, and Russian coins, at the least, all circulating freely at the same time in the United States. Try paying your income tax in Euros this year and see how far that gets you now.

MARKET OVERVIEW

As with any market, world coin values are in a constant state of flux, with some coins going up in price while others correspondingly drop or remain about the same from year to year. Why is that? Why do coin values fluctuate? What makes a series like Swiss shooting talers or Victorian pennies remain hot for many years and then level off or even bottom out?

Obviously there are multiple factors that affect coin pricing but as with most commercial markets, the biggest movers of coin value (besides bullion content) are supply and demand. A rare coin will always be rare; a common coin will always be common. Thus, mintage (or rarity) is one of the key components to a coin's value. Rare coins are always worth more than common coins and will always be more in demand. It is self-evident, yet it is surprising how often collectors forget that when fixating on obtaining a specific coin, especially a common coin, price be damned.

As director and curator of your own museum, you can play both sides of this coin, so to speak, to your own advantage. If the common stuff is readily available—great, fill up the museum shelves with low-cost examples (types) of world coins. Going to a single large coin show could lead to scores if not hundreds of new coins for your museum collection, each entirely different for less than a dollar each; often for less than a quarter. But if you are going after a single high-value, high-dollar coin, the old adage "buy the highest valued coin you can afford" usually proves true.

So if rarity equals the "supply" side of the supply/demand equation, what about demand? Who is buying the coins that is driving up or at least stabilizing the price? Demand for world coins, either new issues from national mints or old type coins from distant regimes, is created by people with discretionary income: extra money they can spend on their hobby. It is very closely tied to national economies. Thus, there are very few coin collectors in countries with terrible economies like Chad or Bangladesh and far more collectors in countries with strong markets like Germany or the United States. For the past few years, countries with a growing middle class, like Russia and China, have proven to be dynamic new markets, with thousands of expatriated coins now returning to their country of origin to satisfy new collector demand. China in particular remains a hot market for most types of post-revolution Chinese coins.

By that logic, emerging nations with long histories of coinage, such as Turkey, Brazil, Norway and especially India, could prove to be the next vibrant markets if their economies continue to improve. Even countries like Cuba and Venezuela, which have been economically repressed due to leadership issues, could see significant changes in their collector base if their national economies were to jumpstart under new forms of government.

Finally, there is the one-out-of-a-hundred new coin type that is issued, becomes an instant hit in the marketplace and soon becomes far more valuable than its issue price would suggest. Picking this coin in advance is as much luck as talent, but a common denominator is collector appeal—how does the coin look? Is it "pretty" (back to Neanderthals picking up rocks!)? Ultimately, coins are symbols of power and authority disguised as works of art. Nicely designed coins stand on their own merit. Beautiful coins will be recognized as such in the marketplace. Develop your artistic eye by looking at other coins that have appreciated greatly in value. But above all, buy it because you like it, because it fits your museum's collection policy, not because you are trying to make money off it.

To continue that thought and finish out this introduction, as a collector (versus an investor or dealer) you must remember that your objective is not to make money on your coin collection, but to enjoy yourself. You are buying this or that particular coin because it gives you pleasure, not so you can retire. True, you don't want to throw your money away and that is why this guide comes in so handy. But museums are not in business to make money—they are in fact usually nonprofit institutions. You might think of your own finances that way as well—nonprofit. So, say a particular coin cost you $50 when you bought it but when you go to sell (de-accession) it, you only get $25. Were you ripped off? Not necessarily. Think of some special event or celebration where you spent $50 on a nice dinner. Do you expect three years later to still be able to recoup that money? No, it is the pleasure of the experience that you savor, not the cost. Just so when selling a coin after it no longer has that special appeal that caused you to buy it in the first place. You don't have to make money to come out ahead on every coin transaction. That's why they call it discretionary income.

By now you are probably tired of reading about world coins and instead want to dig in to your own new pile. By all means, jump in and enjoy. Use this guide to help you identify, organize and appraise your collect. Welcome to your own personal museum.

And let me know if you need help with your hidden cabinet.

Dr. Lawrence J. Lee, private curator
Lincoln, NE
January 9, 2013

BUYING AND SELLING WORLD COINS

Intelligent coin buying is the key to building a good collection at a reasonable cost. Today, with the added confusion of grading and the questionable practices of some coin sellers, it is more necessary than ever to be a skilled buyer.

In the interest of supplementing the coin pricing and identification in this book with practical advice on astute buying, the editors present the following article. It reviews major pitfalls to which an uninformed buyer might succumb and gives specific suggestions on getting the most for your money when buying coins.

The editors wish to state clearly that the exposure of questionable practices by some coin sellers, as detailed below, is not intended as a general indictment of the coin trade. The vast majority of professional coin dealers are ethical and try to please. Moreover, it can be safely stated that if the hobbyist restricts his buying exclusively to well-established coin dealers, he runs very little risk.

QUESTIONABLE SOURCES FOR BUYING COINS

Unsatisfactory sources of coins—those entailing a higher than necessary degree of risk—include flea markets, antique shops, garage sales, private parties who are unknown to you, auction sales in which coins are offered along with non-numismatic merchandise, and advertisements in magazines and newspapers published for a general readership rather than for coin collectors. This advice is given to benefit the non-expert buyer and especially the beginner. Advanced collectors with full confidence in their coin-buying skills will sometimes shop these sources to find possible bargains.

Mail-Order Ads in National Magazines

The sharp rise in coin values during 1979 and 1980 encouraged many promoters to deal in coins. (Promoters are persons who aren't coin dealers in the accepted sense of the term, but who utilize coins for

7

large-scale mail-order promotions.) The objective, nearly always, is to sell coins to buyers of limited knowledge and thereby succeed in promising more, and charging more, than would a legitimate professional coin dealer. Undoubtedly such promotions are extremely successful, to judge from the number of such ads that appear regularly.

The ads look and sound impressive. They show enlargement of the merchandise. They quote facts and figures, often with historical data. They present a variety of guarantees about the coins, and there is no misrepresentation in those guarantees. But the price you pay is twice to three times as much as it would be if you bought from a *real* coin dealer. In the legitimate coin trade, the coins sold via these ads are looked upon as "junk coins." They command a very small premium over their bullion value. They are not only the most common dates but are usually in undesirable condition.

To lend credibility, the promoters will normally use a company name, which gives the appearance of being that of a full-time coin dealer. There is nothing illegal in doing this, but it does contribute to the misleading nature of such ads.

Let's examine some of the specific methods used in today's ever-increasing deceptive coin ads. You will soon see why coins, especially silver coins, have become a favorite of mail-order promoters: they can be "hyped" in a most convincing manner, without making statements that are patently false. Thus, the advertisers skirt around—though narrowly—allegations of mail fraud. (Fraud cannot be alleged on the basis of price, as a merchant is free to charge what he pleases for whatever he sells.)

1. Creating the impression that the coins offered originate from a hidden sequestered cache not previously available to the public. This is accomplished by use of such phrases as "just found 2,367 specimens," "now released to the public. . . ." The assertion that they were "just found" is not wholly inaccurate, however. The advertiser has more than likely located a dealer who could supply wholesale quantities of junk coins. The coins themselves were never lost or hidden. "Now released to the public" has nothing to do with official release. It simply means the advertiser is selling them now.

2. Leading the potential customer to believe the coins are scarcer or more valuable than they really are. This is done via numerous techniques. Among the favorites is to compare the advertiser's selling price against prices for other coins of the same series. They are rare, desirable dates in UNC condition, not the common, circulated coins you receive from the advertiser.

When coins are offered, it will be said that "you just can't find them in circulation any longer." It's entirely true that they cannot be found in day-to-day circulation. But coin dealers have them and sell them for less than you will pay through such an ad. The fact that these coins are not found in circulation is not an indication of rarity.

Many coins carrying very little premium value over their face value cannot be found in day-to-day circulation.

3. Emphatic guarantee that the coins are genuine. On this point the advertiser can speak with no fear of legal repercussion. His coins are genuine and nobody can say otherwise. But, even where absolute truth is involved, it can be—and is—presented in such a manner as to give a false impression. By strongly stressing the coins' authenticity, the message is conveyed that many non-authentic specimens exist and that you run a risk in buying from someone else. Such is far from the case. Any large coin dealer can sell you quantities of perfectly genuine coins.

4. Implication that the coins offered are "special," as opposed to specimens of the same coins available at coin shops. This presents an obvious difficulty for the advertiser, as his coins are just the opposite of special; usually heavily circulated, often with actual damage such as nicks, gouges, etc. This problem is not, however, insurmountable. The advertiser can keep silent about the condition of his coins and present them as some sort of special government issue. Usually this is done by selling them in quantities of four or five and referring to them as "Sets," "Government Mint Sets," or something similar. The uninformed reader believes he is ordering a set assembled and packaged by various mints. Mints do assemble and package sets, as everyone knows. But they had no part in these! Assembling and packaging was done by the advertiser. Regardless of how attractive the box or case may be, it is not of official nature and lends absolutely nothing to the value.

5. Failure to state actual silver content. This falls under the heading of deception by silence. The potential customer is left to draw his own conclusions and the advertiser knows full well that those conclusions will be wrong; provided, of course, the ad is worded in such a way that it lends itself to incorrect conclusions. When silver coins are advertised collectors automatically think in terms of 90% silver. Yet the advertiser is legally within his rights in referring to 40% silver coins as silver. As the 40% silver coins look just like their 90% silver predecessors, few purchasers will suspect they've overpaid. Until they have them appraised.

6. Creation of gimmicked names for coins. By calling a coin something different than its traditional numismatic name, it is made to seem more unusual or special.

7. False references. Advertisements of this type are sometimes accompanied by doubtful or fairly obvious fake references on the advertiser's behalf. Taking his cue from legitimate coin dealers, whose ads nearly always refer to their membership in coin organizations and often carry other easily verifiable references as well, he feels he must present similar assurances of his background and reliability. Since he has nothing too convincing to offer in the way of genuine references, he manufactures them. He invents the name of a mythical coin organization, of which he is either a member in good standing, an officer, or perhaps even president. If he chooses not to go quite that far, since he might be caught in the deception, he can take a less volatile course and claim membership in "leading coin collector and dealer organizations" without, of course, naming them.

MAIL ORDER COINS

As stated previously, purchasing world coins through mail order will provide you with the greatest opportunity of finding exactly the coins that you are looking for to add to your collection. While working on this book, we have had the opportunity of coming in contact with many dealers as well as collectors.

RECOMMENDED SOURCES FOR BUYING COINS

As a general rule, coin purchasing should be confined to the following sources:

1. Professional coin dealers who sell coins at a shop and/or by mail order.
2. Auction sales conducted by professional coin dealers or auction houses making a specialty of coins.
3. Shows and conventions for coin collectors.

Another acceptable source, though unavailable to many coin hobbyists, is the fellow collector with duplicate or surplus specimens to sell or trade. This source is acceptable only if the individual is known to you, as transactions with strangers can result in problems.

If a coin shop is located in your area, this is the best place to begin buying. By examining the many coins offered in a shop you will become familiar with grading standards. Later you may wish to try buying at auction. When buying from dealers, be sure to do business only with reputable parties. Be wary of rare coins offered at bargain prices, as they could be counterfeit or improperly graded. Some bargain coins are specimens that have been amateurishly cleaned and are not considered desirable by collectors. The best "bargains" are popular coins in good condition, offered at fair prices.

The dangers of buying from sources other than these are overgraded and consequently overpriced coins; non-graded and likewise overpriced coins; and coins that have been doctored, "whizzed," chemically treated, artificially toned, or otherwise altered. Buying from legitimate, recommended sources greatly reduces but does not absolutely eliminate these risks. The buyer himself is the ultimate safeguard, if he has a reasonably thorough working knowledge of coins and the coin market. In this respect experience is the best teacher, but it can sometimes be costly to learn from bad coin-buying experiences.

COIN-BUYING GUIDELINES

Smart coin buyers follow certain basic strategies or rules. They will not buy a rare coin that they know little or nothing about. They will do some checking first. Has the coin been frequently counterfeited? Are counterfeits recorded of that particular date and mint mark? What are the specific grading standards? What key portions of the design should be examined under magnification to detect evidence of circulation wear?

The smart coin buyer may be either a hobbyist collecting mainly for the sport of it or an investor. In either case he learns not just about coins but the workings of the coin trade: its dealers and auctioneers and their methods of doing business. It's essential to always keep up to date, as the coin market is a continual hotbed of activity.

When buying from the recommended sources there is relatively little danger of fakes, doctored coins, or other obviously unwanted material. If such a coin does slip through and escape the vigilance of an ethical professional dealer, you are protected by his guarantee of authenticity. It is highly unlikely that you will ever be "stuck" with a counterfeit, doctored, or otherwise misrepresented coin bought from a well-established professional.

Merely avoiding fakes is, however, not the sole object of intelligent coin buying. It is, in fact, a rather minor element in the overall picture. Getting the absolute most for your money in terms of properly graded coins at fair prices is the prime consideration. Here the responsibility shifts from seller to buyer. It is the dealer's responsibility not to sell fakes or misidentified coins. But it is the buyer's responsibility to make certain of getting the best deal by comparing prices and condition grades of coins offered by different dealers. Quite often you can save by comparison shopping, even after your incidental expenses are tabulated. The very unique nature of the coin market makes this possible.

Prices do vary from one dealer to another on many coins. That is precisely the reason—or at least one of the primary reasons—for the *Blackbook*. If you could determine a coin's value merely by checking one dealer's price, or even a few dealers' prices, there would be minimal need for a published price guide. The editors review prices charged by hundreds of dealers to arrive at the median or average market prices that are listed in the *Blackbook*. Prices are matched condition grade by condition grade, from UNC down the line. The results are often little short of astounding. One dealer may be asking $50 for a coin priced at $30 by another. And there are sure to be numerous other offerings of the coin at $35, $40, $45, and various midpoint sums.

It is important to understand why prices vary and how you can utilize this situation to your advantage.

Some readers will remark, at this juncture, that prices vary because of inaccurate grading.

It is unquestionably true that personal applications of the grading standards do contribute to price differences. It is one reason for non-uniform prices. *It is not the only one.*

Obviously the lower-priced specimens are not always those to buy. Smart numismatic buying calls for knowing when to take a bargain and when to pass. A low price could result from something directly concerning the coins. Or it may be tied to matters having nothing to do with the coin or coins. A dealer could be oversupplied, or he may be offering coins in which he does not normally deal and wants to move them quickly. He may have a cash flow imbalance and need to raise funds, in which case he has probably reduced most of his prices. He may be pricing a coin low because he made a fortunate purchase in which the coin cost him very little. In all of these cases—and examples of all can be found regularly in the coin trade—the lower than normal price is not a reflection upon the coin's quality or desirability. These coins, if properly graded, are well worth buying. They do save you some money and cause no problems.

Personal circumstances of the dealer are, to one degree or another, reflected in the prices of most of his coins. If the dealer has substantial operating costs to meet, such as shop rent and employee salaries, his overall pricing structure will reflect this. Yet his prices are not likely to be too much higher than the average, as this class of dealer is intent on quick turnover. Also, there is a certain degree of competitiveness between dealers, particularly those whose advertisements run in the same periodicals. Unfortunately, this competitiveness is sometimes carried to extremes by some dealers, resulting in "bargains" that are sometimes overgraded.

Condition has always played a major role in U.S. coin prices. As of this writing there are no accepted international grading standards for foreign coins.

PUTTING YOUR COIN-BUYING KNOWLEDGE TO WORK

1. Deal with someone in whom you can have confidence. The fact that a dealer has been in the business a long period of time may not be an absolute guarantee of his reliability, but it is definitely a point in his favor. Is he a member of coin collector or coin dealer organizations? You do not have to ask about this to find out. If he does hold membership in good standing in any of the more prestigious organizations, that fact will be prominently displayed in his ads, his sales literature, and on the walls of his shop. The leading organization for coin dealers is the PNG, or Professional Numismatists' Guild. Its members are carefully screened and must, after gaining admittance, comply with its code of ethics. Complaints against PNG members are investigated. Those that cannot be easily resolved are brought before an arbitration panel. You are on the safest possible ground when dealing with a PNG member. As the PNG is rather a select group, however, your local dealer may not be a member. This in itself should not make him suspect. One of the requirements of PNG membership is to carry at least $100,000 retail value in coins, and many dealers simply do not maintain that large an inventory. Is your dealer an American Numismatic Association member? A member of the local Chamber of Commerce?

2. Don't expect the impossible, either in a dealer or his coins. The dealers are in business to make a profit and they could not do this by offering bargains on every coin they sell. Treat the dealers fairly. Look at things from their point of view. For example, a long "layaway" on an expensive coin may not be in the dealer's best interest. Dealers will go out of their way for established customers but, even then, they cannot be expected to place themselves at a disadvantage.

BUYING IN PERSON AT A COIN SHOP

1. Plan your visits in advance. Don't shop in a rush or on the spur of the moment. Give yourself time to look, think, examine, and decide.

2. Before entering the shop have a clear idea of the specific coins, or at least the type of coins, you want to see. If more than a few dates and mint marks are involved, do not trust it all to memory. Write a list.

3. Look at everything that interests you before deciding to buy anything.

4. When shopping for rarities, bring along your own magnifier. A small one with attached flashlight is the most serviceable. You may not be able to conduct really in-depth examinations in a shop, but you'll learn more with a magnifier than without one. Don't be reticent about using it. The dealers will not be insulted.

5. If the shop has more than one specimen of the coin that interests you, ask to see them all. Even if all are graded identically and priced identically, you may discover that one seems a shade nicer than the rest.

6. If this is your first visit to the shop, you will want to give some attention to whether or not the shop inspires confidence. An experienced collector tends to get different vibrations from each shop, to the point where he can form an opinion—almost immediately— sometimes before entering. Some coin shops give the distinct impression of being more professional than others. And that impression is usually correct! There are various points on which this can be judged. Do all coins, with the exception of bullion items, have their prices marked on the holder? Is the price accompanied by a statement of condition? Are the holders, and the style of notations on them, fairly uniform from coin to coin? If the coins are housed in various different kinds of holders, with notations that seem to have been made by a dozen different people, they are most likely remnants from the stocks of other dealers or so-called "odd lots." Their condition grades should have been verified and they should have been transferred to uniform holders before being placed for sale. Since the shopkeeper failed to do this, he probably knows very little about their actual condition grades. He merely took the previous owners' word for it. Does the shopkeeper impress you as a person with intimate knowledge of coins? He need not love coins, as his business is selling and not collecting them. But he should appear to regard them a little higher than "just merchandise." He ought to be appreciative of and perhaps even enthusiastic over the finer aspects of a rare coin. Under no circumstances should he treat coins as if he cares nothing about them, such as by handling them roughly or sloppily or touching their surfaces with his fingers.

7. Buying in person gives you an opportunity to converse with the dealer and this can have its advantages. Upon expressing interest in a coin you may discover that the dealer offers a verbal discount from the market price—even without asking for one. If this does not occur, you do, of course, have the right to at least hint at the matter. Just a modest savings can often turn a borderline item into a sound purchase. Don't get the reputation of asking for a discount on every coin you buy. Let the circumstances guide you, and be diplomatic. You are always in a better position to receive a discount when purchasing a number of coins at the same time. Dealers like volume buyers. Never say, "Will you take $300 for this?" or anything that could be construed as making the dealer an offer. The dealers make offers when they buy from the public, and the right to make an offer is something they like to reserve for themselves. You can broach the subject in a more subtle fashion. Instead of mentioning what you would be willing to give for the coins, ask if there is a savings (savings is a much better word than discount) on large purchases. If you pay in cash, you have a better bargaining position as you're saving the dealer the time required in collecting the funds. That is the essence of reasonable discounts; playing fair, not becoming a nuisance, and being willing to accept a small consideration, even if just 5%. At least with the small discounts you are, or should be, getting good coins. If anyone is willing to discount a coin by 50% you can be virtually certain it is a problem item.

BUYING COINS BY MAIL ORDER

There is no reason to shun mail orders. Most coin dealing is done by mail. There are at least a dozen mail-order coin dealers for every one who operates a shop. Your local shop may not specialize in your type of coins, but in dealing by mail you can reach any coin dealer in the country and obtain virtually any coin you may want.

Consider the following before doing any mail-order buying:

1. Compare ads and prices, compare descriptions, compare everything from one ad to another running in the same publication. Look for evidence of the advertiser's professional standing, such as PNG membership. Read his terms of sale. There should be unqualified guarantee of authenticity plus a guarantee of satisfaction. If you are not satisfied with your purchase for any reason, you should have the option of returning it within a specific time period. This time period should be stated in the dealer's terms of sale. (It will usually be ten days or two weeks.) It should likewise be clearly stated that if you do choose to return the coins, you can receive a full refund or credit as you prefer (not as the dealer prefers). Full refund means the sum paid for the coins, with postage and registration fees deducted. Few dealers will refund postage charges. Consequently, when you return a shipment you are paying the postage both ways.

2. Send a small trial order if you haven't previously done business with the advertiser. This will give you the opportunity to judge what sort of coins he supplies. You will also discover how prompt and attentive he is. The results of this trial order should give you a fairly good idea of what you can expect from that dealer when placing large orders.

3. Do not photocopy an ad and circle numbers. Write out your order, simply and plainly. Mention the publication and issue date. The dealer probably has different ads running in different publications.

4. Give second choices only if this is necessary to qualify for a discount. Otherwise don't. Most dealers will send you your first choice if it's available. Some will send the second choice, even if they do still have your first choice. This is called "stock balancing." If they have two remaining specimens of your first choice, and twenty of your second choice, they would much prefer sending you the second choice. Only a relatively small proportion of dealers will ignore your wishes in this manner, but our suggestion still applies: no second choices if you can avoid them. To speed things up, make payment by money order or credit card. A personal check may delay shipment by as much as three weeks.

5. Examine the coins as soon as possible upon receiving them. If a return is necessary, this must be done promptly to be fair to the dealer. Most likely you will not be permitted to remove a coin from its protective holder to examine it. The coins will be in clear mylar (an inert plastic) holders known as "flips" or "flipettes," with a staple at the top. The staple must be in place for return to be honored. While this may seem harsh, it is necessary as a way for the dealer to protect himself against unscrupulous collectors who would switch coins on him. These individuals would replace a high-grade coin with one of lower grade from their collection, and return the lower-grade specimen, asking for a refund. In the unlikely event you receive a coin in a holder which does not permit satisfactory examination, the best course is to simply return it. In making your examination be fair to yourself and to the dealer. Should you have the least doubt about its authenticity, submit the coin to the American Numismatic Association for its opinion and inform the dealer of your action. If the ANA finds the coin to be fake or doctored, you can return it even if the grace period for returns has expired. Under these circumstances many dealers will reimburse you for the ANA's evaluation cost. Chances are, however, that you will never receive a suspect coin.

6. Do not file a complaint against the dealer unless he is clearly in violation of his printed "terms of sale." When it is absolutely necessary to do so, a report of the transaction may be forwarded to the organizations in which he maintains membership, as well as the publications in which he advertises. But even if you place hundreds of mail orders, it is unlikely that the need will ever arise to register a formal complaint against a dealer.

SELLING COINS TO A DEALER

All coin dealers buy from the public. They must replenish their stock and the public is a much more economical source of supply than buying from other dealers. Damaged, very worn, or common coins are worthless to a dealer. So, too, usually, are sets in which the "key" coins are missing. If you have a large collection or several valuable coins to sell, it might be wise to check the pages of coin publications for addresses of dealers handling major properties, rather than selling to a local shop.

Visit a coin show or convention. There you will find many dealers at one time and place, and you will experience the thrill of an active trading market in coins. You will find schedules of conventions and meetings of regional coin clubs listed in the various trade publications.

To find your local coin dealer, check the Yellow Pages under "Coin Dealers."

Coin collecting offers infinite possibilities as an enjoyable hobby or profitable investment. It need not be complex or problem-laden. But anyone who buys and sells coins—even for the most modest sums—owes it to himself to learn how to buy and sell wisely.

NUMISMATIC INVENTORY SOFTWARE

By Tom Bilotta
Carlisle Development Corporation

During the past year, the trend toward computing platforms other than the traditional desktop PC has continued to accelerate. Tablet computers such as the iPad and its Windows-based competitors have exploded in use and are now commonly used for functions previously performed on traditional PCs. Microsoft has now entered this market with the new Surface tablet and Windows 8 RT. Smartphones and e-readers also continue to become more useful and will play an increased roll in collector applications.

2012 has seen the emergence of some applications (apps) for numismatists on the iPhone and iPad. These apps go beyond the functionality of simple browsers accessing web content to fully functional mobile applications. Initial applications have focused on educational information such as coin identification and grading. Also some applications to educate young numismatists have appeared in the app store. 2013 should bring a substantial new suite of applications targeting core collector functions.

BULLION VALUATION AND ANALYSIS

Over the past several years, the volatility of spot bullion prices has sparked collector interest in understanding the bullion value of their collection. Collectors of gold and silver coins have experienced the complex relationship between bullion and numismatic values. Often numismatic premiums diminish as bullion values rise. This has increased the importance of understanding the bullion value in your collection as well as its impact on the overall value of your collection and projected cost to purchase new items.

PORTABLE COMPUTING

Portable computing has much to offer, especially when supported by access to your data via the Internet. For collectors, use of portable devices is in its infancy. Most available collector-oriented applications are primarily Internet browsers, often enhanced to present content optimally on the mobile device. But apart from browsing web content, there are very few numismatic software applications available on these devices.

One of the challenges of mobile computing particular to the coin collecting market is the basic demographic. The average age of coin collectors is quite high and many collectors suffer from eyesight limitations. On home PCs this can be addressed by very affordable, large-screen monitors. Small mobile devices tend to use small fonts to allow maximum content. In the future, flexible, expandable screens may help address this issue.

CLOUD COMPUTING

The real benefits of mobile devices for collectors will be realized when user data can be maintained in the cloud and accessed anywhere. In such an environment, a collector could maintain his collection on his PC at home and access it from his cellphone or tablet while attending a show or traveling by airplane. The collector's ability to work with his collection would not be limited to time spent at home. Synchronization of data would be automatic. It is expected that during 2013, cloud computing will find its way into core applications intended to assist collectors in working with their collections.

Cloud Computing: Security

There are a number of issues to be resolved before these benefits are attainable. One of the major ones is security. There are daily reports of security breaches on the Internet. These affect governments, major financial institutions, and corporations and individuals alike. The willingness of collectors to place their sensitive collection data in the cloud will depend on their confidence in the security of their data. It is clear that today we do not understand enough about internet security to build truly robust and impenetrable defenses. Even major institutions such as the Department of Defense are "hacked."

Cloud Computing: Applications Availability

Another issue is the development of collector applications software intended to exploit mobile computing. Such software has to present the capabilities of robust PC–based collectibles software optimized for the smaller viewing area and touch interface of the mobile device. These applications must also perform well in the more limited resource environments available on mobile devices.

The smaller screen areas of mobile devices make it more difficult to present a large amount of information on one screen as well as manipulate it for analytical purposes. Mobile devices currently address this by allowing the user to employ virtual pages which are larger than the device and which can be accessed by simple hand motions.

Cloud Computing: Standards

Several major corporations are setting up resources for cloud computing, these include Apple, Google, and Microsoft. It remains to be seen how these environments will interact. Ideally for the user, data would seamlessly be shared between these environments. A user on a Windows-based PC at home should be able to access their data without regard to the specifics of the servers on which it is maintained. The same user should be able to access the same data on an iPhone at a remote location.

Cloud Computing: Reliability of Access

Early users of cloud computing have experienced significant periods during which their data was not accessible. This unreliability will be an impediment to widespread dependence on the cloud. Cloud infrastructure must approach the uptime of other utilities such as your telephone and electric power, which are expected to be up and running very close to 100% of the time. This will require substantial buildup of infrastructure that is not commonly employed for Internet computing currently. Redundant data centers and communications paths will be required throughout the entire network.

Choosing the Right Portable Device for You

The choice of a portable device is a personal one and is driven as much by your typical usage, physical limitations, and other considerations. Many users will employ multiple portable devices for different purposes. Many coin collectors are older and would have difficulty with the small screen size and keys on an e-reader or smartphone and would be better served by a traditional laptop or tablet computer. If you find an affordable e-reader or tablet computer that provides adequate viewing quality for you, it will likely be a very convenient choice for all sorts of Internet activity associated with your collecting pursuits.

THE INTERNET

As in recent years, Internet activity by collectors continues to grow. The trend toward cloud computing is one of the newest growth areas of Internet activity.

COIN COLLECTING SOFTWARE

Coin collecting software that runs on your own computer avoids the problems of Internet catalogs and provides you with rich functionality to work with your collection.

Collectors who adopt computer inventory programs increase their enjoyment of collecting, provide the needed documentation to protect their collection, gain insight into the value of their collection and better prepare their families to deal with their collection if the need arises.

In order to exploit the power that computers bring to collecting, the collector must acquire a base level of knowledge sufficient to harness this capability in a safe and productive manner. The remainder of this article will focus on some of the more important points of using numismatic inventory software.

Coin & Paper Money Inventory Software

One of the first applications of a computer is to organize a collection. This activity requires cataloguing what you have, deciding how it will be grouped, and determining what kind of reports you will need. Reports will assist you in defining your collecting objectives, tracking value, and assuring your collection is adequately protected and insured.

Organizing Your Collection with Coin & Paper Money Inventory Software

Collectors of coins and currency fall into several categories. There is the serious coin collector who enjoys the hobby and pursues personally defined collecting objectives. Accumulators retain many of the coins that they receive in normal commerce and build up large quantities of unsorted coins. Investors use coin collecting to build portfolios intended to produce profits.

Inheritors receive a coin collection or accumulation from their families and must decide how they will handle a potentially valuable asset.

All of these collectors have a common need to catalog their items and understand their value. Most collectors also have accumulated many items with a very wide range of values.

A modern inventory program can adapt to meet the needs of all types of users from novice collectors to experienced experts. It will incorporate a comprehensive database of coin and or paper money to assist the user in identifying and defining their collections as well as a flexible set of functionality to enable them to organize their collection in a manner consistent with their collection methodology.

Most collectors will want to organize their collections into several groupings. The collector will want to create collections that mirror their physical collection. For example, someone with coin albums of common series such as Mercury dimes, statehood quarters, or buffalo nickels will want to have software albums organized in similar fashion. Other coins might be grouped into coins for sale, duplicates, partial collections for other family members, or any other categorization which suits the collector.

Using Your Time Wisely

When using computer software to catalog a coin or paper money collection it is important to use it in a manner consistent with your purposes and which will enhance your enjoyment. You should spend your time, therefore, working with the portions of your collection in which you have the most interest or where the primary financial value exists.

For example, if you are collecting a complete set of Mercury dimes, you may wish to scan an image of each individual piece so that you can print picture catalogs of your collection. For these coins, you might choose to enter in complete information including purchase price, source, certification information, origin, etc. For this type of grouping you will also likely want to include coins that you don't have that are required to complete your collection, enabling you to generate want lists. This will also assist you in identifying the cost to complete your collection and planning your approach.

For large quantities of relatively inexpensive items or coins worth only bullion content and where you have no particular collecting interest, you might choose to only enter a single line item and not bother to take the time to list each coin individually. For example, if you have several hundred silver Washington quarters in circulated condition from the 1950s and 1960s you might enter a single line item 225 Washington Quarters with a date range and average value. In this way, large accumulations can be tracked with minimum effort and your attention can be focused on your real collecting interests. Your coin inventory program should adapt to all of these possible approaches to organizing your collection.

Evaluating Coin and Paper Money Inventory Software

The quality of the software that you purchase will greatly impact the success of your efforts.

One of the most important parts of a coin inventory program is the database. The database contains standard information about coins and paper money and saves the user from having to type this information manually. The greater the amount of information in the standard database, the easier the task of data entry. A modern coin collecting program, at a minimum, should include coin type, date, mint mark, denomination and variety. Comprehensive programs, such as those made by Carlisle Development Corporation, also include such information as designer/engraver, coinage metal, size, weight, edge, and mintage. The organization of the database should reflect commonly used groupings and thereby provide users with guidance in organizing their collection.

Some inventory programs include current market values. It is important that these are updated frequently and produced by reliable sources. Coin values should evolve to include areas of high market interest. For example, over the past year, the market interest in high grade recent coin issues has become very high. It is also important to allow the user the ability to extend the database to include items that are not listed. These may be specialized varieties, private mint products, or other coin-related collectibles.

Ability to share data with other programs and people is also very important. Most computerized collectors are connected to the Internet and will want to share some information with other collectors and dealers. The ability to export listings in common text readable formats for transmission over the internet or for input into a word processor or spreadsheet is of great value in buying and selling coins and paper money.

Carlisle Development's inventory software, Collector's Assistant, provides a comprehensive database of all coins ever minted by the United States Mint. This includes all types of coins by date and mint mark, bullion coins, sets, old and new commemoratives. Recent additions to the database are the 50 states circulating quarters and the new Sacagawea Dollar. Coin values are licensed from Coin World, Inc., an industry leader in providing coin valuations. Quarterly updates are available by subscription allowing collectors to maintain trends of their values. Carlisle Development's Currency Collector's Assistant has a complete database based on *Friedberg's Paper Money of the United States,* 19th Edition. This database includes all U.S. paper money, including Confederate notes and Encased postage stamps. A relationship with CDN, publisher of the Greensheet, makes value information available to the paper money collector in electronic format.

For collectors of ancient coins, Carlisle offers an add-on database containing color images of several hundred ancient coins and a specialized interface containing data entry fields appropriate for ancient coins. For example, the date field can handle and sort mixed AD/BC dates and has long fields for obverse and reverse inscriptions. The most recent additions to Carlisle Development's databases include the Euro Coin Database and World Currency Database.

Report Generation

Once you have entered your coin collection into an inventory program, the most important function will become its ability to generate a wide array of reports and/or exports for informational purposes.

You will probably want to have a detailed listing, identifying items, their value, and where they are stored for insurance purposes. You will want to generate partial lists of your collections for sales and trading. You may want to generate labels to aid in identifying your coins. You may want to look at your collection in many different ways such as sorted by value or metal content or collection completeness.

One common need of coin collectors is the printing of inserts for 2" flips. Once catalogued, computer software can allow you to produce customized flip inserts in a standard format of your own design.

Report generation is the subset of an inventory program that produces the listings that you view on the screen, print on paper, or export to other computer applications. Its flexibility will greatly impact its utility. For example, you may want to generate two listings of coins that you have for sale, one which includes your cost and target price (your copy) and one which does not include this information for general distribution to prospective buyers.

At various times, you will probably want to be able to list any subset of the information fields, filter based on a wide array of parameters, and sort using different criteria.

As mentioned at the beginning of this article, report generation may be used to output PDF files which may be viewed using a portable device such as an e-book reader.

Other Functionality You Should Expect from Your Inventory Software

Inventory software should be able to store all of the information in which a collector is interested. Specific fields will vary based on collector interest and purpose. Some will require detailed certification and descriptive information, others comprehensive purchase and sales history. Some collectors will want to have comprehensive recording of storage location and insurance information. Modern programs provide sufficient information fields to meet all of these needs.

Backup and restore functionality should allow the user to easily protect the data they have meticulously entered. History charting enables the user to track the changes of value of a part of their collection over time.

Good software must be easy to use and supported by context sensitive help that provides the user with detailed instructions in a "how-to" format on all of the basic functions that they will wish to perform.

Availability of Timely Updates

Once you have taken the time to catalog your collection in a computer program, you will want to preserve your investment by having access to database updates incorporating information on new coin releases as well as changes in value. Your supplier of inventory software should have a timely program for availability of annual database and value updates.

Educational Software for Collectors

Adding significantly to your enjoyment of collections are electronic information sources that exploit the power of the computer to present you with high quality information in an easily accessible format. These programs can provide comprehensive knowledge of all aspects of coin collecting, detailed information on grading coins, and specialized information such as collecting coin varieties.

COIN GRADING

Most coin collectors will want to be able to grade their coins, at least to an approximate grade. This enables them to have an understanding of value as well as identify coins that might be appropriate for certification. Coin grading skill is built up through time and experience.

The Grading Assistant, offered by Carlisle Development, is based on the official Grading Guide of the American Numismatic Association, now published by Whitman Publishing. It enables the user to view side-by-side images of their own coins along with various grades from the ANA grading set. These images are supported by detailed descriptions of the wear points for each grade. Using software such as the Grading Assistant, a user can develop their skill in grading coins and establish approximate grades for their collection.

VARIETY COLLECTING

The collecting of coin varieties is an exciting area of the hobby currently experiencing some growth. Varieties are the result of differences in the minting process or dies that produce design differences and or errors. These include such effects as doubling of some of features or letters, extra pieces of metal on the coin surface and die breaks. Variety collecting requires the collector to identify subtle differences in coin designs.

The Morgan dollar series is one of the most commonly collected and is categorized by many varieties. Carlisle Development offers a Top 100 Morgan Dollar CD, based on the book written by Michael Fey and Jeff Oxman. This work provides pictures, identification information, and values for the most sought after and valuable Morgan dollar varieties. It provides a spectacular set of high quality pictures to assist you in identifying these coins and also the full text and information provided in this work.

BULLION ANALYSIS

The increase in bullion prices has made understanding of bullion value much more important and significantly impacts the cost of acquiring new items. Carlisle Development offers the Bullion Analyzer to assist collectors in understanding bullion values and their impact on your collecting pursuits.

MOBILE APPLICATIONS FOR NUMISMATISTS

During 2012, Carlisle Development introduced its two first iPhone/iPad apps, the Coin Identification/Mint Mark Locator and Top 100 Morgan Varieties. Both tools are available at the Apple app store (visit www.carlisledevelopment.com/mobileapps.html for a link to the app store). The Coin Identification/Mint Mark Locator assists a collector in identifying U.S. coin types and also locating the mint mark. It covers all coins from 1793–present and includes basic numismatic data. The Top 100 Morgan Varieties provides high resolution images and supporting numismatic data to assist collectors in identifying more valuable Morgan dollar varieties.

GENERAL EDUCATIONAL WORKS ON COLLECTING

There is much to learn about coin collecting, whether it is technical knowledge such as grading and authentication or practical knowledge such as buying and selling coins, attending trade shows, or participating in auctions. Educational computer software offers advantages over printed works in that the contents may be searched and indexed, allowing the user to rapidly retrieve valuable information.

Carlisle Development offers the *Coin Collector's Survival Manual,* Sixth Edition, an interactive edition of the work by Scott Travers. This work provides a set of information that every collector of coins should have. The entire contents of this book are provided in a searchable, interactive format. This allows the user to easily locate information based on word searching, topics, illustrations, bookmarks, a table of contents, or index. The most recent edition of this work, released in 2008, contains the contents of *How to Make Money in Coins Right Now*, covering such topics as cracking-out coins for upgrade and premium coins. In addition to the contents of the book, a set of high quality grading images have been included for such topics as identifying MS-63, MS-65, MS-67 coins and toning. An interactive grading calculator brings to life the grading methods described in the book.

WELL DESIGNED COMPUTER SOFTWARE WILL ADD TO YOUR ENJOYMENT OF COLLECTING

Carlisle Development Corporation publishes the most comprehensive line of collector software available, especially regarding coins and paper money.

Central to Carlisle's product line is the Collector's Assistant, the most advanced and comprehensive collection software available. It is sold in a variety of configurations to serve collectors of over thirty collectible types from autographs to toys. Most extensive is support for coins and paper money. The Collector's Assistant family includes:

- United States Coin Database—complete listings of all U.S. coinage from 1793 to the present. 50 State quarter program and the Presidents Dollar program are recent additions. This also includes Colonial and Hawaiian coinage.

- World Coin Database—A listing of over 5,000 coin types from over forty-five countries, which may be extended by the user. Also includes comprehensive listings of Canada, Australia, Euro coinage, and world bullion gold and silver coins.

- Ancient Coin Database—includes several thousand listings of Byzantine, Judaic, Roman and Greek coinage along with several hundred images. Data entry screens are optimized for ancient coin collectors including long fields for inscriptions and preloaded choice lists of rulers, ancient denominations, towns, mints, and others.

- United States Currency Database—A complete listing of all United States currency based on Friedberg's 18th Edition, Paper Money of the United States. This also includes 120 high quality color images of early U.S. currency.

To learn more about Carlisle Development's product line, visit our website at www.carlisledevelopment.com. You will find current product information and may also place orders. You can reach us by e-mail at support@carlisledevelopment.com or by phone at 800-219-0257.

INTERNATIONAL RATES OF EXCHANGE TABLE

Courtesy of The Monetary Research Institute, "MRI Bankers' Guide to Foreign Currency"

The following 2013 list of the international exchange fixed rates as of January. The right-hand column indicates the number of units (in that country's currency) that equal $1 USA. Please use these rates as only a guide. Rates may vary, so please check with your local bank before making a transaction.

ISO Code Country / Currency Rates against USD (9 January 2013)	Official rate[1]	Parallel Market
AFN Afghanistan/ New Afghani	51.23	(*)
ALL Albania/Lek	107.00	(*)
DZD Algeria/Dinar	78.94	90.00
EUR Andorra → Euro		
AOA Angola/(new) kwanza[2]	95.86	(*)
XCD Anguilla → East Carib dollar	2.67	(*)
XCD Antigua & Barbuda → E.C.$	2.67	(*)
ARS Argentina/Peso	4.93	7.10
AMD Armenia/Dram	406.00	(*)
AWG Aruba/Florin	1.79	(*)
AUD Australia/Dollar	.9516	(*)
EUR Austria → Euro		
AZN Azerbaijan/(New) manat	0.7667	(*)
BSD Bahamas/Dollar	1.00	(*)
BHD Bahrain/Dinar	.3770	(*)
BDT Bangladesh/Taka	79.71	(*)
BBD Barbados/Dollar	1.98	(*)
BYB Belarus/(new) rubel[2]	8,670	(*)
EUR Belgium → Euro		
BZD Belize/Dollar	1.98	(*)
XOF Benin → CFA franc West	502.90	(*)
BMD Bermuda/Dollar	1.00	(*)
BTN Bhutan/Ngultrum	54.85	(*)
BOB Bolivia/Boliviano	6.91	(*)
USD Bonaire → U.S. dollar		
BAM Bosnia-Herzegovina/ K.Marka	1.4990	(*)

ISO Code Country / Currency Rates against USD (9 January 2013)	Official rate[1]	Parallel Market
BWP Botswana/Pula	7.8550	(*)
BRL Brazil/Real	2.0400	2.08
USD British Virgin Isl → U.S. dollar	1.00	(*)
BND Brunei/Ringgit	1.2270	(*)
BGN Bulgaria/(New) lev	1.4990	(*)
XOF Burkina Faso → CFA franc West	502.90	(*)
BIF Burundi/Franc	1,552	
KHR Cambodia/Riel	3,996	(*)
XAF Cameroon → CFA franc Central	502.90	(*)
CAD Canada/Dollar	.9873	(*)
CVE Cape Verde/Escudo	84.05	(*)
KYD Cayman Islands/Dollar	1.2345[M]	(*)
XAF Ctrl.African Rep. → CFA fr Ctrl	502.90	(*)
XAF CFA franc-Central	502.90	(*)
XOF CFA franc-West	502.90	(*)
XPF CFP franc	91.49	(*)
XAF Chad → CFA franc Central	502.90	(*)
CLP Chile/Peso	471.00	(*)
CNY China Peoples Rep/ Yuan	6.20	(*)
COP Colombia/Peso	1,767	(*)
KMF Comoros/Franc	377.10	(*)
CDF Congo, D.R./Franc Congolaise	916.70	(*)
XAF Congo, Rep. → CFA Central	502.90	(*)
NZD Cook Islands/Dollar	1.1920	(*)

ISO Code Country / Currency Rates against USD (9 January 2013)	Official rate[1]	Parallel Market	ISO Code Country / Currency Rates against USD (9 January 2013)	Official rate[1]	Parallel Market
CRC Costa Rica/Colón	501.90	(*)	INR India/Rupee	54.85	(*)
HRK Croatia/Kuna	5.8040	(*)	IDR Indonesia/Rupiah	9,660	(*)
CUP Cuba/Peso	1.00	25.00	IRR Iran/Rial	12,270	22,000
CUC Cuba/Peso convertible	1.00	(*)	IQD Iraq/Dinar	1,163	1,180
CMD Curaçao+St. Maarten /Caribbean dollar	1.79		EUR Ireland → Euro		
EUR Cyprus/Euro			GBP Isle of Man → Sterling pound	1.60[M]	(*)
CZK Czech Republic/Koruna	19.56	(*)	ILS Israel/New sheqel	3.7780	(*)
DKK Denmark/Krona	5.72	(*)	EUR Italy → Euro		
DJF Djibouti/Franc	175.90	(*)	XOF Ivory Coast → CFA franc West	502.90	(*)
XCD Dominica → East Carib dollar	2.67	(*)	JMD Jamaica/Dollar	92.45	(*)
DOP Dominican Republic/ Peso	40.40	(*)	JPY Japan/Yen	87.84	(*)
XCD Eastern Caribbean/ Dollar	2.67	(*)	GBP Jersey → Sterling pound	1.60[M]	(*)
USD Ecuador → U.S. dollar		(*)	JOD Jordan/Dinar	.7087	(*)
EGP Egypt/Pound	6.5120		KZT Kazakhstan/Tenge	150.80	(*)
SVC El Salvador/Colón[3]	8.75	(*)	KES Kenya/Shilling	86.60	(*)
GBP England → Sterling pound	1.60[M]	(*)	AUD Kiribati → Australian dollar		
XAF Equatorial Guinea → CFA franc Ctrl	502.90	(*)	KPW Korea PDR/Won	131.70	1,000
ERN Eritrea/Nakfa	15.00	35.00	KRW Korea Republic/Won	1,061	(*)
EEK Estonia → Euro			KWD Kuwait/Dinar	.2824	(*)
ETB Ethiopia/Birr	18.29	(*)	KGS Kyrgyzstan/Som	47.40	(*)
EUR European Union/Euro	1.3040[M]	(*)	LAK Lao PDR/Kip	7,923	
FKP Falkland-Malvinas/ Pound	1.60[M]	(*)	LVL Latvia/Lat	.5343	(*)
DKK Faroes/Krona	5.72	(*)	LBP Lebanon/Pound	1,505	(*)
FJD Fiji Is/Dollar	1.7730	(*)	LSL Lesotho/Maloti	8.5940	(*)
EUR Finland → Euro			LRD Liberia/Dollar	73.50	(*)
EUR France → Euro			LYD Libya/Dinar	1.2530	(*)
XPF French Polynesia → CFP franc	91.49	(*)	CHF Liechtenstein → Swiss franc		
XAF Gabon → CFA franc Central	502.90	(*)	LTL Lithuania/Litas	2.6470	(*)
GMD Gambia/Dalasi	33.00	(*)	EUR Luxembourg → Euro		
GEL Georgia/Lari	1.6560	(*)	MOP Macao/Pataca	7.9840	(*)
EUR Germany → Euro			MKD Macedonia/New denar	47.20	(*)
GHS Ghana/New Cedi	1.8850	(*)	MGA Madagascar/Ariary	2,258	(*)
GIP Gibraltar/Pound	1.60[M]	(*)	MWK Malawi/Kwacha	348.10	370.00
EUR Greece → Euro			MYR Malaysia/Ringgit	3.0380	(*)
DKK Greenland → Denmark	5.72	(*)	MVR Maldives/Rufiya	15.39	(*)
XCD Grenada → East Caribbean dollar	2.67	(*)	XOF Mali → CFA franc West	502.90	(*)
GTQ Guatemala/Quetzal	7.93	(*)	EUR Malta → Euro		(*)
GBP Guernsey → Sterling pound	1.60[M]	(*)	USD Marshall Isl → U.S. dollar		
XOF Guinea-Bissau/CFA franc West	502.90	(*)	MRO Mauritania/Ouguiya	303.50	(*)
GNF Guinea Conakry/Franc	6,990	8,500	MUR Mauritius/Rupee	30.65	(*)
GYD Guyana/Dollar	201.20	(*)	MXN Mexico/(New) Peso	12.75	(*)
HTG Haïti/Gourde	42.15	(*)	MDL Moldova/Leu	12.20	(*)
HNL Honduras/Lempira	19.90	(*)	EUR Monaco → Euro		
HKD Hong Kong/Dollar	7.7520	(*)	MNT Mongolia/Tugrik	1,393	(*)
HUF Hungary/Forint	222.30	(*)	EUR Montenegro → Euro		
ISK Iceland/Krona	129.70	(*)	XCD Montserrat → East Carib dollar	2.67	(*)
			MAD Morocco/Dirham	8.5350	
			MZN Mozambique/(New) Metical	29.90	(*)
			MMK Myanmar/Kyat	857.00	(*)
			NAD Namibia/Dollar	8.5940	(*)

ISO Code	Country / Currency Rates against USD (9 January 2013)	Official rate[1]	Parallel Market
AUD	Nauru → Australian dollar		
NPR	Nepal/Rupee	87.76	(*)
EUR	Netherlands → Euro		
ANG	Neth Antilles → Curaçao &St. Maarten		
XPF	New Caledonia → CFP franc	91.49	(*)
NZD	New Zealand/Dollar	1.1920	(*)
NIO	Nicaragua/Córdoba	24.15	(*)
XOF	Niger → CFA franc		
	West	502.90	(*)
NGN	Nigeria/Naira	156.40	(*)
GBP	Northern Ireland → Sterling pound	1.60[M]	(*)
NOK	Norway/Krone	5.60	(*)
OMR	Oman/Rial	.3850	(*)
PKR	Pakistan/Rupee	97.32	(*)
USD	Palau → U.S. dollar		
PAB	Panama/Balboa → U.S. dollar		
PGK	Papua New Guinea/ Kina	2.810	(*)
PYG	Paraguay/Guaraní	4,252	4,150
PEN	Peru/Nuevo sol	2.5490	(*)
PHP	Philippines/Piso	40.80	(*)
PLN	Poland/New złoty	3.1310	(*)
EUR	Portugal → Euro		
QAR	Qatar/Riyal	3.64	(*)
RON	Romania/New leu	3.3680	(*)
RUB	Russia/(New) ruble	30.39	(*)
RWF	Rwanda/Franc	630.80	(*)
USD	Saba → U.S. dollar		
USD	St. Eustatius → U.S. dollar		
SHP	St. Helena/Pound	1.60[M]	(*)
XCD	St. Kitts & Nevis → E.Carib $	2.67	(*)
XCD	St. Lucia → East Caribbean $	2.67	(*)
CMD	St. Maarten/Caribbean dollar		
XCD	St. Vincent → East Caribbean $	2.67	(*)
WST	Samoa/Tala	2.2610	(*)
EUR	San Marino → Euro		
STD	São Tome e Principe/ Dobra	18,200	
SAR	Saudi Arabia/Riyal	3.75	(*)
GBP	Scotland → Sterling pound	1.60[M]	(*)
XOF	Senegal → CFA franc West	502.90	(*)
RSD	Serbia/Dinar	85.79	(*)
SCR	Seychelles/Rupee	13.09	
SLL	Sierra Leone/Leone	4,334	(*)
SGD	Singapore/Dollar	1.2270	(*)
EUR	Slovakia → Euro		
EUR	Slovenia → Euro		
SBD	Solomon Is/Dollar	7.0070	(*)
SOS	Somalia/Shillin	1575	10,000
	Somaliland/Shilin	6,500	(*)

ISO Code	Country / Currency Rates against USD (9 January 2013)	Official rate[1]	Parallel Market
ZAR	South Africa/Rand	8.5940	(*)
SSP	South Sudan/Pound	3.15	5.00
EUR	Spain → Euro		
LKR	Sri Lanka/Rupee	126.30	(*)
SDG	Sudan/(New) pound	4.4150	2.80
SRD	Surinam/Dollar	3.30	(*)
SZL	Swaziland/Lilangeni	8.5940	(*)
SEK	Sweden/Krona	6.5720	(*)
CHF	Switzerland/Franc	.9271	(*)
SYP	Syria/Pound	70.85	95.00
TWD	Taiwan/NT Dollar	29.00	(*)
TJS	Tajikistan/Somoni	4.7580	(*)
TZS	Tanzania/Shilling	1,593	(*)
THB	Thailand/Baht	30.38	(*)
XOF	Togo → CFA franc West	502.90	(*)
TOP	Tonga/Pa'anga	1.7270	(*)
	Transdniester/ Ruble (2001)	11.10	(*)
TTD	Trinidad & Tobago/ Dollar	6.3890	(*)
TND	Tunisia/Dinar	1.5710	(*)
TRY	Turkey/New lira[5]	1.776	(*)
TMT	Turkmenistan/ (New) manat[9]	2.84	(*)
USD	Turks & Caicos → U.S. dollar		
AUD	Tuvalu → Australian dollar		
UGX	Uganda/Shilling	2,710	(*)
UAH	Ukraine/Hryvnia	8.0990	(*)
AED	United Arab Emirates/ Dirham	3.6730	(*)
USD	U.S.A./Dollar	1.00	(*)
UYU	Uruguay/Peso uruguayo	19.35	(*)
UZS	Uzbekistan/Som- Currency	1,985	2,500
VUV	Vanuatu/Vatu	93.29	(*)
EUR	Vatican City → Euro		
VEF	Venezuela/Bolívar (fuerte)[8]	4.2940	9.20
VND	Vietnam/Đồng	20,840	(*)
YER	Yemen/Rial	214.90	(*)
RSD	Yugoslavia → Serbia & Montenegro		
ZMW	Zambia/Kwacha [11]	5.27	(*)
ZWD	Zimbabwe/(2009) dollar[10]		(*)

[1]	Fixed or free market rate.
[2]	U.S. Dollars co-circulate.
[6]	AYM1 = AZM5,000
[8]	VEF1 = VEB1,000
[9]	TMT1 = TMM 5,000
[10]	Currency suspended as of 16 April 2009.
[11]	ZMW1 = ZMK1,000
(*)	Free, parallel market not needed, or parallel market very close to official rate.
[M]	Multiplication rate

INTERNATIONAL COIN MINTS AND DISTRIBUTORS

Foreign countries sell their current coinage directly through the government of issue and/or through official U.S. distributors. The following is a list of countries and/or distributors from which current coins can be purchased. Ask to be placed on their mailing lists to receive notification of the most current releases. Website Resource: www.mintsoftheworld.com

ANDORRA
Servei D' Emissions Episcopal
C/. Prat de la Creu
96 4t 5a
Andorra La Vella
PRINCIPAT D' ANDORRA
Telephone: 00376-869-099
Fax: 00376-869-099
email: andorramint@andorramint.ad
website: www.andorra.ad
(silver coins)

AUSTRALIA
Royal Australian Mint
Denison Street
Deakin, ACT 2600
AUSTRALIA
Telephone: 0061-2-6202-6800
Fax: 0061-2-6202-6953
email: info@ramint.gov.an
website: www.ramint.gov.an
The Royal Australian Mint in Canberra is the home of Australia's coins and was officially opened by His Royal Highness, The Duke of Edinburgh, on Monday, February 22, 1965.

Commissioned to produce Australia's decimal coinage, introduced into circulation on February 14, 1966, the Royal Australian Mint holds a place in history as the first mint in Australia not to be a branch of the Royal Mint in London.

Since its opening in 1965 the Mint has produced over eight billion circulating coins and currently has the capacity to produce over two million coins per day or over six hundred million coins per year, with staff working a single shift only.

Coins are not the only products of the Mint. Medals, medallions, seals, and tokens are produced for a wide range of government, business, sporting, and tourist needs in Australia and overseas. A small selection includes The Order of Australia, Vietnam Medal, New Zealand Commonwealth Games Victory Medals, Third Pacific Conference Games Medallion, Anzac Peace Medallion, Sydney Monorail Token, and Queensland's Jupiters Casino Token.

The Royal Australian Mint strikes coins for a number of South Pacific nations. Export coins were first struck in 1969 for New Zealand, and since then coins have been produced for Papua New Guinea, Tonga, Western Samoa, Cook Islands, Fiji, Malaysia, Thailand, Nepal, Bangladesh, and Tokelau.

Perth Mint (Western Australia Mint)
P.O. Box 6297
300–310 Hay Street
East Perth, Western Australia 6004
AUSTRALIA
Telephone: 0061-8-9421-7218
Fax: 0061-8-9225-5012
email: info@perthmint.com.au
website: www.perthmint.com.au

AUSTRIA (silver coins)
North American office:
Euro Collections International Inc.
621 Discovery Street
Ste. 727
Victoria, BC Canada V8W 2P9
Telephone: (888) 904-5544
Fax: (250) 658-1455
email: info@eurocollections.com
website: www.eurocollections.com

Austrian Mint
Munze Osterreich AG
A-1031 Wien Postfach 181
Am Heumarkt I
AUSTRIA
Telephone: 0043-1-717-15-0
Fax: 0043-1-715-40-70
email: marketing@austrian-mint.com
website: www.austrian-mint.com

Royal Belgian Mint
Monnaie Royale de Belgique
Bd. Pacheco laan 32
1000 Bruxelles
BELGIUM
Telephone: 0032-(0)2-221-07-30
Fax: 0061-(0)8-9225-5012
email: mrb.kmb@minfin.fed.be

website: www.treasury.fgov.be/
Internet

BERMUDA
Bermuda Monetary Authority
26 Burnaby Street
Hamilton, HM 11
BERMUDA
Telephone: 001-441-295-5278
Fax: 001-441-292-7471
email: info@bma.bm
website: www.bma.bm

BRAZIL (silver & gold coins)
Casa de Moeda do Brasil
Rua Rene Bitten-Court 371
23565–200 Distrito Industrial de
Santa Cruz
Rio de Janeiro RJ,
BRAZIL
Telephone: 0055-021-2414-2222
Fax: 0055-021-2418-1122
email: csocial@casadamoeda.com.br
website: www.casadamoeda.com.br

BULGARIA (silver coins)
Bulgarian Mint
1 Alexander Battenberg Sq.
Sofia 1000
BULGARIA
Telephone: (+3592) 807-1855
Fax: (+3592) 973-8161
email: mint@omega.bg
website: www.mint.bg

CANADA (silver & gold coins)
Royal Canadian Mint
320 Promenade Sussex Drive
Ottawa, Ontario K1A 0G8
CANADA
Telephone: 800-267-1871
email: info@mint.ca
website: www.mint.ca

CHINA, PEOPLE'S REPUBLIC OF
(silver & gold coins)
18/F, Agricultural Bank of China,
No. 188

West Liberation Road,
Shenzhen, China
Post Code 518001
Telephone: 0086-(0)10-63102266
Fax: 0086-(0)10-63101570
email: webmaster@chinagoldcoin.net
website: www.chinagoldcoin.net

CYPRESS
Central Bank of Cypress
P.O. Box 5529
Nicosia, Cyprus

CZECH REPUBLIC *(silver coins)*
Czech Mint
Bizuterie Ceska Mincovna
U prehrady 61,
466 23 Jablonec nad Nisou
CZECH REPUBLIC
Telephone: 00420-483-513-111
email: mince@mint.cz
website: www.mint.cz

DENMARK *(silver & gold coins)*
Danish Central Bank
Havnegade 5
1093 Copenhagen
DENMARK
email: info@nationalbanken.dk
website: www.nationalbanken.dk

EGYPT *(silver & gold coins)*
Central Bank of Egypt
31 Kasr Elnil St.
Cairo
EGYPT
website: www.cbe.org.eg

(silver coins)
Egyptian Coin Center
41 Ramses Street
P.O. Box 77
Mohamed Farid
Cairo
EGYPT

FINLAND *(silver coins)*
Mint of Finland
P.O. Box 100
(Suometsantie 1)

FIN-01741 Vantaa
FINLAND
Telephone: 00-358-9-894-31
email: info@rahapajamoneta.fi
website: www.mint.fi

FRANCE
Monnaie de Paris
11 quai de Conti
75270 Paris Cedex 06
FRANCE
Telephone: 0033-(0)1-40-46-56-66
Fax: 0033-(0)1-40-46-57-00
website: www.monnaiedeparis.fr

GERMANY
German Mint
Bahnhofstrasse 16–18
D-6380 Bad Homburg 1
GERMANY
Telephone: 0049(0)6172/108-0
website: www.bwpv.de

IRELAND
Official Irish Central Bank
Sandyford
Dublin 16
IRELAND
Telephone: 353 01 2955666
Fax: 353 01 2956536
email: enquiries@centralbank.ie
website: www.centralbank.ie

ISRAEL *(gold coins)*
Israel Government Coins &
Metals Corp.
P.O. Box 7900
Jerusalem 91078
ISRAEL
website: www.isragift.co.il

ITALY *(silver & gold coins)*
Instituto Poligrafico e
Zecca Dello Stato
Piazza Verdi, 10
00198 Roma
ITALY
Telephone: 0039-06-85081

Fax: 0039-06-8508251
email: grafico@ipzs.it
website: www.ipzs.it

NETHERLANDS *(silver & gold coins)*
Dutch Mint
Leidsweg 90, 3531 BG
Leidseweg 90
Utrecht
THE NETHERLANDS
Telephone: 0031(0)30-2910410
Fax: 0031(0)30-2946179
website: www.knm.nl

NEW ZEALAND
Royal Mint of New Zealand
P.O. Box 9260
Newmarket, Auckland 1031
NEW ZEALAND
Telephone: 0064-9-377-6837
Fax: 0064-9-377-6836
email: sals@newzealandmint.com
website: www.nzmint.com

NORWAY *(silver & gold coins)*
Royal Mint of Norway
P.O. Box 53
N-3602 Kongsberg
NORWAY
Telephone: 0047-32-29-95-30
Fax: 0047-32-29-95-50
email: post@dkm.no
website: www.dkm.no

POLAND *(silver & gold coins)*
Polish State Mint
MINT-POL S.A.
Pereca Street, 21
00 958 Warsaw
POLAND
Telephone: 0048-22-656-40-00
Fax: 0048-22-620-52-22
email: mennica@mennica.com.pl
website: www.mennica.com.pl

PORTUGAL *(silver coins)*
Portugal State Mint

Casa da Moeda
Av. Dr. Antonio Jose de Almeida
P-1092 Lisboa, Codex
PORTUGAL

SINGAPORE *(silver coins)*
BCCS Depot Singapore
10 Depot Walk
SINGAPORE 04 10

(gold coins)
Singapore Mint
249 Jalan Boon Lay
SINGAPORE 2261
REPUBLIC OF SINGAPORE
Singapore Mint
20 Teban Gardens Crescent
Singapore 608928
Telephone: +65 6565 2626
Fax: +65 6565 2626
email: scnm@singaporemint
.com.sg
website: www.singaporemint.com

SOUTH AFRICA
(silver & gold coins)
South African Mint Company
Old Johannesburg RD,
Gateway, Centurion
P.O. Box 464
Pretoria 0001
SOUTH AFRICA
Telephone: 0027-12-677-2777
Fax: 0027-12-677-2690
email: samint@samint.co.za
website: www.samint.za

SPAIN *(silver & gold coins)*
Spanish Royal Mint
Fabrica Nacional de Moneda y
Timbre
Jorge Juan, 106
28071 Madrid
SPAIN
Telephone: 0034-91-566-65-56
Fax: 0034-91-504-29-43
website: www.fnmt.es

SWEDEN *(silver & gold coins)*
AB Tumba Bruk Myntverket
Official Swedish Mint
Smedjegatan 19
S-63 1 06 Eskilstuna
SWEDEN
Telephone: 0046-016-42-81-00
Fax: 0046-016-42-81-20
website: www.myntverket.se

SWITZERLAND *(silver & gold coins)*
Offical Swiss Mint
Bernastrasse 28
CH-3003 Bern
SWITZERLAND
Telephone: 0041-(0)31-322-60-68
Fax: 0041-(0)31-322-60-07
email: info@swissmint.ch
website: www.swissmint.ch

THAILAND *(silver coins)*
Royal Decorations & Coins Div.
Royal Grand Palace
Chakrapong RD
Bangkok 10200
THAILAND
Telephone: 02-901-4901-44
Fax: 02-901-2617
website: www.royalthaimint.net

TURKEY *(silver & gold coins)*
Turkish State Mint
email: info@mint.gov.tr
website: www.mint.gov.tr

UNITED KINGDOM
(silver & gold coins)
British Royal Mint
Llantrisant, Pontyclun
Mid-Glamorgan CF7 8YT
UNITED KINGDOM
Telephone: 0044(0)845-60-88-300
Fax: 0044(0)1443-62-33-30
website: www.royalmint.com

UNITED STATES OF AMERICA
(silver & gold coins)
United States Mint
Customer Care Center
801 9th St. NW
Washington, D.C. 20220
USA
Telephone: 800-872-6468
website: www.usmint.gov

VATICAN CITY
Filatelico e Numismatico
I-00120 Vatican City
ITALY

INTERNATIONAL ASSOCIATION OF PROFESSIONAL NUMISMATISTS

OBJECT OF THE ASSOCIATION

The I.A.P.N. was constituted at a meeting held in Geneva in 1951 to which the leading international numismatic firms had been invited. There were 28 foundation members. The objects of the Association are the development of a healthy and prosperous numismatic trade conducted according to the highest standards of business ethics and commercial practice, the encouragement of scientific research and the propagation of numismatics, and the creation of lasting and friendly relations amongst professional numismatists throughout the world.

Membership is vested in numismatic firms, or in numismatic departments of other commercial institutions, and *not* in individuals. Today there are more than 114 numismatic firms in membership, situated in five continents and twenty-three countries. The General Assembly is the supreme organ of the Association, and this is convened annually, normally in a different country.

The Executive Committee is composed of twelve to fifteen persons from at least six different countries and includes the President, two Vice-Presidents (one from each Hemisphere), the General Secretary, and the Treasurer. There are subcommittees dealing with membership, discipline, publications, and anti-forgery work.

In pursuit of the objective to encourage numismatic research the Association has published or assisted in the publication of a number of important numismatic works. In particular it maintains a close liaison with the International Numismatic Commission, and individual members take an active interest in the work of their national numismatic organizations.

In 1965 the I.A.P.N. held an international congress in Paris to consider the study of and defense against counterfeit coins, and in 1975 the Association established the International Bureau for the Suppression of Counterfeit Coins (I.B.S.C.C.) in London. This Bureau maintains close links with mints, police forces, museums, collectors, and dealers, publishing both a half-yearly Bulletin on Counterfeits and specialized reports on counterfeits. It will give an opinion as to authenticity and further details may be had on application to the Bureau.

The members of the I.A.P.N. guarantee the authenticity of all the coins and medals which they sell—this is a condition of membership—so collectors may purchase numismatic material from any of the firms listed in the following pages in the full knowledge that if any item does prove to be counterfeit or not as described the piece can be returned and the purchase price will be refunded, without regard to date of purchase.

Membership in the Association is not lightly acquired as applicants have to be sponsored by three members, and the vetting of applications involves a rigorous and sometimes protracted procedure. In order to be admitted the applicants must have been established in business as numismatists for at least four years and must be known to a number of members, and the Committee need to be satisfied that they have carried on their business in an honorable manner and that they have a good general knowledge of numismatics as well as expertise in whatever field is their speciality.

The Medal of Honour of the Association was established in 1963 in memory of its first president, Leonard S. Forrer, and is awarded by the President to persons of distinction whom the Association wishes to honor or for distinguished services to the Association.

The Association is a non-profit-making organization established within the terms of paras. 60 *et seq* of the Swiss Civil Code. Its registered office is at P.O. Box 3647, CH-4002 Basle (Switzerland). Further inquiries about the Association may be made to the General Secretary.

Secretary:
Jean-Luc Van der Schueren
14, Rue de la Bourse, BE-1000 Bruxelles (Belgium)
Tel.: +32-2-513 3400 — Fax: +32-2-512 2528
e-Mail: *iapnsecret@iapn-coins.org*

AUSTRALIA
Downies Coins Pty. Ltd.
(Mr. Ken Downie; Chris Meallin,
John Freestone)
Australia
P.O. Box 3131
NUNAWADING, VIC. 3131
Street Address:
3 Redland Drive
Mitcham, Vic. 3132
Telephone: (61) 3-8456 8456
FX: (61) 3-8456 8401
info@downies.com
www.downies.com
Specialties:Australian, British
Commonwealth and
world coins and
banknotes; medals,
tokens, militaria

NOBLE NUMISMATICS Pty Ltd
169 Macquarie Street
SYDNEY NSW 2000
Telephone: (61)-(2) 9223 4578
FX: (61)-(2) 9233 6009
info@noble.com.au
www.noble.com.au
Auctions
Specialties: Australian and world
coins, banknotes,
commemorative and
war medals, tokens.

AUSTRIA
HERINEK, Gerhard
Josefstädterstrasse 27
1080 WIEN
Telephone: (43) (01) 40 64 396
FX: (43) (01) 40 64 396
Publications
Specialties: Antike Münzen,
Römisch Deutsches
Reich

BELGIUM
FRANCESCHI Mr. Druso
B. Franceschi & Fils, Numismates
10, Rue Croix-de-Fer
B-1000 BRUXELLES
Telephone: (32) (02) 217 9395
FX: +32-2-217 93 95
List Publications Auctions
drusofranceschi@hotmail.com

VAN DER SCHUEREN, Jean-Luc
14, Rue de la Bourse,
B-1000 BRUXELLES (Belgium)
Telephone: (32) (02) 513 3400
FX: (32) (02) 512 2528
iapnsecret@compuserve.com
www.coins.be
List
Specialties: Ancient and medieval
coins, Low Countries,
world coins and tokens

CANADA
WEIR NUMISMATICS LTD., Randy
PO Box 64577, UNIONVILLE,
Ont. L3R 0M9
Telephone: (905) 503 0052
FX: (905) 503 0051
List Mail Bid Sales
randy.weir@rogers.com
Specialties: British Colonial coins,
Canadian tokens

EGYPT
BAJOCCHI JEWELLERS
(Comm. Pietro Bajocchi)
45 Abdel Khalek Sarwat Street
11511 CAIRO
Telephone: (20) (02) 2391 9160 /
2390 0030
FX: (20) (02) 2393 1696
Specialties: Ptolemaiques,
Greco, Romaines
d'Alexandrie
bajocci@bajocchi.com.eg

FRANCE
VINCHON-NUMISMATIQUE
(Mme Françoise Berthelot-Vinchon)
75002 Paris
77, rue de Richelieu
Telephone: (33) 142 97 50 00
FX: (33) 142 86 06 03
vinchon@wanadoo.fr
www.vinchon.com
Specialties: coins, medals and
orders; engraved
stones, cylinders,
ancient jewels, and
antiquities

BOURGEY, Sabine
7, Rue Drouot, F-75009 PARIS
Telephone: (33) (01) 47 70 88 67;
1 47 70 35 18
FX: (33) (01) 42 46 58 48
bourgey@club-internet.fr
www.franceantiq.fr/sna/bourgey
List Publications Auctions
Specialties: Monnaies, médailles,
jetons, éditions
numismatiques

Burgan Numismatique - Maison
Florange
(Mr. Claude Burgan;
Isabelle Burgan)
75002 Paris
8, rue du 4 Septembre
Telephone: (33) 142 96 95 57
FX: (33) 142 86 92 43
burgan@wanadoo.fr
www.numisonline.com
Specialties: coins of the French
kingdom; ancient
coins; numismatic
literature

MAISON PLATT SAS (Gérard Barré,
Daniel Renaud Sandrine Barré)
49, Rue de Richelieu, F-75001
PARIS
Telephone: (33) (01) 42 96 50 48
FX: (33) (01) 42 61 13 99
maisonplatt@club-internet.fr
www.maisonplatt.com

List Publications Auctions
Specialties: Monnaies antiques,
françaises, médailles,
jetons, papier-
monnaie. Ordres et
décorations, librairie
numismatique

NUMISMATIQUE et CHANGE DE
PARIS
(Annette Vinchon)
3, Rue de la Bourse, F-75002 PARIS
avinchon@club-internet.fr
www.vinchon.net
Telephone: (33) (01) 42 97 53 53 /
42 97 46 85
FX: (33) (01) 42 97 44 56
Publications Mail Bid Sales
Auctions
Specialties: Monnaies modernes.
Monnaies d'or cotées
en bourse. Lingots.
Billets, assignats.
Ourvages de
Référence

O.G.N.
(Pierre Crinon, François Mervy)
64, Rue de Richelieu, F-75002 Paris
Telephone: (33) (01) 42 97 47 50
FX: (33) (01) 42 60 01 37
ogn.numismatique@wanadoo.fr
www.ogn-numismatique.com
List Publications Auctions
Specialties: Monnaies antiques,
françaises, étrangères,
médailles, jetons

Patrick Guillard Eurl
(M. Patrick Guillard)
75261 Paris, Cedex 06
B.P. 41
Telephone: (33) 145 48 18 37
FX: (33) 145 48 29 65
pg@patrickguillard.com
www.patrickguillard.com
Specialties: French coins, from
Carolingians to today;
ancient Roman and

Greek coins; French banknotes and Euro-zone

LA PARPAÏOLLE
(Mr. Rober Le Guen)
13191 Marseille Cedex 20
10, rue Bernex - B.P. 30006
Telephone: (33) 491 62 74 00
info@monnaies-parpaiolle.com
www.monnaies-parpaiolle.com
Specialties: ancient, French Royal, and world coins; tokens and medals; banknotes

POINSIGNON-NUMISMATIQUE
4, Rue des Francs Bourgeois,
F-67000 STRASBOURG
Telephone: (33) (03) 88 32 10 50
FX: (33) (03) 88 75 01 14
contact@poinsignon-numismatique
.com
www.poinsignon-numismatique
.com
List   Auctions
Specialties: Monnaies antiques, françaises, alsaciennes et islamiques, librairie numismatique

Maison Platt S.A.S.
75001 Paris
49, rue de Richelieu
Telephone: (33) 142 96 50 48
FX: (33) 142 61 13 99
maisonplatt@club-internet.fr
www.maisonplatt.com
Specialties: ancient and French coins; medals, tokens, and paper money; orders and decorations; numismatic literature

PHILIPPE SAIVE NUMISMATIQUE
(M. Philippe Saive)
57000 Metz
18, rue Dupont des Loges
Telephone: (33) 387 74 17 10

FX: (33) 387 36 39 62
contact@saivenumismatique.com
www.saivenumismatique.com
Specialties: ancient, Royal, French, and foreign coins; Lorraine coins; tokens and medals; emergency money; banknotes; books

VINCHON-NUMISMATIQUE, Jean
(Jean Vinchon et Françoise Berthelot-Vinchon)
77, Rue de Richelieu, F-75002
PARIS
Telephone: (33) (01) 42 97 50 00
FX: (33) (01) 42 86 06 03
vinchon@wanadoo.fr
www.vinchon.com
List   Publications   Auctions
Specialties: Monnaies, médailles, décorations, pierres gravées, cylindres, bijoux anciens, antiquités

GERMANY
DILLER, Johannes
(Ohlstadter Str. 21)
D-81373 MÜNCHEN
Telephone: (49) (089) 760 3550
FX: (49) (089) 769 8939
muenzen-diller@t-online.de
www.muezen-diller.de
Specialties: Münzen (900-1800), Medaillen (1500-1933), Kelten von Süddeutschland, Numism. Antiquariat

WESTFÄLISCHE AUKTIONSGESELLSCHAFT
(Herr Udo Gans; Heinz-Günther Hild)
59821 Arnsberg
Nordring 22
Telephone: (49) 2931 20 42 (Gans)
               (49) 2921 22 11 (Hild)
FX: (49) 2931 21 28 4
info@wag-auktionen.de
www.wag-auktionen.de

Specialties: German coins and
medals, especially
Saxony, Bruswick-
Lüneberg, and
Brandenburg-Prussia;
European coins

GIESSENER MÜNZHANDLUNG
DIETER GORNY GmbH
Maximiliansplatz 20
D-80333 MÜNCHEN
Telephone: (49) (089) 24-22-64-30
FX: (49) (089) 2285513
info@gmcoinart.de
www.gmcoinart.de
Specialties: Münzen und Medaillen
der Antike und der
Neuzeit

Leipziger MÜNZHANDLUNG und
Auktion Heidrun HÖHN e.K.
(Frau Heidrun Höhn)
04109 Leipzig
Nikolaistraße 25
Telephone: (49) 341 960 23 86
FX: (49) 341 211 72 45
info@numismatik-online.de
www.numismatik-online.de

JACQUIER, Paul-Francis
Honsellstrasse 8, D-77694 KEHL
am Rhein
Telephone: (49) (07851) 12 17
FX: (49) (07851) 73 074
coinsjacquier@aol.com
www.coinsjacquier.com
Specialties: Celtic, Greek, Roman,
Byzantine coins.
Classical art.

KAISER, Herr Rüdiger
Münzfachgeschäft
Mittelweg 54, D-60318 FRANKFURT
Telephone: (49) (069) 597 11 09
FX: (49) (069) 55 38 16
kaiserruediger@t-online.de
Specialties: Antike, Europäische
Münzen und Medaillen
bis 1900

KRICHELDORF Nachf., H.H.
(Volker Kricheldorf)
Günterstalstrasse 16
D-79102 FREIBURG im Breslau
Telephone: (49) (0761) 739 13
FX: (49) (0761) 70 96 70
ainp@kricheldorf.de
www.kricheldorf.de

KÜNKER, Fritz Rudolf,
Münzenhandlung
(F.R. Künker, H.-R. Künker,
Oliver Köpp)
Gutenbergstrasse 23
D-49076 OSNABRÜCK
Telephone: (49) (0541) 96 20 20
FX: (49) (0541) 96 20 222
service@kuenker.de
www.kueker.de
Specialties: Antike, Mittelalter und
Neuzeit, Goldmünzen

Numismatik LANZ (Dr. Hubert Lanz,
Ingrid Franke, Walter Schantl,
Florian Eggers)
Luitpoldblock-Maximiliansplatz 10
D-80333 MÜNCHEN
Telephone: (49) (089) 29 90 70
FX: (49) (089) 22 07 62
info@lanz.com
www.numislanz.de
Auctions
Specialties: Antike, Mittelalter,
Neuzeit, Literatur,
Münzen und Medaillen

Manfred OLDING Münzenhandlung
(Herr Manfred Olding)
49078 Osnabrück
Goldbreede 14
Telephone: (49) 541 44 22 77
FX: (49) 541 44 22 67
info@manfred-olding.de
www.manfred-olding.de
Specialties: German coins and
medals, especially
Brandenburg-Prussia,
Saxony and North
Germany; European coins

MEISTER Münzenhandlung
(Herr Michael Meister)
71634 Ludwigsburg
Moltkestrasse 6
Telephone: (49) 7141 92 05 18
FX: (49) 7141 92 47
info@muenzenmeister.de
Specialties: *Austria, Germany,*
Europe, especially
medals

MÜNZEN-UND
MEDAILLENHANDLUNG
STUTTGART
(Stefan Sonntag)
Charlottenstrasse 4, D-70182
STUTTGART
stefan.sonntag@coinsmedals.de
www.coinsmedals.de
Telephone: (49) (0711) 24 44 57
FX: (49) (0711) 23 39 36
List   Publications

NEUMANN GmbH (Ernst)
(Herr Ernst Neumann; Erika Neumann)
89312 Günzburg
Wätteplatz 6
ernst@neumann-muenzen.de
www.neumann-muenzen.de
Telephone: (49) 8221 321 87
FX: (49) 8221 321 75

PEUS NACHF., Dr. Busso (Dieter Raab,
Wilhelm Müseler, Christian Stoess)
Bornwiesenweg 34, D-60322
FRANKFURT/M.
Telephone: (49) (069) 959 6620
FX: (49) (069) 55 59 95
info@peus-muenzen.de
www.peus-muenzen.de

Münzhandlung RITTER GmbH
(E. & J. Ritter und
Klaus Fleissner)
Immermannstr. 19,
D-40210 DÜSSELDORF
Telephone: (49) (211) 367 80-0
FX: (49) (211) 367 80-25
info@muenzen-ritter.com

www.muenzen-ritter.com
List
Specialties: *Münzen der Antike*
und Deutschlands.
Grosshandel/Wholesale

TIETJEN + CO.
Spitalerstrasse 30, D-20095
HAMBURG
Telephone: (49) (040) 33 03 68
FX: (49) (040) 32 30 35
info@tietjien-hamburg.de
www.tietjien-hamburg.de
Publications   Auctions
Specialties: *Coins, medals, paper*
money and books

HUNGARY
Numismatica Erembolt
(Mr. Làszló Nudelman; Làszló
Fejszès)
1051 Budapest
Vörösmarty Tèr 6
Telephone: 1 337 4908
FX: 1 337 4908
Nudel-numis@freemail.hu
www.numismatica.hu
Specialties: *Hungarian and*
Transylvanian coins
and medals from
medieval to present;
orders

IRELAND
I.C.E. Ltd
(Jerome Lacroix)
Charter House,
5 Pembroke Row, DUBLIN 2
Telephone: +353-1-6768-775
auctionice@gmail.com
www.auctionice.com

ITALY
CARLO CRIPPA s.n.c.
(Carlo e Paolo Crippa)
Via Cavalieri del S. Sepoicro, 10
I-20121 MILANO
Telephone: (39) (02) 878 680
FX: (39) (02) 890 163 54
info@crippanumis-matica.it

www.crippanumis-matica.it
List   Publications
*Specialties: Grecques et romaines.
Italiennes médiévales
et modernes, surtout
de l'atelier de Milan*

DE FALCO (Alberto de Falco)
Corso Umberto 24, I-80138 NAPOLI
Telephone: (39) (081) 55 28 245
FX: (39) (081) 55 17 645
info@albertodefalco.com
www.albertodefalco.com
List
*Specialties: Monete dell'Italia
meridionale e della
Sicilia*

FALLANI (Dr. Carlo-Maria Fallani)
Via del Babuino 58a, I-00187 ROMA
Telephone: (39) (06) 320 7982
FX: (39) (06) 320 7645
*Specialties: Grecques, romaines
et byzantines.
Archéologie*

BARANOWSKY S.A.S.
(Dott. Vincenzo Filonardi)
00187 Roma
Via del Corso 184
Telephone: 390 6 679 1502
FX: 390 6 679 1502
*Specialties: Greek, Romans, and
medieval Italian coins*

Mr. Walter MUSCHETTI
33100 Udine
Galleria Astra, P.O. Box 125
Telephone: 390 43 25 51 14 31
FX: 390 43 25 05 754

PAOLUCCI, Raffaele
Via San Francesco 154
I-35121 PADOVA
Telephone: (39) (049) 651 997
FX: (39) (049) 651 552
raffypd@libero.it
*Specialties: Medieval Italian coins,
especially Venetian*

RANIERI NUMISMATICA SRL
(Mr. Marco Ranieri; Egidio Ranieri)
40124 Bologna
Piazza Calderini 2/2
Telephone: 390 51 26 77 36
FX: 390 33 81 24 05 42
info@numismaticaranieri.it
www.numismaticaraniere.it
*Specialties: Italian coins; medieval
and papal coinage*

RATTO, Mario
Via A. Manzoni 14 (Palazzo
Trivulzio), I-20121 MILANO
Telephone: (39) (02) 79 93 80
FX: (39) (02) 79 64 93
List   Publications   Auctions
*Specialties: Grecques, romaines,
italiennes, médiévales
et modernes*

RINALDI O. & Figlio,
(Alfio e Marco Rinaldi)
Via Cappello 23 (Casa di Giulietta)
I-37121 VERONA
Telephone: (39) (045) 803 40 32
FX: (39) (045) 803 40 32
info@numismaticarinaldi.it
www.numismaticarinaldi.it
List   Publications
*Specialties: Greche, romane,
italiane, estere e
medaglie*

Livio SANTAMARIA
00197 Rom
Via Giacinta Pezzana 15
Telephone: 390 68 08 35 48

VARESI NUMISMATICA S.A.S.
(Sign. Alberto Varesi)
27100 Pavia
Viale Montegrappa 3
Telephone: 390 38 257 06 85
FX: 390 38 248 92 34
info@varesi.it
www.varesi.it
*Specialties: Italian coins (medieval
and modern), Marenghi*

JAPAN

DARUMA INTERNATIONAL
GALLERIES
(Yuji Otani)
2-16-32-701, Takanawa,
Minato-ku, JP-TOKYO 108-0074
Telephone: (81) (03) 3447 5567
FX: (81) (03) 3449 3344
sales@darumacoin.co.jp
www.darumacoin.co.jp
List   Publications   Auctions
Specialties: World gold and silver
                coins, Japanese
                coins and banknotes,
                Chinese coins

WORLD COINS JAPAN
(Mr. Eiichi Ishii;
Katsunosuke Ishii)
Tokyo 105-0013
1-15-5 Hamamatsu-cho, Minato-ku
Telephone: (81) 3 5777 0351
FX: (81) 3 5777 0352
info@coins.co.jp
www.coins.co.jp
Specialties: Japanese coins and
                banknotes; world
                coins, ancient to
                modern; Japanese
                stamps

LUXEMBOURG

LUX NUMIS (Romain Probst)
Galerie Mercure, 41, Av. de la Gare,
6988 Hostert 20, rue J.P. Kommes
L-1611 LUXEMBOURG
Telephone: (352) 34 04 87 /
                34 04 87
FX: (352) 34 82 17
List   Publications   Auctions
Specialties: Luxembourg,
                Monnaies du
                monde, Monnaies de
                nécessité, gauloises

MONACO

EDITIONS VICTOR GADOURY
(M. Francesco Pastrone; Frederico
Pastrone)

98000 Monte Carlo
57 rue Grimaldi
Telephone: 377 93 25 12 96
FX: 377 93 50 13 39
contact@gadoury.com
www.gadoury.com
Specialties: gold and silver
                coins; coins of
                Monaco, France,
                Italy, Europe, and the
                world; numismatic
                publications

NETHERLANDS

MEVIUS NUMISBOOKS
INTERNATIONAL BV
(Johan Mevius, Gabriel Munoz)
Oosteinde 97,
NL-7671 AT VRIEZENVEEN
Telephone: (31) (0546) 561 322
FX: (31) (0546) 561 352
info@mevius.nl
www.mevius.nl
List   Publications
Specialties: Numismatic books,
                coins & medals of the
                Netherlands

VAN DER DUSSEN BV, A.G.
(Pauline van der Dussen)
6211 JB MAASTRICHT
Witmakersstraat 14A
Telephone: (31) (043) 321 51 19
FX: (31) (043) 321 60 14
info@vanderdussen.com
www.vanderdussen.com
Publications   Auctions
Specialties: Coins of the world,
                medals, numismatic
                books

VERSCHOOR Munthandel
(Mr. Dim Verschoor; Henk
Verschoor)
3291 TB Strijen
Binnensingel 3
Telephone: 31 78 674 7712
FX: 31 78 674 4424
info@verschoor.com
www.verschoor.com

Specialties: *Dutch historical and*
family medals in both
silver and gold; Dutch
provincial, colonial,
and kingdom coins;
numismatic literature
and sales catalogues
pertaining to Dutch
numismatics

WESTERHOF, Jille Binne
Trekpad 38-40,
NL-8742 KP BURGWERD
Telephone: (31) (0515) 573 364
FX: (31) (0515) 573 364
info@westernumis.nl
www.westernumis.nl
Auctions
Specialties: *Coins of the*
Netherlands,
Europe, historical
medals

NORWAY
OSLO MYNTHANDEL AS
(Mr. Ronny Hatletvedt)
0256 Oslo
Inkognitogata 33
Sentrum, N-0101 Oslo 1
Telephone: +47-23 10 00 00
FX: +47-23 10 00 01
kontakt@oslomynthandel.no
www.oslomynthandel.no
List   Publications   Auctions
Specialties: *Scandinavian coins,*
Thailand, Ancient
coins

SINGAPORE
TAISEI STAMPS & COINS (S) PTE
LTD.
(B.H. Lim, Mr. Samuel Chua)
116 Middle Road #09-02
ICB Enterprise House
SINGAPORE 188972
Telephone: (65) 63 36 85 85
FX: (65) 63 39 50 01
coin@taisei.com.sg
www.taisei.com.sg

Auctions
Specialties: *Chinese coins, coins of*
Asia, banknotes, world
gold and silver coins

SPAIN
CALICO, X. & F. (Xavier Jr. Calicó)
Plaza del Angel 2,
E-08002 BARCELONA
Telephone: 00 349-3310 5512 /
00 349-3310 5516
FX: 00 349-3310 2756
subasías.numismatics@aureo.com
www.aureo.com
Publications   Auctions
Specialties: *Espagne, possessions*
espagnoles en Europe,
Amérique latine,
Editeurs de médailles

CAYON, Juan R., JANO S.L.
Alcala 35, E-28014 MADRID
Telephone: +349-1-308 2310
FX: +349-1-319 4206
www.cayon.com
cayon@cayon.com
List   Publications
Specialties: *Spanish world, ancient*
coins, crowns and
numismatic books

SEGARRA Numismatica
(Don Fernando P. Segarra; Fernando
P. Segarra Koester)
28012 Madrid
Calle Mayor, 31, Entreplanta
Derecha
Telephone: 349 1366 4272
FX: 349 1366 3531
info@segarranumismatica.com
www.segarranumismatica.com
Specialties: *rare Spanish, Latin*
American, Roman,
Greek, and Visigothic
coins; Spanish
banknotes

VICO SA, Jesus
(Jesus Vico and Julio Chico)
E-28009 MADRID

Telephone: (34) 9(1) 431 88 07
FX: (34) 9(1) 431 01 04
jesusvico@jesusvico.com
www.jesusvico.com
Publications   Auctions
Specialties: Spain, Latin America,
                       Roman, banknotes

SRI LANKA
Mr. D. V. PERRY
Colombo 6
8/3 Balapokuna Place
Telephone: 94 18 20 504
FX: 94 15 00 544
Dave_sue@sti.ik

SWEDEN
ULF NORDLINDS MYNTHANDEL AB
(Hans Hirsch, Ulf Nordlind)
Karlavägen 46, 10243 STOCKHOLM
Telephone: (46) (08) 662 62 61
FX: (46) (08) 661 62 13
info@nordlindsmynt.se
www.nordlindsmynt.se
List
Specialties: Scandinavian coins,
                       medals, numismatic
                       literature

SWITZERLAND
HESS-DIVO AG
Löwenstrasse 55, CH-8001 ZÜRICH
Telephone: (41) (01) 225 4090
FX: (41) (01) 225 4099
mailbox@hessdivo.com
www.hessdivo.com
List   Auctions   Publications
Specialties: Swiss coins, coins of
                       the world, medals,
                       ancient coins

NUMISMATICA ARS CLASSICA AG
(Arturo Russo)
P.O. Box 2655
CH-8022 ZÜRICH
Telephone: (41) (44) 261 1703
FX: (41) (44) 261 5324
zurich@arsclassicacoins.com

List   Publications   Mail   Bid
Sales   Auctions
Specialties: Greek, Roman,
                       Byzantine and
                       medieval coins

THAILAND
HOUSE OF THE COINS, LTD. PART.
(Mr. Jan Olav Aamlid)
Chonburi 20150
391/110 Moo 10, Thappraya Road
and Soi 13, Thambon, Nongprue,
Ampur Banglamung
Telephone: (66) 818 455 404
FX: (66) 382 313 70
coin@loxinfo.co.th
www.thaicoins.com
Specialties: coins, medals, and
                       banknotes of Thailand
                       and Scandinavia; world
                       coins and medals in
                       all metal

UNITED KINGDOM
BALDWIN & SONS LTD., A.H.
(A.H.E. Baldwin)
11 Adelphi Terrace
GB-LONDON WC2N 6BJ
Telephone: (44) 20-7930-6879 /
                       7930 9808 (auctions)
FX: (44) 20-7930-9450
coins@baldwin.co.uk
www.baldwin.co.uk
Publications   Auctions

DAVIES Paul Ltd.
(Mr. Paul Davies; Catherine Davies;
Phil Maunsell)
Ilkley, West Yorksire, LS29 8TZ
P.O. Box 17
Telephone: (44) 1943 603 116
FX: (44) 1943 816 326
paul@pauldaviesltd.co.uk
Specialties: gold coins of the world,
                       1800 to date

DIX NOONAN WEBB
(Mr. Christopher Webb; Peter
Preston-Morley; Michael Sharp; Jim
Brown; I. Vecchi; P. Mitchell)
London, W1J 8BQ

16 Bolton Street, Piccadilly
Telephone: (44) 20 7016 1700
FX: (44) 20 7016 1799
chris@dnw.co.uk
www.dnw.co.uk

EIMER Christopher
(Mr. Christopher Eimer)
London, NW11 7RF
P.O. Box 352
Telephone: (44) 20 8458 9933
FX: (44) 20 8455 3535
art@christophereimer.co.uk
www.christophereimer.co.uk
Specialties: historical and
commemorative
medals; portrait
plaques and cameos;
medallic art

FORMAT OF BIRMINGHAM LTD.
(Garry Charman, David Vice)
18, Lower Temple St. Burlington
Ct. Unit K
BIRMINGHAM B2 4JD
Telephone: (44) (0121) 643 2058
FX: (44) (0121) 643 2210
formatcoins@btconnect.com
List
Specialties: World coins and
medals 1500–1960

KNIGHTSBRIDGE COINS
(Stephen C. Fenton)
43, Duke Street, St. James's
LONDON SW1Y6DD
Telephone: (44) (207) 930 7597 /
930 8215
FX: (44) (207) 930 8214
stephcf232@aol.com
Specialties: English coins, coins
from USA, Australia
and Thailand

RUDD Chris
(Mrs. Elizabeth Cottam;
Chris Rudd)
Aylsham, Norfold, NR11 6TY
P.O. Box 222
Telephone: (44) 1263 73 50 07
FX: (44) 1263 73 17 77

liz@celticcoins.com
www.celticcoins.com
Specialties: Celtic coins

Douglas SAVILLE Numismatic
Books
(Mr. Douglas Sa Ville)
Reading, RG4 7DH
Chiltern Thameside, 37c St. Peters
Avenue, Caversham
Telephone: (44) 118 918 7628;
(44) 7823 323 100
(mobile)
FX: (44) 118 946 1067
info@douglassaville.com
www.douglassaville.com
Specialties: rare, out-of-print,
and secondhand
numismatic books

SPINK & SON LTD.
(Phillip Skingley)
69 Southampton Row. Bloomsbury,
LONDON WCIB 4GT
Telephone: 44 020. 7563-4000
FX: 44-20-7563-4068
info@spink.com
www.spink.com
Auctions   List (10 a year)
Publications
Specialties: Ancient, British, and
world coins

WILKES Tim
(Mr. Tim Wilkes)
Tonbridge Kent TN9 9LR
P.O. Box 566
Telephone: (44) 7538-476-757
tim@wilkescoins.com
www.wilkescoins.com
Specialties: medieval, Indian, and
Islamic coins

UNITED STATES OF AMERICA
BERK, LTD., Harlan J.
31 North Clark Street
CHICAGO, IL 60602
Telephone: (001) (312) 609 0016
FX: (001) (312) 609 1309
info@harlanjberk.com
www.harlanjberk.com

List (bimonthly)
Specialties: All coins 700 BC
to 1990s; classical
antiquities

BULLOWA, C.E. (Mrs. Earl E. Moore)
COINHUNTER
1608 Walnut Street, Ste. 1600
PHILADELPHIA, PA 19103
Telephone: (001) (215) 735 5517
FX: (001) (215) 735 5722
cebullowa@yahoo.com
List Auctions
Specialties: U.S., ancient and
foreign coins and
books.

DAVISSON'S LTD.
(Allan Davisson, Ph.D.,
Marnie Davisson)
17862 Big Fish Lake Rd.
COLD SPRING, MN 56320
Telephone: (001) (320) 685 3835
FX: (001) (320) 685 8636
coins@davissons.net
www.britishcoins.com
List (bimonthly) Publications
Mail Bid Sales
Specialties: British, ancient and
classical European
coins, books

FREEMAN + SEAR (David R. Sear,
Robert D. Freeman,
Tory Fleming Freeman)
PO Box 641352, LOS ANGELES,
CA 90064-6352
Telephone: (001) (310) 450-9755
FX: (001) (310) 450-8865
info@freemanandsear.com
www.freemanandsear.com
List Mail Bid Sales Auctions
Specialties: Ancient Greek, Roman
and Byzantine coins

FROSETH INC., K.M. (Kent Froseth)
PO Box 23116
MINNEAPOLIS, MN 55423
Telephone: (001) (800) 648 7662

FX: (001) (952) 835 3903
fm26@quest.net
www.kmfroseth.com
E-mail: Kmfcoi19@mail.idt.net
Specialties: US, foreign gold and
silver coins

GILLIO INC., Ronald J.
(Ronald Gillio)
Goldmünzen International
1103 State Street
SANTA BARBARA, CA 93101
Telephone: (001) (805) 963 1345
FX: (001) (805) 962 6659
rjgillio@verizon.net
www.gillio.com
List Publications Auctions
Specialties: U.S. Gold, especially
rare dates and proofs,
US type coins. All
Oriental and Asian
numismatics,
especially Japan,
Korea and Taiwan

MARGOLIS, Richard
(Richard and Sara Margolis)
PO Box 2054, TEANECK, NJ 07666
Telephone: (001) (201) 848 9379
FX: (001) (201) 847 0134
remoulade5@aol.com
Publications
Specialties: Foreign coins, medals,
tokens, patterns

PONTERIO & ASSOCIATES, Inc.
(Richard Ponterio, Kent Ponterio)
18061 Fitch
IRVINE, CA 92614
Telephone: (001) (619) 299 0400
FX: (001) (619) 299 6952
Auctions
Specialties: Coins, medals and
banknotes of Mexico
and Latin America,
world paper money,
gold coins and
crowns, ancient
coins

HLS STACKS RARE COINS
(Lawrence Stack)
18 Arlington Lane
BAYVILLE, NY 11709
List   Publications   Auctions
Specialties: United States,
                European, ancient,
                medieval

STEPHENS Inc., Karl (Karl Stephens)
PO Box 3038
FALLBROOK, CA 92088
Telephone: +1-760-731-6138
FX: +1-760-731-9132
karlstephens@earthlink.net
www.karlstephensinc.com
List
Specialties: Foreign coins, medals,
                tokens, Eastern
                Europe, US type and
                copper coins

SUBAK Inc.
(Carl and Jon Subak, Peter Klem)
22 West Monroe Street, Room 1506
CHICAGO, IL 60603
Telephone: (001) (312) 346 0609 /
                346 0673
FX: (001) (312) 346 0150
Specialties: Roman, Byzantine,
                medieval

TELLER NUMISMATIC
ENTERPRISES
(M. Louis Teller, Ph.D., A. Wing)
16055 Ventura Blvd., Suite 635
ENCINO, CA 91436
Telephone: (001) (818) 783 8454
FX: (001) (818) 783 9083

mlt@tellercoins.com
www.tellercoins.com
Specialties: Gold and silver coins
                of the world. Specialist
                in Russia, China, 19th-
                century Oriental coins
                and choice foreign
                paper money

WADDELL, Ltd., Edward J.
(Edward J. Waddell Jr.)
PO Box 3759
FREDERICK, MD 21702
(Suburb of Washington, D.C.)
FX: (001) (301) 473 8716
ed@coin.com
www.coin.com
List
Specialties: Greek, Roman,
                Byzantine and
                medieval coins;
                numismatic literature

VENEZUELA
NUMISMATICA GLOBUS
(Señor Antonio Alessandrini)
Caracas 1050
Calle Paraiso, Edf. Perla, Ofic. 12,
Sabana Grande
Telephone: 58 212 762 6442 or 762
                8076
FX: 58 212 762 9039
alessandrini@globuscoins.com
www.globuscoins.com
Specialties: coins, medals, and
                paper money of
                Venezuela; coins and
                medals of the world in
                all metals, 1500 to date

INTERNATIONAL NUMISMATIC ORGANIZATIONS

The following is a list of international numismatic organizations. This information is current as of the publication date. It is suggested that you write, call, or fax for more up-to-date membership information. If your organization is not listed, please send information to the author for inclusion in subsequent editions.

AUSTRALIA

• NUMISMATIC ASSOCIATION OF AUSTRALIA INC, P.O. Box 3664, Norwood SA 5067 AUSTRALIA. Email: pnj.lane@bigpond .org, Website: naa-online.com

• TASMANIAN NUMISMATIC SOCIETY, INC., P.O. Box 12, Clarmont, Tasmania 7011 AUSTRALIA. Telephone: 036249 1369. Email: misteeth@bigpond.net.au, Website: www.vision.net.au/ ~pwood/tns.html

BELGIUM

• INTERNATIONAL ASSOCIATION OF PROFESSIONAL NUMISMATICS (IAPN-AINP), 14, Rue de la Bourse, BE-1000 Bruxelles, BELGIUM. Telephone: +32-2-513-3400, Fax: +32-2-512-2528, Email: iapnsecret@iapn-coins.org, Website: www .iapn-coins.org
   IAPN's membership includes more than 114 numismatic firms in all five continents and twenty-three countries.
• SOCIETE ROYALE DE NUMISMATIQUE DE BELGIQUE, c/o Cabinet de Médailles, Bibliothéque Royale de Belgique, Boulevard de l'Empereur 4 á 1000 Bruxelles, BELGIUM. Contact: Luc Smolderen, Website: www.numisbel.be

CANADA

• THE ROYAL CANADIAN NUMISMATIC ASSOCIATION, 5694 Highway #7 East, Suite 432, Markham ON CANADA L3P 1B4. Telephone: 647-401-4014, Fax: 905-472-9645, Email: info@rcna.ca

The CNA is a nonprofit educational and social body incorporated by Dominion Charter in 1963. It has grown by leaps and bounds from an idea of dedicated numismatists to form the world's second largest numismatic association.

Their present membership is basically located in Canada and the United States but they do have additional members around the world. They all have one common interest and that is Canadian numismatics.

As a member of the Association you will be eligible to receive the CNA/NESA Numismatic Correspondence Course at a reduced cost. You will receive the Journal, *which carries articles, advertisements by dealers/members, and information about other CNA activities.*

The Journal *has been published since 1966 and has carried many of the most important papers relating to Canadian numismatics.*

CHINA

• ORIENTAL NUMISMATIC SOCIETY (ONS), c/o Dept. of Coins & Medals, British Museum, Great Russell St., London WC1B 3DG. Website: http://orientalnumismaticsociety.org, Email: robert@orientalnumismaticsociety.org

The aims of the Society are to promote the systematic study of the coins, medals, and currency, both ancient and modern, of India, the Far East, the Islamic countries and their non-Western predecessors. It was founded in 1970 and its membership of some 650 people is spread over 40 countries.

CROATIA

• CROATIAN NUMISMATIC SOCIETY, Croatian Numismatic DRUŠTVO, 10000 ZAGREB, MARGARETSKA 3, tel/fax 00 3851 492 0520.

A current price list for Bosnian, Croatian, Macedonian, Serbian, Slovenian, and Yugoslavian bank notes and coins is available from the society. This list is free to all interested collectors when accompanied by a stamped, self-addressed envelope from the U.S.A., or cost of postage from other countries. Also available from the society is a limited number of large geographic maps of the Independent State of Croatia, 1941–45, in color.

DENMARK

• DANISH TOKEN CLUB, fl.eis@mail.dk

• DANISH NUMISMATIC SOCIETY, Galionsvej 12.2 th DK, 1437 Copenhagen, Denmark. Email: preben.nielsen@youmail .dk, Website: numismatik.dk

FRANCE

• LA SOCIETE FRANCAISE DE NUMISMATIQUE 58 rue de Richelieu, 75 002 PARIS, FRANCE. Telephone: 01-53-79-86-26; Email: secretariat@sfnum.asso.fr; Website: www.sfnum .asso.fr

GERMANY

• DEUTSCHE NUMISMATISCHE GESELLSCHAFT, GERMANY Email: info@numismatische-gesellshaft.de; Website: www .numismatische-gesellschaft.de

GREECE

• HELLENIC NUMISMATIC SOCIETY, ELINIKOS COSMOS, Piraeos 254, Tavros (Athens) GR-177 78 GREECE. Telephone: +30-212-254-2930; Fax: +30-212-254-0123

ISRAEL

• AMERICAN ISRAEL NUMISMATIC ASSOCIATION, P.O. Box 20255, Fountain Hills, AZ 85269. Telephone: (818) 225-1348; Website: amerisrael.com

• ISRAEL NUMISMATIC SOCIETY, c/o The Israel Museum, P.O. Box 71117, Jerusalem 91710, ISRAEL. Telephone: +972-2-6708831

INDIA

• NUMISMATIC SOCIETY OF INDIA, P.O. Box Banaras Hindu University, Varanasi, 221-005 (U.P.) INDIA. Website: www.bhu .ac.in/aihc/ins.htm#9.htm

LITHUANIA

• LITHUANIAN NUMISMATIC ASSOCIATION—The Knight, P.O. Box 22696, Baltimore, MD 21203. Email: Lithnumis @hotmail.com

MALAYSIA

• MALAYSIA NUMISMATIC SOCIETY, P.O. Box 12367, Kuala Lumpur, 50776 MALAYSIA. Email: info@money.org.my, Website: www.money.org.my

MEXICO

• SOCIEDAD NUMISMATICA DE MEXICO A. C., Eugene No. 13-301, Col. Nápoles, C. P. 03810, MEXICO. Telephone: 5536-4440, FX: 5543-1791

The society publishes a trimestral bilingual journal. The society periodically organizes auctions. Members receive catalogs and prices realized of these auctions and may also place numismatic items of their own for auction sale.

NEW ZEALAND

• ROYAL NUMISMATIC SOCIETY OF NEW ZEALAND, G.P.O., Box 2023, Wellington, 6140 NEW ZEALAND. Website: www .msnz.com

PORTUGAL

• CLUBE NUMISMATIC DE PORTUGAL, Rua Angelina Vidal 40, 1170-020 Lisbon, PORTUGAL

• SOCIEDADE PORTUGUESA DE NUMISMATICA, Rua De Costa Cabral, 664, 4200-211 Porto PORTUGAL

RUSSIA

• RUSSIAN NUMISMATIC SOCIETY, P.O. Box 3684 Santa Rosa, CA, 95402. Contact: Sec. Treas., Telephone: 707-527-1007, FX: 707-527-1204, Email: RNSJournals@gmail.com, Website: russiannumismaticsociety.org.

The Society was established in 1979. Since 1981 the Society's journal, the JRNS, is published three times a year and is the principle element holding the Society to its course. In support of its editorial work, the Society maintains a very compre-

hensive library of standard and specialized works on Russian numismatics, many of which are available on loan to the members. The Society provides advice and support on research resources.

SOUTH AFRICA

• SOUTH AFRICAN NUMISMATIC SOCIETY, P.O. Box 1689, Cape Town, 8000 SOUTH AFRICA

SPAIN

• ASOCIACION NUMISMATICA ESPAÑOLA, Gran via de les Corts Catalanes, 627 08010 Barcelona, SPAIN. Telephone: +34-933-188-245, FX: +34-933-189-062, Email: ane@numisane .org, Website: www.numisane.org

SWITZERLAND

• NUMISMATISCHER VEREIN ZURICH, Postfach 2647, CH-8022, Zurich SWITZERLAND. Website: www.nvz-ch.org

• SWISS NUMISMATIC SOCIETY, Email: contact@numisuisse. ch, Website: www.numisuisse.ch

THAILAND

• NUMISMATIC ASSOCIATION OF THAILAND, P.O. Box 31, Jomtien Post Office THAILAND. Telephone: (038)231-370

TURKEY

• TURKISH NUMISMATIC SOCIETY, Haci Emin Efenoi Sokak Murat, Apt NO 7 D: 4 Tesvikiye, Istanbul, TURKEY. Telephone: +90-212-234-2268, Fax: +90-212-234-2567, Email: tnd @turknumismatik.org.tr, Website: www.turknumismatick.org.tr

UKRAINE

• UKRAINIAN PHILATELIC & NUMISMATIC SOCIETY, 157 Lucinda Ln, Wyomissing, PA 19610-1026 Website: www.upns.org
   The Society was founded in 1952 and concentrates on collectibles (coins, banknotes, stamps, etc.) of Ukrainian themes. The Society publishes a bimonthly newsletter and quarterly journal.

UNITED KINGDOM

• BRITISH ASSOCIATION OF NUMISMATIC SOCIETIES, c/o Manchester Museum, Oxford RD, Manchester M13 9PL, UK, Telephone: 0161-275-2643, Website: www.coinclubs.freeserve .co.uk

• BRITISH NUMISMATIC SOCIETY, c/o The Warburg Institute, Woburn Square, LONDON, WCIH OAB, United Kingdom, Website: britnumsoc.org

The British Numismatic Society was founded in 1903. The Society's terms of reference extend to cover all coins struck or used in Great Britain and Ireland from the introduction of coinage into Britain in the first century B.C. down to modern times. It also concerns itself with medals, tokens, etc., and with coinage of present or former British overseas territories and dependencies.

The British Numismatic Journal, *published annually by the Society and distributed to all paid-up members, provides the results of the most recent scholarly research into the history of the coinage, and records significant new numismatic discoveries. It is issued cloth-bound.*

• ROYAL NUMISMATIC SOCIETY, Dept. Coins/Medals, The British Museum, Great Russell Street, London WC1B 3DG, ENGLAND. Contact: ms_secretary@hotmail.co.uk

The Society was founded in 1836 as the Numismatic Society of London and received the title of the Royal Numismatic Society by Royal Charter in 1904. The Society is an academic body of charitable status concerned with research into all branches of numismatics. Its lectures and publications deal with classical, oriental, medieval, and modern coins, as well as paper money, tokens, and medals.

U.S.A.

• AMERICAN NUMISMATIC ASSOCIATION, 818 North Cascade Avenue, Colorado Springs, CO 80903-3279. Telephone: 719-632-2646, FX: 719-634-4085, Email: ana@money.org, Website: www.money.org

• AMERICAN NUMISMATIC SOCIETY, 75 Varick St., Floor 11, New York, NY 10013, Telephone: 212-571-4470, FX: 212-571-4479

• ANCIENT COIN CLUB OF LOS ANGELES, c/o L. Friedman, 16255 Ventura Blvd., Ste 1200, Encino, CA 91436-2363, Website: www.accla.org.

This club was established in 1966 and features highly informative and enjoyable programs on ancient Greek or Roman numismatics and cultures, as well as afternoons of coin trading exhibits and door prizes. Visitors are cordially invited to attend their meetings and meet others who share the same numismatic interests.

• CALIFORNIA EXONUMIST SOCIETY, 611 Oakwood Way, El Cajon, CA 91436

• INTERNATIONAL NUMISMATIC SOCIETY OF SAN DIEGO, Email: INSSDclub@gmail.com, Website: www.INSSD.org

The International Numismatic Society of San Diego pursues the interest of foreign numismatics.

• NUMISMATICS INTERNATIONAL, P.O. Box 570842, Dallas, TX 75357-0842. Website: www.numis.org

Numismatics International was formed in Dallas, Texas, in July 1964 and now has well over 800 members worldwide.

Their objectives are to encourage and promote the science of numismatics by specializing in areas and nations other than the United States; to cultivate fraternal relations among collectors and numismatic students; to encourage and assist new collectors; to foster the interest of youth in numismatics; to stimulate and advance affiliations among collectors and kindred organizations; and to acquire, share, and disseminate numismatic knowledge.

• SOCIETY FOR ANCIENT NUMISMATICS (SAN), P.O. Box 4085, Panarama City, CA 91412-4095. Contact: Dr. Lawrence A. Adams.

The Journal of the Society for Ancient Numismatics (SAN) is published twice yearly. The SAN Journal supports the field of ancient numismatics with its wide range of articles and illustrations by scholars, professional numismatists, collectors, and amateurs with special perspectives. The Journal may be found in many of the world's foremost university and museum libraries.

• SOCIETY FOR INTERNATIONAL NUMISMATICS, P.O. Box 943, Santa Monica, CA 90406. Contact: Barry Lapes, Telephone: 310-399-1085

The Society for International Numismatics is an international organization dedicated to the promotion of serious numismatic studies, endeavoring to bring to the collecting fraternity special items of interest and fundamental information. They hope their work will stimulate the individual study of numismatics from a practical as well as historical and economic viewpoint.

The Society's publications are: SINformation, *the Society's news journal;* COIN *(Compendium of International Numismatics), composed of original articles by Society members;* and NUMOGRAM, *a "Reader's Digest" of numismatic articles.*

The Society also publishes papers from its various bureaus on a periodic basis and presents educational forums and lecture programs for the collecting fraternity.

• WORLD PROOF NUMISMATIC ASSOCIATION, P.O. Box 4094, Pittsburgh, PA 15201. Contact: Gail P. Gray, Telephone: 412-782-4477, FX: 412-782-0227

INTERNATIONAL NUMISMATIC PUBLICATIONS

AUSTRALIA

• TASMANIAN NUMISMATIST, Newsletter of the Tasmanian Numismatic Society, Inc., PO Box 12, Claremont, Tasmania 7011, AUSTRALIA. Telephone: 036249-1369.

CANADA

• THE CN JOURNAL, The Royal Canadian Numismatic Association, Contact: Dan Gosling, 49 Sierra Grande Estates, Sherwood Park AB, Canada T8G 1A2, Telephone: 780-922-5743, Email: dan @gosling.ca. **Summary of content:** Aims to encourage and promote the science of numismatics by the study of coins, paper money, medals, tokens, and all other numismatic items, with special emphasis on material pertaining to Canada.

• CANADIAN COIN NEWS, PO Box 28103 Lakeport PO, 600 Ontario Street, St. Catharines, ONL2N 7P8 CANADA. Telephone: 905-646-7744, FX: 905-646-0995. Website: www.canadiancoinnews .com, Subscription/Book Orders 1-800-408-0352 **Summary of content:** Whether numismatist or novice, it brings the collector the most complete, most authoritative, and most timely news available, with features on tokens and paper money to the finest coverage of Canadian decimal coinage.

CZECH REPUBLIC

• NUMISMATICKE LISTY, Narodni Muzeum, Vaclavske nan.68, 115 79 Prague 1, CZECH REPUBLIC. Text in Czech; summaries in English, French, German, and Russian. Subscription available through Amazon.com.

DENMARK

• NORDISK NUMISMATISK UNION MEDLEMSBLAD, Nordisk Numismatisk Union, c/o Royal Collection of Coins and Medals, National Museum, Frederiksholms Kanal 12, DK-1220 Copenhagen K, DENMARK. FX: 45-33-15-55-21. Website: http://nnunion.net/

ENGLAND

• COIN NEWS, Token Publishing, Ltd., Orchard House, Duchy RD, Heath Park, Honiton, Devon EX 14 1YD, ENGLAND. Telephone: +44(0) 1404-44166, Fax: +44(0) 1404-44788, Email: subs @tokenpublishing.com, Website: www.tokenpublishing.com. **Summary of content:** General magazine for collectors covering coins, medals, and banknotes. The UK's best-selling coin magazine.

• COIN NEWS COIN YEARBOOK, Token Publishing, Ltd, Orchard House, Duchy RD, Heath Park, Honiton, Devon EX 14 1YD ENGLAND. Telephone: +44(0) 1404-44166, Fax: +44(0) 1404-44788, Email: subs@tokenpublishing.com, Website: www.tokenpublishing .com. **Summary of content:** Yearbook covering all aspects of coin collecting, and price guide to coins, banknotes, and medallions.

FINLAND

• NUMISMAATIKKO, Suomen Numismaatikkoliitto, P.O. Box 895, FIN-00101 Helsinki, FINLAND. Telephone: 358-31-631-480, FX: 358-31-631-480.

FRANCE

• NUMISMATIQUE & CHANGE, SEPS, 10, avenue Victor-Hugo 55800 Revigny-sur-Ornain, FRANCE. Telephone: 0-825-82-63-63, FX 03-29-70-57-44.

• REVUE NUMISMATIQUE (Societe Francaise de Numismatique), Societe d'Edition les Belles Lettres, 95 Boulevard Raspail, 75006 Paris, FRANCE. Telephone: 1-45485826, FX: 1-45485860. **Document type:** Academic/scholarly publication.

GERMANY

• DER GELDSCHEINSAMMLER, H. Gietl Verlag and Publikations Service GmbH, Postfach 166, 93122 Regenstauf, GERMANY. Telephone: 49-9402-5856, FX: 49-9402-6635. **Document type:** Newsletter.

• NUMISMATISCHES NACHRICHTENBLATT, Deutsche Numismatische Gesellschaft, Hans-Purrmann-Allee 26, 67346 Speyer, GERMANY. Telephone: 49-6232-35752. **Document type:** Newsletter.

GREECE

• NOMISMATIKA KHRONIKA, Hellenic Numismatic Society-Elleniki Nomismatiki Etaireia, Didotou 106 80 Athens, GREECE. Telephone: 30-1-3615-585, FX: 30-1-3634-296. **Document type:** Academic/scholarly publication, monographic series. **Summary of content:** Covers Greek and related numismatics of all periods. Translations or summaries in English.

INDIA

• JOURNAL NUMISMATIC SOCIETY OF INDIA, Numismatic Society of India, Banaras Hindu University, Varanasi 221005, INDIA. Telephone: 311074. Email: pnsingh-bhu@yahoo.com, Website: www.bhu.ac.in. Text in English.

ISRAEL

• ISRAEL NUMISMATIC JOURNAL, Israel Numismatic Society, c/o The Israel Museum, P.O. Box 711117, Jerusalem 91710, ISRAEL. Telephone: +972-2-6708831. Website: INS.org.il. **Document type:** Academic/scholarly publication. Text in English.

ITALY

• ISTITUTO ITALIANO DI NUMISMATICA, Istituto Italiano di Numismatica, Palazzo Barberini, Via Quattro Fontane 13, 00184 Rome, ITALY. Telephone: 39-6-4743603, FX: 39-6-4743603. Website: www. istitutoitaliannonumismatica.it. **Document type:** Academic/scholarly publication. **Summary of content:** Presents research on numismatic subjects.

• NUMISMATICA, Gino Manfredini, Ed. & Pub., Via Ferramola 1-A, 25121 Brescia, ITALY. Telephone: 030-3756211. **Document type:** Newsletter.

• PANORAMA NUMISMATICO, 75000, Via Grimau 6-A, 46029 Suzzara (MN), ITALY. Telephone: 39-376-532063, FX: 39-376-521304. **Document type:** Academic/scholarly publication. **Summary of content:** Covers ancient and Italian numismatics for collectors and scholars.

NETHERLANDS

• EUROPEAN NUMISMATICS, Uitgeverij Numismatica Nederland N.V., Darwinplantsoen 26, Amsterdam 6, NETHERLANDS. Text in Dutch and English.

• JAARBOEK VOOR MUNT-EN PENNINGKUNDE, Koninklijk Nederlands Genootschap voor Munt-en Penningkunde-Royal Dutch Society of Numismatics, c/o The Netherlands Bank, Postbus 98, 1000 AB Amsterdam, NETHERLANDS. **Document type:** Academic/scholarly publication. Text in Dutch, occasionally in English, French, German; summaries in English.

POLAND

• LODZKI NUMIZMATYK, Polskie Towarzystwo Archeologiczne i Numizmatyczne, Oddzial w Lodzi, Plac Wolnosci 14, Lodz, POLAND.

• WIADOMOSCI NUMIZMATYCZNE/NUMISMATIC NEWS, Ossolineum Publishing House, Foreign Trade Department, Rynek 9, 50-106 Wroclaw, POLAND.

SLOVAKIA

• SLOVENSKA NUMIZMATIKA (Slovenska Akademia Vied) Veda, Publishing House of the Slovak Academy of Sciences, Klemensova 19, 814, 30 Bratislava, SLOVAKIA. Text in Slovak.

SPAIN

• GACETA NUMISMATICA, Asociacion Numismatica Espanola, Gran Via de les Corts Catalanes, 627, 08010 Barcelona, SPAIN. Telephone: +34-933-188-245, Fax: +34-933-189-062, Email: ane @numisane.org, Website: www.numisane.org. **Document type:** Academic/scholarly publication.

SWEDEN

• NUMISMATISKA MEDDELANDEN NUMISMATIC COMMUNICATIONS, Svenska Numismatiska Foereningen, Banergatan 17 nb, S-115 22 Stockholm, SWEDEN. Telephone: 46-8-667-55-98, FX: 46-8-6670771. **Document type:** Academic/scholarly publication.

SWITZERLAND

• GAZETTE NUMISMATIQUE SUISSE/SCHWEIZER MUENZBLAETTER, Alexander Wild, Rathausgasse 30, CH-3011 Bern, SWITZERLAND. **Document type:** Newsletter.

• HAUTES ETUDES NUMISMATIQUES (Ecole Pratique des Hautes Etudes, Centre de Recherches d'Histoire et de Philologie, FR), Librairie Droz S.A., 11, rue Massot, CH-1211 Geneva 12, SWITZERLAND. Telephone: 41-22-3466666, FX: 41-22-3472391,

Website: www.ephe.sorbonne.fr, circ. 500. **Document type:** Monographic series. **Summary of content:** Examines ancient coins.

• MUENZEN-REVUE, International Coin Trend Journal, Verlag Muenzen-Revue AG, Blotzheimerstr.40, CH-4055 Basel, SWITZERLAND. Telephone: 41-61-3825504, FX: 41-61-3825542. **Document type:** Trade publication. **Summary of content:** Feature news, history, values, new coins, trade, as well as reports of events and auctions for coin hobbyists. Subscriptions available on Amazon.com.

• NUMISMATICA E ANTICHITA CLASSICHE, Amici dei Quaderni Ticinesi di Numismatica e Antichita Classiche, Secretariat, C.P.3157, CH-6901 Lugano, SWITZERLAND. Telephone: 41-91-6061606. **Document type:** Academic/scholarly publication. Text in English, French, German, and Italian.

• REVUE SUISSE DE NUMISMATIQUE/SCHWEIZERISCHE NUMISMATISCHE RUNDSCHAU, Societe Suisse de Numismatique-Schweizerische Numismatische Gesellschaft, Niederdorfstr. 43, CH-8001 Zurich, SWITZERLAND. Website: numisuisse.ch. **Document type:** Newsletter.

USA

• AMERICAN JOURNAL OF NUMISMATICS, American Numismatic Society, 75 Varick St., 11th FLR, NY, NY 10013, Telephone: 212-571-4470, Fax: 212-571-4479, Website: http://numismatics.org, Email: numlit@numismatics.org. **Summary of content:** Academic analysis of numismatic objects contributing to the understanding and interpretation of history, political science, archaeology, and art history.

• CLASSICAL NUMISMATIC REVIEW, Classical Numismatic Group, Inc., P.O. Box 479, Lancaster, PA 17608-0479. Telephone: 717-390-9194, FX: 717-390-9978. Website: www.cngcoins.com.

• COIN WORLD, P.O. Box 4315, Sidney, OH 45365, Telephone: 1-800-253-4555. **Document type:** Weekly newspaper. **Summary:** Editorials on U.S. and world coinage, price listing, and dealer advertisements.

• PROOF COLLECTORS CORNER, World Proof Numismatic Association, Box 4094, Pittsburgh, PA 15201. Telephone: 412-782-4477, FX: 412-782-0227. Website: www.coinmall.com, Email: worldproofna@aol.com. **Document type:** Trade publication. **Summary of content:** Provides current coverage of numismatic issues, with information on the history and background of coins.

• SHEKEL, American Israel Numismatic Association, P.O. Box 940277, Rockaway Park, NY 11694-0277. Telephone: 718-634-9266, FX: 718-318-1455. **Document type:** Academic/scholarly publication. **Summary of content:** Presents collection of Israel and Judaic coins, medals, and currency from antiquity to the present.

• SINFORMATION, Society for International Numismatics, PO Box 5207, Sherman Oaks, CA 91413. Telephone: 818-788-1129, Website: www.coinbooks.org. **Document type:** Newsletter.

• THE CELATOR, P.O. Box 10607, Lancaster, PA 17605-0607, Telephone: 717-656-8557, Email: Kerry@celator.com, Website: www.celator.com. **Document type:** Consumer publication. **Summary of content:** Articles and features about ancient and medieval coins and artifacts, and antiquities.

HOW TO USE
THIS BOOK

This book was written as a guide to the world's most popular coins. To list every coin that was ever minted by every country in the world would fill a book many times this size. We, therefore, have chosen to list the coins that are readily available to the average collector, with prices that would accommodate the largest number of collectors. Considerable effort was expended to consolidate and verify the information listed. Should you have any questions or corrections, the authors would be grateful to hear your comments. Please write to: *Blackbooks,* P.O. Box 690312, Orlando, FL 32869.

The prices listed in this book represent the current collector values at the time of printing. Since some of the types and varieties of coinage fluctuate in price more than others, it would be wise to consult several sources, i.e. coin dealers and trade publications, before any transaction.

Apart from the chapter immediately following titled "Ancient Coins," each coin listing in this guide contains the following information:

DATE or DATE RANGE—Date ranges were used to conserve space. Likewise, listings for coins later than 1980 were generally omitted because of their minimal collector value.

COIN TYPE—This is the unit of measure on the face value of the coin.

VARIETY—This information usually describes the images that appear on either the obverse (front) or the reverse (back) of the coin. Please note that some varieties of the same denomination may command a higher price than others of the same denomination.

METAL—When known, the metallic content of the coin is listed.

ABP—This is the average buy price that coin dealers are buying from the public. Readers should understand that the actual prices paid by any given dealer will vary based on the dealer's inventory and the market demand in the dealer's specific area. Remember that this book is presented merely as a guide.

There are two reasons for not listing an ABP price for a particular coin. The first concerns *coins that* are not *made from a precious metal* (gold, silver, or platinum). If there is no price listed for this kind of coin, it means that the price that a dealer would pay would be minimal.

ABP prices are also not listed for *coins that* are *made of gold, silver, or platinum.* The reason for this is that the dealers usually buy this kind of coin based on its bullion value. In most cases they will pay you for the amount of gold, silver, or platinum that the coin contains plus a premium, i.e. the bullion "spot" price plus a percentage. When determining the melt or bullion value of the coin, the dealer not only will have to consider the weight of the coin, but he will also have to determine the purity level of the gold, silver, or platinum, i.e. pure silver (.999), sterling silver (.925), etc. These variables make it difficult for an inexperienced dealer to calculate the bullion value of a coin. We recommend contacting dealers that have experience in dealing in bullion coinage. We have included a bullion value chart in this book which you can use to approximate the bullion value, assuming the coin is made from gold, silver, or platinum. Don't forget that the purity level of the gold, silver, or platinum will affect the bullion value.

CURRENT RETAIL VALUES—These prices are listed in either average fine or average UNC (uncirculated) condition. It is of utmost importance that a coin be accurately graded before a value can be determined. Although *there is no universally accepted grading standards for world coinage,* we have adopted the two U.S. grading conditions of AVERAGE FINE and AVERAGE UNC for the purposes of this book.

AVERAGE FINE condition would be represented by a coin that exhibited a moderate amount of wear, but still had visible signs of all of the detail that could be found on a coin of UNC condition. Usually the higher relief areas on the coin show the most wear.

AVERAGE UNC condition or uncirculated condition would be a coin that was never in general circulation. Current issues of uncirculated coins can be purchased directly from the mints where they are made, or from dealers or other collectors. Usually the finish of an uncirculated coin is much brighter, with very few surface scratches. When building a collection with the more current issues, you should try to collect UNC specimens when possible.

PRICES—The prices that are listed are average prices for coins that were minted in that particular date range. The price for a coin of a specific date in that particular date range will vary slightly from the price indicated. This variation in price is based on several variables. Some of the factors that affect the price of a coin are: 1) the amount of coins that were minted, 2) the amount of coins in circulation, 3) the demand for that coin in your geographic area, and 4) the condition in which the coin is generally found.

INVENTORY CHECKLIST—For the purposes of record keeping, we have included a ☐ at the beginning of each listing. Write a check mark or darken the ☐ in front of each coin in your collection. By doing this you will have a portable record of your collection to take with you to coin shows and dealers.

We hope that you enjoy using this book and invite you to become familiar with the other books in the *Official Blackbook Price Guide* series.

There is the best-selling *Official Blackbook Price Guide of U.S. Coins* which lists more than 16,000 prices for every U.S. coin minted, including colonial tokens, farthings, halfpennies, and gold pieces, plus sections on varieties and errors. It is fully illustrated.

There is also the *Official Blackbook Price Guide of U.S. Paper Money* which lists more than 6,000 prices for every national note issued from 1861 to date, including demand notes, national bank notes, silver and gold certificates, treasury notes, federal reserve notes, and confederate currency. It too is fully illustrated.

And finally, there is the *Official Blackbook Price Guide of U.S. Postage Stamps* which lists more than 20,000 prices for general U.S. postage stamps issued from 1847 to date, plus revenue, stock transfer and hunting permit stamps, United Nations issues, mint sheets, and first day covers. It is fully illustrated in color.

These books are available from your local bookstores, coin shops, and from the publisher.

PNG—THE PROFESSIONAL NUMISMATISTS GUILD

The Professional Numismatists Guild, founded in 1955, had its inception in 1950 with Abe Kosoff. At the time, Kosoff was in partnership with Abner Kreisberg in Numismatic Gallery, a firm that was well known for handling major collections and rarities.

Kosoff and several other coin dealers believed that the hobby of coin collecting could be better served if a professional group was organized. After much effort, the Professional Numismatists Guild was established. Its motto, "Knowledge, Integrity, Responsibility" continues to reflect the aims of the not-for-profit organization.

For the first decade, membership in the Professional Numismatists Guild (PNG) was by invitation, and only a small number of dealers were asked to join. As time passed, the PNG achieved stature, experience, and wisdom, and the membership rolls were expanded.

Today, the PNG comprises a membership across the United States and abroad of virtually all leading professional numismatists. The depth and breadth of the membership brings a rich diversity to the group and has made its progress possible.

MEMBERSHIP IN THE GUILD

To join the PNG, a dealer must have experience in the field, must certify that he or she has significant financial worth, and must be elected by a majority of the present members. All the PNG members are subject to the rules and regulations of the Guild, which include an arbitration procedure for resolving disagreements between buyers and sellers of numismatic properties.

The Professional Numismatists Guild looks forward to many more years of enhancing the field of numismatics through adherence to strict ethical and professional standards, cooperative projects with the American Numismatic Association, educational efforts geared to hobbyists, and other programs to benefit what has rightfully been called the world's greatest hobby.

AAMLID, Jan Olav
(PNG #356)
OSLO MYNTHANDEL AS
Ovre Slottsgate 6
House of the Golden Coin
193/119 Moo 10,
South Pattaya Road
Nangprue
Banglamung, Chonburi
Thailand 20230
Tel: (+66) 818 45504
Fax: (+66) 384 20090
Hours: By appointment
e-mail: *coin@loxinfo.co.th*
website: *www.tahicoins.com*
Specialties: *Scandinavian
coins & banknotes. Thai coins
& banknotes. Ancient Roman &
Greek coins. Coins of the world
in all medals.*

ABBOTT, John T.
(PNG #669)
ABBOTT'S CORPORATION
33700 Woodward Avenue
Birmingham, MI 48009
Tel: (248) 644-8565
Fax: (248) 644-7038
Hours: 9–6 Mon.–Fri., 9–4 Sat.
e-mail: *John@abbottscorp.com*
website: *www.abbottscorp.com*
Specialties: *Buying & selling
collections, appraisals &
portfolios.*

ABBOTT, Michael
(PNG #670)
MICHAEL D. ABBOTT NUMIS-
MATICS
4501 Cartwright Rd
STE 502
Missouri City, TX 77459
Tel: (281) 222-2646
(281) 437-9334
Fax: (281) 969-8943
e-mail:
vopalensky281@yahoo.com

ABEL, Tony
(PNG #621)
SILVERTOWNE
120 East Union City Pike
Winchester, IN 47394
Tel: (765) 584-7481
Fax: (765) 584-1246
e-mail: *sales@silvertowne.com*
website: *silvertowne.com*

ADKINS, Gary
(PNG #352)
Gary Adkins Associates, Inc
5151 Edina Industrial Blvd
STE 200
Minneapolis, MN 55439
Tel: (952) 835-2244
(877) 264-6383
Fax: (952) 835-2266
Hours: 9–5 Mon.–Fri. or
by appointment
Fixed price list. PCGS, NGC,
ANACS authorized dealer.
Appraisals, liquidations.
e-mail: *gary@coinbuys.com*
website: *www.coinbuys.com*
Specialties: *Rare coins and
currency. Gold, silver, and
platinum bullion. Collections and
estate appraisals, liquidations,
and auctions.*

ADKINS, Tony
(PNG #A632)
SUMMIT RARE COINS
P.O. Box 390508
Minneapolis, MN 55439-0508
Tel: (952) 767-3800
Fax: (952) 835-1246
By appointment only
e-mail:
tony@srcnumismatics.com
Specialties: *All U.S. coins,
including rare gold, silver, and
copper coins, bust and seated
coinage, patterns, currency, 20th-
century rarities, gold and silver
bullion; PCGS and NGC; estates, liquidations, and appraisal.*

AKERS, David W.
(PNG #279)
DAVID AKERS NUMISMATICS, INC.
P.O. Box 373
Stuart, FL 34995-0373
Tel: (772) 219-4557
Fax: (772) 223-1964
Hours: By appointment only
e-mail: *DWA38@aol.com*

ALBANESE, John
(PNG #686)
CERTIFIED ACCEPTANCE CORP.
P.O. Box 1776
Far Hills, NJ 07931
Tel: (908) 781-9101
Fax: (908) 781-0746
websites: *www.caccoin.com,
www.stopcoinfraud.org,
www.coinplex.com*
e-mail: shield30@aol.com
Hours: By appointment only

ALLEVA, Buddy
(PNG #441)
Long Island Rare Coins
& Currency/Numismatics
Unlimited, Inc.
187 Veterans Blvd., STE. 2
Massapequa, NY 11758
Tel: (866) 355-2646
Fax: (516) 797-8421
e-mail: *nuicoins@optonline
.net*
website: *www.longislandrarecoins
.com*
Specialties: *Want list
specialist. Assistance
in building collections
& sets of all U.S. coins.
Specializing in appraisals,
U.S. commemoratives, U.S.
currency, U.S. gold coins,
patterns, type coins & silver
dollars. "Always customer
friendly!"*

ANKERMAN, Walt
(PNG #401)
CARLSBAD VILLAGE COINS
2977 State St
Carlsbad, CA 92008
Tel: (760) 434-6601
Hours: By appointment only
Fixed price lists.
Specialties: *Buying and selling
all types of United States
& foreign coins; all grading
services available.*

ATKINS, Gary
(PNG # 606)
EAGLE HILLS COINS
P.O. Box 399
Eagle, ID 83616
Tel: (208) 455-9559
Fax: (208) 455-9565
e-mail: *ronnierosen@qwest.net*
website:
www.eaglehillscoins.com

AVENA, Daniel J., Sr.
(PNG #376)
ARC INC. T/A AVENA RARE COIN
2581 E. Chestnut Ave., Ste. B
Vineland, NJ 08361
Tel: (800) 272-2646
(856) 794-1600
Fax: (856) 794-8818
Hours: 8AM-5PM
e-mail: *info@avenararecoin.com*
website: *www.avenararecoin.com*
Specialties: *Buyers and sellers
of all U.S. rare coins.*

AVENA, Daniel J. Jr.
(PNG #500)
ARC INC. T/A AVENA RARE COIN
2581 E. Chestnut Ave., Ste. B
Vineland, NJ 08361
Tel: (800) 272-2646
(856) 794-1600
Fax: (856) 794-8818
Hours: 8AM–5PM

e-mail: *info@avenararecoin.com*
website:
www.avenararecoin.com
Specialties: *Buyers and sellers of all U.S. rare coins.*

AVENA, Robert L.
(PNG #377)
ARC INC. T/A AVENA RARE COIN
2581 E. Chestnut Ave., Ste. B
Vineland, NJ 08361
Tel: (800) 272-2646
(856) 794-1600
Fax: (856) 794-8818
Hours: 8AM–5PM
e-mail:
info@avenararecoin.com
website:
www.avenararecoin.com
Specialties: *Buyers and sellers of all U.S. rare coins.*

BAGG, Richard A., Ph.D.
(PNG #R586)
NUMISMATIC ADVISOR, LLC
Newburyport, MA 01950
Tel: (978) 255-1127
website:
linkedin.com/in/richardbagg
e-mail: *rickbagg@hotmail.com*
Hours: By appointment
Notes: For over 40 years, served as negotiator and agent for thousands of clients with several hundred millions of dollars in coins who have sold their holdings through public auction or by outright sale
Specialty: *I am available to buy and sell coins and currency of all types, assemble and appraise collections, construct investment portfolios and I consult with those who wish to auction their material as to which auction house to choose and how to go about negotiating commissions.*

BARNETT, Loren D.
(PNG #427)
BARNETT RARITIES CORP.
P.O. Box 2277
Birmingham, MI 48012
Tel: (248) 644-1124
Fax: (248) 644-3739
e-mail: *BarnettRarities@aol.com*
Specialties: *U.S. gold coins, to the trade.*

BART, Frederick J.
(PNG #585)
BART, INC.
P.O. Box 2
Roseville, MI 48066
Tel: (586) 979-3400
Fax: (586) 979-7976
e-mail: *BartIncCor@aol.com*
website: *executivecurrency.com*
Hours:10–6 EST
Specialties: *United States paper money, gold and silver coins.*

BATTAGLIA, Joseph C.
(PNG #A-517)
GOLDLINE INTERNATIONAL
100 Wilshire Blvd., 3rd floor
Santa Monica, CA 90401
Tel: (310) 319-0205
Fax: (310) 319-0265
Hours: M–F 7–5 PST
e-mail: *clientservices@ goldlinecoins.com*
website: *www.goldline.com*
Specialties: *U.S. gold and silver coins, Saint Gaudens, Morgan Dollars, Peace Dollars, and French and Swiss Francs.*

BATTINO, Mitchell
(PNG #662)
HUDSON RARE COINS, INC.
P.O. Box 7177
Princeton, NJ 08543
Tel: (212) 819-0737
Fax: (212) 819-9127
Hours: By appointment

e-mail: *hudsonrc@att.net*
website:
www.hudsonrarecoins.com
Specialties: *U.S. and world
coins in gold and silver, appraisals of collections and estates; certified member of
Appraisers Association of America (AAA), numismatic consultant, author, and cataloguer.*

BEEGLE, Allan P.
(PNG #696)
LIBERTY COIN SERVICE
400 Frandor Ave.,
Lansing, MI 48912
Tel: (517) 351-4720
Fax: (517) 351-3466
Website: *libertycoinservice.com*
E-mail:
allanb@libertycoinservice.com
Hours: M–F 10–6, Sat. 10–2

BELLISARIO, Lee J.
(PNG #402)
BELLISARIO RARE COIN
GALLERY, LLC
5 Cameron Street
Wellesley, MA 02482
Tel: (781) 235-1949
(617) 513-4450
Fax: (781) 235-9179
e-mail:
bellisariorarecoins@gmail.com
Hours: M–F 10–5
Specialties: *Rare U.S. gold
and silver coins. Contributor
to guide book of U.S. Coins,
dealer #4 for PCGS. In business since 1968.*

BERG , David
(PNG #258)
DAVE BERG, LTD.
P.O. Box 348
Portersville, PA 16051
Tel: (724) 452-4586
Fax: (724) 452-0276

e-mail: *davbergltd@aol.com*
Free price list upon request.
Specialties: *United States
paper money.*

BERGELT, Jeffrey P.
(PNG #403)
BERGELT INTERNATIONAL,
INC.
P.O. Box 1627
Ft. Lee, NJ 07024
Tel: (201) 592-8599
(201) 592-8587
Fax: (201) 592-9219
Hours: 9:30–4:00 Mon.–Fri. by
appointment only.
e-mail: *jbergelt@msn.com*
Specialties: *U.S. gold coins,
World gold coins, U.S. silver
dollars.*

BERK, Aaron
(PNG #607)
HARLAN J BERK, LTD.
31 N. Clark Street
Chicago, IL 60602
Tel: (312) 609-0016
Fax: (312) 609-1305
Hours: 9-5
Bimonthly buy or bid sales.
e-mail: *aaron@hjbltd.com*
website: *www.hjbltd.com*
Specialties: *Ancient Greek,
Roman and Byzantine coinage
of the finest quality. U.S. coins
& bullion, antiquities, stamps &
autographs.*

BERK, Harlan J.
(PNG #178)
HARLAN J BERK, LTD.
31 North Clark Street,
Chicago, IL 60602
Tel: (312) 609-0016
Fax: (312) 609-1309
Website: *hjbltd.com*
E-mail: *info@hjbltd.com*
Hours: 9–5

Bimonthly buy or bid sales.
Specialties: *Ancient Greek, Roman, and Byzantine coinage of the finest quality. U.S. coins & bullion, antiquities, stamps, & autographs.*

BERK-SCHMIDT, Shanna
(PNG #671)
HARLAN J. BERK, LTD.
31 N. Clark Street
Chicago, IL 60602
Tel: (312) 609-0026
Fax: (312) 609-1309
e-mail: shanna@hjbltd.com
website: *www.hjbltd.com*
Specialties: *ancient coins, U.S. coins, world coins, paper money, antiquities.*

BERNBERG, Jeffrey F.
(PNG #297)
RARE COIN COMPANY OF AMERICA, INC., RARCOA, INC.
7550 S. Quincy St.
Willowbrook, IL 60527
Tel: (630) 654-2580
Fax: (630) 654-3556
Hours: 8-4 by appointment
e-mail: *jbernberg@rarcoa.com*
website: *www.rarcoa.com*
HESS-DIVO LTD.
Zurich, Switzerland.
Specialties: *All U.S. coins in gold, silver & copper. Ancient & foreign coins in gold, silver & copper; auctions, major market maker & importer of U.S. gold coins. Contact us for a free copy of the Rarcoa Gold Sheet.*

BEYMER, Jack H.
(PNG #259)
JACK BEYMER, INC.
2490 West 3rd St.
Santa Rosa, CA 95401
Tel: (707) 544-1621

Fax: (707) 575-5304
Hours: 9–5 Mon.–Sat.
Fixed price lists.
Specialties: *Early U.S. Copper coins, Barber series, seated coins, type coins.*

BIANCO, Mike
(PNG #535)
MIKE BIANCO RARE COIN
P.O. Box 231878
Encinitas, CA 92023
Tel: (760) 436-3637
Fax: (760) 436-3784
Hours: 9–5 Mon.–Fri.
Specialties: *Highgrade gold, type, gold & silver commemoratives. Pre-1930 cigar box labels.*

BOHNERT, Brad
(PNG #442)
THE NUMISMATIC EMPORIUM, INC.
P.O. Box 929
Woodland Hills, CA 91367
Tel: (818) 887-2723
Fax: (818) 887-0301
Hours: Wholesale to the trade only.
Specialties: *U.S. gold coins.*

BONHAM, Mike
(PNG #658)
MIKE BONHAM, LLC
TANGIBLE INVESTMENTS
1910 S. Coast Hwy.,
Laguna Beach, CA 92651
Tel: (949) 715-5333
Fax: (949) 715-6703
Cell: (949) 878-0393
e-mail: *mike@gocoins.com*
website: gocoins.com
Hours: 8–5 pm
Specialty: *Auction advice, rare U.S. gold coins, rare type coins, top 100 U.S. coins, bullion, appraisals,*

buying, consulting/rare coin portfolios. Gold, silver, platinum, palladium, pre-1933 gold, evaluations.

BOZARTH, Victor
(PNG #661)
BOZARTH NUMISMATICS, INC.
P.O. Box 771
Brenham, TX 77833
Tel: (979) 421-9814
Fax: (979) 421-9815
eBay: *bozarthnumismaticsinc*
e-mail: *bozarthnumismatics @sbcglobal.net*
website: *bozarthcoins.com*
Specialties: *always buying high-grade, U.S. coinage.*

BROWN, Nicholas
(PNG #652)
MAJESTIC RARITIES, LLC
501 N. Clinton, Unit 2503
Chicago, IL 60654
Tel: (888) 714-1776
Fax: (312) 879-1776
e-mail: *npb@majesticrarities.com*
website: *www.majesticrarities.com*
Specialties: *modern Chinese, U.S. key date, U.S. error coins.*

BROWNE, Charles
(PNG #610)
CHARLES BROWNE CO.
P.O. Box 369
East Derry, NH 03041
Tel: (603) 479-3935
(603) 432-0823
Fax: (603) 432-0823
e-mail: *cbbiscuit51@yahoo.com*
Specialties: *type coin specialist, copper-nickel silver-gold; appraisals and consultations for attorneys, banks, and collectors; professional coin grader.*

BRUSH, John Stanford
(PNG #A619)
DAVID LAWRENCE RARE COINS
P.O. Box 9174
Virginia Beach, VA 23450
Tel: (800) 776-0560
Fax: (866) 581-2254
Hours: 9 a.m.–5 p.m. (EST)
e-mail: *john.brush@davidlawrence.com*
website: *www.davidlawrence.com*
Specialties: *U.S. coins.*

BULLOWA, Mrs. C.E.
(PNG #LM3)
COINHUNTER
1616 Walnut Street, Suite 2112
Philadelphia, PA 19103-5364
Tel: (215) 735-5517
Fax: (215) 735-5722
Appointment preferred; Mon-Fri 9-4
Specialties: *U.S., foreign, numismatic books, appraisals.*
Established 1952.

BURD, William A.
(PNG #539)
CHICAGO COIN CO., INC
6455 W. Archer Avenue
Chicago, IL 60638
Tel: (773) 586-7666
Fax: (773) 586-7754
Mon-Fri 8-4:30, Sat 8-1
e-mail: *chicagocoin@att.net*
website: *www.chicagocoin.com*
Specialties: *U.S. coins, gold coins, currency; wholesale bullion to the trade*

Executive Director
BRUEGGEMAN, Robert
(PNG #AF526)
POSITIVE PROTECTION, INC.
28441 Rancho California Rd #106
Temecula, CA 92590
(760) 728-1300

Fax: (760) 728-8507
e-mail: *bob@ppius.com*
website: *www.ppius.com*
Specialties: *Security.*

CALDWELL, Tom
(PNG #646)
NORTHEAST NUMISMATICS
INC.
10 Concord Crossing
Suite 220
Concord, MA 01742
Tel: (978) 369-9155
(800) 449-2646
Fax: (978) 369-9619
By appointment
e-mail: *tom@northeastcoin.com*
website:
www.northeastcoin.com
Specialties: *buying and selling all U.S. and world coinage, appraisals and estate liquidations.*

CAMPBELL, Randy
(PNG #709)
INDEPENDENT COIN
GRADERS
P.O. Box 267000
Tampa, FL 33688
Tel: (813) 963-2401
(877) 221-4424
Fax: (813) 969-2890
e-mail: *customersatisfaction @icgcoin.com*
website: *icgcoin.com*

CAMPBELL, H. Robert (Bob)
(PNG #537)
ALL ABOUT COINS, INC.
1123 E. 2100 South
Salt Lake City, UT 84106
Tel: (801) 467-8636
Fax: (801) 467-4471
Hours: Tues.-Fri. 10-6, Sat.
10-5, MST Closed Sun. Mon.
We are an old fashioned type of coin shop. We also sell metal detectors.

e-mail:
allaboutcoins@qwestoffice.net
Specialties: *Rainbow toning on coins, western trade tokens and medals. Mormon gold coins, tokens, & medals. 200+ different books and a complete line of supplies for sale. Past ANA president.*

CARR, David G.
(PNG #593)
RARE COINS OF NORTH
AMERICA, LLC
P.O. Box 246
North Reading, MA 01864
Tel: (978) 771-1995
Specialties: *All rare U.S. coins; buy, sell, or trade.*

CARTER, Jason L.
(PNG #554)
CARTER NUMISMATICS, INC.
1218 E. 33rd Street
Tulsa, OK 74105
Tel: (918) 583-2646
(800) 817-2646
Fax: (918) 583-9533
Hours: 9:00 a.m.–5:30 p.m. CT
High-end certified U.S. coins, rare bust and seated material.
e-mail:
jason@carternumismatics.com
website:
www.carternumismatics.com
Specialties: *Liberty seated rarities, early type coins, gold rarities.*

CASPER, Michael I.
(PNG #576)
MICHAEL I. CASPER, RARE
COINS, INC.
P.O. Box 40
Ithaca, NY 14851
Tel. (607) 257-5349
Fax: (607) 266-7904
Hours: 24/7
e-mail: *michael@caspercoin.com*

website: *www.caspercoin.com*
Specialties: *Morgan Silver Dollars, bullion, and United States stamps.*

CAWLEY, John
(PNG #544)
DILLON GAGE, INC. OF DALLAS
P.O. Box 171
Hamilton, Montana 59840
Tel: (406) 363-7490
Cell: (214) 213-5084
Hours: By appointment & all major coin conventions.
e-mail: *railman@cybernet1.com*
Specialties: *Primarily U.S. gold— circs, slabs, large lots—including rarities & branch mint coins in all grades, damaged to proof.*

CAYON FERNANDEZ, Juan Ramon   (PNG #306)
JANO S.L.
Augusto Figueroa 4-baijo
Madrid 28004, Spain
Tel: (0034) 91 5210832
Fax: (0034) 91 5233585
Publications, catalogs, auctions and lists.
e-mail: *juanr@moncayon.com*
website: *monayon.com*
Specialties: *Spanish world & ancient world.*

CHANG, Wei T.
(PNG #624)
THE WTC GROUP INC.
1712 Miramonte Ave., Suite A
Mountain View, CA 94040
Tel: (650) 619-9228
Fax: (408) 255-1949
Hours: By appointment only.

CHRAMOSTA, Robert
(PNG #638)
TIMES PAST
6222 Richmond Ave #540

Houston, TX 77057
Tel: (713) 977-7296
Fax: (713) 977-7297
Hours: Mon–Thurs 9–5; Fri 9–1; Sat by appointment
e-mail: *rob@timespast.us*
website: *www.timespastcollections.com*
Specialties: *U.S. gold and silver coins, type coins, proof and mint, and mint state and U.S. currency.*

CHARVILLE, Brett
(PNG #712)
STANDARD NUMISMATICS, LLC
Chicago, IL
Tel: (888) 331-2646
Fax: (312) 257-3075
e-mail: *brett @standardnumismatics.com*
website: *standardnumismatics.com*
Specialties: *Type and gold rarities. Certified dollars.*

COOK, Howard C., JR
(PNG #563)
HCC, INC.
7151 Spring Meadows Drive West
P.O. Box 560
Holland, OH 43528
Tel: (419) 865-8461
(800) 422-4405
Hours: 9–5 Mon.–Fri.
e-mail: *howard@hcc-coin.com*
website: *www.hcc-coin.com*
Specialties: *Investment grade rare coins. Banking coin program services.*

COULSON, Thomas W.
(PNG #697)
LIBERTY COIN SERVICE
400 Frandor Ave.,
Lansing, MI 48912
Tel: (517) 351-4720

Fax: (517) 351-3466
e-mail:
coulsontw69@yahoo.com
website: *libertycoinservice.com*
Hours: M–F 10–6, Sat. 10–2

COUNTS, Mary
(PNG #639)
WHITMAN PUBLISHING, LLC
301 Clairmont Rd.
STE C
Atlanta, GA 30329
Tel. (404) 235-5317
Fax: (404) 214-4398
e-mail:
mary.counts@whitmanbooks.com
website: *www.whitmanbooks.com.*

CRANE, Marc
(PNG #565)
MARC ONE NUMISMATICS,
INC
P.O. Box 8048
Newport Beach, CA 92658
Tel: (800) 346-2721
(714) 258-0954
Fax: (888) 440-6441
9–5 by appt. M–F
e-mail: *marc@marconeinc.com*
website: *www.marconeinc.com*
Specialties: *U.S. gold and
all U.S. coins including
patterns. Instant payment
for all coins, paper money,
collections & estates, etc.
Portfolio management including
acquisitions & liquidations.
Numerous references upon
request.*

CROSS, William K.
(PNG #181)
CHARLTON PRESS
P.O. Box 820, Station
Willowdale B
North York, Ontario,
Canada M2K 2R1
Tel: (800) 442-6042 or
(416) 488-1418

Fax: (800) 442-1542
Call for appointment.
e-mail:
chpress@charltonpress.com
website:
www.charltonpress.com

CRUM, Adam J.
(PNG #620)
MONACO FINANCIAL, LLC
4900 Birch St.
Newport Beach, CA 92660
(949) 752-1933
Fax: (949) 251-0139
e-mail: *acrum@fea.net*
website:
www.monacorarecoin.com
Specialties: *high-end rare
coins.*

DANNREUTHER, John West
(PNG #299)
Box 3330
Memphis, TN 38173-0330
Tel. (901) 523-9687
Fax: (901) 523-2995
Hours: By appointment only
Fixed price lists, publications.
e-mail: *jdrc@mindspring.com*
website: *www.jdrarecoins.com*
Specialties: *PCGS graded rare
& choice U.S. coins.*

DARAY, Dennis A.
(PNG #584)
SOUTHERN COINS &
PRECIOUS METALS
4513 Zenith St.
Metairie, LA 70001
Tel: (504) 887-0000
(800) 535-9704
Fax: (504) 887-0071
Hours: 9–5:30 CDT
e-mail: *Dennis@scpm.com*
website: *www.scpm.com*
Specialties: *U.S. Rarities,
Morgan & Peace dollars. PCGS*

& NGC certified U.S. gold, silver & type coins.

DEEDS, Steve
(PNG #250)
MORGAN GOLD
19900 MacArthur Blvd.,
Suite 150
Irvine, CA 92612
Tel: (800) 585-1773
Fax: (949) 387-5335
e-mail: stevedeeds@coins.com
website: morgangold.com
Hours: 8–5
Specialties: U.S. and European gold coins and bullion coins.

DEGLER, Klaus J.
(PNG #463)
ROCKY MOUNTAIN COIN
EXCHANGE, INC.
538 S. Broadway
Denver, CO 80209
Tel: (303) 777-GOLD
CoinNet CO-01
Fax: (303) 733-4946
Hours: 9:30–5:00 M–F
e-mail:
RMCoin@qwestoffice.net
website: www.RMcoin.com
Specialties: U.S. gold, gem & rare foreign crowns, national currency, U.S. type coins, medals & tokens.

DELOREY, Thomas K.
(PNG #602)
P.O. Box 751
Blue Island, IL 60406
Tel: (708) 362-4053
e-mail: tomdelorey@aol.com
website: www.hjbltd.com

DENLY, Thomas M.
(PNG #358)
DENLY'S COINS OF BOSTON
P.O. Box 51010
10 High Street Room 1107
Boston, MA 02110
Tel: (617) 482-8477
(800) HI-DENLY
Fax: (617) 357-8163
Hours: 9–5 Mon.–Fri. Call by phone; not open to public
Fixed price lists as published in Bank Note Reporter.
e-mail: denlys@aol.com
website: www.denlys.com
Specialties: U.S. paper money both large & small, obsolete currency, colonial currency, Confederate currency, fractional currency, national currency, books on paper money, mylar D currency holders, U.S. coins, Canadian currency, foreign currency. Currency auction representation.

DeROMA, Matthew
(PNG #674)
M. T. DeROMA RARE COINS & STAMPS, INC.
P.O. Box 800
Somers, CT 06071
Tel: (860) 749-4603
Cell: (860) 922-3973
e-mail: matt.mtdrcs@cox.net
Hours: 9 a.m.–7 p.m.
Specialties: U.S. Key Date coins; U.S. Silver Eagles, Chinese Silver Pandas, Australian Silver Zodiacs.

DI GENOVA, Silvano A.
(PNG #378)
Tangible Investments
218 Forest Ave.
Laguna Beach, CA 92651
Tel: (888) 655-9255
(949) 715-5333
Fax: (949) 715-6703
e-mail: info@gocoins.com
website: www.gocoins.com
Specialties: Appraisals, Auctions, Cash Buyers, U.S.

*Coins, Foreign Coins, All
Bullion, Jewelry, Art & Antiques.*

DOMINICK, William
(PNG #479)
WESTWOOD RARE COIN
GALLERY, INC
P.O. Box 31
Tappan, NY 10983
Tel: (201) 768-4433
Fax: (201) 768-8496
e-mail: *wwrc@optonline.net*
Hours: By appointment only
Personalized portfolio
management for individuals,
financial planners, pension
plans, monthly acquisition
plans, free appraisals, want
list service and personal
consultations.
Specialties: *U.S. gold, key
date coins, double die cents,
1856 Eagles, 1895 Morgans.*

DOWNEY, Sheridan
(PNG #502)
SHERIDAN DOWNEY,
NUMISMATIST
4100-10 Redwood Rd. #398
Oakland, CA 94619-2369
Tel: (510) 479-1585
(800) 597-9403
Fax: (650) 948-4019
Hours: 9–6 Pacific Time
e-mail: *sdowney3@aol.com*
website:
www.sheridanscoins.com
Specialties: *Early U.S.
coinage, 1794-1836, with
emphasis on U.S. bust half-
dollars. Consignments
accepted for regular auction
sales of bust half dollars.*

DRAGONI, Augusto
(PNG #287)
AUGUSTO DRAGONI
Via Faentina Sud 12
Russi (Ravenna), Italy 48026

Tel: 39-0544-582163
Fax: 39-0544-580173
Hours: By appointment only
Specialties: *Italian, Vatican,
San Marino, silver & gold
coins.*

DRZEWUCKI, Ron
(PNG #532)
RON DRZEWUCKI RARE
COINS / MODERN COIN
WHOLESALE, INC.
P.O. Box 110159
Lakewood Ranch, FL 34211
Tel: (941) 907-8484
Fax: (941) 907-2232
e-mail: *ron@rondrzewucki.com
sales@moderncoinwholesale
.com*
websites: *rondrzewucki.com
moderncoinwholesale.com*
eBay: *moderncoinwholesale
rondrzewucki*
Hours: 9–5 *office hours by
appointment only
Notes: A professional
numismatist for 28 years.
Owned St. Louis Rare Coins
before joining NGC. Posesses
a discriminating eye and has
taught several grading seminars
and counterfeit detection
classes. He is a Life Member of
the ANA & ANS and many state
associations.
Specialties: *Appraisals.*

DUNCAN, Kathleen
(PNG #518)
PINNACLE RARITIES, INC.
2411 Pacific Ave S.E. 2nd Floor
Olympia, WA 98501
Tel: (360) 786-5721
(800) 432-6467
Fax: (360) 786-6045
Hours: 9-5:30 (By appt. only)
e-mail:
kathleen@pinnacle-rarities.com

website:
www.pinnacle-rarities.com
Fixed price list. Newsletter.
On-line inventory. Auction
representation, free appraisals.
Specialties: *High grade PCGS
& NGC certified U.S. coinage
(1793 and 1950). Full service
firm servicing collector-investor
and dealer community. NGC &
PCGS submissions.*

DUNCAN, Richard, Sr.
(PNG #516)
U.S. COINS, INC.
8435 Katy Freeway
Houston, TX 77024
Tel: (713) 464-6868
Fax: (713) 464-7548
Fixed price lists, publications.
e-mail: *info@buyuscoins.com*
website: *www.buyuscoins.com*
Specialties: *Investment quality
silver & gold certified coins
from $50 to $500,000.00. Type
coins, proof & mint state, gold,
dollars and commemoratives.
Free award winning
consultations, appraisals &
recommendations given with
a smile.*

DUSKIE, Gary
(PNG #649)
COIN GALLERIES ON THE
LAKE
144 Market Place Ave.
P.O. Box 3781
Mooresville, NC 28117
Tel: (704) 662-9719
(704) 651-5332
By appointment only
e-mail:
coingalleries@windstream.net
website: *www.coingalleries.org*
Specialties: *U.S. coins only,
mail bid auctions.*

FAZZARI, Skip
(PNG #710)
INDEPENDENT COIN
GRADERS
P.O. Box 267000
Tampa, FL 33688
Tel: (813) 963-2401
(877) 221-4424
Fax: (813) 969-2890
e-mail:
skip.fazzari@icgcoin.com
website: *icgcoin.com*

FEIGENBAUM, John A.
(PNG #570)
DAVID LAWRENCE RARE
COINS
P.O. Box 9174
Virginia Beach, VA 23450
Tel: (800) 776-0560
(757) 491-1060
Fax: (866) 896-9624
Hours: 9–5 (EST)
e-mail:
info@davidlawrence.com
eBay: davidlawrence.auctions
website:
www.davidlawrence.com
Specialties: *U.S. and World
certified coins and currency;
weekly internet auctions and
retail.*

FELDMAN, Mark R.
(PNG #294)
A COIN EXCHANGE
18631 Ventura Blvd.
Tarzana, CA 91356
Tel: (818) 344-9555
Hours: Mon.-Fri. 10-5, Sat. 11-4
e-mail:
mark@acoinexchange.com
website:
www.acoinexchange.com
Specialties: *Retail coin
shop. All investor & collector
services; buy & sell U.S. coins,
foreign coins; gold, silver &*

platinum bullion; diamonds, jewelry & scrap. Other services include appraisals, estates, pension plans & expert witness testimony. Confidential consultations available at your home, office or bank.

FENTON, Stephen C.
(PNG #577)
KNIGHTSBRIDGE COINS
43 Duke St., St. James
London, SW1Y6DD,
United Kingdom
Tel: 011442079308215
011442079307597
Fax: 011442079308214
Hours: Mon-Fri 10:30-5:30
e-mail: *stephcf232@aol.com*
Specialties: *Great Britain. USA. Austrailia. South Africa.*

FISHMAN, Jason
(PNG #701)
JOHN MABEN RARE COINS
5565 Broadcast Ct.,
Sarasota, FL 34240
Tel: (800) 362-9004, #220
Fax: (941) 907-8833
website: *moderncoinmart.com*
e-mail:
jason@moderncoinmart.com

FITZGERALD, George, IV
(PNG #702)
JOHN MABEN RARE COINS
5565 Broadcast Ct.,
Sarasota, FL 34240
Tel: (800) 362-9004
Fax: (941) 907-8833
e-mail:
george@moderncoinmart.com
website: *moderncoinmart.com*

FORGUE, Dennis J.
(PNG #239)
HARLAN J. BERK, LTD.

31 North Clark Street
Chicago, IL 60602
Tel: (312) 609-0016
Fax: (312) 609-1305
Hours: 9:00-4:45
e-mail: *dennis@hjbltd.com*
website: *www.hjbltd.com*
Specialties: *All kinds U.S. coins & currency, autographs. Past president of Prof. Currency Dealers Association.*

FOSTER, James
(PNG #706)
LIBERTY COIN GALLERY
2201 E. Willow St., Ste. AA
Signal Hill, CA 90755
Tel: (562) 988-1516
Fax: (562) 988-8777
e-mail: *jfoster@libcoin.com*
website: *libertycoin.com*

FRAMPTON, Cory
(PNG #682)
MEXICAN COIN CO., LLC
P.O. Box 5270
Carefree, AZ 85377
Tel: (480) 921-2562
(602) 228-9331
Fax: (480) 563-0713
e-mail:
cory@mexicancoincompany.com
website:
mexicancoincompany.com
Specialties: *Mexican coins and currency.*

FRESE, Leo
(PNG #623)
LEO FRESE COINS AND
COLLECTIBLES
25572 Del Poniente
Laguna Niguel, CA 92677
Tel: (612) 916-0789
e-mail: *lpfrese@gmail.com*
Specialties: *Rare coins, collectibles, bullion.*

FRICKE, Pierre
(PNG #708)
PIERRE FRICKE
P.O. Box 1094
Sudbury, MA 01776
Tel: (404) 895-0672
e-mail: *pficke@csaquotes.com*
website: *csaquotes.com*
eBay: *armynova*
Specialties: *Early American coppers, especially large cents and fugios. Confederate and southern paper money. Northeast obsolete currency, U.S. large type—1860s.*

FRIEDBERG, Arthur L.
(PNG #284)
THE COIN AND CURRENCY
INSTITUTE, INC.
P.O. Box 399
Williston, Vt. 05495
Tel: (802) 878-0822
(800) 421-1866
Fax: (973) 471-1062
Hours: By appointment only
e-mail: *mail@coin-currency.com*
website:
www.coin-currency.com
Fixed price lists, publications, catalogs.
Specialties: *North American representative for numerous government mints. Publisher of reference books.*

FROSETH, Kent Morris
(PNG #406)
K.M. FROSETH, INC.
P.O. Box 23116
Minneapolis, MN 55423
Tel: (952) 831-9550
(800) 648-7662
Fax: (952) 835-3903
Hours: By appointment only
e-mail: *fm26@qwest.net*
website: *www.kmfroseth.com*
Specialties: *World coins,*
specializing in Scandinavia.
Rare foreign gold.

FULJENZ, Michael R.
(PNG #519)
MIKE FULJENZ UNIVERSAL
COIN & BULLION, LTD.
7410 Phelan Blvd.
Beaumont, TX 77706
Tel: (800) 459-2646
(409) 658-4533
Fax: (409) 866-3666
Hours: 8–5 Mon.–Fri.
e-mail:
vickie@universalcoin.com
website: *www.universalcoin*
.com
Specialties: *Silver, gold & platinum American Eagles. PCGS & NGC certified Type II & Type III $20 gold Liberties. FREE newsletter, private reports, books & personal consulting for new inquiries.*

GARRETT, Jeff C.
(PNG #329)
MID-AMERICAN RARE COIN
GALLERIES
1707 Nicholasville Rd.
Lexington, KY 40503
Tel: (859) 276-1551
Fax: (859) 278-8640
Cell: (859) 396-4505
e-mail: *coinman4u@aol.com*
website: *rarecoingallery.com*
SARASOTA RARE COIN
GALLERIES
640 S. Washington Bl., #100
Sarasota, FL 34236
Tel: (941) 366-2191
Specialty: *All U.S. coinage, with special interest in gold coins. Collections wanted with free advice on sale and disposition of estates. Author of* Encyclopedia of U.S. Gold Coinage. *We consider*

knowledge to be the key to serving our clients.

GEHRINGER, Stephen J.
(PNG #480)
Stephen Gehringer Enterprises
P.O. Box 3364
Allentown, PA 18106
Tel: (610) 533-0380
(610) 395-9700
Fax: (610) 330-0300
Hours: 9–5 M–F, Sat. 9–1
e-mail: keycoin@aol.com

GERMANO, Salvatore
(PNG #481)
S.G. RARE COINS, INC.
625 Lafayette Avenue
Hawthorne, NJ 07506
Tel: (973) 304-0520
Fax: (973) 304-0914
Hours: By appointment only
e-mail: sgrarecoins@aol.com
website: sgrarecoins.com
eBay: glass1979,
onionsavenged, taquitochalupa
Specialties: Buy, sell PCGS/
NGC/ANACS/ICG/SEGS
certified coins wholesale.
Also GSA dollars, original BU
rolls, 1936-54 proof sets, U.S.
Patterns, Territorials, and World
Gold.

GILLIO, Dennis M.
(PNG #321)
G & A COINS, INC.
Divisions: Dennis Gillio Rare
Coins, Gillio & Associates,
Rare Coins, Precious Metals,
Loans, Dennis Gillio Rare Coin
Auctions
10113 Riverside Drive
Toluca Lake, CA 91602
3465 State St., #376
Santa Barbara, CA
Tel: (818) 985-3900
Tel: (805) 563-9234 (Santa
Barbara)

Fax: (818) 762-6717
e-mail: gilliocoin@aol.com
website: gandacoins.com
Hours: Toluca Lake: 10–5
Mon.–Sat. Auction dates: Varies
Santa Barbara: By Appointment
only
Specialties: U.S. gold coins,
PCGS gold coins, world gold
coins, Franklin Mint gold coins;
gold, silver, platinum bullion, and
coins. Loans made on coins.

GILLIO, Ronald J.
(PNG #204)
RONALD J. GILLIO, INC.
JOHSON-GILLIO LLC
8 W. Figueroa St.
Santa Barbara, CA 93101
Tel: (805) 963-1345
Fax: (805) 962-6659
Hours: 10–5 Mon.–Fri.
Divisions: Gillio Rare Coins
& Fine Jewelry, Goldmunzen
International, Gillio Coins
International, Gillio Coins Hong
Kong, R.J. Gillio Auctions, Long
Beach Coin, Stamps Collectibles
Expo. Santa Clara Coin, Stamp
& Collectibles Expo.
e-mail: rjgillio@verizon.net
website: www.gillio.com;
www.exposunlimited.com
Specialties: U.S. gold coins,
world gold coins, Far East &
Asian coins, auctions.

GLASSMAN, Andrew
(PNG #644)
SPECTRUM NUMISMATICS
INTERNATIONAL, INC.
1063 McGaw, Suite 100
Irvine, CA 92614
Tel: (949) 955-1250
Fax: (949) 955-1824
e-mail: andrewg@coins.com

GOLDBERG, Ira M.
(PNG #153)

IRA & LARRY GOLDBERG
COINS & COLLECTIBLES, INC.
11400 West Olympic Blvd.
STE 800
Los Angeles, CA 90064
Tel: (310) 551-2646
(800) 978-2646
Fax: (310) 551-2626
Hours: 9–5 M–F
Antiquities
e-mail: *ira@goldbergcoins.com*
website:
www.goldbergcoins.com
Specialties: *Ancient Greek,
Roman, Judean, Byzantine, U.S.
& World coinage.*

GOLDMAN, Kenneth
(PNG #252)
KENNETH GOLDMAN, INC
P.O. Box 920404
Needham, MA 02492
Tel: (781) 449-0058
Fax: (781) 326-6758
Hours: 9–5
We attend all major coin
conventions & auctions in the
U.S.A. Appraiser for the Federal
Trade Commission.
e-mail: *KenGoldman@aol.com*
Specialties: *Choice U.S.
type coins, gold and silver,
pioneer gold, U.S. pattern
coins, investment portfolios for
qualified clients.*

GORNY, Dieter
(PNG #264)
GORNY & MOSCH
GIESSENER
MUNZHANDLUNG GmbH
Maximiliansplatz 20
D-80333 Munchen, Germany
Tel: 0049-89 24226430
Fax: 0049-89 2285513
Hours: M–F 10–1, 2:30–6
Mon–Fri
e-mail: *info@gmcoinart.de*
website: *www.gmcoinart.de*

Specialties: *Ancient, foreign
& German coins & medals,
medieval through modern
times, antiquities.*

GRAHAM, Michael A.
(PNG #254)
MT. HIGH COIN &
COLLECTIBLES—
185 S.E. 3rd Street
Bend, OR 97702
Tel: (541) 385-7113
Fax: (541) 385-7133
Hours: 10-4:30 p.m.
COINET OR11
Fixed price lists, art bar
specialist, catalogs.
e-mail: info@mtnhighcoin.com
website: *www.mtnhighcoin.com*
Specialties: *Rare U.S. coins,
unique collectables, antique
jewelry, estates. Silver, Gold,
and Bronze mint manufacturing,
Sports Memorabilia.*

GREENBERG, Frank
(PNG #313)
FRANK GREENBURG, INC.
P.O. Box 831
Broomall, PA 19008
Tel: (610) 325-9951
Cell: (610) 220-7277
e-mail:
frank@frankgreenberg.com
Hours: By appointment
Specialties: Better U.S. coins
bought, sold and appraised. Full
time Professional Numismatic
since 1969.

GREENSTEIN, David M.
(PNG #A664)
HARLAN J. BERK, LTD.
31 N. Clark St.
Chicago, IL 60602
Tel: (312) 609-0016
Fax: (312) 609-1305
e-mail: *david@hjbltd.com*

website: *www.hjbltd.com*

GREENSTEIN, Robert
(PNG #A601)
HARLAN J. BERK, LTD.
31 N. Clark St.
Chicago, IL 60602
Tel: (312) 609-0016
Fax: (312) 609-1305
e-mail: *bobg@hjbltd.com*
website: *www.hjbltd.com*
Specialties: *U.S. coins.*

GROVICH, Nicholas F.
(PNG #553)
AMERICAN FEDERAL RARE
COIN & BULLION
P.O. Box 5810
Carefree, AZ 85377-5810
Tel: (602) 992-6857
(800) 221-7694
Fax: (480) 493-8158
8-5 MST
e-mail: *nick@amfedcoins.com*
website:
www.americanfederal.com
Specialties: *Gold & silver
commemoratives, high grade
(MS65 & better) U.S. coins. We
purchase all types of coins from
Indian cents thru proof gold.
We will travel to you to inspect
collections and pay on the spot
or you can take advantage of
our Guaranteed Consignment.*

GRUNDY, Ed
(PNG #A484)
P.O. Box 3013
Pueblo, CO 81005
Tel: (719) 252-2792
e-mail: *grundy888@aol.com*

GULLEY, Kent E.
(PNG #455)
SARASOTA RARE COIN
GALLERY
640 S. Washington Blvd., # 100
Sarasota, FL 34236
Tel: (941) 366-2191
(800) 447-8778
Fax: (941) 954-8833
Hours: 9–5 Mon.–Fri., 9–4 Sat.
Catalogs
e-mail: *srcg@hotmail.com*
website: *www.sarasotacoin.com*
Specialties: *U.S. gold, silver
dollars, certified & uncertified
bullion.*

HALPERIN, James L.
(PNG #482)
HERITAGE AUCTION GAL-
LERIES
3500 Maple Ave., 17th Floor
Dallas, TX 75219
Tel: (214) 409-1255
(800) 872-6467
(214) 528-3500
Fax: (214) 409-2255
Hours: Mon–Fri 10–5
e-mail: *jim@ha.com*
website: *www.ha.com*
Specialties: *online auctions,
internet membership community
for collectors and dealers, fixed
price lists, publications, catalogs, auction sales.*

HAMRICK, John B.
(PNG #564)
JOHN B. HAMRICK & CO.
3050 Royal Blvd. S. #100
Alpharetta, GA 30009
Tel. (678) 319-3005
Fax: (678) 319-3006
Hours: 9–6 M–F
e-mail:
john@johnbhamrickcoins.com
website:
www.johnbhamrickcoins.com
Specialties: *Certified U.S.
coins (PCGS & NGC) 1792–
1955. We deal in everything
from 1/2 cents to $50 gold*

coins plus patterns and early commemoratives.

HANKS, Larry
(PNG #241)
HANKS AND ASSOCIATES, INC.
P.O. Box 913
Indian Rocks Bch., FL 33785
Tel: (727) 593-1303
Fax: (727) 517-2905
Hours: 10–5 Mon.–Fri.
Fixed price lists, publications, catalogs, auction sales.
e-mail: *whanks3700@aol.com*
website: *www.rare-coins.net*
Specialties: *U.S. & world gold coins, rare paper money purchases, sales, submissions for PCGS & NGC certified coins, syndication of rare coins, pension plan investments.*

HANLON, Terence F.
(PNG #578)
DILLON GAGE
15301 Dallas Parkway
Suite 200
Addison, TX 75001
Tel: (800) 375-4653
(972) 386-2901
Fax: (972) 490-3218
Hours: 8–6 CT
e-mail:
thanlon@dillongage.com
websites: *www.dillongage.com, fitztrade.com, idsofcanada.com, diamondstateddepository.com*
Specialties: *Precious Metals Refinery. Jewelry closeouts. Commodities trading. Rare date U.S. gold. Bullion trading.*

HANSON, Jon G.
(PNG #87)
P.O. Box 81555
Wellesley, MA 02481
Tel: (781) 235-6628
Fax: (781) 235-1142

Hours: By appointment only
e-mail: *jonontime@aol.com*
Specialties: *Early American coins & medals, U.S. half cents, rare American numismatic books & accumulations, pioneer gold, U.S. assay ingots & horological items.*

HARRISON, Steve
(PNG #693)
KEDZIE KOIN & JEWELRY
5909 S. Kedzie Avenue
Chicago, IL 60629
Tel: (773) 436-0777
Fax: (773) 471-3029
e-mail: *kedziekoin@aol.com*
website: *kedziekoins.net*
eBay: *KEDZIEKOINS*
Hours: Mon.–Sat. 10–5
Specialties: *American coins, U.S. Dollars.*

HARWELL, Robert, II
(PNG #330)
HANCOCK & HARWELL RARE COINS & PRECIOUS METALS
3155 Roswell Rd., Ste 310,
Atlanta, GA 30305
Tel: (404) 261-6565
Fax: (404) 237-6500
e-mail: *bob@raregold.com*
website: *raregold.com*
Hours: 10:00–4:00 EST
Specialties: *Dahlonega & Charlotte gold coins, gold, silver, platinum, slabbed and raw U.S. coins.*

HELLER, Patrick A.
(PNG #651)
LIBERTY COIN SERVICE
400 Frandor Ave.
Lansing, MI 48912
Tel: (517) 351-4720
(800) 933-4720
Fax: (517) 351-3466
e-mail:
path@libertycoinservice.com

website: *libertycoinservice.com*
Hours: M-F 10-6; Sat 10-2
Company founded 1971.
Nationally quoted newsletter.
Specialties: *All U.S., foreign and ancient coins; U.S. paper money; tokens and medals; gold, silver and platinum bullion; PCGS, NGC, ANACS authorized dealer; estates; liquidations and appraisals.*

HENDRICKSON, David J.
(PNG #336)
SILVER TOWNE L.P. COIN SHOP
120 E. Union City Pike
Winchester, IN 47394
Tel: (800) 788-7481
Fax: (765) 584-1246
Hours: 9–5 Mon.–Fri., 9–4 Sat.
e-mail: *david.hendrickson @silvertowne.com*
website: *www.silvertowne.com*
Specialties: *All U.S. coins. All bullion items. All NGC-PCGS graded coins. Coin & jewelry items.*

HENDRICKSON, Leon E.
(PNG #170)
SILVER TOWNE L.P. COIN SHOP
120 East Union City Pike,
Winchester, IN 47394
Tel: (765) 584-7481
Fax: (765) 584-1246
Hours: 9–5 Mon.–Fri., 9–4 Sat.
e-mail: *sales @silvertowne.com*
website: *www.silvertowne.com*
Specialties: *All U.S. coins, all bullion items, all PCGS & NGC graded coin. Gold & silver refining, coin jewelry items.*

HENRY, Gene L.
(PNG #171)

GENE L. HENRY, INC.
P.O. Box 2998
Issaquah, WA 98027
Tel: (425) 392-1485
Fax: (425) 392-1470
Anytime, by appointment only
e-mail: *genelhenry@aol.com*
Specialties: *U.S. silver dollars & gold coins, large stock, U.S. coins, raw & slabbed.*

HERNDON, Wayne
(PNG #655)
WAYNE HERNDON RARE COINS, INC.
P.O. Box 221601
Chantilly, VA 20153
Tel: (703) 385-0058
Fax: (703) 385-0059
Hours: Mon–Fri 10-7; Sat–Sun 9–7
e-mail: *wh@wayneherndon.com*
website: *www.wayneherndom.com*

HERTZBERG, Jack Charles
(PNG #445)
JACK HERTZBERG RARE COINS
Hours: By appointment only
e-mail: *jackchertzberg @comcast.net*
Specialties: *Managed rare coin portfolios.*

HERZOG, John
(PNG #595)
824 Harbor Rd.
South Port, CT 06890
Tel: (347) 413-4098
e-mail: *john@herzogandco.com*

HERZOG, Mary K.
(PNG #676)
DISRUPTEK, LLC
P.O. Box 203
Wallingford, PA 19086

Tel: (347) 413-4098
(877) 347-7785
Fax: (954) 653-4637
e-mail: *mary@disruptek.com*
website: *www.disruptek.com*
Specialties: *U.S. coins.*

HIRTZINGER, Karl
(PNG #608)
KEVDAL NUMISMATICS, LLC.
P.O. Box 2297
Springfield, OH 45501
Tel: (612) 840-6892
Hours: By appointment
e-mail:
khirtzinger@hotmail.com
Specialties: *NGC and PCGS certified high quality gold and silver U.S. coins, 1793-1950; U.S. pattern coinage and Canadian/British.*

HARPER, David C.
(PNG #AF656)
KRAUSE PUBLICATIONS
700 E. State St.
Iola, WI 54990
Tel: (715) 455-2214 ext: 13344
Fax: (715) 445-4087
e-mail:
david.harper@fumedia.com
website:
www.numismaticnews.com

HOSIER, Donald W., Jr.
(PNG #380)
dba D. & E. C. S.
P.O. Box 1346
Point Pleasant Bch, NJ 08742
Tel: (732) 701-0454
Fax: (732) 701-0458

IMHOF, Todd L.
(PNG #525)
HERITAGE AUCTIONS
3500 Maple Ave., 17th Floor
Dallas, TX 75219-3931
Tel: (214) 409-1313

(800) 872-6467
Fax: (214) 409-1696
Hours: 9–5 Mon.–Fri., 9–1 Sat.
e-mail: *todd@ha.com*
website: *www.ha.com*
Note: Collections purchased outright and accepted for auctions.
Specialties: *rare U.S. coins, world coins, ancient coins, medals, currency.*

INGRAFFIA, Victor
(PNG #657)
GIBRALTAR COINS & PRECIOUS METALS, INC.
27001 U.S. 19N
#8520
Clearwater, FL 33761
Tel: (727) 712-8088
Fax: (727) 799-4646
e-mail: *info@gibraltarcoins.com*
website:
www.gibraltarcoins.com
Specialties: *Better date U.S. gold coins, Morgan Dollars, U.S. type coins, precious metals.*

IVY, Steve
(PNG #381)
HERITAGE NUMISMATIC AUCTIONS
3500 Maple Ave., 17th Floor
Dallas, TX 75219
Tel: (214) 528-3500
(800) 872-6467
Fax: (214) 443-8409
Hours: 9–5 Mon.–Fri., Sat. 9–1
HERITAGE NUMISMATIC AUCTIONS, Fixed price lists, publications, catalogs, auction sales, wholesale fax list.
e-mail: *steve@ha.com*
website: *www.ha.com*
Specialties: *Buying, selling, financing, joint ventures. Coin show and Internet auction sales*

*throughout the year. Advances
made on consignment accepted.*

JONES, Harry E.
(PNG #212)
HARRY E. JONES RARE
COINS & CURRENCY
7379 PEARL RD
Cleveland, OH 44130
Tel: (440) 234-3330
Fax: (440) 234-3332
e-mail: hjones6671@aol.com
Specialties: *National currency,
U.S. coins, uncut sheets, error
notes.*

JOYCE, Michael
(PNG #654)
GULFCOAST COIN & JEW-
ELRY BROKERS, INC.
1400 Colonial Blvd., #77
Ft. Meyers, FL 33907
Tel: (239) 939-5636
Fax: (239) 939-5739
e-mail:
mike@gulfcoastcoin.com
website:
www.gulfcoastcoin.com
Specialties: *rare coins, bullion,
and jewelry*

KAGIN, Don
(PNG #526)
KAGIN'S INC.
1550 Tiburon Blvd. #201
Tiburon, CA 94920
Tel: (415) 435-2601
Fax: (415) 435-1627
Hours: 9–5pm M–F
e-mail: info@kagins.com
website: www.kagins.com
Specialties: *Pioneer gold,
patterns, Calif. Fractional gold,
U.S. silver, gold, copper, paper
currency.*

KARLER, Charles R.
(PNG #408)

SOUTHWESTERN GOLD, INC.
6909 Menaul Blvd. NE, Suite F
Albuquerque, NM 87110
Tel: (505) 881-3636
Fax: (505) 883-8957
e-mail:
southwesterngold@msn.com
website:
www.southwesterngold.com
Specialties: *U.S. gold coins.*

KAROLEFF, Bradley S.
(PNG #A678)
COINS + LLC
225 E. 6th St., Suite 1
Cincinnati, OH 45202
Tel: (513) 621-1996
(859) 371-1414
Fax: (513) 621-1996
e-mail: bkaroleff@yahoo.com
website: coinspluscincy.com
Specialties: *U.S. coins and
currency. Full line of supplies
and numismatic literature. Four
locations in greater Cincinnati.*

KARSTEDT, Christine
(PNG #A587)
STACK'S BOWERS
GALLERIES
P.O. Box 1804
Wolfeboro, NH 03894
Tel. (603) 569-0823
(866) 811-1804
Fax: (603) 569-3875
Hours: 9–5
e-mail:
ckarstedt@stacksbowers.com
website:
www.stacksbowers.com
Specialties: *U.S. Coins,
Auctions. Licensed auctioneer.*

KEMP, Linda
(PNG #612)
OSSIE'S RARE COINS
4560 Hamilton Blvd.
Allentown, PA 18103

Tel: (610) 530-1588
Fax: (610) 530-1589
Hours: 9–5
e-mail: kempl@earthlink.net
Specialties: *rare U.S. coins; collections and estates; U.S. currency.*

KETTERLING, Don
(PNG #409)
DH Ketterling Numismatic Consulting
3535-R East Thousand Oaks Blvd. #136
Westlake Village, CA 91362
Tel: (805) 418-7455
(818) 632-2352
Fax: (805) 418-7455
Hours: By appointment only
e-mail:
dhkconsulting@verizon.net
website: www.dhkrcc.com
Specialties: *High grade U.S. rare coins and currency. Wholesale service to marketers and dealers. Co-managing the RCA, Ltd. rare coin trading fund. Estate and insurance appraisals along with expert testimony services.*

KIERSTEAD, Jeff
(PNG #699)
MINTPRODUCTS.COM
P.O. Box 10592
Bedford, NH 03110
Tel: (603) 622-2922
Fax: (603) 622-8257
e-mail: jeff@mintproducts.com
website: mintproducts.com
Hours: M–F 9–5
Notes: MintProducts.com—your Internet coin store has been one of the most popular numismatic sites on the web since 1999.
Specialties: *Modern coins, bullion coins, collector coins. Buying all coins.*

KIMMEL, Andrew W.
(PNG #675)
PARAGON NUMISMATICS, INC.
1425 W. Mequon Rd., Ste E
Mequon, WI 53092
Tel: (262) 240-9975
(262) 893-2436 (mobile)
Hours: 9–5 Mon–Fri
e-mail: ak@paragoncoins.com
website:
www.paragoncoins.com
Specialties: *buying and selling all U.S. and foreign coins.*

KLIMAN, Myron M.
(PNG #147)
NUMISMATIC ENTERPRISES
P.O. Box 9365
South Laguna, CA 92652
Tel: (949) 496-8589
Fax: (949) 496-8589
Hours: 9–5 Mon.–Sat., by appointment only
e-mail: mikekliman@gmail.com
website: www.home.earthlink
.net/-numivision
Appraisals and consultations.
Specialties: *U.S. type coins.*

KNIGHT, Lyn F.
(PNG #194)
LYN F. KNIGHT
P.O. Box 7364
Overland Park, KS 66207-0364
Tel: (913) 338-3779
(800) 243-5211
Fax: (913) 338-4754
Hours: By appointment only
Fixed price lists, auction sales, catalogs.
e-mail: lyn@lynknight.com
websites: www.lynknight.com,
lkcaworldpapermoney.com
Specialties: *U.S. & Canadian paper money & coins.*

KONIG, Kenneth
(PNG #A626)
GREATER MILWAUKEE COIN
& JEWELRY
615 N. Barstow
Waukesha, WI 53186
Tel: (262) 896-8955
Fax: (262) 896-9317
e-mail:
konigk1@yahoo.com
website:
www.milwaukeecoin.com

KONIG, Russell
(PNG #625)
GREATER MILWAUKEE COIN
& JEWELRY
4040 N. Calhoun Rd.
Brookefield, WI 53005
Tel: (262) 781-4200
Fax: (262) 781-2883
e-mail:
konigk1@yahoo.com
website:
www.milwaukeecoin.com

KOPPENHAVER, Paul L.
(PNG #LM5)
THE COIN HAVEN
P.O. Box 34056
Granada Hills, CA 91394-9056
Tel: (818) 832-8068
Fax: (818) 832-8987
Former PNG Executive Director
1978-1994. Recipient of Abe
Kosoff Founder's Award.
e-mail: plkopp@as.net
Specialties: *Charlotte,
Dahlonega, & Carson City
gold, U.S. type coins, tokens,
medals, currency & western
Americana. Mail order only,
token and medal auctions.*

KRAH, Kenneth C.
(PNG #530)
NUMISMATIC GUARANTY
CORP.

1500 Independence Blvd.,
Ste. 220
Sarasota, FL 34234
Tel: (800) 642-2646
Hours: 9-6 EST
e-mail: kkrah@ngccoin.com
Specialties: *U.S. English
colonial, European coins and
numismatic literature.*

KRILL, Gregory
(PNG #557)
NORTH BAY RARE COIN &
JEWELRY
1241 Adams St. #1002
St. Helena, CA 94574
Tel: (707) 287-1919
Fax: (949) 857-5128
Bu roll deals, all denominations.
e-mail:
greg@northbayrarecoin.com
Specialties: *B.U. U.S. gold,
dated U.S. gold, B.U. silver
dollars.*

KUTCHER, Bruce
(PNG #360)
BRUCE KUTCHER, INC.
P.O. Box 101
Nahant, MA 01908
Tel: (781) 581-0631
Fax: (781) 581-9683
By appointment only
Specialties: *U.S. gold &
certified coins.*

LAIBSTAIN, Harry
(PNG #536)
HARRY LAIBSTAIN RARE
COINS & JEWELRY
P.O. Box 3596
Norfolk, VA 23514
Tel: (757) 622-6760
(800) 869-1869
Fax: (757) 622-6764
Hours: 9–5:30
HLRC mailing list & newsletter;
Coin World advertiser.
e-mail: harry@hlrc.com

website: *www.hlrc.com*
Specialties: *Early type coins, large cents, Colonials & half cents, key date coins, commemoratives, gold & silver better date U.S. gold, Diamonds.*

LECCE, Robert B.
(PNG #347)
ROBERT B. LECCE, NUMISMATIST, INC.
17761 Southwick Way
Boce Raton, FL 33498
Tel: (561) 483-4744
(561) 213-2667
Fax: (561) 483-2660
e-mail: *(Business)*
Rareusgold@aol.com,
(Personal)
artglass2000@aol.com
website: *www.rareusgold.com*

LEE, Larry L.
(PNG #350)
COIN AND BULLION RESERVES
2621 East 15th Street
Panama City, FL 32405
Tel: (850) 785-9546
Fax: (850) 763-1134
Hours: 9–6 Mon.–Sat.
e-mail:
coinandbullion@knology.net
website:
www.coinandbullion.com
Specialties: *U.S. coins & currency.*

LEIDMAN, Julian M.
(PNG #195)
JULIAN M. LEIDMAN/
BONANZA COINS
940 Wayne Avenue
Silver Spring, MD 20910
Tel: (301) 585-8467
(301) 585-0690
Hours: By appointment
Fixed price lists, occasionally.
e-mail: *julian@juliancoin.com*

website: *www.juliancoin.com*
Specialties: *Choice U.S. rare coins & patterns. Attends most major coin shows & auctions; consultant to quality minded collectors. Available for appraisal & as consultant, any aspect of numismatics; services want lists.*

LEIFER, Bret
(PNG #513)
BRET LEIFER NUMISMATICS
Box 5225
Wayland, MA 01778
Tel: (508) 655-1125
(800) 331-2646 (COIN)
Fax: (508) 650-1847
Hours: By appointment only
e-mail: *coins@coinguy.com*
website: *www.coinguy.com*
Specialties: *Certified gold pieces. High quality type coins. Assistance in building world class collections; will act as a broker for qualified clients; buying and selling. Free consultation and/or appraisal. Grading services provided. Always buying coins & accumulations.*

LERNER, Jonathan
(PNG #633)
SCARSDALE COIN
135 Summerfield St.
Scarsdale, NY 10583
Tel: (914) 722-3606
Fax: (801) 516-7761
e-mail: *coinhelp@yahoo.com*
website: *www.coinhelp.com*
Specialties: *Three cent silver "Trimes."*

LEVINE, Stuart
(PNG #412)
P.O. Box 806
Marblehead, MA 01945

Tel: (781) 477-0552
Fax: (781) 477-0827
e-mail:
stuartlevine@comcast.net
Specialties: *Rare United States regular issue, proof & pattern coinage. U.S. related colonial & territorial issues.*

LEVINSON, Robert A.
(PNG #AF561)
LEVINSON & KAPLAN,
A PROFESSIONAL
CORPORATION
15303 Ventura Blvd., #1650
Sherman Oaks, CA 91403
Tel: (818) 382-3434
Fax: (818) 382-3433
e-mail:
Bob@levkaplawyers.com
website: *www.levkaplaw.com*
Specialties: *Legal representation for coin dealers, auction houses & parties engaging in numismatic transactions, including issues with interpretation of contracts, auctions, sales, disputes, etc. Attorney is also a collector, and author in several publications regarding numismatic subjects and is general counsel to various numismatic related firms.*

LIPTON, Kevin
(PNG #383)
KEVIN LIPTON RARE COIN,
INC.
9478 W. Olympic Blvd.
Ste. 202
Beverly Hills, CA 90212
Tel: (310) 712-8118
Fax: (310) 772-0122
Hours: 9–5
Specialties: *8:00 a.m.–5:30 p.m.*

LISOT, David
(PNG #AF627)

COINTELEVISON.COM
908 Audelia Rd., #200-330
Richardson, TX 75081
Tel: (800) 876-2320
e-mail:
dlisot@cointelevision.com
website:
www.cointelevision.com
Specialties: *video production, DVD distribution, visual media consulting, specialist in coin and collectible productions.*

LOBEL, Richard
(PNG #229)
COINCRAFT
44 & 45 Great Russell Street
London, England, WC1B 3LU
Tel: (0207) 636-1188
(0207) 637-8785
Fax: (0207) 323-2860
Hours: 9–5 Mon.–Fri., 10–2:30
Sat.
e-mail: *info@coincraft.com*
website: *www.coincraft.com*
Specialties: *Publishers of "The Phoenix" every 3 weeks, "The Banknote Bulletin," "The Coin Collector," "Bluecard Flyer." Books published: Coincraft's Standard Catalogue of English & U.K. Coins 1066 to Date, Coincraft's Standard Catalogue of the Coins of Scotland, Ireland, Channel Islands & The Isle of Man, Medallions of The Great Exhibition/Choice British coins, banknotes, ancient coins & antiquities.*

LONG, James E.
(PNG #637)
J.E.L. COINS
P.O. Box 3003
Baltimore, MD 21229
Tel: (410) 674-9380
Fax: (410) 674-0073
e-mail: *jelcoins@aol.com*

LOPRESTO, Samuel L.
(PNG #362)
PMB 410
21517 Linda Dr.
Torrance, CA 90503
Tel: (310) 540-4984
e-mail: *lopresto@flash.net*
Specialties: *U.S. & foreign coins, tokens, medals, jewelry.*

LUSTIG, Andrew
(PNG #614)
P.O. Box 806
New York, NY 10960
Tel: (845) 321-0249
e-mail: *andylustig@earthlink.net*
Specialties: *patterns, pioneer gold, worldwide auction representation.*

MABEN, John
(PNG #363)
JOHN MABEN RARE COINS, INC.
5565 Broadcast Court
Sarasota, FL 34240
Tel: (941) 907-8050
Fax: (941) 907-8833
Hours: By appoinment only
e-mail:
john@moderncoinmart.com
Specialties: *modern coins, all other areas of U.S. coins; buying individual coins, coin collections, and estates.*

MANDERSCHEID, Paul
(PNG #468)
LIBERTY COIN SERVICE
400 Frandor Ave.
Lansing, MI 48912
Tel: (800) 933-4720
Fax: (517) 351-3466
website: *libertycoinservice.com*
e-mail:
paulm@libertycoinservice.com
Hours: M–F 10–6, Sat 10–2

MANLEY, Dwight N.
(PNG #522)
FULLERTON COINS
123 N. Raymond
Fullerton, CA 92831
Tel: (714) 526-5460
Hours: Tues.–Sat. 10–4
e-mail: *dmanleyinc@aol.com*
Specialties: *U.S. coins—buy, sell, and trade.*

MARKOFF, Steven C.
(PNG #289)
AMAG, INC.
233 Wilshire Blvd. Ste 200
Santa Monica, CA 90401
Tel: (310) 587-1470
Fax: (310) 319-0310
Hours: 8–5
e-mail: *scmarkoff@aol.com*
website: *www.amark.com*
Specialties: *Wholesaling, trading, marketing & financing of precious metals in coin, bar, plate & grain form, refining of precious metals scrap. Bullion coins.*

MARTIN, James F.
(PNG #AF618)
JAMES F. MARTIN CO.
Jamaica, NY 11434
Tel: (917) 414-0229 (mobile)
e-mail: *jmart29@banet.net*
Specialties: *Research of U.S. currency.*

MASSIE, Dustin E.
(PNG #643)
DUSTIN MASSIE NUMISMATIST, INC.
P.O. Box 234
Madison, IL 62060
Tel: (618) 444-2442
Fax: (618) 452-7095
Hours: 8–5
e-mail: *dustinem@aol.com*
website: *www.dustinem.com*

Specialties: *world gold, U.S. gold, silver type, key, and semi key coins in high grades, and classic commemorative gold and silver.*

MATTHEWS, James
(PNG #A673)
STACK'S-BOWERS
GALLERIES
1063 McGaw #100
Irvine, CA 92614
Tel: (540) 335-3288
e-mail:
jmatthews@stacksbowers.com
website:
www.stacksbowers.com
Specialties: *Die varieties of federal coinage.*

MCBRIDE, Art
(PNG #645)
ART MCBRIDE RARE COINS
P.O. Box 956
Sherwood, OR 97140
Tel: (503) 925-8230
Fax: (503) 925-8230
Hours: By appointment
e-mail: artmcbride@aol.com
website:
www.coinclub.com/artmcbride

MCCAWLEY, Chris Victor
(PNG #397)
CVM / M&G AUCTIONS
P.O. Box 5250
Frisco, TX 75035
Tel: (972) 668-1575
Fax: (972) 668-2126
e-mail: cmccawley@aol.com
websites: www.earlycents.com,
friscomint.com,
colonialsonline.com
Specialties: *Early American copper coin, half cents, large cents & colonials. Specialty auctions of early copper.*

McCORMICK, Mark
(PNG #713)
MISSOURI COIN CO.
11718 Manchester Road
Des Peres, MO 63131
Tel: (314) 965-9797
e-mail: mark@mocoin.com
website: mocoin.com

MCGUIGAN, James R.
(PNG #384)
JIM MCGUIGAN
P.O. Box 133
No. Versailles, PA 15137
Tel: (412) 247-4484
Fixed price lists.
e-mail: jimmcguigan@verizon
.net
Specialties: *Early U.S. copper, silver & gold coins. Attendance at most major shows & auctions. Services offered to collectors, dealers & investors include: auction representation, numismatic counseling, appraisals, solicitation of want lists.*

MEHALKO, Diane
(PNG #683)
DAVID BERZON CO., INC.
2069 S. 108th St.
West Allis, WI 53227
Tel: (414) 543-8833
Fax: (414) 543-2014
Hours: Mon–Fri 10–5
e-mail: derzon@ameritech.net
website: www.derzoncoins.com

MELAMED, Richard
(PNG #604)
SPECTRUM NUMISMATICS
18061 Fitch
Irvine, CA 92614
Tel: (949) 955-1250
Fax: (949) 955-1824
Hours: Mon–Fri 8–5

e-mail:
richardm@coloradorarities.com

MERCER, Daryl L.
(PNG #314)
TEBO COIN COMPANY, INC.
2863 28th Street
P.O. Box 4900
Boulder, CO 80306
Tel: (303) 444-2646
(877) 750-2646
Fax: (303) 449-4653
Hours: M–F 9:30–5:30,
Sat. 9:30-2:00
e-mail: tebocoin@hotmail
.com
Specialties: *U.S. coins &
currency, appraisals, foreign &
ancient, collector coins & sets.
All rare coins/currency.*

MERENA, Raymond
(PNG #LM231)
RETIRED
1085 Harbor Island Lane
Vero Beach, FL 32967-7412
(772) 564-8611
Fax: (772) 567-1119
e-mail: pmerena@verizon.net

MERRILL, Bruce
(PNG #A571)
BRUCE MERRILL, INC.
Box 572
Olathe, KS 66061
Tel: (913) 764-8554
Fax: (913) 780-0692
e-mail:
midastouch6025@yahoo.com

MILAS, Edward
(PNG #157)
RARE COIN COMPANY OF
AMERICA, INC. RARCOA, INC.
7550 S. Quincy St.
Willowbrook, IL 60527
Tel: (630) 654-2580
Fax: (630) 654-3556
Hours: 8-4 By Appointment

e-mail: *info@rarcoa.com*
website: *www.rarcoa.com*

MILAS, Wayde
(PNG #611)
RARCOA, INC.
7550 S. Quincy St.
Willowbrook, IL 60527
Tel: (630) 654-2580
Fax: (630) 654-3556
e-mail: wmilas@rarcoa.com
website: www.rarcoa.com

MILLER, Wayne
(PNG #547)
WAYNE MILLER COINS
38 N. Last Chance Gulch
Helena, MT 59601
Tel: (406) 442-0713
Fax: (406) 442-0789
e-mail: waynemiller
@waynemillercoins.com
website:
www.waynemillercoins.com
Specialties: *Morgan & Peace
dollars, generic certified $20
gold.*

MILLS, Warren T.
(PNG #505)
RARE COINS OF NEW
HAMPSHIRE
28 Jones Road, Suite 1
People's United Bank Bldg
Milford, NH 03055
Tel: (603) 673-9311
(800) 225-7264
Fax: (603) 673-9539
Hours: 9–7 Mon.–Fri.
e-mail: warrenprcnh.com
website: www.rcnh.com
Specialties: *All United States
coins; rarities purchased &
sold; auction representation;
liquidation services. We
specialize in all key & semi key
collector coins. Call us regarding
coins, currency or tokens. Free*

appraisals & want list service for raw or certified coins.

MINSHULL, Lee S.
(PNG #540)
LEE MINSHULL R.C., INC.
P.O. Box 4389
Palos Verdes, CA 90274
Tel: (310) 377-1299
Fax: (310) 320-6660
Hours: 9–6
e-mail: *lmrcinc@msn.com*
website:
www.goldcoinbuyer.com
Specialties: *U.S. gold cal gold patterns.*

MOLINE, Michael
(PNG #385)
HERITAGE AUCTION GAL-
LERIES
9478 W. Olympic Blvd.
Beverly Hills, CA 90210
Tel: (310) 492-8612
Fax: (310) 492-8622
e-mail: *mmoline@ha.com*
website: *www.ha.com*
Specialties: *rare U.S. coins, world coins, currency, vintage watches, jewelry, historic news-papers, manuscripts, books, po-litical memorabilia, and sports collectibles.*

MOLINE, Michael
(PNG #385)
HERITAGE AUCTIONS
9478 W. Olympic Blvd.,
First Floor
Beverly Hills, CA 90212
Tel: (310) 492-8612
(800) 872-6467
Fax: (310) 492-8622
e-mail: *mmoline@ha.com*
website: *ha.com/bh*
Hours: 9–5 Mon–Fri, Sat by appointment
Specialties: *Rare U.S. coins,*

world coins, ancient coins, medals currency, political memorabilia, rare comic books, pop culture & illustration art, movie posters & sports collectibles.

MONTGOMERY, Paul
(PNG #549)
AMERICAN PRECIOUS
METALS EXCHANGE
226 Dean A. McGee Ave.
Oklahoma City, OK 73102
Tel: (405) 595-2100 x140
Fax: (603) 569-5319
Hours: 8:30-5 Mon.–Fri.
Rare coin auction firm with frequent auction sales in NYC, Baltimore, Los Angeles and other major metropolitan cities.
e-mail:
paul.montgomery@apmex.com
website: *www.apmex.com*
Specialties: *All U.S. coins, world coins, ancient coins, paper money, medals & tokens.*

MORAN, Christopher
(PNG #714)
THE HAPPY COIN
P.O. Box 1108
Hopewell Junction, NY 12533
Tel: (800) 544-3750
Fax: (845) 622-4700
e-mail:
chris@thehappycoin.com
website: *thehappycoin.com*

MOROWITZ, Arthur
(PNG #613)
CHAMPION STAMP COMPANY
432 West 54th St.
New York, NY 10019
Tel: (212) 489-8130
Fax: (212) 581-8130

MUNZNER, Richard T.
(PNG #278)

LAUREL CITY COINS AND ANTIQUES
462 Main Street
P.O. Box 1093
Winsted, CT 06098
Tel: (860) 379-0325
Fax: (860) 379-0325
Hours: Tue.–Fri. 10–4:30; Sat. 9:30–4:00
Specialties: *Collector coins, Proof & Mint sets, Coin supplies.*

NACHBAR, Richard N.
(PNG #493)
RICHARD NACHBAR RARE COINS
5820 Main Street, Suite 601
Williamsville, NY 14221
Tel: (716) 635-9700
(877) 622-4227
Fax: (716) 635-9762
Hours: 10–4 M–F by Appointment
e-mail: *nachbar@coinexpert.com*
website: *www.coinexpert.com*
Specialties: *Expert appraisals & leading national buyer of coin collections and estates, especially U.S. Gold Coins, Type Coins, Silver Dollars, U.S. Commemoratives, Pioneer Gold, Territorials and U.S. Currency. We travel to purchase collections & have also attended all major national shows for our clients since 1973.*

NAPOLITANO, Chris
(PNG #528)
STACK'S-BOWERS NUMISMATICS
1063 McGaw #100
Irvine, CA 92614
Tel: (949) 955-1250
Fax: (949) 955-1824
Hours: 8–5 M–F
e-mail: *cnapolitano@bowersandmerena.com*
Specialties: *All U.S. coins & currency, from junk to certified gem rarities. PCGS, NGC, ANACS, ICG.*

NOXON, Casey
(PNG #431)
TEXAS NUMISMATIC INVESTMENTS, INC.
P.O. Box 26625
Austin, TX 78755
Tel: (512) 343-0343
Fax: (512) 343-6923
Hours: By appointment only
e-mail: *TNII@flash.net*
Specialties: *Patterns, rare date gold, silver dollars, pioneer gold.*

NUGGET, Paul
(PNG #317)
STACK'S-BOWERS NUMISMATICS
123 W 5th Street
New York, NY 10019
Tel: (212) 582-2580
Fax: (516) 505-9193
Hours: 9–5 by appointment only
e-mail: *pnugget@stacksbowers.com*
Fixed price lists.
Specialties: *United States coins & currency, rare date gold, auction work.*

OAKES, Dean
(PNG #127)
DEAN OAKES COINS & CURRENCY
P.O. Box 1456
Iowa City, IA 52244
Tel: (319) 338-1144
Hours: By appointment only

O'CONNOR, Joseph
(PNG #692)

O'CONNOR NUMISMATICS, LLC
P.O. Box 638
New Lenox, IL 60451
Tel: (815) 462-9433
Fax: (815) 462-9434
e-mail: *joe@ocnumis.com*
website: *ocnumis.com*

OLMSTEAD, David
(PNG #545)
ALPINE NUMISMATICS, INC.
P.O. Box 5071
Buena Vista, CO 81211
Tel: (719) 395-5800
Hours: 9–6 M–F MT
e-mail: *alpinenum@aol.com*
website:
www.alpinenumismatics.com
Specialties: *U.S. coins
1793-1950. Early type. Rare
date seated, barber & 20th
century. Early and rare date
gold.*

OSWALD, Vernon H., Sr
(PNG #158)
OSSIE'S COIN SHOP
4560 Hamilton Blvd.
Allentown, PA 18103
Jan.-June: (561) 483-9626
June-Dec. (610) 965-9485
Fax: (610) 530-1589
Hours: 10–6 M–F
e-mail: *ossievh@msn.com*
Specialties: *Gold coins. Proof
coins, U.S. patterns, all U.S.
coins. NGC & PCGS graded
coins US type notes (large to
sm.) Nat'l currency (Large &
sm.) No. 1 type Notes & Nat'l
bank notes & rare currency
documents, appraisals &
estates coins or paper money.*

PANITCH, William S.
(PNG #685)
WILLIAM S. PANITCH RARE
COINS

3 Computer Drive West, #122
Albany, NY 12205
Tel: (518) 489-4400
Hours: By appointment
e-mail: *wpanitch@gmail.com*
website: *www.wspcoin.com*
Specialties: *U.S. & foreign
coins and paper money.*

PAPPACODA, Andrew
(PNG #551)
FLORIDA COIN & JEWELRY,
INC.
P.O. Box15835
Clearwater, FL 33766-5835
Tel. (727) 669-2646
Fax: (727) 723-1956
Hours: 9–6 M–F; or call for
appointment.
e-mail: *floridacoin@aol.com*
website: *www.floridacoin.com*
Specialties: *U.S. gold coins,
key dates in all series. Ebay
Power Seller: Florida Coin.*

PARRELLA, Joseph
(PNG #667)
EASTERN NUMISMATICS, INC.
642 Franklin Avenue
Garden City, NY 11530
Tel: (516) 746-6460
(800) 835-0008
Fax: (516) 746-6467
e-mail: *jdp@uscoins.com*
website: *www.uscoins.com*
Twitter: *jdparrela*
Hours: M–F 10–5, Sat 10–2
Specialties: *U.S. gold, rare
coins & currency, ancient &
foreign coins, precious metals.
Expert appraisals & portfolio
evaluation service.*

PEARLMAN, Donn
(PNG #AF498)
H.S. PERLIN CO., INC.
4491 Via Bianca Ave.
Las Vegas, NV 89141

Tel: (702) 868-5777
e-mail: *info@goldendures.com*
Specialties: *Public relations & communications counsel to the profession.*

PERLIN, Joel D.
(PNG #391)
H.S. PERLIN CO., INC.
1110 Silverado St.
La Jolla, CA 92037-4524
Tel: (858) 459-4409
(858) 459-7803
Fax: (858) 459-7804
Hours: M–F 10–6 by
appointment only
e-mail: *info@parlincoins.com*
website: *goldendures.com*
Specialties: *U.S. rare coins, gold coins of the world, high quality ancient coins; rare coin estates & collections appraised & purchased. 28th year in rare coin business in La Jolla, California.*

PIENTA, Peter
(PNG #283)
NORTHSHORE
NUMISMATICS, INC.
358 Main Street
Wakefield, MA 01880
Tel: (781) 246-4500
Hours: Mon.–Fri. 9–4, Sat. 9–1
e-mail: *png283@aol.com*
website: *www.nscoins.com*
Specialties: *New England's largest display of collector coins.*

PIRET, Diane Augusty
(PNG #A-424)
I.C.T.A
P.O. Box 316
Belle Chasse, LA 70037
Tel: (504) 392-0023
Fax: (504) 392-0305
e-mail: *dapiret@aol.com*
website: *ictaonline.org*

Specialties: *Government Relations.*

PONTERIO, Richard H.
(PNG #308)
PONTERIO & ASSOCIATES,
INC. (A DIVISION OF STACKS-
BOWERS)
1063 McGaw #100
Irvine, CA 92614
Tel. (800) 458-4646
Tel. (800) 854-2888
Fax: (949) 253-4091
Hours: By appointment only
Mexican coins, medals & paper
money.
e-mail:
rponterio@stacksbowers.com
website:
www.bowersandmerena.com
Specialties: *Ancients, Appraisals, Auctions, World coins and World Currency.*

PRATALI, Wayne A.
(PNG #R599)
USCOIN.NET
827 Union Pacific Blvd.
PMB 71-463
Laredo, TX 78045
Tel: (213) 985-0519
Hours: 24 hours
e-mail:
waynepratali@uscoin.net
website: *www.uscoin.net*
Specialties: *Rare gold coins.*

QUAN, Kitty
(PNG #694)
PANDA AMERICA CORP.
19675 Mariner Ave.
Torrance, CA 90503
Tel: (310) 373-9647
Fax: (310) 378-6024
e-mail:
kitty@pandaamerica.com
website: *pandaamerica.com*
Hours: 9–5 M–F

Specialties: *Panda coins, new modern issue coins from Australia, Canada, China, France, Great Britain, Israel, Mexico, and other countries and areas.*

QUITMEYER, Richard
(PNG #A681)
YELLOW RIVER RARE COINS
P.O. Box 26276
Minneapolis, MN 55462
Tel: (612) 986-2566
Fax: (952) 929-8036
Hours: By appointment
e-mail:
sales@yellowriverrarecoins.com
website:
www.yellowriverrarecoins.com

RATNER, Daniel N.
(PNG #496)
RATNER RARE COIN
INVESTMENTS, INC.
P.O. Box 2125
Rockville, MD 20847-2125
Tel: (301) 770-1799
Fax: (301) 770-1869
By appointment only
e-mail:
danratner1@comcast.net
Specialties: *U.S. Gold, dollar rolls, original commems, all high grade U.S. coins.*

RETTEW, Joel D., Sr.
(PNG #163)
SOEL RETTEN COINS
P.O. Box 1466
Lake Forest, CA 92609
Tel: (800) 473-9155
Fax: (949) 609-0120
Hours: By appointment
Fixed price lists, catalogs, publications, auction sales, newsletters.
e-mail: *fastcoin@gmail.com*
website: *www.fastcoin.com*
Specialties: *Collector coins,*
investment grade certified U.S. rare coins, PCGS & NGC dealer; appraiser for the Federal Trade Commission.

RINKOR, Don
(PNG #663)
DON RINKOR RARE COINS
2600 Mendolino Ave., Suite C
Santa Rosa, CA 95403
Tel: (707) 546-2575
Fax: (707) 546-2545
e-mail: *donrinkor@sonic.net*
website: *www.dmpldollar.com*

ROBERTS, Greg
(PNG #414)
SPECTRUM NUMISMATICS
1063 McGaw #100
Irvine, CA 92614
Tel. (949) 955-1250
Fax: (949) 955-1824
Hours: 8–5 M–F

ROBINS, Douglas
(PNG #261)
DOUGLAS ROBINS, INC
(541) 757-1177
Specialties: *Canada: coins & tokens. World coins.*

RODGERS, Brad
(PNG #448)
THE NUMISMATIC
EMPORIUM, INC.
P.O. Box 929
Woodland Hills, CA 91367
Tel: (818) 887-2723
(800) 530-3050
Fax: (818) 887-0301
Specialties: *U.S. gold coins.*

ROHAN, Gregory J.
(PNG #449)
HERITAGE AUCTIONS
445 Park Ave. (near 57th St.)
New York, NY 10022
Tel: (212) 466-3500

(800) 872-6467
Fax: (214) 528-2596
Hours: 10–6 Mon.–Fri.
Auction sales, collections
purchased.
e-mail: *greg@ha.com*
website: *www.ha.com*
Specialties: *Buying, selling,
financing, joint ventures, coin
show and Internet auction
sales throughout the year.
Consignments accepted.*

ROSE, Jonathan
(PNG #A653)
CAPITAL GOLD GROUP, INC.
5850 Canoga Ave, Suite 400
Woodland Hills, CA 91367
Tel: (800) 510-9594
Fax: (800) 830-0863
e-mail: *j.rose@safeasgold.com*
website: *safeasgold.com*
Specialties: *Pre-1933 gold
coins, rarities, bullion.*

ROSEN, Maurice
(PNG #523)
NUMISMATIC COUNSELING,
INC.
P.O. Box 38
Plainview, NY 11803
Tel: (516) 433-5800
Fax: (516) 433-5801
Hours: 9–5
e-mail: *MauriceRosen@aol.com*
Specialties: *U.S. coins.
Investment counseling
& portfolio management;
publisher & editor of* The Rosen
Numismatic Advisory.

ROSSMAN, Will
(PNG #A-533)
COINSTARZ, LLC
300 E. Miller Ct. #2229
Castle Rock, CO 80104
Tel: (970) 404-1937
Fax: (772) 460-8805

Hours: 11–5 M–F, 10–2 Sat.
e-mail: *coinstarz6@gmail.com*
website: *www.coinstarz.com*
Specialties: *Estates, trusts
and collections purchased/
appraised. Auction Services
available. Want lists serviced.
Will travel to consult.*

ROWE, Allen
(PNG #634)
NORTHERN NEVADA COIN
601 N. Carson St.
Carson City, NV 89701
Tel:(888) 836-5527
(775) 884-1660
Fax: (775) 884-1644
Hours: Mon–Fri 9–5:30; Sat
10–4
e-mail: *arowe@brokencc.com*
website: *www.brokencc.com*
Specialties: *Pre-33 U.S. gold
coins, silver dollars, Carson City
coins.*

ROWE, John N. III
(PNG #65)
SOUTHWEST NUMISMATIC
CORP.
6116 N. Central Expy., Suite 921
Dallas, TX 75206
Tel: (214) 823-9202
(214) 826-3036
Fax: (214) 823-1923
Hours: By appointment only
Specialties: *Appraisals, U.S.
coins, U.S. and obsolete paper
money, Texas currency.*

RUBENSTEIN, M.H.
(PNG #186)
MARTIN RUBENSTEIN
COMPANY
1750 Sunrise Highway
Bay Shore, NY 11706
Tel: (631) 665-8924
Fax: (631) 665-8945
Hours: 9–5:30 Tues.–Sat.

Fixed price lists, monthly, FREE for the asking; catalogs; United States, world and wholesale price list.
Specialties: *Coins & currency of U.S., Canada; ancients & world bought & sold; same day jet service since 1961.*

RUDDY, James
(PNG #50)
12 Nebulae Way
Rancho Mirage, CA 92270
Tel: (760) 321-4408
Specialties: *NASA equipment that was on the surface of the moon, Robbins space medals.*

RUDO, Jay
(PNG #680)
JOHN MABEN RARE COIN
5565 Broadcast Court
Sarasota, FL 34240
Tel: (800) 362-9004
Fax: (941) 907-8833
e-mail:
jay@moderncoinmart.com
website:
www.moderncoinmart.com
Specialties: *Modern certified coins.*

RUNZE, Paul
(PNG #660)
GROVE COIN CO.
8306 Tamarack Village, #401
Woodbury, MN 55125
Tel: (651) 738-8352
Fax: (651) 731-6659
e-mail: *paul@grovecoin.com*
website: *www.grovecoin.com*

SALZBERG, Andrew
JOHN MABEN RARE COINS
5565 Broadcast Ct.
Sarasota, FL 34240
Tel: (941) 907-8050 #224
Fax: (941) 907-8833

e-mail:
andy@moderncoinmart.com
website: *moderncoinmart.com*

SALZBERG, Mark
(PNG #596)
NUMISMATIC GUARANTY
CORPORATION
P.O. Box 4776
Sarasota, FL 34230
Tel: (941) 360-3990
Fax: (941) 360-2553
e-mail: *mark@ngccoin.com*
website: *www.ngccoin.com*

SAMUELSON, Dana
(PNG #650)
AMERICAN GOLD
EXCHANGE, INC.
P.O. Box 9426
Austin, TX 78766
Tel: (800) 613-9323
Fax: (512) 323-0194
Hours: M–F 8:30–6:30 (CST)
e-mail: *dana@amergold.com*
website: *www.amergold.com*
Specialties: *U.S. gold coins, modern bullion, and classic European gold bullion.*

SAYLOR III, Byrd
(PNG #640)
LOUISVILLE NUMISMATIC
EXCHANGE, INC.
527 S. Third St.
Louisville, KY 40202
Tel: (502) 584-9879
Hours: 9–5 M–F
e-mail: *byrd@louisvillenumismatic
.com*
website: *louisnumismatic.com*

SCHELL, Thomas F.
(PNG #506)
SECURITY RARE COINS
1513 Lititz Pike
Lancaster, PA 17601
Tel: (717) 291-9621

Fax: (717) 291-9685
Hours: 10–6 M–F, 10–2 Sat.
Specialties: *All U.S. coins & bullion items. Authorized PCGS, NGC dealer.*

SCHINKE, Glenn
(PNG #520)
GLENN SCHINKE
P.O. Box 52
Montrose, CA 91021
Tel. (626) 446-6775
Cell: (626) 221-4606
e-mail:
schinke4-bzzz@yahoo.com
Fixed price lists
Specialties: *Ancient, medieval & foreign coins; tokens & medals; broken banknotes.*

SCHMIDT, Dean
(PNG #451)
DEAN SCHMIDT RARE COIN
P.O. Box 532–104 N. 5th St.
Atchison, KS 66002
Tel: (913) 367-3314
(800) 543-6720
Fax: (913) 367-4106
Hours: M–F 10–5
e-mail: *dsrc01@aol.com*
Specialties: *Collections & estates appraised & purchased. All major U.S. rarities especially wanted.*

SCHMIDT, Gerald A.
(PNG #566)
IMPERIAL COINS
P.O. Box 6479
Glen Valley, VA 23058
Tel: (804) 360-5684
Hours: 9:30 a.m.–1:00 p.m.
T–S
Specialties: *U.S. & World General.*

SCHROEDER, David
(PNG #695)
DSS COIN AND BULLION

1906 So. 13th St.
Omaha, NE 68108
Tel: (402) 342-9153
Fax: (402) 614-5101
e-mail:
david@dsscoinandbullion.com
website:
dsscoinandbullion.com
Hours: M 9–4, T–F 9–5, Sat. 9–3
Specialties: *All NGC PCGS certified collector coins, copper, bullion, certified foreign, tokens, gold.*

SCHUCH, John L.
(PNG #560)
JOHN L. SCHUCH R.C
898 Douglas Blvd.
Roseville, CA 95678
Tel: (916) 780-7097
(916) 780-7063
Fax: (916) 780-6780
Hours: 9–5 Mon.–Thur., 9–2 Fri.
e-mail: *jlssr@surewest.net*
Specialties: *Franklin halves Full bell lines. Jefferson Nickels Full Steps.*

SCHWARY, Richard Joseph
(PNG #365)
CALIFORNIA NUMISMATIC INVESTMENTS, INC.
525 West Manchester Blvd.
Inglewood, CA 90301-1627
Tel: (310) 674-3330
(800) 225-7351
Fax: (310) 330-3766
Free 24-Hour Quote Line: (888) 443-GOLD Free info. package, authorized PCGS/NGC dealer.
e-mail: *rschwary@aol.com*
website: *www.golddealer.com*
Specialties: *All gold, silver & platinum bullion; investment quality, certified rare coins. Buy & sell collections, large or small, & guarantee the best prices in the nation.*

SEGO, James
(PNG #690)
JMS COINS
P.O. Box 9643
Naperville, IL 60567
Tel: (630) 701-8801
(888) 252-7997
e-mail: *jsego@jmscoins.com*
websites: *jmscoins.com,*
eliginsinvestments.com

SHAPIRO, Larry
(PNG #687)
LARRY SHAPIRO RARE
COINS
P.O. Box 4942
Palos Verdes, CA 90274
Tel: (310) 710-2869
e-mail: *larry@lsrarecoins.com*
website: *lsrarecoins.com*
Hours: M–Sat. 9–6
Specialties: *Morgans, Peace,*
Walker, proof type toned coins.

SIMEK, James A.
(PNG #319)
NUMISGRAPHIC
ENTERPRISES
P.O. Box 7157
Westchester, IL 60154-7157
Tel: (630) 889-8207
Fax: (708) 345-8207
Hours: By appointment only
Specialties: *Quality U.S. coins,*
U.S. large & small size currency,
Nationals, Hawaiiana, black
& white & color numismatic
photography, catalog
production.

SIMMONS, Van
(PNG #542)
DAVID HALL'S RARE COINS
P.O. Box 6220
Newport Beach, CA 92658
Tel: (800) 759-7575
Fax: (949) 477-5874
Hours: 7-5 PST

e-mail: *info@davidhall.com*
website: *www.davidhall.com*
Specialties: *High quality U.S.*
rare coins.

SKRABALAK, Andrew
William   (PNG #591)
ANGEL DEE'S
COINS & COLLECTIBLES
P.O. Box 5234
Woodbridge, VA 22194
Tel: (703) 580-6969
Fax: (703) 580-6969
Hours: 10 a.m.–10 p.m. EST
7 days a week.
e-mail:
buycoins@angeldees.com
website: *www.angeldees.com*
Specialties: *Small cents and*
nickels, primarily mint state and
proof.

SMITH, Thomas J.
(PNG #527)
THE NUMISMATIC
EMPORIUM, INC.
P.O. Box 234
Glen Ellyn, IL 60138
Tel: (630) 790-1564
Fax: (630) 790-0486
Specialties: *Importer and*
marketmaker in all U.S. gold
coins.

SNOW, Richard
(PNG #707)
EAGLE EYE RARE COINS,
INC.
P.O. Box 32891 (mail)
6464 E. Grant, #105
Tuscon, AZ 85751
Tel: (520) 498-4615
(866) 323-2646
Fax: (520) 529-1299
e-mail: *rick@indiancent.com*
websites: *indiancent.com*
greatcoins.com
eBay: *eerc*

eBay: EERC
Hours: 9–5 M–F in store
Specialties: *Flying Eagle and Indian Cents, Eagle Eye Photo Seal.*

SONG, Paul
(PNG #631)
BONHAMS & BUTTERFIELDS
7601 Sunset Boulevard
Los Angeles, CA 90046
Tel: (323) 436-5455
Cell: (310) 633-4170
Fax: (323) 850-5843
e-mail:
paul.song@bonhams.com
website:
www.bonhams.com/uscoins
Specialties: *U.S. 19th and 20th century coins; Greek, Roman, and world coinage; Auctions; U.S. gold; Ancients; Latin American; jewelry and time pieces.*

SPANIER, Kurt
(PNG #366)
P.O. Box 37
Las Rozas, Madrid, 28230
Tel: 011-3491-6302690
Hours: By appointment only
e-mail: *kurtspa@sapo.pt*
Specialties: *Expertise, counseling & estimation on Roman coins, Spanish & colonial coins, Portuguese coins.*

SPENCE, Larry Gerald
(PNG #301)
LARRY SPENCE RARE COINS
P.O. Box 26
Rosanky, TX 78953
Tel: (512) 657-6335
Fax: (830) 839-4537
Hours: By appointment

STACK, Harvey G.
(PNG #291)

STACK'S
P.O. Box 0401
Green Vale, NY 11548
Tel: (516) 551-7388
Fax: (516) 484-4403
Hours: By appointment only
66 years of selling at public auction—1935 to present.
Fixed price lists, catalogs, publications, auction sales.
e-mail: *hgs1919@gmail.com*
website: *www.stacks.com*
Specialties: *United States gold, silver & copper coins; ancient & foreign gold, silver & copper coins; Coin Galleries—Stack's foreign department.*

STACK, Lawrence R.
(PNG #355)
HSL STACK'S
P.O. Box 803
New York, NY 10021
Tel: (516) 456-1326
Fax: (516) 624-7125
65 years of selling at public auction—1935 to present.
Fixed price lists, catalogs, publications, auction sales.
e-mail:
lawrencerstack@gmail.com
website: *www.stacks.com*
Specialties: *United States gold, silver & copper coins; ancient & foreign gold, silver & copper coins. English hammered coins. Coin galleries—Stack's foreign department.*

STAGG, David C., III
(PNG #392)
DAVID C. STAGG III, INC
P.O. Box 640
Santa Rosa, CA 95402
Tel: (707) 938-4901
Fax: (707) 591-0902
Hours: By appointment only
e-mail: *dcstagg@msn.com*

Specialties: *Quality U.S. material.*

STEINBERG, Eric
(PNG #590)
BROWARD COUNTY COINS &
COLLECTIBLES, INC.
P.O. Box 770727
Coral Springs, FL 33077
Tel. (954) 721-9247
Fax: (954) 721-9237
Hours: M–F 10–4. By
Appointment
e-mail: *Browardcc@aol.com*
website:
www.browardcountycoins.com

STEINMETZ, Dennis E.
(PNG #302)
STEINMETZ COINS &
CURRENCY
350 Centerville Road
Lancaster, PA 17601
Tel: (717) 299-1211
(800) 334-3903
Cell: (717) 371-5000
Fax: (717) 299-0289
Hours: 9:30–5:30 M/T/Th/F,
9–12 Sat., Closed Wed.
Facts Teletype D-13, Other
hours by appointment.
e-mail: *dsteinco@aol.com*
website:
www.steinmetzcoins.com
Specialties: *Numismatic collecting, U.S. coins & currency.*

STUPPLER, Barry S
(PNG #334)
BARRY STUPPLER &
COMPANY, INC.
5855 Topanga Canyon Blvd.
#330
Woodland Hills, CA 91367
Tel: (818) 592-2800
Fax: (818) 594-8599
Hours: 9–5 M–F
e-mail: *barry@stuppler.com*
website: *www.stuppler.com*

Specialties: *High grade U.S. gold & silver singles, gold, platinum & silver bullion & coins.*

SUNDERLAND, James
(PNG #548)
JAMES & SONS, LTD.
3474 Vollmer Rd.
Olympia Fields, IL 60461
Tel: (708) 481-1500
Fax: (708) 226-0074
Hours: Tues.–Sat. 10–4
website:
www.jamesandsons.com
Specialties: *U.S. gold & type coins, PCGS dealer.*

SUNDMAN, David M
(PNG #510)
LITTLETON COIN COMPANY,
INC.
1309 Mt. Eustis Rd.
Littleton, NH 03561
Tel. (603) 444-5386
(800) 645-3122
Fax: (603) 444-3512
Hours: 8–4 M–F
Catalogs and fixed price lists
sent on request.
e-mail: *info@littletoncoin.com*
website: *www.littletoncoin.com*
Specialties: *All U.S. coins & paper money. Littleton Coin is a family-owned firm offering friendly service to collectors for over 55 years. Extensive color catalogs available FREE. U.S. coins and currency sent on approval to qualified applicants. With over 100,000 customers, we always need to buy U.S. coins and paper money!*

SWEENEY, Fred
(PNG #629)
FRED SWEENEY RARE
COINS
P.O. Box 936
Shawnee Mission, KS 66201

Tel: (913) 962-2100
Fax: (913) 962-2451
e-mail:
fred@sweeneyrarecoins.com
website:
www.sweeneyrarecoins.com

SWIATEK, Anthony
(PNG #511)
MINERVA C & J, LTD.
P.O. Box 684
Saratoga Springs, NY 12866
Tel: (518) 587-9451
Fax: (518) 587-9452
Hours: 9–7 EST
Free coin grading service.
e-mail: *uscoinguru@aol.com*
website:
www.anthonyswiatek.com
Specialties: *U.S.
commemoratives, U.S. type,
U.S. gold, U.S. currency.*

TANCER, Gary
(PNG #659)
GARY TANCER RARE COINS
INC.
2500 N. Military Trail, Suite 100
Boca Raton, FL 33431
Tel: (561) 981-8533
Fax: (561) 981-8535
Hours: M–F 10–6
e-mail: *gtrci@aol.com*
website: *www.cgobr.com*
Specialties: *U.S. rare coins*

TELLER, M. Louis
(PNG #415)
M. LOUIS TELLER
NUMISMATIC COMPANY
16055 Ventura Blvd., Ste. 635
Encino, CA 91436
Tel. (818) 783-8454
Fax: (818) 783-9083
Hours: By appointment only
e-mail: *mlt@tellercoins.com*
website: *www.tellercoins.com*
Specialties: *Rare world gold &*

*silver coins, fine quality world
banknotes.*

TERRANOVA, Anthony
(PNG #327)
ANTHONY TERRANOVA, INC.
P.O. Box 985, FDR Station
New York, NY 10150
Tel. (212) 787-5682
Specialties: *U.S colonial, state
coinage issues, early U.S. mint
issues & rare gold. Historical
American medals. TO THE
TRADE ONLY.*

THOMAS, Tom
(PNG #700)
JOHN MABEN RARE COINS
5565 Broadcast Ct.
Sarasota, FL 34240
Tel: (941) 907-8050
Fax: (941) 907-8833
e-mail: *tom@moderncoinmart
.com*
website: *moderncoinmart.com*

TODD, Mark (Ben)
(PNG #615)
SARASOTA RARE COIN GAL-
LERY
640 S. Washington Blvd., Suite
100
Sarasota, FL 34236
Tel: (941) 366-2191
Fax: (941) 954-8833
e-mail: *sarararecoin@aol.com*
website: www.*sarasotacoin.com*

TOMASKA, Rick J.
(PNG #589)
R & I COINS
P.O. Box 230009
Encinitas, CA 92023
Tel: (858) 792-1219
(800) 753-2646
Fax: (858) 792-8758

Hours: 9–5 Mon.–Fri,
10–3 Sat.
website: www.ricoins.com
Specialties: Cameo coinage,
mint state Franklin halves. U.S.
Proof Coins.

TREGLIA, Jerry
(PNG #A-588)
JERRY TREGLIA RARE COINS
P.O. Box 295
Ridgewood, NJ 07451
Tel: (201) 825-9737
(201) 665-8111-CELL
Fax: (201) 825-4055
Hours: 9–5
Specialties: U.S. gold coins &
Pioneer gold.

TUBBS, Hayden
(PNG #703)
JOHN MABEN RARE COINS
5565 Broadcast Ct.
Sarasota, FL 34240
Tel: (941) 907-8050
Fax: (941) 907-8833
e-mail: hayden
@moderncoinmart.com
website: moderncoinmart.com

TUCKER, Warren
(PNG #622)
HERITAGE AUCTIONS
3500 Maple Ave., 17th floor
Dallas, TX 75219
Tel: (214) 528-3500
Fax: (214) 443-8425
Hours: 9–5 M–F, 9–1 Sat.
e-mail: warren@ha.com
Specialties: Heritage World
Coin auctions.

USKALI, Roxana
(PNG #665)
HARLAN J. BERK, LTD.
31 N. Clark Street
Chicago, IL 60602
Tel: (312) 609-0016

Fax: (312) 609-1305
e-mail: roxana@hjbltd.com
website: www.hjbltd.com

VAN BEBBER, Robert
(PNG #556)
RARE COIN GALLERIES OF
GLENDALE
228 S. Brand Blvd
Glendale, CA 91204
Tel. (818) 243-2900
(818) 243-1169
Hours: Tues.–Sat. 9–5
Specialties: U.S. coins, world
coins, banknotes, medals,
antiques & jewelry. World gold
& silver coin specialists.

VARNER, Mal
(PNG #270)
ALHAMBRA COIN CENTER,
INC.
254 East Main Street
Alhambra, CA 91801
Tel: (626) 282-1151
(800) 932-COIN
Fax: (626) 282-4694
Hours: Mon.–Thur. 9–5:30, Fri.
9–6, Sat. 10–3
e-mail: malcolm@alhambra.com
Specialties: Rare U.S. &
foreign gold & silver coins;
PCGS & NGC certified coins;
estate jewelry, diamonds,
watches.

VARTIAN, Armen R.
(PNG #AF515)
ATTORNEY AT LAW
1601 N. Sepulveda Blvd. #581
Manhattan Beach, CA 90266
Tel: (310) 372-1355
Fax: (866) 427-3820
e-mail: avartian@gmail.com

VYZAS, Evangelos
(PNG ##581)
P.O. Box 450
Pully, Switzerland 1009

Tel: 01141796580909
011306944148080
Fax: 01141217294615
Hours: Office Hours
e-mail: *e.vyzas@bluewin.ch*
Specialties: *Ancient Greek, Byzantine, Modern Greek coins and medals. Greek currency. All Greek world.*

WADE, Vincent
(PNG #711)
PINEHURST COIN EX-
CHANGE, INC.
1420 Highway 5
Pinehurst, NC 28374
Tel: (910) 235-2646
Fax: (910) 687-0340
e-mail: *contact@pinehurstcoins .com*
website: *pinehurstcoins.com*
Hours: 10–6 M–F, 10–3 Sat.
EST
Specialties: *Wholesale and retail dealer, modern certified coins, appraisals, buying collections & estates.*

WEAVER, Richard
(PNG #598)
DELAWARE VALLEY RARE
COIN
2835 West Chester Pike
Broomall, PA 19008
Tel: (610) 356-3555
Fax: (610) 325-0468
e-mail: *rweaver@dvrcc.com*

WEINBERG, Fred C.
(PNG #257)
FRED WEINBERG & CO.
16311 Ventura Blvd.
Ste. #1298
Encino, CA 91436
Tel: (818) 986-3733
(818) 986-3800
Fax: (818) 986-2153
Hours: 8–4 with appointment

Fixed price lists.
e-mail: *fred@fredweinberg.com*
website:
www.fredweinberg.com
Specialties: *Major Mint Errors Coins & Currency, PCGS Certified coins, & U.S. Gold. Marketing experience & consulting.*

WEISS, Martin
(PNG #579)
MARTIN WEISS
73900 Dinah Shore Dr. Ste 201
Palm Desert, CA 92211
Tel: (424) 247-3162
(760) 832-7707
Hours: 9–5 M–F
Winner of the 2002 Sol Kaplan
Award for "helping in cleansing
our profession of theivery and
for upholding the ethics that the
PNG stands for."
e-mail:
martynweiss@aol.com
website:
www.pandaamerica.com
Specialties: *Major market maker of modern world coins, official distributor for leading world mints. Wholesale and retail for gold & silver foreign coins, United States gold commemoratives, etc. Custom minting coins & medals.*

WEITZ, Harold B.
(PNG #375)
HAROLD B. WEITZ, INC
6315 Forbes Avenue, Suite 208
Pittsburgh, PA 15217
Tel: (412) 521-1879
(800) 245-4807
Fax: (412) 521-1750
Hours: 8:30–4:30
Fixed price lists, catalogs.
e-mail: *hw@weitzcoins.com*
website: *www.weitzcoins.com*

WEITZ, Saul
(PNG #393)
HAROLD B. WEITZ, INC.
6315 Forbes Avenue, Suite 208
Pittsburgh, PA 15217
Tel: (412) 521-1879
(800) 245-4807
Fax: (412) 521-1750
Hours: 8:30–4:30
Fixed price lists, catalogs.
e-mail: www.*saul@aol.com*
website: *www.thinkcoins.com*

WEYGANT, David J.
(PNG #600)
DAVID J. WEYGANT RARE
COINS
P.O. Box 1067
Lake Placid, FL 33862
Tel: (863) 699-1586
Fax: (863) 699-6165
e-mail: *dalias13@hotmail.com*
website: *www.djwcoin.com*
Specialties: *Numismatics.*

WHITE, Harlan
(PNG #132)
2425 El Cajon Blvd
San Diego, CA 92104
Tel: (619) 298-0137
Fax: (619) 298-7966
Hours: 9–4:30, Sat 9–12
Specialties: *$5,000, $10,000,
$500, $1,000 notes. Territorial
& pioneer gold, U.S. coins,
Hawaiian coins.*

WHITNAH, Paul R.
(PNG #AF440)
M&M WORLD TRAVEL
SERVICE
5801 West I-20, Suite 325
Arlington, TX 76017-1078
Tel: (817) 561-1252
Fax: (800) 426-8326
e-mail: *pwhitnah
@mmworldtravel.com*
website:
www.mmworldtravel.com

WILKISON, John
(PNG #351)
WILKISON INTERNATIONAL
P.O. Box 158839
Nashville, TN 37215
Tel: (615) 613-5809
Hours: 10–5 M–F
e-mail: *admin
@wilkinsoninternational.com*
website:
www.wilkinsoninternational.com

WILLIAMS, Dale L.
(PNG #432)
WILLIAMS GALLERY, INC.
29 South Tracy
Bozeman, MT 59715
Tel:(406) 586-4343
(800) 422-0787
Fax: (406) 586-3921
Hours: 9–5 M–F
e-mail: *coins@collectorusa.com*
website: *www.collectorusa.com*
Specialties: *Buying coin
collections & estates, selling
high quality U.S. rare coins.*

WING, Augusto
(PNG #A-423)
M. LOUIS TELLER
NUMISMATIC CO.
16055 Ventura Blvd., Ste. 635
Encino, CA 91436
Tel: (818) 783-8454
Fax: (818) 783-9083
Hours: By appointment only
e-mail: *gus@tellercoins.com*
website:
www.tellercoins.com
Specialties: *Chinese, South
American crowns & patterns,
world gold.*

WINTER, Douglas A.
(PNG #399)
DOUGLAS WINTER
NUMISMATICS
P.O. Box 4383
Portland, OR 97208

Tel: (503) 241-6056
Cell: (214) 675-9897
Fax: (503) 241-6056
Hours: By appointment only
Fixed price lists, appraisals,
consulting, writing projects.
e-mail: *DWN@ont.com*
website:
www.raregoldcoins.com
Specialties: *18th & 19th
century U.S. gold with an
emphasis on choice & rare
branch mint issues; pre-1850
proof silver coinage.*

WINTERSTEIN, Christian
(PNG #315)
UBS AG
CH-4002 Basel,
Aeschenvorstadt,
Tel: (061) 288-2703
Fax: (061) 288-6673
Hours: 8:15–4:30 M–F
Fixed price lists, publications,
catalogs, auction sales.

WOODSIDE, John J.
(PNG #543)
SCOTSMAN COIN &
JEWELRY
11262 Olive Blvd.
St. Louis, MO 63141
Tel: (800) 642-4305
Fax: (314) 692-0410
Hours: 8–5 M–Sat.
Buying guide, selling catalog.
e-mail: *jay@scoins.com*
website: *www.scoins.com*
Specialties: *Coins, currency,
jewelry.*

WRUBEL, Gordon J.
(PNG #316)
COLLECTORS UNIVERSE
PROFESSIONAL
COINGRADING SERVICE
P.O. Box 11777
Newport Beach, CA 92658
Tel: (800) 458-4646

Fax: (603) 569-5319
Hours: 9–5 M–F
e-mail: *gwrubel@collectors.com*
Specialties: *U.S. and
Canadian coins, specializing
in early copper, high quality
U.S. gold and type coins. Rare
phonograph records.*

WNUCK, David J.
(PNG #642)
HLRC
61 N. Plains Industrial Rd.
Wallingford, CT 06492
Tel: (800) 264-6799
e-mail: *dave@hlrc.com*
website: *www.hlrc.com*
Specialties: *Buyer/seller of
rare/historic early American
coins and related items: Colonial coins/tokens, U.S. coins in
copper/silver/gold, rare types/
key dates, pattern coins, pri-
vate/territorial gold coins, eso-
teric numismatic items.*

YOUNGERMAN, William J.
(PNG #236)
WILLIAM YOUNGERMAN, INC.
150 E. Palmetto Pk. Rd. #101
Bank of America Bldg.
Boca Raton, FL 33432
Tel. (561) 368-7707
Tel. (800) 327-5010
Fax: Fax: (561) 394-6084
Hours: 9:30-5:00 M-F
e-mail: *bill@youngermans.com*
website:
www.williamyoungerman.com
Specialties: *Rare U.S. and
world gold coins; collections
bought and sold, paper money.
Appraisals.*

YUTZY, Brian
(PNG #605)
LONE STAR NUMISMATICS,
LLC

8556 Katy Freeway, Suite 101
Houston, TX 77024
Tel: (713) 465-6777
Fax: 465-6778
e-mail: briman36@yahoo.com

ZARIT, Jeffrey S.
(PNG #388)
P.O. Box 2137
Wylie, TX 75098
Tel: (972) 881-2701
(800) 654-7527
Fax: (972) 881-2702
Hours: By appointment only
Fixed price lists (3–5 per year).

e-mail: jeff@klippes.com
website: www.klippes.com
eBay: Jeffone
Specialties: Foreign silver &
copper coins, 1500-date. Ebay
Internet Auctions.

ZURAWSKI, Jr., Stanley M.
(PNG #AF237)
NEVADA COIN MART, INC.
P.O. Box 46110
Las Vegas, NV 89114
Tel: (702) 369-0500
(800) 634-6732

ANCIENT COINS: COLLECTING HISTORICAL COINS

Courtesy of Victor England, Jr., Senior Director of Classical Numismatic Group, Inc.

Coins are the most important form of money. For over 2,000 years these small pieces of metal have represented units of intrinsic value.

Today we take coins for granted; but since coinage emerged in the late 7th century B.C. it has played an important role in the economics of many cultures. Today we are fortunate to have coins as records of past history.

Through the collecting of coins you can acquire significant historical artifacts that can lead you down many paths of research and exploration. If only these small objects could talk—I am sure they would tell many interesting tales.

The collecting of historical coins from the Greek, Roman, and Byzantine periods is an affordable pastime that can provide many hours of enjoyment. The collecting of ancient coins is perhaps the oldest part of numismatics. Once only the hobby of kings, it is now a rewarding field readily open to all.

A recently published book series, *Ancient Coin Collecting* by Wayne G. Sayles, is a must for anyone wanting to look over this fascinating area of numismatics. These books are available from your favorite bookstore or numismatic bookseller.

Over the next few pages I will introduce you to 32 ancient coins that might form the beginnings of your collection. Condition, strike, and style play important roles in the price of ancient coins. I have provided price ranges you might expect to pay for some of these coins. The price categories in the order they appear on the following pages are as follows:

Fine–Very Fine   Very Fine–Good   Very Fine—Extremely Fine

Over 2,600 years ago in Lydia (Western Turkey), small lumps of metal were stamped with a simple design. These lumps of metal, made from a natural alloy of silver and gold, were called electrum. They represent one of the earliest coins.

1. Uncertain Kings of Lydia. Before 561 B.C. Electrum Third Stater. Obverse: Head of a roaring lion, knob on forehead. Reverse: Double incuse punch. Average weight 4.70 grams.

500–700	1000–1400	1500–2400

Croesus, the last King of the Lydians, lived from 560–546 B.C. He was an extremely powerful ruler who subjected many lands in the area. From the spoils of successful war and a rich supply of bullion in his native land, he became fabulously wealthy. The expression "rich as Croesus" still has meaning today. Croesus introduced us to coins made of refined metals of gold and silver.

2. LYDIA, King Croesus. 560–546 B.C. Silver Siglos. Obverse: Confronted foreparts of lion and bull. Reverse: Double incuse punch. Average weight 5.30 grams.

250–400	500–700	750–1200

Over the next hundred years that followed, coinage became the accepted medium of exchange. People in Greece and other nearby countries soon started making use of coins. The designs on the coins reflected the heritage of the many diverse cities that surrounded the Mediterranean. As a result of commerce and war the coinage of the greatest cities of the ancient world became the trade coins of the day. Many Greek coins were very skillfully made and extremely beautiful. Designs often incorporated the patron deity of the city or the badge of the city itself.

Tarentum was the most important city in Southern Italy in the 5th and 4th centuries before Christ. The foundation myth of the city relates the story of a dolphin saving Taras from a shipwreck at sea. In the place where he came ashore, the city of Tarentum was founded.

3. TARENTUM in Calabria. Circa 334–330 B.C. Silver Nomos. Obverse: Naked horseman on horse left. Taras astride of dolphin right. Average weight 7.80 grams.

150–200   250–400   700–1200

On the island of Sicily, Syracuse became the dominant city. Coinage developed on the island in the 6th century B.C. and reached its height in the 5th century. Some of the finest examples of the engravers' art are found on the coins of Syracuse.

4. SYRACUSE on the island of Sicily. Circa 480–475 B.C. Silver Tetradrachm. Obverse: Charioteer driving slow quadriga to the right, Nike above placing a wreath on the horse's head. Diademed head of Arethusa right, four dolphins swimming around. Average weight 17.00 grams.

400–600   600–800   1500–3000

Throughout most of the 5th century B.C. after the defeat of the Persians, Athens was mistress of the Aegean. She became the cultural and political center of the Greek world.

5. ATHENS in Attica. After 449 B.C. Silver Tetradrachm. Obverse: Helmeted head of Athena. Reverse: Owl standing right in shallow incuse, olive spray behind. Average weight 17.00 grams.

200–300   400–700   900–1500

Aegina was an island off the coast of Athens. The Aeginetans were exceptional maritime merchants. Aegina was the central staging depot for Black Sea grain on its way to the Peloponnisos. These early trade coins circulated throughout the Mediterranean.

6. AEGINA. Circa 525–480 B.C. AR Stater. Obverse sea turtle, with T-back dots, seen from above. Reverse. Skew incuse. Average weight 12.25 grams.

100–250   300–500   800–1500

7. AEGINA. Circa 457–431 B.C. AR Tater. Land tortoise, with segmented shell, seen from above. Reverse: Skew pattern incuse. Average weight 12.25 gm.

200–300   500–650   900–1200

Corinth, situated in central Greece, was one of the great commercial centers in her day. Coins of Corinth were widely imitated by other cities. The flying Pegasus is seen on the coins of many of her trading partners.

8. CORINTH in Corinthia. Circa 345–307 B.C. Silver Stater. Obverse: Pegasus flying left. Reverse: Helmeted head of Athena left. Average weight 8.50 grams.

150–200	300–400	500–1000

In Asia Minor we find the important port and naval base of Aspendos. Her coins depict two naked wrestlers grappling in contest. Sporting events were an integral part of life in ancient Greece. The modern day Olympics trace their origins to Greece and her culture.

9. ASPENDOS in Pamphylia. Circa 370–330 B.C. Silver Stater. Obverse: Two wrestlers grappling. Reverse: Slinger standing right in throwing pose, triskeles in the field. Average weight 10.50 grams.

150–250	250–400	600–1200

Along the north coast of Africa we find the important maritime trading city of Carthage. Due to the great natural harbor and favorable geographical location, Carthage became one of the great powers of the Greek world.

10. CARTHAGE in Zeugitania. Circa 350–260 B.C. Gold/Electrum Stater. Obverse: Wreathed head of Tanit left. Reverse: Horse standing right. Average weight 7.50 grams.

500–600	750–900	1400–2000

In the late 4th century a ruler came to power who would change the shape of the world as it was known at the time. At the age of 20, in 336 B.C., Alexander III (the Great) became ruler of the small kingdom of Macedonia. By the time he died 13 years later at the age of 33, he had conquered an empire that stretched from Greece to India. Alexander's coinage played an important role in his eastern conquests. Local coinages were replaced with his tetradrachms. Over 200 mints produced coins in his name.

11. Alexander III, King of Macedon. 336–323 B.C. Silver Tetradrachm. Obverse: Head of Herakles right, wearing a lion skin. Reverse: Zeus enthroned left, holding an eagle in his outstretched hand. Average weight 17.00 grams.

150–200	250–425	500–800

Alexander was one of the most successful generals who ever lived. Upon his death his kingdom was divided amongst several of his generals. Many of the kings who came after Alexander put his picture on their coins. They believed he was a god.

12. Lysimachos, King of Thrace. 323–281 B.C. Silver Tetradrachm. Obverse: Head of deified Alexander the Great right. Reverse: Athena seated left holding Nike in her outstretched hand. Average weight 17.00 grams.

200–250   300–450   900–1500

As the successors of Alexander established power in their own rights, several powerful kingdoms formed. One of the most powerful of the new kingdoms was the Ptolemaic kingdom in Egypt. Under Ptolemy and his successors, this kingdom would survive until the death of Cleopatra VII, lover of Julius Caesar and Mark Antony. The coins of Ptolemaic Egypt provide us with portraits of important historical rulers.

13. Ptolemy I, King of Egypt. 323–283 B.C. Silver Tetradrachm. Obverse: Diademed bust of Ptolemy right. Reverse: Egyptian eagle standing left on thunderbolt. Average weight 14.50 grams.

100–250   250–350   500–800

14. Cleopatra VII, Queen of Egypt. 51–30 B.C. Bronze 80 Drachmae. Obverse: Diademed bust of Cleopatra right. Reverse: Eagle standing left on thunderbolt. Average weight 18.00 grams.

| 100–200 | 300–600 | 1200–1600 |

To the east of Egypt was the province of Judaea. The area was under the rule first of the Persians, then Alexander the Great, and later the Ptolemaic kings followed by the Seleucids. During the late 2nd century B.C., Judaea achieved a measure of independence under the Hasmoneans and finally under Alexander Jannaeus, 103–76 B.C., full autonomy. This impoverished area gave birth to two of the world's greatest religions—Judaism and later Christianity.

15. Alexander Jannaeus, Hasmonean King of Judaea. 103–76 B.C. Bronze Prutah. Obverse: Anchor, legend around. Reverse: Wheel with eight spokes. Average weight 1.00 gram.

| 20–30 | 40–75 | 200–400 |

Late in the 2nd century B.C., the port city of Tyre regained her autonomy in the waning days of Ptolemaic and Seleucid influence. A remarkable silver coinage was struck at Tyre from about 126 B.C. until well into Roman times. The famous tetradrachms (shekels) of this series have achieved some notoriety as the most likely coinage with which Judas was paid his "30 pieces of silver" for the betrayal of Christ.

16. TYRE in Phoenicia. After 126 B.C. Silver Tetradrachm (shekel). Obverse: Laureate bust of Melkart. Reverse: Eagle standing left on prow. Average weight 14.00 grams, declining later to 13.00 grams.

250–400   500–600   750–1200

"And when they had bound him, they led him away, and delivered him to Pontius Pilate the governor." Matthew 27:2

This coin speaks for itself.

17. Pontius Pilate, Roman Prefect of Judaea under Tiberius, Emperor of Rome. 26–29 A.D. Bronze Prutah. Obverse: Lituus with inscription around. Reverse: Date within wreath. Average weight 1.00 gram.

30–50   75–125   400–600

While the Hellenistic kingdoms were vying for control in the east, another power was slowly emerging in the west. On the banks of the river Tiber in Italy in a small village called Rome, a new empire was taking shape. According to legend, twins called Romulus and Remus founded Rome in the middle of the 8th century B.C. By the 3rd century B.C. this small agricultural community had grown and began building one of the greatest empires the world has ever seen.

At first the Romans used coins that were struck on the Greek system that was already in place in Italy.

18. ROMAN REPUBLIC. Circa 225–212 B.C. Silver Didrachm (Quadrigatus). Obverse: Laureate head of Janus. Reverse: Jupiter in a quadriga moving to the right being driven by Victory. Average weight 6.50 grams.

100–200   300–400   700–1200

One of the main reasons the Romans struck coins was to pay the soldiers. As the Roman army expanded the boundaries of the

Empire, a new denomination emerged that would become the standard for many centuries. The Roman silver denarius was struck from the 2nd century B.C. until the 3rd century A.D. In the latter days of the Republic and early days of the Empire a Roman soldier received an annual salary of 225 denarii.

19. ROMAN REPUBLIC. After 200 B.C. Issued by various moneyers. Silver Denarius. Obverse: Helmeted head of Roma right, X below chin. Reverse: The Dioscuri riding right. Average weight 3.85 grams.

50–75	100–150	3500–4500

As the Empire expanded, the political system in Rome suffered. Rome was no longer able to govern itself under rules of just a Senate, and influential people began to try and take control of the reins of power. In 59 B.C., Caius Julius Caesar was elected to be a governing consul. He spent the next eight years campaigning in Britain and Gaul. A power struggle ensued amongst other ruling members of the ruling Roman triumvirate, and, after defeating Pompeii in 48 B.C. Caesar marched into Rome as her undisputed master. After only a short period of supreme power he was assassinated on the Ides (15th) of March in 44 B.C.

20. Julius Caesar. Struck 49 B.C. Silver Denarius. Obverse: Elephant right trampling a serpent, CAESAR below. Reverse: Priestly implements. Average weight 4.00 grams.

150–200	300–400	600–1000

After the assassination of Caesar, another triumvirate was formed to try and govern Rome. Two of the members of this group, Mark Antony and Octavian (Augustus), were to play important roles in the advancement of the Roman empire. Antony was given command of the province of Asia. It was here that he met and was captivated by the last of the Ptolemaic dynasty, Cleopatra VII. Antony then quarrelled with Octavian in a struggle for ultimate power. He was defeated at the battle of Actium and fled with Cleopatra to Egypt where he committed suicide in 30 B.C. During this struggle with Octavian he struck a series of denarii for each of the legions under his command.

21. Mark Antony. 32–31 B.C. Silver Legionary Denarius. Obverse: Manned galley right. Reverse: Aquila surmounted by an eagle and flanked by two standards, the legend LEG followed by a Roman numeral representing the legion. Average weight 3.50 grams.

| 75–100 | 150–200 | 500–700 |

Having achieved undisputed mastery of the Roman world in 30 B.C., Octavian returned stability to the Roman state. In 27 B.C. the Senate acknowledged his mastery and bestowed upon him the title of Augustus, by which he is best known. Augustus ruled long and prosperously, dying at the age of 77. He left behind the foundations for one of the world's greatest empires.

22. Augustus. 27 B.C.–14 A.D. Silver Denarius. Obverse: Laureate head of Augustus right. Reverse: Caius and Lucius Caesars standing facing, shields and spears between them. Average weight 3.60 grams.

| 75–100 | 150–200 | 400–600 |

Augustus' long life and treachery within his household resulted in his stepson Tiberius succeeding him. Tiberius proved himself an able administrator. The ministry and crucifixion of Jesus Christ occurred during his reign.

The Tribute Penny. *"Is it lawful to give tribute to Caesar, or not? Shall we give or shall we not give? But he knowing their hypocrisy, said unto them, Why tempt ye me? Bring me a penny, that I may see it. And they brought it. And He said unto them, Whose is this image and superscription? And they said unto Him, Caesar's. And Jesus, answering, said unto them, Render to Caesar the things that are Caesar's, and to God the things that are God's."* Mark 12:14–17

23. Tiberius. 14–37 A.D. Silver "Tribute" Denarius. Obverse: Laureate head right, inscription around. Reverse: Livia as pax seated right on throne. Average weight 3.60 grams.

| 125–200 | 250–300 | 600–750 |

When no clear line of succession to an emperor was apparent, it was often the Praetorian guard who helped choose a successor. Upon the death of the infamous Caligula, the guard raised Claudius to the purple giving him the title of Augustus. The story of these turbulent times has been re-created on video under the title of *I, Claudius.*

24. Claudius. 41–54 A.D. Bronze As. Obverse: Bare head of Claudius left. Reverse: Minerva standing right hurling javelin. Average weight 11.00 grams.

| 100–175 | 250–350 | 600–800 |

Nero, the adopted son of Claudius, was one of Rome's most colorful emperors. His unbridled enthusiasm, love of the finer things in life, passion for sporting events, and rumored love of fire, led him to commit suicide.

25. Nero. 54–68 A.D. Bronze As. Obverse: Laureate head of Nero right. Reverse: View of the front of the Temple of Janus. Average weight 11.00 grams.

100–175   250–350   700–1200

By the 2nd century A.D. the Roman Empire had reached gargantuan proportions. One of Rome's best administrators was the emperor Hadrian. He spent much of his career travelling the vast empire. His most lasting legacy is Hadrian's Wall in northern England.

26. Hadrian. 117–138 A.D. Silver Denarius. Obverse: Laureate head of Hadrian right. Reverse: Concordia seated left. Average weight 3.35 grams.

50–75   100–200   400–600

In 248 A.D. Rome celebrated the 1000th anniversary of its foundation. Philip I, emperor of Rome, celebrated this anniversary with magnificent games featuring many wild beasts collected especially for this celebration. By the middle of the 3rd century, the denarius had lost much of its value. A larger silver piece was introduced called the antoninianus.

27. Philip I. 244–249 A.D. Silver Antoninianus. Obverse: Radiate bust of Philip right. Reverse: SAECVLARES AVG around various different animals used in the celebration of the 1000th anniversary. Average weight 3.65 grams.

30–50   75–100   125–225

Christianity was a persecuted religion for much of its first 300 years. The first Roman emperor to embrace Christianity was Constantine I, the Great. It is said that he converted on his deathbed.

28. Constantine I, the Great. 307–337 A.D. Bronze Follis. Obverse: Helmeted and cuirassed bust right. Reverse: Roma seated right holding shield. (Many obverse and reverse variations). Average weight 3.00–4.00 grams.

20–30   40–60   150–250

Christianity did not gain immediate acceptance after the death of Constantine. The "Philosopher" Julian II outlawed Christianity 30 years after the death of Constantine, preferring the old pagan religions.

29. Julian II, the Philosopher. 360–363 A.D. Bronze (uncertain denomination). Obverse: Diademed, draped, and cuirassed bust right. Reverse: Apis bull standing right, two stars above. Average weight 8.50 grams.

150–200   300–500   800–1200

By the 5th century A.D., the Roman empire had split into two empires. The empire in the west was tangled in political upheaval. The center of the empire had moved from Rome to Constantinople. In contrast to the problems in the West, the Eastern division of the Empire enjoyed comparative peace under the leadership of Theodosius II. His most notable achievement was the compilation of the legal code known as the Codex Theodosianus. By the 5th century, silver and bronze coins had been replaced by the gold solidus as the coin of the realm.

30. Theodosius II. 402–450 A.D. Gold Solidus. Obverse: Helmeted and cuirassed three-quarter facing bust, spear over far shoulder. Reverse: Constantinopolis enthroned right, holding globus cruciger and sceptre. Average weight 4.45 grams.

200–300	350–500	700–1200

By the 6th century the last vestiges of the Roman Empire had faded into obscurity. While the west was still in turmoil the east found leadership under the religious successors to the Romans. The Byzantine Empire would last until the fall of Constantinople in 1453.

The Byzantine Empire found solid leadership under Justinian I. He ruled for almost four decades. He consolidated the empire, regaining territory lost to the Goths and Vandals. At home in Constantinople, he built the great church of St. Sophia. This is still standing as one of the great architectural achievements of its time in modern day Istanbul. Justinian is also remembered for his final codification of Roman law. He consolidated the best of Roman law for generations to come.

31. Justinian I. 527–565 A.D. Bronze Follis. Obverse: Helmeted facing bust of Justinian holding globus cruciger. Reverse: Large M, flanked by ANNO on the left, numbers on the right indicating the year of his reign and a mint mark below. Average weight 22.00 grams declining to 15.00 grams.

20–30   75–100   400–600

By the 7th century, new nations were emerging in the west and the Byzantine Empire was locked in perpetual struggle with the Arab world. Justinian II showed his devotion to God by placing the image of Christ on his coinage. He was the first emperor to do this. However, his attempts at introducing his doctrines into the policies of the Church were rejected. In the old city of Rome, the papacy was in its infancy. But once again a gradual shift of power was beginning to occur.

32. Justinian II. 685–695 A.D. Gold Solidus. Obverse: Facing bust of bearded Christ imposed over a cross, hand raised in benediction. Reverse: Justinian standing crowned, wearing loros and holding cross potent on steps. Average weight 4.30 grams.

600–800   900–1200   1800–2200

This is only an abbreviated list of the many thousands of different coins one can purchase. Hopefully this list will start you on the road to discovery and collecting in this fascinating field.

The following is a list of six suggested titles for further reading:

Foss, Clive. *Roman Historical Coins.* 1990
Howgego, Christopher. *Ancient History from Coins.* 1995
Jenkins, G. K. *Coins in History—Ancient Greek Coins.* 1990
Lorber, Cathy. *Treasures of Ancient Coinage: From the Private Collections of American Numismatic Society Members.* 1996
Sayles, Wayne G. *Ancient Coin Collecting.* 1996.
Sear, David. *Byzantine Coins and Their Values.* 1987

One of the best general publications on ancient coins is *The Celator,* ed. Kerry Wetterstrom, published monthly. Contact the publication at P.O. Box 859, Lancaster, PA 17608.

Two organizations that are active in the field of ancient numismatics are the American Numismatic Society (ANS) (contact at Broadway at 155th

St., New York, NY 10032), and the Society for Ancient Numismatics (SAN) (contact at P.O. Box 4095, Panorama City, CA 91412).

I am one of the Directors of the Classical Numismatic Group, Inc. (CNG). For the past 22 years we have been quietly building a full-service numismatic firm dedicated to serving the needs of our customers in the fields of ancient, world, and British numismatics. Each year we conduct three auctions, publish three fixed-price lists, attend numerous shows around the world, and even occasionally publish a book. If you would like to know more about us or the field of ancient numismatics, please get in touch. We would like to be of service. Write, call, or e-mail us at Classical Numismatic Group, Inc., P.O. Box 479, Lancaster, PA 17608-0479. Phone (717) 390-9194, fax (717) 390-9978, e-mail: cng@cngcoins.com. We invite you to learn more about ancient coins at www.cngcoins.com.

ANTILLES (NETHERLANDS)

Key to Grading: Lion

DATE	COIN TYPE/VARIETY/METAL	ABP FINE	AVERAGE FINE
☐ 1952–1970	1 Cent, Lion, Bronze	$ .47	$ .78

Key to Grading: Shield

☐ 1970–1978	1 Cent, Bronze	.23	.39

Key to Grading: Lion

DATE	COIN TYPE/VARIETY/METAL	ABP FINE	AVERAGE FINE
☐ 1956–1965	2½ Cents, Lion, Bronze	$ .30	$ .49
Key to Grading: Shield			
☐ 1970–1978	2½ Cents Bronze	.29	.48

Key to Grading: Scallop			
☐ 1957–1970	5 Cents, Juliana, Cupro-Nickel	.30	.49
Key to Grading: Shield			
☐ 1971–1985	5 Cents Copper Nickel	.19	.32

Key to Grading: Bust of Queen			
☐ 1954–1970	1/10 Gulden, Juliana, Silver	.85	1.42
Key to Grading: Shield			
☐ 1970–1985	10 Cents Nickel	.30	.49

Key to Grading: Bust of Queen			
☐ 1954–1970	1/4 Gulden, Juliana, Silver	.56	.94
Key to Grading: Shield			
☐ 1970–1985	25 Cents Nickel	.23	.39
Key to Grading: Flower			
☐ 1989–2000	50 Cents Steel	.30	.49

Key to Grading: Shield			
☐ 1952–1970	1 Gulden, Juliana, Silver	1.10	1.85
Key to Grading: Shield			
☐ 1970–1980	1 Gulden Nickel	.55	.91

DATE	COIN TYPE/VARIETY/METAL	ABP FINE	AVERAGE FINE

Key to Grading: Shield

| ☐ 1964 | 2¹/₂ Gulden, Juliana, Silver | $3.85 | $6.75 |

Key to Grading: Shield

☐ 1978–1980	2¹/₂ Gulden	1.45	2.45
☐ 1981–1988	2¹/₂ Gulden	1.45	2.40
☐ 1989–2000	2¹/₂ Gulden	1.15	1.90

ARGENTINA

The first coins were used in 1813, followed by silver reales in 1815, and the copper centavos and gold pesos in the mid-1800s. Cupro-nickel pesos and aluminum-bronze pesos were used in the 1900s. Decimal coins were used in 1881. The currency today is the peso.

Argentina—Type Coinage

Key to Grading: Shield

DATE	COIN TYPE/VARIETY/METAL	ABP FINE	AVERAGE FINE
☐ 1882–1896	1 Centavo, Bronze	$ .88	$1.45
☐ 1939–1944	1 Centavo, Bronze	.18	.32
☐ 1945–1948	1 Centavo, Copper	.26	.44

Key to Grading: Shield

DATE	COIN TYPE/VARIETY/METAL	ABP FINE	AVERAGE FINE
☐ 1882–1896	2 Centavos, Bronze	$ .63	$1.05
☐ 1939–1947	2 Centavos, Bronze	.30	.49
☐ 1947–1950	2 Centavos, Copper	.30	.49
Key to Grading: Bust			
☐ 1896–1942	5 Centavos, Cupro-Nickel	.38	.53

☐ 1942–1950	5 Centavos, Aluminum-Bronze	.20	.34
☐ 1950	5 Centavos, Death of San Martin Centennial, Cupro-Nickel	.30	.49
☐ 1951–1953	5 Centavos, Cupro-Nickel	.30	.49
☐ 1953–1956	5 Centavos, Copper-Nickel Clad Steel	.30	.49
☐ 1957–1959	5 Centavos, Nickel Clad Steel	.30	.49
Key to Grading: Bust			
☐ 1881–1883	10 Centavos, Silver	—	12.00

☐ 1896–1942	10 Centavos, Cupro-Nickel	.34	.56
☐ 1942–1950	10 Centavos, Aluminum-Bronze	.30	.49
☐ 1950	10 Centavos, Death of San Martin Centennial, Cupro-Nickel	.25	.42
☐ 1951–1953	10 Centavos, Cupro-Nickel	.25	.42

DATE	COIN TYPE/VARIETY/METAL	ABP FINE	AVERAGE FINE
☐ 1952–1956	10 Centavos, Copper-Nickel Clad Steel	$ .30	$ .49
☐ 1957–1959	10 Centavos, Nickel Clad Steel	.30	.49
Key to Grading: Bust			
☐ 1881–1883	20 Centavos, Silver	10.70	17.85
☐ 1896–1942	20 Centavos, Cupro-Nickel	.30	.49

☐ 1942–1950	20 Centavos, Aluminum-Bronze	.26	.44
☐ 1950	20 Centavos, Death of San Martin Centennial, Cupro-Nickel	.26	.44
☐ 1951–1953	20 Centavos, Cupro-Nickel	.03	.50
☐ 1952–1956	20 Centavos, Copper-Nickel Clad Steel	.26	.44
☐ 1957–1961	20 Centavos, Nickel Clad Steel	.26	.44
Key to Grading: Bust			
☐ 1881–1883	50 Centavos, Silver	—	42.50

☐ 1941	50 Centavos, Nickel	.03	.53
☐ 1952–1956	50 Centavos, Copper-Nickel Clad Steel	.23	.39
☐ 1957–1961	50 Centavos, Nickel Clad Steel	.17	.28
Key to Grading: Bust			
☐ 1881–1883	1 Peso, Silver	—	146.50

☐ 1957–1962	1 Peso, Nickel Clad Steel	.30	.49
☐ 1960	1 Peso, Sesquicentennial of Provisional Government, Nickel Clad Steel	.30	.49
Key to Grading: Bust			
☐ 1884	1/2 Argentino, Gold	—	1050.00
☐ 1881–1896	Argentino, Gold	—	240.00

Key to Grading: Ship

DATE	COIN TYPE/VARIETY/METAL	ABP FINE	AVERAGE FINE
☐ 1961–1968	5 Pesos, Nickel Clad Steel	$ .25	$ .42

Key to Grading: Rider

☐ 1962–1968	10 Pesos, Nickel Clad Steel	.25	.42
☐ 1966	10 Pesos, Sequicentennial of Independence, Nickel Clad Steel	.23	.39

Key to Grading: Shield

☐ 1964–1968	25 Pesos, Nickel Clad Steel	.30	.49

Key to Grading: Bust

☐ 1968	25 Pesos, Death of Sarmiento, Nickel Clad Steel	.28	.46

Argentina—Current Coinage

Key to Grading: Bust

☐ 1970–1975	1 Centavo, Aluminum	.26	.42
☐ 1983	1 Centavo, Aluminum	.26	.42
☐ 1970–1975	5 Centavos, Aluminum	.23	.39
☐ 1985–1988	5 Centavos, Brass	.25	.42

Key to Grading: Bust

DATE	COIN TYPE/VARIETY/METAL	ABP FINE	AVERAGE FINE
☐ 1970–1976	10 Centavos, Brass	$ .30	$ .49
☐ 1983	10 Centavos, Aluminum	.28	.46

Key to Grading: Bust

☐ 1970–1976	20 Centavos, Brass	.23	.39
☐ 1970–1976	50 Centavos, Brass	.25	.42
☐ 1983–1984	50 Centavos, Aluminum	.25	.42

Key to Grading: Sun Burst

☐ 1974–1976	1 Peso, Aluminum-Brass	.23	.39
☐ 1984	1 Peso, National Congress, Aluminum	.25	.42
☐ 1976–1977	5 Pesos, Aluminum-Bronze	.25	.42
☐ 1977	5 Pesos, Bicentennial of Admiral Brown, Aluminum-Bronze	.25	.42
☐ 1984–1985	5 Pesos, Buenos Aires City Hall, Brass	.25	.42
☐ 1976–1978	10 Pesos, Aluminum-Bronze	.25	.42
☐ 1977	10 Pesos, Bicentennial of Admiral Brown, Aluminum-Bronze	.25	.42
☐ 1984–1985	10 Pesos, Independence Hall, Brass	.25	.42
☐ 1978	50 Pesos, Birth of San Martin 200th Anniversary, Aluminum-Bronze	.25	.42
☐ 1979	50 Pesos, Jose de San Martin, Aluminum-Bronze	.25	.42

Key to Grading: Soccer Ball

DATE	COIN TYPE/VARIETY/METAL	ABP FINE	AVERAGE FINE
☐ 1977–1978	50 Pesos, World Soccer Championship, Aluminum-Bronze	$ .26	$ .44
☐ 1980–1981	50 Pesos, Jose de San Martin, Brass-Steel	.23	.39

Key to Grading: Rider & Horse

☐ 1980–1981	50 Pesos, Conquest of Patagonia Centennial, Aluminum-Bronze	.23	.39
☐ 1985	50 Pesos, Central Bank 50th Anniversary, Aluminum-Bronze	.18	.30

Key to Grading: Soccer Ball or Bust

☐ 1977–1978	100 Pesos, World Soccer Championship, Aluminum-Bronze	.25	.42
☐ 1978	100 Pesos, Death of San Martin 200th Anniversary, Aluminum-Bronze	.23	.39
☐ 1979	100 Pesos, Conquest of Patagonia Centennial, Aluminum-Bronze	.23	.39
☐ 1979–1981	100 Pesos, San Martin, Aluminum-Bronze	.20	.33
☐ 1980–1981	100 Pesos, Brass-Steel	.19	.32
☐ 1977	1000 Pesos, World Soccer Championship, Silver	—	7.50
☐ 1978	1000 Pesos, World Soccer Championship, Silver	—	6.25
☐ 1977	2000 Pesos, World Soccer Championship, Silver	—	7.15
☐ 1978	2000 Pesos, World Soccer Championship, Silver	—	7.15
☐ 1977	3000 Pesos, World Soccer s Championship, Silver	—	12.75
☐ 1978	3000 Pesos, World Soccer Championship, Silver	—	12.75

Argentina—Latest Coinage

☐ 1985	1/2 Centavo, Brass	.23	.39
☐ 1985–1987	1 Centavo, Ostrich, Brass	.23	.39
☐ 1992	1 Centavo, Brass	.23	.39

Key to Grading: Animals or Sun Burst

DATE	COIN TYPE/VARIETY/METAL	ABP FINE	AVERAGE FINE
☐ 1985–1988	5 Centavos, Wildcat, Brass	$ .26	$ .44
☐ 1992	5 Centavos, Radiant Sun, Brass	.19	.32

Key to Grading: Sun Burst or Building

☐ 1985–1988	10 Centavos, Radiant Sun, Brass	.23	.39
☐ 1992	10 Centavos, Radiant Sun, Aluminum-Bronze	.23	.39
☐ 1992	25 Centavos, Building, Brass	.25	.42

Key to Grading: Bust or Building

☐ 1985–1988	50 Centavos, Brass	.25	.42
☐ 1992	50 Centavos, Tucuman Capitol Building, Brass	.25	.42
☐ 1989	1 Austral, Buenos Aires City Hall, Aluminum	.25	.42

Key to Grading: Building

DATE	COIN TYPE/VARIETY/METAL	ABP FINE	AVERAGE FINE
☐ 1989	5 Australes, Tucuman Independence Hall, Aluminum	$ .25	$ .42

Key to Grading: Building or Shield

DATE	COIN TYPE/VARIETY/METAL	ABP FINE	AVERAGE FINE
☐ 1989	10 Australes, Casa del Acuerdo, Aluminum	.26	.44
☐ 1990–1991	100 Australes, Aluminum	.26	.44
☐ 1990–1991	500 Australes, Aluminum	.26	.44

Key to Grading: Shield

DATE	COIN TYPE/VARIETY/METAL	ABP FINE	AVERAGE FINE
☐ 1990–1991	1000 Australes, Aluminum	.23	.39
☐ 1991	1000 Australes, Ibero-American Series, Silver	—	92.50

AUSTRALIA

Australia's currency is based on the decimal system: one hundred cents (100c) equals one Australian dollar ($1). Decimal currency was introduced in Australia on 14 February 1966 and replaced the imperial system of pounds, shillings, and pence.

Like most national currencies, Australia's currency consists of both coins and currency notes. At various times Australian coins have been made in San Francisco, London, Birmingham, Bombay, and Calcutta, but, today, all Australian circulating coins are produced at the Royal Australian Mint in Canberra.

All Australian currency notes are produced by Note Printing Australia, an autonomous division of the Reserve Bank of Australia, located at Craigieburn, just outside Melbourne.

BRIEF HISTORY OF AUSTRALIA'S COINS

The early inhabitants of the penal colony of New South Wales brought with them English coins as well as those from ports of call on the long voyage. Many different coins and tokens were traded in the colony for differing values, sometimes based vaguely on the value of the coin's metal content.

As this was an unsatisfactory way of conducting transactions, Governor King, in 1800, issued a proclamation to establish a uniform value for the most common coins. The lowest value of two pence was given to a copper coin of one ounce. Various other coins such as rupees, ducats, guilders, and guineas were assigned higher values.

Front: Portuguese Johanna
Back: Ducat

The chronic shortage of coin bedevilled several of the colony's early governors (namely, Phillip, Hunter, King, and Bligh). Rum was more freely available and became the common medium of exchange, earning for New South Wales the name, "the rum colony."

Governor Lachlan Macquarie recognized the role of rum in the colony's affairs but also realized that something had to be done about the acute shortage of coin. He overcame the problem, at least partially, when His Majesty's Sloop *Samarang* arrived in 1812 carrying 40,000 Spanish dollars. Macquarie had the ingenious idea of cutting the center out of the dollars and overstamping the two separate pieces with "New South Wales 1813" to make coins of two different denominations, the so-called "holey dollar" and its centerpiece, the "dump." These coins remained in circulation until 1829. Silver coins from England were used from about 1824.

Holey dollar

The Gold Rush of the 1850s led to the belief that some of Australia's coins could be locally produced. In 1855 the Sydney Mint opened—its first coin was the Sydney gold sovereign. Mints were also established in Melbourne (1872) and Perth (1899).

The first federally commissioned coins were issued in 1910. In 1916, numbers of threepence, sixpence, one shilling, and two shilling (florin) coins were minted in Melbourne.

The Sydney Mint closed in 1926 and the Melbourne Mint closed in 1968 when its functions were transferred to the newly established Royal Australian Mint in Canberra. The Royal Australian Mint is the first Australian mint not to be a branch of the Royal Mint in London. It has produced more than 10 billion Australian coins. It has also made circulating coins or collector (numismatic) coins for such countries as Bangladesh, the Cook Islands, Tonga, New Zealand, Papua New Guinea, and Thailand.

TYPE OF COINS

Australia produces three categories of coins:

Circulating Coins: Standard day-to-day currency and used in normal commercial transactions.

Adelaide ingot

Collector Coins: Commemorative or other coins not in general circulation. They are, however, legal tender and may be used for commercial transactions. Collector coins are classified as "proof" or "uncirculated" coins.

Bullion Coins: Gold, silver, or platinum coins. The bullion value of the metal used in the manufacture of each coin is greater than its face value. These are classified as "non-circulating legal tender" (NCLT).

Circulating coins

The denominations of the new decimal currency coins introduced in 1966 were: 1c, 2c, 5c, 10c, 20c, and 50c. All were round in shape.

Round 50c coin (reverse)

There were no mintings of the 50c coin in the next two years and, when it next appeared, in 1969, its shape was changed to dodecagonal (12 sided). The round 50c was made in a silver alloy (80%). As the price of silver rose in the late 1960s, the metal value of the coin rose above its face value. It was a loss-maker for the government as well as confusing to consumers because of its size similarity to the 20c coin.

A $1 coin was introduced in 1984 and a $2 coin was introduced in 1988 to replace $1 and $2 currency notes which were gradually withdrawn.

Composition of circulating coins

The 1c and 2c (bronze) coins are made from copper (97%), zinc (2.5%), and tin (0.5%).

The 5c, 10c, 20c, and 50c coins are made of cupro-nickel; that is, 75% copper and 25% nickel.

The $1 and $2 coins are aluminum-bronze: 92% copper, 6% aluminum, and 2% nickel.

Withdrawal of coins

In 1990 the Australian government announced that from 1992 all 1c and 2c coins would be withdrawn. This is because of the changing worth of small denominations generally. These two coins, however, remain legal tender.

The demand for circulating coins has dropped steadily since the 1970s due mainly to the wider availability and acceptance of credit cards. As a result, the Royal Australian Mint has not only stopped making some coins (for instance, 1c and 2c pieces) but also it has reduced production of others. An unexpected side effect of the withdrawal of 1c and 2c coins, as from February 1992, has been the large number of other coins that have been returned to banks, most particularly 5c and 10c coins. This phenomenon has been called the "money box effect"—because of people emptying their money boxes on bank counters and handing in all their "loose change."

Dodecagonal 50c coin (obverse)

Coin designs

Coins have an obverse side and a reverse side. The obverse side of all Australian decimal coins carries an effigy of Her Majesty Queen Elizabeth II, as she is the Queen of Australia. This side of all coins also carries the year the coin was minted. Designs are approved by the Australian Treasurer.

The theme selected in 1966 for Australia's first decimal coins was Australian native fauna (except for the 50c coin which shows the Australian Coat of Arms). Later coins have featured different subjects.

*from left to right, 1c coin: the feather-tail glider (a type of possum)
also known as the "flying squirrel"*

2c coin: the frill-necked lizard

5c coin: the echidna or spiny anteater

10c coin: the lyrebird

(below) 20c coin: the platypus

*(above) 50c coin: Australia's Coat of Arms with a kangaroo on the
left side of the coin and an emu on the right. The Coat of Arms
shows a shield with six parts, each containing the badge of one of
Australia's six states. The same design applies to the 1966 round
version of this coin and the later 12-sided one.*

$1 coin: the kangaroo

*The 1993 $1 coin has water quality as its theme. It
features a tree sculpted in flowing water to show
the link between water and the environment.*

$2 coin: a bust of an Aborigine, taken from an engraving by Ainslie Roberts and set against a background of the Southern Cross and Australian flora. The flora is Xanthorrhoea, commonly known as the grass tree, which is found throughout Australia.

Collector coins

In addition to proof and uncirculated sets of coins, which are issued each year, the Royal Australian Mint issues commemorative coins on a regular basis.

The $5 coin is aluminium-bronze: 92% copper, 6% aluminum, and 2% nickel. The first $5 coin was issued to commemorate the opening of Australia's new federal Parliament building. Parliament House in Canberra was officially opened on 9 May 1988 by Her Majesty Queen Elizabeth II. Two $5 coins were released in 1990 in a joint program with New Zealand to celebrate the 75th anniversary of the landing at Gallipoli by Australian and New Zealand forces in 1915. In 1992 a $5 commemorative coin was issued to mark the International Year of Space.

The $10 coin is made of sterling silver (that is, 92.5% silver and the balance made up of copper). The first $10 coin was released in 1982 to commemorate the XII Commonwealth Games, held in Brisbane. Subsequent designs have carried the theme of the Coat of Arms of each of Australia's six states and two territories: Victoria (1985); South Australia (1986); New South Wales (1987); First Fleet Bicentennial design (1988); Queensland (1989); Western Australia (1990); Tasmania (1991), and Northern Territory (1992). The Australian Capital Territory is featured on the 1993 coin.

Tasmania's $10 commemorative coin

A "Birds of Australia" series was introduced in 1989 on a double thickness (piedfort) $10 coin and on a standard proof $10 coin. The first bird featured was a kookaburra—others in the series are a sulphur-crested cockatoo (1990), a jabiru (1991), an emperor penguin (1992), and a palm cockatoo for 1993.

The $200 coin is manufactured from 22K gold (that is, 91.66% gold).

The first $200 coin showed a koala on the reverse and was minted in 1980. Subsequent $200 coins have depicted the wedding of the Prince of Wales and Lady Diana Spencer in 1981; the Commonwealth Games in Brisbane (1982); the embarkation of the First Fleet to Australia in 1787 (1987); and the landing by Captain Arthur Phillip at Sydney Cove in 1788 (1988).

Australia's first $250 coin

The "Pride of Australia" series, which began in 1989, adopted Australia's unique wildlife as its theme and has so far shown a frilled-neck lizard (1989), platypus (1990), emu (1991), echidna (1992), and feather-tail glider (1993).

Bullion (or investment) coins

The Perth Mint is Australia's specialist precious metals mint and one of the world's oldest mints still operating from its original premises. Established in 1899 as a branch of Britain's Royal Mint, The Perth Mint became a statutory authority of the Western Australian Government in 1970.

Since then, the Mint's bullion coin programs have established a formidable reputation for Australia as a leader in international precious metals markets. In 1997, The Perth Mint, in a joint venture with the Royal Australian Mint, was granted approval to mint the commemorative precious metal coins for the Sydney 2000 Olympic Games, a most prestigious proof coin program.

THE 1999 CENTENARY AUSTRALIAN BULLION COIN COLLECTION

The Perth Mint—A Century of Minting Excellence

The Perth Mint celebrates its centenary on June 20, 1999, representing a significant milestone in the history of Western Australia and in the development of Australia's gold industry.

Originally opened in 1899 as a branch of the British Royal Mint, The Perth Mint was established to turn the gold from the Western Australian gold rush into sovereigns for the British Empire, which it did until Britain came off the gold standard in 1931. Ownership of the Mint was transferred to the Western Australian government in 1970. Since then, through the introduction of the Australian Family of Precious Metal Coins in gold, platinum, silver, and palladium, The Perth Mint has established a formidable reputation for Australia as a leader in international precious metal investment markets.

Renowned for excellence and innovation, The Perth Mint, together with the Royal Australian Mint, was granted approval to mint the commemorative precious metal coins for the Sydney 2000 Olympic Games, a four-year program which commenced in 1997 and ran through the end of 2000.

In its Centenary year, The Perth Mint was proud to recall its achievements and planned a range of activities and coin issues to commemorate this historic milestone.

As part of the celebrations, the 1999 bullion coins bear their own special commemoration with the incorporation in their design, for the first time, of the "P100" mintmark, encompassing the traditional Perth Mint "P" mintmark and the numerals "100."

The Australian Nugget Gold Bullion Coins

Gold Bullion Collector Coins

The Australian Kangaroo Nugget bullion coin is the only major legal tender, pure gold coin to change its design each year and to limit its mintages annually.

As such, it is the only legal tender, gold bullion coin that offers investors the potential for numismatic appreciation over time, in addition to an investment in the precious metal itself.

The 1999 Nugget design captures the innocence of a baby gray kangaroo, commonly known as a "Joey," and is the tenth design in the internationally acclaimed and remarkably successful Kangaroo series.

In 1999, no more than 350,000 1 oz coins, 100,000 ½ oz coins, 150,000 ¼ oz coins, 200,000 ⅒ oz coins, and 200,000 ⅟₂₀ oz coins were produced.

Gold Bullion Investor Coins

The Australian Nugget Large Bullion Coins (LBCs) are universally recognized as being the most affordable means of purchasing gold bullion in the secure form of official, legal tender coins. The Nugget LBCs feature the Australian Red Kangaroo design, which remains constant from year to year. Only the year of mintage changes.

Technical Specifications of the Australian Nugget

SIZE		KILO	10 OZ	2 OZ	1 OZ	½ OZ	¼ OZ	¹⁄₁₀ OZ	¹⁄₂₀ OZ
Gold Content	Troy oz	32.151	10	2	1	½	¼	¹⁄₁₀	¹⁄₂₀
Denomination	A$	3000	1000	200	100	50	25	15	5
Fineness	% purity	99.99	99.99	99.99	99.99	99.99	99.99	99.99	99.99
Standard Weight	gms	1000.35	311.317	62.265	31.162	15.594	7.807	3.133	1.571
Remedy Allowance	gms	0.25	0.25	0.05	0.055	0.040	0.030	0.022	0.015
Maximum Diameter	mm	75.30	60.30	40.60	32.10	25.10	20.10	16.10	14.10
Maximum Thickness	mm	13.90	7.90	4.00	2.80	2.40	2.00	1.50	1.40
Milled Edge Serrations	no.	320	283	250	180	150	130	120	108

The Australian Koala Platinum Bullion Coins

Platinum Bullion Collector Coins

The Australian Koala is the only legal tender, pure platinum bullion coin to carry a different design each year.

It is also the only platinum bullion coin with a preannounced, limited mintage.

In 1999, no more than 100,000 1 oz coins, 5,000 ½ oz coins, 20,000 ¼ oz coins, 20,000 ⅒ oz coins, and 20,000 ⅟₂₀ oz coins were produced.

The 1999 design features a young koala clinging to a fallen log, chewing a favored eucalyptus leaf. It is the twelfth design in the series.

Platinum Bullion Investor Coins

The Australian Koala Large Bullion Coins (LBCs) are the most affordable means of buying platinum in the secure form of official, legal tender coins. They feature an unchanging design, depicting a koala sitting in a tree. Only the year of mintage changes annually.

Platinum's critical role in pollution control sees its importance to everyday life increasing each year, yet only about 140 tonnes of newly mined platinum reach Western markets in a typical year, which makes it 17 times rarer than gold and 120 times rarer than silver.

Technical Specifications of the Australian Koala

SIZE		KILO	10 OZ	2 OZ	1 OZ	½ OZ	¼ OZ	⅟₁₀ OZ	⅟₂₀ OZ
Platinum									
Content	Troy oz	32.151	10	2	1	½	¼	⅟₁₀	⅟₂₀
Denomination	A$	3000	1000	200	100	50	25	15	5
Fineness	% purity	99.95	99.95	99.95	99.95	99.95	99.95	99.95	99.95
Standard									
Weight	gms	1001.00	311.691	62.313	31.185	15.605	7.815	3.137	1.571
Remedy									
Allowance	gms	0.50	0.50	0.075	0.065	0.045	0.035	0.025	0.015
Maximum									
Diameter	mm	75.30	60.30	40.60	32.10	25.10	20.10	16.10	14.10
Maximum									
Thickness	mm	13.90	7.90	3.80	2.70	2.30	1.90	1.32	1.40
Milled Edge									
Serrations	no.	320	283	250	180	150	130	120	108

The Australian Kookaburra Silver Bullion Coins

Silver Bullion Collector Coins

The Australian Kookaburra is the only major legal tender, pure silver coin to change its design yearly.

The 1999 design features a pair of kookaburras, an adult and a juvenile, perched in their most favored habitat, the branch of a eucalyptus tree, and is the tenth design in the series.

Only 300,000 of these coins are produced annually for sale worldwide compared with the millions of its competitors.

Silver Bullion Investor Coins

The Australian Kookaburra Large Bullion Coins (LBCs) are unique. They are the world's largest bullion coins. They are also more affordable per ounce than any other silver bullion coins and provide investors with the security only official, legal tender coins can provide. The distinctive kookaburra design changes every year.

Technical Specifications of the Australian Kookaburra

SIZE		KILO	10OZ	2OZ	1OZ
Silver Content	Troy oz	32.151	10	2	1
Denomination	A$	30	10	2	1
Fineness	% purity	99.9	99.9	99.9	99.9
Standard Weight	gms	1002.502	312.347	62.77	31.635
Remedy Allowance	gms	1.50	1.00	0.50	0.50
Maximum Diameter	mm	101.00	75.50	50.30	40.60
Maximum Thickness	mm	14.60	8.70	4.50	4.00
Milled Edge Serrations	no.	160*	120*	80*	250

*Interrupted

THE 1998 PROOF SETS

The Australian Family of Precious Metals 1998 Proof Sets

The Perth Mint's three-metal proof sets have always been a popular annual release, with back issues now scarce. Their popularity is partly due to the unique opportunity they offer to secure examples of the Mint's world-renowned proof coins in gold, silver, and platinum. Minted to the highest proof standards and beautifully presented in solid jarrah cases with numbered certificates of authenticity, the 1998 Proof Sets are offered in three handsome formats with very limited mintages.

Endearing Designs

The 1998 Proof Nugget coin, individually struck from 99.99% pure gold, captures the innocence of a baby gray kangaroo, or "Joey." The 1998 Proof Kookaburra features a pair of kookaburras, an adult and juvenile perched in the branch of a eucalyptus tree, and is struck from the finest 99.9% silver. Minted in the rarest of all precious metals, 99.95% pure platinum, the 1998 Proof Koala features a young koala clinging to a fallen log, chewing a favored eucalyptus leaf.

Each coin is an outstanding example of the coin maker's art, minted with painstaking attention to detail at every stage.

As with all Perth Mint proof issues, the "P" mint mark is incorporated into the design, denoting a proud tradition of quality and innovation.

Mintage Limits

PROOF SET	FORMAT	MINTAGE
Mini Three-Metal	1 oz silver Kookaburra, ¹⁄₂₀ oz gold Nugget ¹⁄₂₀ oz platinum Koala	700
Midi Three-Metal	1 oz silver Kookaburra, ½ oz gold Nugget ½ oz platinum Koala	250
1 oz Three-Metal	1 oz silver Kookaburra, 1 oz gold Nugget 1 oz platinum Koala	150

Coins shown actual size

Technical Specifications

		NUGGET			**KOALA**			**KOOKABURRA**
Metal Content	Troy oz	1	½	⅟₂₀	1	½	⅟₂₀	1
Denomination	A$	100	50	5	100	50	5	1
Fineness	%	99.99	99.99	99.99	99.95	99.95	99.95	99.9
Standard Weight	gms	31.162	15.594	1.571	31.185	15.605	1.571	31.635
Remedy Allowance	gms	0.055	0.040	0.015	0.065	0.045	0.015	0.50
Max Diameter	mm	32.10	25.10	14.10	32.10	25.10	14.10	40.60
Max Thickness	mm	2.80	2.40	1.40	2.70	2.30	1.40	4.00
Milled Edge Serrations	no.	180	150	108	180	150	108	250

Australia—Type Coinage

Key to Grading: Busts

DATE	COIN TYPE/VARIETY/METAL	ABP FINE	AVERAGE FINE
☐ 1911–1936	½ Penny, George V, Bronze	$ .72	$ 1.20
☐ 1938–1939	½ Penny, George VI, Bronze	.24	.42
☐ 1939–1948	½ Penny, George VI, Bronze	.30	.49
☐ 1949–1952	½ Penny, George VI, Bronze	.30	.49
☐ 1953–1956	½ Penny, Elizabeth II, Bronze	.30	.49
☐ 1959–1964	½ Penny, Elizabeth II, Bronze	.24	.42

Key to Grading: Busts

☐ 1911–1936	1 Penny, George V, Bronze	.44	.78
☐ 1938–1948	1 Penny, George VI, Bronze	.31	.55
☐ 1949–1952	1 Penny, George VI, Bronze	.26	.44
☐ 1953	1 Penny, Elizabeth II, Bronze	.24	.42
☐ 1955–1964	1 Penny, Elizabeth II, Bronze	.24	.42
☐ 1910	3 Pence, Edward VII, Silver	—	8.50
☐ 1911–1936	3 Pence, George V, Silver	—	5.00

Key to Grading: Busts

☐ 1938–1944	3 Pence, George VI, Silver	—	2.50
☐ 1947–1948	3 Pence, George VI, Silver	—	2.50
☐ 1949–1952	3 Pence, George VI, Silver	—	2.50

DATE	COIN TYPE/VARIETY/METAL	ABP FINE	AVERAGE FINE
☐ 1953–1954	3 Pence, Elizabeth II, Silver	—	$5.80
☐ 1955–1964	3 Pence, Elizabeth II, Silver	—	3.40

Key to Grading: Busts

☐ 1910	6 Pence, Edward VII, Silver	—	16.50
☐ 1911–1936	6 Pence, George V, Silver	—	6.80
☐ 1938–1945	6 Pence, George VI, Silver	—	4.50
☐ 1946–1948	6 Pence, George VI, Silver	—	4.50
☐ 1950–1952	6 Pence, George VI, Silver	—	4.50
☐ 1953–1954	6 Pence, Elizabeth II, Silver	—	4.00
☐ 1955–1963	6 Pence, Elizabeth II, Silver	—	4.00
☐ 1910	1 Shilling, Edward VII, Silver	—	10.25
☐ 1911–1936	1 Shilling, George V, Silver	—	12.50

Key to Grading: Busts

☐ 1938–1944	1 Shilling, George VI, Silver	—	8.10
☐ 1946–1948	1 Shilling, George VI, Silver	—	7.00
☐ 1950–1952	1 Shilling, George VI, Silver	—	7.00
☐ 1953–1954	1 Shilling, Elizabeth II, Silver	—	7.00
☐ 1955–1963	1 Shilling, Elizabeth II, Silver	—	7.00
☐ 1910	1 Florin, Edward VII, Silver	—	55.50
☐ 1911–1936	1 Florin, George V, Silver	—	36.50

Key to Grading: Busts

DATE	COIN TYPE/VARIETY/METAL	ABP FINE	AVERAGE FINE
☐ 1938–1945	1 Florin, George VI, Silver	—	$8.40
☐ 1946–1947	1 Florin, George VI, Silver	—	7.50
☐ 1951–1952	1 Florin, George VI, Silver	—	3.25
☐ 1953–1954	1 Florin, Elizabeth II, Silver	—	7.10
☐ 1956–1963	1 Florin, Elizabeth II, Silver	—	7.10

Key to Grading: Busts

DATE	COIN TYPE/VARIETY/METAL	ABP FINE	AVERAGE FINE
☐ 1937–1938	1 Crown, George VI, Silver	—	22.00
☐ 1871–1887	½ Sovereign, Victoria, Young Head, Gold	—	206.50
☐ 1887–1893	½ Sovereign, Victoria, Jubilee Head, Gold	—	206.50
☐ 1893–1901	½ Sovereign, Victoria, Old Head, Gold	—	156.50
☐ 1902–1910	½ Sovereign, Edward VII, Gold	—	125.50
☐ 1911–1918	½ Sovereign, George V, Gold	—	125.50
☐ 1871–1887	1 Sovereign, Victoria, Young Head, Rev: Shield, Gold	—	—
☐ 1871–1887	1 Sovereign, Victoria, Young Head, Rev: St. George, Gold	—	230.00
☐ 1887–1893	1 Sovereign, Victoria, Jubilee Head, Gold	—	206.50
☐ 1893–1901	1 Sovereign, Victoria, Old Head, Gold	—	206.50
☐ 1902–1910	1 Sovereign, Edward VII, Gold	—	206.50
☐ 1911–1931	1 Sovereign, George V, Gold	—	380.00

Australia—Commemorative Coinage

Key to Grading: Busts

DATE	COIN TYPE/VARIETY/METAL	ABP FINE	AVERAGE FINE
☐ 1927	Commemorative Florin, Establishment of Parliament at Canberra, Silver	—	7.75
☐ 1934	Commemorative Florin, Victoria & Melbourne Centennial, Dated 1934–35, Silver	—	196.50
☐ 1951	Commemorative Florin, Fifty-year Jubilee, Silver	—	9.40
☐ 1954	Commemorative Florin, Royal Visit, Silver	—	9.40

Australia—Decimal Coinage

Key to Grading: Bust

DATE	COIN TYPE/VARIETY/METAL	ABP FINE	AVERAGE FINE
☐ 1966 to Date	1 Cent, Elizabeth II, Ring-tailed Opossum, Bronze	$ .23	$ .39
☐ 1966 to Date	2 Cents, Elizabeth II, Frilled Lizard, Bronze	.23	.39

Key to Grading: Bust

☐ 1966 to Date	5 Cents, Elizabeth II, Spiny Anteater, Cupro-Nickel	.23	.39

Key to Grading: Bust

☐ 1966 to Date	10 Cents, Elizabeth II, Lyre Bird, Cupro-Nickel	.23	.39

Key to Grading: Bust

☐ 1966 to Date	20 Cents, Elizabeth II, Duckbill Platypus, Cupro-Nickel	.23	.39

Key to Grading: Bust

DATE	COIN TYPE/VARIETY/METAL	ABP FINE	AVERAGE FINE
☐ 1966	50 Cents, Elizabeth II, Silver	—	$6.75
☐ 1969–1984	50 Cents, Elizabeth II, Cupro-Nickel	.47	.78
☐ 1970	50 Cents, Elizabeth II, Cook's Voyage—200th Anniversary, Cupro-Nickel	.47	.78
☐ 1977	50 Cents, Elizabeth II, Queen's Silver Jubilee, Cupro-Nickel	.43	.71
☐ 1981	50 Cents, Elizabeth II, Wedding of Prince Charles and Lady Diana, Cupro-Nickel	.33	.55
☐ 1982	50 Cents, Elizabeth II, 12th Commonwealth Games, Cupro-Nickel	.53	.88
☐ 1985 to Date	50 Cents, Elizabeth II, Cupro-Nickel	.40	.66
☐ 1988	50 Cents, Elizabeth II, Australian Bicentennial, Cupro-Nickel	.40	.66
☐ 1988	50 Cents, Elizabeth II, Australian Bicentennial, Silver	—	76.50
☐ 1989	50 Cents, Elizabeth II, 12th Commonwealth Games, Silver	—	76.50
☐ 1989	50 Cents, Elizabeth II, Cook's Voyage—200th Anniversary, Silver	—	76.50
☐ 1989	50 Cents, Elizabeth II, Wedding of Prince Charles & Lady Diana, Silver	—	76.50
☐ 1989	50 Cents, Elizabeth II, Queen's Silver Jubilee, Silver	—	75.00
☐ 1991	50 Cents, Elizabeth II, Decimal Currency—25th Anniversary, Cupro-Nickel	.53	.88

Key to Grading: Bust

☐ 1984 to Date	1 Dollar, Elizabeth II, Kangaroos, Nickel-Aluminum-Copper	1.10	1.80

DATE	COIN TYPE/VARIETY/METAL	ABP FINE	AVERAGE FINE
☐ 1986	1 Dollar, Elizabeth II, International Year of Peace, Aluminum-Bronze	$1.15	$1.90
☐ 1988	1 Dollar, Elizabeth II, Aboriginal Art, Aluminum-Bronze	1.30	2.20
☐ 1988–1990	1 Dollar, Elizabeth II, Masterpieces in Silver—Aboriginal Art, Silver	—	106.50
☐ 1990	1 Dollar, Elizabeth II, Masterpieces in Silver—International Year of Peace, Silver	—	106.50
☐ 1990	1 Dollar, Elizabeth II, Masterpieces in Silver—Kangaroos, Silver	—	106.50
☐ 1992	1 Dollar, Elizabeth II, Olympics—Javelin Thrower, Aluminum-Bronze	1.40	2.30

Key to Grading: Bust

DATE	COIN TYPE/VARIETY/METAL	ABP FINE	AVERAGE FINE
☐ 1988–1991	2 Dollars, Elizabeth II, Male Aborigine, Aluminum-Bronze	3.55	5.90
☐ 1988	5 Dollars, Elizabeth II, House of Parliament, Aluminum-Bronze	—	12.50
☐ 1988	5 Dollars, Elizabeth II, House of Parliament, Silver	—	42.50
☐ 1990	5 Dollars, Elizabeth II, ANZAC Memorial, Aluminum-Bronze	9.90	16.50
☐ 1992	5 Dollars, Elizabeth II, Australian Space Industry, Aluminum-Bronze	9.90	16.50
☐ 1982	10 Dollars, Elizabeth II, 12th Commonwealth Games, Silver	—	34.50
☐ 1985	10 Dollars, Elizabeth II, State of Victoria—150th Anniversary, Silver	—	34.50
☐ 1986	10 Dollars, Elizabeth II, South Australia—150th Anniversary, Silver	—	34.50
☐ 1987	10 Dollars, Elizabeth II, New South Wales, Silver	—	34.50
☐ 1988	10 Dollars, Elizabeth II, Governor Philip Landing, Silver	—	31.50
☐ 1989	10 Dollars, Elizabeth II, Queensland, Silver	—	26.75
☐ 1989	10 Dollars, Elizabeth II, Kookaburra, Silver	—	38.50
☐ 1990	10 Dollars, Elizabeth II, Cockatoo, Silver	—	32.50
☐ 1990	10 Dollars, Elizabeth II, Western Australia, Silver	—	27.50

DATE	COIN TYPE/VARIETY/METAL	ABP FINE	AVERAGE FINE
☐ 1991	10 Dollars, Elizabeth II, Birds of Australia—Jabiru Stork, Silver	—	$48.50
☐ 1991	10 Dollars, Elizabeth II, Tasmania, Silver	—	48.50
☐ 1992	10 Dollars, Elizabeth II, Northern Territory, Silver	—	30.50
☐ 1992	10 Dollars, Elizabeth II, Emperor Penguin, Silver	—	46.50
☐ 1992	25 Dollars, Elizabeth II, Queen's 40th Anniversary of Reign—Princess Diana, Silver	—	69.50
☐ 1992	25 Dollars, Elizabeth II, Queen's 40th Anniversary of Reign—Queen Mother, Silver	—	69.50
☐ 1992	25 Dollars, Elizabeth II, Queen's 40th Anniversary of Reign—Princess Margaret, Silver	—	54.50
☐ 1980	200 Dollars, Elizabeth II, Koala, Gold	—	305.50
☐ 1981	200 Dollars, Elizabeth II, Wedding of Prince Charles & Lady Diana, Gold	—	305.50
☐ 1982	200 Dollars, Elizabeth II, 12th Commonwealth Games, Gold	—	305.50
☐ 1985	200 Dollars, Elizabeth II, Koala, Gold	—	305.50
☐ 1986	200 Dollars, Elizabeth II, Koala, Gold	—	305.50
☐ 1987	200 Dollars, Elizabeth II, Arthur Philip, Gold	—	290.00
☐ 1988	200 Dollars, Elizabeth II, Australia Bicentennial, Gold	—	290.00
☐ 1989	200 Dollars, Elizabeth II, Pride of Australia—Frilled-neck Lizard, Gold	—	328.50
☐ 1990	200 Dollars, Elizabeth II, Pride of Australia—Platypus, Gold	—	352.50
☐ 1991	200 Dollars, Elizabeth II, Pride of Australia—Emu, Gold	—	352.50
☐ 1992	250 Dollars, Elizabeth II, Queen's 40th Anniversary of Reign—Princess Diana, Gold	—	810.00
☐ 1992	250 Dollars, Elizabeth II, Queen's 40th Anniversary of Reign—Princess Anne, Gold	—	805.50
☐ 1992	250 Dollars, Elizabeth II, Queen's 40th Anniversary of Reign—Queen Mother, Gold	—	805.50
☐ 1992	250 Dollars, Elizabeth II, Queen's 40th Anniversary of Reign—Princess Margaret, Gold	—	805.50

BELGIUM

The first coins appeared in the 2nd century. The silver denier was popular through the 12th century. During the 1400s, most of the coins produced were gold. In the 1500s, large copper coins were introduced. A new coin system was established in 1612. Most of the coins then included liards, patards, schellings, patagons, ducatons, and sovereigns. The currency used today is based on the franc.

Belgium—Type Coinage

Key to Grading: Lion

DATE	COIN TYPE/VARIETY/METAL	ABP FINE	AVERAGE FINE
☐ 1869–1907	1 Centime, Leopold II— 1st Coinage, Copper	$1.40	$2.30
☐ 1912–1914	1 Centime, Albert I, Copper	.69	1.15
☐ 1869–1909	2 Centimes, Leopold II— 1st Coinage, Copper	1.15	1.90
☐ 1910–1919	2 Centimes, Albert I, Copper	.69	1.15
☐ 1894–1901	5 Centimes, Leopold II—1st Coinage, Cupro-Nickel	1.15	1.95

Key to Grading: Crown

DATE	COIN TYPE/VARIETY/METAL	ABP FINE	AVERAGE FINE
☐ 1901–1907	5 Centimes, Leopold II—2nd Coinage, Cupro-Nickel	$ .30	$ .49
☐ 1910–1932	5 Centimes, Albert I, Cupro-Nickel	.23	.39
☐ 1915–1916	5 Centimes, German Occupation, Zinc	.23	.39
☐ 1930–1932	5 Centimes, Albert I, Nickel-Brass	.23	.39
☐ 1938–1940	5 Centimes, Leopold III—Belgie-Belgique, Nickel-Brass	.30	.49
☐ 1941–1943	5 Centimes, German Occupation, Zinc	.30	.49
☐ 1894–1901	10 Centimes, Leopold II—1st Coinage, Cupro-Nickel	1.40	2.35

Key to Grading: Crown

☐ 1901–1906	10 Centimes, Leopold II—2nd Coinage, Cupro-Nickel	.16	.27
☐ 1915–1917	10 Centimes, German Occupation, Zinc	.40	.66
☐ 1920–1929	10 Centimes, Albert I, Cupro-Nickel	.40	.66
☐ 1930–1932	10 Centimes, Albert I, Nickel-Brass	2.85	4.73
☐ 1938–1939	10 Centimes, Leopold III—Belgie-Belgique, Nickel-Brass	.40	.66
☐ 1941–1946	10 Centimes, German Occupation, Zinc	.33	.55

Key to Grading: Crown

DATE	COIN TYPE/VARIETY/METAL	ABP FINE	AVERAGE FINE
☐ 1953–1963	20 Centimes, Baudouin I, Bronze	$ .23	$ .39
☐ 1908–1909	25 Centimes, Leopold II— 2nd Coinage, Cupro-Nickel	.69	1.15
☐ 1910–1929	25 Centimes, Albert I, Cupro-Nickel	.21	.36
☐ 1915–1918	25 Centimes, German Occupation, Zinc	.43	.71
☐ 1938–1939	25 Centimes, Leopold III— Belgie-Belgique, Nickel-Brass	.33	.55
☐ 1942–1947	25 Centimes, German Occupation, Zinc	.30	.49

Key to Grading: Crown

☐ 1964–1976	25 Centimes, Cupro-Nickel	.18	.30
☐ 1866–1899	50 Centimes, Leopold II— 1st Coinage, Silver	—	8.25
☐ 1901	50 Centimes, Leopold II— 2nd Coinage, Silver	—	3.60
☐ 1907–1909	50 Centimes, Leopold II— 2nd Coinage, Silver	—	3.60
☐ 1910–1914	50 Centimes, Albert I, Silver	—	3.60
☐ 1918	50 Centimes, German Occupation, Zinc	1.50	2.50
☐ 1922–1934	50 Centimes, Albert I, Nickel	.39	.61

Key to Grading: Crown

☐ 1952–1980	50 Centimes, Baudouin I, Bronze	.33	.55
☐ 1866–1887	1 Franc, Leopold II—1st Coinage, Silver	—	8.10
☐ 1880	1 Franc, Leopold II—50th Anniversary of Independence, Silver	—	19.50
☐ 1904–1909	1 Franc, Leopold II—2nd Coinage, Silver	—	6.50
☐ 1910–1918	1 Franc, Albert I, Silver	—	2.65

Key to Grading: Figure

DATE	COIN TYPE/VARIETY/METAL	ABP FINE	AVERAGE FINE
☐ 1922–1935	1 Franc, Albert I, Nickel	$ .16	$ .27
☐ 1939–1940	1 Franc, Leopold III—Belgie-Belgigue, Nickel	.28	.46
☐ 1941–1947	1 Franc, German Occupation, Zinc	.28	.46
☐ 1950–1988	1 Franc, Postwar Issue, Cupro-Nickel	.14	.24
☐ 1991–1993	1 Franc, Leopold III	.28	.46
☐ 1994	1 Franc, Alber II	.28	.46
☐ 1866–1887	2 Francs, Leopold II—1st Coinage, Silver	—	32.50
☐ 1880	2 Francs, Leopold II—50th Anniversary of Independence, Silver	—	70.50
☐ 1904–1909	2 Francs, Leopold II—2nd Coinage, Silver	—	21.50
☐ 1910–1912	2 Francs, Albert I, Silver	—	8.45
☐ 1923–1930	2 Francs, Albert I, Nickel	5.45	9.10

Key to Grading: Leaf

☐ 1944	2 Francs, Allied Issue, Steel	.33	.55

Key to Grading: Bust

☐ 1865–1876	5 Francs, Leopold II—1st Coinage, Silver	—	15.50
☐ 1930–1934	5 Francs, 1 Belga, Albert I, Nickel	2.90	4.85
☐ 1938–1939	5 Francs, Leopold III—Belgie-Belgigue, Nickel	2.90	4.85

DATE	COIN TYPE/VARIETY/METAL	ABP FINE	AVERAGE FINE
☐ 1941–1947	5 Francs, German Occupation, Zinc	$3.55	$5.93
☐ 1948–1981	5 Francs, Postwar Issue, Cupro-Nickel	.28	.46
☐ 1986–1993	5 Francs, Leopold III	.28	.46
☐ 1994–1997	5 Francs, Albert II	.28	.46
☐ 1930	10 Francs, 2 Belgas, Albert I: Independence Centennial, Nickel	21.85	36.40
☐ 1969–1979	10 Francs, Leopold III	.22	.37
☐ 1867–1882	20 Francs, Leopold II—1st Coinage, Gold	—	376.50
☐ 1914	20 Francs, Albert I, Gold	—	248.50
☐ 1931–1932	20 Francs, 4 Belgas, Albert I, Nickel	31.75	52.90
☐ 1933–1934	20 Francs, Albert I, Silver	—	75.00
☐ 1934–1935	20 Francs, Leopold III, Silver	—	6.50
☐ 1949–1955	20 Francs, Postwar Issue, Silver	—	8.10

Key to Grading: Bust

DATE	COIN TYPE/VARIETY/METAL	ABP FINE	AVERAGE FINE
☐ 1980–1992	20 Francs, Bronze	1.30	2.20
☐ 1984–1997	20 Francs, Bronze Albert II	.82	1.35
☐ 1987–1988	5 ECU, European Currency Units, Silver	—	49.50
☐ 1935	50 Francs, Brussels Exposition/ Railway Centennial, Silver	—	102.00

Key to Grading: Bust

DATE	COIN TYPE/VARIETY/METAL	ABP FINE	AVERAGE FINE
☐ 1939–1940	50 Francs, Leopold III, Silver	—	24.00
☐ 1948–1954	50 Francs, Postwar Issue, Silver	—	6.50
☐ 1958	50 Francs, Brussels Fair, Silver	—	7.50
☐ 1960	50 Francs, Marriage Commemorative, Silver	—	9.45
☐ 1987–1993	50 Francs, Leopold III, Nickel	2.80	4.65
☐ 1994–1997	50 Francs, Albert II	2.80	4.65
☐ 1989–1990	10 ECU, European Currency Units, Gold	—	290.00
☐ 1948–1954	100 Francs, Postwar Issue, Silver	—	7.50
☐ 1990–1991	20 ECU, European Currency Units, Gold	—	510.00
☐ 1989	25 ECU, European Currency Units, Gold	—	352.00

DATE	COIN TYPE/VARIETY/METAL	ABP FINE	AVERAGE FINE
☐ 1976	250 Francs, Jubilee of King Baudouin, Silver	—	$13.50
☐ 1987–1988	50 ECU, European Currency Units, Gold	—	312.50
☐ 1980	500 Francs, Independence—150th Anniversary, Silver Clad	4.50	7.50
☐ 1989	100 ECU, European Currency Units—Maria Theresa, Gold	—	958.00
☐ 1990	500 Francs, King Baudouin—60th Birthday, Silver	—	56.50

BERMUDA

The first coins were used in 1616. The copper sixpence was followed by the copper penny in the 1700s and the silver crown and bronze cent in the 1900s. The first decimal coins were used in 1970. Today's currency is the dollar.

Bermuda—Bullion/Bermuda*

Key to Grading: Bust

☐ 1987	5 Dollars, Sailing Ship—Sea Venture Wreck, Silver	—	235.00
☐ 1988	5 Dollars, Sailing Ship—San Antonio, Silver	—	235.00
☐ 1992	5 Dollars, Olympic Rings, Silver	—	250.00

*Since these coins were manufactured and sold primarily for their bullion value, their current value is determined by the current spot price of gold.

DATE	COIN TYPE/VARIETY/METAL	ABP FINE	AVERAGE FINE
☐ 1987	25 Dollars, Ship—Sea Venture, Palladium	—	$495.00
☐ 1988	25 Dollars, Ship—San Antonio Wreck, Palladium	—	500.00

Bermuda—Type Coinage

Key to Grading: Bust

☐ 1970–1985	1 Cent, Wild Boar, Bronze	.26	.44
☐ 1986–1991	1 Cent, Wild Boar, Bronze	.26	.44

Key to Grading: Bust

☐ 1991–1997	1 Cent, Wild Boar, Zinc	.23	.39

Key to Grading: Bust

☐ 1970–1985	10 Cents, Bermuda Lily, Cupro-Nickel	.26	.44
☐ 1986–1997	10 Cents, Bermuda Lily, Cupro-Nickel	.26	.44

Key to Grading: Bust

☐ 1970–1985	25 Cents, Tropical Bird, Cupro-Nickel	.23	.39
☐ 1984	25 Cents, 375th Anniversary, Cupro-Nickel	.37	.60
☐ 1959	1 Crown, 350th Anniversary, Silver	4.57	7.62
☐ 1964	1 Crown, Silver	4.03	6.72

Key to Grading: Bust

DATE	COIN TYPE/VARIETY/METAL	ABP FINE	AVERAGE FINE
☐ 1970–1985	50 Cents, Arms of the Bermudas, Cupro-Nickel	$ .43	$ .71
☐ 1970	1 Dollar, Elizabeth II, Silver	—	29.50

Key to Grading: Bust

DATE	COIN TYPE/VARIETY/METAL	ABP FINE	AVERAGE FINE
☐ 1972	1 Dollar, Silver Wedding Anniversary, Silver	—	12.50
☐ 1981	1 Dollar, Royal Wedding, Cupro-Nickel	5.35	8.90
☐ 1981	1 Dollar, Royal Wedding, Silver	—	24.50
☐ 1983	1 Dollar, Cahow Over Bermuda, Brass	2.65	4.40
☐ 1985	1 Dollar, Cruise Ship Tourism, Silver	—	34.50
☐ 1985	1 Dollar, Cruise Ship Tourism, Copper-Nickel	3.30	5.50
☐ 1986	1 Dollar, World Wildlife Fund— Sea Turtle, Cupro-Nickel	5.30	8.80
☐ 1986	1 Dollar, World Wildlife Fund— Sea Turtle, Silver	—	39.50
☐ 1986	1 Dollar, World Wildlife Fund— Sea Turtle, Brass	9.90	16.55
☐ 1987	1 Dollar, Commercial Aviation— 50th Anniversary, Cupro-Nickel	5.45	9.05
☐ 1987	1 Dollar, Commercial Aviation— 50th Anniversary, Silver	—	39.50
☐ 1988	1 Dollar, Railroad, Silver	—	49.50
☐ 1988	1 Dollar, Sailboat, Brass	1.65	2.73
☐ 1988	1 Dollar, Railroad, Cupro-Nickel	4.30	7.15
☐ 1989	1 Dollar, Monarch Conservation Project, Silver	—	42.00

DATE	COIN TYPE/VARIETY/METAL	ABP FINE	AVERAGE FINE
☐ 1989	1 Dollar, Monarch Conservation Project, Cupro-Nickel	$4.95	$8.25
☐ 1990	1 Dollar, 90th Birthday of Queen Mother, Silver	—	75.50
☐ 1990	1 Dollar, 90th Birthday of Queen Mother, Cupro-Nickel	3.45	5.30
☐ 1992	1 Dollar, Olympic Rings, Bronze	23.15	38.60
☐ 1990	2 Dollars, Cicada Insects, Silver	—	58.75
☐ 1990	2 Dollars, Tree Frog, Silver	—	64.25
☐ 1991	2 Dollars, Yellow-crowned Night Heron, Silver	—	58.75
☐ 1991	2 Dollars, Spiny Lobster, Silver	—	58.75
☐ 1992	2 Dollars, Cedar Tree, Silver	—	58.75
☐ 1992	2 Dollars, Bluebird, Silver	—	58.75
☐ 1983–1986	5 Dollars, Onion Over Map of Bermuda, Brass	3.55	5.90
☐ 1983–1986	10 Dollars, Hogge Money—Ship, Gold	—	93.50
☐ 1983–1986	10 Dollars, Wildlife—Tree Frog, Gold	—	85.50
☐ 1983–1986	10 Dollars, Hogge Money—Wild Pig, Gold	—	134.50
☐ 1970	20 Dollars, Seagull in Flight, Gold	—	424.00
☐ 1975	25 Dollars, Royal Visit, Cupro-Nickel	47.00	78.55
☐ 1977	25 Dollars, Queen's Silver Jubilee, Silver	—	54.50
☐ 1989	25 Dollars, Hogge Money—Ship, Gold	—	202.00
☐ 1990	25 Dollars, Hogge Money—Wild Pig, Gold	—	200.00
☐ 1977	50 Dollars, Queen's Silver Jubilee, Gold	—	160.50
☐ 1989	50 Dollars, Hogge Money—Wild Pig, Gold	—	438.50
☐ 1990	50 Dollars, Hogge Money—Ship, Gold	—	538.00
☐ 1975	100 Dollars, Royal Visit, Gold	—	114.00
☐ 1977	100 Dollars, Queen's Silver Jubilee, Gold	—	130.50
☐ 1989	100 Dollars, Hogge Money—Ship, Gold	—	1150.00
☐ 1990	100 Dollars, Hogge Money—Wild Pig, Gold	—	1150.00
☐ 1981	250 Dollars, Wedding of Prince Charles & Lady Diana, Gold	—	748.00

BOLIVIA

The first coins were used in 1574, and nearly all were silver for the following 250 years. The silver "cob" Spanish reales were in use in the 1700s, followed by the silver melgarejo. The cupro-nickel centavos were in evidence in the 1800s, and the cupro-nickel pesos bolivianos in the 1970s. Decimal coins were used in 1864. The currency today is the peso boliviano.

Boliva—Type Coinage

Key to Grading: Coat of Arms

DATE	COIN TYPE/VARIETY/METAL	ABP FINE	AVERAGE FINE
☐ 1864	1 Centecimo, 1st Coinage, Copper	$59.70	$99.50
☐ 1878	1 Centavo, 3rd Coinage, Obv: Date, Rev: Wreath Containing 1, Copper	107.00	178.45
☐ 1878	1 Centavo, 3rd Coinage, Obv: Value, Rev: Wreath Containing Legend, Copper	155.60	259.00
☐ 1883	1 Centavo, 3rd Coinage, Obv: Value, Rev: Wreath Containing Legend, Bronze	4.05	6.70

Key to Grading: Coat of Arms

DATE	COIN TYPE/VARIETY/METAL	ABP FINE	AVERAGE FINE
☐ 1864	2 Centecimos, 1st Coinage, Copper	109.15	181.90
☐ 1878	2 Centavos, 3rd Coinage, Obv: Value, Rev: Wreath Containing Legend, Copper	56.25	93.75
☐ 1878	2 Centavos, 3rd Coinage, Obv: Date, Rev: 2 cent Value Under Condor	232.85	388.00

DATE	COIN TYPE/VARIETY/METAL	ABP FINE	AVERAGE FINE
☐ 1883	2 Centavos, 3rd Coinage, Obv: Value, Rev: Wreath Containing Legend, Bronze	$8.40	$14.00
☐ 1864–1865	1/20 Boliviano, 1st Coinage, Silver	—	26.50

Key to Grading: Coat of Arms

DATE	COIN TYPE/VARIETY/METAL	ABP FINE	AVERAGE FINE
☐ 1871–1872	5 Centavos, 2nd Coinage, Obv: 11 Stars at Bottom, Rev: Without Weight, Silver	—	32.75
☐ 1871	5 Centavos, 2nd Coinage, Obv: 11 Stars at Bottom, Rev: With Weight, Silver	—	32.75
☐ 1872–1884	5 Centavos, 3rd Coinage, La Union Es La Fuerza, Silver	—	6.50
☐ 1872	5 Centavos, 2nd Coinage, Obv: 9 Stars at Bottom, Rev: Without Weight, Silver	—	16.25
☐ 1883	5 Centavos, 3rd Coinage, Center Hole; Obv: Value, Rev: Wreath Containing Legend, Cupro-Nickel	9.75	16.25
☐ 1883	5 Centavos, 3rd Coinage, Obv: Value, Rev: Wreath Containing Legend, With Hole, Cupro-Nickel	2.95	4.90
☐ 1885–1900	5 Centavos, 3rd Coinage, La Union Es La Fuerza, Silver	—	7.50
☐ 1892	5 Centavos, 3rd Coinage, Obv: Value, Rev: Wreath Containing Legend, Cupro-Nickel	3.25	5.40
☐ 1893–1919	5 Centavos, 3rd Coinage, Cupro-Nickel	3.25	5.40

Key to Grading: Coat of Arms

DATE	COIN TYPE/VARIETY/METAL	ABP FINE	AVERAGE FINE
☐ 1864–1866	1/5 Boliviano, 1st Coinage, Silver	—	$20.00
☐ 1864–1867	1/10 Boliviano, 1st Coinage, Silver	—	20.00
☐ 1870–1871	10 Centavos, 2nd Coinage, Obv: 11 Stars at Bottom, Rev: With Weight, Silver	—	7.20
☐ 1871	10 Centavos, 2nd Coinage, Obv: 11 Stars at Bottom, Rev: Without Weight, Silver	—	9.75
☐ 1872	10 Centavos, 2nd Coinage, Obv: 9 Stars at Bottom, Rev: Without Weight, Silver	—	7.20
☐ 1872–1884	10 Centavos, 3rd Coinage, La Union Es La Fuerza, Silver	—	7.20
☐ 1883	10 Centavos, 3rd Coinage, Obv: Value, Rev: Wreath Containing Legend, Cupro-Nickel	10.40	17.35
☐ 1883	10 Centavos, 3rd Coinage, Center Hole; Obv: Value, Rev: Wreath Containing Legend, Cupro-Nickel	3.55	5.90
☐ 1885–1900	10 Centavos, 3rd Coinage, La Union Es La Fuerza, Silver	3.55	5.90

Key to Grading: Coat of Arms

☐ 1892	10 Centavos, 3rd Coinage, Obv: Value, Rev: Wreath Containing Legend, Cupro-Nickel	2.95	4.90
☐ 1893–1919	10 Centavos, 3rd Coinage, Cupro-Nickel	2.95	4.90
☐ 1870–1871	20 Centavos, 2nd Coinage, Obv: 11 Stars at Bottom, Rev: With Weight, Silver	—	58.45
☐ 1871	20 Centavos, 2nd Coinage, Obv: 11 Stars at Bottom, Rev: Without Weight, Silver	—	58.45
☐ 1871–1872	20 Centavos, 2nd Coinage, Obv: 9 Stars at Bottom, Rev: Without Weight, Silver	—	16.75

DATE	COIN TYPE/VARIETY/METAL	ABP FINE	AVERAGE FINE
☐ 1872–1885	20 Centavos, 3rd Coinage, La Union Es La Fuerza, Silver	—	$6.50
☐ 1879	20 Centavos, Daza, President 1876–1880, Silver	—	32.75

Key to Grading: Coat of Arms

☐ 1885–1907	20 Centavos, 3rd Coinage, La Union Es La Fuerza, Silver	—	11.50
☐ 1870–1871	Boliviano-2nd Coinage obv: 11 stars at bottom, rev: with weight, Silver	—	39.50
☐ 1871–1872	Boliviano, 2nd Coinage, obv: 9 stars at bottom, rev: without weight, Silver	—	28.50
☐ 1872–1893	Boliviano, 3rd Coinage, La Union Es La Fuerza, Silver	—	32.25

BRAZIL

The first coins were used in 1645 and included the gold guilders, followed by the gold "Johannes," gold reis, silver reis, and the copper reis. The stainless-steel centavos were issued in 1975. The decimal system was established in 1942. Today's currency is the cruzeiro.

Brazil—Type Coinage

Key to Grading: Bust

☐ 1868–1870	10 Reis, Pedro II, Bronze	.66	1.10

Key to Grading: Bust

DATE	COIN TYPE/VARIETY/METAL	ABP FINE	AVERAGE FINE
☐ 1868–1870	20 Reis, Pedro II, Bronze	$1.70	$2.85
☐ 1889–1912	20 Reis, Republic, Bronze	1.70	2.85
☐ 1918–1935	20 Reis, Republic, Cupro-Nickel	1.15	1.90

Key to Grading: Bust

☐ 1873–1880	40 Reis, Pedro II, Bronze	1.40	2.30
☐ 1889–1912	40 Reis, Republic, Bronze	2.80	4.65

Key to Grading:

☐ 1886–1888	50 Reis, Pedro II, Cupro-Nickel	1.50	2.50
☐ 1918–1935	50 Reis, Republic, Cupro-Nickel	3.36	.60
☐ 1871–1875	100 Reis, Pedro II, Cupro-Nickel	1.60	2.65

DATE	COIN TYPE/VARIETY/METAL	ABP FINE	AVERAGE FINE
☐ 1886–1889	100 Reis, Pedro II, Cupro-Nickel	$ .52	$ .87
☐ 1889–1900	100 Reis, Republic, Cupro-Nickel	1.10	1.80
☐ 1901	100 Reis, Republic, Cupro-Nickel	.34	.57
☐ 1918–1935	100 Reis, Republic, Cupro-Nickel	.25	.42
☐ 1932	100 Reis, Republic, Colonization 400th Anniversary, Cupro-Nickel	.38	.63
☐ 1936–1938	100 Reis, Republic, National Heroes Series—Tamandare, Cupro-Nickel	.28	.46
☐ 1938–1942	100 Reis, Republic, Vargas, Cupro-Nickel	.28	.46
☐ 1942–1943	10 Centavos, Republic, Cupro-Nickel	.28	.46

Key to Grading: Bust

DATE	COIN TYPE/VARIETY/METAL	ABP FINE	AVERAGE FINE
☐ 1947–1955	10 Centavos, Republic, Obv: Bonifacio, Aluminum-Bronze	.28	.46
☐ 1956–1962	10 Centavos, Republic, Aluminum	.28	.46
☐ 1854–1867	200 Reis, Pedro II, Silver	—	6.50
☐ 1867–1869	200 Reis, Pedro II, Silver	—	7.65
☐ 1871–1874	200 Reis, Pedro II, Cupro-Nickel	1.50	2.45
☐ 1886–1889	200 Reis, Pedro II, Cupro-Nickel	1.50	2.45
☐ 1889–1900	200 Reis, Republic, Cupro-Nickel	2.60	4.35
☐ 1901	200 Reis, Republic, Cupro-Nickel	.52	.86

Key to Grading: Bust

DATE	COIN TYPE/VARIETY/METAL	ABP FINE	AVERAGE FINE
☐ 1918–1935	200 Reis, Republic, Cupro-Nickel	.30	.49
☐ 1932	200 Reis, Republic, Colonization 400th Anniversary, Silver	—	2.10
☐ 1936–1938	200 Reis, Republic, National Heroes Series—Maua, Cupro-Nickel	.26	.44
☐ 1938–1942	200 Reis, Republic, Vargas, Cupro-Nickel	.26	.44
☐ 1942–1943	20 Centavos, Republic, Cupro-Nickel	.26	.44

DATE	COIN TYPE/VARIETY/METAL	ABP FINE	AVERAGE FINE
☐ 1948–1956	20 Centavos, Republic, Obv: Barbosa, Aluminum-Bronze	$ .25	$ .42
☐ 1948–1956	20 Centavos, Republic, Obv: Dutra, Aluminum-Bronze	.25	.42

Key to Grading: Coat of Arms

☐ 1956–1962	20 Centavos, Republic, Aluminum	.25	.42

Key to Grading: Bust

☐ 1936–1938	300 Reis, Republic, National Heroes Series—Carlos Gomes, Cupro-Nickel	.18	.30
☐ 1938–1942	300 Reis, Republic, Vargas, Cupro-Nickel	.32	.54
☐ 1900	400 Reis, Republic, Discovery 400th Anniversary, Silver	10.50	17.50
☐ 1901	400 Reis, Republic, Cupro-Nickel	1.40	2.30
☐ 1918–1935	400 Reis, Republic, Cupro-Nickel	.50	.81
☐ 1932	400 Reis, Republic, Colonization 400th Anniversary, Cupro-Nickel	1.55	2.55

Key to Grading: Bust

☐ 1936–1938	400 Reis, Republic, National Heroes Series—Oswaldo Cruz, Cupro-Nickel	1.60	2.65

DATE	COIN TYPE/VARIETY/METAL	ABP FINE	AVERAGE FINE
☐ 1938–1942	400 Reis, Republic, Vargas, Cupro-Nickel	$ .39	$ .65
☐ 1922	500 Reis, Republic, Independence Centennial, Aluminum-Bronze	.39	.65
☐ 1932	500 Reis, Republic, First Settler, Aluminum-Bronze	1.45	2.40
☐ 1939	500 Reis, Republic, Famous Men Series—de Assis, Aluminum-Bronze	.52	.87
☐ 1849–1852	500 Reis, Pedro II, Silver	—	18.45
☐ 1853–1867	500 Reis, Pedro II, Silver	—	18.45
☐ 1867–1868	500 Reis, Pedro II, Silver	—	9.25
☐ 1876–1889	500 Reis, Republic, Silver	—	11.10

Key to Grading: Bust

☐ 1906–1913	500 Reis, Republic, Silver	—	6.10
☐ 1924–1930	500 Reis, Republic, Aluminum-Bronze	.33	.55
☐ 1935	500 Reis, Republic, National Heroes Series—Diego Feijo, Aluminum-Bronze	1.45	2.42
☐ 1942–1943	50 Centavos, Republic, Cupro-Nickel	.34	.57

Key to Grading: Bust

☐ 1956	50 Centavos, Republic, Aluminum-Bronze	.16	.27
☐ 1849–1852	1000 Reis, Pedro II, Silver	—	12.50
☐ 1853–1866	1000 Reis, Pedro II, Silver	—	12.50
☐ 1869	1000 Reis, Pedro II, Silver	—	34.50
☐ 1876–1889	1000 Reis, Pedro II, Silver	—	26.75
☐ 1889	1000 Reis, Republic, Silver	—	26.75
☐ 1900	1000 Reis, Republic, Discovery 400th Anniversary, Silver	—	86.50

DATE	COIN TYPE/VARIETY/METAL	ABP FINE	AVERAGE FINE
☐ 1922	1000 Reis, Republic, Independence Centennial, Aluminum-Bronze	$1.40	$2.35

Key to Grading: Bust

DATE	COIN TYPE/VARIETY/METAL	ABP FINE	AVERAGE FINE
☐ 1906–1913	1000 Reis, Republic, Silver	—	6.50
☐ 1924–1930	1000 Reis, Republic, Aluminum-Bronze	.85	1.40
☐ 1932	1000 Reis, Republic, First Governor, Aluminum-Bronze	2.75	4.55
☐ 1935	1000 Reis, Republic, National Heroes Series—Jose de Anchieta, Aluminum-Bronze	.88	1.45
☐ 1939	1000 Reis, Republic, Famous Men Series—Barreto, Aluminum-Bronze	.34	.57

Key to Grading: Map & Bust

DATE	COIN TYPE/VARIETY/METAL	ABP FINE	AVERAGE FINE
☐ 1942–1956	Cruzeiro, Republic, Aluminum-Bronze	.28	.46
☐ 1956	Cruzeiro, Republic, Aluminum-Bronze	.28	.46
☐ 1957–1961	Cruzeiro, Republic, Aluminum	.28	.46
☐ 1851–1852	2000 Reis, Pedro II, Silver	—	24.50
☐ 1853–1867	2000 Reis, Pedro II, Silver	—	24.50
☐ 1868–1869	2000 Reis, Pedro II, Silver	—	32.50
☐ 1886–1889	2000 Reis, Pedro II, Silver	—	24.50
☐ 1891–1897	2000 Reis, Republic, Silver	—	745.00
☐ 1900	2000 Reis, Republic, Discovery 400th Anniversary, Silver	—	128.50

Key to Grading: Bust

DATE	COIN TYPE/VARIETY/METAL	ABP FINE	AVERAGE FINE
☐ 1906–1913	2000 Reis, Republic, Silver	—	$9.20
☐ 1924–1934	2000 Reis, Republic, Silver	—	6.65
☐ 1932	2000 Reis, Republic, King John III, Aluminum-Bronze	3.10	5.20
☐ 1935	2000 Reis, Republic, National Heroes Series—Caxias, Aluminum-Bronze	.82	1.37
☐ 1936–1938	2000 Reis, Republic, National Heroes Series—Duke of Caxias, Aluminum-Bronze	.52	.87
☐ 1939	2000 Reis, Republic, Famous Men Series—Peixoto, Aluminum-Bronze	.52	.87

Key to Grading: Maps or Bust

DATE	COIN TYPE/VARIETY/METAL	ABP FINE	AVERAGE FINE
☐ 1942–1956	2 Cruzeiros, Republic, Aluminum-Bronze	.32	.53
☐ 1956	2 Cruzeiros, Republic, Aluminum-Bronze	.32	.53
☐ 1957–1961	2 Cruzeiros, Republic, Aluminum	.32	.53
☐ 1900	4000 Reis, Republic, Discovery 400th Anniversary, Silver	—	230.00
☐ 1854–1869	5000 Reis, Pedro II, Gold	—	165.00

Key to Grading: Bust

DATE	COIN TYPE/VARIETY/METAL	ABP FINE	AVERAGE FINE
☐ 1936–1938	5000 Reis, Republic, National Heroes Series—Santos Dumont, Silver	—	$2.50
☐ 1942–1943	5 Cruzeiros, Republic, Aluminum-Bronze	.54	.89
☐ 1849–1851	10000 Reis, Pedro II, Gold	—	280.00
☐ 1853–1889	10000 Reis, Pedro II, Gold	—	280.00
☐ 1889–1922	10000 Reis, Republic, Gold	—	228.50
☐ 1965	10 Cruzeiros, Republic, Aluminum	.28	.47
☐ 1849–1851	20000 Reis, Pedro II, Gold	—	585.00
☐ 1851–1852	20000 Reis, Pedro II, Gold	—	585.00
☐ 1853–1889	20000 Reis, Pedro II, Gold	—	585.00
☐ 1889–1922	20000 Reis, Republic, Gold	—	520.00
☐ 1965	20 Cruzeiros, Republic, Aluminum	.28	.47
☐ 1965	50 Cruzeiros, Republic, Cupro-Nickel	.28	.47

CANADA

The first coins, sols, and deniers in silver, bullion, and copper were used in 1670. In the 1800s the bronze penny token was in use. The first decimal coins were used in 1858. The currency today is the dollar.

THE ROYAL CANADIAN MINT
Courtesy of the Royal Canadian Mint

In many ways, the history of the Royal Canadian Mint mirrors that of Canada itself.

As Canada struggled toward independence, its first settlers used a rich and sometimes confusing mix of French, American, Spanish, and British currency to support its rapid development and growth. But to a young and vigorous country, national pride demanded that it be able to produce its own coins. At the same time, gold mining in British Columbia and the Yukon had reached unprecedented levels with much of this precious metal exported to the United States. Promoters believed a Canadian Mint would stabilize the price of gold and that a policy of keeping government and banking reserves in domestic coinage should be encouraged. At this time, reserves were held in foreign gold coins or bullion.

Following demands for a Canadian Mint as early as 1880, the new Mint's location on Sussex Drive in Ottawa was purchased from a private land owner for $21,000 and construction began in 1905. Arthur H.W. Cleave, having served at the Royal Mint in London, was appointed Superintendent of the Canadian branch of the Royal Mint. Dr. James Bonar, who had been on the Board of Civil Examiners in London since 1876, became the first Deputy Master of the Mint.

January 2, 1908, marked the historic date of the official opening of the Ottawa Branch of Britain's Royal Mint with the striking of a fifty-cent piece. This historic site on Sussex Drive is still in use today.

The early years saw the Mint efficiently producing gold sovereigns, Canadian coins, and millions of ounces of refined gold. The Mint even produced gun parts for Britain during World War I.

The Royal Canadian Mint was officially placed in Canadian hands on December 1, 1931, reporting to the Department of Finance. After many years of establishing new coinage and refining records, the Canadian government gave the Mint the authority needed to respond more quickly to the changing conditions of a modern world by making it a Crown corporation on April 1, 1969.

Other Important historic dates:

April 30, 1976: A branch of the Mint, dedicated to the high-speed production of domestic and foreign circulation coins, is inaugurated in Winnipeg.

December 17, 1987: The Royal Canadian Mint is financially restructured, allowing it to apply its net earnings to meet operational requirements, replace capital assets, ensure its overall financial stability, and pay a reasonable dividend to the shareholder, the Canadian government.

The Refinery

Fashioned after its British counterpart, the Canadian Branch faced an unusual dilemma in its early history. In Britain there was any number of local, privately owned refineries to choose from so it was not necessary for a refinery to be built as part of the Royal Mint's operations. This was not the case in Canada. The problem came to light in late 1906. Canada must have a refinery. After much debate, construction began in 1909. Until the completion of the refinery in 1911, the Ottawa Mint's Assay Department was given the task of purifying incoming gold, a job that kept the Chief Assayer working long into the night to keep up with demand.

The Mint Today

Today's modern Mint, with its unsurpassed standards of craftsmanship in minting circulation and commemorative collector coins and its reputation as a premier refiner of gold, is known and respected around the globe. As a profit-making Crown corporation, the Mint is run much like any other company, with a mandate to produce a fair return on investment for its sole shareholder, the Canadian government. The President and Master of the Mint is the senior executive officer of the organization, reporting to a Board of Directors appointed by the Minister of Public Works and Government Services. All Royal Canadian Mint stocks are owned by the government, and they are not traded on the stock market.

With its headquarters in Ottawa and a state-of-the-art production facility in Winnipeg, the Royal Canadian Mint today employs some 500 highly skilled and dedicated individuals involved in all aspects of coin design, production, and marketing in one of the largest and most complex minting facilities in operation today.

Refinery and Assay

Since 1908, the Royal Canadian Mint has been assaying and refining gold for mining companies, foreign governments, and private interests. The Mint runs one of the largest gold refineries in the Western Hemisphere, refining an average of 2 million Troy ounces per year.

The Royal Canadian Mint hallmark is recognized worldwide as a guarantee of honest weight and purity. That guarantee is on every gold product produced, including:

- 400 oz. London Good Delivery bars
- 100 oz. Comex bars
- Kilo bars
- Granular gold

Like the Gold Maple Leaf, all Royal Canadian Mint gold products can be traded anywhere gold is bought and sold.

Custom Products

The Royal Canadian Mint produces custom medals, tokens, and trade dollars for a wide number of uses. The Mint is also able to customize some existing numismatic products by transferring an organization's logo or any other print specification onto the coin packaging (available in Canada only).

Bullion Coins

Bullion coins are struck in the purest of precious metals (gold, platinum, or silver), and are not only an attractive coin, but also a means for the general public to buy, own, and invest in precious metals.

Because the Royal Canadian Mint is so well known and respected, the Maple Leaf bullion coins are bought and sold around the world.

Circulation Coins

All circulation coins supplied by the Royal Canadian Mint are manufactured at a high-speed production facility in Winnipeg, Manitoba. This highly automated facility covers 160,000 square feet and has a total production capacity of up to 150 coins per second.

NUMISMATIC COINS

Numismatic coins, produced by the Royal Canadian Mint for collecting or gift giving, are miniature works of fine art that reflect the Canadian identity. Original works by famous Canadian artists are painstakingly reproduced by the Mint's master engravers in the minute detail you see portrayed on each coin. Every coin tells a story of discovery, adventure, and natural beauty unique to Canada, and reflects the Royal Canadian Mint's pride in their great heritage.

2001 Releases

2001 CHINESE LUNAR SERIES—
THE YEAR OF THE SNAKE

The centre of the Year (2001) of the Snake coin features an octagonal 24-karat gold covered cameo depicting the Snake. In each year of the series, the design on the gold cameo will change to depict the animal for the year of issue. The twelve animals of the Chinese lunar calendar appear around the circumference of the reverse of the sterling silver coin. Canadian artist Harvey Chan created the design of the Chinese symbols. The obverse of the coin portrays an effigy of her Majesty Queen Elizabeth II by Dora de Pédery-HUNT, surrounded by the inscription 15 DOLLARS, CANADA, 2001.

The Chinese lunar calendar follows a twelve-year cycle and each year is associated with an animal. The twelve animals of the Chinese lunar calendar are the rat, ox, tiger, rabbit, dragon, snake, horse, sheep, monkey, rooster, dog and pig. According to the Chinese astrology, those born in the year of the Snake are regarded as wise and contemplative, but inwardly naïve. They are prudent.

The mint produced 68,888 of the Year of the Snake coins. The coins come in an embossed red velvet box with gold moiré sides.

Coin Specifications:

Composition:	Coin: 92.5% silver, 7.5% copper.
	Cameo: 24 karat gold covered
Weight:	34 grams
Diameter:	Coin: 40 mm Cameo: 17.5 mm
Edge:	Reeded
Face Value:	$15.00
Finish:	Proof: frosted relief on brilliant background
Mintage:	68,888
Collector Value:	$125.00

2001 CHINESE LUNAR SERIES—
THE YEAR OF THE SNAKE HOLOGRAM COIN

To celebrate the arrival of the Year of the Snake in the Chinese lunar calendar, the Royal Canadian Mint has introduced the Year of the Snake Hologram Gold Coin. This is the second hologram coin commemorating the Chinese Lunar calendar produced by the Royal Canadian Mint.

Designed by Canadian artist Harvey Chan, the 2001—$150 18-karat Gold Coin features a snake entwined around a bamboo stalk. The 18-karat gold (75% gold and 25% silver) coin has a diameter of 28 mm and weighs 13.61 grams. The coin has a serrated edge and is 1.81 mm thick. The face value is $150 and the mintage is limited to 6,888 coins worldwide.

Collector Value: $350.00

2001 THE FIRST TRANSATLANTIC WIRELESS
TRANSMISSION—100th ANNIVERSARY
Marconi Sterling Silver Two Coin Set

Produced in partnership with the British Royal Mint, this set commemorates the 100th Anniversary of the first transatlantic wireless transmission. Marconi's achievement marked the beginning of wireless communication era and sparked a technological revolution that continues to transform the world. Canada received the first transmission at Signal Hill in St. Johns, Newfoundland, and is today one of the world leaders in the wireless telecommunications industry.

This set features coins by the Royal Canadian Mint and the Royal British Mint. The reverse of the $5 Royal Canadian Mint coin depicts sound waves travelling from Poldhu near Cornwall in England to St. John's, Newfoundland in Canada. This bi-metallic coin is sterling silver with a 24-karat gold-plated cameo of Guglielmo Marconi. The reverse of the £2 British Royal Mint coin features an elegant symbolic rendition of radio waves emanating from a sundial bearing the year 2001. This coin is presented as a bi-metallic coin in sparkling sterling silver—with the golden outer ring coated in 22 carat gold. The Canadian coin was designed by artist Cosme Saffloti, while the British Coin was designed by Robert Evans.

Collector Value: $50.00 set of 2

2001 The Gold Maple Leaf Five-Coin Hologram Set

The 2001 GML Five-Coin Set represents only the second time such a set has been issued by the Royal Canadian Mint. The first was issued as a 20th anniversary set in 1999. In this set, the distinctive maple leaf appears as a high-resolution dot matrix hologram, which has been struck directly onto each of the five coins. The maple leaf hologram design features hues of red, green, blue, and yellow. Each set includes a 1, 1/2, 1/4, 1/10 and 1/20 troy ounce gold coin.

As with the 1/4 ounce Gold Maple Leaf, each coin is characterized by two finishes. The reverse features the hologram Maple Leaf design on a brilliant background. The obverse maintains the traditional bullion coin finish (brilliant relief on matte field) with the effigy of Her Majesty Queen Elizabeth II by artist Dora de Pédery-Hunt.

Each coin is 99.99% pure gold and mintage has been limited to 600 sets worldwide. The set comes in a mahogany box with a brass plaque featuring the Royal Canadian Mint logo and a numbered certificate of authenticity.

Coin Specifications:

SIZE (TROY OZ.)	GOLD PURITY	TOTAL WEIGHT	DIAMETER	THICKNESS	LEGAL TENDER VALUE
1	99.99%	31.150 g	30 mm	2.87 mm	$50
1/2	99.99%	15.584 g	25 mm	2.23 mm	$20
1/4	99.99%	7.797 g	20 mm	1.78 mm	$10
1/10	99.99%	3.131 g	16 mm	1.13 mm	$5
1/20	99.99%	1.581 g	14.1 mm	0.92 mm	$1

Edge: Reeded
Finish: Traditional bullion coin finish (brilliant relief on a matte field)
Mintage: 600 sets
Collector Value: $2650.00 set

2001 The Gold Maple Leaf 1/4 Ounce Hologram Coin

Guaranteed by the Government of Canada to contain 99.99% pure gold, the 2001 1/4 ounce Gold Maple Leaf Hologram joins the existing family of Royal Canadian Mint's Gold Maple Leaf products unsurpassed for their purity throughout the world.

In this 1/4 ounce GML coin, the high-resolution dot matrix hologram which has been struck directly on the coin, depicts three maple leaves on a branch imbued with hues of red, green, blue, and yellow.

Two finishes characterize each coin. The reverse features the hologram Maple Leaf design on a brilliant background. The obverse maintains the traditional bullion coin finish (brilliant relief on matte field) with the effigy of Her Majesty Queen Elizabeth II by artist Dora de Pédery-Hunt.

Mintage has been limited to 150,000 coins worldwide.

Since Canada's Maple Leaf Bullion Coins were first introduced in 1979, they have become the standard for superior quality as the purest gold coin in the world. The Mint was the first to produce 99.99% pure gold coins in 1982, and has diversified its bullion line with the creation of a guaranteed value gold bullion coin in 1997 as well as a gold bullion wafer and a 99.999% pure gold coin, which set a new standard of purity for Canada and the world.

Collector Value: $225.00

2001 The "Harlequin Duck" Platinum Four Coin Set

The Harlequin Duck (Histrionicus histrionicus) featured on the 2001 Platinum Coin Set of the Royal Canadian Mint is one of the most unique ducks in the world. Designed by Royal Canadian Mint engravers, the four platinum Harlequin Duck coins are the twelfth addition to the platinum wildlife series begun in 1990.

The platinum set consists of a 1/10 ounce $30 coin that features the profile of a Harlequin Duck head, a 1/4 ounce $75 coin that features the duck in flight, a 1/2 ounce $150 coin that features a female duck with chick and a one ounce $300 coin that features a group of ducks. The 2001 platinum coins are available only as a four coin set.

Collector Value: $2500.00 set of 4

2001 LAND SEA AND RAIL SERIES—
The Russell 'Light Four' Model L Touring Car

The Russell 'Light Four' Model L Touring Car was built by the Canadian Cycle & Motor Company Ltd. The Russell was the first mass-produced Canadian car with a Canadian-built engine and chassis. Specially engineered for Canadian driving conditions, the Russell quickly became Canada's first successful selling automobile.

The Model L of 1908 was an affordable car with a hand horn, brass side and tail lamps, acetylene headlamps and a 4-cylinder, 24-hp engine. Its extra 56.5-inch wheel tread prevented it from slipping into carriage ruts in the roads.

After 1910, the Russell became a luxury car. The Canada Cycle & Motor Company Ltd., along with McLaughlin and Ford, became one of the three tycoons of the Canadian automobile industry due to the success of The Russell Model L.

Coin Specifications:

Composition:	92.5% silver, 7.5% copper
Weight:	31.103 grams
Diameter:	38 mm
Thickness:	3.5 mm
Edge:	Interrupted serration
Face Value:	$20
Finish:	Proof (frosted relief on a brilliant background)
Mintage:	15,000 each coin
Collector Value:	$100.00

2001 LAND SEA AND RAIL SERIES—
The Marco Polo 150th Anniversary

Built in Saint John, New Brunswick in 1851 by James Smith, the Marco Polo for a time was considered to be the fastest ship in the world and named the "Queen of the Seas." The Marco Polo beat the world record run from England to Australia by a full week and reached England from Canada in 15 days on her record breaking maiden voyage. Furthermore, the Marco Polo was the first ship to circumnavigate the world in less than 6 months.

The ship was designed to carry a crew of 60 and 960 passengers. The 1625-ton vessel with three complete decks carried emigrants and timber across the oceans. In 1883, while transporting a load of pine to England, the Marco Polo encountered a storm in the Gulf of the St. Lawrence and the ship ran ashore.

Coin Specifications:

Composition:	92.5% silver, 7.5% copper
Weight:	31.103 grams

Diameter:	38 mm
Thickness:	3.5 mm
Edge:	Interrupted serration
Face Value:	$20
Finish:	Proof (frosted relief on a brilliant background)
Mintage:	15,000 each coin
Collector Value:	$115.00

2001 LAND SEA AND RAIL SERIES—The Scotia

Built in Hamilton, Ontario in 1861, The Scotia was the first loco-motive in Canada to be built with a steel boiler in order to reduce heat loss and generate more power.

Coin Specifications:

Composition:	92.5% silver, 7.5% copper
Weight:	31.103 grams
Diameter:	38 mm
Thickness:	3.5 mm
Edge:	Interrupted serration
Face Value:	$20
Finish:	Proof (frosted relief on a brilliant background)
Mintage:	15,000 each coin
Collector Value:	$100.00

2001 The Library of Parliament—125th Anniversary

With a commanding presence on the shores of the Ottawa River, it is difficult to imagine that the Library of Parliament was once a tran-sient collection of books traveling between Canada's early political centers. This was precisely the case until Queen Victoria selected Ottawa as Canada's capital and prompted the establishment of a permanent library there.

Construction began in December 1859 and continued for 17 years before the library was completed in 1876, opening with a grand ball on February 28th of that year.

From its inception, the library incorporated the very best that architecture had to offer. Inspiration was found in London and Paris, and the innovative design was immensely popular. Its elaborate iron doors and roof proved their worth when fire threatened the library in 1916 and 1952.

Despite the ravages of history and time, many of the library's original features remain, evoking the grandeur of another age for everyone who visits there.

DESIGN

Reverse: The reverse of the coin features an inside view of the Library of Parliament. The focal point of the coin depicts the statue of Her Majesty Queen Victoria.

Obverse: The obverse features a contemporary effigy of Her Majesty Queen Elizabeth II by artist Dora de Pédery-HUNT.

ARTIST

Robert-Ralph Carmichael was born in Sault Ste. Marie, Ontario. Mr. Carmichael is a graduate of both The Ontario College of Art in Toronto and Carleton University in Ottawa.

Coin Specifications:

Composition:	14 karat gold: 58.33% gold - 41.67% silver
Weight:	13.338 grams
Diameter:	27 mm
Thickness:	2.15 mm
Edge:	Reeded
Face Value:	$100
Mintage:	10,000
Collector Value:	$275.00

2001 The "Mayflower" 99.999% Gold Coin

The Royal Canadian Mint issues its fourth floral coin from the 99.999% Gold Coin Series, with the 2001 $350 gold coin depicting the Trailing Arbutus (Epigaea repens), more commonly known as the Mayflower. So profound was this flower's springtime appearance that Nova Scotia's early residents quickly adopted it as a celebrated patriotic symbol. The Mayflower was praised by songwriters and poets. It was showcased on the province's early stamps and coins, as well as the decorative brass of its militia. The Mayflower became the floral emblem of Nova Scotia after an act of legislature in 1901.

The design was created by Canadian artist Bonnie Ross. The obverse of the coin depicts and effigy of Her Majesty Queen Elizabeth II by Dora de Pédery-HUNT surrounded by the inscription "Elizabeth II Canada D.G. Regina Fine Gold 350 Dollars Or Pure," with the year of issue to the left of the Queen and .99999 to the right. The mintage of this new 99.999 percent gold coin is limited to 2,001.

Collector Value: $850.00

2001 NATIONAL BALLET
OF CANADA 50th ANNIVERSARY

The National Ballet of Canada, a company with more than 50 dancers and its own full symphony orchestra, is Canada's premier dance company which ranks as one of the world's top international companies. Founded in 1951 by English dancer Celia Franca, the company was established as a classical company and it is the only Canadian company to present a full range of traditional full evening ballet classics. The company also embraces contemporary works and encourages the creation of new ballets from Canadian choreographers.

The first performance of the company was performed on November 12, 1951 at the Eaton Auditorium in Toronto. The program included Les Sylphides and the Polovtsian Dances from Prince Igor. The principal dancers with the company were Celia Franca, Irene Alpine, Lois Smith, David Adams, and Jury Gotshalks.

The National Ballet of Canada earned its international reputation in 1970 when it was the only classical ballet company to be invited to perform at the Expo '70 in Osaka, Japan. In 1972, the company undertook its first European Tour to Britain, France, Belgium, Monaco, Switzerland, and Germany. Also in 1972, Rudolf Nureyev performed the production of Sleeping Beauty with the company. With this ballet, the National Ballet of Canada made a debut at the New York Metropolitan Opera House in 1973. Since then, the company has made numerous appearances at the New York Opera House.

In 1983, the legendary Erik Bruhn, considered one of the greatest male classical dancers of this century, took over the position of

Artistic Director. Bruhn added many new famous ballets to the company's repertoire including The Merry Widow, and The Blue Snake. After having traditionally natured Artistic Directors, James Kudelka was appointed the National Ballet of Canada's Artistic Director in 1996. A world-renowned choreographer, Mr. Kudelka transformed the company to the forefront on the international dance scene as a first-class creative organization.

DESIGN

Reverse: The reverse of the coin depicts a scene from the company's debut performance of the classical ballet Les Sylphides, designed by Canadian artist Scott McKowen. The ballerina is being held in an arabesque pose by her partner in the foreground with the corps de ballet in the background.

Obverse: The obverse of the coin features an effigy of Her Majesty, Queen Elizabeth II, by artist Dora de Pédery-HUNT.

ARTIST

Scott McKowen received a Bachelor of Fine Arts from the University of Michigan School of Art in 1978. McKowen has combined his skills as a graphic designer and his longtime theater background to establish a career specializing in theater posters and graphics for the performing arts. Residing in Stratford, Ontario, Mr. McKowen is an active participant of the Stratford Festival designing their promotional material.

The 2001 Silver Dollar Coin is the 38th in a series celebrating Canadian Historical Events, People and Places begun in 1935. The 2001 coin is available in proof finish or brilliant uncirculated finish. For 2001, the silver dollar will have a limited mintage: 125,000 for the proof coin, and 65,000 for the brilliant uncirculated coin. The proof finish coin is encapsulated and presented in a green display case lined with green flock. The protective sleeve features graphics representative of the theme. The proof finish includes a numbered certificate of authenticity. The brilliant uncirculated coin is presented in a plastic capsule and protected with matchbox style packaging

Coin Specifications:

Composition:	Sterling Silver
	92.5% silver, 7.5% copper
Weight:	25.175 grams
Diameter:	36.07 mm
Thickness:	3.02 mm
Edge:	Reeded
Face Value:	$1.00
Collector Value:	$30.00 brilliant uncirculated
	$65.00 cased proof

2001 THE ROYAL MILITARY COLLEGE OF CANADA—125th ANNIVERSARY

Located in Kingston, Ontario, the Royal Military College is Canada's only national military university. Steeped in tradition, it boasts an impressive alumni of Canada's military leaders, political figures and captains of industry that have served Canada well. Mr. Gerald T. Locklin of the Royal Military College was the artist of record for the coin's design.

The proof finish coin is encapsulated and presented in a blue display case lined with blue flock. The protective sleeve features graphics representative of the theme. The proof finish includes a numbered certificate of authenticity. The brilliant uncirculated coin is presented in a plastic capsule and protected with matchbox style packaging.

Coin Specifications:

Composition:	92.5% silver
	07.5% copper
Finish:	Proof
Weight:	5.35 grams
Diameter:	21.20 mm
Thickness:	1.93 mm
Certificate:	included
Mintage:	40,000 coins
Face Value:	5 cents
Artist:	Gerald T. Locklin
Price:	16.95 CAD / 11.95 USD
Collector Value:	$28.00

The Spirit of Canada
25-cent Silver Maple Leaf Coloured Coin

Since Canada's Maple Leaf Bullion Coins were first introduced in 1979, they have become the standard for superior quality as the purest silver coin in the world. In 2001, the coin is available in a beautiful new design of three leaves in brilliant fall colours. The design was created by Canadian artist Debbie Adams, which suggests a palette of muted earth neutrals and stunning arboreal reds and yellows. Designed by artist Silke Ware of Kitchener, Ontario, this coin is only one of three colorised coins ever issued by the Royal Canadian Mint. At the centre is a red maple leaf, Canada's distinctive emblem.

"This new Spirit of Canada coin is a powerful symbol of the values that have made Canada strong," said the Honourable Alfonso Gagliano, Minister of Public Works and Government Services Canada and Minister responsible for the Royal Canadian Mint. "It supports our constant desire to promote tradition and pride among Canadians."

Collector Value: $26.00

2000 Releases

2000 Millennium Sterling Silver
Proof 25-cent Coins

The monthly coins issued in the 2000 Millennium coin series are available individually in sterling silver, presented in a deluxe display case. Designed by individual Canadians from all walks of life, these coins celebrate a future full of promise.

January 2000

Canada's first coin of the year 2000 showcases the artistic talents of Winnipeg freelance graphic designer Donald F. Warkentin, whose passion for his country and optimism about its future shines through his inspiring design "Pride."

Mr. Warkentin's design honors our country's vibrant character and expresses Canadians' celebration of life, of our people, of peace, stability, and a flourishing bounty. It sends a signal, from east to west, that Canada is a nation looking forward to a future filled with promise.

Collector Value: $2.00

February 2000

The February 2000 coin, Ingenuity, features the work of John Jaciw of Windsor, Ontario. The coin celebrates Canadian ingenuity, representing a model society—prosperous farms, innovative cities, rapid safe transportation, and an eye toward space.

John immigrated to Canada in 1949. After studies at the Creative School of Art in Edmonton, and the Meizinger Art School in Detroit,

Michigan, John worked as a graphic designer for Hiram Walker and Sons Limited for thirty years.

The Ingenuity coin was launched on February 4, 2000, at an event at DaimlerChrysler Canada's Windsor Assembly Plant. DaimlerChrysler Canada is responsible for the creation of the minivan, considered one of the past century's most innovative and commercially successful vehicles.

Collector Value: $2.00

March 2000

Collector Value: $2.00

April 2000

Collector Value: $2.00

May 2000

Collector Value: $2.00

June 2000

Collector Value: $2.00

July 2000

Collector Value: $2.00

August 2000

Collector Value: $2.00

September 2000

Collector Value: $2.00

October 2000

Collector Value: $2.00

November 2000

Collector Value: $2.00

December 2000

Collector Value: $2.00

Commemorative Set

2000 Sterling Silver 25-cent Coins

Designed by individual Canadians from all walks of life, these Millennium 25-cent coins celebrate a future full of promise. This exclusive set brings together all twelve 25-cent coins issued in 2000 to celebrate this nation's future. The coins feature the initials of their designer. This deluxe collector set of twelve sterling-silver 25-cent coins comes in a flawless proof finish and is presented in a sleek display case.

Collector Value: $175.00

Proof Set

2000 Uncirculated Gift Set

This prestigious set features Canada's circulation coins struck in a proof finish. All coins except the one-cent and one-dollar circulation coin are sterling silver. The Proof Set includes the 2000 Proof Silver Dollar: the Voyage of Discovery. The coins are displayed in specially designed acrylic lenses that allow two-sided viewing, all housed in a dark green Nabuka case.

Collector Value: $120.00

Souvenir Set

2000 Nickel 25-cent Coins

Designed by individual Canadians from all walks of life, these Millennium 25-cent coins celebrate a future full of promise. The Millennium souvenir set features all twelve coins in nickel with brilliant relief on brilliant background. The coins are displayed in a map of Canada seen from space. Also included in this set is the exclusive Millennium medallion—available only in this Royal Canadian Mint Millennium souvenir set.

Collector Value: $45.00

Specimen Set

2000 Uncirculated Gift Set

The Specimen set features a superb collection of Canada's circulation coins, struck with new dies and hand-selected to guarantee the highest quality finish with brilliant relief on a lined matte background. The two-dollar coin features frosted relief on a brilliant background. The alloys are the same as found in circulation coins.

Collector Value: $40.00

Uncirculated Set

2000 Uncirculated Gift Set

Coins are individually sealed in plastic and presented in a keep-sake envelope. The uncirculated set features the two-dollar coin with the polar bear and an envelope with a striking image of a polar bear in the Canadian arctic.

Collector Value: $30.00

Tiny Treasures

2000 Uncirculated Gift Set

Uncirculated Tiny Treasures coin set features a finish with a brilliant field on a brilliant relief. The two-dollar coins offered in these sets feature the brilliant field and maintain the frosted polar bear re-lief. The alloys are the same as found in circulation coins.

Ideal for young children, this set comes in a display case illus-trated with cute and cuddly teddy bears and includes a special card that children can mail back to receive a special surprise gift from the Royal Canadian Mint on their next birthday.

Collector Value: $25.00

The Adventures of Zachary and Penny Money

Based on the 1999 Millennium Coins

Have fun reading, playing, and discovering our heritage with Zachary and Penny Money!

Zachary and Penny are first cousins who love to explore. On their journey of discovery, they meet wonderful heroes and memorable characters who help them discover Canada's rich and remarkable history.

The Adventures of Zachary and Penny Money come to you in twelve beautifully illustrated stories based on each of Canada's 25-cent 1999 Millennium coins.

The Adventures of Zachary and Penny Money includes:

- Twelve stories and games in six superb booklets, representing all twelve Millennium coins.
- A nifty display card to collect your twelve 1999 25-cent Millennium coins.

Collector Value: $18.00

First Recorded Modern Hockey Game—
125th Anniversary (1875)

2000 50¢ Sterling Silver Proof Coin

The first recorded hockey game that was played with regulations similar to those that rule the ice today was played on March 3, 1875, at the Victoria Skating Rink in Montreal.

This design evokes the speed and skill of the sport as a modern hockey player maneuvers a puck across the ice.

The coins for the 2000 issue in this series were designed by Canadian artist Brian Hughes.

Coin Specifications:

Composition:	Sterling silver (.925 silver, .075 copper)
Edge:	Reeded
Weight:	9.30 grams
Diameter:	27.13 mm
Face Value:	50 cents
Collector Value:	$20.00

Introduction of Curling to North America—
240th Anniversary (1760)

2000 50¢ Sterling Silver Proof Coin

Although there are no official records, the winter of 1759–60 is often cited as curling's North American debut. History recalls how Scottish soldiers stationed in Quebec City during the Seven-Year War transformed a French cannon into curling irons.

This design captures the precision and technique modern curlers must exercise to propel a curling stone toward its target.

The coins for the 2000 issue in this series were designed by Canadian artist Brian Hughes.

Coin Specifications:

Composition:	Sterling silver (.925 silver, .075 copper)
Edge:	Reeded
Weight:	9.30 grams
Diameter:	27.13 mm
Face Value:	50 cents
Collector Value:	$20.00

Mother and Child

2000 $200 22-Karat Gold Coin

It is a mother's love and devotion that enable the Inuit to thrive in one of the world's harshest environments. Here, mothers are an endless source of security, warmth, and beauty in an unforgiving land.

The gaze between an Inuit woman and her child speaks the universal language of a mother's love. Her hand-crafted parka and boots reveal the care that is taken to transform life's necessities into works of art.

Designed by celebrated Inuit artist Germaine Arnaktauyok, whose work also appears on the 1999 $2 Canadian Coin, entitled Drum Dance.

This coin is the final issue in the four-coin "Native Cultures and Traditions" series (1997–2000).

Coin Specifications:

Purity:	22-karat or 91.67% gold, 8.33% silver
Edge:	Reeded
Weight:	17.135 grams
Gold Content:	15.552 grams (minimum ½ Troy ounces)
Diameter:	29 mm
Face Value:	$200.00
Mintage:	10,000
Collector Value:	$365.00

Northwest Passage

2000 $100 14-Karat Gold Coin

Sir John Franklin's disappearance in the Arctic prompted dozens of search-and-rescue expeditions. While the 1850 rescue attempt by Robert McClure failed to locate Franklin, it did succeed in unlocking the final link to the coveted Northwest Passage.

McClure's crew struggles against harsh frozen terrain while their ship, the HMS Investigator, remains locked in ice.

John Mardon was born in Welland, Ontario, and has received international acclaim for his work.

Coin Specifications:

Content:	58.33% gold, 41.67% silver
Edge:	Reeded
Weight:	13.338 grams
Diameter:	27 mm
Face Value:	$100.00
Mintage:	15,000
Collector Value:	$250.00

Voyage of Discovery

2000 Proof Silver Dollar

The next millennium promises to be an era of profound exploration as the boundaries of science, medicine, technology, and space continue to be challenged.

Highlights the newest frontier unlocked during the last millennium—

space. Internationally recognized symbols including the space shuttle, solar panels, the earth's atmosphere, and a robotic arm are brought together to create a stylized maple leaf to celebrate Canada's continued contribution to the space program.

Designed by artist and designer Donald F. Warkentin of Winnipeg, Manitoba.

Coin Specifications:

Composition:	Sterling silver, 92.5% silver, 7.5% copper
Edge:	Reeded
Weight:	25.175 grams
Diameter:	36.07 mm
Face Value:	$1.00
Collector Value:	$45.00
Also available:	Brilliant uncirculated sterling-silver dollar

1999 Releases

1999 225th Anniversary of the Voyage of Juan Pérez and the Sighting of the Queen Charlotte Islands

The Royal Canadian Mint salutes the spirit of explorers by commemorating the discovery of the Queen Charlotte Islands by Juan Pérez on a sterling-silver dollar coin.

"The Queen Charlotte Islands are a beautiful part of Canada's natural and cultural heritage," said Danielle Wetherup, President of the Royal Canadian Mint. "The 1999 Silver Dollar celebrates their discovery and the historic meeting of Europeans and Native Canadians."

The reverse of the silver dollar coin, designed by Canadian artist David Craig, portrays Haida canoes approaching the Santiago, a 225-ton Spanish frigate. Captain Juan Pérez and his crew of 86 sailed from Monterrey to explore the northern coast of North America and discovered Queen Charlotte Islands. The obverse of the coin features an effigy of Her Majesty Queen Elizabeth II by Canadian artist Dora de Pedery-Hunt.

The 1999 silver dollar coin is the 35th in a series celebrating Canadian Historical Events, People, and Places begun in 1935. They are available proof finish or brilliant uncirculated finish. The proof finish coin is encapsulated and presented in a green display case lined with green flock. The protective sleeve features Queen Charlotte Islands and the Santiago. The proof finish includes a numbered certificate of authenticity. The brilliant uncirculated coin is presented in a plastic capsule and protected with matchbox-style packaging that doubles to display the coin.

Coin Specifications:

Composition:	Sterling silver, 92.5% silver, 7.5% copper
Weight:	17.135 grams
Diameter:	36.07 mm
Thickness:	2 mm
Edge:	Reeded
Face Value:	$1.00
Collector Value:	Proof $36.00
Brilliant UNC:	$40.00

1999 Aviation Series—Part II

The de Havilland DHC-8 Dash 8

In the early 1980s, the rapidly expanding market for small, 30- to 40-seat airliners for the commuter trade gave rise to this elegant turboprop aircraft. Designed to operate economically at crowded airports with short runways, the DHC-8 Dash 8 is a fast, quiet high-wing, multipurpose regional transport aircraft. The sleek airframe enables the aircraft to reach cruising speeds rapidly and to climb fast and steep to flying altitude. The Dash 8 made its first official flight on June 20, 1983.

With the development of the Dash 8's older cousins—the Twin Otter and the Dash 7, smaller and larger respectively than the Dash 8—de Havilland had already established a stronghold in the area of STOL; with the Dash 8, de Havilland entered the fast-growing regional transport field. During the design phase, the manufacturers sent teams far and wide to collect information on the requirements of small airlines so that the Dash 8 could be tailor-made to satisfy the market. The resulting aircraft has sold briskly both to regional airlines and corporate clients.

The cameo portrays Robert H. Fowler, OC. Mr. Fowler, who joined de Havilland in 1952 as a test pilot, contributed to the development of flight control and propeller systems which helped de Havilland to become a world leader in the STOL concept. Later, he performed the first flights of the Dash 8.

Coin Specifications:

Composition:	92.5% sterling silver, with a 24-karat gold-covered cameo
Edge:	Interrupted serrations
Diameter:	38 mm
Reverse:	The de Havilland DHC-6 Twin Otter
Obverse:	Effigy of Her Majesty Queen Elizabeth II
Designed By:	Neil Aird
Face Value:	$20.00
Finish:	Proof (frosted relief on brilliant background)
Mintage:	50,000
Packaging:	Single coin: Aluminum case modeled after the wing of an aircraft with a propeller embossed on the cover. Comes with a numbered certificate of authenticity.
	Complete series: a ten-coin case is available for the entire series of ten coins.
Collector Value:	$100.00

The de Havilland DHC-6 Twin Otter

The appearance of a new power plant in the late 1950s (a propeller turbine that gave more power for a much lower installed weight than any equivalent piston engine) cleared the way for the design of a new, twin-prop aircraft that would equal the STOL performance of its predecessor and exceed its speed and capacity. De Havilland also worked closely with the military in the late 1950s to refine its STOL technology. The DHC-6 Twin Otter, the result of these efforts, made its first test flight on May 20, 1965.

Though developed mainly for the bush plane market, the Twin Otter has become one of the most lauded commuter aircraft in the world today, and it is also used for military operations. Able to land and take off from short runways, water, and snow, the aircraft is superbly versatile. A total of 844 Twin Otters were built between 1965 and 1988 and sold all over the world. As of 1990, more than 600 of these planes were still in service, reaching out to previously inaccessible areas.

The cameo portrays George Neal, Chief Test Pilot and Flight Operations Director with de Havilland. Mr. Neal participated in the testing of the Twin Otter and its predecessor, the Otter. In 1989 he received the McKee trophy and in 1995 was elected to the aviation Hall of Fame.

Coin Specifications:

Composition:	92.5% sterling silver, with a 24-karat gold-covered cameo
Edge:	Interrupted serrations
Diameter:	38 mm
Reverse:	The de Havilland DHC-6 Twin Otter
Obverse:	Effigy of Her Majesty Queen Elizabeth II
Designed By:	Neil Aird
Face Value:	$20.00
Finish:	Proof (frosted relief on brilliant background)
Mintage:	50,000
Packaging:	Single coin: Aluminium case modeled after the wing of an aircraft with a propeller embossed on the cover. Comes with a numbered certificate of authenticity.
	Complete series: A ten-coin case is available for the entire series of ten coins
Collector Value:	$100.00

1999 "The Butterfly" $200 22-Karat Gold Coin

The Royal Canadian Mint has introduced a $200 22-karat gold coin featuring Mi'kmaq art. The coin depicts a butterfly in a design incorporating the traditional Mi'kmaq double curve symbol of the balance between the physical and spiritual worlds.

"Our Native Cultures and Traditions gold coin series features beautiful original works by Canada's finest artists," said Danielle Wetherup, president of the Royal Canadian Mint. "The Butterfly coin reflects the richness of Mi'kmaq traditions and the fine talent the Mi'kmaq bring to Canada's artistic heritage."

Mi'kmaq artist Alan Syliboy of Nova Scotia drew his inspiration for the design on the reverse of the coin from the rock drawings or petroglyphs of Kejimkujik Park, Nova Scotia. The double curve butterfly design is surrounded by other ancient petroglyph symbols such as the five-pointed star symbolizing eternity, and the fir branch representing prosperity. The obverse depicts an effigy of Her Majesty Queen Elizabeth II by Canadian artist Dora de Pédery-Hunt, surrounded by the inscription 200 Dollars, Canada, 1998, Elizabeth II.

The 1999 Butterfly $200 gold coin is the third in a series of four coins celebrating Canada's Native Cultures and Traditions. The Mint will produce 25,000 of the Butterfly coins which are available encapsulated, in a no-frills shipper, or encapsulated and presented in an elegant metal-trimmed case and protective box. Both packaging options for the coins include a numbered certificate of authenticity from the Mint. The Royal Canadian Mint also commissioned a collector box created by native artist Mary Anne Barkhouse to house all four coins and their accompanying certificates. The coins are available directly from the Mint by calling 1-800-267-1871 in Canada, 1-800-268-6468 in the United States, for $414.95 ($274.95 U.S.) with the case, $409.95 ($271.95 U.S.) without the case. The four-coin case is available for $79.95 ($52.95 U.S.). The coins are also available from the Royal Canadian Mint's global network of dealers and distributors.

The Royal Canadian Mint is the Crown Corporation responsible for the minting and distribution of Canada's circulation coins. The Royal Canadian Mint is recognized as one of the largest and most versatile mints in the world, offering a wide range of specialized, high-quality coinage products and related services on an international scale.

Coin Specifications:

Purity:	22-karat or 91.67% gold, 8.33% silver
Weight:	17.135 grams
Gold Content:	15.552 grams (minimum Troy ounce of fine gold)
Diameter:	29 mm
Thickness:	2 mm
Edge:	Reeded
Face Value:	$200
Mintage:	25,000
Collector Value:	$355.00

1999 Millennium Sterling Silver
Proof 25-Cent Coins

Each of the Millennium Sterling Silver Proof 25-Cent Coins is available separately and has its own mark of distinction, especially since it features the month it was issued.

The individual coins are presented in a deluxe display case accompanied by a Certificate of Authenticity. Whatever the occasion, celebrate it with a 1999 Millennium Sterling Silver Coin.

Coin Specifications:

Composition:	Sterling silver (92.5% Ag; 7.5% Cu)
Finish:	Frosted relief on brilliant background
Edge:	Reeded
Weight:	5.9 grams
Diameter:	23.88
Thickness:	1.66 mm
Obverse:	Contemporary effigy of Her Majesty Queen Elizabeth II, by artist Dora de Pédery-Hunt.
Face Value:	25 cents
Collector Value:	$38.00

1999 90th Anniversary Coin Set

Struck to commemorate the opening of the Mint on January 2, 1908, the specimen sets were the first numismatic products to be offered by the Royal Mint, Ottawa. They were presented in a handsome red leather box stamped with these words in gold lettering: "First Coinage in Canada/1908/Royal Mint Ottawa." In 1998, to commemorate the ninetieth anniversary of the Royal Canadian Mint, the Mint's master engravers reproduced the original 1908 designs with an antique finish. The obverse of each coin bears the effigy of her Majesty Queen Elizabeth II by artist Dora de Pédery-Hunt.

Coin Specifications:

Denomination:	50 cents	25 cents	10 cents	5 cents	1 cent
Reverse:	Maple Leaves with Imperial State Crown	Maple Leaves with Imperial State Crown	Maple Leaves with Imperial State Crown	Maple Leaves with Imperial State Crown	Circle of Maple Leaves
Composition:	.925 silver .075 copper	.925 silver .075 copper	.925 silver .075 copper	.925 silver .075 copper	Copper-plated on .925 silver .075 copper
Weight (g):	11.62	5.81	2.32	1.167	5.67
Diameter (mm):	29.72	23.62	18.034	15.494	25.4
Edge:	Reeded	Reeded	Reeded	Reeded	Plain
Collector Value:	$150.00				

1999 Royal Canadian Mint
One-Ounce Gold Wafers

The Royal Canadian Mint launched a new gold investment product in the form of a 24-karat One-Ounce Gold Wafer.

"The Royal Canadian Mint strives to serve the needs of its customers with a variety of innovative products. Our gold wafer provides investors with a new investment vehicle made of the same high purity gold as our world-famous Gold Maple Leaf bullion investment coins," said Danielle Wetherup, president of the Royal Canadian Mint.

The One-Ounce Gold Wafer is rectangular (40.20 mm long by 24.20 mm wide) with a thickness of 1.717 mm and weighs 31.160 gm. The obverse of the wafer features a brilliant raised Hallmark of the Royal Canadian Mint and the inscription 1 oz .9999 and FINE GOLD OR PUR on a parallel finish field with a frosted edge. The reverse design is comprised of a repetitive series of frosted Mint logos with a brilliant logo in the center of the wafer.

As with other Royal Canadian Mint investment products, the One-Ounce Gold Wafer is available through the Royal Canadian Mint North American network of bullion dealers and distributors at a cost based on the price of gold on the open market, plus a small premium. The gold wafers are offered individually in a blister pack.

Over the years, the Royal Canadian has built a reputation for its innovative approach in the world of investment. The Mint was the first to introduce a bullion coin of 24-karat-gold purity in 1982 and in 1997, it was the first to introduce a guaranteed value gold investment coin. In 1998, the Mint also introduced a limited edition .99999 pure gold coin.

The Royal Canadian Mint is the Crown Corporation responsible for the minting and distribution of Canada's circulation coins. The Royal Canadian Mint is recognized as one of the largest and most versatile mints in the world. It has successfully diversified its operations and extended the scope of its marketing activities beyond Canada's borders and now offers a wide range of specialized, high-quality coinage products and related services on an international scale.

Wafer Specifications:

Composition:	.9999 gold
Weight:	1 ounce
	31.160 grams
Width:	24.20 mm
Length:	40.20 mm
Thickness:	1.717 mm
Shape:	Rectangular
Finish:	Field: Parallel lines
	Lettering and hallmark: Brilliant relief
	Design and edge: Frosted
Packaging:	Blister pack

1999 Sporting Firsts

Basketball

Springfield, Massachusetts, USA: The YMCA Training School was exceptionally clean that day—not a box to be found anywhere. Nothing to toss balls into as a stay-in-shape winter exercise. However, the janitor did find some peach baskets, which Canadian James Naismith (1861–1939) promptly mounted to the gymnasium balconies.

No rackets nor bats, just skill and aim to sink the ball into the basket, just like his childhood game of "duck on a rock." Remove the original target from above. Technique, not force.

In December 1891, eighteen students grabbed a soccer ball and sampled Naismith's game according to his set of thirteen rules. It was the indoor exercise that drew a crowd. A student suggested the name "Naismith ball" but the inventor preferred "basket ball." Within a year of its creation, two of Naismith's students were teaching the game at the YMCA in Montreal and St. Stephen, New Brunswick. Eight years later, the peach basket was replaced by a bottomless net.

Coin Specifications:

Composition:	Sterling silver (92.5% silver, 7.5% copper)
Weight:	9.30 grams
Diameter:	27.13 mm
Edge:	Reeded
Obverse:	Effigy of Her Majesty Queen Elizabeth II

Face Value:	50 cents
Designed By:	Donald Curley
Finish:	Proof (frosted relief on a brilliant background)
Packaging:	Single coin: Encapsulated coin housed in an innovative metal box
	Twelve-coin set: Individual metal boxes are displayed within a collectible metal box
Collector Value:	$22.00

Football

Who would have guessed that a move to promote sports in Canada would emerge as an icon in Canadian and North American football? It was June 1, 1909, when the Governor General of Canada, Lord Earl Grey, donated the Grey Cup for the amateur Rugby Football Championship of Canada.

The trophy was originally produced by Birks Jewellers at a cost of $48.00. The first Grey Cup game was played on December 4, 1909. On June 19, 1963, Lord Earl Grey was inducted into the Canadian Football Hall of Fame for his contribution to Canadian sports.

Coin Specifications:

Composition:	Sterling silver (92.5% silver, 7.5% copper)
Weight:	9.30 grams
Diameter:	27.13 mm
Edge:	Reeded
Obverse:	Effigy of Her Majesty Queen Elizabeth II
Face Value:	50 cents
Designed By:	Donald Curley
Finish:	Proof (frosted relief on a brilliant background)
Packaging:	Single coin: Encapsulated coin housed in an innovative metal box
	Twelve-coin set: Individual metal boxes are displayed within a collectible metal box
Collector Value:	$22.00

Golf

The coin shows golfers at play in period costume and commemorates the first Canadian Open Golf Championship, held during Dominion Day weekend, July 1, 1904. Hosted by North America's oldest golf organization, the Royal Montreal Golf Club, twelve contenders teed up for this premiere. It is believed to be the third oldest professional golf tournament in the world after the British Open (1860) and the U.S. Open (1895).

The one-day, 36-hole tournament was sponsored by the Royal Canadian Golf Association. J. H. Oke of the Royal Ottawa Golf Club, who claimed the $60 purse, played the winning score of 156. Donald H. Curley, a fine artist of Nova Scotia, created this unique design.

Coin Specifications:

Composition:	Sterling silver (.925 silver, .075 copper)
Weight:	9.30 grams
Diameter:	27.13 mm
Edge:	Reeded
Reverse:	Commemorates the first Canadian Open Golf Championship (1904)
Obverse:	Effigy of Her Majesty Queen Elizabeth II
Face Value:	50 cents
Designed By:	Donald H. Curley
Finish:	Proof: Frosted relief on a brilliant background
Packaging:	Single coin: Encapsulated coin housed in an innovative metal box
	Twelve-coin set: Single boxed coins housed within a collectible metal case
Collector Value:	$22.00

Yachting

The coin features a racing yacht at full sail. The first international yacht race held between Canada and the United States took place over a 30-mile course on Lake St. Clair: racers were required to finish the course within seven hours. With a twenty-six-minute lead in the third race and her captain and designer Alexander Cuthbert at the helm, Ontario's Annie Cuthbert sailed past the finish line on Monday, August 10, 1874, beating her American challenger, the Cora of Chicago.

Captain Cuthbert then proudly accepted the Fisher Cup—known as the Goodwin Cup until 1882—believed to be the oldest trophy in international freshwater yachting. Donald H. Curley, a fine artist of Nova Scotia, created this unique design.

Composition:	Sterling silver (.925 silver, .075 copper)
Weight:	9.30 grams
Diameter:	27.13 mm
Edge:	Reeded
Reverse:	Commemorates the first international yacht race between Canada and the United States (1874)
Obverse:	Effigy of Her Majesty Queen Elizabeth II
Face Value:	50 cents
Designed By:	Donald H. Curley
Finish:	Proof: Frosted relief on a brilliant background
Packaging:	Single coin: Encapsulated coin housed in an innovative metal box
	Twelve-coin set: Single boxed coins housed within a collectible metal case
Collector Value:	$22.00

Nunavut

1999 Millennium Two-Dollar Coin

In June 1999, the Royal Canadian Mint introduced the Nunavut 1999 Millennium $2 coin to celebrate the birth of Canada's youngest territory on April 1, 1999. The coin features an Inuit man completely absorbed in his spiritual, almost hypnotic drum dance—an age-old ritual that remains highly visible throughout Nunavut today. The new design will temporarily replace the polar bear that has graced the

$2 coin since 1996. The Nunavut 1999 Millennium $2 coin was designed by the Inuit artist Germaine Arnaktauyok and is available in 22-karat gold (shown above), sterling silver, and as part of a complete, uncirculated set or specimen set.

Composition: Gold: 22-karat-gold inner core with 4.1-karat-gold outer ring
Sterling silver: 92.5% sterling silver (inner core 22-karat gold plated)
Finish: Proof (frosted relief on brilliant background)
Designed By: Inuit artist Germaine Arnaktauyok
Mintage: Gold: 10,000 worldwide
Sterling silver: 40,000 worldwide
Includes numbered certificate of authenticity
Collector Value: Gold: $875.00, Proof Silver: $50.00

Cameo for Macau

1999 Sterling Silver Coin with Gold Cameo

This extraordinary sterling-silver coin with its gold cameo inset was produced for the Autoridade Monetaria e Cambial de Macau (AMCM—the Macau minting authority). It celebrates the establishment of the Macau Special Administrative Region of China on December 20, 1999.

The design features a Portuguese ship and a Chinese barque, portraying Macau as a city where cultures of the East and West become one. The oval-shaped 24-karat-gold cameo depicts a historic temple in Macau. The reverse of the coin bears the Coat of Arms of the city of Macau. It is presented in a deluxe red velvet case with gold moiré sides inside a red presentation box with gold lining. A numbered Certificate of Authenticity is included.

Collector Value: $85.00

The Path of Life

1999 Sterling Silver Dollar

This is the first Canadian coin design to be inspired by a commemorative postage stamp. The design features a couple in their golden years travelling the road of life. The trees symbolize the passage of time as they progress from spring blossoms to fall foliage. A collaborative effort by illustrator Shelagh Armstrong-Hodgson and designer Paul Hodgson, the design evokes a sense of movement—the new vitality of this colorful period of life.

The United Nations declared 1999 the International Year of Older Persons to increase awareness of the world's aging population and a shift in perceptions and policies. Signed October 1, 1998, the resolution calls for solidarity, respect, and mutual exchange between generations. As a founding UN member-state, Canada has generated a domestic initiative to create a society for all ages.

Collector Value: $75.00

1998 RELEASES

$200 22-Karat-Gold Coin Featuring the Legend of the White Buffalo

The design depicts the white buffalo coming alive and leaping into action. The legend of the white buffalo tells of the healing and regeneration of the Chipewyan people of Western Canada. It states that when a white buffalo calf is born, people will awaken to the light and Mother Earth will be healed. This powerful message for the people of the First nations is captured in a striking gold issue, designed by Canadian native artist Alex Janvier.

The 1999 $200 gold coin featuring the Harmony design is one of a series celebrating Canadian native cultures and traditions. This series was developed in collaboration with the Canadian Museum of Civilization.

Coin Specifications:

Purity:	22-karat or 91.67% gold, 8.33% silver
Weight:	17.135 grams
Gold Content:	15.552 grams (minimum Troy ounce of fine gold)
Diameter:	29 mm
Thickness:	2 mm
Edge:	Reeded
Face Value:	$200
Mintage:	25,000
Collector Value:	$800.00

1998 Canada's Ocean Giants

With Killer whales leaping in the background, the Royal Canadian Mint launched the "Canada's Ocean Giants" series of four fifty-cent sterling-silver coins featuring the Killer, Humpback, Beluga, and Blue whales at the Vancouver Aquarium. A contest with a grand prize of a family whale-watching adventure in Victoria, British Columbia, was also announced during the show.

The whales found in Canada's oceans are fascinating creatures and visitors from around the world come to Canada for whale-watching. "Our coins show the grace and beauty of these majestic animals," said Mint president Danielle Wetherup. "We are proud to offer Canadians and visitors to Canada a chance to win an exciting whale-watching adventure."

The 1998 "Canada's Ocean Giants" coins are available individually or as a four-coin set, and continue the Discovering Nature series featuring Canadian wildlife began in 1995. The coins are encapsulated and come in a presentation box with a protective sleeve. The four-coin set comes with an illustrative booklet featuring a photo and profile of the artist as well as information on the four whales featured on the coins. All designs were created by Québec wildlife artist Pierre Leduc. The obverse of each coin features an effigy of Her Majesty Queen Elizabeth II by artist Dora de Pédery-Hunt.

The coins are available worldwide through the Royal Canadian Mint's network of dealers and distributors or directly from the Mint in North America by calling 1-800-267-1871 (Canada), 1-800-268-6468 (U.S.). Individual coins cost $19.95 in Canadian funds ($14.65 U.S.). The four-coin set is available for the price of three individual coins at $59.95 Canadian ($44.45 U.S.).

The Royal Canadian Mint is the Crown Corporation responsible for the minting and distribution of Canada's circulation coins. The Royal Canadian Mint is recognized as one of the largest and most versatile mints in the world. Over the years, the Mint has successfully diversified its operations and extended the scope of its marketing activities beyond Canada's borders and now offers a wide range of specialized, high-quality coinage products and related services on an international scale.

Killer Whale

Although the black-and-white Killer whale is off all Canadian ice-free coasts, it is most common on Canada's west coast. On the east coast and in the eastern Arctic, it is an unpredictable visitor in most localities. Killer-whale schools have been studied in the coastal waters around Vancouver Island and their short-term and seasonal movements are well known. Adult males (8–10 m and 7–8 tons) are easily identified by the tall, upright dorsal fin. The species is highly social and nearly always seen in schools comprised of long-lasting kinship groups. Despite years of scientific observation, the Killer whale retains some of its secrets, and the length and timing of the reproductive cycle is not completely understood. Killer whales feed on fish, including salmon, and are also partial to seals.

Humpback

Humpback whales are common off eastern Canada during summer, particularly in the coastal waters off southwestern Nova Scotia and southeastern Newfoundland. They have little fear of ships and will often come to whale-watching boats, rolling on their backs or lying on their sides, with long flippers waving in the air and arching the tail flukes out of the water. Humpbacks are not large by baleen whale standards; the calves are born in the tropics and are about 4.5 m in length. Adult males may reach 15–16 m and weigh 15–25 tons and migrate for thousands of kilometers between the warm-water breeding areas and the rich feeding zones of the temperate and sub-Arctic North Atlantic and North Pacific. Humpback whales eat primarily oceanic shrimp and small fish, capturing the food in their huge mouths and straining out the water through the two rows of their baleen plates.

Beluga or White Whale

The Beluga is relatively abundant in several regions of the Arctic and thousands of animals move inshore after the ice-break in Hudson's Bay. Many can be seen near Churchill, Manitoba. The Belugas of the small population (approximately 600) in the estuary of the St. Lawrence are often easily viewed from tour boats or sometimes from the lighthouse at the mouth of the Saguenay River in Quebec. There is concern about the future status of this isolated population, so regulations for viewing Belugas are strict. The species is relatively small; adults reach only 4–4.5 meters in length, but Belugas are easily seen when they surface and some can be quite curious, making close approaches to boats if not alarmed. Beluga calves are harder to see because they are bluish gray or brownish for the first two years of life.

Blue Whale

The Blue whale is much rarer than the Humpback in Canadian waters. Occasionally seen off the west coast and the Atlantic Provinces, this gigantic, mottled blue-gray whale is best viewed in the waters off the Sept-Iles region of Quebec where up to 300 mammals are known to range in the summer months, feeding on large shoals of pelagic shrimp called "krill." This species is the largest mammal that the earth has ever known, dwarfing most dinosaurs. Adult Blue whales attain lengths of more than 30 m and may weigh over 150 tons, especially in Antarctic months. The female gives birth to a single calf, about 6–8 meters in length, every two or three years. The Blue whale is a highly migratory species but, because most of its movements are offshore, they are not as well understood as other species.

Coin Specifications:

Composition:	Sterling silver (.925 silver, .075 copper)
Weight:	9.3 grams
Diameter:	27.13 mm
Edge:	Reeded
Face Value:	50 cents
Collector Value:	$22.00 each

1998 Fine Silver Two-coin Set
Norman Bethune Commemorative Coin Set

This set of two silver coins, jointly issued by the Royal Canadian Mint and the China Gold Coin Incorporation, honors an extraordinary Canadian—Dr. Norman Bethune. Bethune, who was born in Gravenhurst, Ontario, in 1890, served humanity during three wars—the First World War, the Spanish Civil War, and the Sino-Japanese War. In 1938, Bethune went to China to become chief surgeon for the Eighth Route Army during the Sino-Japanese War. As well as designing a Model Hospital, writing text books, and training young Chinese doctors, Bethune served on the battlefield, invented a collapsible operating table, and organized medical supply units that could be transported on mule back. The 49-year-old doctor died in 1939, while still in China.

Coin Specifications:

Composition:	.9999 Fine silver
Finish:	Proof (frosted relief on brilliant background)
Edge:	Reeded
Weight:	31.39 grams
Diameter:	38 mm
Thickness:	3.3 mm
Reverse:	Depicts Norman Bethune travelling with the mobile surgery unit (Canadian coin)
Designed By:	Harvey Chan (Canadian coin)
Obverse:	Effigy of Her Majesty Queen Elizabeth II
Face Value:	$5.00
Mintage:	Maximum of 80,000 sets worldwide
Collector Value:	$90.00

1998 Proof Silver Dollar
125th Anniversary of the Creation
of the North-West Mounted Police

In 1873, the NWMP was created as part of Prime Minister Sir John A. MacDonald's National Policy. It was to replace the militia in Manitoba and to maintain law and order in Canada's unruly and unpatrolled northwestern frontier. The NWMP force was conceived and established to administer Canadian law, to end the whiskey trade and the lawlessness that accompanied it, and to establish peaceful relations with natives before CPR workers and settlers arrived.

The "pill-box" hat was the first forage cap approved for use by the North-West Mounted Police. Its design reflects the British military style of the era. In 1902, the now familiar wide-brimmed Stetson was officially introduced.

The scarlet tunic and red serge jacket that are part of the uniform worn today by the Royal Canadian Mounted Police are identical to those worn by the North-West Mounted Police 125 years ago.

1998 Proof Silver Dollar Specifications:

Composition:	92.5% sterling silver
Finish:	Proof (frosted relief on brilliant background)
Edge:	Reeded
Weight:	25.175 grams
Diameter:	36.07 mm
Thickness:	2.95 mm
Reverse:	125th anniversary of the creation of the North-West Mounted Police
Designed By:	Adeline Halvorson
Obverse:	Effigy of Her Majesty Queen Elizabeth II
Face Value:	$1.00
Collector Value:	$120.00

1998 Fifty-cent Sterling-Silver Coins
Canadian Sports' Firsts

These coins are the first issued in a three-year program. The series commemorates important Canadian sporting events. Four sports per year will be honored. The first two chosen themes for this year are as follows:

The First Canadian to Win the Grand Prix of Canada for F1 Auto Racing (1978)

This coin commemorates that thrilling moment on October 8, 1978, in Montreal, when a red Ferrari, driven by Gilles Villeneuve, roared into the lead and over the finish line. It was the first time that a Canadian had won a Formula One Grand Prix race, and the crowd exploded in wild national pride. Since then, many young Canadians have been inspired by Villeneuve's victory to participate in this demanding sport.

The First Overseas Canadian Soccer Tour (in Ireland, England, and Scotland) in 1888

This coin commemorates Canada's first overseas soccer tour in 1888. The final match of the 23-game rout of Britain was played at the Kennington Oval, London. Ten thousand spectators watched skeptically to see how the colonials played Britain's national game. Though the British scored a narrow victory, the cliff-hanger left them surprised and respectful, calling the Canadians "truly formidable opponents." In Canada today, soccer is second only to hockey in popularity.

The First Official Amateur Figure-Skating Championships Held by The Amateur Skating Association of Canada (1888)

This coin, designed by Friedrich Peter, commemorates Canada's first national figure-skating championships, held in Toronto in 1888. It was a time when the so-called "fancy skating" was beginning to take off, with amateur skaters thronging the rinks of skating clubs all over Canada. Organized competition, however, was in its infancy. Though the national championships lapsed in the years immediately after 1888, it was nevertheless the beginning of a competitive tradition that has since taken Canadians to the highest levels worldwide.

The First Canadian Ski-Running and Ski-Jumping Championships (1898)

This coin, designed by Friedrich Peter, commemorates the first Canadian Ski Racing and Ski Jumping Championships, held in Rossland, B.C. in 1898. Imagine being there in the crowd and watching, breathless, as pioneer ski racers zoomed down the icy slopes. Ski racing—or "running"—was new to Canada in the 19th century. Brought here by Scandinavian immigrants, skiing quickly became part of life in Canada. Today, more than five million Canadians ski.

Coin Specifications:

Composition:	Sterling silver (92.5%)
Finish:	Proof (frosted relief on brilliant background)
Edge:	Reeded
Weight:	9.30 grams
Thickness:	2.11 mm
Diameter:	27.13 mm
Reverse:	Four designs depicting Canadian Sports Firsts
Designed By:	Friedrich G. Peter

Obverse: Effigy of Her Majesty Queen Elizabeth II
Face Value: 50 cents
Collector Value: $24.00 each

1998 Twelve-Year Lunar Series
Year of the Tiger

Centuries ago, the Chinese invented a calendar based on the lunar—rather than the solar—cycle. These symbols roughly approximate the signs of the zodiac in Western culture; however, they denote years instead of months. In 1998, the Royal Canadian Mint began production of the twelve-year annual series with a coin commemorating the Year of the Tiger. All twelve of the Lunar animals—the Rat, the Ox, the Tiger, the Rabbit, the Dragon, the Snake, the Horse, the Sheep, the Monkey, the Rooster, the Dog, and the Pig—appear in a circular arrangement around the rim of each coin, with a different animal highlighted each year in a central cameo. The coin's obverse bears the effigy of Her Majesty Queen Elizabeth II by artist Dora de Pédery-Hunt.

Coin Specifications:

Composition: 92.5% silver, 7.5% copper
Finish: Proof (frosted relief on brilliant background)
Edge: Reeded
Weight: 34 grams
Diameter: Coin: 40 mm; Cameo: 17.5 mm
Reverse: Year of the Tiger
Designed By: Harvey Chan
Obverse: Effigy of Her Majesty Queen Elizabeth II
Face Value: $15.00
Mintage: 68,888
Collector Value: $475.00

1998 Platinum Proof Coin Set
The Gray Wolf

The gray wolves are the largest wild members of the dog family. Because of vigorous efforts to eliminate them in other parts of the world, Canada is their last and most important stronghold; however, even here they are in retreat. Yet the gray wolf has a vital role to play in preserving the Canadian wilderness. As the country's largest predator, the wolf helps to maintain an ecological balance between the animal populations and habitat capacity. Most of Canada's wolves—some 58,000 strong—live in the far north.

Coin Specifications:

	1 oz.	½ oz.	¼ oz.	¹⁄₁₀ oz.
Purity (%)	99.95	99.95	99.95	99.95
Weight (g)	31.16	15.59	7.80	3.132
Diameter (mm)	30	25	20	16
Face Value	$300.00	$150.00	$75.00	$30.00
Finish:	Proof (frosted relief on brilliant background)			
Edge:	Reeded			
Designed By:	Kerri Burnett			
Obverse:	Effigy of Her Majesty Queen Elizabeth II			
Collector Value:	$3600.00.			

1998 Aviation Series—Part II
The Canadair (Bombardier) CP-107 Argus

Coin 7—The Canadair CP-107 Argus

Built for antisubmarine maritime reconnaissance, the Canadair CP-107 Argus navigated and fought more effectively than any other aircraft in its class. Powered by huge piston engines, the airframe was strengthened for the rigors of low-level flying over the open sea. The heart of the Argus was the Air Navigation and Tactical Control System (ANTAC). It became the world's most advanced ASW aircraft. The Argus entered squadron service with the RCAF in 1958 and flew its last mission in 1981.

The Argus was flown by a unique team: the pilot and the flight engineer. It was the flight engineer's responsibility to control all power settings from his position behind the copilot. The pilot determined the power setting and the flight engineer set the exact amount of power requested.

Coin Specifications:

Composition:	92.5% sterling silver, with a 24-karat-gold-covered cameo
Finish:	Proof (frosted relief on brilliant background)
Edge:	Interrupted serrations
Weight:	31.103 grams
Diameter:	38 mm
Thickness:	3.50 mm
Reverse:	The Canadair (Bombardier) CP-107 Argus
Designed By:	Peter Mossman
Obverse:	Effigy of Her Majesty Queen Elizabeth II
Face Value:	$20.00
Mintage:	50,000
Price:	$57.95 per coin
Packaging:	Aluminum case modeled after the wing of an aircraft with a propeller embossed on the cover
Collector Value:	$120.00

1998 Aviation Series—Part II
The Canadair (Bombardier) CL-215 Waterbomber

Coin 8—The Canadair CL-215 Waterbomber

Designed primarily for forest protection and fire control, the Canadair CL-215 can spray chemical retardants and water while still in flight. In just 10 seconds, this twin-engined amphibian aircraft will scoop enough water to spray an area of 12 by 100 meters. Probes scoop up the water as the aircraft skims across the surface of a suitable body of water. In June of 1978, a CL-215 in Manitoba made 160 drops in one day, spraying nearly 1,000 tons of water. This aircraft can spray and reload as many as 30 times an hour.

Forest fires could be fought with CL-215s in three ways. One method involves the spraying of pre-mixed long-term chemical fire retardants pumped into the tanks at the base. The second involves the use of short-term retardants that are mixed with water during scooping. The third is the use of plain water scooped up from any ¾-mile stretch of lake or ocean.

Coin Specifications:

Composition:	92.5% sterling silver, with a 24-karat-gold-covered cameo
Finish:	Proof (frosted relief on brilliant background)
Edge:	Interrupted serrations
Weight:	31.103 grams
Diameter:	38 mm
Thickness:	3.50 mm
Reverse:	The Canadair (Bombardier) CL-215 Waterbomber
Designed By:	Peter Mossman
Obverse:	Effigy of Her Majesty Queen Elizabeth II
Face Value:	$20.00
Mintage:	50,000
Price:	$57.95 per coin
Packaging:	Aluminum case modeled after the wing of an aircraft with a propeller embossed on the cover.
Collector Value:	$95.00

1998 Pure Gold Coin
.99999 Gold Coin

The Royal Arms of Canada were established by proclamation of the King in 1921. They signify national sovereignty and are used by Canada on federal government possessions (such as buildings, official seals, money, passports, proclamations, etc.) as well as rank badges of some members of the Canadian Forces. The current version of the Arms of Canada was drawn by Mrs. Cathy Bursey-Sabourin and approved in 1994.

At the base of the Coat of Arms are the four floral emblems: the English Rose, the Scottish Thistle, the Irish Shamrock, and the French Fleur-de-lis. Of particular interest is the fact that the English Rose is not a cultivated flower. Rather, it is a combination of the white Tudor rose of the House of York and the red rose of the House of Lancaster. The Scottish Thistle is Onopordum acanthium, the traditional bull thistle. The Irish Shamrock has three petals, as does the French Fleur-de-lis (Lilium candidum or Lily).

Coin Specifications:

Composition:	.99999 pure gold
Finish:	Proof (frosted relief on brilliant background)
Edge:	Reeded
Weight:	38.05 grams
Diameter:	34 mm
Thickness:	2.7 mm
Reverse:	Depicts an arrangement of the floral emblems found on the Canadian Coat of Arms
Designed By:	Pierre Leduc
Obverse:	Effigy of Her Majesty Queen Elizabeth II
Face Value:	$350.00
Mintage:	Maximum of 1,998 coins worldwide
Collector Value:	$1650.00

1998 Proof Set

A proof finish means the relief (raised part of the design) is given a frosted texture, while the background remains brilliant (shiny).

The Royal Canadian Mint Proof Set is the premium collector set for people interested in Canada's circulation coin designs. In addition to the current silver dollar, each year the set features the proof numismatic variety of the current selection of circulation coins, most of these struck in precious metals exclusively for this set.

Coin Specifications:

Denomination:	Proof Dollar	2 dollars	1 dollar	50 cents	25 cents	10 cents	5 cents	1 cent
Reverse:	125th Anniversary of the founding of the North-West Mounted Police	Polar Bear	Common Loon	Coat of Arms of Canada	Caribou	Fishing Schooner	Beaver	Maple Leaf
Alloy:	92.5% sterling silver	92.5% sterling silver	Nickel electro-plated with bronze	92.5% sterling silver	92.5% sterling silver	92.5% sterling silver	92.5% sterling silver	Bronze
			24 kt. gold-plated inner core					
Weight (g):	25.175	8.83	7.00	9.30	5.90	2.40	5.35	2.50
Diameter (mm):	36.07	28.07	26.50 11-sided	27.13	23.88	18.03	21.20	19.10
Edge:	Reeded	Interrupted serrations	Plain	Reeded	Reeded	Reeded	Plain	Plain

Collector Value: $38.00

1998 Specimen Set

The Specimen Set is a collection including one example of each Canadian circulation coin, struck with numismatic dies onto specially prepared coin blanks. The finish is a threefold combination of brilliant and frosted relief on a line finish background. The alloys are the same as found in circulation coins, except for the one-cent coin, which is solid bronze instead of reflecting the plated composition of the circulating one-cent coin.

Coin Specifications:

Denomination:	2 dollars	1 dollar	50 cents	25 cents	10 cents	5 cents	1 cent
Reverse:	Polar Bear	Common Loon	Coat of Arms of Canada	Caribou	Fishing Schooner	Beaver	Maple Leaf
Alloy:	Outer ring: 99⁺% Nickel Inner core: 92% Copper	Nickel electro-plated with bronze	Nickel	Nickel	Nickel	Cupro-nickel	Bronze
Weight (g):	7.30	7.00	8.10	5.05	2.07	4.60	2.50
Diameter (mm):	28 26.50	27.13 11-sided	23.88	18.03	21.20	19.10	
Edge:	Interrupted serrations	Plain	Reeded	Reeded	Reeded	Plain	Plain
Collector Value:	$38.00						

1998 Uncirculated Sets

The finish of the 1998 coins offered in the Uncirculated, O Canada!, and Tiny Treasures coin sets is a brilliant field on a brilliant relief. The two-dollar coins offered in these sets feature the brilliant field but maintain the frosted polar bear relief introduced in the 1997 Uncirculated Set. The alloys are the same as found in circulation coins.

As of 1998, all Uncirculated Sets are produced at the Royal Canadian Mint's Winnipeg plant, using numismatic dies and specially prepared blanks. All Uncirculated Sets include a mint mark on the obverse of each coin to indicate from which plant they originate.

People wishing to collect an uncirculated version of Canadian circulation coins will usually purchase the Uncirculated Set, while the "O Canada!" Gift Set and Tiny Treasures Gift Set are attractively presented for use as gifts.

Coin Specifications:

Denomination	2 dollars	1 dollar	50 cents	25 cents	10 cents	5 cents	1 cent
Reverse:	Polar Bear	Common Loon	Coat of Arms of Canada	Caribou	Fishing Schooner	Beaver	Maple Leaf

Alloy:	Outer ring: 99⁻% Nickel Inner core: 92% Copper	Nickel electro-plated with bronze	Nickel	Nickel	Nickel	Cupro-nickel zinc	Copper-plated-zinc
Weight (g):	7.30	7.00	8.10	5.05	2.07	4.60	2.25
Diameter (mm):	28	26.50	27.13 11-sided	23.88	18.03	21.20	19.05
Edge:	Interrupted serrations	Plain	Reeded	Reeded	Reeded	Plain	Plain
Collector Value:	$45.00						

1997 RELEASES

1997 500th Anniversary
Proof Silver Ten-Cent Coin

The theme of the 1997 proof silver ten-cent coin commemorates the momentous voyage from Bristol, England, to the east coast of Canada, made in 1497 by John Cabot (Giovanni Caboto). Caboto was an Italian but he sailed under the English flag, sanctioned by the King of England.

On May 2, 1497, navigator and cartographer John Cabot departed from Bristol, England, aboard the Matthew, a small ship with a crew of 18 men, in search of westward routes to the Far East.

On June 24, 1497, they made landfall somewhere on what is today the coast of Newfoundland, naming it "Buena Vista." Cabot sailed briefly along the coast exploring what he called "the country of the Great Khan," believing it to be Asia. Upon his return to England in August 1497, Cabot reported waters rich with fish and a land of plenty.

Coin Specifications:

Composition:	Sterling silver (92.5% silver, 7.5% copper)
Finish:	Proof (frosted relief on brilliant background)
Edge:	Reeded
Weight:	2.4 grams

Diameter:	18.03 mm
Thickness:	1.2 mm
Reverse:	Depicts the historic voyage of John Cabot's boat, the Matthew, approaching land
Designed By:	Donald H. Curley
Obverse:	Contemporary effigy of Her Majesty Queen Elizabeth II, by artist Dora de Pédery-Hunt
Face Value:	10 cents
Mintage:	50,000 worldwide
Collector Value:	$30.00

1997 Fifty-Cent Sterling-Silver Proof Coins, Canada's Best Friends

Nova Scotia Duck Tolling Retriever

"Tolling" is a hunting expression, meaning "to lure game by appealing to their curiosity." In nature, it is the fox who entices ducks to shore by playing and gambolling on the waterfront: the canine equivalent is a dog developed in the 1860s in Yarmouth, Nova Scotia. Hunters, observing the behavior of the fox, developed a new breed by crossing several retrievers, including the Irish Setter which gives the Duck Tolling Retriever its characteristic red or orange color. This alert and lively animal works with a concealed hunter, fetching sticks and luring the curious ducks shoreward with its playful antics. Originally limited to Nova Scotia, the breed is now known across Canada and internationally.

Coin Specifications:

Composition:	Sterling silver (92.5% silver, 7.5% copper)
Finish:	Proof (frosted relief on brilliant background)
Edge:	Reeded
Weight:	9.30 grams
Diameter:	27.13 mm

Reverse: Nova Scotia Duck Tolling Retriever
Designed By: Arnold A. Nogy
Obverse: Effigy of Her Majesty Queen Elizabeth II
Face Value: 50 cents
Collector Value: $24.00

Canadian Eskimo Dog

This strong northern breed goes back some 2,000 years in Canada. Brought here by Mongolian migrants from Asia, for centuries the Eskimo Dog served northern peoples as a sled dog in winter and as a pack animal in summer. This breed is known for its toughness and endurance. Its thick coat protects it in even the coldest of temperatures. It can pull weights of up to 80 kilos and, even when food is scarce, it can travel as much as 100 kilometers a day. In recent years, the Eskimo Dog has been largely replaced by the snowmobile in northern life. From a population of 20,000 animals in the 1920s, its numbers fell to a low of some 200 in the 1970s. Since then, efforts to reestablish the breed have begun to find success.

Coin Specifications:

Composition: Sterling silver (92.5% silver, 7.5% copper)
Finish: Proof (frosted relief on brilliant background)
Edge: Reeded
Weight: 9.30 grams
Diameter: 27.13 mm
Reverse: Canadian Eskimo Dog
Designed By: Arnold A. Nogy
Obverse: Effigy of Her Majesty Queen Elizabeth II
Face Value: 50 cents
Collector Value: $24.00

Labrador Retriever

The Labrador, whose ancestors were discovered in Newfoundland and Labrador by 18th-century colonists, is probably descended from dogs abandoned there by European fishermen almost two centuries earlier. Left on their own, the dogs developed into skillful hunters. In the early 1800s a few specimens were taken back to Britain where they soon proved their worth as retrievers of fish and game. The British further developed the breed by crossing it with a number of existing retrievers. Soon, the Labrador had become the most valued game dog in Britain. Recognized by the Kennel Club of Britain in 1903 and a few years later by Canada, the black, yellow, and chocolate-colored Labradors are known for their intelligence and for their gentle, affectionate natures.

Coin Specifications:

Composition: Sterling silver (92.5% silver, 7.5% copper)
Finish: Proof (frosted relief on brilliant background)

Edge:	Reeded
Weight:	9.30 grams
Diameter:	27.13 mm
Reverse:	Labrador Retriever
Designed By:	Arnold A. Nogy
Obverse:	Effigy of Her Majesty Queen Elizabeth II
Face Value:	50 cents
Collector Value:	$26.00

Newfoundland

This massive dog is the "gentle giant" of Canadian breeds. The origins of the Newfoundland are lost in time but may go back nearly a thousand years to the crossing of indigenous breeds with the giant bear dogs of Viking explorers. Literature is full of heroic tales of this brave and affectionate dog. The Newfoundland seems to have a life-saving instinct and is known to have rescued many children, fishermen, and shipwrecked sailors from drowning. The dog's thick, water-repellent coat, rudderlike tail, and webbed feet make it a water dog par excellence, and for centuries it has worked side by side with the Newfoundland fisherman. Its large size and strength have combined with intelligence and character to produce an exceptionally loyal and good-natured dog.

Coin Specifications:

Composition:	Sterling silver (92.5% silver, 7.5% copper)
Finish:	Proof (frosted relief on brilliant background)
Edge:	Reeded
Weight:	9.30 grams
Diameter:	27.13 mm
Reverse:	Newfoundland
Designed By:	Arnold A. Nogy
Obverse:	Effigy of Her Majesty Queen Elizabeth II
Face Value:	50 cents
Collector Value:	$26.00

1997 Commemorative Proof Silver Dollar, 1972 Canada/Russia Hockey Series

The theme of the 1997 commemorative silver dollar celebrates more than the 25th anniversary of the 1972 Canada/USSR Hockey Series. It also celebrates the qualities of sportsmanship, teamwork, and self-discipline athletic sports such as hockey teaches to young athletes around the world. Such qualities were clearly recognizable in the athletes of both teams throughout the dramatic eight-game series. In Canada, through the dedication of volunteer coaches, the support of businesses, and Canadian Hockey, thousands of young people learn to be the best they can be. The 1997 silver dollar is a tribute to their tireless efforts.

The 1972 Canada/USSR Series began September 2 and concluded September 28, 1972. This special exhibition series was arranged by Hockey Canada, the Canadian Amateur Hockey Association, and the Soviet Hockey Federation. Hockey Canada and the Canadian Amateur Hockey Association have since merged to become Canadian Hockey. The first four games were played in Montreal, Toronto, Winnipeg, and Vancouver. The last four were played in Moscow. When the series was over Canada had four wins, the Soviets three, and one game had been tied. There had been breathtaking displays of athletic excellence, cultural exchanges, and a new adventure in diplomacy.

The series was a turning point in the history of hockey. Until 1972 international rules had prevented Canadian players from the National Hockey League from playing in a world hockey championship. Today players from professional teams can now compete in amateur championships and honor those who stood behind them throughout their career.

1997 Commemorative Proof Silver Dollar Specifications:

Composition:	92.5% sterling silver
Finish:	Proof (frosted relief on brilliant background)
Edge:	Reeded
Weight:	25.175 grams
Diameter:	36.07 mm
Thickness:	2.95 mm
Reverse:	Commemorates the climactic goal of the Canada/Russia series' eighth and final game

Designed By:	Roger Hill
Obverse:	Effigy of Her Majesty Queen Elizabeth II
Face Value:	$1.00
Collector Value:	$45.00

1997 14-Karat Gold Coin, The Telephone

The theme for the 1997 $100 gold coin focuses on Alexander Graham Bell. His invention of the telephone revolutionized the manner in which people communicate across the globe. The satellite view of the world encircled by the telephone wire reinforces the impact this invention has had on our lives. In this design, the artist has carefully paid tribute to Alexander Graham Bell's birthplace in Scotland and to his new home in North America. The following are excerpts from The Telephone Story, courtesy of the Baddeck Public Library "search for Yesterday," April 1981.

In July of 1874, Bell hit upon the principle of the telephone. That summer, while visiting his parents in Brantford, Bell worked on a phonautograph, a somewhat macabre device to translate sounds into visible marking with equipment using the actual ear of a dead man. When the words were spoken, the ear membrane vibrated and moved a lever that etched a wave pattern on a piece of smoked glass.

August 3, 1876	Bell completed the first one-way call of five miles from a store in Mount Pleasant, Ontario, to the telegraph office in Brantford.
August 4, 1876	Bell tested the telephone over a line 3 miles long from the telegraph office in Brantford to the Bell homestead, Tutelo Heights, Brantford, Ontario.
August 10, 1876	Bell made what is considered the world's first long-distance telephone call. He was stationed in Robert White's Boot and Shoe Store, Paris, Ontario, and his father and others were stationed in the Dominion Telegraph Company's office in Brantford, Ontario. The distance was eight miles.
October 9, 1876	The first two-way long-distance call was set

up between Boston and Cambridgeport. Bell and Watson used two miles of private wire that belonged to the Walworth Manufacturing Company.

August 29, 1877   The first telephone was leased in Canada.

Coin Specifications:

Composition:	58.33% gold, 41.67% silver
Finish:	Proof (frosted relief on brilliant background)
Edge:	Reeded
Weight:	13.338 grams
Diameter:	27 mm
Thickness:	2.15 mm
Reverse:	Depicts the profile of a mature Alexander Graham Bell, an old-fashioned telephone, and a satellite view of the world
Designed By:	Donald H. Curley
Obverse:	Effigy of Her Majesty Queen Elizabeth II
Face Value:	$100.00
Mintage:	Maximum of 25,000 coins worldwide
Collector Value:	$650.00

1997 22-Karat-Gold Coin, Haida

This coin features the Haida legend of Raven Bringing Light to the World, a beautiful example of Haida totemic art by British Colombia–based Haida artist Robert Davidson. The design is based on Raven, the Haida cultural hero. An ancient Haida narrative tells the story of the time when Raven took the sun back from the Chief of the Sky and returned it to the people of the earth.

The 1997 $200 gold coin featuring the Haida design is the first of a series celebrating Canadian native cultures and traditions. This series was developed in collaboration with the Canadian Museum of Civilization.

Coin Specifications:

Composition:	91.67% pure gold
Finish:	Proof (frosted relief on brilliant background)
Edge:	Reeded
Weight:	17.135 grams

Diameter:	29 mm
Thickness:	2 mm
Reverse:	"Raven Bringing Light to the World" (1986–87) is an excellent example of totemic art
Designed By:	Robert Davidson
Obverse:	Effigy of Her Majesty Queen Elizabeth II
Face Value:	$200.00
Mintage:	Limited to only 25,000 coins worldwide
Collector Value:	$900.00

1997 Silver Aviation Cameo Series—Part II Powered Flight in Canada Beyond World War II

Coin 6—The Canadair CT-114 Tutor: The Snowbirds

Skill, professionalism, and teamwork describe the key characteristics of the pilots who fly the Snowbirds. Audiences worldwide have enjoyed the aerobatics of the Canadair CT-114 Tutor. The Tutor was designed in 1958 as an all-purpose jet training aircraft for the flight instruction of military pilots. This aircraft is an all-metal, side-by-side, two-seat monoplane with a single jet engine. The high maneuverability and relatively slow speed of the Tutor is ideally suited for aerobatics. A well-tuned engine enhances engine response in low-level flying. The basic Tutor was slightly modified for use by the Snowbirds. Required was a smoke-generating system with a unique paint scheme for added crowd appeal.

Coin 6 features a close-up view of a Canadair CT-114 Tutor, the Snowbirds flying in a "Big Diamond" formation, and the Snowbird squadron crest. The cameo portrays the likeness of Edward Higgins, a former Vice-President of Canadair. Mr. Higgins was the driving force behind the design and construction of the Tutor.

Coin Specifications:

Composition:	92.5% sterling silver, with a 24-karat-gold-covered cameo
Finish:	Proof (frosted relief on brilliant background)
Edge:	Interrupted serrations
Weight:	31.103 grams
Diameter:	38 mm
Thickness:	3.50 mm

Reverse:	Avro Canada CF-105 Arrow with gold cameo of Jim Chamberlin
Designed By:	Ross Buckland (1997 issues)
Obverse:	Effigy of Her Majesty Queen Elizabeth II
Face Value:	$20.00
Mintage:	Maximum of 50,000 of each coin worldwide
Collector Value:	$115.00

1997 Silver Aviation Cameo Series—Part II Powered Flight in Canada Beyond World War II

Coin 5—The Canadair F-86 Sabre:
The Golden Hawks

Innovative and talented, the expertise of the Canadian aviation industry continued to excite the imagination. The technology of the Canadair F-86 Sabre was world renowned. The Sabre became one of the top military aircraft in Europe during the 1950s. Chosen to fulfill Canada's fighter aircraft commitment to NATO, a team of Sabres went on to become famous as the Golden Hawks. Painted gold with a red-and-white hawk emblazoned on each side, the Golden Hawks thrilled audiences with their aerobatic maneuvers.

Over the years Canadair built over 1,800 Sabres in six variants. Air forces in several countries, as well as the RCAF and RAF, flew the Sabre. The Canadian-built Mk. 6, powered by an Orenda engine, was the finest variant of the Sabre line.

This aerobatic team was formed in 1959 to commemorate two milestones in Canadian aviation history: the 50th Anniversary of powered flight in Canada, and the 35th Anniversary of the RCAF.

Coin 5 features a close-up view of a Canadair Mk. 6 Sabre, four Golden Hawks in their "Diamond" formation, and the Golden Hawk insignia. The cameo portrays the likeness of Fern Villeneuve, the first leader of the Golden Hawks.

Coin Specifications:

Composition:	92.5% sterling silver, with a 24-karat-gold-covered cameo
Finish:	Proof (frosted relief on brilliant background)
Edge:	Interrupted serrations

Weight:	31.103 grams
Diameter:	38 mm
Thickness:	3.50 mm
Reverse:	Avro Canada CF-105 Arrow with gold cameo of Jim Chamberlin
Designed By:	Ross Buckland (1997 issues)
Obverse:	Effigy of Her Majesty Queen Elizabeth II
Face Value:	$20.00
Mintage:	Maximum of 50,000 of each coin worldwide
Collector Value:	$125.00

1997 Platinum Proof Coins, The Wood Bison

The wood bison is a unique part of Canada's natural history. Wood bison once roamed the meadows of the boreal forests of northwestern Canada by the thousands, providing food, shelter, and clothing for native peoples. Under hunting pressure that accompanied early exploration and the fur trade, the wood bison population was cut down to a mere 250 by 1900. Active protection by the Government of Canada reversed this trend. By the time Wood Buffalo Park was established in 1922, wood bison numbers had recovered to at least 1500.

Unfortunately a release of surplus plains bison—a much smaller animal—from southern Canada into Wood Buffalo National Park in the late 1920s resulted in the mixing of the two subspecies and the introduction of serious cattle diseases. Since then, seven healthy, free-roaming populations most representative of the original wood bison have been established as part of a national recovery program. Thanks to an environmental campaign that began at the turn of the century, the wood bison will likely continue to be part of Canada's natural heritage.

Coin Specifications:

	1 oz.	$1/2$ oz.	$1/4$ oz.	$1/10$ oz.
Purity (%):	99.95	99.95	99.95	99.95
Weight (g):	31.16	15.59	7.80	3.132
Diameter (mm):	30	25	20	16
Face Value:	$375.00	$185.00	$100.00	$45.00

Finish:	Proof (frosted relief on brilliant background)
Edge:	Reeded
Reverse:	Depicts the wood bison in four different scenes: a mother and father guarding their calf; a majestic wood bison in full profile; two calves at play; and a stately portrait of the wood bison.
Designed By:	Chris Bacon
Obverse:	Effigy of Her Majesty Queen Elizabeth II
Mintage:	Maximum of 1,000 sets; 1,000 $1/2$ oz. coins; 1,000 $1/10$ oz. coins worldwide

Collector Value: $3250.00 set

1996 Releases

1996 Silver Aviation Cameo Series—Part II
Powered Flight in Canada Beyond World War II

Coin 3—Avro Canada CF-105 Arrow

One of the finest achievements in Canadian aviation history, the Avro Canada CF-105 Arrow was never allowed to fulfill its mission. Intended to replace the Avro Canada CF-100 Canuck as a supersonic all-weather interceptor, the Arrow incorporated advanced technical innovations. A source of national pride, this aircraft became a symbol of Canadian excellence.

For various reasons, mostly due to high costs, the Federal Government cancelled the Avro Arrow program on February 20, 1959. Almost everything connected to the program was destroyed. Fortunately, the forward fuselage of the first MK. 2 Arrow was saved and is on display at the National Aviation Museum in Ottawa (Canada).

Coin Specifications:

Composition:	92.5% sterling silver, with a 24-karat-gold-covered cameo
Finish:	Proof (frosted relief on brilliant background)
Edge:	Interrupted serrations
Weight:	31.103 grams
Diameter:	38 mm
Thickness:	3.50 mm
Reverse:	Avro Canada CF-105 Arrow with gold cameo of Jim Chamberlin
Designed By:	Robert Bradford (1995 issues), Jim Bruce (1996 issues)
Obverse:	Effigy of Her Majesty Queen Elizabeth II
Face Value:	$20.00
Mintage:	Maximum of 50,000 of each coin worldwide
Collector Value:	$85.00

Coin 4—Avro Canada CF-100 Canuck

Determined to eliminate reliance on foreign manufactured aircraft, the RCAF commissioned Avro Canada to design and build the Avro Canada CF-100. A fledgling company, Avro attracted experienced Canadian aviation personnel employed during the Second World War. The Avro CF-100 Canuck became a major Canadian aviation success.

Designed to patrol the Canadian frontier, the CF-100 excelled in its mission as a sub-sonic all-weather interceptor. Nicknamed the "Clunk," this aircraft is a twin engine, two-seat fighter. The first of the two CF-100 prototypes was flown in January 1950. Powerful Canadian designed-and-built Orenda engines replaced the British Rolls-Royce Avon engines in 1952. Today, two RCAF CF-100 Mk. 5s are part of the collection at the National Aviation Museum in Ottawa (Canada).

Coin Specifications:

Composition: 92.5% sterling silver, with a 24-karat-gold-covered cameo
Finish: Proof (frosted relief on brilliant background)
Edge: Interrupted serrations
Weight: 31.103 g
Diameter: 38 mm
Thickness: 3.50 mm
Reverse: Avro Canada CF-100 Canuck with gold cameo of Jan Zurakowski
Designed By: Robert Bradford (1995 issues), Jim Bruce (1996 issues)
Obverse: Effigy of Her Majesty Queen Elizabeth II
Face Value: $20.00
Mintage: Maximum of 50,000 of each coin worldwide
Collector Value: $85.00

Canadian Art Series—$200 Gold Coin

The first $200 22-karat gold coin in a new Canadian Art Series. The first coin in the series features the famous painting The Habitant Farm, by Canadian Artist Cornelius Krieghoff.

The Habitant Farm, one of Cornelius Kreighoff's famous depictions of life in rural Quebec during the 19th century, is featured on the reverse of the coin. The obverse features a contemporary effigy of Her Majesty Queen Elizabeth II by artist Dora de Pédery-HUNT.

The $200 22-karat gold coin series will continue an exploration of the development of Canadian art as it travels through our history. The Royal Canadian Mint first introduced the $200, 22-karat gold coin series in 1990 to commemorate Canadian culture and heritage. From 1997 to 2000, the series featured art from Canada's Native peoples in a series called Native Cultures and Traditions. The development of art in Canada and its journey across the country's history form the subject for this new 4 years series dedicated to Canadian Art. The coins of this new series will feature works of Canadian artists from the permanent exhibition at the National Gallery of Canada.

The coin is available in two different packaging options, the encapsulated coin comes with a numbered Certificate of Authenticity or the encapsulated coin is presented in a slick metal die-cast case with a gold plated logo and a pakka wood interior in a protective box, accompanied by a numbered Certificate of Authenticity.

The reverse design, the Habitant Farm, c. 1856, features a typical farmhouse scene in rural Quebec during the mid-1800s. The obverse of the coin features a contemporary effigy of Her Majesty Queen Elizabeth II by artist Dora de Pédery-HUNT.

Coin Specifications:

Purity:	22-karat or 91.67% gold & 8.33% silver
Weight:	17.135 grams
Gold Content:	15.552 grams (Minimum 1/2 Troy ounce of fine gold)
Diameter:	29 mm
Thickness:	2 mm
Edge:	Reeded
Face Value:	$200
Mintage:	10,000
Collector Value:	$775.00

Canadian Festivals Series

In 2001, the Royal Canadian Mint launched a new series of sterling silver 50-cent coins commemorating Canadian festivals from coast to coast.

Themes of Canadian Festivals

2001
Quebec Winter Carnival (Quebec)
Toonik Tyme (Nunavut)
Newfoundland and Labrador Folk Festival (Newfoundland)
Festival of the Fathers (Prince Edward Island)

2002
Annapolis Valley Blossom Festival (Nova Scotia)
Stratford Festival of Canada (Ontario)
Folklorama (Manitoba)
Calgary Stampede (Alberta)
Squamish Days Logger Sports (British Columbia)

2003
Yukon International Storytelling Festival (Yukon Territory)
Festival acadien de Caraquet (New Brunswick)
Back to Batoche (Saskatchewan)
Great Northern Arts Festival (Northwest Territories)

Canadian Festivals #1—50 cent sterling silver coin—Quebec Winter Carnival Folk Festival

The first in a series of 13 coins celebrating Canadian Festivals
  Coin Specifications:

Composition:	Sterling Silver
	92.5% silver, 7.5% copper
Weight:	9.30 grams
Diameter:	27.13 mm
Thickness:	2.08 mm
Edge:	Reeded
Face Value:	50 Cents
Mintage:	Singles—unlimited; Full 13 coin set—20,00
Collector Value:	$45.00

Canadian Festivals #2—50 cent sterling silver coin—Toonik Tyme Folk Festival

The second in a series of 13 coins celebrating Canadian Festivals. Nunavut's biggest festival, now in its 37th season, celebrates the coming of Spring and honours special people in the community. The people of Iqaluit come together to enjoy traditional Inuit games, snowmobiling, dog team races, entertainment and a wide variety of traditional dishes.

The reverse of the coin designed by Canadian artist John Mardon depicts events that are characteristic of the Toonik Tyme celebration such as dog sled racing, drum dancing and ski-doo racing. The obverse features the portrait of Her Majesty Queen Elizabeth II by Dora de Pédery-Hunt.

Individual coins in the Canadian Festivals series are encapsulated and housed in folder-style packaging with full colour graphics.

Coin Specifications:

Composition:	Sterling Silver
	92.5% silver, 7.5% copper
Weight:	9.30 grams
Diameter:	27.13 mm
Thickness:	2.08 mm
Edge:	Reeded
Face Value:	50 Cents
Mintage:	Singles—unlimited; Full 13 coin set—20,00
Collector Value:	$55.00

Canadian Festivals #3—50 cent sterling silver coin—Newfoundland and Labrador Folk Festival

The third in a series of 13 coins celebrating Canadian Festivals. The design is the work of Saskatchewan born David Craig who has already produced a number of coin designs for the Royal Canadian Mint.

Individual coins in the Canadian Festivals series are encapsulated and housed in folder-style packaging with full colour graphics.

Coin Specifications:

Composition:	Sterling Silver
	92.5% silver, 7.5% copper
Weight:	9.30 grams
Diameter:	27.13 mm
Thickness:	2.08 mm
Edge:	Reeded
Face Value:	50 Cents
Mintage:	Singles—unlimited; Full 13 coin set—20,00
Collector Value:	$55.00

Canadian Festivals #4—50 cent sterling silver coin—Prince Edward Island's Festivals of the Fathers

The fourth in a series of 13 coins celebrating Canadian Festivals. The design is the work of Montague born artist Brenda Artist Brenda Whiteway who currently resides in Charlottetown.

Individual coins in the Canadian Festivals series are encapsulated and housed in folder-style packaging with full colour graphics.

Coin Specifications:

Composition:	Sterling Silver
	92.5% silver, 7.5% copper
Weight:	9.30 grams
Diameter:	27.13 mm
Thickness:	2.08 mm
Edge:	Reeded
Face Value:	50 Cents
Mintage:	Singles—unlimited; Full 13 coin set—20,00
Collector Value:	$55.00

NUMISMATIC NETWORK CANADA— ASSOCIATED COIN CLUBS AND SOCIETIES

Numismatic Network Canada is the Internet network designed for those interested in coins, tokens, paper money, and related numismatic material. It is sponsored and created by the principal nonprofit organizations in Canada to meet the needs of collectors, historians, researchers, and other people interested in numismatics, wherever their location.

British Columbia

RCNA Area Director for British Columbia and Yukon
E-mail: AlTebworthALVINU.54@hotmail.com

Alberni Valley Coin Club
E-mail: rustynbetty@telus.net

North Shore Numismatic Society
P.O. Box 44009, 6518 E. Hastings, Burnaby, BC V5B 4Y2

Vancouver Numismatic Society
4645 West 6th Ave., Vancouver, BC V6R 1V6

Victoria Numismatic Society
P.O. Box 39028, James Bay PO, Victoria, BC V8V 4X8
E-mail: victoriacoinclub@yahoo.com
Internet: victoriacoinclub.vndv.com/

Mid-Island Coin Club
West Coast Stamp and Coin
4061 Norweel Dr, Nanaimo, British Columbia V9T1Y8

Alberta

RCNA Area Director for Alberta and the Northwest Territories
James Williston
E-mail: *jawilliston@shaw.ca*

Calgary Numismatic Society
P.O. Box 633, Calgary AB T2P 2J3
E-mail: info@calgarynumismaticsociety.org
Internet: www.calgarynumismaticsociety.org

Edmonton Numismatic Society
P.O. Box 78057, R.P.O. Callingwood, Edmonton, Alberta T5T 6A11
E-mail: Grove_ra@shaw.ca
Internet: www.edmontoncoinclub.com

Medicine Hat Coin & Stamp Club
22 Park Meadows Dr. SE Suite #104, Medicine Hat, Alberta T1B 4E8

Saskatchewan

RCNA Area Director for Saskatchewan
Vic Schoff
E-mail: *v.schoff@sasktel.net*

Regina Coin Club
P.O. Box 174, Regina, Saskatchewan S4P 2Z6
Internet: www.reginacoinclub.com
E-mail: info@reginacoinclub.com

Saskatoon Coin Club
P.O. Box 1674, Saskatoon, Saskatchewan S7K 7E8

Manitoba and Nunavut

Manitoba Coin Club
P.O. Box 321, Winnipeg, Manitoba R3C 2H6
James McLeod
E-mail: mbcoin@shaw.ca
Internet: www.manitobacoinclub.org

Ontario

RCNA Area Director for Eastern Ontario (postal codes K & P)
Steve Woodland
E-mail: *swoodland@xpornet.com*

RCNA Area Director for Western Ontario (postal code N)
Brent W. J. Mackie
E-mail: *bwjmackie@rcna.ca*

RCNA Area Director for Central Ontario (postal codes L & M)
Robert (Bob) Forbes
E-mail: *rforbes@mccarthy.ca*

Brantford Numismatic Society
P.O. Box 28015, N. Park Plaza, Brantford, Ontario N3R 7K5

Chedoke Numismatic Society
c/o: Dorte Brace
E-mail: *brace@cogeco.ca*

Ingersoll Coin Club
c/o: Thomas Masters, 823 Van St. London, ON N5Z 1M8

Kent Coin Club
27 Peter St., Chatham ON N7M 5B2

Lake Superior Coin Club
P.O. Box 10245, Thunder Bay, Ontario P7B 6T7

London Numismatic Society
c/o: Ted Leitch, 543 Kininvie Dr., London, Ontario N2G 1P1

Niagara Falls Coin Club
c/o: Todd Hume, 41 Radford Avenue, Fort Erie ON L2A 5H6
Contact Todd Hume (905) 871-2451
E-mail: *humebl@aol.com*

Nickel Belt Coin Club (Sudbury)
E-mail: *admin@nickelbeltcoinclub.com*
Internet: *www.nickelbeltcoinclub.com*

North York Coin Club
E-mail: *info@northyorkcoinclub.ca*
Internet: *www.northyorkcoinclub.ca*

Oshawa & District Coin Club
P.O. Box 30557, Oshawa Centre, Oshawa, Ontario L1J 8L8
E-mail: papman@idirect.com

City of Ottawa Coin Club
P.O. Box 42004, R.P.O. St. Laurent, Ottawa, Ontario K1K 4L8
E-mail: *info@ons-sno.ca*
Internet: *www.ons-sno.ca*
Pembroke Centennial Coin Club
c/o: J. Baird, 596 Apple Blossom Dr., Pembroke, Ontario K8A 8G2

Peterborough Numismatic Society
c/o: Don Hurl, 1331 Buckhorn Rd, R.R. #1, Lakefield, Ontario, K0L 2H0

Scarborough Coin Club
P.O. Box 562, Pickering, Ontario L1V 2R7
E-mail: cpms@idirect.com

South Wellington Coin Society
c/o: Scott Douglas, 273 Mill St. East, Acton, Ontario, L7J 1J7
E-mail: scott.douglas@sympatico.ca

Stratford Coin Club
P.O. Box 21031, Stratford, Ontario N5A 7V4
E-mail: Larry Walker lswalker@cyg.net

Timmins Coin Club
Kevin M.
E-mail: *nifinoer@hotmail.com*

Toronto Coin Club
128 Silverstone Drive, Toronto ON M9V 3B7
E-mail: info@torontocoinclub.ca
www.torontocoinclub.ca

Waterloo Coin Society
P.O. Box 40044, Waterloo Square, 75 King St. South, Waterloo, Ontario N2J 4V1
Peter Becker—Secretary and Newsletter Editor
E-mail: secretary@waterloocoinsociety.com
Web site: www.waterloocoinsociety.com

Windsor Coin Club
5060 Tecumseh Road East, Box 505, Windsor, Ontario N8T 1C1
Web site: www.windsorcoinclub.com

Woodstock Coin Club
Box 20128, Woodstock, Ontario N4S 8X8

Quebec

RCNA Area Director for Montreal (postal code H)
Louis Chevrier
E-mail: *monnaie@videotron.ca*

RCNA Area Director for Quebec (postal codes J & G)
Regent St. Hilaire
E-mail: *regent@globetrotter.net*

Association des Numismates et des Philatelliste de Boucherville Inc.
(A.N.P.B. Inc.)
C.P. 1111, Boucherville, Quebec J4B 5E6
visitez notre site WEB a www.anpb.net

Club de Numismates du Bas St-Laurent
C.P. 1475, Rimouski, Quebec G5L 8M3
www.cnbsl.org

Lakeshore Coin Club
P.O. Box 1137, Pointe Claire Postal Stn., Pointe Claire, Quebec,
H9S 4H9

Societe Numismatique de Quebec
C.P. 56036, Quebec City, Quebec G1P 2W0

New Brunswick

RCNA Area Director for New Brunswick & Prince Edward Island
Tim Henderson, Box 467, Florenceville, New Brunswick E7L 1Y9
E-mail: *tgh@nbnet.nb.ca*

Fredericton Numismatic Society
89 Bellflower St., New Maryland NB E3C 1C2

Moncton Coin Club
P.O. Box 54, Moncton, New Brunswick E1C 8R9
E-mail: coincbnt@nbnet.nb.ca

St. John Coin Club
Tom Craig, 10 Robys Road, Quispamsis, New Brunswick E2G/G8
E-mail: ycart@nb.sympatico.ca

Nova Scotia

RCNA Area Director for Newfoundland & Nova Scotia
Douglas B. Shand
E-mail: *shawimm@ns.sympatico.ca*

Atlantic Provinces Numismatic Association
c/o: Dartmouth Seniors' Service Centre, 45 Ochterloney Street,
Dartmouth NS B2Y 4M7
E-mail: *apna@apnaonline.ca*
Web site: www.apnaonline.ca

Halifax Coin Club
c/o: Dartmouth Seniors' Service Centre, 45 Ochterloney Street,
Dartmouth, NS, B2Y 4M7
E-mail: *bronan@halifaxcoinclub.ca*
Web site: www.halifaxcoinclub.ca

Sou'West Coin Club
c/o: Douglas B. Shand, P.O. Box 78, Shag Harbour, Shelbourne
County NS B0W 3B0
E-mail: shawimm@klis.com

Prince Edward Island

RCNA Area Director for New Brunswick & Prince Edward Island
Tim Henderson, Box 467, Florenceville, New Brunswick E7L 1Y9
E-mail: *tgh@nbnet.nb.ca*

PEI Numismatic Association
10 Edinburgh Dr., Charlottetown PE, C1A 3E8

Newfoundland

RCNA Area Director for Newfoundland & Nova Scotia
Jeff Wilson
E-mail: *j.wilson@ns.sympatico.ca*

Apprenp'tits Numismates
C.P. 41021, Succ Le Mesnil, Quebec QC G2K 2E3
E-mail: *info@apprenptits.org*
Web site: *www.apprentits.org*

CANADIAN COIN ORGANIZATIONS

The following information is printed with the permission of the organizations listed and was obtained from the Numismatic Network of Canada.

Assoc. des Numismates Francophones du Canada
C.P. 31, Dorion QC JMV 5V8
E-mail: anfc@cam.org
Internet: http://www.cam.org/~anfc/anfc.html

Canadian Association of Numismatic Dealers
Box 10272, Winona PO, Stoney Creek ON L8E 5R1
E-mail: *info@cand.org*
Web site: *www.cand.org*

Canadian Association of Wooden Money Collectors
c/o: Ross Kingdon, 12 Peter St., R.R. #1, Grand Valley ON L0N 1G0
E-Mail: nbelsten@sympatico.ca
Web site: *www.nunetcan.net/cawmc.htm*

The Royal Canadian Numismatic Association
5694 Highway #7 East, Suite 432, Markham ON Canada L3P 1B4
E-mail: info@rcna.ca
Web site: *www.rcna.ca*

Canadian Numismatic Research Society
c/o: Ron Greene, Box 1351, Victoria, British Columbia V8W 2W7
E-mail: ragreene@telus.net
Web site: *www.nunetcan.net/cnrs.htm*

Canadian Tire Coupon Collectors Club
c/o: Roger Fox, 382 Selby Cres., Newmarket, Ontario L3Y 6E1
Web site: www.ctccc.ca

Classical & Medieval Numismatic Society
P.O. Box 956, Station "B," Toronto, Ontario M2K 2T6
E-mail: billmcdo@idirect.com
Web site: *www.cmns.ca*

Enthusiasts of Newfoundland Numismatics
Bill Kamb
E-mail: nfld_h@siscom.net
Web site: www.nunet.ca/nne

Ontario Numismatic Association
P.O. Box 40033, Waterloo Square P.O., 75 King St., Waterloo, Ontario N2J 4V1
E-mail: rmcph@internet.look.ca
Web site: *www.ontario-numismatic.org*

Atlantic Provinces Numismatic Association

The APNA is a nonprofit numismatic organization consisting of members located mainly throughout Canada's Eastern Maritime provinces. Seven coin clubs and organizations also hold membership in the Association. The objectives of APNA are to encourage and promote the collection and study of all numismatic material and dispense numismatic information wherever possible. Its aim is also to cultivate fraternal relations among members at meetings, conventions, and other gatherings.

The Association assists in the formation of new coin clubs and aids those that may be losing ground. It acts as an advisory board, if called upon, to adjudicate unfair practices and generally provides a strong and united voice when needed in the interests of numismatics generally.

APNA publishes a quarterly newsletter in which it offers free advertising to members. It organizes a biannual convention in various locations through the maritimes. Membership is open to anyone of good repute, regardless of their location.

APNA dues are:

$15 Regular membership
$10 Junior membership (first year free)
$15 Corporate membership (clubs, libraries, etc.)

You may contact the APNA by writing to Treasurer, Atlantic Provinces Numismatic Association, Attn: Doug Dahr, 131 Stillwater Lake, Nova Scotia, B3Z IG2, CANADA

E-mail address is cjdahaeastlink.ca

The editor of The Atlantic Numismatist is Rick Chalmers. Our editor will welcome comments, suggestions, member ads and articles, etc. via e-mail: g.chalmers@ns.sympatico.ca or at our mailing address: c/o The Dartmouth Seniors Service Center, 45 Ochterloney Street, Dartmouth, N.S., B2Y 4M7, CANADA

The Royal Canadian Numismatic Association

The RCNA is a nonprofit educational organization formed in 1950 and incorporated by Canada Charter in 1963. It has grown by leaps and bounds from an idea of a few dedicated numismatists to become one of the world's largest numismatic associations. Present membership is basically located in Canada and the United States of America but we do have additional members around the world. They all have one common interest and that is Canadian numismatics.

RCNA Services and Advantages Offered

Being a member of RCNA offers a great opportunity to meet other people with similar interests, correspond with them, and cultivate new friendships. As a member of the Association you will be eligible to receive the RCNA/NESA Numismatic Correspondence Course at a reduced cost.

You will receive the RCNA Journal which carries articles and papers on Canadian coins, tokens, and other numismatic subjects, advertisements by dealers and members, and information about other RCNA activities. The Journal has been published since 1956 and has carried many of the most important papers relating to Canadian numismatics. A number of these articles have been published in French. In the Journal you will be able to advertise your coins, and buy from or sell to other members. Advertising rates are published in the Journal.

The highlight of the year is the RCNA Annual Convention, which has been held in various cities across Canada since 1954. The Convention is Canada's oldest continuing numismatic event where people with a common interest come together. An auction at every Convention helps collectors build their collections and provides a basis for determining values when buying or selling all kinds of numismatic material. Dealers from across Canada and the United States take bourse space at the Convention to offer a great variety of material for sale.

At the RCNA Convention, other numismatic organizations hold their annual meetings or conduct educational programs. These include the Canadian Numismatic Research Society, the Canadian Paper Money Society, the Canadian Association of Token Collectors, the Canadian Association of Wooden Money Collectors, the Love Token Society, the Classical and Medieval Numismatic Society, and others. Delegates from coin clubs across Canada meet and exchange views on common problems to help the hobby and the collector. Members of the RCNA exhibit items from their collections in competition for display awards, thus sharing their knowledge with everyone. Once you attend a RCNA Convention and join in the activities you will come back again and again.

Members have access to the Association's extensive library. A catalogue is available to all members on request. The catalogue is available in either a written version or on a computer disc. There is a charge to assist in mailing the catalog or disc. The library has both books and slide programs. Members may borrow books for a period of one month. Slides and films may be borrowed for two weeks. On valuable shipments the borrower is required to pay the postage and registration both ways. Inside Canada a special postage rate is available. For further information, contact the librarian: Dan Gosling, 49 Sierra Grande Estates, 52131 Range Road 210, Sherwood Park AB Canada T8G 1A2, Phone: (780) 922-5743 or E-mail: dan@gosling.ca.

Note: The RCNA does not buy, sell, or evaluate numismatic material, with the exception that it sells its own publications and medals, etc., which are advertised in the Journal.

Reduced rates, broad coverage, and numismatic insurance in Canada and the United States are also available to members. Details on request.

RCNA Correspondence Course

The Royal Canadian Numismatic Association and Numismatic Educational Services Association have recently launched an exceptional, inexpensive correspondence course for Canadian coin collectors of all ages. Whether you're just beginning to collect coins or have been involved in the hobby for some time, this course is for you! Renowned Canadian coin experts lead you through the stages of coin production and the history of Canadian coins, tokens, medals, and paper money. Through a series of 12 easy-to-read modules and self-paced tests you'll learn the ABC's of coin collecting, including tips on what to collect, how to build a collection, housing and handling your coins, grading coins, the organized hobby, "extinct" Canadian coins, the "coining" process, Canadian commemorative coins, and how to join formal organizations geared toward collectors like yourself. This course is an absolute must for anyone interested in Canadian coins and collecting.

For further information or an application form to sign up for the course, please contact the Executive Secretary of the RCNA.

RCNA Membership/Subscription

Regarding the cost of membership/subscription in the RCNA, the following rules apply:

- Dues are payable in Canadian dollars to Canadian addresses and, because of high postal costs, in U.S. dollars to all other addresses.
- Payment may be made by money order, bank draft, or personal check.
- We regret that we are unable to offer credit card services.
- Postage stamps are not acceptable.
- Currency (U.S. or Canadian only) is acceptable and should be sent by security-registered mail only.
- Membership is not GST taxable.
  Various memberships offered are:

REGULAR—Applicants 18 years of age or over $39.00
JUNIOR—Applicants under 18 years of age $22.50
    Must be sponsored by a parent or guardian
FAMILY—Husband, wife, and children at home, under 18 years of
    age, One Journal only $44.00

CORPORATE—Clubs, societies, libraries, and other nonprofit organizations $39.00
LIFE MEMBERSHIP...Upon request
After one year of regular membership. Details on deferred-payment plan available on request.

First-class mailing of the Journal is available on remittance of $9 (Cdn.) to Canadian addresses, $7.50 (U.S.) to USA addresses, and $15 (U.S.) to all other addresses.

For membership/subscription information or a free sample copy of our publication, contact: The Royal Canadian Numismatic Association, 5694 Highway #7 East, Suite 432, Markham ON Canada L3P 1B4, Telephone (647) 401-4014, or Fax: (905) 472-9645. E-mail: info@rcna.ca

Canadian Numismatic Research Society

The Canadian Numismatic Research Society (CNRS) was founded in 1963 by a group of respected Canadian numismatists who wished to stimulate public awareness and understanding of numismatics related to Canada, through the promotion of research and study, and the dissemination of knowledge.

Membership in the CNRS is by invitation only. The main criteria are that a prospective member be actively engaged in numismatic research and has published the results of his/her research in a widely distributed journal or book. Current members have a wide range of interests from ancient coins to Canadian banking history and include coins, tokens, medals, paper money and numismatic literature.

The society does not evaluate or grade material.

The Society publishes a quarterly in conjunction with the Canadian Association of Token Collectors. This quarterly, Numismatica Canada, is available to non-members on an annual basis for Can. $20.00 within Canada or U.S. $20.00 elsewhere, postpaid. The content is primarily concerned with Canadian tokens and their histories, but there are numerous articles on medals, modern municipal trade dollars and other numismatic topics. Please contact the editor: Harry James, P.O. Box 22022, Elmwood Sq. P.O., 2024 First Avenue, St. Thomas, Ontario, Canada N5R 4W1. E-mail: *harryjames6@gmail.com*

Back issues of our former publication, The Transactions, are still available for some years. Please contact the editor.

Ronald Greene, Secretary Canadian Numismatic Research Society, P.O. Box 1351, Victoria, BC, Canada V8W 2W7, Fax: 250-598-5539 E-mail: ragreene@telus.net, www.nunet.ca/cnrs.htm

Edmonton Numismatic Society

The Edmonton Numismatic Society is a not-for-profit organization dedicated to the needs of fellow numismatists in our local area of Edmonton, Alberta, Canada, as well as the northern Alberta area, the rest of Canada, and the world! It was formerly known as The Edmonton Coin Club and was formed in 1953.

All members receive a newsletter as part of their dues. The newsletter supplies information on current events, as well as articles on coins, paper money, tokens, and medals.

MEMBERSHIP (Canadian funds unless noted otherwise): Family: $15, Regular: $15 Junior (16 AND UNDER): $5. U.S. addresses in U.S. funds, overseas add $5. Dues apply for one (1) calendar year membership in the Edmonton Numismatic Society (Jan. to Dec.)—(half price if joining from Sept. to Dec.). Subject to approval by the Membership, an official receipt and membership card will be issued.

For more information: Edmonton Numismatic Society, P.O. Box 78057, R.P.O. Callingwood, Edmonton AB Canada T5T 6A1, Telephone: (780) 433-7288, www.edmontoncoinclub.com

Ontario Numismatic Association

In 1962 the idea for this Association originated at a meeting of delegates from various numismatic clubs of Ontario. The meeting took place at the Waterloo Coin Society's annual banquet and from this the ONA was born. The delegates at the first meeting recognized the need for an organization to serve the educational and social needs of the Ontario clubs and hobbyists. The ONA was incorporated in 1962 as a nonprofit educational and social organization dedicated to the collector.

Since that time, the Executive has grown to include 11 Regional Directors, an Editor-Librarian, an Audio-Visual Service Director, and a Speakers Circuit and Convention Coordinator. Appeals were made throughout Ontario clubs for memberships, numismatic books for the library, and for audio-visual programs that the member clubs could use at their meetings. The appeals proved very successful and to date over 50 audio-visual programs and 500 books and pamphlets are in the library. Membership to date stands at over 35 clubs and numismatic organizations, over 65 life members, and varying membership from both Canada and the United States. Appeals for all these mentioned above are still in effect and the donations to the audio-visual service and the library would be gratefully received.

From the first convention held at Prudhommes Garden Hotel near St. Catharines, where over 1,700 attended and 250 were at the banquet, and conventions held in most major cities across Ontario from Windsor to Ottawa and from Sudbury to Niagara Falls, the ONA is active and prosperous. One of the excellent initiatives put into effect was the Award of Merit. Another was the establishment of the Speakers Circuit.

The conventions held annually offer numismatic groups the opportunity to get together and hold annual meetings. Also, the Club Delegates Meeting provides each club representative an opportunity to voice opinions, share ideas, and benefit from the experience and ideas of the other clubs. Displays in many numismatic categories at the convention offer the collectors an opportunity to not only see exceptional and often very rare material, but to gain knowledge from the research done by the exhibitor to create the display.

In the future the ONA will continue to search out new ideas that will improve the hobby for the clubs and the individual collector. The ONA will also continue:

- to encourage clubs and members to participate in all activities of the Association;
- to expand the audio-visual and numismatic library;
- to provide liability insurance coverage in the amount of $2,000,000 for all participating member clubs and individual members;
- to expand the Speakers Circuit;
- to select active clubs in Ontario towns and cities to host successful future conventions.

The ONA motto is "VIRES ACQUIRIT EUNDO." It means "AS IT GROWS, IT GATHERS STRENGTH." The accomplishments of the ONA over the years since 1962 serve to prove the validity of this motto for our organization. Finally, it is a pleasure to invite all who are not now members of the ONA to join so we can share the many pleasures and benefits of numismatics together in future years.

ONA dues per calendar year are:

$15 Regular membership
$10 Junior membership (up to age 18)
$22 Husband and wife (one journal)
$35 Club or association
$600 Life membership (subject to by-laws)

For further information contact: Ontario Numismatic Association, P.O. Box 40033, Waterloo Sq. P.O., 75 King Street South, Waterloo, ON, N2J 4V1, CANADA. E-mail: president@the-ona.ca. Website: http://the-ona.ca/

Publication—*Canadian Coin News*

Canadian Coin News has been around for more than 30 years and in that time it has become the definitive source for information about coin collecting and numismatics from a Canadian perspective.

Although we cover the entire world of numismatics, the majority of our readers are Canadians, and we concentrate on the unique circumstances surrounding collecting in our native land. Our editorial pages include information on new and old issues, as well as commentary, investment tips, and Canada's most up-to-date listings of prices.

We haven't put the entire magazine online, but we have included an archive of interesting and relevant articles and pictures. We have also included information on how to subscribe or how to reach us. We are eager to hear your comments, suggestions, advice, and even a few flames. Our aim is to give you some of the basic information and contacts you need as a collector. We have also completed the first version of our Canadian Numismatic FAQ.

If you offer products or services of interest to Canadian numismatists, the best way to reach them is through Canadian Coin News, either online or in print.

For more information, or to receive a sample copy of Canadian Coin News along with our media kit and rate card, please contact: Advertising Manager, Canadian Coin News, 103 Lakeshore Rd., St. Catharines, ON, L2N 2T6, Canada, (905) 646-7744. E-mail: advertising@trajan.ca, Website: www.canadiancoinnews.ca

Have Canadian Coin News delivered directly to your door every two weeks! Here are our subscription rates, which offer a significant savings off the cover price of $2.50 per issue: Basic rates: 1 year (26 issues) Canada (includes GST): $46.27. United States and possessions: $43.95. Foreign: $172.00.

To order by telephone using a credit card: Call 1-800-408-0352, Monday through Friday, 9:00 A.M. to 5 P.M. Eastern Time.

To order by mail: Send your request to Trajan Publishing Corporation, P.O. Box 28103, Lakeport P.O., St. Catharines, ON, L2N 7P8, Canada.

To order by fax: Fax your order 24 hours a day to 1-905-646-0995.

To order by E-mail: Send E-mail to orders@trajan.com.

For mail, fax, and E-mail orders please include your name, mailing address, and daytime telephone number. For credit-card orders, please include your card number, type of card, and expiration date.

CAND (Canadian Association of Numismatic Dealers)

What Is CAND?

The Canadian Association of Numismatic Dealers is a nonprofit association of professional numismatists organized in 1975 under letters patented as Canada 70,067 Inc. CAND's function is to ensure a high degree of professionalism by its members. Each CAND member has signed a strict code of ethics, which is enforceable by our by-laws.

CAND members are engaged in the retail numismatic trade, primarily in Canadian numismatics, and may conduct business from anywhere in the world. CAND members include coin dealers, show operators, publishers, supply manufacturers, bullion dealers, foreign exchange dealers, auctioneers, paper money dealers, and foreign coin and paper money dealers.

CAND features a mechanism for redress of grievances against members, and a performance fund for at least partial compensation to wronged collectors should the dealer be unable to fulfill his obligation.

How to Reach CAND
Telephone: (905) 643-4988 (with answering machine)
Facsimile: (905) 643-6329
E-mail: email@cand.org
Website: www.cand.org/
Mail: CAND, Attn: Jo-Anne Simpson, Executive Secretary, Box 10272, Winona PO, Stoney Creek, Ontario L8E 5R1

List of Members

Albern Coins and Foreign
Exchange Ltd
1511 Centre Street NW
Calgary, AB
CANADA T2E 2S1
Tel: (403) 276-8938
Fax: (403) 276-5415
E-mail: info@albern.com.
www.albern.com

Armstrong, Mr. Robert
Bob Armstrong Coins
P.O. Box 333
Owen Sound, Ontario
N4K 5P5 Canada
Tel: (519) 371-8021

Bailey, Mr. Ted
Ted's Collectibles
281-A Grand River Street
North
Paris, ON
CANADA N3L 2N9
Tel: (519) 442-3474
Fax: (519) 442-2969
E-mail: tedscollectibles@
bellnet.ca

Bell, Mr. Brian
The Coin Cabinet
118 Cameron Street
Moncton, NB E1C 5Y6
Tel: (506) 857-9403
Fax: (506) 857-9403
E-mail: coincbnt@nbnet.nb.ca
The Coin Cabinet
154 Waterloo St.
Saint John, NB E2L 3R1
E-mail: Coins118@hotmail.com

Bell, Mr. Geoffrey
84 King St.
Saint John, NB E2L 1G4

Bromberg, Mr. Steven
Canadian Coin & Currency
10211 Yonge Ave.
Richard Hill, ON L4C 3B3
Tel: (905) 883-6339
Fax: (905) 883-5929
E-mail: steven@cdncoin.com
www.cdncoin.com

Burrell, Mr. John
Halton Coins and Collectibles
The Numis Store, Unit 4
2500 Wiliams Parkway
Brampton, ON L6S 5M9
E-mail:
johnhaltoncoins@cogeco.ca

Burton, Mr. Willard
B & W Coins
Unit #8, 345 Queen St. West
Brampton, ON L6Y 3A9
Tel: (905) 450-2870
Fax: (905) 450-3170
E-mail: b_and_w@sympatico.ca
www.bwcoin.com

Charlton, Mr. James
Retired, Honorary Member
Tel: (905) 562-5567

Chicoine, Mr. Yvon
Member, Dealer Control Com-
mittee
Monnaie de Versailles
7275 Sherbrooke Est,
local 2219
Montreal, Quebec
H1N 1E9 Canada
Tel: (514) 352-9101
Fax: (514) 352-0057

Cross, Mr. William K.
The Charlton Press
Honouary Life Member
P.O. Box 820
Station Willowdale B,
North York, ON M2K 2R1

Tel: (416) 488-1418
Fax: (416) 488-4656
E-mail: chpress@charltonpress
.com
www.charltonpress.com

Doucett, Mr. Rayburn [a, d, e]
P.O. Box 1032
Belledune, New Brunswick
E8G 2X9
Tel: (506) 237-4107
Fax: (506) 237-4105
E-mail: delray@nbnet.nb.ca

Dowsett, Mr. Bob
B.C. Coins
Stratford, ON
Tel: (519) 271-8884
Fax: (519) 275-2684
E-mail: bccoins@rogers.com

Evans, Mr. Bret
Trajan Publishing Corp.
103 Lakeshore Suite No. 202
St. Catharines, ON L2N 2T6
Tel: (905) 646-7744
Fax: (905) 646-0995
E-mail:
Editor, Bret Evans:
bret@trajan.ca
office@trajan.ca

Fedore, Mr. Gary
Select Currency
P.O. Box 91519
47 Main Street
Georgetown, ON L7G 3G2
Tel: (416) 705-4068
E-mail: gwfedora@sympatico.ca

Feehan, Mr. Gerhard
Citadel Coins
1903 Barrington Street
Halifax, NS B3L 3L7
Tel: (902) 492-0130
E-mail: citadelcoins@eastlink.ca

Findlay, Mr. Michael
Certified Coins of Canada
CAND President
P.O. Box 2043

Angus, ON L0M 1B0
Tel: (705) 423-1140
Fax: (705) 423-1069
E-mail: ccdn@bconnex.net

Frick, Mr. Theodore
Icecube Enterprises
Box 85
Remer, MN 56662 USA

Garrison, Mr. Harry
Colonial Valley Coins
4343 South Broad Street
Hamilton, NJ 08650 USA
Tel:(609)585-8104,
585-0254
Fax: (609) 581-1261
E-mail: HWG2@verizon.net

Graham, Mr. Ian
Royal Canadian Mint [c]
320 Sussex Dr.
Ottawa, Ontario
K1A 0G8 Canada
Tel: (613) 993-0805
Tel: (800) 496-6660
Fax: (613) 998-1330
E-mail: graham@mint.ca

Grant-Duff, Mr. Brian
Coins & Stamps
5630 Dunbar St.
Vancouver, BC V6N 1W7
Tel: (604) 684-4613
Fax: (604) 684-4618
E-mail: collect@direct.ca
http://www.downtownstamps.
bc.ca

Grecco, Mr. Andy
Andy Grecco Coins
Tel: (905) 227-3534
Cell: (905) 931-4632

Hill, Mr. David
Dave's Numismatics
Tel: (705) 440-0394
E-mail: dave@coinsnmore.com

Hoare, Wendy
Jeffrey Hoare Auctions, Inc.

CAND Secretary/Treasurer
319 Springbank Drive
London, ON N6J 1G6
Tel: (519) 473-7491
Fax: (519) 473-1541
E-mail: jhoare@jeffreyhoare.on.ca
http://www.jeffreyhoare.on.ca

Hoskins, Mr. Vern
Cameo Coins
PO Box 879
Port Dover, ON N0A 1N0
Tel: (519) 583-2526

Iorio, Mr. Joseph
J & M Coin & Jewelry
127 East Broadway
Vancouver, British Columbia
V5T 1W1 Canada
Tel: (604) 876-7181
Fax: (604) 876-1518
E-mail: jandm@jandm.com
http://www.jandm.com

Isaacs, Sean
Alliance Coin & Banknote
88 Mill St., Box 1806
Almonte, ON K0A 1A0
Tel: (613) 256-6785
Fax: (613) 256-7319
E-mail: sean@alliance
coin.com
http://www.alliancecoin.com/

Jenner, Mr. Brian
Brian Jenner Inc.
PO Box 2466
Pasco, WA 99302, USA
Tel: (509) 735-2172
Fax: (509) 783-8042

Jones, Mr. Greg
Lighthouse Numismatics
Suite 37
2625 Joseph Howe Drive
Halifax, NS B3L 4G4
E-mail: the1936dot@hotmail.com

Kennedy, Mr. Tom
TLC Coin Show
P.O. Box 23032
Stratford, ON N5A 2M0

King, Ross
Box 571
Chesley, Ontario
N0G 1L0 Canada
Tel: (519) 363-3143
Fax: (519) 363-3143
E-mail: rdking@bmts.com

Kokotailo, Mr. Robert
Calgary Coin Gallery
Box 1608 Station M
Calgary, AB T2P 2L7
Store: 1404 Center Street S.E.
Tel: (403) 266-5262
Fax: (403) 266-6527
E-mail: robert@calgarycoin.com
www.calgarycoin.com

Koolhaas, Mr. Paul
CAND Vice President
P.O. Box 404
Tottenham, ON L0G 1W0
Tel: (416) 909-6442
E-mail:
paul.koolhaas@sympatico.ca

Laing, Mr. Ian
Gatewest Coin & Stamp
1711 Corydon Ave.
Winnipeg, Manitoba
R3N 0J9 Canada
Tel: (204) 489-9112
Fax: (204) 489-9118
E-mail:
internet@gatewestcoin.com
http://www.gatewestcoin.com

Lawson, Mr. James
The Lawson Gallery
1 Crossing Bridge Ct.
Stittsville, Ontario
K2S 1S2 Canada
Tel: (613) 831-2815
Fax: (613) 831-6106

Leardi, Mr. Frank
Frank Leardi Coins
P.O. Box 361, Station T
Toronto, Ontario
M6B 4A3 Canada
Tel: (416) 781-3170
Fax: (416) 781-3170

Lockwood, Mr. Peter
c/o Guardian Intl. Gold
Ste# 812, 27 Dundas Square
Toronto, ON M5B 1B7
Tel: (416) 861-1888
E-mail: peter@guardiangold.com

Manz, Mr. George
George Manz Coins
P.O. Box 3626
Regina, SK S4P 3L7
Tel: (306) 352-2337
E-mail: george@georgemanz
coins.com
www.GLStampsandcoins.com

McDonald, Mr. Peter
PO Box 171
Kirkland, PQ H9H 0A3
Tel: (514) 231-4106
Fax: (514) 426-0100
E-mail: pmcoins@total.net

McKaig, Mr. Andrew
Canadian Currency Grading
Service
Calgary, AB
Tel: (403) 717-2646
Fax: (403) 251-9518
E-mail:
mckaigm@cal.cybersurf.net

Merkley, Mr. William
London Coin Centre
[a, b, c, d, e, f, j, k]
345 Talbot St.
London, Ontario
N6A 2R5 Canada
Tel: (519) 663-8099
Fax: (519) 663-8019
E-mail: coins.coins@rogers.ca
http://www.coins.on.ca

Merritt, Tom
TCM World Currency
P.O. Box 430
Smithville, ON L0R 2A0

Miller, Gary
Londinivm
Tel: (416) 953-2465
E-mail: romancoins@rogers.com

Olmstead, Mr. Don
Olmstead Currency
Member, Dealer Control
Committee
PO Box 487
St. Stephen, NB E3L 3A6
Tel: (506) 466-2078
Fax: (506) 466-5726
E-mail:
banknote@nbnet.nb.ca

Osaduke, Mr. Ron
The Coin Shop & Currency
Exchange
1100 Burnhamthorpe Road W, #14
Mississauga, ON L5C 4G4
Tel: (905) 949-2646
Fax: (289) 232-7296

Powell, Mr. Hugh
Newcan Coins & Currency
Box 220
Enderby, BC V0E 1V0
Tel: (250) 838-0100
Fax: (250) 515-3808
E-mail: newcancc@shaw.net

Preece, Mr. Kenneth
N & K Coin Shop
Brantford, ON
Tel: (519) 758-5424

Richardson, Mr. Jim
Western Coins & Stamps Ltd.
#2-6380 No. 3 Rd.
Richmond, BC V6Y 2B3
Tel: (604) 278-3235
Fax: (604) 278-3246
E-mail: westerncns@telus.net

Schaffer, Mr. Dale
Schaffer's Inc.
7107 South Yale Ave., No. 199
Tulsa, OK 74136 U.S.A.
Tel: (918) 496-3008
E-mail: dale.schaffer@home.com

Shores, Mr. David
Canadian Coin Company
P.O. Box 894
Lynden, WA 98264 U.S.A.

Simpson, Mr. Richard
R & S Coins
P.O. Box 10272, Winona PO
Stoney Creek, Ontario
L8E 5R1 Canada
Tel: (905) 643-4988
Fax: (905) 643-6329
E-mail: rscoins@cogeco.ca

Thompson, Mr. Ron
Canada Coin & Paper Money
P.O. Box 425
St. Albert, AB T8N 7A2
Tel: (780) 459-6868
E-mail: ronscoins@shaw.ca
www.members.shaw.ca/
ronscoins

Wright, Mr. Stan
Diverse Equities Inc.,
Member, Dealer Control
Committee
Box 61144 KPO
Calgary, AB T2N 4S6
Tel: (403) 230-9321
Fax: (403) 274-3828
Cell: (403) 650-1928
E-mail: *stan@diverseequities
.com*
www.diverseequities.com

CHINA

The first coins, cast in molds, were used in the 6th century B.C. Imitation coins were made of cast bronze. Hoe-shaped coins were produced in the mid-3rd century B.C. Round coins with holes were made at a few mints. The round coins and the tool coins were issued in different denominations, based on the weight of the metal in each coin. The bronze 5-grain coin was introduced in 118 B.C. and was the standard until the early 7th century A.D. Bronze coins with square holes remained through the 13th century. The silver dirhem was in evidence in the 13th century, followed by the brass coin and the silver dollar in the 18th and 19th centuries. Decimal coins appeared in the 1st century A.D. The currency today is the yuan.

China—People's Republic

Key to Grading: Coat of Arms

DATE	COIN TYPE/VARIETY/METAL	ABP FINE	AVERAGE FINE
☐ 1955–2000	1 Fen, People's Republic, Aluminum	$ .28	$ .46

Key to Grading: Coat of Arms

DATE	COIN TYPE/VARIETY/METAL	ABP FINE	AVERAGE FINE
☐ 1955–2000	2 Fen, People's Republic, Aluminum	$ .28	$ .46

Key to Grading: Coat of Arms

DATE	COIN TYPE/VARIETY/METAL	ABP FINE	AVERAGE FINE
☐ 1955–2000	5 Fen, People's Republic, Aluminum	.19	.32
☐ 1980–2000	Jiao, People's Republic, Copper-Zinc	.42	.70
☐ 1987	Jiao, People's Republic, 6th National Games—Soccer, Brass	.42	.70
☐ 1987	Jiao, People's Republic, 6th National Games—Volleyball, Brass	.30	.49

Key to Grading: Coat of Arms or Figures

DATE	COIN TYPE/VARIETY/METAL	ABP FINE	AVERAGE FINE
☐ 1987	Jiao, People's Republic, 6th National Games—Gymnast, Brass	.34	.57
☐ 1980–1986	2 Jiao, People's Republic, Copper-Zinc	.52	.87
☐ 1980–1986	5 Jiao, People's Republic, Copper-Zinc	.52	.87
☐ 1983	5 Jiao, People's Republic, Marco Polo, Silver	52.53	87.55
☐ 1991–1996	5 Jiao, People's Republic, Brass	.34	.57
☐ 1980	Yuan, People's Republic, 1980 Olympics—Alpine Skiing, Brass	5.75	9.55
☐ 1980	Yuan, People's Republic, 1980 Olympics—Equestrian, Brass	5.75	9.55
☐ 1980	Yuan, People's Republic, 1980 Olympics—Wrestling, Brass	5.75	9.55
☐ 1980	Yuan, People's Republic, 1980 Olympics—Archery, Brass	5.75	9.55
☐ 1980	Yuan, People's Republic, 1980 Olympics—Biathlon, Brass	5.75	9.55
☐ 1980	Yuan, People's Republic, 1980 Olympics—Figure Skating, Brass	5.75	9.55

DATE	COIN TYPE/VARIETY/METAL	ABP FINE	AVERAGE FINE
☐ 1980	Yuan, People's Republic, 1980 Olympics—Soccer, Brass	$5.85	$9.75
☐ 1980	Yuan, People's Republic, 1980 Olympics—Speed Skating, Brass	5.85	9.75
☐ 1980–1986	Yuan, People's Republic, Cupro-Nickel	.52	.87
☐ 1982	Yuan, People's Republic, World Cup Soccer, Copper	4.65	7.80
☐ 1983	Yuan, People's Republic, Panda, Brass	11.05	18.40
☐ 1984	Yuan, People's Republic, Panda, Brass	11.05	18.40
☐ 1984	Yuan, People's Republic, 35th Anniversary, Cupro-Nickel	3.40	5.65
☐ 1985	Yuan, People's Republic, Tibet 20th Anniversary, Cupro-Nickel	3.40	5.65

Key to Grading: Figures or Buildings

DATE	COIN TYPE/VARIETY/METAL	ABP FINE	AVERAGE FINE
☐ 1985	Yuan, People's Republic, Sinkiang 30th Anniversary, Cupro-Nickel	1.45	2.40
☐ 1986	Yuan, People's Republic, Year of Peace, Cupro-Nickel	2.85	4.75
☐ 1987	Yuan, People's Republic, Mongolian 40th Anniversary, Cupro-Nickel	1.45	2.40
☐ 1988	Yuan, People's Republic, Ninghsia 30th Anniversary, Cupro-Nickel	3.45	5.70
☐ 1988	Yuan, People's Republic, People's Bank 40th Anniversary, Cupro-Nickel	2.85	4.75
☐ 1988	Yuan, People's Republic, Kwangsi 30th Anniversary, Cupro-Nickel	2.85	4.75
☐ 1989	Yuan, People's Republic, 40th Anniversary, Nickel-clad Steel	2.85	4.75
☐ 1990	Yuan, People's Republic, XI Asian Games—Female Archer, Nickel-clad Steel	2.85	4.75
☐ 1990	Yuan, People's Republic, XI Asian Games—Sword Dancer, Nickel-clad Steel	2.85	4.75
☐ 1991	Yuan, People's Republic, 1978 Party Conference, Nickel-plated Steel	2.85	4.75

DATE	COIN TYPE/VARIETY/METAL	ABP FINE	AVERAGE FINE
☐ 1991	Yuan, People's Republic, Women's Soccer Championship—Player, Nickel-plated Steel	$ .52	$ .87
☐ 1991	Yuan, People's Republic, Planting Trees Festival—Seedling, Cupro-Nickel	.38	.63
☐ 1991	Yuan, People's Republic, Chinese Communist Party 1st Meeting, Nickel-plated Steel	.52	.87
☐ 1991	Yuan, People's Republic, Planting Trees Festival—Globe, Cupro-Nickel	.57	.94
☐ 1991	Yuan, People's Republic, Women's Soccer Championship—Goalie, Nickel-plated Steel	.45	.76
☐ 1991	Yuan, People's Republic, Planting Trees Festival—Portrait, Cupro-Nickel	.52	.87
☐ 1991	Yuan, People's Republic, Party Meeting, Nickel-plated Steel	.45	.76
☐ 1983	5 Yuan, People's Republic, Marco Polo, Silver	—	105.00
☐ 1984	5 Yuan, People's Republic, Olympics—High Jumper, Silver	—	52.50
☐ 1984	5 Yuan, People's Republic, Soldier Statues, Silver	—	48.50
☐ 1985	5 Yuan, People's Republic, Founders of Chinese Culture—Lao-Tse, Silver	—	48.50
☐ 1985	5 Yuan, People's Republic, Founders of Chinese Culture—Wu Guang, Silver	—	48.50
☐ 1985	5 Yuan, People's Republic, Founders of Chinese Culture—Qu Yuan, Silver	—	48.50
☐ 1985	5 Yuan, People's Republic, Founders of Chinese Culture—Sun Wu, Silver	—	48.50
☐ 1986	5 Yuan, People's Republic, Chinese Culture—Chemist, Silver	—	48.50
☐ 1986	5 Yuan, People's Republic, Chinese Culture—Mathematician, Silver	—	48.50
☐ 1986	5 Yuan, People's Republic, Soccer—2 Players, Silver	—	38.50
☐ 1986	5 Yuan, People's Republic, Chinese Culture—Historian, Silver	—	52.50
☐ 1986	5 Yuan, People's Republic, Great Wall, Silver	—	38.00
☐ 1986	5 Yuan, People's Republic, Wildlife—Giant Panda, Silver	—	48.50
☐ 1986	5 Yuan, People's Republic, Year of Peace, Silver	—	310.00

DATE	COIN TYPE/VARIETY/METAL	ABP FINE	AVERAGE FINE
☐ 1986	5 Yuan, People's Republic, Soccer, Silver	—	$64.50
☐ 1986	5 Yuan, People's Republic, Chinese Culture—Paper Making, Silver	—	64.50
☐ 1987	5 Yuan, People's Republic, Poet Du Fu, Silver	—	85.50
☐ 1987	5 Yuan, People's Republic, Princess Cheng Wen & Song Zuan Gan Bu, Silver	—	85.50
☐ 1987	5 Yuan, People's Republic, Poet Li Bai, Silver	—	85.50
☐ 1987	5 Yuan, People's Republic, Bridge Builder Li Chun, Silver	—	85.50
☐ 1988	5 Yuan, People's Republic, Olympics—Downhill Skier, Silver	—	85.50
☐ 1988	5 Yuan, People's Republic, Olympics—Sailboat Racing, Silver	—	85.50
☐ 1988	5 Yuan, People's Republic, Poetess Li Qing-zhao, Silver	—	79.50
☐ 1988	5 Yuan, People's Republic, Yue Fei—Military Hero, Silver	—	79.50
☐ 1988	5 Yuan, People's Republic, Olympics—Woman Hurdler, Silver	—	85.50
☐ 1988	5 Yuan, People's Republic, Poet Su Shi, Silver	—	85.50
☐ 1988	5 Yuan, People's Republic, Olympics—Fencing, Silver	—	80.00
☐ 1988	5 Yuan, People's Republic, Bi Sheng Inventor of Movable Type Printing, Silver	—	74.50
☐ 1989	5 Yuan, People's Republic, Soccer Players, Silver	—	62.50
☐ 1989	5 Yuan, People's Republic, Playwright Guan Hanging, Silver	—	74.50
☐ 1989	5 Yuan, People's Republic, Kublai Khan, Silver	—	86.50
☐ 1989	5 Yuan, People's Republic, Huang Daopo—Invented Water Wheel, Silver	—	86.50
☐ 1989	5 Yuan, People's Republic, Save the Children Fund, Silver	—	86.50
☐ 1989	5 Yuan, People's Republic, Scientist Guo Shousing, Silver	—	86.50
☐ 1990	5 Yuan, People's Republic, Bronze Archaeological Finds—Elephant Pitcher, Silver	—	86.50
☐ 1990	5 Yuan, People's Republic, Historian Luo Guan Zhong, Silver	—	70.50

DATE	COIN TYPE/VARIETY/METAL	ABP FINE	AVERAGE FINE
☐ 1990	5 Yuan, People's Republic, Soccer—Goalie, Silver	—	$65.50
☐ 1990	5 Yuan, People's Republic, Seafarer Zeng He, Silver	—	84.00
☐ 1990	5 Yuan, People's Republic, Bronze Archaeological Finds—Rhinocerus, Silver	—	66.50
☐ 1990	5 Yuan, People's Republic, Soccer Players, Silver	—	55.00
☐ 1990	5 Yuan, People's Republic, Revolutionary Li Zicheng, Silver	—	83.00
☐ 1990	5 Yuan, People's Republic, Bronze Archaeological Finds—Mythical Creature, Silver	—	82.50
☐ 1990	5 Yuan, People's Republic, Bronze Archaeological Finds—Leopard, Silver	—	74.50
☐ 1990	5 Yuan, People's Republic, Naturalist Li Shi Zhen, Silver	—	74.50
☐ 1991	5 Yuan, People's Republic, Scientist Song Ying Xing, Silver	—	82.50
☐ 1991	5 Yuan, People's Republic, Writer Cao Xue Qin, Silver	—	89.00
☐ 1991	5 Yuan, People's Republic, Official—Lin Ze Xu, Silver	—	89.00
☐ 1991	5 Yuan, People's Republic, Revolutionary Hong Xu Quan, Silver	—	84.00
☐ 1992	5 Yuan, People's Republic, Ancient Kite Flying, Silver	—	74.50
☐ 1992	5 Yuan, People's Republic, Metal Working Scene, Silver	—	82.50
☐ 1992	5 Yuan, People's Republic, First Compass, Silver	—	74.50
☐ 1992	5 Yuan, People's Republic, Great Wall, Silver	—	82.50
☐ 1992	5 Yuan, People's Republic, First Seismograph, Silver	—	65.50

CUBA

Cuba was never provided with its own coinage. Spanish coins were used, with the silver peso in 1915, the gold peso in 1916, the silver centavo in 1920, and the aluminum centavo in 1981. The decimal system was established in 1915. Today's currency is the peso.

Cuba—Type Coinage

Key to Grading: Bust or Coat of Arms

DATE	COIN TYPE/VARIETY/METAL	ABP FINE	AVERAGE FINE
☐ 1953	1 Centavo, Marti Centennial, Brass	$ .25	$ .42
☐ 1915–1938	1 Centavo, Cupro-Nickel	.25	.42
☐ 1943	1 Centavo, Brass	.22	.37
☐ 1946–1961	1 Centavo, Cupro-Nickel	.22	.37

Key to Grading: Bust

☐ 1958	1 Centavo, Cupro-Nickel	.28	.46

Key to Grading: Coat of Arms

☐ 1915–1916	2 Centavos, Cupro-Nickel	.28	.46

Key to Grading: Coat of Arms

DATE	COIN TYPE/VARIETY/METAL	ABP FINE	AVERAGE FINE
☐ 1915–1920	5 Centavos, Cupro-Nickel	$ .85	$1.40
☐ 1943	5 Centavos, Brass	.52	.87
☐ 1946–1961	5 Centavos, Cupro-Nickel	.52	.87
☐ 1952	10 Centavos, Republic 50th Anniversary, Silver	.52	.87

Key to Grading: Coat of Arms

☐ 1915–1949	10 Centavos, Silver	—	6.50

Key to Grading: Coat of Arms

☐ 1952	20 Centavos, Republic 50th Anniversary, Silver	—	4.50
☐ 1915–1949	20 Centavos, Silver	—	7.60
☐ 1953	25 Centavos, Marti Centennial, Silver	—	4.50

Key to Grading: Coat of Arms

DATE	COIN TYPE/VARIETY/METAL	ABP FINE	AVERAGE FINE
☐ 1952	40 Centavos, Republic 50th Anniversary, Silver	—	$8.40
☐ 1915–1920	40 Centavos, Silver	—	12.25
☐ 1953	50 Centavos, Marti Centennial, Silver	—	9.25
☐ 1898	1 Peso, Silver	—	610.00
☐ 1953	1 Peso, Marti Centennial, Silver	—	12.25

Key to Grading: Coat of Arms

☐ 1915–1934	1 Peso, Silver	—	33.50
☐ 1915–1916	1 Peso, Gold	—	105.00
☐ 1934–1939	1 Peso, Silver	—	56.50
☐ 1915–1916	2 Pesos, Gold	—	122.50
☐ 1915–1916	4 Pesos, Gold	—	205.00
☐ 1915–1916	10 Pesos, Gold	—	420.00
☐ 1915–1916	20 Pesos, Gold	—	575.00

EGYPT

The first coins were used in the 4th century B.C. The earliest coins were silver pieces and gold coins. The silver "owl" drachmas appeared in the 5th century B.C., followed by bronze coins, gold drachmas, and gold solidi. The copper fals was in evidence in the 760s, then the gold dinar, silver ghirsh, the cupro-nickel, gold piastres, and bronze milliemes. The decimal system was established in 1916. Today's currency is the Egyptian pound.

Egypt—Type Coinage

DATE	COIN TYPE/VARIETY/METAL	ABP FINE	AVERAGE FINE
☐ 1917	½ Millieme, Hussein Kamil, Bronze	$1.95	$3.25
☐ 1924	½ Millieme, Fuad I, Bronze	1.95	3.25
☐ 1929–1932	½ Millieme, Fuad I, Bronze	3.90	6.50
☐ 1938	½ Millieme, Farouk I, Bronze	2.60	4.35
☐ 1917	1 Millieme, Hussein Kamil, Cupro-Nickel	1.85	3.00
☐ 1924	1 Millieme, Fuad I, Bronze	1.85	3.00
☐ 1929–1935	1 Millieme, Fuad I, Bronze	1.85	3.00
☐ 1938–1950	1 Millieme, Farouk I, Bronze	1.85	3.00

DATE	COIN TYPE/VARIETY/METAL	ABP FINE	AVERAGE FINE
☐ 1954–1958	1 Millieme, Republic, Aluminum-Bronze	.54	.89

DATE	COIN TYPE/VARIETY/METAL	ABP FINE	AVERAGE FINE
☐ 1916–1917	2 Milliemes, Hussein Kamil, Cupro-Nickel	1.30	2.20
☐ 1924	2 Milliemes, Fuad I, Cupro-Nickel	1.30	2.20

DATE	COIN TYPE/VARIETY/METAL	ABP FINE	AVERAGE FINE
☐ 1929	2 Milliemes, Fuad I, Cupro-Nickel	1.15	1.90
☐ 1938	2 Milliemes, Farouk I, Cupro-Nickel	1.75	2.95
☐ 1933	2½ Milliemes, Fuad I, Cupro-Nickel	1.75	2.95

Key to Grading: Bust

DATE	COIN TYPE/VARIETY/METAL	ABP FINE	AVERAGE FINE
☐ 1916–1917	5 Milliemes, Hussein Kamil, Cupro-Nickel	$3.00	$4.95
☐ 1924	5 Milliemes, Fuad I, Cupro-Nickel	3.00	4.95
☐ 1929–1935	5 Milliemes, Fuad I, Cupro-Nickel	3.00	4.95

Key to Grading: Bust

☐ 1938–1941	5 Milliemes, Farouk I, Cupro-Nickel	1.60	2.65
☐ 1938–1943	5 Milliemes, Farouk I, Bronze	1.60	2.65
☐ 1954–1958	5 Milliemes, Republic, Aluminum-Bronze	2.80	4.60
☐ 1916–1917	10 Milliemes, Hussein Kamil, Cupro-Nickel	2.80	4.60
☐ 1924	10 Milliemes, Fuad I, Cupro-Nickel	2.80	4.60
☐ 1929–1935	10 Milliemes, Fuad I, Cupro-Nickel	1.50	2.45

Key to Grading: Bust

☐ 1938–1941	10 Milliemes, Farouk I, Cupro-Nickel	1.50	2.45
☐ 1938–1943	10 Milliemes, Farouk I, Bronze	1.50	2.45
☐ 1954–1958	10 Milliemes, Republic, Aluminum-Bronze	1.50	2.45
☐ 1916–1917	2 Piastres, Hussein Kamil, Silver	—	6.00
☐ 1920	2 Piastres, Fuad, Silver	—	6.00

Key to Grading: Lettering

DATE	COIN TYPE/VARIETY/METAL	ABP FINE	AVERAGE FINE
☐ 1885–1910	1/40 Ghirsh, Abdul Hamid II, Minted in Europe, Bronze	$1.48	$2.50
☐ 1910–1914	1/40 Ghirsh, Mohammed V, Bronze	1.10	1.80
☐ 1885–1910	1/20 Ghirsh, Abdul Hamid II, Minted in Europe, Bronze	1.10	1.80
☐ 1910–1914	1/20 Ghirsh, Mohammed V, Bronze	1.50	2.50

Key to Grading: Lettering

☐ 1916–1917	5 Piastres, Hussein Kamil, Silver	—	9.00
☐ 1920	5 Piastres, Fuad, Silver	—	40.50
☐ 1864	4 Para, Abdul Aziz, Minted in Europe, Bronze	3.70	6.15
☐ 1885–1910	1/10 Ghirsh, Abdul Hamid II, Minted in Europe, Cupro-Nickel	1.55	2.55
☐ 1910–1914	1/10 Ghirsh, Mohammed V, Cupro-Nickel	1.55	2.55

Key to Grading: Lettering

☐ 1916–1917	10 Piastres, Hussein Kamil, Silver	—	10.75
☐ 1920	10 Piastres, Fuad, Silver	—	48.00
☐ 1885–1910	2/10 Ghirsh, Abdul Hamid II, Minted in Europe, Cupro-Nickel	1.55	2.55

DATE	COIN TYPE/VARIETY/METAL	ABP FINE	AVERAGE FINE
☐ 1910–1914	²/₁₀ Ghirsh, Mohammed V, Cupro-Nickel	$3.45	$5.80
☐ 1916–1917	20 Piastres, Hussein Kamil, Silver	—	28.50
☐ 1862–1876	10 Para, Abdul Aziz, Silver	—	33.50
☐ 1864–1870	10 Para, Abdul Aziz, Minted in Europe, Bronze	3.25	5.40
☐ 1868–1871	10 Para, Abdul Aziz, Copper	3.25	5.40
☐ 1876–1878	10 Para, Abdul Hamid II, Silver	—	122.50
☐ 1861–1875	20 Para, Abdul Aziz, Silver	—	45.25

Key to Grading: Lettering

DATE	COIN TYPE/VARIETY/METAL	ABP FINE	AVERAGE FINE
☐ 1863–1870	20 Para, Abdul Aziz, Minted in Europe, Bronze	3.90	6.50
☐ 1868–1871	20 Para, Abdul Aziz, Copper	10.70	17.85
☐ 1876–1878	20 Para, Abdul Hamid II, Silver	—	132.00

Key to Grading: Lettering

DATE	COIN TYPE/VARIETY/METAL	ABP FINE	AVERAGE FINE
☐ 1885–1910	⁵/₁₀ Ghirsh, Abdul Hamid II, Minted in Europe, Cupro-Nickel	1.55	2.55
☐ 1910–1914	⁵/₁₀ Ghirsh, Mohammed V, Cupro-Nickel	1.55	2.55
☐ 1868–1871	40 Para, Abdul Aziz, Copper	519.00	865.00
☐ 1870	40 Para, Abdul Aziz, Minted in Europe, Bronze	3.45	5.70
☐ 1861–1876	1 Ghirsh, Abdul Aziz, Silver	—	16.50
☐ 1876	1 Ghirsh, Mohammed V, Minted in Europe, Silver	—	7.00
☐ 1876–1880	1 Ghirsh, Abdul Hamid II, Silver	—	7.00
☐ 1885–1908	1 Ghirsh, Abdul Hamid II, Minted in Europe, Silver	—	7.00
☐ 1897–1908	1 Ghirsh, Abdul Hamid II, Minted in Europe, Cupro-Nickel	1.40	2.30

DATE	COIN TYPE/VARIETY/METAL	ABP FINE	AVERAGE FINE
☐ 1910–1911	1 Ghirsh, Mohammed V, Silver	—	$6.60
☐ 1910–1914	1 Ghirsh, Mohammed V, Cupro-Nickel	4.22	7.04
☐ 1916	100 Piastres, Hussein Kamil, Gold	—	130.00
☐ 1885–1908	2 Ghirsh, Abdul Hamid II, Minted in Europe, Silver	—	10.00
☐ 1910–1911	2 Ghirsh, Mohammed V, Silver	—	10.00
☐ 1864	2$1/2$ Ghirsh, Abdul Aziz, Minted in Europe, Silver	—	100.00
☐ 1868–1875	2$1/2$ Ghirsh, Abdul Aziz, Silver	—	535.00
☐ 1861–1870	5 Ghirsh, Abdul Aziz, Silver	—	505.00
☐ 1862–1876	5 Ghirsh, Abdul Aziz, Gold	—	65.50
☐ 1864	5 Ghirsh, Abdul Aziz, Minted in Europe, Silver	—	130.00

Key to Grading: Lettering

DATE	COIN TYPE/VARIETY/METAL	ABP FINE	AVERAGE FINE
☐ 1877–1882	5 Ghirsh, Abdul Hamid II, Gold	—	535.00
☐ 1885–1908	5 Ghirsh, Abdul Hamid II, Minted in Europe, Silver	—	18.00
☐ 1891–1909	5 Ghirsh, Abdul Hamid II, Gold	—	100.00
☐ 1910–1914	5 Ghirsh, Mohammed V, Silver	—	18.00
☐ 1862–1871	10 Ghirsh, Abdul Aziz, Silver	—	380.00
☐ 1864	10 Ghirsh, Abdul Aziz, Minted in Europe, Silver	—	130.00
☐ 1870–1874	10 Ghirsh, Abdul Aziz, Gold	—	174.50
☐ 1885–1908	10 Ghirsh, Abdul Hamid II, Minted in Europe, Silver	—	66.50
☐ 1892–1909	10 Ghirsh, Abdul Hamid II, Gold	—	89.50
☐ 1910–1914	10 Ghirsh, Mohammed V, Silver	—	45.50
☐ 1861–1862	20 Ghirsh, Abdul Aziz, Silver	—	650.00
☐ 1876–1880	20 Ghirsh, Abdul Hamid II, Silver	—	1400.00
☐ 1885–1908	20 Ghirsh, Abdul Hamid II, Minted in Europe, Silver	—	36.50
☐ 1910–1914	20 Ghirsh, Mohammed V, Silver	—	36.50
☐ 1868–1875	25 Ghirsh, Abdul Aziz, Gold	—	128.50
☐ 1871–1876	50 Ghirsh, Abdul Aziz, Gold	—	289.50
☐ 1861–1876	100 Ghirsh, Abdul Aziz, Gold	—	289.50
☐ 1864	100 Ghirsh, Abdul Aziz, Minted in Europe, Gold	—	575.00

DATE	COIN TYPE/VARIETY/METAL	ABP FINE	AVERAGE FINE
☐ 1876–1883	100 Ghirsh, Abdul Hamid II, Gold	—	$765.00
☐ 1887	100 Ghirsh, Abdul Hamid II, Minted in Europe, Gold	—	380.00
☐ 1868–1875	500 Ghirsh, Abdul Aziz, Gold	—	RARE
☐ 1876–1881	500 Ghirsh, Abdul Hamid II, Gold	—	RARE
☐ 1955	1 Pound, Republic, Revolution 3rd & 5th Anniversaries, Gold	—	275.50
☐ 1955	5 Pounds, Republic, Revolution 3rd & 5th Anniversaries, Gold	—	1100.00

Egypt—United Arab Republic

Key to Grading: Eagle

☐ 1960–1966	Millieme, UAR, Aluminum-Bronze	.28	.47

Key to Grading: Eagle

☐ 1962–1966	2 Milliemes, UAR, Aluminum-Bronze	.28	.47

Key to Grading: Eagle

☐ 1960–1966	5 Milliemes, UAR, Aluminum-Bronze	.28	.47

Key to Grading: Eagle

DATE	COIN TYPE/VARIETY/METAL	ABP FINE	AVERAGE FINE
☐ 1958–1966	10 Milliemes, UAR, Aluminum-Bronze	$.59	$ .98
☐ 1958	20 Milliemes, UAR, Agriculture & Industry Fair, Aluminum-Bronze	.59	.98
☐ 1958	1/2 Pound, UAR, Founding of the United Arab Republic, Gold	—	238.00
☐ 1960	Pound, UAR, Aswan Dam, Gold	—	248.00
☐ 1960	5 Pounds, UAR, Aswan Dam, Gold	—	1050.00

FINLAND

Evidence of coinage became common late in the Middle Ages. The first coins were used around 1410. Most were silver ortugs, and nearly all bore the king's name. In the 1800s, the ruble was declared Finland's monetary unit, then the penni and the markka. In 1963, the new 1 penni equaled the old 1 markka.

Finland—Type Coinage

Key to Grading: Crown & Lettering

DATE	COIN TYPE/VARIETY/METAL	ABP FINE	AVERAGE FINE
☐ 1864–1917	1 Penni, Copper	$.40	$ .67
☐ 1919–1924	1 Penni, Copper	.40	.67

Key to Grading: Lettering

☐ 1963–1969	1 Penni, Copper	.26	.43
☐ 1969–1979	1 Penni, Aluminum	.26	.43

Key to Grading: Crown & Lettering

☐ 1865–1917	5 Pennia, Copper	.40	.67
☐ 1918–1940	5 Pennia, Copper	.35	.59
☐ 1941–1943	5 Pennia, Copper	.23	.39
☐ 1963–1977	5 Pennia, Copper	.27	.45
☐ 1977–1990	5 Pennia, Aluminum	.27	.45

Key to Grading: Crown & Lettering

DATE	COIN TYPE/VARIETY/METAL	ABP FINE	AVERAGE FINE
☐ 1865–1917	10 Pennia, Copper	$.63	$1.10
☐ 1919–1940	10 Pennia, Copper	.26	.43
☐ 1941–1943	10 Pennia, Copper	.26	.43
☐ 1943–1945	10 Pennia, Iron	.26	.43
☐ 1865–1917	25 Pennia, Silver	.84	1.40
☐ 1921–1940	25 Pennia, Cupro-Nickel	.36	.60
☐ 1940–1943	25 Pennia, Copper	.36	.60
☐ 1943–1945	25 Pennia, Iron	.36	.60

Key to Grading: Coat of Arms

☐ 1864–1917	50 Pennia, Silver	1.05	1.75
☐ 1921–1940	50 Pennia, Cupro-Nickel	.26	.43
☐ 1940–1943	50 Pennia, Copper	.26	.43
☐ 1943–1948	50 Pennia, Iron	.33	.55
☐ 1963–1982	10 Pennia, Aluminum-Bronze	.33	.55
☐ 1983–1990	10 Pennia, Aluminum	.23	.39
☐ 1990–2001	10 Pennia, Cupro-Nickel	.26	.43
☐ 1864–1915	Markka, Silver	2.70	4.50
☐ 1921–1924	Markka, Cupro-Nickel	2.60	4.35
☐ 1928–1940	Markka, Cupro-Nickel	.26	.43
☐ 1940–1951	1 Markka, Copper	.26	.43
☐ 1943–1952	1 Markka, Iron	.26	.43
☐ 1952–1962	1 Markka, Iron	.26	.43

Key to Grading: Coat of Arms

DATE	COIN TYPE/VARIETY/METAL	ABP FINE	AVERAGE FINE
☐ 1964–1968	1 Markka, Silver	—	$2.50
☐ 1969–1993	1 Markka, Cupro-Nickel	.33	.55
☐ 1993–2001	Markka, Aluminum-Bronze	.33	.55
☐ 1865–1908	2 Markkaa, Silver	—	12.50
☐ 1928–1946	5 Markkaa, Aluminum-Bronze	.52	.87

Key to Grading: Lettering

☐ 1946–1952	5 Markkaa, Brass	.33	.55
☐ 1952–1962	5 Markkaa, Iron	.33	.55
☐ 1972–1978	5 Markkaa, Aluminum-Bronze	.98	1.65
☐ 1979–1993	5 Markkaa, Aluminum-Bronze	.98	1.65
☐ 1992–1997	5 Markkaa, Aluminum-Bronze	.98	1.65

Key to Grading: Coat of Arms

☐ 1878–1913	10 Markkaa, Gold	83.45	139.05
☐ 1928–1939	10 Markkaa, Aluminum-Bronze	1.45	2.40
☐ 1952–1962	10 Markkaa, Aluminum-Bronze	.85	1.40

Key to Grading: Coat of Arms & Bust

☐ 1967–1977	10 Markkaa, Commemorative, Silver	—	8.35
☐ 1963–1990	20 Pennia, Aluminum-Bronze	.25	.42

Key to Grading: Coat of Arms

DATE	COIN TYPE/VARIETY/METAL	ABP FINE	AVERAGE FINE
☐ 1878–1913	20 Markkaa, Gold	—	$280.00
☐ 1931–1939	20 Markkaa, Aluminum-Bronze	3.45	5.70
☐ 1952–1962	20 Markkaa, Aluminum-Bronze	.33	.55

Key to Grading: Coat of Arms or Building

☐ 1978–1979	25 Markkaa, Commemorative, Silver	—	10.00
☐ 1963–1990	50 Pennia, Aluminum-Bronze	.28	.46
☐ 1990 to Date	50 Pennia, Cupro-Nickel	.28	.46

Key to Grading: Coat of Arms

| ☐ 1952–1962 | 50 Markkaa, Aluminum-Bronze | 3.10 | 5.15 |

Key to Grading: Bust

| ☐ 1981–1985 | 50 Markkaa, Commemorative, Silver | — | 37.50 |
| ☐ 1926 | 100 Markkaa, Gold | — | 720.00 |

DATE	COIN TYPE/VARIETY/METAL	ABP FINE	AVERAGE FINE
☐ 1956–1960	100 Markkaa, Silver	—	$23.75
☐ 1989–1992	100 Markkaa, Commemorative, Silver	—	56.75
☐ 1926	200 Markkaa, Gold	—	1075.00
☐ 1956–1959	200 Markkaa, Silver	—	23.50

Key to Grading: Lettering

☐ 1951–1952	500 Markkaa, Commemorative Coin Issued on the Occasion of the Olympic Games in Helsinki, Silver	—	44.50
☐ 1960	1000 Markkaa, Commemorative Coin Issued on the Occasion of the Centenary of the Finnish Mint, Silver	—	12.00

FRANCE

The earliest coins date from about 500 B.C. The silver drachma was the typical coin from the 4th century B.C., with the gold stater prominent in the 2nd century B.C. The silver denier became popular around 600 A.D. The Middle Ages saw a great amount of feudal coinage, followed by coins influenced by the French Revolution. By the First World War, paper money was substituted for gold. In 1961, the new franc was introduced and used until France transitioned to the euro between 1999 and 2002.

France—Type Coinage

Key to Grading: Bust

DATE	COIN TYPE/VARIETY/METAL	ABP FINE	AVERAGE FINE
☐ 1848–1852A			
Un Centime, Second Republic, Copper		$3.45	$5.70
☐ 1853–1862	Un Centime, Second Empire, Bronze	4.10	6.85
☐ 1872–1920	Un Centime, Third Republic, Bronze	3.45	5.70
☐ 1962–1993	Un Centime, Fifth Republic, Chrome-Steel	.28	.47
☐ 1853–1862	Deux Centimes, Second Empire, Bronze	1.40	2.30
☐ 1877–1920	Deux Centimes, Third Republic, Bronze	3.45	5.70
☐ 1808BB	Cinq Centimes, Copper	84.35	140.60

Key to Grading: Bust & Eagles

DATE	COIN TYPE/VARIETY/METAL	ABP FINE	AVERAGE FINE
☐ 1853–1865	Cinq Centimes, Second Empire, Bronze	3.50	5.85
☐ 1871–1921	Cinq Centimes, Third Republic, Bronze	3.50	5.85
☐ 1914–1938	Cinq Centimes, Third Republic, Copper-Nickel	.28	.46
☐ 1938–1939	Cinq Centimes, Third Republic, Nickel-Bronze	.28	.46
☐ 1961–1964	Cinq Centimes, Fifth Republic, Chrome-Steel	.28	.46
☐ 1966–1993	Cinq Centimes, Fifth Republic, Aluminum-Bronze	.28	.46
☐ 1814–1815BB	Decime, Strasbourg Provisional Issue, Bronze	16.20	27.00
☐ 1807–1809	Dix Centimes, Buillon	4.55	7.60

Key to Grading: Bust

DATE	COIN TYPE/VARIETY/METAL	ABP FINE	AVERAGE FINE
☐ 1852–1864	Dix Centimes, Bronze	$3.12	$5.20
☐ 1870–1921	Dix Centimes, Third Republic, Bronze	3.12	5.20
☐ 1914	Dix Centimes, Third Republic, Nickel	308.00	515.00
☐ 1917–1938	Dix Centimes, Third Republic, Copper-Nickel	.28	.46
☐ 1938–1939	Dix Centimes, Third Republic, Nickel-Bronze	.28	.46
☐ 1941–1945	Dix Centimes, Third Republic, Zinc	.28	.46
☐ 1962–1993	Dix Centimes, Fifth Republic, Aluminum-Bronze	.28	.46

Key to Grading: Bust

☐ 1849–1850	Vingt Centimes, Second Republic, Silver	—	26.50
☐ 1853–1889	Vingt Centimes, Second Empire, Silver	—	26.50
☐ 1941–1945	Vingt Centimes, Second Empire, Zinc	.49	.81
☐ 1962–1993	Vingt Centimes, Fifth Republic, Aluminum-Bronze	.36	.60
☐ 1806–1807	Quart Franc, Silver	—	120.00
☐ 1807	Quart Franc, Negro Head, Silver	—	238.00
☐ 1807–1845	Quart Franc, Laureate Head, Silver	—	238.00
☐ 1845–1846	25 Centimes, Silver	—	23.50

Key to Grading: Bust

DATE	COIN TYPE/VARIETY/METAL	ABP FINE	AVERAGE FINE
☐ 1903–1917	25 Centimes, Third Republic, Nickel	$.55	$ .92
☐ 1917–1937	25 Centimes, Third Republic, Copper-Nickel	.34	.57
☐ 1938–1940	25 Centimes, Third Republic, Nickel-Bronze	.34	.57
☐ 1807	Demi Franc, Negro Head, Silver	—	250.00
☐ 1807–1845	Demi Franc, Laureate Head, Silver	—	36.50
☐ 1845–1846	50 Centimes, Silver	—	24.50
☐ 1849–1850	50 Centimes, Second Republic, Silver	—	66.50
☐ 1852	50 Centimes, Second Republic, President Louis Napoleon, Silver	—	66.50
☐ 1853–1867	50 Centimes, Second Empire, Silver	—	18.50

Key to Grading: Bust

☐ 1871–1920	50 Centimes, Third Republic, Silver	—	6.60
☐ 1921–1939	50 Centimes, Third Republic, Aluminum-Bronze	.28	.46
☐ 1941–1945	50 Centimes, Third Republic, Aluminum	.28	.46
☐ 1962–1964	50 Centimes, Third Republic, Aluminum-Bronze	.28	.46

Key to Grading: Figure

☐ 1965–1993	$\frac{1}{2}$ Franc, Nickel	.35	.59
☐ 1807	1 Franc, Negro Head, Silver	—	665.00
☐ 1807–1848	1 Franc, Laureate Head, Silver	—	38.00
☐ 1849–1868	1 Franc, Second Republic, Silver	—	72.50

Key to Grading: Figure or Bust

DATE	COIN TYPE/VARIETY/METAL	ABP FINE	AVERAGE FINE
☐ 1871–1920	1 Franc, Third Republic, Silver	—	$7.00
☐ 1920–1941	1 Franc, Third Republic, Chamber of Commerce, Aluminum-Bronze	.28	.47
☐ 1941–1959	1 Franc, Third Republic, Aluminum	.28	.47
☐ 1943	1 Franc, Third Republic, Zinc	584.00	973.00
☐ 1960–1999	1 Franc, Fifth Republic, Nickel	.28	.47
☐ 1807	2 Francs, Negro Head, Silver	—	1000.00
☐ 1807–1846	2 Francs, Laureate Head, Silver	—	135.00
☐ 1849–1850	2 Francs, Second Republic, Silver	—	289.00
☐ 1853–1868	2 Francs, Second Empire, Silver	—	289.00

Key to Grading: Bust or Figure

☐ 1870–1920	2 Francs, Third Republic, Silver	—	15.75
☐ 1920–1941	2 Francs, Third Republic, Chamber of Commerce, Aluminum-Bronze	1.39	2.30
☐ 1941–1946	2 Francs, Third Republic, Aluminum	.28	.47
☐ 1979–1999	2 Francs, 5 Republic	.28	.47
☐ 1814–1815	5 Francs, First Restoration, Silver	—	110.00
☐ 1815	5 Francs, The Hundred Days, Silver	—	375.00
☐ 1816–1830	5 Francs, Second Restoration, Silver	—	82.50
☐ 1830–1846	5 Francs, Second Restoration, Louis Phillipe, Silver	—	82.50
☐ 1848–1852	5 Francs, Second Republic, Silver	—	56.50
☐ 1854–1860	5 Francs, Second Empire, Gold	—	88.50
☐ 1861–1870	5 Francs, Second Empire, Silver	—	88.50
☐ 1862–1869	5 Francs, Second Empire, Gold	—	66.50

Key to Grading: Figures or Busts

DATE	COIN TYPE/VARIETY/METAL	ABP FINE	AVERAGE FINE
☐ 1870–1878	5 Francs, Third Republic, Silver	—	$62.50
☐ 1871	5 Francs, Third Republic, Trident, Silver	—	335.00
☐ 1933–1939	5 Francs, Third Republic, Nickel	1.40	2.30
☐ 1938–1946	5 Francs, Third Republic, Aluminum-Bronze	2.80	4.60
☐ 1945–1952	5 Francs, Third Republic, Aluminum	.28	.47
☐ 1960–1969	5 Francs, Fifth Republic, Silver	—	6.60
☐ 1970–1999	5 Francs, Fifth Republic, Copper-Nickel	1.80	3.00
☐ 1989	5 Francs, Fifth Republic, Eiffel Tower Centennial, Platinum	220.65	368.00
☐ 1989	5 Francs, Fifth Republic, Eiffel Tower Centennial, Gold	—	358.00
☐ 1989	5 Francs, Fifth Republic, Eiffel Tower Centennial, Copper-Nickel	2.95	4.90
☐ 1989	5 Francs, Fifth Republic, Eiffel Tower Centennial, Silver	—	35.00
☐ 1850–1914	10 Francs, Gold	—	38.50
☐ 1929–1939	10 Francs, Silver	—	6.60
☐ 1945–1949	10 Francs, Copper-Nickel	.26	.43
☐ 1950–1958	10 Francs, Aluminum-Bronze	.26	.43

Key to Grading: Figures

DATE	COIN TYPE/VARIETY/METAL	ABP FINE	AVERAGE FINE
☐ 1965–1973	10 Francs, Fifth Republic, Silver	—	7.50
☐ 1974–1987	10 Francs, Fifth Republic, Nickel-Brass	1.50	2.45
☐ 1982	10 Francs, Fifth Republic, Leon Gambetta—100th Anniversary, Copper-Nickel	1.50	2.45

DATE	COIN TYPE/VARIETY/METAL	ABP FINE	AVERAGE FINE
☐ 1983	10 Francs, Fifth Republic, Montgolfier Balloon—200th Anniversary, Nickel-Bronze	$1.30	$2.20
☐ 1983	10 Francs, Fifth Republic, Birth of Stendhal—200th Anniversary, Nickel-Bronze	2.95	4.90
☐ 1984	10 Francs, Fifth Republic, Birth of Francois Rudei—200th Anniversary, Nickel-Bronze	2.95	4.90
☐ 1985	10 Francs, Fifth Republic, Victor Hugo Centennial, Silver	—	36.50
☐ 1986	10 Francs, Fifth Republic, Robert Schumann—100th Anniversary, Gold	—	210.00
☐ 1986	10 Francs, Fifth Republic, Robert Schumann—100th Anniversary, Silver	—	40.00
☐ 1986	10 Francs, Fifth Republic, Robert Schumann—100th Anniversary, Nickel-Bronze	1.65	2.75
☐ 1987	10 Francs, Fifth Republic, French Millennium, Silver	—	40.00
☐ 1987	10 Francs, Fifth Republic, French Millennium, Platinum	195.00	324.00
☐ 1987	10 Francs, Fifth Republic, French Millennium, Nickel-Bronze	3.25	5.40
☐ 1987	10 Francs, Fifth Republic, French Millennium, Gold	—	284.00
☐ 1988	10 Francs, Fifth Republic, Rolland Garros—100th Anniversary, Aluminum-Bronze	3.25	5.40
☐ 1988–1997	10 Francs, Fifth Republic, Bastille, Dual Metal	3.25	5.40
☐ 1988	10 Francs, Fifth Republic, Rolland Garros—100th Anniversary, Silver	—	19.50
☐ 1988	10 Francs, Fifth Republic, Rolland Garros—100th Anniversary, Gold	—	—
☐ 1989	10 Francs, Fifth Republic, Montesquieu—300th Anniversary, Dual Metal	3.25	5.40
☐ 1990–1990	European Currency Units, Charlemagne, Silver	—	328.00
☐ 1991–1991	European Currency Units, Descartes, Silver	—	105.00
☐ 1992–1992	European Currency Units, Monet, Silver	—	65.50
☐ 1814	20 Francs, Gold	—	94.00

Key to Grading: Bust

DATE	COIN TYPE/VARIETY/METAL	ABP FINE	AVERAGE FINE
☐ 1929–1939	20 Francs, Silver	—	$7.50
☐ 1950–1954	20 Francs, Aluminum-Bronze	.26	.43
☐ 1992–1997	20 Francs, Mont St. Michel, Tri Metal	2.95	4.90

Key to Grading: Rooster

☐ 1855–1904	50 Francs, Gold	—	448.00

Key to Grading: Rooster

DATE	COIN TYPE/VARIETY/METAL	ABP FINE	AVERAGE FINE
☐ 1950–1954	50 Francs, Aluminum-Bronze	.49	.81
☐ 1974–1980	50 Francs, Silver	—	12.00
☐ 1990	European Currency Units, Charlemagne, Gold	—	485.00
☐ 1990	European Currency Units, Charlemagne, Platinum	324.00	541.00
☐ 1991	European Currency Units, Descartes, Gold	—	665.00
☐ 1991	European Currency Units, Descartes, Platinum	42.20	70.30
☐ 1992	European Currency Units, Monet, Platinum	42.20	70.30

DATE	COIN TYPE/VARIETY/METAL	ABP FINE	AVERAGE FINE
☐ 1992	European Currency Units, Monet, Gold	—	$1125.00
☐ 1855–1936	100 Francs, Gold	—	1000.00

Key to Grading: Busts or Figures

DATE	COIN TYPE/VARIETY/METAL	ABP FINE	AVERAGE FINE
☐ 1954–1958	100 Francs, Copper-Nickel	3.25	5.40
☐ 1982–1993	100 Francs, Pantheon, Silver	—	36.75
☐ 1984	100 Francs, Marie Curie—50th Anniversary, Silver	—	238.00
☐ 1984	100 Francs, Marie Curie—50th Anniversary, Gold	—	800.00
☐ 1985	100 Francs, Germinal Centennial, Gold	—	815.00
☐ 1985	100 Francs, Germinal Centennial, Silver	—	220.00
☐ 1986	100 Francs, Statue of Liberty Centennial, Platinum	247.00	411.00
☐ 1986	100 Francs, Statue of Liberty Centennial, Gold	—	495.00
☐ 1986	100 Francs, Statue of Liberty Centennial, Silver	—	100.00
☐ 1986	100 Francs, Statue of Liberty Centennial, Palladium	171.95	286.60
☐ 1987	100 Francs, Lafayette—230th Anniversary, Platinum	308.00	514.00
☐ 1987	100 Francs, Lafayette—230th Anniversary, Gold	—	595.00
☐ 1987	100 Francs, Lafayette—230th Anniversary, Palladium	155.75	260.00
☐ 1987	100 Francs, Lafayette—230th Anniversary, Silver	—	75.50
☐ 1988	100 Francs, Fraternity, Gold	—	9.15
☐ 1988	100 Francs, Fraternity, Platinum	406.00	676.00
☐ 1988	100 Francs, Fraternity, Silver	—	82.50
☐ 1988	100 Francs, Fraternity, Palladium	152.00	254.00
☐ 1989	100 Francs, Olympics—Ice Skating, Silver	—	82.50
☐ 1989	100 Francs, Olympics—Alpine Skating, Silver	—	75.70
☐ 1989	100 Francs, Human Rights, Palladium	195.00	324.00
☐ 1989	100 Francs, Human Rights, Gold	—	1350.00

DATE	COIN TYPE/VARIETY/METAL	ABP FINE	AVERAGE FINE
☐ 1989	100 Francs, Human Rights, Platinum	$616.00	$1027.00
☐ 1990	100 Francs, Olympics—Speed Skating, Silver	—	68.50
☐ 1990	100 Francs, Charlemagne, Silver	—	85.50
☐ 1990	100 Francs, Olympics—Bobsledding, Silver	—	85.50
☐ 1990	100 Francs, Olympic—Slalom Skier, Silver	—	56.50
☐ 1990	100 Francs, Olympic—Freestyle, Silver	—	72.00
☐ 1991	100 Francs, Olympic—Hockey Player, Silver		78.50
☐ 1991	100 Francs, Olympic—Ski Jumper, Silver	—	67.50
☐ 1991	100 Francs, Basketball—100th Anniversary, Silver		120.00
☐ 1991	100 Francs, Descartes, Silver	—	80.00
☐ 1991	100 Francs, Olympic—Cross Country Skier, Silver		74.50
☐ 1992	100 Francs, Paralympics, Silver	—	205.00
☐ 1993	100 Francs, Louvre Bicentennial—Victory, Silver		75.50
☐ 1993	100 Francs, Louvre Bicentennial—Mona Lisa, Silver		75.50
☐ 1993	100 Francs, Louvre Bicentennial—Victory, Gold		725.00
☐ 1993	100 Francs, Louvre Bicentennial—Liberty, Silver		74.50
☐ 1993	100 Francs, Louvre Bicentennial—Liberty, Gold		855.00
☐ 1989	500 Francs, Olympic—Alpine Skiing, Gold	—	560.00
☐ 1989	500 Francs, Olympic—Ice Skating, Gold	—	560.00
☐ 1990	500 Francs, Olympic—Freestyle Skier, Gold		380.00
☐ 1990	500 Francs, Olympic—Bobsledding, Gold	—	574.00
☐ 1990	500 Francs, Olympic—Slalom Skier, Gold	—	600.00
☐ 1990	500 Francs, Olympic—Speed Skating, Gold		300.00
☐ 1991	500 Francs, Olympic—Coubertin, Gold	—	695.00
☐ 1991	500 Francs, Olympic—Hockey Player, Gold		738.00
☐ 1991	500 Francs, Olympic—Cross Country Skier, Gold		689.00
☐ 1991	500 Francs, Basketball—100th Anniversary, Gold	—	610.00

DATE	COIN TYPE/VARIETY/METAL	ABP FINE	AVERAGE FINE
☐ 1991	500 Francs, Olympic—Ski Jumpers, Gold	—	$802.50
☐ 1993	500 Francs, Louvre—Mona Lisa, Gold	—	RARE

*BV—These coins are relatively current so their collector value is minimal. Since these coins were minted and sold primarily for their bullion value, their current value is determined by the current "spot" price of the precious metal indicated. For accurate prices, contact your local coin dealer.

GERMANY (FED. REP.)

The first coins were used in the 3rd century B.C. as gold staters. In the 1st century B.C., small silver coins were produced. A local gold coin, known as a rainbow-cup, came to an end in the mid-1st century B.C. The silver denar was produced in the 800s. The bracteates became popular in the 1100s, as did pfennigs. A larger silver piece was used in the 14th century, along with other gold coinage. In the 1600s, good coinage had to be restored, with medallic taler being produced. The first decimal coins were used in 1871. Today's currency is the euro.

GERMANY (DEM. REP.)

The first coins were used in 1949 when the German Democratic Republic was formed. Its coinage was based on 100 pfennig to the mark, some in aluminum and some in brass. The mark was cupronickel or silver.

Germany—German Empire Coinage

Key to Grading: Eagle

DATE	COIN TYPE/VARIETY/METAL	ABP FINE	AVERAGE FINE
☐ 1873–1889	1 Pfennig (1st Coinage), Rev: Small Eagle, Copper	$3.45	$5.80
☐ 1890–1916	1 Pfennig (2nd Coinage), Rev: Large Eagle, Copper	.40	.67

Key to Grading: Eagle

DATE	COIN TYPE/VARIETY/METAL	ABP FINE	AVERAGE FINE
☐ 1873–1877	2 Pfennig (1st Coinage), Rev: Small Eagle, Copper	.55	.92
☐ 1904–1916	2 Pfennig (2nd Coinage), Rev: Large Eagle, Copper	.52	.86

Key to Grading: Eagle

DATE	COIN TYPE/VARIETY/METAL	ABP FINE	AVERAGE FINE
☐ 1874–1889	5 Pfennig (1st Coinage), Rev: Small Eagle, Cupro-Nickel	.82	1.35
☐ 1890–1915	5 Pfennig (2nd Coinage), Rev: Large Eagle, Cupro-Nickel	.52	.86

Key to Grading: Eagle

DATE	COIN TYPE/VARIETY/METAL	ABP FINE	AVERAGE FINE
☐ 1873–1889	10 Pfennig (1st Coinage), Rev: Small Eagle, Cupro-Nickel	$.88	$1.45
☐ 1890–1915	10 Pfennig (2nd Coinage), Rev: Large Eagle, Cupro-Nickel	.52	.86
☐ 1873–1877	20 Pfennig (1st Coinage), Rev: Small Eagle, Silver	—	18.75
☐ 1887–1888	20 Pfennig (1st Coinage), Rev: Small Eagle, Cupro-Nickel	—	24.00
☐ 1890–1892	20 Pfennig (2nd Coinage), Rev: Large Eagle, Cupro-Nickel	—	28.50
☐ 1909–1912	25 Pfennig (2nd Coinage), Rev: Large Eagle, Nickel	—	10.25
☐ 1877–1878	50 Pfennig (1st Coinage), Rev: Small Eagle, Silver	—	40.50
☐ 1875–1877	50 Pfennig (1st Coinage), Rev: Small Eagle, Silver	—	40.50
☐ 1896–1901	50 Pfennig (2nd Coinage), Rev: Large Eagle, Silver	—	240.00

Key to Grading: Eagle

☐ 1905–1919	1/2 Mark (2nd Coinage), Rev: Large Eagle, Silver	—	8.25

Key to Grading: Eagle

DATE	COIN TYPE/VARIETY/METAL	ABP FINE	AVERAGE FINE
☐ 1873–1887	1 Mark (1st Coinage), Rev: Small Eagle, Silver	—	$10.25

Key to Grading: Eagle

☐ 1891–1916	1 Mark (2nd Coinage), Rev: Large Eagle, Silver	—	10.25

Germany—World War I Coinage

Key to Grading: Eagle

DATE	COIN TYPE/VARIETY/METAL	ABP FINE	AVERAGE FINE
☐ 1916–1918	1 Pfennig, WWI, Rev: Large Eagle, Aluminum	.49	.81
☐ 1915–1922	5 Pfennig, WWI, Rev: Large Eagle, Iron	.26	.43
☐ 1915–1922	10 Pfennig, WWI, Rev: Small Eagle, Iron	.26	.43
☐ 1916–1917	10 Pfennig, WWI, Rev: Small Eagle, Zinc	55.15	92.00
☐ 1916	1 Kopek, WWI, Iron	3.00	5.00
☐ 1916	2 Kopeks, WWI, Iron	3.00	5.00
☐ 1916	3 Kopeks, WWI, Iron	3.00	5.00

Germany—Weimar Republic Coinage

Key to Grading: Wheat Heads

DATE	COIN TYPE/VARIETY/METAL	ABP FINE	AVERAGE FINE
☐ 1923–1929	1 Rentenpfennig, Weimar Republic, Bronze	.26	.43
☐ 1924–1936	1 Reichspfennig, Weimar Republic, Bronze	.26	.43
☐ 1923–1924	2 Rentenpfennig, Weimar Republic, Bronze	.26	.43
☐ 1924–1936	2 Reichspfennig, Weimar Republic, Bronze	.26	.43
☐ 1932–1933	4 Reichspfennig, Weimar Republic, Rev: Large Eagle, Bronze	3.15	5.25

Key to Grading: Wheat Heads

DATE	COIN TYPE/VARIETY/METAL	ABP FINE	AVERAGE FINE
☐ 1923–1925	5 Rentenpfennig, Weimar Republic, Aluminum-Bronze	$.28	$ .47
☐ 1924–1936	5 Reichspfennig, Weimar Republic, Rev: Large Eagle, Aluminum-Bronze	.28	.47

Key to Grading: Wheat Head

☐ 1923–1925	10 Rentenpfennig, Weimar Republic, Aluminum-Bronze	.31	.51
☐ 1924–1936	10 Reichspfennig, Weimar Republic, Rev: Large Eagle, Aluminum-Bronze	.31	.51

Key to Grading: Wheat Heads

☐ 1919–1922	50 Pfennig, Weimar Republic, Aluminum	.31	.51

Key to Grading: Wheat Heads

DATE	COIN TYPE/VARIETY/METAL	ABP FINE	AVERAGE FINE
☐ 1923–1924	50 Rentenpfennig, Weimar Republic, Aluminum-Bronze	$9.75	$16.20
☐ 1924–1925	50 Reichspfennig, Weimar Republic, Aluminum-Bronze	561.30	935.50
☐ 1924–1925	Mark, Weimar Republic, Rev: Large Eagle, Silver	—	11.75
☐ 1925–1927	1 Reichsmark, Weimar Republic, Rev: Large Eagle, Silver	—	19.50
☐ 1925–1931	2 Reichsmark, Weimar Republic, Rev: Large Eagle, Silver	—	29.50
☐ 1922–1923	3 Mark, Weimar Republic, 3rd Anniversary—Weimar Constitution, Aluminum	3.25	5.40
☐ 1925	3 Reichsmark, Weimar Republic, Commemorative—Millenium Unification of Rhineland, Silver	—	35.00
☐ 1926	3 Reichsmark, Weimar Republic, Commemorative—700th Anniversary of the Freedom of Lubeck, Silver	—	128.50
☐ 1927	3 Reichsmark, Weimar Republic, Commemorative—Bremhaven Centennial, Silver	—	152.50
☐ 1927	3 Reichsmark, Weimar Republic, Commemorative—University of Marburg 400th Anniversary, Silver	—	136.50
☐ 1927	3 Reichsmark, Weimar Republic, Commemorative—University of Tubingen 450th Anniversary, Silver	—	302.00
☐ 1927	3 Reichsmark, Weimar Republic, Commemorative—Nordhausen Millenium, Silver	—	136.50
☐ 1928	3 Reichsmark, Weimar Republic, Commemorative—City of Naumburg—900th Anniversary, Silver	—	152.50
☐ 1928	3 Reichsmark, Weimar Republic, Commemorative—City of Dinkelsbuhl Millenium, Silver	—	530.00
☐ 1928	3 Reichsmark, Weimar Republic, Commemorative—Death of Durer—400th Anniversary, Silver	—	295.00
☐ 1929	3 Reichsmark, Weimar Republic, Commemorative—Birth of Lessing Bicentennial, Silver	—	74.50
☐ 1929	3 Reichsmark, Weimar Republic, Commemorative—Waldeck-Prussia Union, Silver	—	165.50

DATE	COIN TYPE/VARIETY/METAL	ABP FINE	AVERAGE FINE
☐ 1929	3 Reichsmark, Weimar Republic, Commemorative—City of Meissen Millenium, Silver	—	$70.50
☐ 1929	3 Reichsmark, Weimar Republic, Commemorative—Constitution 10th Anniversary, Silver	—	55.50
☐ 1930	3 Reichsmark, Weimar Republic, Commemorative—End of Rhineland Occupation, Silver	—	58.50
☐ 1930	3 Reichsmark, Weimar Republic, Commemorative—Flight of Graf Zeppelin, Silver	—	100.00
☐ 1930	3 Reichsmark, Weimar Republic, Commemorative—Death of Vogelweide 700th Anniversary, Silver	—	72.50
☐ 1931	3 Reichsmark, Weimar Republic, Commemorative—Death of von Stein Centennial, Silver	—	120.00
☐ 1931	3 Reichsmark, Weimar Republic, Commemorative—Magdeburg Rebuilding 300th Anniversary, Silver	—	245.00
☐ 1931–1933	3 Reichsmark, Weimar Republic, Rev: Large Eagle, Silver	—	265.00
☐ 1932	3 Reichsmark, Weimar Republic, Commemorative—Death of Goethe, Silver	—	82.50

Key to Grading: Eagle

DATE	COIN TYPE/VARIETY/METAL	ABP FINE	AVERAGE FINE
☐ 1922	3 Mark, Weimar Republic, Obv: Large Eagle, Aluminum	1.35	2.20
☐ 1924–1925	3 Mark, Weimar Republic, Rev: Large Eagle, Silver	—	52.50
☐ 1925	5 Reichsmark, Weimar Republic, Commemorative—Millennium Unification of Rhineland, Silver	—	100.00
☐ 1927–1933	5 Reichsmark, Weimar Republic, Rev: Large Eagle, Silver	—	100.00

DATE	COIN TYPE/VARIETY/METAL	ABP FINE	AVERAGE FINE
☐ 1927	5 Reichsmark, Weimar Republic, Commemorative—University of Tubingen 450th Anniversary, Silver	—	$365.00
☐ 1929	5 Reichsmark, Weimar Republic, Commemorative—Birth of Lessing Bicentennial, Silver	—	130.50
☐ 1929	5 Reichsmark, Weimar Republic, Commemorative—Constitution 10th Anniversary, Silver	—	130.50
☐ 1929	5 Reichsmark, Weimar Republic, Commemorative—City of Meissen Millennium, Silver	—	295.00
☐ 1930	5 Reichsmark, Weimar Republic, Commemorative—End of Rhineland Occupation, Silver	—	158.00
☐ 1930	5 Reichsmark, Weimar Republic, Commemorative—Flight of Graf Zeppelin, Silver	—	158.00
☐ 1932	5 Reichsmark, Weimar Republic, Commemorative—Death of Goethe, Silver	—	1000.00

Key to Grading: Eagle

☐ 1923	200 Mark, Weimar Republic, Obv: Large Eagle, Aluminum	.55	.92

Key to Grading: Eagle

☐ 1923	500 Mark, Weimar Republic, Obv: Large Eagle, Aluminum	.55	.92

Germany—Third Reich Coinage

Key to Grading: Eagle

DATE	COIN TYPE/VARIETY/METAL	ABP FINE	AVERAGE FINE
☐ 1936–1940	1 Reischspfennig, Third Reich, Obv: Hindenburg, Bronze	$1.20	$2.00
☐ 1940–1945	1 Reischspfennig, Third Reich, Zinc	.66	1.10

Key to Grading: Eagle

☐ 1936–1940	2 Reischspfennig, Third Reich, Obv: Hindenburg, Bronze	.88	1.45

Key to Grading: Eagle

☐ 1936–1939	5 Reischspfennig, Third Reich, Obv: Hindenburg, Aluminum-Bronze	.98	1.65
☐ 1940–1941	5 Reischspfennig, Third Reich, German Army, Zinc w/o White Spots	31.15	51.90
☐ 1940–1944	5 Reischspfennig, Third Reich, Zinc w/o White Spots	.98	1.65

Key to Grading: Eagle

DATE	COIN TYPE/VARIETY/METAL	ABP FINE	AVERAGE FINE
☐ 1936–1939	10 Reichspfennig, Third Reich, Obv: Hindenburg, Aluminum-Bronze	$1.80	$3.00
☐ 1940–1941	10 Reichspfennig, Third Reich, German Army, Zinc w/o white spots	38.95	64.90
☐ 1940–1945	10 Reichspfennig, Third Reich, Zinc w/o White Spots	1.65	2.75

Key to Grading: Eagle

DATE	COIN TYPE/VARIETY/METAL	ABP FINE	AVERAGE FINE
☐ 1935	50 Reichspfennig, Third Reich, Aluminum	1.65	2.75
☐ 1938–1939	50 Reichspfennig, Third Reich, Nickel	10.40	17.35
☐ 1939–1944	50 Reichspfennig, Third Reich, Aluminum	3.90	6.50
☐ 1933–1939	1 Reichsmark, Third Reich, Nickel	16.90	28.15
☐ 1933	2 Reichsmark, Third Reich, Commemorative—Birth of Martin Luther 450th Anniversary, Silver	—	17.50
☐ 1934	2 Reichsmark, Third Reich, Commemorative—Anniversary of Nazi Rule, Silver	—	17.50
☐ 1934	2 Reichsmark, Third Reich, Commemorative—Birth of Schiller 175th Anniversary, Silver	—	68.50
☐ 1936–1939	2 Reichsmark, Third Reich, Obv: Hindenburg, Silver	—	12.75
☐ 1933	5 Reichsmark, Third Reich, Commemorative—Birth of Martin Luther 450th Anniversary, Silver	—	136.50

DATE	COIN TYPE/VARIETY/METAL	ABP FINE	AVERAGE FINE
☐ 1934	5 Reischsmark, Third Reich, Commemorative—Anniversary of Nazi Rule, Silver	—	$23.50
☐ 1934	5 Reischsmark, Third Reich, Commemorative—Birth of Schiller 175th Anniversary, Silver	—	168.50
☐ 1934–1935	5 Reischsmark, Third Reich, Silver	—	9.25
☐ 1935–1936	5 Reischsmark, Third Reich, Obv: Hindenburg, Silver	—	14.75
☐ 1936–1939	5 Reichsmark, Third Reich, Obv: Hindenburg, Silver	—	14.75

Germany—Allied Occupation Coinage

Key to Grading: Eagle

☐ 1944	1 Reichspfennig, Allied Occ, Zinc	1512.00	2520.00
☐ 1944–1946	1 Reichspfennig, Allied Occ, Zinc	34.40	57.35

Key to Grading: Leaves

☐ 1948–1949	1 Pfennig, Allied Occ, Bank Deutscher Lander, Bronze-Steel	.26	.43
☐ 1944–1946	5 Reichspfennig, Allied Occ, Zinc	10.40	17.35

Key to Grading: Leaves

☐ 1949	5 Pfennig, Allied Occ, Bank Deutscher Lander, Brass-Steel	.26	.43
☐ 1945–1948	10 Reichspfennig, Allied Occ, Zinc	17.65	29.45

Key to Grading: Leaves

DATE	COIN TYPE/VARIETY/METAL	ABP FINE	AVERAGE FINE
☐ 1949	10 Pfennig, Allied Occ, Bank Deutscher Lander, Brass-Steel	$.29	$ .48

Key to Grading: Figure

☐ 1949–1950	50 Pfennig, Allied Occ, Bank Deutscher Lander, Cupro-Nickel	42.20	70.30

Germany—German Federal Republic Coinage

☐ 1950 to Date
1 Pfennig, Federal Republic,
Bundesrepublik Deutschland, Bronze-Steel   .29   .48

DATE	COIN TYPE/VARIETY/METAL	ABP FINE	AVERAGE FINE
☐ 1950–1968	2 Pfennig, Federal Republic, Bundesrepublik Deutschland, Bronze	$31.15	$51.90
☐ 1969 to Date	2 Pfennig, Federal Republic, Bundesrepublik Deutschland, Bronze-Steel	31.15	51.90

Key to Grading: Leaves

☐ 1950 to Date	5 Pfennig, Federal Republic, Bundesrepublik Deutschland, Brass-Steel	.27	.45

Key to Grading: Leaves

☐ 1950 to Date	10 Pfennig, Federal Republic, Bundesrepublik Deutschland, Brass-Steel	.27	.45

Key to Grading: Leaves

☐ 1950–1971	50 Pfennig, Federal Republic, Bundesrepublik Deutschland, Cupro-Nickel	.27	.45
☐ 1972 to Date	50 Pfennig, Federal Republic, Bundesrepublik Deutschland, Cupro-Nickel	.27	.45

Key to Grading: Eagle

DATE	COIN TYPE/VARIETY/METAL	ABP FINE	AVERAGE FINE
☐ 1950–2001	1 Deutsche Mark, Federal Republic, Bundesrepublik Deutschland, Cupro-Nickel	$1.05	$1.75
☐ 1951	2 Deutsche Mark, Federal Republic, Bundesrepublik Deutschland, Cupro-Nickel	24.65	41.10
☐ 1957–1971	2 Deutsche Mark, Federal Republic, Bundesrepublik Deutschland, Cupro-Nickel	1.60	2.65
☐ 1957–1971	2 Deutsche Mark, Federal Republic, Bundesrepublik Deutschland, Rev: Max Planck, Cupro-Nickel	1.60	2.65
☐ 1968–1991	2 Deutsche Mark, Federal Republic, Bundesrepublik Deutschland, Rev: Ludwig Erhard, Cupro-Nickel	1.60	2.65
☐ 1969–1987	2 Deutsche Mark, Federal Republic, Bundesrepublik Deutschland, Rev: Konrad Adenauer, Cupro-Nickel	1.60	2.65
☐ 1970–1987	2 Deutsche Mark, Federal Republic, Bundesrepublik Deutschland, Rev: Theodor Heuss, Cupro-Nickel	1.70	2.85
☐ 1979–1991	2 Deutsche Mark, Federal Republic, Bundesrepublik Deutschland, Rev: Kurt Schumacher, Cupro-Nickel	1.70	2.85
☐ 1990–1991	2 Deutsche Mark, Federal Republic, Bundesrepublik Deutschland, Rev: Franz Strauss, Cupro-Nickel	1.70	2.85

Key to Grading: Eagle

DATE	COIN TYPE/VARIETY/METAL	ABP FINE	AVERAGE FINE
☐ 1951–1974	5 Deutsche Mark, Federal Republic, Bundesrepublik Deutschland, Silver	—	$11.75
☐ 1975–2001	5 Deutsche Mark, Federal Republic, Rev: Large Eagle, Cupro-Nickel	4.90	8.15
☐ 1952	5 Deutsche Mark, Federal Republic, Commemorative—Nurnberg Museum Centennial, Silver	—	875.00
☐ 1955	5 Deutsche Mark, Federal Republic, Commemorative—von Schiller 150th Anniversary of Death, Silver	—	538.00
☐ 1955	5 Deutsche Mark, Federal Republic, Commemorative—Birth of Ludwig von Baden 300th Anniversary, Silver	—	400.00
☐ 1957	5 Deutsche Mark, Federal Republic, Commemorative—Death of von Eichendorff Centennial, Silver	—	400.00
☐ 1964	5 Deutsche Mark, Federal Republic, Commemorative—Death of Fichte 150th Anniversary, Silver	—	240.00
☐ 1966	5 Deutsche Mark, Federal Republic, Commemorative—Death of Leibniz 250th Anniversary, Silver	—	52.50
☐ 1967	5 Deutsche Mark, Federal Republic, Commemorative—Wilhelm & Alexander von Humboldt, Silver	—	38.50
☐ 1968	5 Deutsche Mark, Federal Republic, Commemorative—Birth of Ralfellsen 150th Anniversary, Silver	—	10.00
☐ 1968	5 Deutsche Mark, Federal Republic, Commemorative—Death of von Pettenkoffer 150th Anniversary, Silver	—	7.75
☐ 1969	5 Deutsche Mark, Federal Republic, Commemorative—Birth of Fontana 150th Anniversary, Silver	—	7.75
☐ 1969	5 Deutsche Mark, Federal Republic, Commemorative—Death of Mercator 375th Anniversary, Silver	—	7.75
☐ 1970	5 Deutsche Mark, Federal Republic, Commemorative—Birth of Beethoven 200th Anniversary, Silver	—	10.00
☐ 1971	5 Deutsche Mark, Federal Republic, Commemorative—Birth of Durer 500th Anniversary, Silver	—	7.75
☐ 1971	5 Deutsche Mark, Federal Republic, Commemorative—German Unification, Silver	—	10.50

DATE	COIN TYPE/VARIETY/METAL	ABP FINE	AVERAGE FINE
☐ 1973	5 Deutsche Mark, Federal Republic, Commemorative—Birth of Copernicus 500th Anniversary, Silver	—	$10.25
☐ 1973	5 Deutsche Mark, Federal Republic, Commemorative—Frankfurt Parliament 125th Anniversary, Silver	—	10.25
☐ 1974	5 Deutsche Mark, Federal Republic, Commemorative—Birth of Kant 250th Anniversary, Silver	—	10.25
☐ 1974	5 Deutsche Mark, Federal Republic, Commemorative—Constitutional Law 25th Anniversary, Silver	—	10.25
☐ 1975	5 Deutsche Mark, Federal Republic, Commemorative—Birth of Schweitzer Centenary, Silver	—	10.75
☐ 1975	5 Deutsche Mark, Federal Republic, Commemorative—Death of Ebert 250th Anniversary, Silver	—	10.25
☐ 1975	5 Deutsche Mark, Federal Republic, Commemorative—European Monument Protection, Silver	—	10.75
☐ 1976	5 Deutsche Mark, Federal Republic, Commemorative—Death of von Grimmelshausen 300th Anniversary, Silver	—	10.00
☐ 1977	5 Deutsche Mark, Federal Republic, Commemorative—Birth of Stresemann 100th Anniversary, Silver	—	10.00
☐ 1977	5 Deutsche Mark, Federal Republic, Commemorative—Birth of von Kleist 200th Anniversary, Silver	—	10.00
☐ 1977	5 Deutsche Mark, Federal Republic, Commemorative—Birth of Gauss 200th Anniversary, Silver	—	10.00
☐ 1978	5 Deutsche Mark, Federal Republic, Commemorative—Death of Neumann 275th Anniversary, Silver	—	10.00
☐ 1979	5 Deutsche Mark, Federal Republic, Commemorative—Birth of Hahn 100th Anniversary, Cupro-Nickel	—	7.30
☐ 1979	5 Deutsche Mark, Federal Republic, Commemorative—Birth of Hahn 100th Anniversary, Silver	—	RARE
☐ 1979	5 Deutsche Mark, Federal Republic, Commemorative—German Archaeological Institute Anniversary, Silver	—	10.25

DATE	COIN TYPE/VARIETY/METAL	ABP FINE	AVERAGE FINE
☐ 1980	5 Deutsche Mark, Federal Republic, Commemorative—Cologne Cathedral 100th Anniversary, Cupro-Nickel	$4.40	$7.35
☐ 1980	5 Deutsche Mark, Federal Republic, Commemorative—Death of Vogelwelde 750th Anniversary, Cupro-Nickel	4.40	7.35
☐ 1981	5 Deutsche Mark, Federal Republic, Commemorative, Death of von Stein 150th Anniversary, Cupro-Nickel	4.35	7.25
☐ 1981	5 Deutsche Mark, Federal Republic, Commemorative—Death of Lessing 200th Anniversary, Cupro-Nickel	2.80	4.65
☐ 1982	5 Deutsche Mark, Federal Republic, Commemorative—Death of von Goethe 150th Anniversary, Cupro-Nickel	3.60	6.00
☐ 1982	5 Deutsche Mark, Federal Republic, Commemorative, U.N. Environmental Conference 10th Anniversary, Cupro-Nickel	3.60	6.00
☐ 1983	5 Deutsche Mark, Federal Republic, Commemorative—Death of Karl Marx 100th Anniversary, Cupro-Nickel	3.60	6.00
☐ 1983	5 Deutsche, Mark, Federal Republic, Commemorative—Birth of Martin Luther 500th Anniversary, Cupro-Nickel	3.60	6.00
☐ 1984	5 Deutsche Mark, Federal Republic, Commemorative—Birth of Bartholdy 175th Anniversary, Cupro-Nickel	3.60	6.00
☐ 1984	5 Deutsche Mark, Federal Republic, Commemorative—German Customs Union 150th Anniversary, Cupro-Nickel	3.60	6.00
☐ 1985	5 Deutsche Mark, Federal Republic, Commemorative—German Railroad 150th Anniversary, Cupro-Nickel	3.60	6.00
☐ 1985	5 Deutsche Mark, Federal Republic, Commemorative—European Year of Music, Cupro-Nickel	3.60	6.00
☐ 1986	5 Deutsche Mark, Federal Republic, Commemorative—Death of Frederick the Great 200th Anniversary, Cupro-Nickel	3.60	6.00

DATE	COIN TYPE/VARIETY/METAL	ABP FINE	AVERAGE FINE
☐ 1986	5 Deutsche Mark, Federal Republic, Commemorative—Heidenberg University 600th Anniversary, Cupro-Nickel	$2.75	$4.60
☐ 1972	10 Deutsche Mark, Federal Republic, Commemorative—Munich Olympics—Stadium, Silver	—	12.75
☐ 1972	10 Deutsche Mark, Federal Republic, Commemorative—Munich Olympics—Munchen, Silver	—	15.75
☐ 1972	10 Deutsche Mark, Federal Republic, Commemorative—Munich Olympics—Deutschland, Silver	—	15.75
☐ 1972	10 Deutsche Mark, Federal Republic, Commemorative—Munich Olympics—Athletes, Silver	—	15.75
☐ 1972	10 Deutsche Mark, Federal Republic, Commemorative—Munich Olympics—Flame, Silver	—	15.75
☐ 1972	10 Deutsche Mark, Federal Republic, Commemorative—Munich Olympics—Knot, Silver	—	16.75
☐ 1987	10 Deutsche Mark, Federal Republic, Commemorative—Berlin 750 Anniversary, Silver	—	15.75
☐ 1987	10 Deutsche Mark, Commemorative—European Unity, Silver	—	15.75
☐ 1988	10 Deutsche Mark, Commemorative—Death of Zeiss 100th Anniversary, Silver	—	10.75
☐ 1988	10 Deutsche Mark, Federal Republic, Commemorative—Birth of Schopenhauer, Silver	—	12.85
☐ 1989	10 Deutsche Mark, Federal Republic, Commemorative—Port of Hamburg 800th Anniversary, Silver	—	12.85
☐ 1989	10 Deutsche Mark, Federal Republic, Commemorative—Republic 40th Anniversary, Silver	—	15.85
☐ 1989	10 Deutsche Mark, Federal Republic, Commemorative—City of Bonn 200th Anniversary, Silver	—	15.85
☐ 1990	10 Deutsche Mark, Federal Republic, Commemorative—Teutonic Order 800th Anniversary, Silver	—	15.85

DATE	COIN TYPE/VARIETY/METAL	ABP FINE	AVERAGE FINE
☐ 1989	10 Deutsche Mark, Federal Republic, Commemorative—Port of Hamburg 800th Anniversary, Silver	—	$12.75
☐ 1989	10 Deutsche Mark, Federal Republic, Commemorative—Republic 40th Anniversary, Silver	—	12.75
☐ 1989	10 Deutsche Mark, Federal Republic, Commemorative—City of Bonn 2000th Anniversary, Silver	—	12.75
☐ 1990	10 Deutsche Mark, Federal Republic, Commemorative—Teutonic Order 800th Anniversary, Silver	—	12.75
☐ 1990	10 Deutsche Mark, Federal Republic, Commemorative—Death of Barbarossa, Silver	—	12.75
☐ 1991	10 Deutsche Mark, Federal Republic, Commemorative—Brandenburg Gate, Silver	—	12.75
☐ 1992	10 Deutsche Mark, Federal Republic, Commemorative—Civil Pour le Merite Order, Silver	—	16.50
☐ 1992	10 Deutsche Mark, Federal Republic, Commemorative—Kathe Kollwitz Artist, Silver	—	12.75

Germany—Democratic Republic Coinage

Key to Grading: Wheat Head

DATE	COIN TYPE/VARIETY/METAL	ABP FINE	AVERAGE FINE
☐ 1948–1950	1 Pfennig, Democratic Republic, Aluminum	.66	1.10
☐ 1952–1953	1 Pfennig, Democratic Republic, Aluminum	.40	.67

Key to Grading: Wheat Head

DATE	COIN TYPE/VARIETY/METAL	ABP FINE	AVERAGE FINE
☐ 1948–1950	5 Pfennig, Democratic Republic, Aluminum	.82	1.35
☐ 1952–1953	5 Pfennig, Democratic Republic, Aluminum	1.15	1.95

Key to Grading: Wheat Head

DATE	COIN TYPE/VARIETY/METAL	ABP FINE	AVERAGE FINE
☐ 1948–1950	10 Pfennig, Democratic Republic, Aluminum	$.63	$1.05
☐ 1952–1953	10 Pfennig, Democratic Republic, Aluminum	.63	1.05

Key to Grading: Buildings

☐ 1949–1950	50 Pfennig, Democratic Republic, Aluminum-Bronze	1.30	2.15

GREECE

The first coins were used in mid-6th century B.C. Except for a few white-gold coins, early Greek coins were silver. The first gold coins were produced toward the end of the Peloponnesian War. The first bronze coins appeared in the late 5th century B.C. Roman coins were introduced in Greece around the mid-1st century B.C. Bronze coins became more popular, though all coins varied from period to period. Independent coinage was begun in 1827, and the first Greek coinage was struck in Aegina, including copper and silver coins. All had a phoenix rising from the ashes to symbolize the rebirth of the nation and the date of the Greek Revolt (1821). The first decimal coins were used in 1831. The currency today is the euro.

Greece—Type and Democratic Republic Coinage

Key to Grading: Bust

DATE	COIN TYPE/VARIETY/METAL	ABP FINE	AVERAGE FINE
☐ 1869–1870	1 Lepton, Georgios I, Young Head, Copper	$3.80	$6.35
☐ 1878–1879	1 Lepton, Georgios I, Older Head—Second Coinage, Copper	3.80	6.35
☐ 1869	2 Lepta, Georgios I, Young Head, Copper	2.75	4.60
☐ 1878	2 Lepta, Georgios I, Older Head—Second Coinage, Copper	2.75	4.60
☐ 1869–1870	5 Lepta, Georgios I, Young Head, Copper	2.75	4.60
☐ 1878–1882	5 Lepta, Georgios I, Older Head—Second Coinage, Copper	4.95	8.25
☐ 1894–1895	5 Lepta, Georgios I, Third Coinage, Cupro-Nickel	3.10	5.15
☐ 1912	5 Lepta, Georgios I, Third Coinage, Nickel	3.10	5.15

Key to Grading: Bust or Crown

DATE	COIN TYPE/VARIETY/METAL	ABP FINE	AVERAGE FINE
☐ 1954–1971	5 Lepta, Aluminum	.34	.57
☐ 1869–1870	10 Lepta, Georgios I, Young Head, Copper	5.60	9.30
☐ 1878-1882	10 Lepta, Georgios I, Older Head—Second Coinage, Copper	6.85	11.40
☐ 1894–1895	10 Lepta, Georgios I, Third Coinage, Cupro-Nickel	3.40	5.65

Key to Grading: Owl, Bust or Crown

DATE	COIN TYPE/VARIETY/METAL	ABP FINE	AVERAGE FINE
☐ 1912	10 Lepta, Georgios I, Third Coinage, Nickel	$1.75	$2.90
☐ 1922	10 Lepta, Konstantinos I, Second Reign, Aluminum	1.75	2.90
☐ 1954–1971	10 Lepta, Aluminum	.34	.57
☐ 1973–1978	10 Lepta, Aluminum	.34	.57
☐ 1869–1883	20 Lepta, Georgios I, Young Head, Silver	—	8.10
☐ 1893–1895	20 Lepta, Georgios I, Older Head— Third Coinage, Cupro-Nickel	2.80	4.60

Key to Grading: Figure or Bust

DATE	COIN TYPE/VARIETY/METAL	ABP FINE	AVERAGE FINE
☐ 1912	20 Lepta, Georgios I, Third Coinage, Nickel	.44	.74
☐ 1926	20 Lepta, Republic, Cupro-Nickel	.27	.45
☐ 1954–1971	20 Lepta, Aluminum	.27	.45
☐ 1973–1978	20 Lepta, Aluminum	.27	.45
☐ 1868–1883	50 Lepta, Georgios I, Young Head, Silver	—	6.45
☐ 1921	50 Lepta, Konstantinos I, Second Reign, Cupro-Nickel	208.00	346.00
☐ 1926	50 Lepta, Republic, Cupro-Nickel	.50	.84

Key to Grading: Bust

DATE	COIN TYPE/VARIETY/METAL	ABP FINE	AVERAGE FINE
☐ 1954–1965	50 Lepta, Paulos I, Cupro-Nickel	.26	.43
☐ 1973–1986	50 Lepta, Brass	.26	.43
☐ 1868–1883	1 Drachma, Georgios I, Young Head, Silver	—	36.50
☐ 1910–1911	1 Drachma-Georgios I, Third Coinage, Silver	—	9.25
☐ 1926	1 Drachma, Republic, Cupro-Nickel	.66	1.10

Key to Grading: Bust

DATE	COIN TYPE/VARIETY/METAL	ABP FINE	AVERAGE FINE
☐ 1954–1965	1 Drachma, Paulos 1, Cupro-Nickel	$.26	$ .43
☐ 1973–1986	1 Drachma, Brass	.26	.43
☐ 1988–1990	Drachma, Copper	.26	.43
☐ 1868–1883	2 Drachmai, Georgios I, Young Head, Silver	—	70.50
☐ 1911	2 Drachmai, Georgios I, Third Coinage, Silver	—	12.75

☐ 1926	2 Drachmai, Republic, Cupro-Nickel	.39	.65
☐ 1954–1965	2 Drachmai, Paulos I, Cupro-Nickel	.39	.65
☐ 1973–1980	2 Drachmai, Brass	.26	.43
☐ 1982–1986	2 Drachmai, Brass	.26	.43
☐ 1988–1990	2 Drachmai, Copper	.26	.43
☐ 1875–1876	5 Drachmai, Georgios I, Older Head—Second Coinage, Silver	—	62.50
☐ 1876	5 Drachmai, Georgios I, Young Head, Gold	—	460.00

Key to Grading: Eagle, Bust

DATE	COIN TYPE/VARIETY/METAL	ABP FINE	AVERAGE FINE
☐ 1930	5 Drachmai, Republic, Nickel	$.98	$1.65
☐ 1954–1965	5 Drachmai, Paulos I, Cupro-Nickel	.26	.43
☐ 1973–1980	5 Drachmai, Cupro-Nickel	.26	.43
☐ 1982–1990	5 Drachmai, Cupro-Nickel	.26	.43
☐ 1876	10 Drachmai, Georgios I, Young Head, Gold	—	330.00
☐ 1930	10 Drachmai, Republic, Silver	—	10.00

Key to Grading: Bust

DATE	COIN TYPE/VARIETY/METAL	ABP FINE	AVERAGE FINE
☐ 1959–1965	10 Drachmai, Paulos I, Nickel	.26	.43
☐ 1973–1980	10 Drachmai, Cupro-Nickel	.26	.43
☐ 1982–1990	10 Drachmai, Cupro-Nickel	.26	.43
☐ 1876	20 Drachmai, Georgios I, Young Head, Gold	—	190.00
☐ 1884	20 Drachmai, Georgios I, Older Head—Second Coinage, Gold	—	130.00
☐ 1930	20 Drachmai, Republic, Silver	—	10.25
☐ 1935	20 Drachmai, Georgios II, Restoration Commemorative, Gold	—	RARE

Key to Grading: Bust

DATE	COIN TYPE/VARIETY/METAL	ABP FINE	AVERAGE FINE
☐ 1960–1965	20 Drachmai, Paulos I, Silver	—	4.50
☐ 1973–1980	20 Drachmai, Cupro-Nickel	.26	.43
☐ 1982–1988	20 Drachmai, Cupro-Nickel	.26	.43
☐ 1963	30 Drachmai, Paulos I, Centennial of Royal Greek Dynasty, Silver	—	7.50
☐ 1876	50 Drachmai, Georgios I, Older Head—Second Coinage, Gold	—	3000.00
☐ 1980	50 Drachmai, Cupro-Nickel	.39	.65
☐ 1982	50 Drachmai, Cupro-Nickel	.39	.65
☐ 1986–1990	50 Drachmai, Brass	.66	1.10

DATE	COIN TYPE/VARIETY/METAL	ABP FINE	AVERAGE FINE
☐ 1876	100 Drachmai, Georgios I, Older Head—Second Coinage, Gold	—	RARE
☐ 1935	100 Drachmai, Georgios II, Restoration Commemorative, Gold	—	RARE
☐ 1935	100 Drachmai, Georgios II, Restoration Commemorative, Silver	—	1475.00
☐ 1978–1982	100 Drachmai, Silver	14.27	23.50
☐ 1988	100 Drachmai, 28th Chess Olympics, Cupro-Nickel	14.27	23.50
☐ 1990–1991	100 Drachmai, Alexander the Great, Brass	.98	1.65
☐ 1981–1982	250 Drachmai, Pan-European Games, Silver	—	12.10
☐ 1979	500 Drachmai, Common Market Membership, Silver	—	368.50
☐ 1981–1982	500 Drachmai, Pan-European Games, Silver	—	22.50
☐ 1984	500 Drachmai, Olympics—Torch, Silver	—	126.50
☐ 1988	500 Drachmai, 28th Chess Olympics, Silver	—	189.00
☐ 1991	500 Drachmai, XI Mediterranean Games, Silver	—	90.50
☐ 1985	1000 Drachmai, Decade for Women, Silver	—	122.50
☐ 1990	1000 Drachmai, Italian Invasion of Greece—50th Anniversary, Silver	—	136.50
☐ 1981–1982	2500 Drachmai, Pan-European Games, Gold	—	220.50
☐ 1981–1982	5000 Drachmai, Pan-European Games, Gold	—	420.00
☐ 1984	5000 Drachmai, Olympics—Apollo, Gold	—	685.00
☐ 1979	10,000 Drachmai, Common Market Membership, Gold	—	985.00
☐ 1985	10,000 Drachmai, Decade for Women, Gold	—	545.00
☐ 1991	10,000 Drachmai, XI Mediterranean Games, Gold	—	545.00
☐ 1990	20,000 Drachmai, Italian Invasion of Greece—50th Anniversary, Gold	—	2450.00

HUNGARY

The first coins were used in the 3rd century B.C. and were of silver. In the 2nd century B.C., bronze coins were produced. The silver denar appeared in the 11th century, followed by copper denars, gold ducats, and silver talers. The decimal system was established in 1857. Today's currency is the forint.

Hungary—Type Coinage

Key to Grading: Bust

DATE	COIN TYPE/VARIETY/METAL	ABP FINE	AVERAGE FINE
☐ 1882	⁵/₁₀ Krajczar, Franz Joseph, Rev: Shield, Copper	$3.35	$5.60
☐ 1868–1892	1 Krakczar, Franz Joseph, Rev: Shield, Copper	4.20	7.05
☐ 1892–1906	1 Filler, Franz Joseph, Rev: Crown, Bronze	3.35	5.60

Key to Grading: Crown

DATE	COIN TYPE/VARIETY/METAL	ABP FINE	AVERAGE FINE
☐ 1926–1938	1 Filler, Horthy Regency, Crown, Bronze	.34	.57

Key to Grading: Crown

DATE	COIN TYPE/VARIETY/METAL	ABP FINE	AVERAGE FINE
☐ 1892–1915	2 Filler, Franz Joseph, Rev: Crown, Bronze	$.33	$ .55
☐ 1926–1938	2 Filler, Horthy Regency, Crown, Bronze	.28	.46
☐ 1940–1944	2 Filler, Horthy Regency, Stainless Steel	.33	.55
☐ 1946–1947	2 Filler, Republic, Hungarian Arms, Bronze	.28	.46
☐ 1950–1989	2 Filler, Republic, Rev: Spray, Aluminum	.28	.46
☐ 1948–1951	5 Filler, Republic, Rev: Spray, Aluminum	.28	.46

Key to Grading: Bust

DATE	COIN TYPE/VARIETY/METAL	ABP FINE	AVERAGE FINE
☐ 1868–1889	10 Krajczar, Franz Joseph, Rev: Shield, Silver	—	28.50
☐ 1892–1896	10 Filler, Franz Joseph, Rev: Crown, Cupro-Nickel	.49	.81
☐ 1906–1916	10 Filler, Franz Joseph, Rev: Crown, Nickel	.28	.46
☐ 1926–1938	10 Filler, Horthy Regency, Crown, Cupro-Nickel	.57	.95
☐ 1940–1944	10 Filler, Horthy Regency, Stainless Steel	.41	.68

Key to Grading: Bust

DATE	COIN TYPE/VARIETY/METAL	ABP FINE	AVERAGE FINE
☐ 1946–1947	10 Filler, Republic, Dove, Copper-Aluminum	.28	—
☐ 1948–1951	10 Filler, Republic, Rev: Spray, Aluminum	.28	—
☐ 1868–1872	20 Krajczar, Franz Joseph, Rev: Shield, Silver	9.30	15.45
☐ 1892–1894	20 Filler, Franz Joseph, Rev: crown, Cupro-Nickel	1.65	2.75

DATE	COIN TYPE/VARIETY/METAL	ABP FINE	AVERAGE FINE
☐ 1906–1914	20 Filler, Franz Joseph, Rev: Crown, Nickel	$1.65	$2.75
☐ 1926–1938	20 Filler, Horthy Regency, Crown, Cupro-Nickel	2.90	4.80
☐ 1940–1944	20 Filler, Horthy Regency, Center Hole, Stainless Steel	.57	.95
☐ 1946–1947	20 Filler, Republic, Ears of Wheat, Copper-Aluminum	.57	.95
☐ 1948–1950	20 Filler, Republic, Rev: Spray, Aluminum	.57	.95
☐ 1926–1938	50 Filler, Horthy Regency, Crown, Cupro-Nickel	.76	1.25
☐ 1948–1950	50 Filler, Republic, Rev: Spray, Aluminum	.76	1.25

Key to Grading: Bust or Coat of Arms

DATE	COIN TYPE/VARIETY/METAL	ABP FINE	AVERAGE FINE
☐ 1926–1939	1 Pengo, Horthy Regency, Arms, Silver	—	2.30
☐ 1941–1944	1 Pengo, Horthy Regency, Hungarian Arms, Aluminum	.35	.58
☐ 1892–1916	1 Korona, Franz Joseph, Rev: Crown, Silver	—	8.25
☐ 1946–1949	1 Forint, Republic, Hungarian Arms, Aluminum	2.80	4.60
☐ 1929–1938	2 Pengo, Horthy Regency, Madonna, Silver	—	—
☐ 1935	2 Pengo, Horthy Regency, Rakoczi, Silver	—	—
☐ 1935	2 Pengo, Horthy Regency, University of Budapest, Silver	—	—
☐ 1936	2 Pengo, Horthy Regency, Liszt, Silver	—	3.45
☐ 1941	2 Pengo, Horthy Regency, Hungarian Arms, Aluminum	.50	.84
☐ 1912–1914	2 Korona, Franz Joseph, Silver	—	7.40
☐ 1946–1947	2 Forint, Republic, Hungarian Arms, Aluminum	2.95	4.90

Key to Grading: Bust

DATE	COIN TYPE/VARIETY/METAL	ABP FINE	AVERAGE FINE
☐ 1950–1952	2 Forint, Republic, Star With Rays, Hammer and Wheat, Rev: Wreath, Cupro-Nickel	$1.65	$2.75
☐ 1938	5 Pengo, Horthy Regency, Death of St. Stephen 900th Anniversary, Silver	—	11.65
☐ 1943	5 Pengo, Horthy Regency, 75th Birthday of Admiral Horthy, Aluminum	1.80	3.00
☐ 1939	5 Pengo, Horthy Regency, Bust of Admiral Horthy, Silver	—	9.25
☐ 1945	5 Pengo, Horthy Regency, Parliament Building, Aluminum	1.80	3.00
☐ 1948	5 Forint, Republic, Revolution Commemorative, Silver	—	4.25
☐ 1900–1909	5 Korona, Franz Joseph, Rev: Angels Holding Crown, Silver	—	24.50
☐ 1907	5 Korona, Franz Joseph, Jubilee Coronation Scene, Silver	—	39.50
☐ 1930	5 Pengo, Horthy Regency, Bust, Silver	—	10.00
☐ 1946–1947	5 Forint, Republic, Head of Kossuth, Silver	—	6.20
☐ 1948	10 Forint, Republic, Revolution Commemorative, Silver	—	8.25
☐ 1948	20 Forint, Republic, Revolution Commemorative, Silver	—	9.50

ICELAND

Iceland's coinage was originally that of its neighbors, Norway and Denmark. Although an independent republic, Iceland did not have its own currency, the krona, until 1922. In 1944, new denominations were added. In 1981, a new krona was introduced that was equal to 100 old kronur. The currency today is the euro.

Iceland—Type Coinage

Key to Grading: Crown

DATE	COIN TYPE/VARIETY/METAL	ABP FINE	AVERAGE FINE
☐ 1926–1942	1 Eyrir, Kingdom, Bronze	$1.40	$2.35
☐ 1946–1966	1 Eyrir, Republic, Bronze	.33	.55

Key to Grading: Crown

☐ 1926–1942	2 Aurar, Kingdom, Bronze	1.55	2.55

Key to Grading: Crown

DATE	COIN TYPE/VARIETY/METAL	ABP FINE	AVERAGE FINE
☐ 1926–1942	5 Aurar, Kingdom, Bronze	$1.30	$2.20
☐ 1946–1966	5 Aurar, Republic, Bronze	.33	.55
☐ 1981	5 Aurar, Sting Ray, Bronze	.33	.55

Key to Grading: Coat of Arms

☐ 1922–1942	10 Aurar, Kingdom, Cupro-Nickel	3.55	5.90
☐ 1946–1969	10 Aurar, Republic, Cupro-Nickel	.28	.46
☐ 1970–1974	10 Aurar, Republic, Aluminum	.28	.46
☐ 1981	10 Aurar, Cuttlefish, Bronze	.28	.46

Key to Grading: Coat of Arms

☐ 1926–1942	25 Aurar, Kingdom, Cupro-Nickel	1.25	2.10
☐ 1948–1967	25 Aurar, Republic, Cupro-Nickel	.26	.43
☐ 1969–1974	50 Aurar, Republic, Brass	.26	.43
☐ 1981	50 Aurar, Lobster, Bronze	—	—

Key to Grading: Coat of Arms

☐ 1926–1942	1 Krona, Kingdom, Cupro-Nickel	1.75	2.90
☐ 1946	1 Krona, Republic, Aluminum-Bronze	.26	.43
☐ 1957–1975	1 Krona, Republic, Brass	.26	.43
☐ 1976–1980	1 Krona, Republic, Aluminum	.26	.43
☐ 1981–1987	1 Krona, Cod, Cupro-Nickel	.26	.43
☐ 1990	1 Krona, Cod, Stainless Steel	.26	.43

Key to Grading: Coat of Arms

DATE	COIN TYPE/VARIETY/METAL	ABP FINE	AVERAGE FINE
☐ 1925–1940	2 Kronur, Kingdom, Cupro-Nickel	$1.40	$2.30
☐ 1946	2 Kronur, Republic, Aluminum-Bronze	.26	.43
☐ 1958–1966	2 Kronur, Republic, Brass	.26	.43
☐ 1969–1980	5 Kronur, Republic, Cupro-Nickel	.26	.43
☐ 1981–1987	5 Kronur, Dolphins, Cupro-Nickel	.26	.43
☐ 1967–1980	10 Kronur, Republic, Cupro-Nickel	.26	.43
☐ 1984–1987	10 Kronur, Capelins, Cupro-Nickel	.26	.43
☐ 1968	50 Kronur, Sovereignty—50th Anniversary, Nickel	1.15	1.90
☐ 1970–1980	50 Kronur, Parliament, Cupro-Nickel	.26	.43
☐ 1987	50 Kronur, Crab, Brass	.26	.43
☐ 1961	500 Kronur, Sesquicentennial—Sigurdsson, Gold	—	285.00
☐ 1974	500 Kronur, 1st Settlement—1100th Anniversary, Silver	—	22.75
☐ 1986	500 Kronur, Icelandic Bank Notes—100th Anniversary, Silver	—	82.50
☐ 1974	1000 Kronur, 1st Settlement—1100th Anniversary, Silver	—	38.50
☐ 1974	10000 Kronur, 1st Settlement—1100th Anniversary, Gold	—	285.00

INDIA

The first coins were used in the early 4th century B.C., as seen in silver punch-marked coins. Copper-cast coins appeared in 200 B.C., with lead coins in 100 A.D. The silver dramma was in evidence in 190 A.D., and the copper drachmas and gold denara in 350. The gold mohur appeared in the 1500s, and the silver rupees in the 1600s. The copper paisas were in use in the 1800s and the cupro-nickel rupees in 1974. Decimal coins were used in 1957. The currency today is the rupee.

India—Decimal and Non-Decimal Coinage

Key to Grading: Lions

DATE	COIN TYPE/VARIETY/METAL	ABP FINE	AVERAGE FINE
☐ 1957–1962	1 Naye Paisa, Bronze	$.28	$ .46
☐ 1962–1963	1 Naye Paisa, Brass	.28	.46
☐ 1964	1 Paisa, Bronze	.28	.46
☐ 1964	1 Paisa, Brass	.25	.42

Key to Grading: Lions

DATE	COIN TYPE/VARIETY/METAL	ABP FINE	AVERAGE FINE
☐ 1965–1970	1 Paisa, Aluminum	$.28	$ .46

Key to Grading: Lions

DATE	COIN TYPE/VARIETY/METAL	ABP FINE	AVERAGE FINE
☐ 1950–1955	1 Pice, Bronze	.28	.46
☐ 1957–1963	2 Naye Paise, Cupro-Nickel	.28	.46
☐ 1964	2 Paise, Cupro-Nickel	.28	.46

Key to Grading: Lions

DATE	COIN TYPE/VARIETY/METAL	ABP FINE	AVERAGE FINE
☐ 1965–1981	2 Paise, Aluminum	.25	.42

Key to Grading: Lions

DATE	COIN TYPE/VARIETY/METAL	ABP FINE	AVERAGE FINE
☐ 1964–1981	3 Paise, Aluminum	.28	.46
☐ 1950–1955	½ Anna, Cupro-Nickel	.28	.46

Key to Grading: Lions

DATE	COIN TYPE/VARIETY/METAL	ABP FINE	AVERAGE FINE
☐ 1957–1990	5 Naye Paise, Cupro-Nickel	.28	.46
☐ 1964–1966	5 Paise, Cupro-Nickel	.28	.46

Key to Grading: Lions

DATE	COIN TYPE/VARIETY/METAL	ABP FINE	AVERAGE FINE
☐ 1967–1984	5 Paise, Aluminum	$.28	$ .46
☐ 1976	5 Paise, FAO Issues: Food & Work For All, Aluminum	.28	.46
☐ 1977	5 Paise, FAO Issues: Save For Development, Aluminum	.28	.46
☐ 1978	5 Paise, FAO Issues: Food & Shelter For All, Aluminum	.28	.46
☐ 1979	5 Paise, International Year of the Child, Aluminum	.28	.46
☐ 1950–1955	1 Anna, Cupro-Nickel	.28	.46

Key to Grading: Lions

DATE	COIN TYPE/VARIETY/METAL	ABP FINE	AVERAGE FINE
☐ 1957–1963	10 Naye Paise, Cupro-Nickel	.25	.42
☐ 1964–1967	10 Paise, Cupro-Nickel	.25	.42
☐ 1968–1982	10 Paise, Brass	.25	.42

Key to Grading: Figures

DATE	COIN TYPE/VARIETY/METAL	ABP FINE	AVERAGE FINE
☐ 1974	10 Paise, FAO Issue, Brass	.28	.46
☐ 1975	10 Paise, FAO Issue—Woman's Year, Brass	.28	.46
☐ 1976	10 Paise, FAO Issue—Food & Work For All, Brass	.28	.46

DATE	COIN TYPE/VARIETY/METAL	ABP FINE	AVERAGE FINE
☐ 1977	10 Paise, FAO Issue—Save For Development, Brass	$.25	$ .42
☐ 1978	10 Paise, FAO Issue—Food & Shelter For All, Brass	.25	.42
☐ 1979	10 Paise, International Year of the Child, Brass	.25	.42
☐ 1980	10 Paise, Rural Women's Advancement, Brass	.28	.46
☐ 1981	10 Paise, World Food Day, Brass	.28	.46
☐ 1982	10 Paise, IX Asian Games, Brass	.28	.46
☐ 1983–1990	10 Paise, Aluminum	.28	.46
☐ 1950–1955	2 Annas, Cupro-Nickel	.28	.46

Key to Grading: Lions

DATE	COIN TYPE/VARIETY/METAL	ABP FINE	AVERAGE FINE
☐ 1968–1971	20 Paise, Brass	.25	.42
☐ 1969	20 Paise, Aluminum-Bronze	.25	.42
☐ 1970–1971	20 Paise, FAO Issue, Aluminum-Bronze	.25	.42
☐ 1982–1991	20 Paise, Aluminum	.25	.42
☐ 1982	20 Paise, World Food Day, Aluminum	.25	.42
☐ 1983	20 Paise, FAO Issue—Fisheries, Aluminum	.25	.42

Key to Grading: Lions

☐ 1950–1956	¼ Rupee, Nickel	.28	.46

Key to Grading: Lions

DATE	COIN TYPE/VARIETY/METAL	ABP FINE	AVERAGE FINE
☐ 1957–1968	25 Paise, Nickel	$.25	$ .42
☐ 1957–1963	25 Paise, Nickel	.25	.42
☐ 1972–1990	25 Paise, Cupro-Nickel	.25	.42
☐ 1980	25 Paise, Rural Women's Advancement, Cupro-Nickel	.28	.46
☐ 1981	25 Paise, World Food Day, Cupro-Nickel	.28	.46
☐ 1982	25 Paise, IX Asian Games, Cupro-Nickel	.28	.46
☐ 1985	25 Paise, Forestry, Cupro-Nickel	.28	.46
☐ 1988–1991	25 Paise, Rhinoceros, Stainless Steel	.28	.46

Key to Grading: Lions

DATE	COIN TYPE/VARIETY/METAL	ABP FINE	AVERAGE FINE
☐ 1950–1956	½ Rupee, Nickel	.25	.42
☐ 1964–1983	50 Paise, Nickel	.25	.42
☐ 1964	50 Paise, Nehru Death, Nickel	.25	.42
☐ 1969	50 Paise, Centennial—Mahatma Gandhi, Nickel	.25	.42
☐ 1972–1973	50 Paise, Independence— 25th Anniversary, Cupro-Nickel	.25	.42

DATE	COIN TYPE/VARIETY/METAL	ABP FINE	AVERAGE FINE
☐ 1973	50 Paise, FAO Issue—Grow More Food, Cupro-Nickel	.25	.42
☐ 1982	50 Paise, National Integration, Cupro-Nickel	.25	.42
☐ 1984–1990	50 Paise, Cupro-Nickel	.25	.42
☐ 1985	50 Paise, Indira Gandhi—Death, Cupro-Nickel	.28	.46
☐ 1985	50 Paise, Reserve Bank of India— Golden Jubilee, Cupro-Nickel	.28	.46
☐ 1986	50 Paise, FAO—Fisheries, Cupro-Nickel	.28	.46

DATE	COIN TYPE/VARIETY/METAL	ABP FINE	AVERAGE FINE
☐ 1988–1997	50 Paise, Parliament Building, Stainless Steel	$.33	$.55
☐ 1950–1954	1 Rupee, Nickel	.88	1.45
☐ 1962–1974	1 Rupee, Nickel	.72	1.20

Key to Grading: Lions

DATE	COIN TYPE/VARIETY/METAL	ABP FINE	AVERAGE FINE
☐ 1964	1 Rupee, Nehru Death, Nickel	.42	.70
☐ 1969	1 Rupee, Mahatma Gandhi Centennial, Nickel	.42	.70
☐ 1975–1991	1 Rupee, Cupro-Nickel	.25	.42
☐ 1985	1 Rupee, Youth Year, Cupro-Nickel	.25	.42
☐ 1987	1 Rupee, FAO—Small Farmers, Cupro-Nickel	.25	.42
☐ 1989	1 Rupee, FAO—Food & Environment, Cupro-Nickel	.25	.42
☐ 1989	1 Rupee, Nehru's Birth—100th Anniversary, Cupro-Nickel	.25	.42
☐ 1990	1 Rupee, SAARC Year—Care For the Girl Child, Cupro-Nickel	.25	.42
☐ 1990	1 Rupee, ICDS—15th Anniversary, Cupro-Nickel	.25	.42
☐ 1990	1 Rupee, FAO Farming Scene, Cupro-Nickel	.28	.46
☐ 1990	1 Rupee, Dr. Ambedker, Cupro-Nickel	.28	.46
☐ 1991	1 Rupee, Rajiv Gandhi, Cupro-Nickel	.28	.46
☐ 1991	1 Rupee, Parliamentary Conference, Cupro-Nickel	.28	.46
☐ 1982	2 Rupees, IX Asian Games, Cupro-Nickel	.28	.46
☐ 1982–1992	2 Rupees, National Integration, Cupro-Nickel	.25	.42
☐ 1985	2 Rupees, Reserve Bank of India—Golden Jubilee, Cupro-Nickel	$18.90	31.50 Proof
☐ 1985	5 Rupees, Indira Gandhi Death, Cupro-Nickel	.25	.42
☐ 1989	5 Rupees, Nehru's Birth—100th Anniversary, Cupro-Nickel	.49	.81

DATE	COIN TYPE/VARIETY/METAL	ABP FINE	AVERAGE FINE
☐ 1969	10 Rupees, Centennial Birth of Mahatma Gandhi, Silver	—	$3.40

Key to Grading: Lions

DATE	COIN TYPE/VARIETY/METAL	ABP FINE	AVERAGE FINE
☐ 1970	10 Rupees, FAO Issue, Silver	—	6.50
☐ 1972	10 Rupees, Independence—25th Anniversary, Silver	—	4.25
☐ 1973	10 Rupees, FAO Issue, Silver	—	6.50
☐ 1974	10 Rupees, FAO Issue, Cupro-Nickel	1.30	2.20
☐ 1975	10 Rupees, FAO—Women's Year, Cupro-Nickel	1.30	2.20
☐ 1976	10 Rupees, FAO—Food & Work For All, Cupro-Nickel	1.30	2.20
☐ 1977	10 Rupees, FAO—Save For Development, Cupro-Nickel	1.05	1.75
☐ 1978	10 Rupees, FAO—Food & Shelter For All, Cupro-Nickel	1.05	1.75
☐ 1979	10 Rupees, International Year of the Child, Cupro-Nickel	1.05	1.75
☐ 1980	10 Rupees, Rural Women's Advancement, Cupro-Nickel	1.65	2.75
☐ 1981	10 Rupees, World Food Day, Cupro-Nickel	1.65	2.75
☐ 1982	10 Rupees, IX Asian Games, Cupro-Nickel	1.65	2.75
☐ 1982	10 Rupees, National Integration, Cupro-Nickel	1.20	2.00
☐ 1985	10 Rupees, Youth Year, Cupro-Nickel	9.75	16.20
☐ 1985	10 Rupees, Reserve Bank of India—Golden Jubilee, Cupro-Nickel	9.75	16.20

DATE	COIN TYPE/VARIETY/METAL	ABP FINE	AVERAGE FINE
☐ 1973	20 Rupees, FAO Issue, Silver	—	$12.75
☐ 1985	20 Rupees, Death of Indira Gandhi, Cupro-Nickel	15.60	26.00
☐ 1986	20 Rupees, FAO Fisheries, Cupro-Nickel	15.60	26.00
☐ 1987	20 Rupees, FAO—Small Farmers, Cupro-Nickel	15.60	26.00
☐ 1989	20 Rupees, Nehru's Birth—100th Anniversary, Cupro-Nickel	15.60	26.00
☐ 1974	50 Rupees, FAO Issue, Silver	—	11.25
☐ 1975	50 Rupees, FAO—Women's Year, Silver	—	36.50
☐ 1976	50 Rupees, FAO—Food & Work For All, Silver	—	36.50
☐ 1977	50 Rupees, FAO—Save For Development, Silver	—	36.50
☐ 1978	50 Rupees, FAO—Food & Shelter For All, Silver	—	36.50
☐ 1979	50 Rupees, International Year of the Child, Silver	—	36.50
☐ 1980	100 Rupees, Rural Women's Advancement, Silver	—	38.50
☐ 1981	100 Rupees, International Year of the Child, Silver	—	48.50
☐ 1981	100 Rupees, World Food Day, Silver	—	45.50
☐ 1982	100 Rupees, National Integration, Silver	—	54.50
☐ 1982	100 Rupees, IX Asian Games, Silver	—	48.50
☐ 1985	100 Rupees, Youth Year, Silver	—	68.50
☐ 1985	100 Rupees, Death of Indira Gandhi, Silver	—	68.50
☐ 1985	100 Rupees, Reserve Bank of India—Golden Jubilee, Silver	—	76.50
☐ 1986	100 Rupees, FAO—Fisheries, Silver	—	68.50
☐ 1987	100 Rupees, FAO—Small Farmers, Silver	—	68.50
☐ 1989	100 Rupees, Nehru's Birth—100th Anniversary, Silver	—	72.50

IRELAND

The first coins—pennies—appeared in the late 10th century, followed by farthings and halfpennies around 1190. In the mid-1400s, groats were issued, and shillings in the mid-1500s. In the mid-17th century, the Inchiquin was formed. In 1649, half crowns and crowns were issued. Cupro-nickel replaced silver in 1951, and a decimal currency system was set up in 1971. Today Ireland uses the euro.

Ireland—Type Coinage

Key to Grading: Harp

DATE	COIN TYPE/VARIETY/METAL	ABP FINE	AVERAGE FINE
Farthing-Copper			
☐ 1806		$5.90	$9.75
Half Penny-Copper			
☐ 1805		7.80	13.00
☐ 1822		9.75	16.20
☐ 1823		9.75	16.20
Penny-Copper			
☐ 1805		13.00	21.65
☐ 1822		11.70	19.50
☐ 1823		11.70	19.50
Bank of Ireland Tokens			
5 Pence-Silver			
☐ 1805		—	35.00
☐ 1806		—	55.00
10 Pence-Silver			
☐ 1805		—	50.00
☐ 1806		—	42.50
☐ 1813		—	35.50
30 Pence-Silver			
☐ 1808		—	68.50
6 Shilling			
☐ 1804		—	450.00

Key to Grading: Harp

DATE	COIN TYPE/VARIETY/METAL	ABP FINE	AVERAGE FINE
Farthing-Bronze			
☐ 1928		$.55	$ .92
☐ 1930		.80	1.35
☐ 1931		4.20	7.05
☐ 1932		4.55	7.60
☐ 1933		.82	1.35
☐ 1935		4.55	7.60
☐ 1936		4.55	7.60
☐ 1937		.55	.92
☐ 1939		.55	.92
☐ 1940		1.64	2.75
☐ 1941		.52	.86
☐ 1943		.52	.86
☐ 1944		.55	.92
☐ 1946		.42	.70
☐ 1949		.66	1.10
☐ 1953		.36	.60
☐ 1959		.36	.60
☐ 1966		.36	.60

Key to Grading: Harp

Half Penny Bronze

DATE	ABP FINE	AVERAGE FINE
☐ 1928	.88	1.45
☐ 1933	5.20	8.65
☐ 1935	2.60	4.35
☐ 1937	1.15	1.90
☐ 1939	9.75	16.20
☐ 1940	1.15	1.90
☐ 1941	.36	.60
☐ 1942	.36	.60
☐ 1943	.42	.70

DATE	COIN TYPE/VARIETY/METAL	ABP FINE	AVERAGE FINE
☐ 1946		$.98	$1.65
☐ 1949		.42	.70
☐ 1953		.42	.70
☐ 1964		.20	.33
☐ 1965		.29	.48
☐ 1966		.20	.33
☐ 1967		.29	.48

Key to Grading: Harp

Penny-Bronze

DATE	COIN TYPE/VARIETY/METAL	ABP FINE	AVERAGE FINE
☐ 1928		.52	.85
☐ 1931		.66	1.10
☐ 1933		1.30	2.20
☐ 1935		.52	.86
☐ 1937		.52	.86
☐ 1940		3.25	5.40
☐ 1941		.42	.70
☐ 1942		.33	.55
☐ 1943		.72	1.20
☐ 1946		.36	.60
☐ 1948		.36	.60
☐ 1949		.36	.60
☐ 1950		.36	.60
☐ 1952		.36	.60
☐ 1962		.72	1.20
☐ 1963		.36	.60
☐ 1964		.36	.60
☐ 1965		.36	.60
☐ 1966		.36	.60
☐ 1967		.36	.60
☐ 1968		.36	.60

Key to Grading: Harp
3 Pence-Nickel

DATE	COIN TYPE/VARIETY/METAL	ABP FINE	AVERAGE FINE
☐ 1928		$.66	$1.10
☐ 1933		2.95	4.85
☐ 1934		.98	1.65
☐ 1935		2.95	4.85
☐ 1939		9.70	16.20
☐ 1940		1.65	2.75
Copper-Nickel			
☐ 1942		.31	.55
☐ 1943		.66	1.10
☐ 1946		1.15	1.90
☐ 1948		1.15	1.90
☐ 1949		1.34	.60
☐ 1950		.36	.60
☐ 1953		.36	.60
☐ 1956		.36	.60
☐ 1961		.36	.60
☐ 1962		.36	.60
☐ 1963		.36	.60
☐ 1964		.26	.43
☐ 1965		.36	.60
☐ 1966		.36	.60
☐ 1967		.36	.60
☐ 1968		.20	.33

Key to Grading: Harp
6 Pence-Nickel

DATE	COIN TYPE/VARIETY/METAL	ABP FINE	AVERAGE FINE
☐ 1928		.66	1.10
☐ 1934		1.15	1.90
☐ 1935		.98	1.65
☐ 1939		.91	1.50
☐ 1940		.91	1.50
Copper-Nickel			
☐ 1942		.91	1.50
☐ 1945		1.95	3.25
☐ 1946		1.65	2.75
☐ 1947		1.40	2.30
☐ 1948		1.40	2.30
☐ 1949		1.50	2.50

DATE	COIN TYPE/VARIETY/METAL	ABP FINE	AVERAGE FINE
☐ 1950		$1.15	$1.89
☐ 1952		.55	.92
☐ 1953		.55	.92
☐ 1955		1.32	2.20
☐ 1956		.98	1.65
☐ 1958		.82	1.30
☐ 1959		.49	.81
☐ 1960		.49	.81
☐ 1961		.42	.70
☐ 1962		.42	.70
☐ 1963		.42	.70
☐ 1964		.36	.60
☐ 1966		.36	.60
☐ 1967		.36	.60
☐ 1968		.36	.60
☐ 1969		.36	.60

Key to Grading: Harp

Shilling-Silver

DATE	COIN TYPE/VARIETY/METAL	ABP FINE	AVERAGE FINE
☐ 1928		3.25	5.40
☐ 1930		5.50	9.20
☐ 1931		3.90	6.50
☐ 1933		5.20	8.65
☐ 1935		3.25	5.40
☐ 1937		9.75	16.20
☐ 1939		3.25	5.40
☐ 1940		3.25	5.40
☐ 1941		4.55	7.55
☐ 1942		3.90	6.50

Copper-Nickel

DATE	COIN TYPE/VARIETY/METAL	ABP FINE	AVERAGE FINE
☐ 1951		.66	1.10
☐ 1954		.66	1.10
☐ 1955		.98	1.65
☐ 1959		.36	.60
☐ 1962		.49	.81
☐ 1963		.42	.70
☐ 1964		.42	.70
☐ 1966		.42	.70
☐ 1968		.42	.70

Key to Grading: Harp

DATE	COIN TYPE/VARIETY/METAL	ABP FINE	AVERAGE FINE
Florin-Silver			
☐ 1928		—	$15.00
☐ 1930		—	22.00
☐ 1931		—	26.00
☐ 1933		—	20.00
☐ 1934		—	32.00
☐ 1935		—	18.00
☐ 1937		—	38.00
Florin-Silver			
☐ 1939		—	15.00
☐ 1940		—	16.00
☐ 1941		—	16.00
☐ 1942		—	20.00
☐ 1943		—	2400.00
Copper-Nickel			
☐ 1951		1.15	1.90
☐ 1954		.98	1.65
☐ 1955		1.15	1.90
☐ 1959		.55	.92
☐ 1961		.66	1.10
☐ 1962		.49	.81
☐ 1963		.42	.70
☐ 1964		.42	.70
☐ 1965		.49	.81
☐ 1966		.49	.81
☐ 1968		.42	.70
Half Crown-Silver			
☐ 1928		—	18.00
☐ 1930		—	24.00
☐ 1931		—	38.00
☐ 1933		—	22.00
☐ 1934		—	20.00
☐ 1937		—	150.00
☐ 1939		—	20.00
☐ 1940		—	20.00
☐ 1941		—	22.00
☐ 1942		—	22.00
☐ 1943		—	550.00

DATE	COIN TYPE/VARIETY/METAL	ABP FINE	AVERAGE FINE

Copper-Nickel

DATE		ABP FINE	AVERAGE FINE
☐ 1951		$2.60	$4.35
☐ 1954		1.80	3.00
☐ 1955		1.65	2.70
☐ 1959		1.65	2.70
☐ 1961		1.15	1.90
☐ 1962		.66	1.10
☐ 1963		.88	1.45
☐ 1964		.88	1.45
☐ 1966		.66	1.10
☐ 1967		.82	1.35

10 Shillings-Silver

DATE		ABP FINE	AVERAGE FINE
☐ 1966		—	28.50

Decimal Coinage

½ Penny-Bronze

DATE		ABP FINE	AVERAGE FINE
☐ 1971		.30	.49
☐ 1975		.30	.49
☐ 1976		.30	.49
☐ 1978		.30	.49
☐ 1980		.30	.49
☐ 1982		.30	.49
☐ 1985		.30	.49
☐ 1986 Proof only		9.70	16.15

Penny-Bronze

DATE		ABP FINE	AVERAGE FINE
☐ 1971		.30	.49
☐ 1974		.30	.49
☐ 1975		.30	.49
☐ 1976		.30	.49
☐ 1978		.30	.49
☐ 1980		.30	.49
☐ 1982		.30	.49
☐ 1985		.30	.49

DATE	COIN TYPE/VARIETY/METAL	ABP FINE	AVERAGE FINE
☐ 1986		$.26	$ .43
☐ 1988		.26	.43
☐ 1990		.26	.43
Copper-Plated Steel			
☐ 1990		.26	.43
☐ 1992		.26	.43
☐ 1993		.26	.43

Key to Grading: Harp
2 Pence-Bronze

DATE	COIN TYPE/VARIETY/METAL	ABP FINE	AVERAGE FINE
☐ 1971		.29	.48
☐ 1975		.36	.60
☐ 1976		.29	.48
☐ 1978		.29	.48
☐ 1979		.29	.48
☐ 1980		.29	.48
☐ 1982		.29	.48
☐ 1985		.29	.48
☐ 1986		.29	.48
☐ 1988		.29	.48
☐ 1990		.29	.48
Copper-Plated Steel			
☐ 1988		.23	.38
☐ 1992		.23	.38

Key to Grading: Harp
5 Pence-Copper-Nickel

DATE	COIN TYPE/VARIETY/METAL	ABP FINE	AVERAGE FINE
☐ 1969		.39	.65
☐ 1970		.29	.48
☐ 1971		.29	.48
☐ 1974		.29	.48
☐ 1975		.29	.48
☐ 1976		.29	.48
☐ 1978		.29	.48
☐ 1980		.29	.48

DATE	COIN TYPE/VARIETY/METAL	ABP FINE	AVERAGE FINE
☐ 1982		$.29	$ .48
☐ 1985		.29	.48
☐ 1986		.33	.55
☐ 1990		.20	.33
☐ 1992		.33	.55
Reduced Size			
☐ 1992		.23	.38
☐ 1993		.39	.65
☐ 1994		.20	.33
☐ 1995		.29	.48

Key to Grading: Harp

10 Pence-Copper-Nickel

DATE	COIN TYPE/VARIETY/METAL	ABP FINE	AVERAGE FINE
☐ 1969		.49	.81
☐ 1971		.82	1.35
☐ 1973		.49	.81
☐ 1974		.82	1.35
☐ 1975		.33	.55
☐ 1976		.49	.81
☐ 1978		.33	.55
☐ 1980		.39	.65
☐ 1982		.33	.55
☐ 1985		.42	.70
☐ 1986		1.95	3.25
Reduced Size			
☐ 1993		.23	.38

20 Pence-Nickel-Bronze

DATE	COIN TYPE/VARIETY/METAL	ABP FINE	AVERAGE FINE
☐ 1986		1.50	2.45
☐ 1988		1.50	2.45
☐ 1990		.82	1.35
☐ 1992		.82	1.35
☐ 1993		1.50	2.40
☐ 1994		1.50	2.40

Key to Grading: Harp

DATE	COIN TYPE/VARIETY/METAL	ABP FINE	AVERAGE FINE
50 Pence-Copper-Nickel			
☐ 1970		$2.10	$3.50
☐ 1971		2.10	3.50
☐ 1974		1.80	3.00
☐ 1975		1.50	2.45
☐ 1976		.98	1.65
☐ 1977		1.30	2.20
☐ 1978		1.30	2.20
☐ 1979		1.30	2.20
☐ 1981		.82	1.35
☐ 1982		1.30	2.20
☐ 1983		.82	1.35
☐ 1986		3.25	5.40
☐ 1988		.82	1.35
50 Pence-Copper-Nickel			
Dublin—Millennium			
☐ 1988		2.60	4.36
Pound-Copper-Nickel			
☐ 1990		3.25	5.40
Mint Sets			
☐ 1940 & 1950s Mixed Dates in Green-and-Blue Boxes			
Ireland-Issued Sets with Mixed			
Dates to Represent Types			
		42.20	70.30
☐ 1966		19.45	32.45
☐ 1971		7.80	13.00
☐ 1978		5.20	8.65
☐ 1982		5.20	8.65
Proof Sets			
☐ 1928 (8) coins		292.00	486.70
☐ 1951 (3) coins		2425.00	4043.00
☐ 1966 (2) coins		58.40	97.35
☐ 1971 (6) coins		14.30	23.85
☐ 1986 (7) coins		292.00	486.70
☐ 1928–1935	Sixpence, Saorstat Eireann, Nickel	1.65	2.75
☐ 1939–1942	Sixpence, Eire, Nickel	1.65	2.75
☐ 1942–1968	Sixpence, Eire, Cupro-Nickel	.52	.86

ISRAEL

The first coins were used in the 5th century B.C. In 300 B.C. silver tetradrachms and gold staters were produced. Bronze coins appeared in 26 A.D. The copper fals was in evidence in the 600s and 700s, followed by the gold bezant and the base-silver denier. Bronze mils, cupro-nickel prutot, and the silver lira became popular in the 20th century. Today's currency is the livre.

Israel—Type Commemorative and Monetary Reform Coinage

Key to Grading: Wreath

DATE	COIN TYPE/VARIETY/METAL	ABP FINE	AVERAGE FINE
☐ 1948–1949	1 Prutah, Hebrew Date 5709 Anchor, Aluminum	$.48	$ .80

Key to Grading: Lire

DATE	COIN TYPE/VARIETY/METAL	ABP FINE	AVERAGE FINE
☐ 1949	5 Prutot, Hebrew Date 5709 Harp, Bronze	$.28	$ .46

Key to Grading: Pitcher

☐ 1949	10 Prutot, Hebrew Date 5709 Amphora, Bronze	.28	.46
☐ 1952	10 Prutot, Hebrew Date 5712, Aluminum	.28	.46

Key to Grading: Wheat Heads

☐ 1960–1980	1 Agora, Aluminum	.28	.46
☐ 1973	1 Agora, 25th Anniversary of Bank of Israel, Nickel	.28	.46
☐ 1973	1 Agora, 25th Anniversary of Independence, Aluminum	.88	1.45

Key to Grading: Grapes

☐ 1948–1949	25 Mils, Hebrew Date 5708–09 Grape Clusters, Aluminum	20.80	34.65

Key to Grading: Grapes

DATE	COIN TYPE/VARIETY/METAL	ABP FINE	AVERAGE FINE
☐ 1949	25 Prutot, Hebrew Date 5709 Grape Clusters, Cupro-Nickel	$.25	$ .42
☐ 1954	25 Prutot, Hebrew Date 5714, Nickel-clad Steel	.25	.42

Key to Grading: Leaves

| ☐ 1949–1954 | 50 Prutot, Hebrew Date 5709–14 Fig Leaves, Cupro-Nickel | .82 | 1.35 |
| ☐ 1954 | 50 Prutot, Hebrew Date 5714, Nickel-clad Steel | .28 | .46 |

Key to Grading: Design

☐ 1960–1975	5 Agorot, Aluminum-Bronze	1.15	1.90
☐ 1973	5 Agorot, 25th Anniversary of Independence, Cupro-Nickel	1.15	1.90
☐ 1973	5 Agorot, 25th Anniversary of Bank of Israel, Nickel	1.15	1.90
☐ 1974–1979	5 Agorot, Cupro-Nickel	.49	.81
☐ 1976–1979	5 Agorot, Aluminum	.25	.42

Key to Grading: Palm Tree

DATE	COIN TYPE/VARIETY/METAL	ABP FINE	AVERAGE FINE
☐ 1949–1955	100 Prutot, Hebrew Date 5709 Palm Tree, Cupro-Nickel	$.45	$ .76
☐ 1954	100 Prutot, Hebrew Date 5714, Nickel-clad Steel	.38	.63

Key to Grading: Palm Tree

☐ 1960–1977	10 Agorot, Aluminum-Bronze	.23	.38
☐ 1973	10 Agorot, 25th Anniversary of Independence, Cupro-Nickel	.38	.63
☐ 1973	10 Agorot, 25th Anniversary of Bank of Israel, Nickel	.82	1.35
☐ 1974–1979	10 Agorot, Cupro-Nickel	.26	.43
☐ 1977–1980	10 Agorot, Aluminum	.26	.43

Key to Grading: Wheat Head

| ☐ 1949 | 250 Prutot, Hebrew Date 5709 Ears of Wheat, Silver | 1.60 | 2.70 |
| ☐ 1949 | 250 Prutot, Hebrew Date 5709 Ears of Wheat, Cupro-Nickel | .82 | 1.35 |

Key to Grading: Lire

DATE	COIN TYPE/VARIETY/METAL	ABP FINE	AVERAGE FINE
☐ 1960–1979	25 Agorot, Aluminum-Bronze	$.23	$ .39
☐ 1974–1979	25 Agorot, Cupro-Nickel	.49	.81
☐ 1974–1979	25 Agorot, 25th Anniversary of Bank of Israel, Nickel	.82	1.35

Key to Grading: Pomegranates

☐ 1949	500 Prutot, Hebrew Date 5709 Pomegranates, Silver	—	8.25
☐ 1961–1962	1/2 Lira, Feast of Purim, Cupro-Nickel	1.80	3.00

Key to Grading: Menorah

☐ 1963	1/2 Lira, 25th Anniversary of Bank of Israel, Nickel	1.04	1.75
☐ 1963	1/2 Lira, 25th Anniversary of Independence, Cupro-Nickel	.36	.60
☐ 1963–1979	1/2 Lira, Cupro-Nickel	.26	.43
☐ 1958	1 Lira, Law Is Light, Cupro-Nickel	.26	.43
☐ 1960	1 Lira, Henrietta Szold—Hadassa Medical Center, Cupro-Nickel	10.40	17.35
☐ 1960	1 Lira, Deganya, Cupro-Nickel	1.30	2.20

DATE	COIN TYPE/VARIETY/METAL	ABP FINE	AVERAGE FINE
☐ 1961	1 Lirah, Heroism & Sacrifice, Cupro-Nickel	$3.50	$5.90
☐ 1962	1 Lirah, Chanuka—Italian Lamp, Cupro-Nickel	5.75	9.60
☐ 1963	1 Lirah, Chanuka—North African Lamp, Cupro-Nickel	5.75	9.60

Key to Grading: Menorah

☐ 1963–1967	1 Lira, Cupro-Nickel	.28	.46

Key to Grading: Design on Coin

☐ 1958	5 Lirot, Tenth Anniversary of Republic, Silver	—	10.75
☐ 1959	5 Lirot, Ingathering of Exiles, Silver	—	9.25
☐ 1960	5 Lirot, Dr. Theodore Herzi, Silver	—	20.00
☐ 1961	5 Lirot, Bar Mitzvahr, Silver	—	30.25
☐ 1962	50 Lirot, 10th Anniversary— Death of Chaim Weizman, Gold	—	339.00
☐ 1962	5 Lirot, Industrialization of the Negev, Silver	—	52.75
☐ 1963	5 Lirot, Seafaring, Silver	—	445.00
☐ 1964	5 Lirot, Israel Museum, Silver	—	62.50

Key to Grading: Lion's Mane

DATE	COIN TYPE/VARIETY/METAL	ABP FINE	AVERAGE FINE
☐ 1978–1979	5 Lirot, Cupro-Nickel	$.66	$1.10
☐ 1960	20 Lirot, Dr. Theodore Herzi, Gold	—	208.00
☐ 1964	50 Lirot, 10th Anniversary—Bank of Israel, Gold	—	422.50
☐ 1962	100 Lirot, 10th Anniversary—Death of Chaim Weizman, Gold	—	585.50

ITALY

The first coins were used in the 6th century B.C., with an unusual technique called incuse, involving the use of similar designs on both sides of the coin. The early coins were silver, but from about 440 B.C. bronze coins came into evidence, then gold coins appeared toward the end of the 5th century. Julius Caesar's head appeared on coins in 44 B.C., right before his assassination. Around 31 B.C. the Roman coinage system had denominations in gold, silver, and bronze that survived for the next 200 years. The decimal system was set up in 1804, and today's currency is the euro.

Italy—Type and Republic Coinage

☐ 1861–1867	1 Centesimo, Vittorio Emanuel, Copper	$2.80	$4.60
☐ 1895–1900	1 Centesimo, Umberto I, Copper	1.40	2.30
☐ 1902–1908	1 Centesimo, Vittorio III, Bronze	2.80	4.60
☐ 1908–1918	1 Centesimo, Vittorio III, Bronze	1.40	2.30

Key to Grading: Bust

DATE	COIN TYPE/VARIETY/METAL	ABP FINE	AVERAGE FINE
☐ 1861–1867	2 Centesimi, Vittorio Emanuel, Copper	$.82	$1.35
☐ 1895–1900	2 Centesimi, Umberto I, Copper	.82	1.35
☐ 1903–1908	2 Centesimi, Vittorio III, Bronze	.82	1.35
☐ 1908–1917	2 Centesimi, Vittorio III, Bronze	1.30	2.20
☐ 1861–1867	5 Centesimi, Vittorio Emanuel, Copper	1.30	2.20
☐ 1895–1896	5 Centesimi, Umberto I, Copper	12.65	21.10
☐ 1908–1918	5 Centesimi, Vittorio III, Bronze	1.15	1.90

Key to Grading: Bust

☐ 1919–1937	5 Centesimi, Vittorio III, Bronze	.42	.70
☐ 1936–1939	5 Centesimi, Vittorio III, Bronze	.49	.81
☐ 1939–1943	5 Centesimi, Vittorio III, Aluminum-Bronze	.42	.70

Key to Grading: Bust

☐ 1862–1867	10 Centesimi, Vittorio Emanuel, Copper	2.95	4.90
☐ 1893–1894	10 Centesimi, Umberto I, Copper	2.95	4.90
☐ 1908	10 Centesimi, Vittorio III, Bronze	—	Rare
☐ 1911	10 Centesimi, Vittorio III, 50th Anniversary of Kingdom, Bronze	2.60	4.35
☐ 1919–1937	10 Centesimi, Vittorio III, Bronze	.66	1.10
☐ 1939–1943	10 Centesimi, Vittorio III, Aluminum-Bronze	.66	1.10
☐ 1863–1867	20 Centesimi, Vittorio Eman, Silver	—	9.75

Key to Grading: Crown

DATE	COIN TYPE/VARIETY/METAL	ABP FINE	AVERAGE FINE
☐ 1894–1895	20 Centesimi, Umberto I, Cupro-Nickel	$.42	$ .70
☐ 1908–1935	20 Centesimi, Vittorio III, Nickel	.49	.80
☐ 1918–1920	20 Centesimi, Vittorio III, Cupro-Nickel	.39	.65
☐ 1936–1938	20 Centesimi, Vittorio III, Nickel	13.00	21.65
☐ 1939–1943	20 Centesimi, Vittorio III, Stainless Steel	.42	.70
☐ 1902–1903	25 Centesimi, Vittorio III, Nickel	15.60	26.00

Key to Grading: Bust

DATE	COIN TYPE/VARIETY/METAL	ABP FINE	AVERAGE FINE
☐ 1861–1863	50 Centesimi, Vittorio Eman, Silver	—	36.50
☐ 1863–1867	50 Centesimi, Vittorio Eman, Silver	—	10.00
☐ 1889–1892	50 Centesimi, Umberto I, Silver	—	52.50
☐ 1919–1935	50 Centesimi, Vittorio III, Nickel	2.61	4.36
☐ 1936–1938	50 Centesimi, Vittorio III, Nickel	15.59	25.99
☐ 1939–1943	50 Centesimi, Vittorio III, Stainless Steel	—	2.50
☐ 1861–1867	1 Lira, Vittorio Emanuele II, Silver	—	37.50
☐ 1863	1 Lira, Vittorio Emanuele, Silver	—	37.50
☐ 1883–1900	1 Lira, Umberto I, Silver	—	6.00
☐ 1901–1907	1 Lira, Vittorio III, Silver	—	10.00
☐ 1908–1913	1 Lira, Vittorio III, Silver	—	10.00
☐ 1915–1917	1 Lira, Vittorio III, Silver	—	6.75

Key to Grading: Figure

DATE	COIN TYPE/VARIETY/METAL	ABP FINE	AVERAGE FINE
☐ 1922–1935	1 Lira, Vittorio III, Nickel	.82	1.40
☐ 1936–1938	1 Lira, Vittorio III, Nickel	12.65	21.10
☐ 1939–1943	1 Lira, Vittorio III, Stainless Steel	.33	.55
☐ 1946–1950	1 Lira, Republic, Aluminum	3.90	6.50
☐ 1951–1995	1 Lira, Republic, Aluminum	.23	.38
☐ 1861–1863	2 Lire, Vittorio Emanuele I, Silver	—	24.50
☐ 1863	2 Lire, Vittorio Emanuele, Silver	—	24.50

DATE	COIN TYPE/VARIETY/METAL	ABP FINE	AVERAGE FINE
☐ 1881–1899	2 Lire, Umberto I, Silver	—	$9.85
☐ 1901–1907	2 Lire, Vittorio III, Silver	—	24.50
☐ 1908–1912	2 Lire, Vittorio III, Silver	—	12.25
☐ 1911	2 Lire, Vittorio III, 50th Anniversary of Kingdom, Silver	—	33.75
☐ 1914–1917	2 Lire, Vittorio III, Silver	—	9.85

Key to Grading: Bust

DATE	COIN TYPE/VARIETY/METAL	ABP FINE	AVERAGE FINE
☐ 1923–1935	2 Lire, Vittorio III, Nickel	3.25	5.41
☐ 1936–1938	2 Lire, Vittorio III, Nickel	13.00	21.65
☐ 1939–1943	2 Lire, Vittorio III, Stainless Steel	.39	.65
☐ 1946–1950	2 Lire, Republic, Aluminum	8.45	14.10
☐ 1953–1995	2 Lire, Republic, Aluminum	.39	.65
☐ 1861	5 Lire, Vittorio Emanuele I, Italian Unification, Silver	—	715.00
☐ 1861–1878	5 Lire, Vittorio Emanuele I, Silver	—	23.20
☐ 1863–1865	5 Lire, Vittorio Emanuele, Gold	—	13.10
☐ 1878–1879	5 Lire, Umberto I, Silver	—	60.75
☐ 1901	5 Lire, Vittorio III, Silver	—	RARE
☐ 1911	5 Lire, Vittorio III, 50th Anniversary of Kingdom, Silver	—	340.00
☐ 1914	5 Lire, Vittorio III, Silver	—	965.00

Key to Grading: Bust

DATE	COIN TYPE/VARIETY/METAL	ABP FINE	AVERAGE FINE
☐ 1926–1935	5 Lire, Vittorio III, Silver	—	9.85
☐ 1936–1941	5 Lire, Vittorio III, Silver	—	24.50
☐ 1946–1950	5 Lire, Republic, Aluminum	.66	1.10
☐ 1951–1995	5 Lire, Republic, Aluminum	.66	1.10
☐ 1861	10 Lire, Vittorio Emanuele, Gold	—	1850.00
☐ 1863–1865	Vittorio III, Gold	—	192.50
☐ 1910–1927	10 Lire, Vittorio III, Gold	—	995.00
☐ 1926–1934	10 Lire, Vittorio III, Silver	—	68.50

Key to Grading: Bust

DATE	COIN TYPE/VARIETY/METAL	ABP FINE	AVERAGE FINE
☐ 1946–1950	10 Lire, Republic, Aluminum	$.52	$ .87

Key to Grading: Wings

DATE	COIN TYPE/VARIETY/METAL	ABP FINE	AVERAGE FINE
☐ 1951–1995	10 Lire, Republic, Aluminum	.26	.43
☐ 1923	20 Lire, Vittorio III, Anniversary of Fascist Government, Gold	—	386.00
☐ 1928	20 Lire, Vittorio III, End of WWI 10th Anniversary, Gold	—	230.00
☐ 1879–1897	20 Lire, Umberto I, Gold	—	230.00
☐ 1902–1910	20 Lire, Vittorio III, Gold	—	500.00
☐ 1910–1927	20 Lire, Vittorio III, Gold	—	500.00
☐ 1927–1934	20 Lire, Vittorio III, Silver	—	185.00
☐ 1936–1941	20 Lire, Vittorio III, Silver	—	438.00

Key to Grading: Bust

DATE	COIN TYPE/VARIETY/METAL	ABP FINE	AVERAGE FINE
☐ 1957–1959	20 Lire, Republic, Aluminum-Bronze	.26	.43
☐ 1864	50 Lire, Vittorio Emanuele, Gold	—	RARE
☐ 1884–1891	50 Lire, Umberto I, Gold	—	1575.00
☐ 1910–1927	50 Lire, Vittorio III, Gold	—	995.00
☐ 1911	50 Lire, Vittorio III, 50th Anniversary of Kingdom, Gold	—	693.50

DATE	COIN TYPE/VARIETY/METAL	ABP FINE	AVERAGE FINE
☐ 1931–1933	50 Lire, Vittorio III, Gold	—	$368.00
☐ 1936	50 Lire, Vittorio III, Gold	—	1275.00

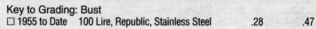

Key to Grading: Bust

DATE	COIN TYPE/VARIETY/METAL	ABP FINE	AVERAGE FINE
☐ 1954–2001	50 Lire, Republic, Stainless Steel	.52	.86
☐ 1864–1878	100 Lire, Vittorio Emanuele, Gold	—	2800.00
☐ 1880–1891	100 Lire, Umberto I, Gold	—	1550.00
☐ 1903–1905	100 Lire, Vittorio III, Gold	—	2375.00
☐ 1910–1927	100 Lire, Vittorio III, Gold	—	2175.00
☐ 1923	100 Lire, Vittorio III, Anniversary of Fascist Government, Gold	—	1250.00
☐ 1925	100 Lire, Vittorio III, 25th Anniversary of Reign & 10th Anniversary of WWI, Gold	—	2375.00
☐ 1931–1933	100 Lire, Vittorio III, Gold	—	295.00
☐ 1936	100 Lire, Vittorio III, Gold	—	2200.00
☐ 1937	100 Lire, Vittorio III, Gold	—	RARE
☐ 1974	100 Lire, Republic, Birth of Marconi 100th Anniversary, Stainless Steel	.28	.47
☐ 1979	100 Lire, Republic, F.A.O. Issue, Stainless Steel	.28	.47
☐ 1981	100 Lire, Republic, Livorno Naval Academy Centennial, Stainless Steel	.28	.47

Key to Grading: Bust

DATE	COIN TYPE/VARIETY/METAL	ABP FINE	AVERAGE FINE
☐ 1955 to Date	100 Lire, Republic, Stainless Steel	.28	.47

Key to Grading: Bust

DATE	COIN TYPE/VARIETY/METAL	ABP FINE	AVERAGE FINE
☐ 1980	200 Lire, Republic, World Food Day, Aluminum-Bronze	$.28	$ .47
☐ 1980	200 Lire, Republic, F.A.O. Issue & International Woman's Year, Aluminum-Bronze	.28	.47

Key to Grading: Bust

DATE	COIN TYPE/VARIETY/METAL	ABP FINE	AVERAGE FINE
☐ 1988	200 Lire, Republic, University of Bologna 900th Anniversary, Silver	10.65	17.75
☐ 1989	200 Lire, Republic, Taranto Naval Yards, Bronzital	.20	.33
☐ 1989	200 Lire, Republic, Christopher Columbus, Silver	—	22.75
☐ 1989	200 Lire, Republic, Soccer, Silver	—	22.75
☐ 1990	200 Lire, Republic, State Council Building, Bronzital	.26	.43
☐ 1991	200 Lire, Republic, Italian Flora & Fauna, Silver	7.45	12.40
☐ 1992	200 Lire, Republic, Genoa Stamp Exposition, Aluminum-Bronze	.26	.43

Key to Grading: Design of Coin

DATE	COIN TYPE/VARIETY/METAL	ABP FINE	AVERAGE FINE
☐ 1958–1989	500 Lire, Republic, Silver	—	$6.50
☐ 1961	500 Lire, Republic, Italian Unification Centennial, Silver	—	9.00
☐ 1965	500 Lire, Republic, Birth of Alighieri 700th Anniversary, Silver	—	9.00
☐ 1974	500 Lire, Republic, Birth of Marconi 100th Anniversary, Silver	—	24.25
☐ 1975	500 Lire, Republic, Birth of Michelangelo 500th Anniversary, Silver	—	24.25
☐ 1981	500 Lire, Republic, Birth of Virgil 2000th Anniversary, Silver	—	24.25
☐ 1982	500 Lire, Republic, Death of Garibaldi 100th Anniversary, Silver	—	24.25
☐ 1982–1995	500 Lire, Republic, Dual Metal	.33	.55
☐ 1982	500 Lire, Republic, Galileo Galilei, Silver	—	24.25
☐ 1984	500 Lire, Republic, Common Market Presidency, Silver	—	36.75
☐ 1984	500 Lire, Republic, Los Angeles Olympics, Silver	—	33.50
☐ 1985	500 Lire, Republic, Etruscan Culture, Silver	—	33.50
☐ 1985	500 Lire, Republic, European Year of Music, Silver	—	36.50
☐ 1985	500 Lire, Republic, Birth of Manzoni 200th Anniversary, Silver	—	39.00
☐ 1985	500 Lire, Republic, Duino College, Silver	—	37.25
☐ 1986	500 Lire, Republic, Birth of Donatello 600th Anniversary, Silver	—	48.50
☐ 1986	500 Lire, Republic, Soccer Championship, Silver	—	52.25
☐ 1986	500 Lire, Republic, Year of Peace, Silver	—	52.25
	Championship, Silver	—	24.25
☐ 1987	500 Lire, Republic, Leopardi, Silver	—	12.10
☐ 1987	500 Lire, Republic, Year of the Family, Silver	—	37.25

DATE	COIN TYPE/VARIETY/METAL	ABP FINE	AVERAGE FINE
☐ 1988	500 Lire, Republic, Constitution 40th Anniversary, Silver	—	$22.50
☐ 1988	500 Lire, Republic, University of Bologna 900th Anniversary, Silver	—	89.50
☐ 1988	500 Lire, Republic, Death of Bosco 100th Anniversary, Silver	—	89.50
☐ 1988	500 Lire, Republic, Summer Olympics—Seoul, Silver	—	56.75
☐ 1989	500 Lire, Republic, Soccer, Silver	—	23.50
☐ 1989	500 Lire, Republic, Christopher Columbus, Silver	—	30.50
☐ 1989	500 Lire, Republic, Fight Against Cancer, Silver	—	68.50
☐ 1990	500 Lire, Republic, Birth of Tizian 500th Anniversary, Silver	—	82.50
☐ 1990	500 Lire, Republic, Columbus— Discovery of America, Silver	—	28.50
☐ 1990	500 Lire, Republic, Ponte Milvio 2100th Anniversary, Silver	—	56.50
☐ 1990	500 Lire, Republic, EEC Council Presidency, Silver	—	36.50
☐ 1991	500 Lire, Republic, Discovery of America, Silver	—	63.00
☐ 1991	500 Lire, Republic, Flora & Fauna, Silver	—	65.00
☐ 1992	500 Lire, Republic, Olympics Building & Track, Silver	—	26.50
☐ 1992	500 Lire, Republic, Christopher Columbus, Silver	—	62.75
☐ 1992	500 Lire, Republic, Rossini, Silver	—	62.75
☐ 1992	500 Lire, Republic, Flora & Fauna, Silver	—	62.75
☐ 1992	500 Lire, Republic, Lorenzo De'Medici, Silver	—	38.00
☐ 1970	1000 Lire, Republic, Centennial of Rome, Silver	—	22.50

JAPAN

The first coins were used in 708 and were silver and copper imitations of Chinese cast-bronze coins. Copper coins were used for the next 250 years. After 958 no copper coins were issued, and by the end of the 10th century they were no longer in use. Imported Chinese bronze coins began circulating in the 13th century. Rectangular-shaped coins were in use in the 17th and 18th centuries. The first decimal coins were produced in 1870. Today's currency is the yen.

Japan—Type Coinage

Key to Grading: Dragon

DATE	COIN TYPE/VARIETY/METAL	ABP FINE	AVERAGE FINE
☐ 1873–1888	½ Sen, Obv: Sun With Rays, Rev: Value in Wreath, Bronze	$3.00	$4.90
☐ 1916–1919	5 Rin, Kiri Crest, Bronze	.55	.92
☐ 1873–1915	1 Sen, Obv: Sun With Rays, Rev: Value in Wreath, Bronze	1.65	2.75

Key to Grading: Flowers

DATE	COIN TYPE/VARIETY/METAL	ABP FINE	AVERAGE FINE
☐ 1916–1937	1 Sen Kiri Crest, Bronze	$.29	$ .48
☐ 1941–1943	1 Sen, Mt. Fuji, Aluminum	.29	.48
☐ 1873–1884	2 Sen, Obv: Sun With Rays, Rev: Value in Wreath, Bronze	1.65	2.75
☐ 1870–1871	5 Sen, Obv: Coiled Dragon, Rev: Sun, Silver	—	338.00
☐ 1873–1880	5 Sen, Obv: Coiled Dragon, Rev: Value in Wreath, Silver	—	38.50
☐ 1897–1905	5 Sen, Obv: Sun With Rays, Rev: Value in Wreath, Cupro-Nickel	8.15	13.55

Key to Grading: Chrysanthemum

DATE	COIN TYPE/VARIETY/METAL	ABP FINE	AVERAGE FINE
☐ 1917–1932	5 Sen, Petaled Flower Around Hole, Cupro-Nickel	2.60	4.35
☐ 1940–1942	5 Sen, Kite, Aluminum	1.50	2.50
☐ 1870–1872	10 Sen, Obv: Coiled Dragon, Rev: Sun, Silver	—	38.50
☐ 1873–1906	10 Sen, Obv: Coiled Dragon, Rev: Value in Wreath, Silver	—	12.25
☐ 1907–1917	10 Sen, Obv: Sun With Rays, Rev: Value in Wreath, Silver	—	4.50
☐ 1920–1932	10 Sen, Petaled Flower Around Hole, Cupro-Nickel	.29	.48
☐ 1940–1943	10 Sen, Chrysanthemum, Aluminum	.29	.48
☐ 1946	10 Sen, Phoenix, Rev: Rice Plants, Aluminum	.26	.43
☐ 1870–1872	20 Sen, Obv: Coiled Dragon, Rev: Sun, Silver	—	38.50
☐ 1873–1905	20 Sen, Obv: Coiled Dragon, Rev: Value in Wreath, Silver	—	141.50
☐ 1906–1911	20 Sen, Obv: Sun With Rays, Rev: Value in Wreath, Silver	—	10.25
☐ 1870–1871	50 Sen, Obv: Coiled Dragon, Rev: Sun, Silver	—	58.25

Key to Grading: Dragon

DATE	COIN TYPE/VARIETY/METAL	ABP FINE	AVERAGE FINE
☐ 1873–1905	50 Sen, Obv: Coiled Dragon, Rev: Value in Wreath, Silver	—	$28.50
☐ 1906–1917	50 Sen, Obv: Sun With Rays, Rev: Value in Wreath, Silver	—	9.00
☐ 1946	50 Sen, Phoenix, Rev: Rice Plants, Bronze	.42	.70
☐ 1947–1948	50 Sen, Chrysanthemum & Blossoms, Brass	.42	.70
☐ 1870–1872	Yen, Obv: Coiled Dragon, Rev: Sun, Silver	—	268.50

Key to Grading: Dragon

☐ 1874–1915	Yen, Obv: Coiled Dragon, Rev: Value in Wreath, Silver	—	—
☐ 1948–1950	Yen, Blossoms, Brass	.49	.81
☐ 1875–1878	Trade Dollar, Obv: Dragon, Rev: Wreath, Silver	—	538.50

LUXEMBOURG

The first coins were used in the late 10th century and were silver deniers. In the 1300s, silver sterlings were in evidence, followed by silver double gros and bronze centimes. The silver franc was popular in the mid-1900s, and the cupro-nickel franc in the latter 1900s. Decimal coins were used in 1854. The currency today is the euro.

Luxembourg—Type Coinage

DATE	COIN TYPE/VARIETY/METAL	ABP FINE	AVERAGE FINE
☐ 1854–1908	2¹/₂ Centimes, Bronze	$3.10	$5.15
☐ 1854–1860	5 Centimes, Bronze	3.60	6.00
☐ 1901	5 Centimes, Adolphe, Cupro-Nickel	.33	.55

Key to Grading: Bust

DATE	COIN TYPE/VARIETY/METAL	ABP FINE	AVERAGE FINE
☐ 1908	5 Centimes, Guillaume IV, Cupro-Nickel	.33	.55
☐ 1915	5 Centimes, "Holed," Zinc	.85	1.45
☐ 1918–1922	5 Centimes, Iron	1.30	2.20
☐ 1924	5 Centimes, Charlotte (1st), Cupro-Nickel	.33	.55
☐ 1930	5 Centimes, Charlotte (1st), Bronze	.33	.55

Key to Grading: Crown or Bust

DATE	COIN TYPE/VARIETY/METAL	ABP FINE	AVERAGE FINE
☐ 1854–1870	10 Centimes, Bronze	$2.95	$4.90
☐ 1901	10 Centimes, Adolphe, Cupro-Nickel	.33	.55
☐ 1915	10 Centimes, "Holed," Zinc	1.10	1.80
☐ 1918–1923	10 Centimes, Iron	2.80	4.60
☐ 1924	10 Centimes, Charlotte (1st), Cupro-Nickel	.29	.48
☐ 1930	10 Centimes, Charlotte (1st), Bronze	.29	.48
☐ 1918–1922	25 Centimes, Iron	1.95	3.25
☐ 1927	25 Centimes, Charlotte (1st), Cupro-Nickel	.36	.60

Key to Grading: Crown or Bust

☐ 1946–1947	25 Centimes, Charlotte (2nd) Letzeburg, Bronze	.29	.48
☐ 1954–1972	25 Centimes, Charlotte (2nd) Letzeburg, Aluminum	.29	.48
☐ 1980	25 Centimes, Charlotte (2nd), Silver	7.45	12.40
☐ 1924–1935	1 Franc, Charlotte (1st), Nickel	.29	.48

Key to Grading: Crown

DATE	COIN TYPE/VARIETY/METAL	ABP FINE	AVERAGE FINE
☐ 1939	1 Franc, Charlotte (1st), Letzeburg, Bronze	$.33	$ .55
☐ 1946–1947	1 Franc, Charlotte (2nd), Letzeburg, Cupro-Nickel	.16	.27
☐ 1952	1 Franc, Charlotte (2nd), Letzeburg, Cupro-Nickel	.26	.43
☐ 1953–1964	1 Franc, Charlotte (2nd), Letzeburg, Cupro-Nickel	.26	.43
☐ 1965–1984	1 Franc, Charlotte (2nd), Millennium Commemorative, Cupro-Nickel	.26	.43
☐ 1980	1 Franc, Charlotte (2nd), Millennium Commemorative, Silver	7.75	12.90
☐ 1986–1987	1 Franc, Charlotte (2nd), Cupro-Nickel	.39	.66
☐ 1988–2001	1 Franc, Charlotte (2nd), Nickel-Steel	.39	.66
☐ 1924	2 Francs, Charlotte (1st), Nickel	.82	1.37
☐ 1929	5 Francs, Charlotte (1st), Silver	1.30	2.10
☐ 1949	5 Francs, Charlotte (2nd), Letzeburg, Cupro-Nickel	.39	.66
☐ 1962	5 Francs, Charlotte (2nd), Cupro-Nickel	.39	.66
☐ 1971–1981	5 Francs, Jean (2nd), Cupro-Nickel	.39	.66

Key to Grading: Bust

☐ 1986–2001	5 Francs, Jean (2nd), Brass	.33	.55
☐ 1929	10 Francs, Charlotte (1st), Silver	2.65	4.40
☐ 1971–1980	10 Francs, Jean (2nd), Nickel	.33	.55
☐ 1946	20 Francs, Charlotte (2nd), 600th Anniversary Death of John the Blind, Silver	—	7.50
☐ 1980	20 Francs, Jean (2nd), Silver	—	40.00

Key to Grading: Bust

DATE	COIN TYPE/VARIETY/METAL	ABP FINE	AVERAGE FINE
☐ 1980–1983	20 Francs, John (2nd), Bronze	$.98	$1.63
☐ 1989	20 Francs, John (2nd), 150th Anniversary of Grand Duchy, Gold	—	212.00
☐ 1990–1991	20 Francs, John (2nd), Bronze	—	—
☐ 1946	50 Francs, Charlotte (2nd), 600th Anniversary Death of John the Blind, Silver	—	12.25
☐ 1987–2001	50 Francs, John (2nd), Nickel	.82	1.37
☐ 1946	100 Francs, John (2nd), 600th Anniversary Death of John the Blind, Silver	—	21.00
☐ 1963	100 Francs, Charlotte (2nd), Silver	—	21.00
☐ 1963	250 Francs, Charlotte (2nd), Millennium Commemorative, Silver	—	62.50

MALTA

The first coins, which were bronze, were used in the 3rd century B.C. The silver tari was in evidence in the 1500s, followed by the copper grano. In the early 1700s, the gold zecchini was in use, and the silver tari appeared in the mid-1700s. The bronze 10 cents was in use in the 1970s since decimal coins came into use in 1972. The currency today is the euro.

Malta—Type Coinage

Key to Grading: Bust

DATE	COIN TYPE/VARIETY/METAL	ABP FINE	AVERAGE FINE
☐ 1827	¹/₃ Farthing, Head of George IV, Copper	$8.45	$14.00
☐ 1835	¹/₃ Farthing, Head of William IV, Copper	5.20	8.60
☐ 1844	¹/₃ Farthing, Head of Victoria, Copper	22.10	36.80
☐ 1866–1885	¹/₃ Farthing, Value in Wreath, Bronze	4.20	7.00
☐ 1902	¹/₃ Farthing, Head of Edward VII, Bronze	4.20	7.00
☐ 1913	¹/₃ Farthing, Head of George V, Bronze	4.20	7.00

MEXICO

The first coins—the silver Spanish reales—were used in 1536. At first coins were struck in silver, gold, and copper but copper was soon discontinued. The silver reales were popular in the 1800s, followed by the brass quartillas, gold pesos, bronze centavos, and silver pesos in the 1900s. The decimal system was established in 1863 and the currency today is the peso.

Mexico—Type and Republic Coinage

Key to Grading: Eagle
Republic 1863–1905
1 Centavo Copper Seated Liberty

☐ 1863	Round 3 Reed Edge	10.50	17.85
☐ 1863	Round 3 Plain Edge	10.40	17.30
☐ 1863	Flat Top 3	10.70	17.85

1 Centavo SLP Mint Mark

☐ 1863		10.70	17.85

1 Centavo Standing Eagle

☐ 1875	Mint Mark As	—	Rare
☐ 1876	Mint Mark As	87.60	146.00
☐ 1880	Mint Mark As	13.00	21.60
☐ 1874–1897	Mint Mark Cn	13.00	21.60

DATE		ABP FINE	AVERAGE FINE
☐ 1879–1891	Mint Mark Do	$8.45	$14.00
☐ 1872–1890	Mint Mark Ga	5.20	8.60
☐ 1875	Mint Mark Ho	324.00	540.75
☐ 1876	Mint Mark Ho	38.95	64.90
☐ 1880–1881	Mint Mark Ho	7.80	13.00
☐ 1869–1897	Mint Mark Mo	3.90	6.50
☐ 1872–1875	Mint Mark Oa	287.40	479.00
☐ 1871–1891	Mint Mark Pi	7.80	13.00
☐ 1872–1881	Mint Mark Zs	5.20	8.60

1 Centavo Copper/Nickel

☐ 1882		5.65	9.45
☐ 1883		1.15	1.90

1 Centavo Copper

☐ 1898		3.25	5.40

1 Centavo Copper

☐ 1899		120.05	200.10
☐ 1900–1905		14.30	23.85

Emperor Maximillian 1864–1867

1 Centavo Copper

☐ 1864		24.70	41.10

Estados Unidos Mexicanos

1 Centavo Bronze 20mm

Key to Grading: Eagle

☐ 1905		2.80	4.85
☐ 1906 Narrow Date		.85	1.40
☐ 1906 Wide Date		.85	1.40
☐ 1910		.98	1.65
☐ 1911		.85	1.40
☐ 1912		.85	1.40
☐ 1913		.85	1.40
☐ 1914		.85	1.40
☐ 1915		8.60	14.35
☐ 1916		29.20	48.65
☐ 1920		12.95	21.60
☐ 1921		3.25	5.40
☐ 1922		7.15	11.90
☐ 1923		.82	1.35

DATE	ABP FINE	AVERAGE FINE
☐ 1924/3	$43.50	$72.50
☐ 1924	2.80	4.60
☐ 1925	2.80	4.60
☐ 1926	1.30	2.20
☐ 1927/6	16.20	27.05
☐ 1927	.36	.60
☐ 1928	.52	.87
☐ 1929	.52	.87
☐ 1930	.52	.87
☐ 1933	.26	.43
☐ 1934	.26	.43
☐ 1935–1942	.26	.43
☐ 1943	.26	.43
☐ 1944–1949	.26	.43

1 Centavo Zapata Issue 16mm

☐ 1915	11.70	19.50

1 Centavo Brass 16mm

☐ 1950–1969	.26	.43

1 Centavo Brass Reduced Size 13mm

☐ 1970	.26	.43
☐ 1972	.26	.43
☐ 1972/2	.45	.76
☐ 1973	1.50	2.50

Republic 1863–1904
2 Centavos Copper/Nickel

☐ 1882–1883	1.50	2.50

Estados Unidos Mexicanos
2 Centavos Bronze 25mm

Key to Grading: Eagle

☐ 1905	81.10	135.20
☐ 1906 Inverted 6 Wide Date	22.70	37.85
	3.25	5.40
☐ 1906 Narrow Date	4.60	7.60
☐ 1920	5.20	8.65
☐ 1921	3.25	5.40
☐ 1922	194.40	324.00
☐ 1924	9.75	16.20

DATE	ABP FINE	AVERAGE FINE
☐ 1925	$2.85	$4.75
☐ 1926	.80	1.35
☐ 1927	.66	1.10
☐ 1928	.66	1.10
☐ 1929	38.95	64.90
☐ 1935	2.90	4.85
☐ 1939	.50	.85
☐ 1941	.50	.85

2 Centavos Bronze Zapata Issue

DATE	ABP FINE	AVERAGE FINE
☐ 1915	4.55	7.60

Republic 1863–1904

5 Centavos Republic Silver

DATE		ABP FINE	AVERAGE FINE
☐ 1868–1870	Mint Mark Ca	—	58.50
☐ 1863	Mint Mark SLP	—	115.00

5 Centavos Republic Silver Cap & Rays

DATE		ABP FINE	AVERAGE FINE
☐ 1867–1868	Mint Mark Mo	—	57.50
☐ 1868	Mint Mark P	—	57.50
☐ 1869	Mint Mark P	—	338.00

5 Centavos Republic Silver Standing Eagle

DATE		ABP FINE	AVERAGE FINE
☐ 1874–1895	Mint Mark As	—	37.50
☐ 1871–1895	Mint Mark CH, Ca	—	7.50
☐ 1873	M. Crude Date Mint Mark CH, Ca	—	168.00
☐ 1871–1897	Mint Mark Cn	—	6.00
☐ 1871P	Mint Mark Cn	—	246.00
☐ 1890D	Mint Mark Cn	—	246.00
☐ 1874–1881	Mint Mark Do	—	246.00
☐ 1887–1894	Mint Mark Do	—	6.00
☐ 1877–1893	Mint Mark Ga	—	10.00
☐ 1877–1893	Mint Mark Go	—	6.00
☐ 1874–1878	Mint Mark Ho	—	168.00
☐ 1880–1894	Mint Mark Ho	—	9.00
☐ 1869–1897	Mint Mark Mo	—	6.00
☐ 1873M	Mint Mark Mo	—	75.50
☐ 1890E	Mint Mark Oa	—	Rare
☐ 1890N	Mint Mark Oa	—	136.50
☐ 1869–1886	Mint Mark Pi	—	115.50
☐ 1887–1893	Mint Mark Pi	—	3.00
☐ 1870–1876	Mint Mark Zs	—	128.50
☐ 1877–1897	Mint Mark Zs	—	6.00

5 Centavos Republic Copper-Nickel

DATE		ABP FINE	AVERAGE FINE
☐ 1882		.66	1.10
☐ 1883		18.20	30.30

5 Centavos Republic Silver

DATE		ABP FINE	AVERAGE FINE
☐ 1898–1904	Mint Mark Cn	—	6.00
☐ 1898–1900	Mint Mark Go	—	3.45

DATE		ABP FINE	AVERAGE FINE
☐ 1898–1904	Mint Mark Mo	$1.65	$2.75
☐ 1898–1904	Mint Mark Zs	2.93	4.90

Emperor Maximillian 1864–1867
5 Centavos Silver

☐ 1864–1866	Mint Mark G	32.45	54.10
☐ 1864–1866	Mint Mark M	16.30	27.05
☐ 1864	Mint Mark P	71.40	118.95
☐ 1865	Mint Mark Z	16.20	27.05

Estados Unidos Mexicanos
5 Centavos Nickel

☐ 1905		3.25	5.40
☐ 1906/5		6.50	10.80
☐ 1906		2.50	4.10
☐ 1907		2.50	4.10
☐ 1909		2.60	4.35
☐ 1910		2.45	4.15
☐ 1911 Wide Date		2.60	4.35
☐ 1911 Narrow Date		2.45	4.10
☐ 1912 Small	Mint Mark	64.90	108.15
☐ 1912 Large	Mint Mark	53.25	88.70
☐ 1913		1.65	2.70
☐ 1914		1.65	2.70

5 Centavos Bronze

☐ 1914		—	—
☐ 1915		2.60	4.35
☐ 1916		11.05	18.45
☐ 1917		38.95	64.90
☐ 1918		16.20	27.05
☐ 1919		88.90	148.20
☐ 1920		3.90	6.50
☐ 1921		6.50	10.80
☐ 1924		35.70	59.50
☐ 1925		4.55	7.60
☐ 1926		4.55	7.60
☐ 1927		2.60	4.35
☐ 1928 Small Date		18.20	30.30
☐ 1928 Large Date		7.80	13.00
☐ 1930 Small Square in O		35.70	59.50
☐ 1930 Oval in O		3.25	5.41
☐ 1931		324.00	541.00
☐ 1933		1.65	2.70
☐ 1934		1.65	2.70
☐ 1935		.80	1.35

5 Centavos Copper-Nickel

☐ 1936		.25	.42

DATE		ABP FINE	AVERAGE FINE
☐ 1937		$ .26	$ .43
☐ 1938		2.90	4.80
☐ 1940		.36	.60
☐ 1942		.49	.81
5 Centavo Bronze Josefa Dominguez			
☐ 1942		8.45	14.10
☐ 1943		.29	.48
☐ 1944		.29	.48
☐ 1945		.29	.48
☐ 1946		.29	.48
☐ 1951		.29	.48
☐ 1952		.49	.81
☐ 1953		.33	.55
☐ 1954		.26	.43
☐ 1955		.69	1.15
5 Centavo Copper/Nickel "White Josefa"			
☐ 1950		.33	.55
5 Centavo Bra40			
☐ 1954 w/Dot		3.25	5.40
☐ 1954 w/o Dot		4.90	8.15
☐ 1955		.26	.43
☐ 1956–1969		.26	.43
5 Centavos Copper-Nickel			
☐ 1960		116.80	194.70
☐ 1962		116.80	194.70
5 Centavos Brass Reduced Size 18mm			
☐ 1970–1976		.23	.38
5 Centavos Stainless Steel			
☐ 1992–1999		.23	.38
Republic 1863–1904			
10 Centavos Silver			
☐ 1864–1870	Mint Mark Ca	—	45.50
☐ 1863	Mint Mark SLP	—	126.50
10 Centavos Silver Cap & Rays			
☐ 1867–1868	Mint Mark Mo	19.50	32.45
☐ 1868–1869	Mint Mark P	—	76.75
10 Centavos Silver			
☐ 1874–1893	Mint Mark As	6.49	10.82
☐ 1871–1895	Mint Mark CH, Ca	—	7.50
☐ 1871–1887	Mint Mark Cn	—	59.50
☐ 1888–1896	Mint Mark Cn	—	9.25
☐ 1878–1886	Mint Mark Do	—	131.00
☐ 1887–1895	Mint Mark Do	—	8.45
☐ 1871–1895	Mint Mark Ga	—	8.45
☐ 1869–1897	Mint Mark Go	—	8.45

DATE		ABP FINE	AVERAGE FINE
☐ 1875S	Mint Mark Go	—	$424.50
☐ 1880S	Mint Mark Go	—	152.50
☐ 1874–1893	Mint Mark Ho	—	12.25
☐ 1868–1897	Mint Mark Mo	—	12.25
☐ 1889E	Mint Mark Oa	—	346.50
☐ 1890E	Mint Mark Oa	—	154.50
☐ 1890N	Mint Mark Oa	—	Rare
☐ 1869–1886	Mint Mark Pi	—	168.00
☐ 1886–1893	Mint Mark Pi	—	9.00
☐ 1885C	Mint Mark Pi	—	Rare
☐ 1870–1877	Mint Mark Zs	—	192.50
☐ 1878–1897	Mint Mark Zs	—	9.00

10 Centavos Silver Restyled Eagle

☐ 1898–1904	Mint Mark Cn	—	7.50
☐ 1898M	Mint Mark Cn	—	100.00
☐ 1898–1900	Mint Mark Go	—	8.50
☐ 1898–1905	Mint Mark Mo	—	8.50
☐ 1898–1905	Mint Mark Zs	—	8.50

Emperor Maximillian 1864–1867
10 Centavos Silver

☐ 1864–1865	Mint Mark G	—	52.50
☐ 1864–1866	Mint Mark M	—	52.50
☐ 1864	Mint Mark P	—	115.00
☐ 1865	Mint Mark Z	—	52.75

Estados Unidos Mexicanos
10 Centavos Silver .0643 ASW

Key to Grading: Eagle

☐ 1905	—	6.60
☐ 1906	—	6.60
☐ 1907/6	—	37.75
☐ 1907	—	3.15
☐ 1909	—	8.00
☐ 1910/00	—	9.25
☐ 1910	—	8.10
☐ 1911 Wide Date	—	8.10
☐ 1911 Narrow Date	—	9.25
☐ 1912	—	9.25

DATE	ABP FINE	AVERAGE FINE
☐ 1912 Low 2	—	$9.25
☐ 1913/2	—	9.25
☐ 1913	—	9.25
☐ 1914	—	9.25
10 Centavos Silver Reduced Size		
☐ 1919	—	8.45
10 Centavos Bronze		
☐ 1919	6.50	10.80
☐ 1920	3.25	5.40
☐ 1921	17.55	29.25
☐ 1935	3.90	6.50
10 Centavos Silver .0384 ASW		
☐ 1925/15	—	20.50
☐ 1925/3	—	12.25
☐ 1925	—	6.20
☐ 1926/16	—	18.50
☐ 1926	—	7.65
☐ 1927	—	7.65
☐ 1928	—	3.10
☐ 1930	—	6.60
☐ 1933	—	2.15
☐ 1934	—	2.15
☐ 1935	—	2.15
10 Centavos Copper-Nickel		
☐ 1936–1946	.33	.55
☐ 1937	1.30	2.20
☐ 1938	.52	.86
10 Centavos Benito Juarez		
☐ 1955	.29	.48
☐ 1956	.29	.48
☐ 1957–1967	.29	.48
10 Centavos Copper/Nickel 5 Rows of Corn		
☐ 1974–1980	.26	.43
☐ 1977	.33	.55
☐ 1980/79	.98	1.65
☐ 1980	.33	.55
10 Centavos 5½ Rows of Corn		
☐ 1974–1980	.26	.43
10 Centavos Stainless Steel		
☐ 1992–1996	.26	.43
Republic 1863–1904		
20 Centavos Silver		
☐ 1898–1904 Mint Mark Cn	—	12.25
☐ 1898–1900 Mint Mark Go	—	12.25
☐ 1898–1905 Mint Mark Mo	—	6.10
☐ 1898–1905 Mint Mark Zs	—	12.25

DATE	ABP FINE	AVERAGE FINE

Estados Unidos Mexicanos
20 Centavos Silver

Key to Grading: Eagle

DATE	ABP FINE	AVERAGE FINE
☐ 1905	—	$11.50
☐ 1906	—	11.50
☐ 1907 Str 7	—	6.60
☐ 1907 crvd 7	—	8.00
☐ 1908	—	75.50
☐ 1910	—	8.10
☐ 1911	—	8.10
☐ 1912	—	33.50
☐ 1913	—	12.25
☐ 1914	—	8.00

20 Centavos Silver Zapata Issue

DATE	ABP FINE	AVERAGE FINE
☐ 1915	—	24.50

20 Centavos Bronze

DATE	ABP FINE	AVERAGE FINE
☐ 1920	16.22	27.04
☐ 1935	3.09	5.15

20 Centavos Silver

DATE	ABP FINE	AVERAGE FINE
☐ 1920	—	7.25
☐ 1921	—	7.25
☐ 1925	—	7.25
☐ 1926/25	—	15.25
☐ 1926	—	7.25
☐ 1927	—	7.25
☐ 1928	—	7.25
☐ 1930	—	7.25
☐ 1933–1943	—	7.25

20 Centavos Bronze

DATE	ABP FINE	AVERAGE FINE
☐ 1943–1946	.39	.65
☐ 1951	.98	1.63
☐ 1952	1.30	2.20
☐ 1954	.33	.55
☐ 1955	.98	1.65

20 Centavos Bronze Restyled Eagle

DATE	ABP FINE	AVERAGE FINE
☐ 1955	.26	.43
☐ 1956	.26	.43
☐ 1957	.26	.43

DATE		ABP FINE	AVERAGE FINE
☐ 1959		$1.35	$2.30
☐ 1960–1971		.26	.43
20 Centavos Bronze Restyled Eagle			
☐ 1971–1973		.26	.43
20 Centavos Copper-Nickel			
☐ 1974–1983		.16	.27
☐ 1977/9 Dbl Die		.39	.65
☐ 1981 clsd 8		.23	.38
☐ 1981/82		10.70	17.85
20 Centavos Bronze			
☐ 1983–1984		.23	.38
Republica Mexicanos			
¼ Real Copper			
☐ 1829–1837		20.80	34.65
¼ Real Silver			
☐ 1834RG	Mint Mark Ca	—	200.00
☐ 1855LR	Mint Mark C	—	152.50
☐ 1842LR	Mint Mark Do	—	60.50
☐ 1843LR	Mint Mark Do	—	38.50
☐ 1842–1862	Mint Mark Ga	—	30.50
☐ 1852LR	Mint Mark Ga	—	210.00
☐ 1854/3LR	Mint Mark Ga	—	210.00
☐ 1842–1863	Mint Mark Mo	—	23.50
☐ 1854	Mint Mark S.L.P.	—	338.50
☐ 1842/1 LR	Mint Mark Zs	—	20.75
☐ 1842 LR	Mint Mark Zs	—	20.75
Republic 1864–1904			
25 Centavos Silver			
☐ 1874–1890	Mint Mark A, As	—	23.75
☐ 1877L	Mint Mark A, As	—	375.00
☐ 1881L	Mint Mark A, As	—	612.00
☐ 1871M	Mint Mark CA, CH, Ca	—	45.50
☐ 1872	M Crude Date Mint Mark CA, CH, Ca	—	84.50
☐ 1883–1889	Mint Mark CA, CH, Ca	—	23.50
☐ 18871–1892	Mint Mark Cn	—	205.50
☐ 1877–1890	Mint Mark Do	—	60.50
☐ 1873	Mint Mark Do	—	Rare
☐ 1878/7E	Mint Mark Do	—	385.50
☐ 1878B	Mint Mark Do	—	Rare
☐ 1880–1889	Mint Mark Ga	—	53.50
☐ 1870–1880	Mint Mark GO	—	22.75
☐ 1881–1890	Mint Mark GO	—	18.25
☐ 1874–1890	Mint Mark Ho	—	22.75
☐ 1883M	Mint Mark Ho	—	210.00
☐ 1869–1890	Mint Mark Mo	—	312.50

DATE		ABP FINE	AVERAGE FINE
□ 1869–1990	Mint Mark Pi	—	$18.50
□ 1870–1890	Mint Mark Zs	—	15.45
Estados Unidos Mexicanos			
25 Centavos Silver			
□ 1950–1953		—	—
25 Centavos Copper-Nickel			
□ 1964		.26	.43
□ 1966 clsd beak		.26	.43
□ 1966 open beak		.49	.81
Republica Mexicanos			
½ Real Silver			
□ 1824JM	Mint Mark Mo	—	84.75
½ Real Silver			
□ 1862PG	Mint Mark A	—	Rare
□ 1844RG	Mint Mark Ca	—	131.50
□ 1845RG	Mint Mark Ca	—	131.50
□ 1846–1869	Mint Mark C, Co	—	27.75
□ 1832–1869	Mint Mark D, Do	—	56.50
□ 1829LF	Mint Mark EoMo	—	250.00
□ 1825–1862	Mint Mark Ga	—	27.50
□ 1844–1851	Mint Mark GC	—	53.50
□ 1826–1868	Mint Mark Go	—	26.75
□ 1826	MJ Mint Mark Go	—	200.00
□ 1839PP	Mint Mark Ho	—	Unique
□ 1862FM	Mint Mark Ho	—	845.00
□ 1867PR/FM	inv 6 & 7/7 Mint Mark Ho	—	191.50
□ 1825–1863	Mint Mark Mo	—	22.50
□ 1831–1863	Mint Mark Pi	—	22.50
□ 1845AM	Mint Mark Pi	—	430.00
□ 1826–1869	Mint Mark Z, Zs	—	23.50
Republic 1863–1904			
50 Centavos Silver Balance Scales			
□ 1875–1885	Mint Mark A, As		30.50
□ 1888L	Mint Mark A, As	—	Counterfeit
□ 1883–1887	Mint Mark Ca, Cha		30.50
□ 1871P	Mint Mark Cn	—	685.00
□ 1873P	Mint Mark Cn	—	685.00
□ 1874P	Mint Mark Cn	—	322.50
□ 1875–1881	Mint Mark Cn	—	27.50
□ 1881G	Mint Mark Cn	—	245.00
□ 1882D	Mint Mark Cn	—	27.25
□ 1882G	Mint Mark Cn	—	191.50
□ 1883–1892	Mint Mark Cn	—	131.50
□ 1888M	Mint Mark Cn	—	Counterfeit
□ 1871P	Mint Mark Do	—	Rare

DATE		ABP FINE	AVERAGE FINE
☐ 1873P–1873P M Mint Mark Do		—	$218.00
☐ 1874–1887	Mint Mark Do	—	58.00
☐ 1869–1888	Mint Mark Go	—	28.50
☐ 1874–1894	Mint Mark Ho	—	25.50
☐ 1888G	Mint Mark Ho	—	Counterfeit
☐ 1895G	Mint Mark Ho	—	360.00
☐ 1869–1873	Mint Mark Mo	—	76.50
☐ 1874/3M	Mint Mark Mo	—	295.00
☐ 1874/2–1887	Mint Mark Mo	—	46.80
☐ 1880	Mint Mark Mo	—	165.00
☐ 1883/2	Mint Mark Mo	—	340.00
☐ 1884M	Mint Mark Mo	—	340.00
☐ 1888M	Mint Mark Mo	—	Counterfeit
☐ 1870–1887	Mint Mark Pi	—	37.75
☐ 1888R	Mint Mark Pi	—	Counterfeit
☐ 1870–1887	Mint Mark Zs	—	37.75
☐ 1876S	Mint Mark Zs	—	167.50
☐ 1886Z	Mint Mark Zs	—	245.00

Emperor Maximillian 1864–1867
50 Centavos Silver

☐ 1866	Mint Mark Mo	—	91.50

Estados Unidos Mexicanos
50 Centavos Silver

Key to Grading: Eagle

☐ 1905	—	11.75
☐ 1906	—	11.45
☐ 1907 str 7	—	11.45
☐ 1907 crvd7	—	11.45
☐ 1908	—	45.50
☐ 1912	—	9.00
☐ 1913/07	—	30.50
☐ 1913/2	—	15.00
☐ 1913	—	10.10
☐ 1914	—	10.10
☐ 1916	—	50.50
☐ 1917	—	9.00
☐ 1918	—	52.50

DATE	ABP FINE	AVERAGE FINE
50 Centavos Reduced Size		
☐ 1918/7	—	$422.50
☐ 1918	—	13.75
☐ 1919	—	13.75
50 Centavos Silver		
☐ 1919	—	13.75
☐ 1920	—	6.00
☐ 1921	—	7.50
☐ 1925	—	12.75
☐ 1937	—	7.60
☐ 1938	—	32.50
☐ 1939	—	9.45
☐ 1942	—	9.45
☐ 1943–1945	—	6.50
50 Centavos Silver		
☐ 1935	—	6.50
50 Centavos Silver Cuauhtemoc		
☐ 1950	—	3.80
☐ 1951	—	3.80
50 Centavos Bronze		
☐ 1955	.66	1.10
☐ 1956	.26	.43
☐ 1957	.39	.65
☐ 1958	.26	.43
50 Centavos Copper-Nickel		
☐ 1964–1969	.26	.43
50 Centavos C/N Stylized Eagle		
☐ 1970–1983	.26	.43
☐ 1972	.33	.55
☐ 1977	1.95	3.25
50 Centavos Stainless Steel		
☐ 1983	.26	.43
50 Centavos Aluminum/Bronze		
☐ 1992–1996	.26	.43
Republica Mexicanos 1824–1864		
1 Real Silver Hooked Neck Eagle		
☐ 1824 RL	—	4200.00
1 Real Silver Upright Eagle		
☐ 1844–1845 Mint Mark Ca	—	750.00
☐ 1855 Mint Mark Ca	—	145.00
☐ 1846–1851 Mint Mark C	—	20.50
☐ 1851–1869 Mint Mark C	—	20.50
☐ 1856 Mint Mark C	—	52.50
☐ 1832–1864 Mint Mark Do	—	23.50
☐ 1862/1CP Mint Mark Do	—	425.00

DATE		ABP FINE	AVERAGE FINE
☐ 1828LF	Mint Mark EoMo	—	$368.00
☐ 1826–1862	Mint Mark Ga	—	23.50
☐ 1830FS	Mint Mark Ga	—	344.50
☐ 1831LP/FS	Mint Mark Ga	—	560.00
☐ 1839JG	Mint Mark Ga	—	365.00
☐ 1848JG		—	675.00
☐ 1844–1851	Mint Mark GC	—	65.50
☐ 1826–1868	Mint Mark Go	—	15.00
☐ 1867–1968	Mint Mark Ho	—	100.00
☐ 1825–1863	Mint Mark Mo	—	17.50
☐ 1831JM	Mint Mark Mo	—	185.00
☐ 1852GC	Mint Mark Mo	—	415.00
☐ 1831–1862	Mint Mark Pi	—	30.00
☐ 1837JS	Mint Mark Pi	—	1175.00
☐ 1838/7JS	Mint Mark Pi	—	365.00
☐ 1826–1869	Mint Mark Zs	—	12.00

Emperor Maximillian 1864–1867
1 Peso Silver

☐ 1866	Mint Mark GO	—	575.00
☐ 1866–1867	Mint Mark Mo	—	68.50
☐ 1868	Mint Mark Pi	—	68.50

Republic 1864–1904
1 Peso Silver Balance Scales

☐ 1872/1–1873	Mint Mark CH	—	52.50
☐ 1872	P/M Mint Mark CH	—	1050.00
☐ 1872P	Mint Mark CH	—	730.00
☐ 1870–1873	Mint Mark Cn	—	44.50
☐ 1870–1873	Mint Mark Do	—	44.50
☐ 1872PT	Mint Mark Do	—	180.00
☐ 1870C	Mint Mark Ga	—	1050.00
☐ 1871–1873	Mint Mark Ga	—	65.50
☐ 1871–1873	Mint Mark Go	—	36.50
☐ 1869–1873	Mint Mark Mo	—	24.50
☐ 1869–1873	Mint Mark Oa	—	47.50
☐ 1869C	Mint Mark Oa	—	Pattern
☐ 1870	OA E Lrg A Mint Mark Oa	—	200.00
☐ 1870–1873	Mint Mark Zs	—	22.50

1 Peso Silver Cap & Rays

☐ 1898–1905	Mint Mark Cn	—	22.50
☐ 1898–1900	Mint Mark Go	—	32.50
☐ 1898–1909	Mint Mark Mo	—	22.50
☐ 1898–1905	Mint Mark Zs	—	22.50

1 Peso Gold

☐ 1888L	Mint Mark As	—	Rare
☐ 1888	AsL/MoM Mint Mark As	—	Rare

DATE	ABP FINE	AVERAGE FINE
☐ 1888Ca/MoM Mint Mark Ca	—	Rare
☐ 1873/1888 Mint Mark Cn	—	$195.000
☐ 1889M Mint Mark Cn	—	Rare
☐ 1891–1905 Mint Mark Cn	—	184.50
☐ 1870–1900 Mint Mark Go	—	184.50
☐ 1875–1888 Mint Mark Ho	—	Rare
☐ 1870–1905 Mint Mark Mo	—	100.00
☐ 1872–1890 Mint Mark Zs	—	205.00

Estados Unidos Mexicanos 1905–Present
1 Peso Silver Caballito

Key to Grading: Eagle		
☐ 1910	—	56.50
☐ 1911 Long Left Low Ray	—	56.50
☐ 1911 Short Left Low Ray	—	75.00
☐ 1912	—	152.50
☐ 1913/2	—	38.00
☐ 1914	—	530.00

1 Peso Silver Cap & Rays

☐ 1918	—	32.50
☐ 1919	—	32.50

1 Peso Silver

☐ 1920–1945	—	9.00
☐ 1920/10	—	72.50

1 Peso Silver

☐ 1947–1948	—	7.50
☐ 1949	—	485.00

1 Peso Silver Jose Morelos y Pavon

☐ 1950	—	3.50

1 Peso 100th Anniv. of Constitution

☐ 1957	—	4.15

1 Peso Jose Morelos y Pavon

☐ 1957–1962	—	.41
☐ 1959	—	.57
☐ 1963–1967	—	.41

1 Peso Copper/Nickel

☐ 1970–1983	.26	.43
☐ 1970 Wide Date	.33	.55

DATE		ABP FINE	AVERAGE FINE
☐ 1977 Thin Date		$ .39	$ .65
1 Peso Stainless Steel			
☐ 1984–1988		.26	.43

Key to Grading: Eagle
1 New Peso Bimetallic

☐ 1992–1996		.26	.43

Republica Mexicanos 1824–1864
2 Reales Silver Hooked Neck Eagle

☐ 1824 DO RL	Mint Mark D, Do	—	84.50
☐ 1824 D RL	Mint Mark D, Do	—	190.50
☐ 1824 JM	Mint Mark Mo	—	52.50

2 Reales Sliver Facing Eagle

☐ 1872	AM Mint Mark A	—	76.50
☐ 1863ML	Mint Mark Ce	—	190.50
☐ 1832–1855	Mint Mark Ca	—	37.50
☐ 1846–1869	Mint Mark C	—	26.50
☐ 1826–1834	Mint Mark Do	—	38.50
☐ 1835/4 RM/RL	Mint Mark Do	—	338.50
☐ 1841–1861	Mint Mark Do	—	24.50
☐ 1846/36	Mint Mark Do	—	192.50
☐ 1855CP	Mint Mark Do	—	395.50
☐ 1856CP	Mint Mark Do	—	174.50
☐ 1828 LF	Mint Mark EoMo	—	650.00
☐ 1825–1862	Mint Mark Ga	—	24.50
☐ 1851JG	Mint Mark Ga	—	545.00
☐ 1854/3JG	Mint Mark Ga	—	545.00
☐ 1857JG	Mint Mark Ga	—	360.00
☐ 1844–1851	Mint Mark GC	—	74.50
☐ 1850MP	Mint Mark GC	—	195.00
☐ 1825–1868	Mint Mark Go	—	26.50
☐ 1848PF	Mint Mark Go	—	150.50
☐ 1861	Mint Mark Ho	—	340.00
☐ 1825–1868	Mint Mark Mo	—	23.50
☐ 1832JM	Mint Mark Mo	—	195.00
☐ 1840ML	Mint Mark Mo	—	265.00
☐ 1829–1869	Mint Mark Pi	—	32.75
☐ 1863RO	Mint Mark Pi	—	168.00
☐ 1825–1870	Mint Mark Zs	—	24.00

DATE	ABP FINE	AVERAGE FINE

Estados Unidos Mexicanos
2 Pesos Gold

| ☐ 1919–1948 | — | $56.50 |

2 Pesos Silver 100th Anniv. of Independence

| ☐ 1921 | — | 38.50 |

Key to Grading: Eagle
2 New Pesos Bimetallic

| ☐ 1992–1995 | .36 | .60 |

2 Pesos Bimetallic Denom w/o N

| ☐ 1996–1999 | .36 | .60 |

Republic 1864–1905
2 ½ Peso Restyled Eagle Gold

Key to Grading: Eagle

☐ 1888 As/MoL	Mint Mark As	—	Rare
☐ 1893M	Mint Mark Cn	—	2650.00
☐ 1888C	Mint Mark Do	—	Rare
☐ 1871S	Mint Mark Go	—	2650.00
☐ 1888	Go/MoR Mint Mark Go	—	2650.00
☐ 1874R	Mint Mark Ho	—	Rare
☐ 1888G	Mint Mark Ho	—	Rare
☐ 1870–1892	Mint Mark Mo	—	450.00
☐ 1872–1890	Mint Mark Zs	—	450.00

Estados Unidos Mexicanos 1905–Present
2 ½ Pesos Gold

| ☐ 1918–1948 | — | 44.50 |
| ☐ 1947 | — | 338.00 |

Republica Mexicanos 1824–1864
4 Reales Upright Eagle Silver

| ☐ 1863ML | Large C Mint Mark Ce | — | 355.00 |

DATE		ABP FINE	AVERAGE FINE
☐ 1863ML	Small C Mint Mark Ce	—	$560.00
☐ 1846CE	Mint Mark C	—	600.00
☐ 1850CE	Mint Mark C	—	121.00
☐ 1852CE	Mint Mark C	—	325.00
☐ 1857CE	Mint Mark C	—	Rare
☐ 1858CE	Mint Mark C	—	152.50
☐ 1860PV	Mint Mark C	—	38.50
☐ 1843–1850	Mint Mark Ga	—	65.50
☐ 1852JG	Mint Mark Ga	—	Rare
☐ 1854JG	Mint Mark Ga	—	Rare
☐ 1856JG	Mint Mark Ga	—	Rare
☐ 1855–1863	Mint Mark Ga	—	228.00
☐ 1844–1850	Mint Mark GC	—	2785.00
☐ 1835–1870	Mint Mark Go	—	38.50
☐ 1841/31PJ	Mint Mark Go	—	230.00
☐ 1861FM	Mint Mark Ho	—	410.00
☐ 1867/1PR/FM	Mint Mark Ho	—	410.00
☐ 1827–1855	Mint Mark Mo	—	410.00
☐ 1850GC	Mint Mark Mo	—	Rare
☐ 1852GC	Mint Mark Mo	—	Rare
☐ 1854GC	Mint Mark Mo	—	Rare
☐ 1859–1868	Mint Mark Mo	—	52.50
☐ 1861FR	Ornamental Edge Mint Mark O	—	365.00
☐ 1861FR	Herringbone Edge Mint Mark O	—	495.00
☐ 1861FR	Obliquely Reed Edge Mint Mark O	—	335.00
☐ 1837–1853	Mint Mark Pi	—	45.50
☐ 1854–1860	Mint Mark Pi	—	538.00
☐ 1859MC	Mint Mark Pi	—	Scarce
☐ 1861–1869	Mint Mark Pi	—	74.50
☐ 1863–1870	Mint Mark ZS	—	74.50

Republic 1864–1905
5 Pesos Restyled Eagle Gold

☐ 1878L	Mint Mark As	—	1775.00
☐ 1888M	Mint Mark Ca	—	Rare
☐ 1873–1903	Mint Mark CN	—	450.00
☐ 1873–1879	Mint Mark Do	—	1050.00
☐ 1871S	Mint Mark Go	—	1000.00
☐ 1887R	Mint Mark Go	—	980.00
☐ 1888R	Mint Mark Go	—	Rare
☐ 1893R	Mint Mark Go	—	Rare
☐ 1874R	Mint Mark Ho	—	Scarce
☐ 1877R	Mint Mark Ho	—	1200.00
☐ 1887A	Mint Mark Ho	—	1200.00
☐ 1888G	Mint Mark Ho	—	Rare
☐ 1870–1905	Mint Mark Mo	—	420.00

DATE	ABP FINE	AVERAGE FINE
Estados Unidos Mexicanos		
5 Peso Gold		
☐ 1918–1944	—	$68.50
5 Peso Silver Cuauhtemoc		
☐ 1947–1948	—	9.00
5 Pesos Silver Railroad		
☐ 1950	—	25.50
5 Pesos Silver Miguel Costilla		
☐ 1951–1953	—	8.50
☐ 1954	—	29.50
5 Pesos Silver 200th Anniv. Hiadalgo's Birth		
☐ 1953	—	6.75
5 Pesos Silver Costilla Reduced Size		
☐ 1955–1957	—	6.75
5 Pesos Silver 100th Anniv. Constitution		
☐ 1957	—	6.75
5 Pesos Silver 100th Anniv. Carranza's birth		
☐ 1959	—	6.75
5 Pesos C/N Guerrero		
☐ 1971–1978	.29	.48
5 Pesos C/N Quetzalcoatl		
☐ 1980–1985	.33	.55
5 Pesos Brass		
☐ 1985–1988	.26	.33
☐ 1987	2.60	4.35

Key to Grading: Eagle

5 Pesos Bimetallic		
☐ 1992–1995	.55	.92
☐ 1996–1999	.55	.92
Republica Mexicanos 1824–1963		
8 Reales Silver Hooked-Neck Eagle		
☐ 1824RL Mint Mark Do	—	410.00
☐ 1824–1825 Mint Mark Go	—	825.00
☐ 1823–1824 Mint Mark Mo	—	238.00
Republic 1864–1905		
8 Reales Upright Eagle Silver		

Key to Grading: Eagle

DATE		ABP FINE	AVERAGE FINE
☐ 1864PG	Mint Mark A, As	—	$1050.00
☐ 1865PG	Mint Mark A, As	—	695.00
☐ 1866PG	Mint Mark A, As	—	2275.00
☐ 1867DL	Mint Mark A, As	—	1775.00

Key to Grading: Eagle

☐ 1868–1895	Mint Mark A, As	—	38.00
☐ 1863ML	Mint Mark Ce	—	675.00
☐ 1864 CeML/PiMc	Mint Mark Ce	—	700.00
☐ 1831–1841	Mint Mark Ca	—	700.00
☐ 1842–1850	Mint Mark Ca	—	60.00
☐ 1851–1857	Mint Mark Ca	—	250.00
☐ 1858–1895	Mint Mark Ca	—	74.50
☐ 1865FP	Mint Mark Ca	—	1775.00
☐ 1866JC	Mint Mark Ca	—	Rare
☐ 1866FP	Mint Mark Ca	—	1450.00
☐ 1866JG	Mint Mark Ca	—	1350.00
☐ 1846–1854	Mint Mark C, Cn	—	325.00
☐ 1855–1897	Mint Mark C, Cn	—	82.50
☐ 1825–1847	Mint Mark Do	—	82.50
☐ 1848–1853	Mint Mark Do	—	152.50
☐ 1854–1895	Mint Mark Do	—	52.50
☐ 1825–1832	Mint Mark Ga	—	250.00
☐ 1833–1839	Mint Mark Ga	—	115.50
☐ 1840–1865	Mint Mark Ga	—	89.50
☐ 1844–1852	Mint Mark GC	—	395.00
☐ 1825–1828	Mint Mark Go	—	395.00
☐ 1829–1897	Mint Mark Go	—	38.50
☐ 1835PP	Mint Mark Ho	—	Rare

DATE		ABP FINE	AVERAGE FINE
☐ 1836PP	Mint Mark Ho	—	Rare
☐ 1839PR	Mint Mark Ho	—	Unique
☐ 1861FM	Reed Edge Mint Mark Ho	—	Scarce
☐ 1862FM	Plain Edge Mint Mark Ho	—	Rare
☐ 1862FM	Snake Tail Left Mint Mark Ho	—	Scarce
☐ 1862FM	Snake Tail Right Mint Mark Ho	—	Scarce
☐ 1863–1867	Mint Mark Ho	—	$420.00
☐ 1868–1895	Mint Mark Ho	—	68.00
☐ 1824–1897	Mint Mark Mo	—	68.00
☐ 1833ML	Mint Mark Mo	—	745.00
☐ 1847ML	Mint Mark Mo	—	Scarce
☐ 18580 AE	Mint Mark O, Oa	—	Scarce
☐ 18580a AE	Mint Mark O, Oa	—	Unique
☐ 1859–1861	Mint Mark O, Oa	—	300.00
☐ 1862–1893	Mint Mark O, Oa	—	52.50
☐ 1827JS	Mint Mark Pi	—	Rare
☐ 1828/7JS	Mint Mark Pi	—	420.00
☐ 1828JS	Mint Mark Pi	—	330.00
☐ 1829–1848	Mint Mark Pi	—	44.50
☐ 1849–1861	Mint Mark Pi	—	205.00
☐ 1862–1863	Mint Mark Pi	—	38.50
☐ 1863FC	Mint Mark Pi	—	Rare
☐ 1864RO	Mint Mark Pi	—	Rare
☐ 1867CA	Mint Mark Pi	—	950.00
☐ 1867RL	Mint Mark Pi	—	825.00
☐ 1867PS/CA	Mint Mark Pi	—	Rare
☐ 1868–1893	Mint Mark Pi	—	55.00
☐ 1825–1897	Mint Mark Zs	—	55.00
☐ 1866VL	Mint Mark Zs	—	Counterfeit
☐ 1867JS	Mint Mark Zs	—	Rare

½ Escudo Gold Upright Eagle

DATE		ABP FINE	AVERAGE FINE
☐ 1848–1870	Mint Mark C	—	120.00
☐ 1833–1864	Mint Mark Do	—	120.00
☐ 1825–1861	Mint Mark Ga	—	120.00
☐ 1846–1851	Mint Mark GC	—	120.00
☐ 1845–1863	Mint Mark Go	—	120.00
☐ 1825–1869	Mint Mark Mo	—	120.00
☐ 1860–1862	Mint Mark Zs	—	120.00

10 Pesos Balance Scale

DATE		ABP FINE	AVERAGE FINE
☐ 1874–1895	Mint Mark AS	—	720.00
☐ 1874DL	Mint Mark AS	—	Rare
☐ 1884L	Mint Mark AS	—	Rare
☐ 1892 L	Mint Mark AS	—	Rare
☐ 1894/3	Mint Mark AS	—	Rare
☐ 1888M	175 Pcs Mint Mark Ca	—	Rare

DATE		ABP FINE	AVERAGE FINE
☐ 1881–1903	Mint Mark Cn	—	$725.00
☐ 1883D	Mint Mark Cn	—	Rare
☐ 1872–1884	Mint Mark Do	—	725.00
☐ 1882P	Mint Mark Do	—	Rare
☐ 1870–1891	Mint Mark Ga		
	Low Mintage for This MM	—	1100.00
☐ 1872S	Mint Mark Go	—	2800.00
☐ 1887R	Mint Mark Go	—	Rare
☐ 1888R	Mint Mark Go	—	Rare
☐ 1874R	Mint Mark Ho	—	Rare
☐ 1876R	Mint Mark Ho	—	Rare
☐ 1878A	Mint Mark Ho	—	2800.00
☐ 1879A	Mint Mark Ho	—	2800.00
☐ 1880A	Mint Mark Ho	—	2800.00
☐ 1881A	Mint Mark Ho	—	Rare
☐ 1870–1905	Mint Mark Mo	—	875.00
☐ 1870–1895	Mint Mark Oa	—	725.00

Estados Unidos Mexicanos
10 Pesos Gold Miguel Hidago

☐ 1905		—	150.00
☐ 1906–1910		—	120.00
☐ 1916		—	265.00
☐ 1917–1919		—	265.00
☐ 1920		—	225.00
☐ 1959	Restrikes	—	110.00

10 Pesos Silver Hidalgo

☐ 1956–1956		—	12.00

Key to Grading: Eagle

10 Pesos Silver Anniv. Constitution

☐ 1957		—	12.00

10 Pesos Silver Anniv. War of Independence

☐ 1960		—	7.50

DATE	ABP FINE	AVERAGE FINE

Key to Grading: Eagle
10 Pesos C/N Hidalgo

		ABP FINE	AVERAGE FINE
☐ 1974–1977	Thin Flan	$ .66	$1.10

10 Pesos C/N Hidalgo

| ☐ 1978–1985 | Thick Flan | .66 | 1.10 |

10 Pesos Stainless Steel

| ☐ 1985–1990 | | .66 | 1.10 |

10 Pesos Bimetallic

| ☐ 1992–Present | | $2.60 | 4.35 |

Republica Mexicanos
1 Escudo Gold Upright Eagle

☐ 1846–1870	Mint Mark C	—	110.00
☐ 1833–1864	Mint Mark Do	—	110.00
☐ 1825–1860	Mint Mark Ga	—	600.00
☐ 1844–1851	Mint Mark GC	—	180.00
☐ 1845–1862	Mint Mark Go	—	175.00
☐ 1825–1869	Mint Mark Mo	—	120.00
☐ 1853–1862	Mint Mark Zs	—	200.00

Emperor Maximilian 1863–1967
20 Pesos gold

| ☐ 1866 | | — | 825.00 |

Key to Grading: Eagle
Republic 1867–1905
20 Pesos Gold Restyled Eagle

☐ 1876–1888	Mint Mark As	—	Rare
☐ 1872–1895	Mint Mark CH, Ca	—	—
☐ 1870–1905	Mint Mark Cn	—	—
☐ 1870–1877	Mint Mark Do	—	—
☐ 1878	Mint Mark Do	—	Rare

DATE		ABP FINE	AVERAGE FINE
☐ 1870–1900	Mint Mark Go	—	$925.00
☐ 1874–1888	Mint Mark Ho	—	Rare
☐ 1870–1905	Mint Mark Mo	—	825.00
☐ 1870–1871	Mint Mark Oa	—	1250.00
☐ 1871–1889	Mint Mark Zs	—	Scarce

Estados Unidos Mexicanos
20 Pesos Gold

| ☐ 1917–1959 | | — | 600.00 |

Key to Grading: Eagle
20 Pesos C/N

| ☐ 1980–1984 | | .29 | .48 |

20 Pesos Brass

| ☐ 1985–1990 | | .23 | .38 |

20 Pesos Bimetallic

| ☐ 1993–1995 | | 4.60 | 7.60 |
| ☐ 1996 | | 3.90 | 6.50 |

Key to Grading: Eagle
25 Pesos Silver Olympics

☐ 1968	Type I	—	12.75
☐ 1968	Type II	—	12.75
☐ 1968	Type III	—	12.75

25 Pesos Silver Benito Juarez

| ☐ 1972 | | — | 12.75 |

Key to Grading: Eagle

DATE		ABP FINE	AVERAGE FINE
25 Pesos Silver Soccer Games			
☐ 1985 Proof		—	—
Republica Mexicanos 1832–1904			
2 Escudos Gold Upright Eagle			
☐ 1846–1857	Mint Mark C	—	230.00
☐ 1833–1844	Mint Mark Do	—	925.00
☐ 1828LF	Mint Mark EoMo	—	1450.00
☐ 1835–1870	Mint Mark Ga	—	265.00
☐ 1844–1850	Mint Mark GC	—	325.00
☐ 1845MP	Mint Mark GC	—	2650.00
☐ 1846MP	Mint Mark GC	—	2650.00
☐ 1845–1862	Mint Mark Go	—	235.00
☐ 1861FM	Mint Mark Ho	—	1500.00
☐ 1825–1869	Mint Mark Mo	—	250.00
☐ 1860–1964	Mint Mark Zs	—	725.00
Estados Unidos Mexicanos 1905–Present			
50 Pesos Gold Centennial of Independence			
☐ 1921–1947		—	685.00

Key to Grading: Eagle	ABP FINE	AVERAGE FINE
50 Pesos C/N Coyolxauhqui		
☐ 1982–1984	.59	.98
50 Pesos C/N Benito Juarez		
☐ 1984–1988	.26	.43
☐ 1986	194.00	324.00
☐ 1988	2.60	4.35
50 Pesos Stainless Steel		
☐ 1988–1992	.26	.43
50 Pesos Silver Soccer		
☐ 1985	—	9.00
50 Pesos Silver Oil Industry		
☐ ND(1988)	—	22.50
50 Pesos Bimetallic		
☐ 1992	9.10	15.15
Republica Mexicanos 1834–1864		
4 Escudos Gold Upright Eagle		
☐ 1846CE	Mint Mark C	—	2450.00
☐ 1847CE	Mint Mark C	—	975.00
☐ 1848CE	Mint Mark C	—	1200.00
☐ 1832–1852	Mint Mark Do	—	Rare

DATE		ABP FINE	AVERAGE FINE
☐ 1844MC	Mint Mark Ga	—	$1275.00
☐ 1844JC	Mint Mark Ga	—	950.00
☐ 1844–1850	Mint Mark Go	—	625.00
☐ 1861FM	Mint Mark Ho	—	1850.00
☐ 1829–1869	Mint Mark Mo	—	785.00
☐ 1861FR	Mint Mark O, Oa	—	2800.00
☐ 1862VL	Mint Mark Zs	—	1900.00

Estados Unidos Mexicanos 1905–Present
100 Pesos Silver Jose Pavon

Key to Grading: Eagle			
☐ 1977 Low 7's		—	6.75
☐ 1977 High 7's		—	6.75
100 Pesos Silver Jose Pavon			
☐ 1977–1979	Date in Line	—	6.75
100 Pesos Aluminum-Bronze			
☐ 1984–1992		.33	.55
☐ 1986		.66	1.10
100 Pesos Silver (.72 ASW) Soccer			
☐ 1985		—	28.00
100 Pesos Silver (1.0 ASW) Soccer			
☐ 1985		—	28.00
100 Pesos Silver Monarch Butterflies			
☐ 1987		—	65.50
100 Pesos Silver Oil Industry			
☐ 1988		—	56.50
100 Pesos Silver Save the Children			
☐ 1991		—	98.00
100 Pesos Silver Ibero Pillars			
☐ 1991–1992		—	98.00
100 Pesos Silver Save the Harbor Porpoise			
☐ 1992		—	98.00

Republica Mexicanos 1823–1864
8 Escudos Gold Hooked-Neck Eagle

☐ 1823JM	Snake Tail Curved Mint Mark Mo	—	Rare
☐ 1823	JM Snake Tail Looped Mint Mark Mo	—	Rare

8 Escudos Gold Upright Eagle

☐ 1864–1872	Mint Mark A	—	1800.00
☐ 1841–1871	Mint Mark Ca	—	775.00

DATE		ABP FINE	AVERAGE FINE

Key to Grading: Eagle

		ABP FINE	AVERAGE FINE
☐ 1846–1870	Mint Mark C	—	$750.00
☐ 1832–1870	Mint Mark Do	—	750.00
☐ 1828–1829	Mint Mark EoMo	—	4000.00
☐ 1825–1866	Mint Mark Ga	—	975.00
☐ 1844–1852	Mint Mark Gc	—	975.00
☐ 1828–1873	Mint Mark Go	—	785.00
☐ 1863–1873	Mint Mark Ho	—	785.00
☐ 1824–1869	Mint Mark Mo	—	485.00
☐ 1858AE	Mint Mark O	—	2800.00
☐ 1858–1871	Mint Mark Zs	—	625.00

Key to Grading: Eagle
Estados Unidos Mexicanos

	ABP FINE	AVERAGE FINE
200 Pesos C/N Anniv. Independence		
☐ 1985	.25	.41
200 Pesos C/N Anniv. 1910 Revolution		
☐ 1985	.25	.41
200 Pesos C/N Soccer		
☐ 1986	.25	.41
200 Pesos Silver Soccer		
☐ 1986	—	48.00
250 Pesos Gold Soccer		
☐ 1985–1986	—	225.00

Key to Grading: Eagle

DATE	ABP FINE	AVERAGE FINE
500 Pesos Gold Soccer		
☐ 1985–1986	—	$3000.00
500 Pesos Silver Anniv. 1910 Revolution		
☐ 1985	27.90	46.50
500 Pesos C/N Francisco Madero		
☐ 1986–1992	1.32	2.21
500 Peso Gold Oil Industry		
☐ 1988	—	3000.00
1000 Pesos Gold Anniv. of Independence		
☐ 1985	—	485.00
1000 Pesos Gold Soccer		
☐ 1986	—	680.00
1000 Pesos Gold Oil Industry		

DATE	ABP FINE	AVERAGE FINE
Key to Grading: Eagle		
☐ 1988	278.10	463.50
1000 Pesos Aluminum-Bronze		
☐ 1988–1992	.65	1.08
2000 Pesos Gold Soccer		
☐ 1986	—	1550.00
5000 Pesos C/N Oil Industry		
☐ N/D(1988)	19.80	33.00

MOROCCO

The first coins were used in the 2nd century B.C., with the silver denarius in 50 B.C., bronze coins in the 1st century B.C., and copper fals in 731 A.D. The silver dirham was in evidence in the 700s, followed by the gold dinar, silver square dirham, and gold double dinar in the 12th and 13th centuries. The copper double fals was in use in the 1800s and the cupro-nickel francs in the mid-1900s. Decimal coins were used in 1921. The currency today is the dirham.

Key to Grading: Coin Design

Morocco—Type Coinage

DATE	COIN TYPE/VARIETY/METAL	ABP FINE	AVERAGE FINE
☐ 1310	¹/₂ Mazuna, Hasan I, Bronze	$155.60	$259.00
☐ 1310	1 Mazuna, Hasan I, Bronze	120.05	200.00
☐ 1320–1321	1 Mazuna, Abd Al-Aziz 2nd Coinage, Bronze	1.20	4.80
☐ 1330	1 Mazuna, Yusuf: 1st Coinage, Bronze	2.90	4.80
☐ 1320–1321	2 Mazuna, Abd Al-Aziz 2nd Coinage, Bronze	2.90	4.80
☐ 1330	2 Mazuna, Yusuf: 1st Coinage, Bronze	2.90	4.80
☐ 1310	2¹/₂ Mazuna, Hasan I, Bronze	90.70	151.00
☐ 1310	5 Mazuna, Hasan I, Bronze	52.00	86.65
☐ 1320–1322	5 Mazuna, Abd Al-Aziz 2nd Coinage, Bronze	5.20	8.65
☐ 1330–1340	5 Mazuna, Yusuf: 1st Coinage, Bronze	2.80	4.60
☐ 1310	10 Mazuna, Hasan I, Bronze	51.00	86.60
☐ 1320–1323	10 Mazuna, Abd Al-Aziz 2nd Coinage, Bronze	2.85	4.75
☐ 1330–1340	10 Mazuna, Yusuf: 1st Coinage, Bronze	1.40	2.30
☐ 1974	1 Santim, Monetary Reform, Gold	—	725.00
☐ 1974–1975	1 Santim, Monetary Reform, Aluminum	—	2.50
☐ 1299–1314	¹/₂ Dirham, Hasan I, Silver	—	6.50
☐ 1313–1319	¹/₂ Dirham, Abd Al-Aziz 1st Coinage, Silver	—	6.50
☐ 1320–1321	¹/₂₀ Rial, Abd Al-Aziz 2nd Coinage, Silver	—	6.50
☐ 1974	5 Santimat, Monetary Reform, Gold	—	—
☐ 1974–1978	5 Santimat, Monetary Reform, Brass	.23	.39
☐ 1987	5 Santimat, Monetary Reform, Brass	.23	.39

Key to Grading: Bust

☐ 1299–1314	1 Dirham, Hasan I, Silver	—	7.50
☐ 1313–1318	1 Dirham, Abd Al-Aziz 1st Coinage, Silver	—	11.00
☐ 1320–1321	¹/₁₀ Rial, Abd Al-Aziz 2nd Coinage, Silver	—	11.00
☐ 1331	¹/₁₀ Rial, Yusuf: 1st Coinage, Silver	—	60.00

Key to Grading: Coat of Arms

DATE	COIN TYPE/VARIETY/METAL	ABP FINE	AVERAGE FINE
☐ 1974–1978	10 Santimat, Monetary Reform, Brass	$ .23	$ .39
☐ 1974	10 Santimat, Monetary Reform, Gold	—	1200.00
☐ 1974	20 Santimat, Monetary Reform, Gold	—	1125.00
☐ 1974–1978	20 Santimat, Monetary Reform, Brass	.23	.39
☐ 1299–1314	2¹/₂ Dirham, Hasan I, Silver	—	9.00
☐ 1313–1318	2¹/₂ Dirham, Abd Al-Aziz 1st Coinage, Silver	—	13.50
☐ 1320–1321	¹/₄ Rial, Abd Al-Aziz 2nd Coinage, Silver	—	9.00
☐ 1329	¹/₄ Rial, Hafiz, Silver	—	10.50
☐ 1331	¹/₄ Rial, Yusuf: 1st Coinage, Silver	—	52.50
☐ 1921–1924	25 Centimes, Yusuf: 2nd Coinage, Cupro-Nickel	2.80	4.60
☐ 1299–1314	5 Dirham, Hasan I, Silver	—	16.50

Key to Grading: Coin Design

☐ 1313–1318	5 Dirham, Abd Al-Aziz 1st Coinage, Silver	—	18.00
☐ 1320–1323	¹/₂ Rial, Abd Al-Aziz 2nd Coinage, Silver	—	16.50
☐ 1329	¹/₂ Rial, Hafiz, Silver	—	16.50
☐ 1331–1336	¹/₂ Rial, Yusuf: 1st Coinage, Silver	—	18.50

Key to Grading: Star Design

DATE	COIN TYPE/VARIETY/METAL	ABP FINE	AVERAGE FINE
☐ 1921–1924	50 Centimes, Yusuf: 2nd Coinage, Cupro-Nickel	$ .91	$1.50
☐ 1945	50 Centimes, Muhammad V: 2nd Coinage, Aluminum-Bronze	.20	.34
☐ 1974	50 Santimat, Monetary Reform, Gold	478.95	798.25
☐ 1974–1978	50 Santimat, Monetary Reform, Brass	.29	.48
☐ 1987	1/2 Dirham, Monetary Reform, Cupro-Nickel	.29	.48
☐ 1299	10 Durham, Hasan I, Silver	—	30.00

Key to Grading: Star

☐ 1313	10 Durham, Abd Al-Aziz 1st Coinage, Silver	—	142.00
☐ 1320–1321	1 Rial, Abd Al-Aziz 2nd Coinage, Silver	—	45.00
☐ 1329	1 Rial, Hafiz, Silver	—	30.00
☐ 1331–1336	1 Rial, Yusuf: 1st Coinage, Silver	—	24.50

Key to Grading: Star

☐ 1921–1924	1 Franc, Yusuf: 2nd Coinage, Cupro-Nickel	.49	.81
☐ 1945	1 Franc, Muhammad V: 2nd Coinage, Aluminum-Bronze	.26	.43
☐ 1951	1 Franc, Muhammad V: 3rd Coinage, Aluminum	.26	.43
☐ 1960	1 Dirham, Hasan II: Monetary Reform, Silver	.63	1.05
☐ 1965–1969	Dirham, Al Hasan II: Monetary Reform, Nickel	.26	.43
☐ 1974	Dirham, Monetary Reform, Gold	—	1350.00

DATE	COIN TYPE/VARIETY/METAL	ABP FINE	AVERAGE FINE
☐ 1974–1978	Dirham, Monetary Reform, Cupro-Nickel	$ .26	$ .44
☐ 1945	2 Francs, Muhammad V: 2nd Coinage, Aluminum-Bronze	.26	.44
☐ 1951	2 Francs, Muhammad V: 3rd Coinage, Aluminum	.26	.44

Key to Grading: Star

DATE	COIN TYPE/VARIETY/METAL	ABP FINE	AVERAGE FINE
☐ 1347–1352	5 Francs, Muhammad V: 1st Coinage, Silver	—	3.00
☐ 1951	5 Francs, Muhammad V: 3rd Coinage, Aluminum	.33	.55
☐ 1965	5 Dirhams, Al Hasan II: Monetary Reform, Silver	—	6.75
☐ 1975–1980	5 Dirhams, Monetary Reform, Cupro-Nickel	.36	.60
☐ 1975	5 Dirhams, Monetary Reform, Silver	—	130.00
☐ 1975	5 Dirhams, Monetary Reform, Gold	—	1650.00
☐ 1987	5 Dirhams, Monetary Reform, Dual Metal	1.60	2.70

Key to Grading: Star

DATE	COIN TYPE/VARIETY/METAL	ABP FINE	AVERAGE FINE
☐ 1347–1352	10 Francs, Muhammad V: 1st Coinage, Silver	—	6.75
☐ 1366	10 Francs, Muhammad V: 2nd Coinage, Cupro-Nickel	.49	.81
☐ 1371	10 Francs, Muhammad Bin Yusuf: 3rd Coinage, Aluminum-Bronze	.23	.39

Key to Grading: Star

DATE	COIN TYPE/VARIETY/METAL	ABP FINE	AVERAGE FINE
☐ 1347–1352	20 Francs, Muhammad V: 1st Coinage, Silver	—	$12.00
☐ 1366	20 Francs, Muhammad V: 2nd Coinage, Cupro-Nickel	.36	.60
☐ 1371	20 Francs, Muhammad V: 3rd Coinage, Aluminum-Bronze	.26	.44

Key to Grading: Star

☐ 1371	50 Francs, Muhammad V: 3rd Coinage, Aluminum-Bronze	.82	1.40
☐ 1975	50 Dirham, Monetary Reform: 20th Anniversary of Independence, Gold	—	2250.00
☐ 1975	50 Dirham, Monetary Reform: 20th Anniversary of Independence, Silver	—	52.50
☐ 1976–1980	50 Dirham, Monetary Reform: Anniversary of Green March, Gold	—	2650.00
☐ 1976–1980	50 Dirham, Monetary Reform: Anniversary of Green March, Silver	—	95.00
☐ 1979	50 Dirham, Monetary Reform: King Hassan Birthday, Silver	—	65.00
☐ 1979	50 Dirham, Monetary Reform: King Hassan Birthday, Gold	—	2250.00
☐ 1979	50 Dirham, Monetary Reform: Year of the Child, Silver	—	65.00
☐ 1979	50 Dirham, Monetary Reform: Year of the Child, Gold	—	2250.00

Key to Grading: Star

DATE	COIN TYPE/VARIETY/METAL	ABP FINE	AVERAGE FINE
☐ 1953	100 Francs, Muhammad V: 3rd Coinage, Silver	—	$7.00
☐ 1983	100 Dirham, 9th Mediterranean Games, Silver	—	8.25
☐ 1985	100 Dirham, Olympic Games, Silver	—	48.00
☐ 1985	100 Dirham, 25th Year of King Hassan, Silver		54.50
☐ 1986	100 Dirham, Papal Visit, Silver	—	85.00
☐ 1986	100 Dirham, Anniversary of Green March, Silver	—	75.00
☐ 1987	100 Dirham, Rabat Mint Opening, Silver	—	75.00
☐ 1980	150 Dirham, Hejira Calendar Century, Gold	—	2450.00
☐ 1980	150 Dirham, Hejira Calendar Century, Silver	—	78.00
☐ 1981	150 Dirham, King Hassan's Coronation 20th Anniversary, Gold	—	2650.00
☐ 1981	150 Dirham, King Hassan's Coronation 20th Anniversary, Silver	—	75.00
☐ 1953	200 Francs, Muhammad Bin Yusuf: 3rd Coinage, Silver	—	7.25
☐ 1987	200 Dirham, Moroccan American Friendship Treaty, Silver	—	75.00
☐ 1989	200 Dirham, First Francophonie Games, Silver	—	75.00

Key to Grading: Bust

☐ 1956	500 Francs, Mohammed V, Silver	—	12.25
☐ 1979–1985	500 Dirham, King Hassan Birthday, Gold	—	685.00

MOZAMBIQUE

The first coins, crude copper and silver, were used in 1725. The silver onca, a rectangular coin, was in evidence in the 1800s, followed by the silver rupee in the 1860s and the cupro-nickel escudo in the 1930s. Decimal coins appeared in 1935. The currency today is the metical.

Mozambique—Type Coinage

DATE	COIN TYPE/VARIETY/METAL	ABP FINE	AVERAGE FINE
☐ 1975	1 Centimo, Peoples Republic, Aluminum	$33.10	$55.20
☐ 1975	2 Centimos, Peoples Republic, Copper-Zinc	24.70	41.10
☐ 1975	5 Centimos, Peoples Republic, Copper-Zinc	15.60	26.00
☐ 1936	10 Centavos, Bronze	2.80	4.60
☐ 1942	10 Centavos, New Reverse Arms, Bronze	1.40	2.30
☐ 1960–1961	10 Centavos, Reduced Size	.26	.44
☐ 1975	10 Centimos, Peoples Republic, Copper-Zinc	16.20	27.05
☐ 1936	20 Centavos, Bronze	1.65	2.70
☐ 1941	20 Centavos, New Reverse Arms, Bronze	1.65	2.70

Key to Grading: Coat of Arms

DATE	COIN TYPE/VARIETY/METAL	ABP FINE	AVERAGE FINE
□ 1949–1950	20 Centavos, New Reverse Arms, Bronze	$ .39	$ .65
□ 1975	20 Centimos, Peoples Republic, Copper-Zinc	29.20	48.70
□ 1936	50 Centavos, Cupro-Nickel	1.65	2.75
□ 1945	50 Centavos, New Reverse Arms, Bronze	1.85	3.05
□ 1950–1951	50 Centavos, New Reverse Arms, Nickel-Bronze	.36	.60

Key to Grading: Coat of Arms

DATE	COIN TYPE/VARIETY/METAL	ABP FINE	AVERAGE FINE
□ 1953–1957	50 Centavos, Decree of January 21, 1952, Bronze	.23	.39
□ 1975	50 Centimos, Peoples Republic, Copper-Zinc	35.70	59.50
□ 1980–1982	50 Centavos, Monetary Reform: Instrument, Aluminum	.26	.44

Key to Grading: Coat of Arms

DATE	COIN TYPE/VARIETY/METAL	ABP FINE	AVERAGE FINE
□ 1936	1 Escudo, Cupro-Nickel	3.10	5.15
□ 1945	1 Escudo, New Reverse Arms, Bronze	1.40	2.30
□ 1950–1951	1 Escudo, New Reverse Arms, Nickel-Bronze	.49	.80
□ 1953–1974	1 Escudo, Decree of January 21, 1952, Bronze	.22	.37
□ 1975	1 Metical, Peoples Republic, Cupro-Nickel	19.55	32.55
□ 1980–1982	1 Metical, Monetary Reform: Female Student, Brass	3.10	5.15
□ 1986	1 Metical, Monetary Reform: Female Student, Aluminum	.26	.44

Key to Grading: Coat of Arms

DATE	COIN TYPE/VARIETY/METAL	ABP FINE	AVERAGE FINE
☐ 1935	2¹/₂ Escudos, Silver	—	$10.50
☐ 1938–1951	2¹/₂ Escudos, New Reverse Arms, Silver	—	7.50
☐ 1952–1973	2¹/₂ Escudos, Decree of January 21, 1952, Cupro-Nickel	.26	.44
☐ 1975	2¹/₂ Meticais, Peoples Republic, Cupro-Nickel	28.55	47.50
☐ 1980–1986	2¹/₂ Meticais, Monetary Reform: Harbor Scene, Aluminium	.30	.49
☐ 1935	5 Escudos, Silver	—	12.00
☐ 1938–1949	5 Escudos, New Reverse Arms, Silver	—	6.50
☐ 1960	5 Escudos, Decree of January 21, 1952, Silver	—	3.75
☐ 1980–1986	5 Meticais, Monetary Reform: Tractor, Aluminum	.36	.60
☐ 1936	10 Escudos, Silver	—	20.00
☐ 1938	10 Escudos, New Reverse Arms, Silver	—	14.75
☐ 1952–1966	10 Escudos, Decree of January 21, 1952, Silver	—	6.50
☐ 1968–1974	10 Escudos, Copper-Nickel	.23	.39
☐ 1980–1981	10 Meticais, Monetary Reform: Industrial Skyline, Cupro-Nickel	.30	.49
☐ 1986	10 Meticais, Monetary Reform: Industrial Skyline, Aluminum	.26	.44
☐ 1952–1966	20 Escudos, Decree of January 21, 1952, Silver	—	—
☐ 1970–1972	20 Escudos, Nickel	.30	.49
☐ 1980–1982	20 Meticais, Monetary Reform: Panzer Tank, Cupro-Nickel	1.15	1.90
☐ 1986	20 Meticais, Monetary Reform: Panzer Tank, Aluminum	1.15	1.90
☐ 1983	50 Meticais, Monetary Reform: World Fisheries Conference, Cupro-Nickel	1.45	2.40
☐ 1983	50 Meticais, Monetary Reform: World Fisheries Conference, Gold	—	2250.00
☐ 1983	50 Meticais, Monetary Reform: World Fisheries Conference, Silver	—	82.50
☐ 1986	50 Meticais, Monetary Reform: Woman & Soldier, Aluminum	.65	1.10

DATE	COIN TYPE/VARIETY/METAL	ABP FINE	AVERAGE FINE
☐ 1985	250 Meticais, Monetary Reform: 10th Anniversary of Independence, Cupro-Nickel	$7.80	$13.00
☐ 1985	250 Meticais, Monetary Reform: 10th Anniversary of Independence, Silver	—	85.50
☐ 1980	500 Meticais, Monetary Reform: 5th Anniversary of Independence, Silver	—	85.50
☐ 1989	500 Meticais, Monetary Reform: Defense of Nature—Moorish Idol Fish, Silver	—	85.50
☐ 1989	500 Meticais, Monetary Reform: Defense of Nature—Lions, Silver	—	85.50
☐ 1989	500 Meticais, Monetary Reform: Defense of Nature—Giraffes, Silver	—	85.50
☐ 1988	1000 Meticais, Monetary Reform: Papal Visit, Silver	—	85.50
☐ 1985	2000 Meticais, Monetary Reform: 10th Anniversary of Independence, Gold	—	1200.00
☐ 1980	5000 Meticais, Monetary Reform: 5th Anniversary of Independence, Gold	—	925.00

NEPAL

The first coins, used in the 6th century A.D., were of silver and copper. Small gold, silver, and copper coins were used in the 12th to 16th centuries. The silver mohur was used in the 17th century, followed by the gold presentation coin in the 1700s, the copper paisa in the 1800s, and the aluminum paisa in the 1900s. Decimal coins were used in 1932. The currency today is the rupee.

Nepal—Type Coinage

DATE	COIN TYPE/VARIETY/METAL	ABP FINE	AVERAGE FINE
☐ 1953–1957	5 Paisa, Bronze	$ .39	$ .65
☐ 1953–1955	10 Paisa, Hands Praying, Bronze	.16	.27
☐ 1953–1954	20 Paisa, Copper-Nickel	17.50	29.15
☐ 1932–1947	20 Paisa, Trident, Rev: Sword, Silver	—	7.00
☐ 1932–1948	50 Paisa, Trident, Rev: Sword, Silver	—	7.00
☐ 1953–1954	50 Paisa, Head of Tribhubana, Silver	—	2.50
☐ 1950	Rupee, Trident, Rev: Sword, Silver	—	7.00
☐ 1932–1948	Rupee, Trident, Rev: Sword, Silver	—	7.00

NETHERLANDS

The first coins were base-gold tremisses, then silver deniers. A revival of gold coinage occurred in the 14th century. In 1606 a new range of coins was established, including the gold ducat and the silver rijksdaalder. In 1680 gulden pieces were added. In 1830 a decimal system, consisting of 100 cents to the gulden, was established. Today the Netherlands uses the euro.

Netherlands—Type Coinage

☐ 1850–1877	½ Cent, Copper	8.45	14.00

Key to Grading: Lion

DATE	COIN TYPE/VARIETY/METAL	ABP FINE	AVERAGE FINE
☐ 1878–1901	½ Cent, Obv: KONINGRIJK, Bronze	$4.20	$7.05
☐ 1903–1906	½ Cent, Obv: KONINKRIJK, Bronze	.52	.87
☐ 1909–1940	½ Cent, Wilhelmina—3rd Coinage, Bronze	.52	.87
☐ 1860–1877	1 Cent, Copper	4.60	7.70

Key to Grading: Lion

☐ 1877–1901	1 Cent, Obv: KONINGRIJK, Bronze	2.60	4.35
☐ 1901	1 Cent, Obv: KONINKRIJK, Bronze	1.80	3.05
☐ 1902–1907	1 Cent, Obv: KONINKRIJK, Bronze	1.80	3.05
☐ 1913–1941	1 Cent, Wilhelmina—3rd Coinage, Bronze	1.80	3.05
☐ 1941–1944	1 Cent, WWII Occupation, Zinc	1.80	3.05
☐ 1948	1 Cent, Wilhelmina, Bronze	.26	.44
☐ 1950–1980	1 Cent, Juliana, Bronze	.26	.44

Key to Grading: Lion

☐ 1877–1898	2½ Cents, Obv: KONINGRIJK, Bronze	3.35	5.60
☐ 1903–1906	2½ Cents, Obv: KONINKRIJK, Bronze	3.05	5.10
☐ 1912–1941	2½ Cents, Wilhelmina—3rd Coinage, Bronze	3.05	5.10
☐ 1941–1942	2½ Cents, WWII Occupation, Zinc	.66	1.10

DATE	COIN TYPE/VARIETY/METAL	ABP FINE	AVERAGE FINE
☐ 1850–1887	5 Cents, Willem III, Silver	—	$14.00
☐ 1907–1909	5 Cents, Wilhelmina—2nd Coinage, Cupro-Nickel	5.90	9.85
☐ 1913–1940	5 Cents, Wilhelmina—3rd Coinage, Cupro-Nickel	1.30	2.20
☐ 1941–1943	5 Cents, WWII Occupation, Zinc	2.60	4.35
☐ 1948	5 Cents, Wilhelmina, Bronze	.26	.44
☐ 1950–2001	5 Cents, Juliana, Bronze	.16	.27
☐ 1849–1890	10 Cents, Willem III, Silver	—	25.00
☐ 1892–1897	10 Cents, Wilhelmina—1st Coinage, Obv: Child Head, Rev: Value in Wreath, Silver	—	7.50
☐ 1898–1901	10 Cents, Wilhelmina—2nd Coinage, Obv: Young Head, Silver	—	12.00
☐ 1903	10 Cents, Wilhelmina—2nd Coinage, Obv: Large Head, Silver	—	6.50
☐ 1904–1906	10 Cents, Wilhelmina—2nd Coinage, Obv: Small Head, Silver	—	12.00

Key to Grading: Bust

DATE	COIN TYPE/VARIETY/METAL	ABP FINE	AVERAGE FINE
☐ 1910–1925	10 Cents, Wilhelmina—3rd Coinage, Obv: Adult Head, Silver	—	3.50
☐ 1926–1945	10 Cents, Wilhelmina—4th Coinage, Obv: Older Head, Silver	—	2.00
☐ 1941–1943	10 Cents, WWII Occupation, Zinc	.49	.81
☐ 1948	10 Cents, Wilhelmina, Nickel	.26	.44
☐ 1950–2001	10 Cents, Juliana, Nickel	.26	.44
☐ 1849–1890	25 Cents, Willem III, Silver	—	128.50
☐ 1892–1897	25 Cents, Wilhelmina—1st Coinage, Obv: Child Head, Rev: Value in Wreath, Silver	—	17.50
☐ 1898–1906	25 Cents, Wilhelmina—2nd Coinage, Silver	—	12.00
☐ 1910–1925	25 Cents, Wilhelmina—3rd Coinage, Obv: Adult Head, Silver	—	7.50

Key to Grading: Bust

DATE	COIN TYPE/VARIETY/METAL	ABP FINE	AVERAGE FINE
☐ 1926–1945	25 Cents, Wilhelmina—4th Coinage, Obv: Older Head, Silver	—	$7.00
☐ 1948	25 Cents, Wilhelmina, Nickel	.29	.48
☐ 1950–1980	25 Cents, Juliana, Nickel	.29	.48
☐ 1980	25 Cents, Juliana, Aluminum	256.00	420.00
☐ 1982–2001	Juliana, Nickel	.29	.48
☐ 1853–1868	½ Gulden, Willem III, Silver	—	18.50
☐ 1898	½ Gulden, Wilhelmina—2nd Coinage, Silver	—	26.50
☐ 1904–1909	½ Gulden, Wilhelmina—2nd Coinage, Silver	—	18.25
☐ 1910–1919	½ Gulden, Wilhelmina—3rd Coinage, Obv: Adult Head, Silver	—	8.75
☐ 1921–1930	½ Gulden, Wilhelmina—4th Coinage, Obv: Older Head, Silver	—	6.50
☐ 1849–1975	1 Ducat, Trade Coins, Gold	—	222.50
☐ 1851–1866	1 Gulden, Willem III, Silver	—	21.00
☐ 1892–1897	1 Gulden, Wilhelmina—1st Coinage, Obv: Child Head, Rev: Value in Wreath, Silver	—	22.50
☐ 1898–1901	1 Gulden, Wilhelmina—2nd Coinage, Silver	—	38.50
☐ 1904–1909	1 Gulden, Wilhelmina—2nd Coinage, Silver	—	21.50
☐ 1910–1917	1 Gulden, Wilhelmina—3rd Coinage, Obv: Adult Head, Silver	—	35.50

Key to Grading: Bust

DATE	COIN TYPE/VARIETY/METAL	ABP FINE	AVERAGE FINE
☐ 1922–1945	1 Gulden, Wilhelmina—4th Coinage, Obv: Older Head, Silver	—	6.50
☐ 1954–1967	1 Gulden, Juliana, Silver	—	2.45

DATE	COIN TYPE/VARIETY/METAL	ABP FINE	AVERAGE FINE
☐ 1980–2001	1 Gulden, Nickel	$1.04	$1.73
☐ 1989	1 Silver Ducat, Silver Wedding Anniversary, Silver	—	30.00
☐ 1854–1967	2 Ducat, Trade Coins, Gold	—	Rare
☐ 1849–1874	2½ Gulden, Willem III, Silver	—	30.00
☐ 1898	2½ Gulden, Wilhelmina—2nd Coinage, Silver	—	285.50

Key to Grading: Bust

☐ 1929–1940	2½ Gulden, Wilhelmina—4th Coinage, Obv: Older Head, Silver	—	8.00
☐ 1959–1966	2½ Gulden, Juliana, Silver	—	7.00
☐ 1969–1980	2½ Gulden, Juliana, Nickel	2.90	4.90
☐ 1980–2001	Juliana, Nickel	1.65	2.70
☐ 1817–1832	3 Gulden, Willem, Silver	—	475.00

Key to Grading: Bust

☐ 1851	5 Gulden, Willem III, Gold	—	685.00
☐ 1912	5 Gulden, Wilhelmina—3rd Coinage, Obv: Adult Head, Gold	—	82.50
☐ 1987–2001	5 Gulden, Juliana, Clad	—	6.50

Key to Grading: Bust

☐ 1851	10 Gulden, Willem III, Gold	—	1000.00

DATE	COIN TYPE/VARIETY/METAL	ABP FINE	AVERAGE FINE
☐ 1875	10 Gulden, Willem III, Rev: Date at Top, Gold	—	$15.00
☐ 1876–1889	10 Gulden, Willem III, Rev: Date at Bottom, Gold	—	210.00
☐ 1892–1897	10 Gulden, Wilhelmina—1st Coinage, Obv: Child Head, Rev: Value in Wreath, Gold	—	2500.00
☐ 1898	10 Gulden, Wilhelmina—2nd Coinage, Gold	—	2500.00
☐ 1911–1917	10 Gulden, Wilhelmina—3rd Coinage, Obv: Adult Head, Gold	—	128.50
☐ 1925–1933	10 Gulden, Wilhelmina—4th Coinage, Obv: Older Head, Gold	—	128.50
☐ 1850–1853	20 Gulden, Willem III, Gold	—	1850.00
☐ 1982	50 Gulden, Dutch American Friendship, Gold	—	Rare (only 2)
☐ 1982	50 Gulden, Dutch American Friendship, Silver	—	68.50
☐ 1984	50 Gulden, 400th Anniversary of Death of William of Orange, Silver	—	52.50
☐ 1987	50 Gulden, Golden Wedding of Queen Mother, Silver	—	75.50
☐ 1988	50 Gulden, 300th Anniversary of William & Mary, Silver	—	75.50
☐ 1990	50 Gulden, 100 Years of Queens, Silver	—	75.50
☐ 1991	50 Gulden, Silver Wedding Anniversary, Silver	—	52.50

NEW ZEALAND

Various foreign coins including Spanish-American, French, Indian, and British were in use in the early 19th century. In 1859, the copper half penny token was in use, followed by the silver florin in the 1930s. New Zealand's first coinage was issued in 1933 and included silver three pences, six pences, shillings, florins, and half crowns. Decimal coins were used in 1967. The currency today is the dollar.

New Zealand—Type Coinage

Key to Grading: Bust

DATE	COIN TYPE/VARIETY/METAL	ABP FINE	AVERAGE FINE
☐ 1940–1947	½ Penny, George VI, Bronze	$ .29	$ .48
☐ 1949–1952	½ Penny, King George the Sixth, Bronze	.29	.48
☐ 1953–1965	½ Penny, Elizabeth II, Bronze	.29	.48

Key to Grading: Bust

☐ 1940–1947	1 Penny, George VI, Bronze	.29	.48
☐ 1949–1952	1 Penny, King George the Sixth, Bronze	.29	.48
☐ 1953–1965	1 Penny, Elizabeth II, Bronze	.29	.48

Key to Grading: Tiara

☐ 1967–1988	1 Cent, Decimal Coinage: Silver Fern Leaf, Bronze	.29	.48
☐ 1933–1936	3 Pence, George V, Silver	.29	.48

Key to Grading: Bust

DATE	COIN TYPE/VARIETY/METAL	ABP FINE	AVERAGE FINE
☐ 1937–1946	3 Pence, George VI, Silver	—	$2.50
☐ 1947	3 Pence, George VI, Cupro-Nickel	.25	.42
☐ 1948–1952	3 Pence, King George the Sixth, Cupro-Nickel	.36	.60
☐ 1953–1965	3 Pence, Elizabeth II, Cupro-Nickel	.23	.38

Key to Grading: Tiara

☐ 1967–1988	2 Cents, Decimal Coinage: Kowhai Leaves, Bronze	.26	.43

☐ 1933–1936	6 Pence, George V, Silver	—	2.50
☐ 1937–1946	6 Pence, George VI, Silver	—	2.50
☐ 1947	6 Pence, George VI, Cupro-Nickel	.88	1.50
☐ 1948–1952	6 Pence, King George the Sixth, Cupro-Nickel	.49	.81
☐ 1953–1965	6 Pence, Elizabeth II, Cupro-Nickel	.33	.55

Key to Grading: Bust

DATE	COIN TYPE/VARIETY/METAL	ABP FINE	AVERAGE FINE
☐ 1933–1935	1 Shilling, George V, Silver	—	$4.30
☐ 1937–1946	1 Shilling, George VI, Silver	—	2.00
☐ 1947	1 Shilling, George VI, Cupro-Nickel	1.80	3.00
☐ 1948–1952	1 Shilling, King George the Sixth, Cupro-Nickel	.88	1.50
☐ 1953–1965	1 Shilling, Elizabeth II, Cupro-Nickel	.88	1.50

Key to Grading: Tiara

☐ 1967 to Date	5 Cents, Decimal Coinage: Tuatara, Cupro-Nickel	.26	.43

Key to Grading: Bust

☐ 1933–1936	1 Florin, George V, Silver	—	6.50
☐ 1937–1946	1 Florin, George VI, Silver	—	4.20
☐ 1947	1 Florin, George VI, Cupro-Nickel	1.70	3.00
☐ 1948–1951	1 Florin, King George the Sixth, Cupro-Nickel	1.70	3.00
☐ 1953–1965	1 Florin, Elizabeth II, Cupro-Nickel	.26	.43

Key to Grading: Tiara

DATE	COIN TYPE/VARIETY/METAL	ABP FINE	AVERAGE FINE
☐ 1967 to Date	10 Cents, Decimal Coinage: Maori Mask, Cupro-Nickel	$ .26	$ .43

Key to Grading: Bust

DATE	COIN TYPE/VARIETY/METAL	ABP FINE	AVERAGE FINE
☐ 1933–1935	1/2 Crown, George V, Silver	—	7.00
☐ 1937–1946	1/2 Crown, George VI, Silver	—	7.00
☐ 1940	1/2 Crown, George VI: Centennial of British Settlement, Silver	2.80	4.65
☐ 1947	1/2 Crown, George VI, Cupro-Nickel	.39	.65
☐ 1948–1951	1/2 Crown, King George the Sixth, Cupro-Nickel	.39	.65
☐ 1953–1965	1/2 Crown, Elizabeth II, Cupro-Nickel	.39	.65

Key to Grading: Tiara

DATE	COIN TYPE/VARIETY/METAL	ABP FINE	AVERAGE FINE
☐ 1967–1989	20 Cents, Decimal Coinage: Kiwi, Cupro-Nickel	.36	.60
☐ 1990	20 Cents, Decimal Coinage: 1990 Anniversary Celebrations, Silver	—	17.00
☐ 1990	20 Cents, Decimal Coinage: 1990 Anniversary Celebrations, Cupro-Nickel	2.80	4.70

DATE	COIN TYPE/VARIETY/METAL	ABP FINE	AVERAGE FINE
☐ 1935	1 Crown, George V: 25th Year of Reign—Treaty of Waitangi, Silver	—	$1425.00
☐ 1949	1 Crown, King George the Sixth: Proposed Royal Visit, Cupro-Nickel	$1.65	2.70

Key to Grading: Hair Lines

| ☐ 1953 | 1 Crown, Elizabeth II, Cupro-Nickel | 1.65 | 2.70 |

Key to Grading: Tiara

| ☐ 1967–1985 | 50 Cents, Decimal Coinage: Endeavour, Cupro-Nickel | .45 | .76 |
| ☐ 1986 to Date | 50 Cents, Decimal Coinage: Elizabeth II, Cupro-Nickel | .45 | .76 |

Key to Grading: Tiara

☐ 1967–1976	1 Dollar, Decimalization Commemorative, Lettered Edge, Cupro-Nickel	.98	1.65
☐ 1969	1 Dollar, Captain Cook— 200th Anniversary, Cupro-Nickel	.36	.60
☐ 1970	1 Dollar, Cook Islands, Cupro-Nickel	2.80	4.60
☐ 1970	1 Dollar, Royal Visit—Mount Cook, Cupro-Nickel	.82	1.40
☐ 1974	1 Dollar, Commonwealth Games, Cupro-Nickel	.82	1.40

DATE	COIN TYPE/VARIETY/METAL	ABP FINE	AVERAGE FINE
☐ 1974	1 Dollar, Commonwealth Games, Silver	—	$40.00
☐ 1974	1 Dollar, New Zealand Day—Kotuku, Cupro-Nickel	1.64	2.73
☐ 1977	1 Dollar, Waitangi Day—Treaty House, Cupro-Nickel	1.64	2.73
☐ 1977	1 Dollar, Waitangi Day—Treaty House, Silver	—	24.50
☐ 1978	1 Dollar, Coronation 25th Anniversary—Parliament, Silver	—	24.50
☐ 1978	1 Dollar, Coronation 25th Anniversary—Parliament, Cupro-Nickel	1.65	2.80
☐ 1979	1 Dollar, Cupro-Nickel	.82	1.30
☐ 1979	1 Dollar, Silver	—	18.50
☐ 1980	1 Dollar, Fantail, Cupro-Nickel	.82	1.30
☐ 1980	1 Dollar, Fantail, Silver	—	23.00
☐ 1981	1 Dollar, Royal Visit—English Oak, Cupro-Nickel	.82	1.30
☐ 1981	1 Dollar, Royal Visit—English Oak, Silver	—	20.00
☐ 1982	1 Dollar, Takaha, Silver	—	26.75
☐ 1982	1 Dollar, Takaha, Cupro-Nickel	.82	1.30
☐ 1983	1 Dollar, 50 Years of Coinage, Silver	—	18.50
☐ 1983	1 Dollar, Royal Visit, Cupro-Nickel	1.65	2.80
☐ 1983	1 Dollar, Royal Visit, Silver	—	34.75
☐ 1983	1 Dollar, 50 Years of Coinage, Cupro-Nickel	1.80	3.05
☐ 1984	1 Dollar, Chatham Island Black Robin, Cupro-Nickel	1.80	3.05
☐ 1984	1 Dollar, Chatham Island Black Robin, Silver	—	32.75
☐ 1985	1 Dollar, Black Stilt, Silver	—	22.75
☐ 1985	1 Dollar, Black Stilt, Cupro-Nickel	1.65	2.80
☐ 1986	1 Dollar, Royal Visit, Silver	—	28.50
☐ 1986	1 Dollar, Royal Visit, Cupro-Nickel	1.65	2.80
☐ 1986	1 Dollar, Kakapo, Silver	—	28.50
☐ 1986	1 Dollar, Kakapo, Cupro-Nickel	1.65	2.80
☐ 1987	1 Dollar, National Parks Centennial, Cupro-Nickel	1.65	2.80
☐ 1987	1 Dollar, National Parks Centennial, Silver	—	36.50
☐ 1988	1 Dollar, Yellow-eyed Penguin, Cupro-Nickel	1.65	2.80
☐ 1988	1 Dollar, Yellow-eyed Penguin, Silver	—	68.50
☐ 1989	1 Dollar, XIV Commonwealth Games—Runner, Cupro-Nickel	1.65	2.80
☐ 1989	1 Dollar, XIV Commonwealth Games—Swimmer, Silver	—	42.50

DATE	COIN TYPE/VARIETY/METAL	ABP FINE	AVERAGE FINE
☐ 1989	1 Dollar, XIV Commonwealth Games—Weightlifter, Silver	—	$30.00
☐ 1989	1 Dollar, XIV Commonwealth Games—Weightlifter, Cupro-Nickel	1.65	2.70
☐ 1989	1 Dollar, XIV Commonwealth Games—Runner, Silver	—	30.00
☐ 1989	1 Dollar, XIV Commonwealth Games—Swimmer, Cupro-Nickel	1.65	2.70
☐ 1989	1 Dollar, XIV Commonwealth Games—Gymnast, Silver	—	30.00
☐ 1989	1 Dollar, XIV Commonwealth Games—Gymnast, Cupro-Nickel	1.80	3.05
☐ 1990	1 Dollar, Kiwi Bird, Silver	—	38.00
☐ 1990	1 Dollar, Anniversary Celebrations, Silver	—	50.00
☐ 1990	1 Dollar, Anniversary Celebrations, Cupro-Nickel	1.80	3.05
☐ 1990	1 Dollar, Kiwi Bird, Aluminum-Bronze	1.80	3.05
☐ 1990	2 Dollars, White Heron, Silver	—	42.50

Key to Grading: Crown

DATE	COIN TYPE/VARIETY/METAL	ABP FINE	AVERAGE FINE
☐ 1990	2 Dollars, White Heron, Aluminum-Bronze	2.70	4.60
☐ 1990	5 Dollars, ANZAC Memorial, Aluminum-Bronze	$27.00	44.90
☐ 1991	5 Dollars, Rugby World Cup, Cupro-Nickel	5.00	8.35
☐ 1991	5 Dollars, Rugby World Cup, Silver	—	27.50
☐ 1992	5 Dollars, 25th Anniversary of Decimalization, Cupro-Nickel	5.75	9.55
☐ 1992	5 Dollars, 25th Anniversary of Decimalization, Silver	—	42.50
☐ 1990	150 Dollars, Kiwi, Gold	—	575.00

NORWAY

In the 9th century some Anglo-Saxon and Frankish coins were in circulation, but were most likely used as jewelry. Silver pennies were minted in the late 10th century, followed by bracteates and skillings, ducats, and dalers. Anglo-Saxon and German coins were important in the 980s and 990s, but English coins dropped and Danish coins became more important after 1050. The main Norwegian series began around 1047. By the 12th century, the Norwegian penny was a bracteate. The only coins struck in Norway at first were base-silver hvids. Larger silver coins were issued in the 16th century. In 1874 a new decimal system was based on the krone.

Norway—Type Coinage

DATE	COIN TYPE/VARIETY/METAL	ABP FINE	AVERAGE FINE
☐ 1839–1841	½ Skilling, Charles XIV, Rev: Lion, Copper	$5.00	$8.35

Key to Grading: Crown

DATE	COIN TYPE/VARIETY/METAL	ABP FINE	AVERAGE FINE
☐ 1863–1872	½ Skilling, Charles XV, Rev: Lion, Copper	5.75	9.55
☐ 1819–1837	1 Skilling, Charles XIV, Rev: Lion, Copper	24.60	41.10
☐ 1867–1870	1 Skilling, Charles XV, Rev: Lion, Copper	3.25	5.40

Key to Grading: Crown

DATE	COIN TYPE/VARIETY/METAL	ABP FINE	AVERAGE FINE
☐ 1876–1902	1 Ore, Oscar II, Rev: Lion, Bronze	$5.00	$8.45
☐ 1906–1950	1 Ore, Haakon VII, Monograms, Bronze	.98	1.60
☐ 1952–1972	1 Ore, Postwar, Obv: Lion, Rev: Monogram	.23	.38
☐ 1822–1834	2 Skillings, Charles XIV, Rev: Lion, Copper	5.00	8.45
☐ 1876–1902	2 Ore, Oscar II, Rev: Lion, Bronze	3.25	5.40

Key to Grading: Crown

☐ 1906–1952	2 Ore, Haakon VII, Monograms, Bronze	.52	.86
☐ 1952–1972	2 Ore, Postwar, Obv: Lion, Rev: Monogram, Bronze	.23	.38
☐ 1870–1872	2 Skillings, Charles XV, Rev: Lion, Copper	3.00	4.80
☐ 1868–1872	3 Skillings, Charles XV, Rev: Lion, Silver	—	15.00
☐ 1825–1842	4 Skillings, Charles XIV, Rev: Lion, Silver	—	11.50

Key to Grading: Crown

☐ 1875–1902	5 Ore, Oscar II, Rev: Lion, Bronze	3.00	5.00
☐ 1907–1952	5 Ore, Haakon VII, Monograms, Bronze	1.50	2.50
☐ 1952–1973	5 Ore, Postwar, Obv: Lion, Rev: Monogram, Bronze	.26	.43

Key to Grading: Crown

DATE	COIN TYPE/VARIETY/METAL	ABP FINE	AVERAGE FINE
☐ 1819–1827	8 Skillings, Charles, XIV, Rev: Lion, Silver	—	$48.00
☐ 1845–1856	12 Skillings, Oscar I, Rev: Lion, Silver	—	38.50
☐ 1861–1872	12 Skillings, Charles XV, Rev: Lion, Silver	—	765.50
☐ 1874–1903	10 Ore, Oscar II, Rev: Lion, Silver	—	45.50
☐ 1909–1920	10 Ore, Haakon VII, Monograms Around Hole, Silver	—	11.00

Key to Grading: Crown

☐ 1920–1951	10 Ore, Haakon VII, Monograms Around Hole, Cupro-Nickel	.39	.65
☐ 1951–1992	10 Ore, Postwar, Obv: Lion, Rev: Monogram, Cupro-Nickel	.39	.65
☐ 1819–1836	24 Skillings, Charles XIV, Rev: Lion, Silver	—	84.50
☐ 1845–1855	24 Skillings, Oscar I, Rev: Lion, Silver	—	30.50
☐ 1861–1872	24 Skillings, Charles XV, Rev: Lion, Silver	—	Scarce
☐ 1876–1904	25 Ore, Oscar II, Rev: Lion, Silver	—	40.50
☐ 1909–1919	25 Ore, Haakon VII, Monograms, Silver	—	24.50

Key to Grading: Crown

DATE	COIN TYPE/VARIETY/METAL	ABP FINE	AVERAGE FINE
☐ 1920–1950	25 Ore, Haakon VII, Monograms Around Hole, Cupro-Nickel	$.52	$ .86
☐ 1952–1982	25 Ore, Postwar, Obv: Lion, Rev: Monogram, Cupro-Nickel	.23	.38
☐ 1819–1844	1/2 Speciedaler, Charles XI, Rev: Lion, Silver	—	165.50
☐ 1846–1855	1/2 Speciedaler, Oscar I, Rev: Lion, Silver	—	110.50

Key to Grading: Crown

☐ 1861–1872	1/2 Speciedaler, Charles XV, Rev: Lion, Silver	—	Rare
☐ 1874–1904	50 Ore, Oscar II, Rev: Lion, Silver	—	42.50
☐ 1909–1917	50 Ore, Haakon VII, Monograms, Silver	—	38.50

Key to Grading: Crown

☐ 1920–1949	50 Ore, Haakon VII, Monograms Around Hole, Cupro-Nickel	.36	.60
☐ 1953–1996	50 Ore, Postwar, Obv: Lion, Rev: Monogram, Cupro-Nickel	.29	.48

Key to Grading: Bust

DATE	COIN TYPE/VARIETY/METAL	ABP FINE	AVERAGE FINE
☐ 1819–1836	1 Speciedaler, Charles XIV, Rev: Lion, Silver	—	$260.00
☐ 1846–1857	1 Speciedaler, Oscar I, Rev: Lion, Silver	—	260.00
☐ 1861–1872	1 Speciedaler, Charles XV, Rev: Lion, Silver	—	420.00
☐ 1875–1904	Krone, Oscar II, Rev: Lion, Silver	—	75.50
☐ 1908–1917	Krone, Haakon VII, Monograms Around Hole, Silver	—	58.50

Key to Grading: Crown

DATE	COIN TYPE/VARIETY/METAL	ABP FINE	AVERAGE FINE
☐ 1925–1951	Krone, Haakon VII, Monograms Around Hole, Cupro-Nickel	.36	.60
☐ 1951–1991	Krone, Postwar, Obv: Lion, Rev: Monogram, Cupro-Nickel	.29	.48
☐ 1878–1904	2 Kroner, Oscar II, Rev: Lion, Silver	—	—
☐ 1906–1907	2 Kroner, Haakon VII, Rev: St. Olaf Standing, Silver	—	34.50
☐ 1908–1917	2 Kroner, Haakon VII, Rev: Lion & Shields, Silver	—	48.50
☐ 1914	2 Kroner, Haakon VII, Centenary of Constitution, Silver	—	23.00
☐ 1873–1902	10 Kroner, Oscar II, Rev: Lion, Gold	—	345.50
☐ 1910	10 Kroner, Haakon VII, Rev: St. Olaf Standing, Gold	—	245.50
☐ 1873–1902	20 Kroner, Oscar II, Rev: Lion, Gold	—	325.50
☐ 1910	20 Kroner, Haakon VII, Rev: St. Olaf Standing, Gold	—	265.00

PAKISTAN

The first coins were used in the 4th century B.C. and were of silver, followed by copper. The gold stater was in evidence in 130, and the silver dirham in 1028. The silver rupee appeared in 1826. The decimal system was established in 1961. The currency used today is the rupee.

Pakistan—Type Coinage

DATE	COIN TYPE/VARIETY/METAL	ABP FINE	AVERAGE FINE
☐ 1961	1 Pice, Bronze	$.26	$ .43

Key to Grading: Wheat Head

☐ 1961–1965	1 Paisa, Bronze	.29	.48
☐ 1965–1966	1 Paisa, Nickel-Brass	.29	.48
☐ 1967–1979	1 Paisa, Aluminum	.29	.48
☐ 1964–1966	2 Paisa, Bronze	.29	.48

DATE	COIN TYPE/VARIETY/METAL	ABP FINE	AVERAGE FINE
☐ 1966–1976	2 Paisa, Aluminum	$.26	$ .43
☐ 1961	5 Pice, Nickel-Brass	.26	.43

Key to Grading: Wreath

☐ 1961–1974	5 Paisa, Nickel-Brass	.20	.33
☐ 1974–1994	5 Paisa, Aluminum	.20	.33
☐ 1950	1 Pie, Bronze	.25	.42
☐ 1961	10 Pice, Cupro-Nickel	.25	.42
☐ 1961–1974	10 Paisa, Cupro-Nickel	.25	.42
☐ 1974–1990	10 Paisa, Aluminum	.25	.42
☐ 1948–1952	1 Pice, Holed, Bronze	.25	.42
☐ 1953–1959	1 Pice, Nickel-Brass	.25	.42
☐ 1963–1967	25 Paisa, Nickel	.25	.42
☐ 1967 to Date	25 Paisa, Cupro-Nickel	.25	.42
☐ 1976	50 Paisa, Anniversary of Mohammed Ali Jinnah, Cupro-Nickel	.25	.42
☐ 1981	50 Paisa, AH1401—1400th Anniversary of Hegira, Cupro-Nickel	.25	.42
☐ 1948–1951	¹/₂ Anna, Crescent, Cupro-Nickel	.25	.42
☐ 1953–1958	¹/₂ Anna, Nickel-Brass	.14	.23
☐ 1963–1969	50 Paisa, Nickel	.20	.33
☐ 1969 to Date	50 Paisa, Cupro-Nickel	.20	.33
☐ 1948–1949	1 Rupee, Crescent to Right, Nickel	.49	.81
☐ 1977	1 Rupee, Islamic Summit Conference, Cupro-Nickel	.26	.43
☐ 1977	1 Rupee, Centennial of Birth of Allama Mohammad Iqbai, Cupro-Nickel	.26	.43
☐ 1979–1988	1 Rupee, Cupro-Nickel	.26	.43
☐ 1981	1 Rupee, World Food Day, Cupro-Nickel	.26	.43
☐ 1981	1 Rupee, 1400th Hegira Anniversary, Cupro-Nickel	.29	.48
☐ 1948–1952	1 Anna, Crescent to Right, Cupro-Nickel	.29	.48
☐ 1950	1 Anna, Crescent to Left, Cupro-Nickel	2.60	4.30
☐ 1953–1958	1 Anna, Cupro-Nickel	.26	.43
☐ 1948–1952	2 Annas, Crescent to Right, Cupro-Nickel	.26	.43
☐ 1950	2 Annas, Crescent to Left, Cupro-Nickel	2.60	4.30
☐ 1953–1959	2 Annas, Cupro-Nickel	.20	.33
☐ 1948–1951	¹/₄ Rupee, Crescent to Right, Nickel	.25	.41

DATE	COIN TYPE/VARIETY/METAL	ABP FINE	AVERAGE FINE
☐ 1950	¼ Rupee, Crescent to Left, Nickel	$5.73	$9.55
☐ 1948–1951	½ Rupee, Crescent to Right, Nickel	.36	.60
☐ 1976	100 Rupees, Conservation Series—Pheasant, Silver	—	84.50
☐ 1976	100 Rupees, Centennial of Birth of Mohammad Ali Jinnah, Silver	—	84.50
☐ 1977	100 Rupees, Centennial of Birth of Allama Mohammad Iqbai, Silver	—	84.50
☐ 1977	100 Rupees, Islamic Summit Conference, Silver	—	56.50
☐ 1976	150 Rupees, Conservation Series—Crocodile, Silver	—	84.50
☐ 1977	500 Rupees, Centennial of Birth Allama Mohammad Iqbai, Gold	—	200.00
☐ 1977	1000 Rupees, Islamic Summit Conference, Gold	—	420.00
☐ 1976	3000 Rupees, Conservation Series—Astor Markhor, Gold	—	950.00

PALESTINE

The following group of coins were produced during Great Britain's rule of Palestine (1922–1948). In 1948, when Palestine became the state of Israel, the coinage was changed significantly to the coins that you will find listed under the ISRAEL section of this book.

Palestine—Type Coinage

Key to Grading: Plant

DATE	COIN TYPE/VARIETY/METAL	ABP FINE	AVERAGE FINE
☐ 1927–1948	Mil, Hebrew-English-Arabic Legends, Rev: Olive Sprig, Bronze	$2.90	$4.90

Key to Grading: Plant

☐ 1927–1947	2 Mils, Hebrew-English-Arabic Legends, Rev: Olive Sprig, Bronze	3.80	6.30

Key to Grading: Wreath

☐ 1927–1947	5 Mils, Wreath, Cupro-Nickel	3.00	4.90
☐ 1942–1944	5 Mils, Bronze	3.00	4.90
☐ 1927–1947	10 Mils, Wreath, Cupro-Nickel	3.25	5.40

Key to Grading: Wreath

☐ 1942–1943	10 Mils, Bronze	5.20	8.70
☐ 1927–1941	20 Mils, Holed Wreath, Cupro-Nickel	12.70	21.10
☐ 1942–1944	20 Mils, Bronze	10.70	17.85
☐ 1927–1942	50 Mils, Olive Sprig, Silver	—	24.50

Key to Grading: Plant

DATE	COIN TYPE/VARIETY/METAL	ABP FINE	AVERAGE FINE
☐ 1927–1942	100 Mils, Olive Sprig, Silver	—	$30.00

PHILIPPINES

The first small, gold coins known as piloncitos were used before the 13th century, followed by cast-bronze square-holed coins. Silver dollars were issued in 1827. The silver reales and copper quarto were in use in the 1800s, followed by the silver peso and cupro-nickel piso in the 1900s. The decimal system was established in 1861. Today's currency is the piso.

Philippines—Spanish Colonies Coinage

Key to Grading: Bust

DATE	COIN TYPE/VARIETY/METAL	ABP FINE	AVERAGE FINE
☐ 1864–1868	10 Centimos, Isabel II, Silver	—	$58.50
☐ 1880–1885	10 Centimos, Alfonso XII, Silver	—	58.50
☐ 1864–1868	20 Centimos, Isabel II, Silver	—	62.50
☐ 1880–1885	20 Centimos, Alfonso XII, Silver	—	52.50
☐ 1865–1868	50 Centimos, Isabel II, Silver	—	265.00
☐ 1880–1885	50 Centimos, Alfonso XII, Silver	—	52.50
☐ 1861–1868	1 Peso, Isabel II, Gold	—	142.50
☐ 1897	1 Peso, Alfonso XIII, Silver	—	68.50
☐ 1861–1868	2 Pesos, Isabel II, Gold	—	230.00
☐ 1861–1868	4 Pesos, Isabel II, Gold	—	525.00
☐ 1880–1885	4 Pesos, Alfonso XII, Gold	—	1275.00

Philippines—U.S. Territorial Coinage

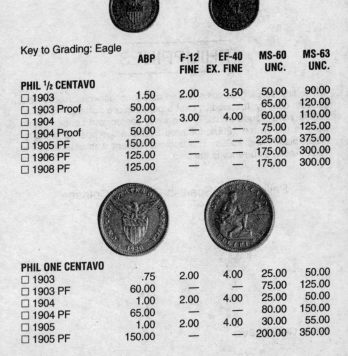

Key to Grading: Eagle	ABP	F-12 FINE	EF-40 EX. FINE	MS-60 UNC.	MS-63 UNC.
PHIL ½ CENTAVO					
☐ 1903	1.50	2.00	3.50	50.00	90.00
☐ 1903 Proof	50.00	—	—	65.00	120.00
☐ 1904	2.00	3.00	4.00	60.00	110.00
☐ 1904 Proof	50.00	—	—	75.00	125.00
☐ 1905 PF	150.00	—	—	225.00	375.00
☐ 1906 PF	125.00	—	—	175.00	300.00
☐ 1908 PF	125.00	—	—	175.00	300.00

PHIL ONE CENTAVO					
☐ 1903	.75	2.00	4.00	25.00	50.00
☐ 1903 PF	60.00	—	—	75.00	125.00
☐ 1904	1.00	2.00	4.00	25.00	50.00
☐ 1904 PF	65.00	—	—	80.00	150.00
☐ 1905	1.00	2.00	4.00	30.00	55.00
☐ 1905 PF	150.00	—	—	200.00	350.00

DATE	ABP	F-12 FINE	EF-40 EX. FINE	MS-60 UNC.	MS-63 UNC.
☐ 1906 PF	125.00	—	—	165.00	325.00
☐ 1908 PF	125.00	—	—	150.00	300.00
☐ 1908 S	2.00	4.00	12.00	45.00	100.00
☐ 1908 S/S Horned S	25.00	32.00	50.00	165.00	310.00
☐ 1908 S/S/S	25.00	32.00	60.00	200.00	350.00
☐ 1909 S	10.00	15.00	30.00	90.00	175.00
☐ 1910 S	4.00	6.00	12.00	35.00	90.00
☐ 1911 S	4.00	6.00	12.00	32.00	85.00
☐ 1911 S over S	25.00	35.00	85.00	125.00	300.00
☐ 1912 S	7.00	10.00	20.00	45.00	165.00
☐ 1912 S over S	20.00	25.00	60.00	120.00	225.00
☐ 1913 S	2.00	4.00	10.00	30.00	90.00
☐ 1914 S	3.00	4.00	15.00	45.00	110.00
☐ 1914 S over S	20.00	28.00	50.00	125.00	240.00
☐ 1915 S	35.00	45.00	85.00	600.00	1500.00
☐ 1916 S	8.00	12.00	30.00	125.00	215.00
☐ 1916 S over S	22.00	30.00	50.00	200.00	400.00
☐ 1917 S	3.50	6.00	12.00	65.00	110.00
☐ 1917/6S	100.00	125.00	165.00	800.00	1950.00
☐ 1918 S	4.00	6.00	12.00	50.00	95.00
☐ 1918 Med S	15.00	18.00	25.00	110.00	185.00
☐ 1918 Large S	350.00	425.00	700.00	1400.00	2500.00
☐ 1919 S	4.00	6.00	10.00	50.00	125.00
☐ 1920	5.00	7.50	12.50	60.00	135.00
☐ 1920 S	15.00	20.00	35.00	175.00	410.00
☐ 1921	1.00	4.00	6.25	40.00	80.00
☐ 1922	1.00	4.00	6.25	40.00	95.00
☐ 1925	1.00	4.00	5.00	25.00	60.00
☐ 1926	1.00	4.00	5.00	22.00	45.00
☐ 1927 M	1.00	4.00	5.00	38.00	55.00
☐ 1928 M	.75	1.00	5.00	35.00	55.00
☐ 1929 M	.75	1.00	5.00	40.00	60.00
☐ 1930 M	.75	1.00	5.00	25.00	50.00
☐ 1930 M/M	8.00	12.00	25.00	100.00	250.00
☐ 1931 M	.75	1.00	5.00	28.00	50.00
☐ 1932 M	.75	1.00	5.00	25.00	50.00
☐ 1933 M	.75	1.00	5.00	25.00	45.00
☐ 1934 M	.75	1.00	5.00	25.00	48.00
☐ 1936 M	.75	1.00	5.00	22.00	40.00
☐ 1937 M	.75	1.00	5.00	22.00	40.00
☐ 1938 M	1.00	1.50	4.00	24.00	40.00
☐ 1939 M	1.00	1.50	4.00	24.00	45.00
☐ 1940 M	1.00	1.50	4.00	17.00	28.00
☐ 1941 M	1.25	2.00	4.00	26.00	55.00
☐ 1944 S	.25	.50	1.00	5.00	9.00
☐ 1944 S Doubled	2.00	4.00	8.00	40.00	75.00

DATE	ABP	F-12 FINE	EF-40 EX. FINE	MS-60 UNC.	MS-63 UNC.
5 CENTAVOS					
☐ 1903	1.00	4.00	6.00	20.00	45.00
☐ 1903 PF	50.00	—	—	70.00	125.00
☐ 1904	2.00	4.00	10.00	35.00	45.00
☐ 1904 PF	55.00	—	—	80.00	150.00
☐ 1905 PF	150.00	—	—	165.00	325.00
☐ 1906 PF	110.00	—	—	150.00	300.00
☐ 1908 PF	115.00	—	—	155.00	300.00
☐ 1916 S	32.00	45.00	100.00	600.00	1400.00
☐ 1917 S	4.00	6.50	15.00	90.00	285.00
☐ 1918 S	4.00	6.50	15.00	100.00	265.00
☐ 1918 S Mule	450.00	550.00	1650.00	7000.00	14000.00
☐ 1919 S	4.00	7.50	17.00	90.00	275.00
☐ 1920	4.00	7.50	14.00	100.00	250.00
☐ 1921	4.00	7.50	14.00	100.00	250.00
☐ 1925	7.00	10.00	26.00	140.00	275.00
☐ 1926	5.00	7.50	16.00	150.00	225.00
☐ 1927	5.00	7.50	16.00	120.00	165.00
☐ 1928	4.00	5.00	12.00	95.00	150.00
☐ 1930	2.00	5.00	8.00	55.00	140.00
☐ 1931	2.00	5.00	8.00	55.00	140.00
☐ 1932	2.00	5.00	8.00	60.00	140.00
☐ 1934	2.00	5.00	8.00	100.00	150.00
☐ 1934 Doubled MM	7.00	12.00	25.00	120.00	275.00
☐ 1935	1.00	2.00	5.00	100.00	165.00
☐ 1937	.70	1.50	4.00	36.00	75.00
☐ 1938	.70	2.00	4.00	28.00	50.00
☐ 1941	1.00	2.00	5.00	30.00	50.00
☐ 1944 P	.70	1.00	2.00	4.00	7.50
☐ 1944 S	.75	1.00	2.00	4.00	7.50
☐ 1945 S	.75	1.00	2.00	4.00	7.50

DATE	ABP	F-12 FINE	EF-40 EX. FINE	MS-60 UNC.	MS-63 UNC.
10 CENTAVOS					
☐ 1903-S	10.00	15.00	42.00	425.00	1200.00
☐ 1903	2.00	3.50	6.00	40.00	100.00

DATE	ABP	F-12 FINE	EF-40 EX. FINE	MS-60 UNC.	MS-63 UNC.
☐ 1903 PF	80.00	—	—	105.00	175.00
☐ 1904	20.00	25.00	45.00	70.00	150.00
☐ 1904 S	3.00	4.00	12.00	55.00	125.00
☐ 1904 PF	80.00	—	—	105.00	175.00
☐ 1905 PF	175.00	—	—	210.00	375.00
☐ 1906 PF	125.00	—	—	165.00	325.00
☐ 1907	2.00	4.00	6.00	50.00	120.00
☐ 1907 S	2.00	4.00	6.00	55.00	135.00
☐ 1908 PF	150.00	—	—	190.00	350.00
☐ 1908 S	2.00	2.75	6.00	75.00	125.00
☐ 1909 S	10.00	15.00	35.00	550.00	1600.00
☐ 1911 S	3.00	8.00	20.00	115.00	400.00
☐ 1912 S	3.00	8.00	18.00	100.00	275.00
☐ 1912 S/S	28.00	35.00	55.00	300.00	575.00
☐ 1913 S	3.00	5.00	18.00	150.00	475.00
☐ 1914 S Long Cross Bar	12.00	17.00	35.00	325.00	700.00
☐ 1914 S	7.00	10.00	22.00	225.00	500.00
☐ 1915 S	12.00	17.00	30.00	300.00	850.00
☐ 1917 S	2.00	3.00	5.00	45.00	100.00
☐ 1918 S	2.00	3.00	5.00	40.00	80.00
☐ 1919 S	2.00	3.00	5.00	45.00	110.00
☐ 1920 M	2.75	3.75	10.00	135.00	265.00
☐ 1921	2.00	3.00	4.00	23.00	55.00
☐ 1929	2.00	3.00	4.00	23.00	50.00
☐ 1935	2.00	3.00	4.00	20.00	50.00
☐ 1937	2.00	2.75	2.00	15.00	35.00
☐ 1938	2.00	2.75	2.00	15.00	35.00
☐ 1941	2.00	3.00	4.00	15.00	30.00
☐ 1944 D	2.00	2.60	3.00	4.00	8.00
☐ 1945 D	2.00	2.60	3.00	4.00	8.00
☐ 1945 D/D	8.00	12.00	20.00	55.00	115.00

TWENTY CENTAVOS

DATE	ABP	F-12 FINE	EF-40 EX. FINE	MS-60 UNC.	MS-63 UNC.
☐ 1903	5.00	6.00	10.00	55.00	135.00
☐ 1903 S	15.00	22.00	60.00	700.00	1850.00
☐ 1903 PF	110.00	—	—	150.00	225.00
☐ 1904	25.00	32.00	45.00	120.00	225.00
☐ 1904 S	5.00	6.00	12.00	85.00	190.00
☐ 1904 PF	110.00	—	—	150.00	220.00
☐ 1905 S	15.00	20.00	50.00	450.00	1350.00
☐ 1905 PF	225.00	—	—	285.00	450.00
☐ 1906 PF	200.00	—	—	275.00	400.00
☐ 1907	4.00	5.00	12.00	125.00	450.00

DATE	ABP	F-12 FINE	EF-40 EX. FINE	MS-60 UNC.	MS-63 UNC.
☐ 1907 S	4.00	5.00	10.00	75.00	350.00
☐ 1908 S	4.00	5.00	12.00	200.00	775.00
☐ 1908 PF	225.00	—	—	275.00	450.00
☐ 1909 S	12.00	25.00	45.00	400.00	1200.00
☐ 1910 S	15.00	22.00	50.00	450.00	1500.00
☐ 1911 S	12.00	19.00	45.00	325.00	1150.00
☐ 1912 S	8.00	15.00	24.00	185.00	525.00
☐ 1913 S	7.00	15.00	24.00	200.00	400.00
☐ 1914 S	10.00	15.00	32.00	225.00	950.00
☐ 1915 S	15.00	22.00	45.00	650.00	1750.00
☐ 1916 S	7.00	18.00	30.00	225.00	450.00
☐ 1917 S	4.00	5.00	12.00	85.00	165.00
☐ 1918 S	4.00	5.00	10.00	85.00	200.00
☐ 1919 S	4.00	5.00	8.00	150.00	300.00
☐ 1920 M	5.00	8.00	10.00	185.00	350.00
☐ 1921	4.00	5.00	7.00	60.00	125.00
☐ 1928/7 Mule	20.00	35.00	125.00	1000.00	2250.00
☐ 1929 Repunch Date	15.00	25.00	60.00	85.00	135.00
☐ 1929	4.00	5.00	9.00	40.00	65.00
☐ 1937	4.00	5.00	6.00	20.00	35.00
☐ 1938	4.00	5.00	6.00	20.00	35.00
☐ 1941	4.00	5.00	5.75	28.00	56.00
☐ 1944 D	4.45	5.00	5.25	6.00	7.00
☐ 1944 D/S	18.00	25.00	50.00	115.00	230.00
☐ 1945 D	4.45	5.00	5.25	6.00	7.00

FIFTY CENTAVOS

DATE	ABP	F-12 FINE	EF-40 EX. FINE	MS-60 UNC.	MS-63 UNC.
☐ 1903	15.00	18.00	20.00	125.00	200.00
☐ 1903 PF	100.00	—	—	135.00	225.00
☐ 1904	25.00	35.00	75.00	175.00	300.00
☐ 1904-S	15.00	20.00	25.00	165.00	265.00
☐ 1904 PF	115.00	—	—	165.00	275.00
☐ 1905 S	22.00	30.00	50.00	575.00	2350.00
☐ 1905 PF	290.00	—	—	365.00	575.00
☐ 1906 PF	250.00	—	—	300.00	475.00
☐ 1907	10.00	12.00	18.00	200.00	500.00
☐ 1907-S	10.00	12.00	32.00	225.00	375.00
☐ 1908-S	10.00	12.00	55.00	250.00	1150.00
☐ 1908 PF	250.00	—	—	325.00	450.00
☐ 1909 S	12.00	15.00	30.00	400.00	1000.00

DATE	ABP	F-12 FINE	EF-40 EX. FINE	MS-60 UNC.	MS-63 UNC.
☐ 1917 S	10.00	12.00	25.00	200.00	550.00
☐ 1917 S Broken 7	15.00	22.00	45.00	500.00	1500.00
☐ 1918 S	10.00	12.00	17.00	115.00	228.00
☐ 1918 Inverted S	35.00	45.00	95.00	250.00	525.00
☐ 1919 S	10.00	14.00	15.00	150.00	225.00
☐ 1920	10.00	14.00	15.00	65.00	125.00
☐ 1921	10.00	12.00	14.00	50.00	100.00
☐ 1944 S	10.00	12.00	12.50	15.00	18.00
☐ 1944 S/S	25.00	35.00	55.00	120.00	175.00
☐ 1945 S	10.00	12.00	12.50	15.00	18.00
☐ 1945 S/S	35.00	50.00	70.00	120.00	200.00

PESO

	ABP	F-12 FINE	EF-40 EX. FINE	MS-60 UNC.	MS-63 UNC.
☐ 1903	30.00	35.00	40.00	200.00	575.00
☐ 1903 S	30.00	35.00	40.00	150.00	425.00
☐ 1903 PF	200.00	—	—	275.00	550.00
☐ 1904	60.00	80.00	125.00	250.00	550.00
☐ 1904-S	30.00	35.00	42.00	175.00	375.00
☐ 1904 PF	200.00	—	—	285.00	585.00
☐ 1905-S	32.00	39.00	45.00	300.00	850.00
☐ 1905-S Straight Serif	50.00	65.00	80.00	700.00	2850.00
☐ 1905 PF	575.00	—	—	900.00	1750.00
☐ 1906 S	1750.00	2500.00	3250.00	21000.00	38500.00
☐ 1906 PF	600.00	—	—	800.00	1500.00
☐ 1907 S	25.00	30.00	32.00	100.00	275.00
☐ 1908 S	25.00	30.00	35.00	100.00	225.00
☐ 1908 S/S	50.00	70.00	135.00	450.00	1250.00
☐ 1908 S Double Diz & Inverted MM	100.00	125.00	185.00	485.00	875.00
☐ 1908 PF	550.00	—	—	675.00	1275.00
☐ 1909 S	25.00	35.00	20.00	100.00	225.00
☐ 1909 S/S	35.00	45.00	65.00	175.00	750.00
☐ 1909 S/S/S	100.00	150.00	200.00	500.00	1500.00
☐ 1910 S	25.00	35.00	40.00	235.00	500.00
☐ 1911 S	30.00	40.00	80.00	1650.00	8000.00
☐ 1912 S	30.00	50.00	100.00	1750.00	11500.00

COMMEMORATIVE

	ABP	F-12 FINE	EF-40 EX. FINE	MS-60 UNC.	MS-63 UNC.
☐ 1936 50 C	40.00	50.00	75.00	125.00	215.00
☐ 1936 Murphy Queyer	70.00	85.00	120.00	200.00	375.00
☐ 1936 Roosevelt Queyer	70.00	85.00	125.00	225.00	425.00

Philippines—Commonwealth Coinage

Key to Grading: Shield

DATE	COIN TYPE/VARIETY/METAL	ABP FINE	AVERAGE FINE
☐ 1937–1944	1 Centavo, Commonwealth, Bronze	$.31	$ .52
☐ 1937–1941	5 Centavos, Commonwealth, Cupro-Nickel	.53	.88

Key to Grading: Shield

☐ 1944–1945	5 Centavos, Commonwealth, Copper-Nickel-Zinc	.28	.46

Key to Grading: Shield

☐ 1937–1945	10 Centavos, Commonwealth, Silver	—	2.50

DATE	COIN TYPE/VARIETY/METAL	ABP FINE	AVERAGE FINE
☐ 1937–1945	20 Centavos, Commonwealth, Silver	—	$4.25
☐ 1936	50 Centavos, Commonwealth Establishment of Commonwealth—Murphy & Quezon, Silver	—	84.50

Key to Grading: Shield

DATE	COIN TYPE/VARIETY/METAL	ABP FINE	AVERAGE FINE
☐ 1944–1945	50 Centavos, Commonwealth, Silver	—	8.75
☐ 1936	1 Peso, Commonwealth, Establishment of Commonwealth—Murphy & Quezon, Silver	—	130.00
☐ 1936	1 Peso, Commonwealth, Establishment of Commonwealth—Roosevelt & Quezon, Silver	—	144.50

Philippines—Republic Coinage

Key to Grading: Shield

DATE	COIN TYPE/VARIETY/METAL	ABP FINE	AVERAGE FINE
☐ 1958–1966	1 Centavo, Republic, Central Bank, Bronze	.31	.52

Key to Grading: Shield

DATE	COIN TYPE/VARIETY/METAL	ABP FINE	AVERAGE FINE
☐ 1958–1966	5 Centavos, Republic, Central Bank, Brass	.31	.52

Key to Grading: Shield

DATE	COIN TYPE/VARIETY/METAL	ABP FINE	AVERAGE FINE
☐ 1958–1966	10 Centavos, Republic, Central Bank, Nickel-Brass	$.22	$ .36

Key to Grading: Shield

☐ 1958–1966	25 Centavos, Republic, Central Bank, Nickel-Brass	.31	.52

Key to Grading: Shield

☐ 1947	50 Centavos, Republic, MacArthur, Silver	—	13.50

Key to Grading: Shield

☐ 1961	1/2 Peso, Republic, Birth of Rizal Centennial, Silver	—	17.50
☐ 1958–1964	50 Centavos, Republic, Central Bank, Nickel-Brass	.34	.57

DATE	COIN TYPE/VARIETY/METAL	ABP FINE	AVERAGE FINE
☐ 1947	1 Peso, Republic, MacArthur, Silver	—	$27.50
☐ 1961	1 Peso, Republic, Birth of Rizal Centennial, Silver	—	25.50
☐ 1963	1 Peso, Republic, Birth of Bonifacio Centennial, Silver	—	25.50
☐ 1964	1 Peso, Republic, Birth of Mabini Centennial, Silver	—	25.50
☐ 1967	1 Peso, Republic, Fall of Bataan & Corregidor—25th Anniversary, Silver	—	25.50

Philippines—Current Coinage

Key to Grading: Shield

☐ 1967–1974	1 Sentimo, Aluminum	.28	.46
☐ 1975–1982	1 Sentimo, Aluminum	.28	.46
☐ 1983–1990	1 Sentimo, Aluminum	.28	.46

Key to Grading: Shield

☐ 1967–1974	5 Sentimos, Brass	.28	.46
☐ 1975–1982	5 Sentimos, Brass	.28	.46
☐ 1983–1991	5 Sentimos, Orchid, Aluminum	.20	.33

Key to Grading: Shield

DATE	COIN TYPE/VARIETY/METAL	ABP FINE	AVERAGE FINE
☐ 1967–1982	10 Sentimos, Orchid, Cupro-Nickel	$.28	$ .46
☐ 1983–1992	10 Sentimos, Aluminum	.28	.46

Key to Grading: Bust

| ☐ 1975–1982 | 25 Sentimos, Cupro-Nickel | .22 | .36 |
| ☐ 1983–1992 | 25 Sentimos, Butterfly, Cupro-Nickel | .22 | .36 |

Key to Grading: Bust

☐ 1967–1975	50 Sentimos, Marcelo del Pilar, Cupro-Nickel	.28	.46
☐ 1983–1990	50 Sentimos, Eagle, Cupro-Nickel	.28	.46
☐ 1992	50 Sentimos, Eagle, Brass	.28	.46
☐ 1969	1 Piso, Birth of Aquinaldo— 100th Anniversary, Silver	—	19.25
☐ 1970	1 Piso, Papal Visit, Silver	—	28.75

Key to Grading: Busts

☐ 1970	1 Piso, Papal Visit, Nickel	.63	1.05
☐ 1970	1 Piso, Papal Visit, Gold	—	1525.00
☐ 1972–1982	1 Piso, Jose Rizal, Cupro-Nickel	.28	.46
☐ 1983–1990	1 Piso, Bull, Cupro-Nickel	.28	.46
☐ 1991	1 Piso, Waterfall, Ship, & Flower, Cupro-Nickel	.28	.46
☐ 1983–1990	2 Piso, Bonifacio, Cupro-Nickel	.28	.46

DATE	COIN TYPE/VARIETY/METAL	ABP FINE	AVERAGE FINE
☐ 1991	2 Piso, Quirino, Cupro-Nickel	$.28	$ .46
☐ 1991–1994	2 Piso, Bonifacio, Stainless Steel	.28	.46
☐ 1975–1982	5 Piso, Ferdinand Marcos, Nickel	.28	.46
☐ 1974	25 Piso, Bank Anniversary—25th, Silver	—	18.60
☐ 1975	25 Piso, Aquinaldo, Silver	—	23.25
☐ 1976	25 Piso, FAO Issue, Silver	—	25.50
☐ 1977	25 Piso, Rice Terraces, Silver	—	27.75
☐ 1978	25 Piso, Birth of Quezon—100th Anniversary, Silver	—	37.00
☐ 1979	25 Piso, UN Conference, Silver	—	37.00
☐ 1980	25 Piso, Birth of MacArthur—100th Anniversary, Silver	—	54.00
☐ 1981	25 Piso, World Food Day, Silver	—	33.50
☐ 1982	25 Piso, Ferdinand Marcos & Ronald Reagan, Silver	—	84.50
☐ 1986	25 Piso, Washington Visit of Aquino, Silver	—	230.00
☐ 1975	50 Piso, New Society Anniversary, Silver	—	30.00
☐ 1976	50 Piso, International Monetary Fund Meeting, Silver	—	34.00
☐ 1977	50 Piso, Mint Inauguration, Silver	—	27.50
☐ 1978	50 Piso, Birth of Quezon—100th Anniversary, Silver	—	32.00
☐ 1979	50 Piso, Year of the Child, Silver	—	32.00
☐ 1981	50 Piso, Papal Visit, Silver	—	37.50
☐ 1982	50 Piso, Bataan-Corregidor 40th Anniversary, Silver	—	30.00
☐ 1983	100 Piso, National University 75th Anniversary, Silver	—	23.00
☐ 1991	150 Piso, Southeast Asian Games, Silver	—	64.50
☐ 1987	200 Piso, Wildlife Fund—Buffalo, Silver	—	115.50
☐ 1990	200 Piso, Save the Children, Silver	—	118.50
☐ 1988	500 Piso, People's Revolution, Silver	—	76.25
☐ 1975	1000 Piso, New Society—3rd Anniversary, Gold	—	424.00
☐ 1976	1500 Piso, International Monetary Fund, Gold	—	1000.00
☐ 1977	1500 Piso, New Society—5th Anniversary, Gold	—	1500.00
☐ 1978	1500 Piso, Mint Inauguration, Gold	—	1275.00
☐ 1981	1500 Piso, Papal Visit, Gold	—	1400.00
☐ 1982	1500 Piso, Bataan-Corregidor 40th Anniversary, Gold	—	1525.00
☐ 1977	2500 Piso, New Society—5th Anniversary, Gold	—	3250.00
☐ 1980	2500 Piso, Birth of MacArthur—100th Anniversary, Gold	—	3250.00

DATE	COIN TYPE/VARIETY/METAL	ABP FINE	AVERAGE FINE
☐ 1986	2500 Piso, Aquino Washington Visit, Gold	—	$1800.00
☐ 1992	10000 Piso, People's Power, Gold	—	2000.00

PITCAIRN ISLANDS

British and New Zealand currency was initially used. The only coins issued in the name of Pitcairn are commemorative pieces, the silver 50 dollar, and the gold 250 dollar produced in 1988.

Key to Grading: Bust

Pitcairn Islands—Type Coinage

DATE	COIN TYPE/VARIETY/METAL	ABP FINE	AVERAGE FINE
☐ 1988	1 Dollar, Elizabeth II: Drafting of Pitcairn Islands Constitution, Silver Proof	—	—
☐ 1988	1 Dollar, Elizabeth II: Drafting of Pitcairn Islands Constitution, Cupro-Nickel	5.86	9.77
☐ 1989	1 Dollar, Elizabeth II: Mutiny on the Bounty, Silver Proof	—	—
☐ 1989	1 Dollar, Elizabeth II: Mutiny on the Bounty, Cupro-Nickel	5.86	9.77
☐ 1990	1 Dollar, Elizabeth II: Burning of the HMAV Bounty, Cupro-Nickel	3.91	6.51
☐ 1990	1 Dollar, Elizabeth II: Burning of the HMAV Bounty, Silver Proof	—	—
☐ 1988	50 Dollars, Elizabeth II: Drafting of Pitcairn Islands Constitution, Silver Proof	—	—
☐ 1989	50 Dollars, Elizabeth II: Mutiny on the Bounty, Silver Proof	—	—
☐ 1990	50 Dollars, Elizabeth II: Burning of the HMAV Bounty, Silver Proof	—	—
☐ 1988	250 Dollars, Elizabeth II: Drafting of Pitcairn Islands Constitution, Gold Proof	—	—
☐ 1989	250 Dollars, Elizabeth II: Mutiny on the Bounty, Gold Proof	—	—

DATE	COIN TYPE/VARIETY/METAL	ABP FINE	AVERAGE FINE
☐ 1990	250 Dollars, Elizabeth II: Burning of the HMAV Bounty, Gold Proof	—	—

POLAND

The first coins, silver denars, were used in the late 10th century and into the 12th century. Then came the silver bracteate denar and the silver schilling in the 1400s. The silver taler, gold ducat, and copper boratinki followed in the 1500s and 1600s. The copper polsgrosz and the silver kopek were in use in the 1800s. The first decimal coins were used in 1923. The currency today is the zloty.

Key to Grading: Eagle

Poland—Type Coinage

☐ 1918	Fenig, WWI Military, Iron	.52	.86
☐ 1923–1939	1 Grosz, Republic, Bronze	.29	.48
☐ 1923	1 Grosz, Republic, Brass	13.00	21.60
☐ 1939	1 Grosz, WWII Occupation, Zinc	.54	.90
☐ 1949	1 Grosz, Republic, Aluminum	.54	.90

Key to Grading: Eagle

☐ 1923	2 Grosze, Republic, Brass	2.80	4.60
☐ 1923–1939	2 Grosze, Republic, Bronze	.29	.48
☐ 1949	2 Grosze, Republic, Aluminum	.29	.48
☐ 1917–1918	5 Fenigow, WWI Military, Iron	.29	.48

Key to Grading: Eagle

DATE	COIN TYPE/VARIETY/METAL	ABP FINE	AVERAGE FINE
☐ 1923	5 Groszy, Republic, Brass	$.36	$ .60
☐ 1923–1939	5 Groszy, Republic, Bronze	.26	.43
☐ 1939	5 Groszy, WWII Occupation, Holed, Zinc	.33	.55
☐ 1949	5 Groszy, Republic, Bronze	.26	.43
☐ 1917	10 Fenigow, WWI Military, Zinc	22.50	37.50

Key to Grading: Eagle

☐ 1923	10 Groszy, WWII Occupation, Zinc	.29	.48
☐ 1923	10 Groszy, Republic, Nickel	.29	.48
☐ 1949	10 Groszy, Republic, Cupro-Nickel	.29	.48
☐ 1949	10 Groszy, Republic, Aluminum	.29	.48
☐ 1917	20 Fenigow, WWI Military, Zinc	35.69	59.50
☐ 1917–1918	20 Fenigow, WWI Military, Iron	.88	1.50

Key to Grading: Eagle

☐ 1923	20 Groszy, Republic, Nickel	.29	.48
☐ 1949	20 Groszy, Republic, Cupro-Nickel	.29	.48
☐ 1949	20 Groszy, Republic, Aluminum	.29	.48

Key to Grading: Eagle

DATE	COIN TYPE/VARIETY/METAL	ABP FINE	AVERAGE FINE
☐ 1923	50 Groszy, Republic, Nickel	$.29	$ .48
☐ 1938	50 Groszy, WWII Occupation, Iron	1.48	2.50
☐ 1949	50 Groszy, Republic, Cupro-Nickel	.36	.60
☐ 1949	50 Groszy, Republic, Aluminum	.36	.60
☐ 1924–1925	1 Zloty, Republic, Silver	—	66.50
☐ 1929	1 Zloty, Republic, Nickel	.45	.76
☐ 1949	1 Zloty, Republic, Aluminum	.29	.48
☐ 1949	1 Zloty, Republic, Cupro-Nickel	.79	1.30
☐ 1924–1925	2 Zlote, Republic, Silver	—	10.85
☐ 1932–1934	2 Zlote, Republic, Silver	—	6.50
☐ 1934–1936	2 Zlote, Republic, Silver	—	7.40
☐ 1936	2 Zlote, Republic, Silver	—	7.40
☐ 1925	5 Zlotych, Republic, Silver	—	230.00
☐ 1928–1932	5 Zlotych, Republic, Silver	—	37.50
☐ 1930	5 Zlotych, Republic, Revolt Against Russians Centennial, Silver	—	34.00
☐ 1932–1934	5 Zlotych, Republic, Silver	—	6.50
☐ 1934	5 Zlotych, Republic, Founding of Rifle Corps 20th Anniversary, Silver	—	9.25
☐ 1934–1938	5 Zlotych, Republic, Silver	—	6.50
☐ 1936	5 Zlotych, Republic, Silver	—	12.25
☐ 1925	10 Zlotych, Republic, Death of Boleslaus I 900th Anniversary, Gold	—	68.50
☐ 1932–1933	10 Zlotych, Republic, Silver	—	6.20
☐ 1933	10 Zlotych, Republic, 250th Anniversary of Relief of Vienna, Silver	—	25.50
☐ 1933	10 Zlotych, Republic, Second Revolt Against Russians 70th Anniversary, Silver	—	25.50
☐ 1934	10 Zlotych, Republic, Founding of Rifle Corps 20th Anniversary, Silver	—	25.50

Key to Grading: Bust

DATE	COIN TYPE/VARIETY/METAL	ABP FINE	AVERAGE FINE
☐ 1934–1939	10 Zlotych, Republic, Silver	—	$7.40
☐ 1925	20 Zlotych, Republic, Death of Boleslaus I 900th Anniversary, Gold	—	187.50

PORTUGAL

The first coins originated in the 2nd century B.C. In 1128 base-silver dinheiros and mealhas were produced, and later the gold morabitino. A range of coins in gold, silver, and base-silver were produced in the 1300s. In the 15th century most coinage was silver leals, with some base-silver reals branco. In the late 15th century the real became the main unit of coinage. In the 1600s systematic dating began appearing on coins. The first decimal coins were used in 1836. The euro is the currency used today.

Portugal—Type Coinage

Key to Grading: Crown

☐ 1868–1875	III Reis, Luis I, Copper	$2.80	4.60
☐ 1867–1879	5 Reis, Luis I, Copper	4.25	7.00
☐ 1882–1886	5 Reis, Luis I, Bronze	.66	1.10
☐ 1890–1906	5 Reis, Carlos I, Bronze	.23	.38
☐ 1910	5 Reis, Emanuel II, Bronze	.26	.43

Key to Grading: Crown

DATE	COIN TYPE/VARIETY/METAL	ABP FINE	AVERAGE FINE
☐ 1867–1877	10 Reis, Luis I, Copper	$3.10	$5.20
☐ 1882–1886	10 Reis, Luis I, Bronze	2.80	4.60
☐ 1891–1892	10 Reis, Carlos I, Bronze	3.25	5.40

Key to Grading: Bust

DATE	COIN TYPE/VARIETY/METAL	ABP FINE	AVERAGE FINE
☐ 1867–1874	20 Reis, Luis I, Copper	7.15	11.90
☐ 1882–1886	20 Reis, Luis I, Bronze	1.45	2.40
☐ 1891–1892	20 Reis, Carlos I, Bronze	3.00	5.10
☐ 1862–1889	50 Reis, Luis I, Silver	3.00	5.10
☐ 1893	50 Reis, Carlos I, Silver	—	9.25
☐ 1900	50 Reis, Carlos I, Cupro-Nickel	.49	.80
☐ 1864–1889	100 Reis, Luis I, Silver	—	7.75
☐ 1890–1898	100 Reis, Carlos I, Silver	—	6.75

Key to Grading: Crown

DATE	COIN TYPE/VARIETY/METAL	ABP FINE	AVERAGE FINE
☐ 1900	100 Reis, Carlos I, Cupro-Nickel	.49	.81
☐ 1909–1910	100 Reis, Emanuel II, Silver	—	2.75

Key to Grading: Bust

DATE	COIN TYPE/VARIETY/METAL	ABP FINE	AVERAGE FINE
☐ 1862–1865	200 Reis, Luis I, Silver	—	$25.50
☐ 1865–1888	200 Reis, Luis I, Silver	—	52.50
☐ 1891–1903	200 Reis, Carlos I, Silver	—	12.75
☐ 1898	200 Reis, Carlos I, 400th Anniversary: Voyages of Discovery, Silver	—	12.75
☐ 1909	200 Reis, Emanuel II, Silver	—	7.50

Key to Grading: Bust or Crown

☐ 1863–1889	500 Reis, Luis I, Silver	—	10.75
☐ 1891–1908	500 Reis, Carlos I, Silver	—	13.25
☐ 1898	500 Reis, Carlos I, 400th Anniversary: Voyages of Discovery, Silver	—	13.25
☐ 1908–1909	500 Reis, Emanuel II, Silver	—	20.75
☐ 1910	500 Reis, Commemorative, Marquis de Pombal, Silver	—	61.75
☐ 1910	500 Reis, Commemorative, Peninsular War Centennial, Silver	—	70.00

Key to Grading: Bust

☐ 1898	1000 Reis, Carlos I, 400th Anniversary: Voyages of Discovery, Silver	—	27.25

DATE	COIN TYPE/VARIETY/METAL	ABP FINE	AVERAGE FINE
☐ 1899	1000 Reis, Carlos I, Silver	—	$22.75
☐ 1910	1000 Reis, Commemorative, Peninsular War Centennial, Silver	—	76.50
☐ 1864–1866	2000 Reis, Luis I, Rev: Arms in Wreath, Gold	—	115.50
☐ 1868–1888	2000 Reis, Luis I, Rev: Mantled Arms, Gold	—	146.50
☐ 1862–1863	5000 Reis, Luis I, Rev: Arms in Wreath, Gold	—	385.50
☐ 1867–1889	5000 Reis, Luis I, Rev: Mantled Arms, Gold	—	275.00
☐ 1878–1889	10000 Reis, Luis I, Rev: Mantled Arms, Gold	—	500.00

Portugal—Port-Republic Coinage

DATE	COIN TYPE/VARIETY/METAL	ABP FINE	AVERAGE FINE
☐ 1917–1921	1 Centavo, 2nd Coinage, Bronze	.29	.48
☐ 1918	2 Centavos, 1st Coinage, World War I Provisional Issue, Iron	17.50	29.80
☐ 1918–1921	2 Centavos, 2nd Coinage, Bronze	.26	.43
☐ 1917–1919	4 Centavos, 2nd Coinage, Cupro-Nickel	.26	.43
☐ 1920–1922	5 Centavos, 2nd Coinage, Bronze	.72	1.25
☐ 1924–1927	5 Centavos, 3rd Coinage, Bronze	.25	.41
☐ 1915	10 Centavos, 1st Coinage, Silver	—	1.75
☐ 1920–1921	10 Centavos, 2nd Coinage, Cupro-Nickel	.52	.86
☐ 1924–1940	10 Centavos, 3rd Coinage, Bronze	.52	.86
☐ 1942–1969	10 Centavos, 3rd Coinage, Bronze	.26	.43
☐ 1969–1979	10 Centavos, 4th Coinage, Aluminum	.26	.43
☐ 1913–1916	20 Centavos, 1st Coinage, Silver	—	5.45
☐ 1920–1922	20 Centavos, 2nd Coinage, Cupro-Nickel	1.60	2.65
☐ 1924–1925	20 Centavos, 3rd Coinage, Bronze	.33	.55
☐ 1942–1969	20 Centavos, 3rd Coinage, Bronze	.23	.38
☐ 1969–1974	20 Centavos, 4th Coinage, Aluminum	.23	.38
☐ 1912–1916	50 Centavos, 1st Coinage, Silver	—	6.85
☐ 1924–1926	50 Centavos, 3rd Coinage, Aluminum-Bronze	.98	1.65
☐ 1927–1968	50 Centavos, 3rd Coinage, Copper-Nickel	.29	.48
☐ 1969–1979	50 Centavos, 4th Coinage, Bronze	.29	.48
☐ 1910	1 Escudo, 1st Coinage, Birth of Republic—October 5th, 1910, Silver	—	22.75

DATE	COIN TYPE/VARIETY/METAL	ABP FINE	AVERAGE FINE
☐ 1915–1916	1 Escudo, 1st Coinage, Silver	—	$20.75
☐ 1924–1926	1 Escudo, 3rd Coinage, Aluminum-Bronze	3.25	5.40
☐ 1927–1968	1 Escudo, 3rd Coinage, Nickel-Bronze	.21	.35
☐ 1969–1980	1 Escudo, 4th Coinage, Bronze	.23	.38

Key to Grading: Shield

☐ 1981–1986	1 Escudo, 5th Coinage, Nickel-Brass	.18	.30
☐ 1986–2001	1 Escudo, 6th Coinage, Nickel-Brass	.23	.38

Key to Grading: Shield

☐ 1932–1951	2¹/₂ Escudos, 3rd Coinage, Silver	—	2.50

Key to Grading: Boat

☐ 1963–1986	2¹/₂ Escudos, 4th Coinage, Cupro-Nickel	.23	.38
☐ 1977	2¹/₂ Escudos, 4th Coinage, 100th Anniversary—Death of Alexandro Herculano, Cupro-Nickel	.23	.38
☐ 1983	2¹/₂ Escudos, 4th Coinage, FAO Issue, Cupro-Nickel	.23	.38
☐ 1983	2¹/₂ Escudos, 4th Coinage, World Roller Hockey Championship, Cupro-Nickel	.23	.38
☐ 1986–2001	2¹/₂ Escudos, 6th Coinage, Nickel-Brass	.23	.38

DATE	COIN TYPE/VARIETY/METAL	ABP FINE	AVERAGE FINE
☐ 1932–1951	5 Escudos, 3rd Coinage, Silver	—	$7.25
☐ 1960	5 Escudos, 3rd Coinage, Death of Henry the Navigator—500th Anniversary, Silver	—	3.15
☐ 1963–1986	5 Escudos, Copper-Nickel	.23	.38
☐ 1928	10 Escudos, 3rd Coinage, Battle of Ourique 1139, Silver	—	17.00
☐ 1932–1948	10 Escudos, 3rd Coinage, Silver	—	17.00
☐ 1954–1955	10 Escudos, 3rd Coinage, Silver	—	6.50
☐ 1960	10 Escudos, 3rd Coinage, Death of Henry the Navigator—500th Anniversary, Silver	—	7.70
☐ 1971–1974	10 Escudos, 4th Coinage, Cupro-Nickel	.20	.33
☐ 1986–2001	10 Escudos, 6th Coinage, Nickel-Brass	.16	.27

Key to Grading: Shield

DATE	COIN TYPE/VARIETY/METAL	ABP FINE	AVERAGE FINE
☐ 1953	20 Escudos, 3rd Coinage, 25 Years of Financial Reform, Silver	—	7.35
☐ 1960	20 Escudos, 3rd Coinage, Death of Henry the Navigator—500th Anniversary, Silver	—	9.25
☐ 1966	20 Escudos, Opening of Salazar Bridge, Silver	—	3.15
☐ 1986–2001	20 Escudos, Cupro-Nickel	.23	.38
☐ 1977–1978	25 Escudos, Cupro-Nickel	.23	.38
☐ 1977–1978	25 Escudos, 100th Anniversary—Death of Alexandre Herculano, Cupro-Nickel	.33	.55
☐ 1980–1986	Increase Size 28.5 MM	.33	.55
☐ 1983	25 Escudos, World Roller Hockey Championship, Cupro-Nickel	.33	.55
☐ 1983	25 Escudos, FAO Issue, Cupro-Nickel	.33	.55
☐ 1984	25 Escudos, Revolution—100th Anniversary, Cupro-Nickel	.26	.43
☐ 1984	25 Escudos, International Year of Disabled Persons, Cupro-Nickel	.26	.43
☐ 1985	25 Escudos, Anniversary—Battle of Aljubarrotta, Cupro-Nickel	.26	.43
☐ 1985	25 Escudos, Anniversary—Battle of Aljubarrotta, Silver	—	38.50

DATE	COIN TYPE/VARIETY/METAL	ABP FINE	AVERAGE FINE
☐ 1986	25 Escudos, Admission to European Common Market, Silver	—	$115.50
☐ 1986	25 Escudos, Admission to European Common Market, Cupro-Nickel	.26	.43
☐ 1968	50 Escudos, Anniversary of Birth of Alvares Cabral, Silver	—	13.50
☐ 1969	50 Escudos, 500th Anniversary—Birth of Vasco de Gama, Silver	—	7.50
☐ 1969	50 Escudos, Centennial—Birth of Marshall Carmone, Silver	—	14.50
☐ 1971	50 Escudos, 125th Anniversary—Bank of Portugal, Silver	—	14.50
☐ 1972	50 Escudos, 400th Anniversary—Heroic Epic "O Lusiadas," Silver	—	14.50
☐ 1986–2001	50 Escudos, Copper-Nickel	.39	.65
☐ 1974	100 Escudos, 1974 Revolution, Silver		9.25
☐ 1984	100 Escudos, International Year of Disabled Persons, Cupro-Nickel	.55	.92
☐ 1985	100 Escudos, 800th Anniversary—Death of King Henriques, Cupro-Nickel	.55	.92
☐ 1985	100 Escudos, 800th Anniversary—Death of King Henriques, Silver	—	34.00
☐ 1985	100 Escudos, 600th Anniversary—Battle of Aljubarrotta, Cupro-Nickel	.52	.86
☐ 1985	100 Escudos, 600th Anniversary—Battle of Aljubarrotta, Silver	—	48.50
☐ 1985	100 Escudos, 50th Anniversary—Death of Fernando Pessoa (Poet), Cupro-Nickel	.39	.65
☐ 1985	100 Escudos, 50th Anniversary—Death of Fernando Pessoa (Poet), Silver	—	208.50
☐ 1986	100 Escudos, World Cup Soccer—Mexico, Silver	—	32.50
☐ 1986	100 Escudos, World Cup Soccer—Mexico, Cupro-Nickel	.52	.86
☐ 1987	100 Escudos, Golden Age of Portuguese Discoveries, Cupro-Nickel	.52	.86
☐ 1987	100 Escudos, Amadeo De Souza Caroso, Cupro-Nickel	.52	.86
☐ 1987	100 Escudos, Golden Age of Portuguese Discoveries, Silver	—	42.50
☐ 1987	100 Escudos, Amadeo De Souza Caroso, Silver	—	42.50
☐ 1987	100 Escudos, Golden Age of Portuguese Discoveries, Gold	—	1000.00

DATE	COIN TYPE/VARIETY/METAL	ABP FINE	AVERAGE FINE
☐ 1988	100 Escudos, Golden Age of Portuguese Discoveries, Platinum	—	$1275.00
☐ 1989	100 Escudos, Discovery of Madeira, Palladium	—	810.00
☐ 1989	100 Escudos, Discovery of Madeira, Silver	—	35.50
☐ 1989	100 Escudos, Discovery of Canary Islands, Cupro-Nickel	3.90	6.50
☐ 1989	100 Escudos, Discovery of Madeira, Gold	—	1275.00
☐ 1989	100 Escudos, Discovery of Canary Islands, Gold	—	1275.00
☐ 1989–2001	100 Escudos, Dual Metal	.39	.65
☐ 1989	100 Escudos, Discovery of Azores, Gold	—	1275.00
☐ 1989	100 Escudos, Discovery of Canary Islands, Silver	—	24.00
☐ 1989	100 Escudos, Discovery of Azores, Silver	—	27.75
☐ 1989	100 Escudos, Discovery of Azores, Cupro-Nickel	3.25	5.40
☐ 1990	100 Escudos, Celestial Navigation, Cupro-Nickel	5.20	8.70
☐ 1990	100 Escudos, Camilo Castelo Branco, Cupro-Nickel	3.90	6.50
☐ 1990	100 Escudos, Celestial Navigation, Gold	—	1000.00
☐ 1990	100 Escudos, Celestial Navigation, Silver	—	25.50
☐ 1990	100 Escudos, Camilo Castelo Branco, Silver	—	30.00
☐ 1990	100 Escudos, 350th Anniversary— Portuguese Independence, Cupro-Nickel	5.20	8.70
☐ 1990	100 Escudos, Celestial Navigation, Platinum	—	2550.00
☐ 1990	100 Escudos, 350th Anniversary— Portuguese Independence, Silver	—	36.50
☐ 1991	200 Escudos, Westward Navigation, Gold	—	1000.00
☐ 1991	200 Escudos, Westward Navigation, Silver	—	36.50
☐ 1991–2001	200 Escudos, Dual Metal	.39	.65
☐ 1991	200 Escudos, Columbus & Portugal, Gold	—	965.00
☐ 1991	200 Escudos, Columbus & Portugal, Silver	—	36.75
☐ 1991	200 Escudos, Columbus & Portugal, Palladium	—	540.00
☐ 1992	200 Escudos, New World America— Columbus & Ships, Gold	—	880.00
☐ 1992	200 Escudos, Cabrilho—Map, Silver	—	42.00
☐ 1992	200 Escudos, Portugal's Presidency of European Community, Cupro-Nickel	5.20	8.70

DATE	COIN TYPE/VARIETY/METAL	ABP FINE	AVERAGE FINE
☐ 1992	200 Escudos, New World America—Columbus & Ships, Silver	—	$40.50
☐ 1992	200 Escudos, Olympics—Runner, Silver	—	40.50
☐ 1992	200 Escudos, Olympics—Runner, Cupro-Nickel	4.59	7.60
☐ 1992	200 Escudos, Portugal's Presidency of European Community, Silver	—	30.00
☐ 1992	200 Escudos, Cabrilho—Map, Cupro-Nickel	4.80	8.20
☐ 1992	200 Escudos, New World America—Columbus & Ships, Cupro-Nickel	4.80	8.20
☐ 1992	200 Escudos, Cabrilho—Map, Platinum	—	Rare
☐ 1992	200 Escudos, Cabrilho—Map, Gold	—	1110.00
☐ 1974	250 Escudos, 1974 Revolution, Silver	—	32.50
☐ 1984	250 Escudos, World Fisheries, Cupro-Nickel	16.22	27.00
☐ 1984	250 Escudos, World Fisheries, Silver	—	130.50
☐ 1988	250 Escudos, Seoul Olympics—Runners, Cupro-Nickel	2.80	4.65
☐ 1988	250 Escudos, Seoul Olympics—Runners, Silver	—	30.00
☐ 1989	250 Escudos, 850th Anniversary—Founding of Portugal, Silver	—	52.50
☐ 1989	250 Escudos, 850th Anniversary—Founding of Portugal, Cupro-Nickel	5.20	8.70
☐ 1983	500 Escudos, XVII European Art Exhibition, Silver	—	82.50
☐ 1983	750 Escudos, XVII European Art Exhibition, Silver	—	24.00
☐ 1980	1000 Escudos, 400th Anniversary—Death of Louis de Camoes, Silver	—	48.50
☐ 1983	1000 Escudos, XVII European Art Exhibition, Silver	—	48.50
☐ 1991	1000 Escudos, Ibero—American Series, Silver	—	90.50

RUSSIA

The first coins were used in the 5th century B.C. and were bronze pieces cast in the shape of dolphins, followed by coin-shaped pieces. In the 4th century, coins were produced in gold, silver, and bronze. Gold staters became popular in 100 A.D., followed by the silver denga in the 15th century, and the silver grossus and silver kopek in the 16th century. The first decimal coins were used in 1704. The currency today is the ruble.

Russia—Type Coinage

Key to Grading: Eagle

DATE	COIN TYPE/VARIETY/METAL	ABP FINE	AVERAGE FINE
☐ 1855–1867	¼ Kopek, Alexander II, Copper	$3.00	$5.10
☐ 1867–1881	¼ Kopek, Alexander II, Copper	1.70	2.80
☐ 1881–1894	¼ Kopek, Alexander III, Copper	3.00	5.10
☐ 1894–1916	¼ Kopek, Nikolai II, Copper	1.70	2.80

Key to Grading: Eagle

DATE	COIN TYPE/VARIETY/METAL	ABP FINE	AVERAGE FINE
☐ 1855–1858	½ Ruble, Czarist Empire, Silver	6.80	11.35
☐ 1859–1885	½ Ruble, Czarist Empire, 2nd Coinage, Silver	21.65	36.05
☐ 1855–1867	½ Kopek, Alexander II, Copper	3.00	5.10
☐ 1867–1881	½ Kopek, Alexander II, Copper	3.00	5.10
☐ 1881–1894	½ Kopek, Alexander III, Copper	1.30	2.20
☐ 1894–1916	½ Kopek, Nikolai II, Copper	.80	1.35

Key to Grading: Eagle

DATE	COIN TYPE/VARIETY/METAL	ABP FINE	AVERAGE FINE
☐ 1855–1858	1 Ruble, Czarist Empire, Silver	—	$68.50
☐ 1859	1 Ruble, Nikolai I, Silver	—	115.50
☐ 1859–1885	1 Ruble, Czarist Empire, 2nd Coinage, Silver	—	52.50
☐ 1883	1 Ruble, Alexander III, Silver	—	68.50
☐ 1886–1894	1 Ruble, Alexander III, Silver	—	52.50
☐ 1895–1915	1 Ruble, Nikolai II, Silver	—	30.00
☐ 1896	1 Ruble, Coronation Comm, Silver	—	54.50
☐ 1898	1 Ruble, Alexander II, Silver	—	230.00
☐ 1912	1 Ruble, Alexander III, Silver	—	375.00
☐ 1912	1 Ruble, Napoleon Defeat, Silver	—	—
☐ 1913	1 Ruble, Romanoff Dynasty, Silver	—	36.50
☐ 1914	1 Ruble, Battle of Gangut, Silver	—	675.00
☐ 1855–1867	1 Kopek, Alexander II, Copper	4.10	6.80

Key to Grading: Eagle

☐ 1867–1916	1 Kopek, Czarist Empire, 2nd Coinage, Copper	3.15	5.20
☐ 1855–1859	2 Kopeks, Czarist Empire, Copper	3.15	5.20
☐ 1859–1867	2 Kopeks, Czarist Empire, 2nd Coinage, Copper	3.15	5.20

Key to Grading: Eagle

DATE	COIN TYPE/VARIETY/METAL	ABP FINE	AVERAGE FINE
☐ 1867–1916	2 Kopeks, Czarist Empire, 2nd Coinage, Copper	$.98	$1.60
☐ 1855–1859	3 Kopek, Czarist Empire, Copper	1.45	2.40
☐ 1859–1867	3 Kopeks, Czarist Empire, 2nd Coinage, Copper	2.80	4.60

Key to Grading: Eagle

DATE	COIN TYPE/VARIETY/METAL	ABP FINE	AVERAGE FINE
☐ 1867–1916	3 Kopeks, Czarist Empire, 2nd Coinage, Copper	1.80	3.00
☐ 1869–1885	3 Rubles, Czarist Empire, 2nd Coinage, Gold	—	338.00
☐ 1855–1858	5 Kopeks, Czarist Empire, Silver	—	6.75
☐ 1855–1859	5 Kopeks, Czarist Empire, Copper	2.80	4.60
☐ 1859–1867	5 Kopeks, Czarist Empire, 2nd Coinage, Copper	2.80	4.60
☐ 1859–1866	5 Kopeks, Czarist Empire, 2nd Coinage, Silver	—	6.75
☐ 1867–1916	5 Kopeks, Czarist Empire, 2nd Coinage, Copper	3.75	6.25
☐ 1867–1915	5 Kopeks, Czarist Empire, 2nd Coinage, Silver	—	9.00
☐ 1855–1858	5 Rubles, Czarist Empire, Gold	—	216.00
☐ 1859–1885	5 Rubles, Czarist Empire, 2nd Coinage, Gold	—	270.00
☐ 1886–1894	5 Rubles, Alexander III, Gold	—	270.00
☐ 1895–1896	5 Rubles, Gold	—	1975.00
☐ 1897–1911	5 Rubles, Reduced Weight Gold	—	102.00
☐ 1897	7½ Rubles, Reduced Weight Gold	—	185.75
☐ 1855–1858	10 Kopeks, Czarist Empire, Silver	—	10.65
☐ 1859–1866	10 Kopeks, Czarist Empire, 2nd Coinage, Silver	—	4.00
☐ 1867–1917	10 Kopeks, Czariest Empire, 2nd Coinage, Silver	—	4.00
☐ 1886–1894	10 Rubles, Alexander III, Gold	—	515.00
☐ 1895–1897	10 Rubles, Gold	—	2250.00
☐ 1898–1911	10 Rubles, Reduced Weight Gold	—	130.50
☐ 1859–1866	15 Kopeks, Czarist Empire 2nd Coinage, Silver	—	9.75

Key to Grading: Eagle

DATE	COIN TYPE/VARIETY/METAL	ABP FINE	AVERAGE FINE
☐ 1867–1917	15 Kopeks, Czarist Empire 2nd Coinage, Silver	—	$4.00
☐ 1897–1897	15 Rubles, Reduced Weight Gold	—	252.50
☐ 1855–1858	20 Kopek, Czarist Empire, Silver	—	7.75
☐ 1859–1866	20 Kopeks, Czarist Empire, 2nd Coinage, Silver	—	6.50
☐ 1867–1917	20 Kopeks, Czarist Empire, 2nd Coinage, Silver	—	4.00

Key to Grading: Eagle

☐ 1855–1858	25 Kopeks, Czarist Empire, Silver	—	10.00
☐ 1859–1885	25 Kopeks, Czarist Empire, 2nd Coinage, Silver	—	30.00
☐ 1886–1894	25 Kopeks, Alexander III, Silver	—	54.50

Key to Grading: Eagle

☐ 1895–1901	25 Kopeks, Nikolai II, Silver	—	20.25
☐ 1876	25 Rubles, Czarist Empire, 2nd Coinage, Gold Proof	—	Rare
☐ 1896–1908	25 Rubles, Gold	—	3250.00
☐ 1902	37$\frac{1}{2}$ Rubles, Reduced Weight Gold, Gold	—	Rare

DATE	COIN TYPE/VARIETY/METAL	ABP FINE	AVERAGE FINE
☐ 1886–1894	50 Kopeks, Alexander III, Silver	—	$40.50
☐ 1895–1914	50 Kopeks, Nikolai II, Silver	—	10.50

Russia—Empire Type Coinage

Key to Grading: Eagle

DATE	COIN TYPE/VARIETY/METAL	ABP FINE	AVERAGE FINE
☐ 1803–1810	1 Poluska, Alexander I, 1st Coinage, Copper	31.82	53.00
☐ 1839–1846	Poluska, Nikolai I, 3rd Coinage, Copper	3.90	6.50
☐ 1849–1855	Poluska, Nikolai I, 4th Coinage, Copper	3.90	6.50
☐ 1855–1861	Poluska, Alexander II, Copper	3.90	6.50
☐ 1867–1881	Poluska, Alexander II, 2nd Coinage, Copper	3.90	6.50
☐ 1882–1891	Poluska, Alexander III, 2nd Coinage, Copper	2.70	4.60
☐ 1894–1916	Poluska, Nikolai II, 2nd Coinage, Copper	.98	1.60
☐ 1804–1808	1 Denga, Alexander I, 1st Coinage, Copper	71.40	118.90
☐ 1810–1825	1 Denga, Alexander I, 2nd Coinage, Copper	6.50	10.80
☐ 1827–1830	1 Denga, Nicholas I, 1st Coinage, Copper	3.15	5.20
☐ 1839–1848	1 Denga, Nicholas I, 3rd Coinage, Copper	3.15	5.20
☐ 1849–1855	1 Denga, Nicholas I, 4th Coinage, Copper	3.15	5.20
☐ 1855–1861	1 Denga, Alexander II, Copper	3.15	5.20
☐ 1855–1861	1 Denga, Alexander II, 1st Coinage, Copper	3.25	5.40
☐ 1882–1894	1 Denga, Alexander III, Copper	2.80	4.70
☐ 1884–1916	1 Denga, Nikolai II, Copper	2.80	4.70
☐ 1804–1810	1 Kopek, Alexander I, 1st Coinage, Copper	22.70	37.85
☐ 1810–1825	1 Kopek, Alexander I, 2nd Coinage, Copper	5.80	9.70
☐ 1826–1830	1 Kopek, Nicholas I, 1st Coinage, Copper	4.00	6.50
☐ 1830–1839	1 Kopek, Nicholas I, 2nd Coinage, Copper	4.00	6.50
☐ 1839–1847	1 Kopek, Nicholas I, 3rd Coinage, Copper	4.00	6.50
☐ 1849–1856	1 Kopek, Nicholas I, 4th Coinage, Copper	4.00	6.50
☐ 1855–1864	1 Kopek, Alexander II, 1st Coinage, Copper	2.80	4.80
☐ 1867–1881	1 Kopek, Alexander II, 2nd Coinage, Copper	1.30	2.20
☐ 1882–1894	1 Kopek, Alexander III, Copper	.10	.38
☐ 1894–1916	1 Kopek, Nicholas II, Copper	.15	.55
☐ 1802–1810	2 Kopeks, Alexander I, 1st Coinage, Copper	28.55	47.60

DATE	COIN TYPE/VARIETY/METAL	ABP FINE	AVERAGE FINE
☐ 1810–1825	2 Kopeks, Alexander I, 2nd Coinage, Copper	$2.00	$5.40
☐ 1826–1830	2 Kopeks, Nicholas I, 1st Coinage, Copper	5.00	8.60
☐ 1830–1839	2 Kopeks, Nicholas I, 2nd Coinage, Copper	4.00	7.10
☐ 1839–1848	2 Kopeks, Nicholas I, 3rd Coinage, Copper	4.00	7.10
☐ 1849–1855	2 Kopeks, Nicholas I, 4th Coinage, Copper	4.00	6.70
☐ 1855–1865	2 Kopeks, Alexander II, 1st Coinage, Copper	3.85	6.70
☐ 1882–1894	2 Kopeks, Alexander III, Copper	.37	.65
☐ 1894–1916	2 Kopeks, Nicholas II, Copper	.46	.80
☐ 1839–1848	3 Kopeks, Nicholas I, 3rd Coinage, Copper	8.00	14.30
☐ 1849–1855	3 Kopeks, Nicholas I, 4th Coinage, Copper	6.00	14.30
☐ 1855–1865	3 Kopeks, Alexander II, 1st Coinage, Copper	6.00	14.30
☐ 1867–1881	3 Kopeks, Alexander II, 2nd Coinage, Copper	.93	1.65
☐ 1882–1894	3 Kopeks, Alexander III, Copper	1.55	2.70
☐ 1894–1916	3 Kopeks, Nicholas II, Copper	1.55	2.70
☐ 1802–1810	5 Kopeks, Alexander I, 1st Coinage, Copper	16.20	27.00
☐ 1810–1825	5 Kopeks, Alexander I, Silver	—	11.60
☐ 1826–1835	5 Kopeks, Nicholas I, Silver	—	12.25
☐ 1830–1839	5 Kopeks, Nicholas I, 2nd Coinage, Copper	4.00	8.90
☐ 1832–1855	5 Kopeks, Nicholas I, Silver	—	12.75
☐ 1849–1855	5 Kopeks, Nicholas I, 4th Coinage, Copper	5.00	8.90
☐ 1855–1881	5 Kopeks, Alexander II, Silver	—	12.75
☐ 1855–1866	5 Kopeks, Alexander II, 1st Coinage, Copper	2.00	5.40
☐ 1867–1881	5 Kopeks, Alexander II, 2nd Coinage, Copper	2.00	4.30
☐ 1881–1892	5 Kopeks, Alexander III, Silver	—	12.45
☐ 1882–1894	5 Kopeks, Alexander III, Copper	1.55	2.70
☐ 1894–1916	5 Kopeks, Nicholas II, Copper	30.00	69.50
☐ 1796–1801	10 Kopeks, Paul I, Silver	—	84.50
☐ 1802–1825	10 Kopeks, Alexander I, Silver	—	16.50
☐ 1826–1832	10 Kopeks, Nicholas I, Silver	—	15.50
☐ 1833–1855	10 Kopeks, Nicholas I, Silver	—	15.50
☐ 1855–1881	10 Kopeks, Alexander II, Silver	—	7.35

DATE	COIN TYPE/VARIETY/METAL	ABP FINE	AVERAGE FINE
☐ 1881–1892	10 Kopeks, Alexander III, Silver	—	$4.00
☐ 1860–1881	15 Kopeks, Alexander II, Silver	—	4.00
☐ 1887–1887	15 Kopeks, Alexander III, Silver	—	4.00
☐ 1810–1825	20 Kopeks, Alexander I, Silver	—	13.50
☐ 1833–1855	20 Kopeks, Nicholas I, Silver	—	12.45
☐ 1855–1881	20 Kopeks, Alexander II, Silver	—	6.65
☐ 1881–1892	20 Kopeks, Alexander III, Silver	—	6.65
☐ 1826–1835	25 Kopeks, Nicholas I, Silver	—	20.75
☐ 1855–1881	25 Kopeks, Alexander II, Silver	—	20.75
☐ 1881–1894	25 Kopeks, Alexander III, Silver	—	54.00
☐ 1886–1904	25 Kopeks, Nicholas II, Silver	—	54.00
☐ 1881–1892	50 Kopeks, Alexander III, Silver	—	54.00
☐ 1896–1904	50 Kopeks, Nicholas II, Silver	—	12.35
☐ 1801–1825	1 Ruble, Alexander I, Silver	—	42.50
☐ 1826–1832	1 Ruble, Nicholas I, Silver	—	42.50
☐ 1833–1855	1 Ruble, Nicholas I, Silver	—	46.50
☐ 1855–1881	1 Ruble, Alexander II, Silver	—	46.50
☐ 1881–1894	1 Ruble, Alexander III, Silver	—	46.50
☐ 1894–1916	1 Ruble, Nicholas II, Silver	—	46.50
☐ 1828–1845	3 Rubles, Platinum	—	424.50
☐ 1826–1855	5 Rubles, Gold	—	230.00
☐ 1829–1845	6 Rubles, Platinum	—	2250.00
☐ 1830–1845	12 Rubles, Platinum	—	2450.00

SOUTH AFRICA

The first coins, the silver guilders, were used in 1802. The silver pence, bronze penny, and gold pound were used in the 1800s. The silver florin was used in the 1900s, as were the cupro-nickel shilling, brass cent, and gold krugerrand. The first decimal coins were used in 1961. Today's currency is the rand.

South Africa—Republic Type Coinage

Key to Grading: Bust

DATE	COIN TYPE/VARIETY/METAL	ABP FINE	AVERAGE FINE
☐ 1892–1898	1 Penny, Paul Kruger, Bronze	$4.35	$7.60
☐ 1892–1897	3 Pence, Paul Kruger, Silver	—	9.25

Key to Grading: Bust

☐ 1892–1897	6 Pence, Paul Kruger, Silver	—	9.25

Key to Grading:

☐ 1892–1897	1 Shilling, Paul Kruger, Silver	—	10.75
☐ 1892–1897	2 Shillings, Paul Kruger, Silver	—	18.50

Key to Grading: Bust

☐ 1892–1897	2$^{1}/_{2}$ Shillings, Paul Kruger, Silver	—	42.00
☐ 1892	5 Shillings, Paul Kruger, Silver	—	115.00
☐ 1892–1897	1/2 Pond, Paul Kruger, Gold	—	252.50
☐ 1892–1900	1 Pond, Paul Kruger, Gold	—	245.00
☐ 1902	1 Pond, Veld, Gold	—	945.00

South Africa—Union Type Coinage

DATE	COIN TYPE/VARIETY/METAL	ABP FINE	AVERAGE FINE
☐ 1923–1931	1 Farthing, George V, Legend SUID-AFRIKA, Bronze	$3.00	$5.05
☐ 1931–1936	1 Farthing, George V, Legend SUID-AFRIKA, Bronze	3.00	5.05
☐ 1937–1947	1 Farthing, George VI, Legend SUID-AFRIKA, Bronze	.36	.60
☐ 1948–1950	1 Farthing, George VI, Obverse Legend GEORGIUS SEXTUS REX, Bronze	.36	.60

Key to Grading: Bust

DATE	COIN TYPE/VARIETY/METAL	ABP FINE	AVERAGE FINE
☐ 1951–1952	1 Farthing, George VI, Reverse Legend SUID-AFRIKA—SOUTH AFRICA, Bronze	.36	.60
☐ 1953–1960	1 Farthing, Elizabeth II, Reverse Legend SUID-AFRIKA—SOUTH AFRICA, Bronze	.19	.32
☐ 1923–1926	¹/₂ Penny, George V, Legend SUID-AFRIKA, Bronze	5.70	9.50
☐ 1931–1936	¹/₂ Penny, George V, Legend SUID-AFRIKA, Bronze	1.80	3.00
☐ 1937–1947	¹/₂ Penny, George VI, Legend SUID-AFRIKA, Bronze	.36	.60
☐ 1948–1952	¹/₂ Penny, George VI, Legend GEORGIUS SEXTUS REX, Bronze	.36	.60

Key to Grading: Bust

DATE	COIN TYPE/VARIETY/METAL	ABP FINE	AVERAGE FINE
☐ 1953–1960	¹/₂ Penny, Elizabeth II, Legend Elizabeth II Regina, Bronze	.33	.55
☐ 1923–1930	1 Penny, George V, Bronze	2.60	4.35

Key to Grading: Bust

DATE	COIN TYPE/VARIETY/METAL	ABP FINE	AVERAGE FINE
☐ 1931–1936	1 Penny, George V, Legend SUID-AFRIKA, Bronze	$.96	$1.60
☐ 1937–1947	1 Penny, George VI, Legend SUID-AFRIKA, Bronze	.36	.60
☐ 1948–1950	1 Penny, George VI, Legend GEORGIUS SEXTUS REX, Bronze	.36	.60
☐ 1951–1952	1 Penny, George VI, Legend SUID-AFRIKA—SOUTH AFRICA, Bronze	.36	.60
☐ 1953–1960	1 Penny, Elizabeth II, Legend SUID-AFRIKA— SOUTH AFRICA, Bronze	.36	.60
☐ 1923–1930	3 Pence, George V, Legend SUID-AFRIKA, Silver	—	3.15
☐ 1931–1936	3 Pence, George V, Legend SUID-AFRIKA, Silver	—	3.15

Key to Grading: Bust

☐ 1937–1947	3 Pence, George VI, Legend SUID-AFRIKA, Silver	—	2.30
☐ 1948–1950	3 Pence, George VI, Legend, GEORGIUS SEXTUS REX, Silver	—	1.00
☐ 1953–1960	3 Pence, Elizabeth II, Silver	—	1.00
☐ 1923–1930	6 Pence, George V, Legend SUID-AFRIKA, Silver	—	6.65
☐ 1931–1936	6 Pence, George V, Legend SUID-AFRIKA, Silver	—	6.65
☐ 1937–1947	6 Pence, George VI, Legend SUID-AFRIKA, Silver	—	2.65

Key to Grading: Bust

DATE	COIN TYPE/VARIETY/METAL	ABP FINE	AVERAGE FINE
☐ 1948–1950	6 Pence, George VI, Legend GEORGIUS SEXTUS REX, Silver	—	$3.00
☐ 1951–1952	6 Pence, George VI, Legend SUID-AFRIKA—SOUTH AFRICA, Silver	—	3.00
☐ 1953–1960	6 Pence, Elizabeth II, Silver	—	3.00
☐ 1923–1930	1 Shilling, George V, Legend SUID-AFRIKA, Silver	—	9.50
☐ 1931–1936	1 Shilling, George V, Legend SUID-AFRIKA, Silver	—	6.65

Key to Grading: Bust

☐ 1937–1947	1 Shilling, George VI, Silver	—	6.65
☐ 1948–1952	1 Shilling, George VI, Legend GEORGIUS SEXTUS REX, Silver	—	3.45
☐ 1953–1960	1 Shilling, Elizabeth II, Silver	—	2.35
☐ 1923–1930	1 Florin, George V, Legend SUID-AFRIKA, Silver	—	9.45
☐ 1931–1936	2 Shillings, George V, Legend SUID-AFRIKA, Silver	—	9.45
☐ 1937–1947	2 Shillings, George VI, Legend SUID-AFRIKA, Silver	—	9.45
☐ 1948–1950	2 Shillings, George VI, Legend GEORGIUS SEXTUS REX, Silver	—	15.45
☐ 1951–1952	2 Shillings, George VI, Legend SUID-AFRIKA—SOUTH AFRICA, Silver	—	7.00
☐ 1953–1960	2 Shillings, Elizabeth II, Silver	—	7.00
☐ 1923–1930	2½ Shillings, George V, Silver	—	7.75
☐ 1931–1936	2½ Shillings, George V, Legend SUID-AFRIKA, Silver	—	20.85

DATE	COIN TYPE/VARIETY/METAL	ABP FINE	AVERAGE FINE
☐ 1937–1947	2½ Shillings, George VI, Legend SUID-AFRIKA, Silver	—	$8.95
☐ 1948–1952	2½ Shillings, George VI, Legend GEORGIUS SEXTUS REX, Silver	—	9.45
☐ 1953–1960	2½ Shillings, Elizabeth I, Silver	—	9.45
☐ 1947	5 Shillings, Royal Visit Co, Silver	—	9.45

Key to Grading: Bust

☐ 1948–1950	5 Shillings, George VI, Silver	—	9.40
☐ 1951	5 Shillings, George VI, Legend SUID-AFRIKA—SOUTH AFRICA, Silver	—	9.40
☐ 1952	5 Shillings, Capetown Comm, Silver	—	9.40
☐ 1953–1959	5 Shillings, Elizabeth II, Silver	—	7.75
☐ 1960	5 Shillings, 50th Anniversary, Silver	—	7.75
☐ 1923–1926	½ Sovereign, George V, Gold	—	100.00
☐ 1952	½ Pound, George VI, Gold	—	169.50
☐ 1953–1960	½ Pound, Elizabeth II, Gold	—	270.00

Key to Grading: Bust

☐ 1923–1932	1 Sovereign, George V, Gold	—	215.00
☐ 1952	1 Pound, George VI, Gold	—	184.50
☐ 1953–1960	1 Pound, Elizabeth II, Gold Proof	—	215.00

South Africa—Republic Coinage

Key to Grading: Bust

DATE	COIN TYPE/VARIETY/METAL	ABP FINE	AVERAGE FINE
☐ 1961–1964	½ Cent, Brass	$.22	$ .38
☐ 1970–1976	½ Cent, Bronze	.22	.38
☐ 1979	½ Cent, Bronze PRF	1.15	2.00
☐ 1982	½ Cent, Bronze PRF	1.15	2.00
☐ 1961–1964	1 Cent, Brass	.25	.43
☐ 1965–1969	1 Cent, Bronze	.25	.43
☐ 1968	1 Cent, Bronze PRF	.63	1.10
☐ 1970–1989	1 Cent, Bronze	.13	.22
☐ 1976	1 Cent, Bronze	.22	.38
☐ 1979	1 Cent, Bronze	.13	.22
☐ 1982	1 Cent, Bronze	.22	.38
☐ 1990 to Date	1 Cent, Copper-Steel	.25	.43
☐ 1965–1969	2 Cents, Bronze	.25	.43
☐ 1968	2 Cents, Bronze	.25	.43
☐ 1970–1990	2 Cents, Bronze	.13	.22

Key to Grading: Bust

☐ 1961–1964	2½ Cents, Silver	—	3.90
☐ 1961–1964	5 Cents, Silver	—	3.90
☐ 1965–1969	5 Cents, Nickel	.25	.43
☐ 1968	5 Cents, Nickel	.13	.22
☐ 1970–1989	5 Cents, Nickel	.28	.48
☐ 1976	5 Cents, Nickel	.28	.48
☐ 1979	5 Cents, Nickel	.28	.48
☐ 1982	5 Cents, Nickel	.28	.48
☐ 1990 to Date	5 Cents, Copper-Steel	.13	.22
☐ 1961–1962	10 Cents, Silver	.43	.74

DATE	COIN TYPE/VARIETY/METAL	ABP FINE	AVERAGE FINE
☐ 1965–1969	10 Cents, Nickel	$.22	$ .38
☐ 1968	10 Cents, Nickel	.31	.55
☐ 1970–1989	10 Cents, Nickel	.28	.48
☐ 1976	10 Cents, Nickel	.28	.48
☐ 1979	10 Cents, Nickel	.16	.28
☐ 1982	10 Cents, Nickel	.20	.35
☐ 1990–1999	10 Cents, Brass-Steel	.17	.30
☐ 1961–1964	20 Cents, Silver	.87	1.55
☐ 1965–1969	20 Cents, Nickel	.17	.32
☐ 1968	20 Cents, Nickel	.93	1.60
☐ 1970–1990	20 Cents, Nickel	.28	.48
☐ 1976	20 Cents, Nickel	.28	.48
☐ 1979	20 Cents, Nickel	.28	.48
☐ 1982–1982	20 Cents, Nickel	.28	.48
☐ 1990 to Date	20 Cents, Brass-Steel	.28	.48

Key to Grading: Bust

DATE	COIN TYPE/VARIETY/METAL	ABP FINE	AVERAGE FINE
☐ 1961–1964	50 Cents, Silver	—	6.50
☐ 1965–1969	50 Cents, Nickel	.34	.60
☐ 1968	50 Cents, Nickel	.34	.60
☐ 1970–1990	50 Cents, Nickel	.34	.60
☐ 1976	50 Cents, Nickel	.34	.60
☐ 1979	50 Cents, Nickel	.34	.60
☐ 1982	50 Cents, Nickel	.34	.60
☐ 1990 to Date	50 Cents, Brass-Steel	.46	.78
☐ 1961–1983	1 Rand, Gold	—	85.00
☐ 1965–1968	1 Rand, Silver	—	6.65

Key to Grading: Coat of Arms

DATE	COIN TYPE/VARIETY/METAL	ABP FINE	AVERAGE FINE
☐ 1970–1989	1 Rand, Silver	—	6.65
☐ 1977–1990	1 Rand, Nickel	.49	.84

DATE	COIN TYPE/VARIETY/METAL	ABP FINE	AVERAGE FINE
☐ 1961–1983	2 Rands, Gold	—	$310.00
☐ 1989	2 Rands, Copper-Nickel	.46	.80

South Africa—Bullion Coinage

DATE	COIN TYPE/VARIETY/METAL	ABP FINE	AVERAGE FINE
☐ 1980	$1/10$ Krugerrand, Gold	—	250.00
☐ 1980	$1/4$ Krugerrand, Gold	—	500.00
☐ 1980	$1/2$ Krugerrand, Gold	—	1100.00
☐ 1967	Krugerrand, Gold	—	1800.00

*BV ≠ These coins are relatively current so their collector value is minimal. Since these coins were minted and sold primarily for their bullion value, their current value is determined by the current "spot" price of the precious metal indicated. For accurate prices, contact your local coin dealer.

SPAIN

The earliest coins from the 4th century B.C. were marked Em. The silver denarius was popular from about 100 B.C. to 45 B.C., with bronze coins and the gold tremissis becoming popular by 600 to 700. Gold coins were popular in the mid-1400s. Decimal coins appeared in 1848, with the euro being the currency used today.

Spain—Type Coinage

Key to Grading: Bust

DATE	COIN TYPE/VARIETY/METAL	ABP FINE	AVERAGE FINE
☐ 1866–1868	$1/2$ Centimo, Isabell II, 2nd Decimal Coinage, Bronze	5.50	9.65
☐ 1866–1868	1 Centimo, Isabell II, 2nd Decimal Coinage, Bronze	7.45	13.00
☐ 1870	1 Centimo, Bronze	.63	1.10
☐ 1906	1 Centimo, Alfonso XIII, 4th Coinage, Bronze	.63	1.10
☐ 1911–1913	1 Centimo, Alfonso XIII, 5th Coinage, Bronze	4.10	7.15

DATE	COIN TYPE/VARIETY/METAL	ABP FINE	AVERAGE FINE
☐ 1904–1905	2 Centimos, Alfonso XIII, 4th Coinage, Bronze	$.37	$ .65
☐ 1911–1912	2 Centimos, Alfonso XIII, 5th Coinage, Bronze	.37	.65

Key to Grading: Bust

DATE	COIN TYPE/VARIETY/METAL	ABP FINE	AVERAGE FINE
☐ 1866–1868	2½ Centimos, Isabell II, 2nd Decimal Coinage, Bronze	5.00	8.65
☐ 1868	25 Milesimas, Provisional, Battle of Alcolea Bridge, Bronze	35.00	70.30
☐ 1854–1864	5 Centimos de Real, Isabell, 2nd Decimal Coinage, Copper	10.00	17.85
☐ 1866–1868	5 Centimos, Isabell II, 2nd Decimal Coinage, Bronze	10.00	17.85

Key to Grading: Lion or Bust

DATE	COIN TYPE/VARIETY/METAL	ABP FINE	AVERAGE FINE
☐ 1870	5 Centimos, Bronze	2.65	4.60
☐ 1875	5 Centimos, Carlos VII, Bronze	12.35	21.50
☐ 1877–1879	5 Centimos, Alfonso XII, 2nd Coinage, Bronze	.78	1.36
☐ 1937	5 Centimos, Republic, 2nd Coinage, Iron	.63	1.10
☐ 1940–1953	5 Centimos, Nationalist Govt, 1st Coinage, Aluminum	.31	.55
☐ 1854–1864	10 Centimos, Isabell II, Decimal Coinage, Copper	10.90	19.00
☐ 1864–1868	10 Centimos, Isabell II, 2nd Decimal Coinage, Silver	—	52.50

Key to Grading: Lion or Bust

DATE	COIN TYPE/VARIETY/METAL	ABP FINE	AVERAGE FINE
☐ 1870	10 Centimos, Bronze	1.55	$2.75
☐ 1875	10 Centimos, Carlos VII, Bronze	12.00	22.70
☐ 1877–1879	10 Centimos, Alfonso XII, 3rd Coinage, Bronze	.31	.52
☐ 1940–1953	10 Centimos, Nationalist Govt, 1st Coinage, Aluminum	.25	.42
☐ 1959	10 Centimos, Kingdom, Aluminum	.25	.42
☐ 1865–1868	20 Centimos, Isabell II, 2nd Decimal Coinage, Silver	—	58.50
☐ 1869–1870	20 Centimos, Obverse Legend: Espana, Silver	—	230.00
☐ 1949	20 Centimos, Nationalist Govt, 2nd Coinage, Cupro-Nickel	.22	.38
☐ 1925	25 Centimos, Alfonso XIII, 6th Coinage, Nickel-Brass	.37	.62
☐ 1927	25 Centimos, Alfonso XIII, 6th Coinage, Cupro-Nickel	.28	.46
☐ 1933	1 Peseta, Republic, 1st Coinage, Silver	—	7.50
☐ 1934	25 Centimos, Republic, 1st Coinage, Nickel-Bronze	.31	.54
☐ 1937	25 Centimos, Nationalist Govt, 1st Coinage, Cupro-Nickel	.31	.54
☐ 1938	25 Centimos, Republic, 2nd Coinage, Copper	.95	1.60
☐ 1864–1868	40 Centimos, Isabell II, 2nd Decimal Coinage, Silver	—	17.00
☐ 1848–1853	1/2 Real, Isabell II, Copper	14.85	24.75
☐ 1869–1870	50 Centimos, Obverse Legend: Espana, Silver	—	37.00
☐ 1880–1885	50 Centimos, Alfonso XII, 3rd Coinage, Silver	—	7.00
☐ 1889–1892	50 Centimos, Alfonso XIII, 1st Coinage, Silver	—	18.60
☐ 1894	50 Centimos, Alfonso XIII, 2nd Coinage, Silver	—	10.00

DATE	COIN TYPE/VARIETY/METAL	ABP FINE	AVERAGE FINE
☐ 1896–1900	50 Centimos, Alfonso XIII, 3rd Coinage, Silver	—	$6.60
☐ 1904	50 Centimos, Alfonso XIII, 4th Coinage, Silver	—	4.30
☐ 1910	50 Centimos, Alfonso XIII, 5th Coinage, Silver	—	4.30
☐ 1926	50 Centimos, Alfonso XIII, 6th Coinage, Silver	—	4.30
☐ 1937	50 Centimos, Republic, 2nd Coinage, Copper	.46	.77
☐ 1949–1963	50 Centimos, Kingdom, Cupro-Nickel	.31	.54
☐ 1966–1975	50 Centimos, Kingdom, Aluminum	.31	.54
☐ 1980	50 Centimos, Kingdom, World Cup Soccer Games, Aluminum	.22	.36
☐ 1850–1855	1 Real, Isabell II, Arms Without Pillars, Silver	—	13.50
☐ 1857–1864	1 Real, Isabell II, 2nd Decimal Coinage, Silver	—	18.50
☐ 1865–1868	1 Escudo, Isabell II, 3rd Decimal Coinage, Silver	—	33.00
☐ 1869–1870	1 Peseta, Obverse Legend: Espana, Silver		18.50
☐ 1869	1 Peseta, Obverse Legend: Gobierno Provisional, Silver	—	6.25
☐ 1876	1 Peseta, Alfonso XII, 2nd Coinage, Silver	—	10.50
☐ 1881–1885	1 Peseta, Alfonso XII, 3rd Coinage, Silver	—	10.50
☐ 1889–1891	1 Peseta, Alfonso XIII, 1st Coinage, Silver	—	24.50
☐ 1893–1894	1 Peseta, Alfonso XIII, 2nd Coinage, Silver	—	18.50
☐ 1896–1902	1 Peseta, Alfonso XIII, 3rd Coinage, Silver	—	6.60
☐ 1903–1905	1 Peseta, Alfonso XIII, 4th Coinage, Silver	—	7.70
☐ 1937	1 Peseta, Republic, 2nd Coinage, Brass	1.25	3.15
☐ 1944	1 Peseta, Nationalist Govt, 1st Coinage, Aluminum-Bronze	2.95	5.00
☐ 1947–1975	1 Peseta, Kingdom, Alluminum-Bronze	2.95	5.00

Key to Grading: Bust

DATE	COIN TYPE/VARIETY/METAL	ABP FINE	AVERAGE FINE
☐ 1947–1963	1 Peseta, Kingdom, 2nd Coinage, Aluminum-Bronze	$.31	$ .52

Key to Grading: Bust

DATE	COIN TYPE/VARIETY/METAL	ABP FINE	AVERAGE FINE
☐ 1980	1 Peseta, Kingdom, World Cup Soccer Games, Aluminum-Bronze	.31	.52
☐ 1982–2001	1 Peseta, Kingdom, Aluminum	.31	.52
☐ 1852–1855	1 Reales, Isabell II, Arms Without Pillars, Silver	—	22.50
☐ 1857–1864	2 Reales, Isabell II, 2nd Decimal Coinage, Silver	—	42.50
☐ 1865–1868	2 Escudos, Isabell II, 3rd Decimal Coinage, Silver	—	45.00
☐ 1865–1868(69)	2 Escudos, Isabell II, 3rd Decimal Coinage, Gold	—	525.00
☐ 1869–1870	2 Pesetas, Provisional, Obverse Legend: Espana, Silver	—	12.35
☐ 1879–1884	2 Pesetas, Alfonso XII, 3rd Coinage, Silver	—	12.35
☐ 1889–1892	2 Pesetas, Alfonso XIII, 1st Coinage, Silver	—	18.60
☐ 1894	2 Pesetas, Alfonso XIII, 2nd Coinage, Silver	—	82.00
☐ 1905	2 Pesetas, Alfonso XIII, 4th Coinage, Silver	—	7.70
☐ 1982–1984	2 Pesetas, Kingdom, Aluminum	.31	.52
☐ 1953	2½ Pesetas, Kingdom, Aluminum-Bronze	.31	.52
☐ 1852–1855	4 Reales, Isabell II, Arms Without Pillars, Silver	—	38.00
☐ 1856–1864	4 Reales, Isabell II, 2nd Decimal Coinage, Silver	—	51.75
☐ 1865–1868	4 Escudos, Isabell II, 3rd Decimal Coinage, Gold	—	92.50
☐ 1869–1870	5 Pesetas, Provisional, Obverse Legend: Espana, Silver	—	50.00
☐ 1871	5 Pesetas, Amadeo I, Obverse Legend: Espana, Silver	—	30.00
☐ 1873	5 Pesetas, Republic, Cartagena Mint, Silver	—	58.00

Key to Grading: Bust

DATE	COIN TYPE/VARIETY/METAL	ABP FINE	AVERAGE FINE
☐ 1875–1876	5 Pesetas, Alfonso XII, 1st Coinage, Silver	—	$34.00
☐ 1877–1882	5 Pesetas, Alfonso XII, 2nd Coinage, Silver	—	42.50
☐ 1882–1885	5 Pesetas, Alfonso XII, 3rd Coinage, Silver	—	32.50
☐ 1888–1892	5 Pesetas, Alfonso XIII, 1st Coinage, Silver	—	30.50
☐ 1892–1894	5 Pesetas, Alfonso XIII, 2nd Coinage, Silver	—	34.00
☐ 1896–1899	5 Pesetas, Alfonso XIII, 3rd Coinage, Silver	—	30.50

Key to Grading: Bust

☐ 1949	5 Pesetas, Kingdom, Nickel	.30	1.05
☐ 1957–1975	5 Pesetas, Kingdom, Cupro-Nickel	.16	.26
☐ 1980	5 Pesetas, Kingdom, World Cup Soccer Games, Cupro-Nickel	9.90	16.50
☐ 1982–1989	5 Pesetas, Kingdom, Cupro-Nickel	.28	.46
☐ 1989–2001	5 Pesetas, Kingdom, Aluminum-Bronze	.28	.46
☐ 1851–1856	10 Reales, Isabell II, Arms Flanked by Pillars, Silver	—	69.50
☐ 1857–1864	10 Reales, Isabell II, 2nd Decimal Coinage, Silver	—	205.00
☐ 1865–1868	10 Escudos, Isabell II, 3rd Decimal Coinage, Gold	—	270.00
☐ 1878–1879	10 Pesetas, Alfonso XII, 2nd Coinage, Gold	—	346.50
☐ 1983–1985	10 Pesetas, Kingdom, Cupro-Nickel	.31	.52
☐ 1845–1855	20 Reales, Isabell II, Silver	—	144.50
☐ 1850–1855	20 Reales, Isabell II, Arms Flanked by Pillars, Silver	—	110.00

DATE	COIN TYPE/VARIETY/METAL	ABP FINE	AVERAGE FINE
☐ 1856–1864	20 Reales, Isabell II, 2nd Decimal Coinage, Silver	—	$115.50
☐ 1861–1863	20 Reales, Isabell II, 2nd Decimal Coinage, Gold	—	128.50
☐ 1887–1890	20 Pesetas, Alfonso XIII, 1st Coinage, Gold	—	2.50
☐ 1892	20 Pesetas, Alfonso XIII, 2nd Coinage, Gold	—	1400.00
☐ 1896–1899	20 Pesetas, Alfonso XIII, 3rd Coinage, Gold	—	248.00
☐ 1904	20 Pesetas, Alfonso XIII, 4th Coinage, Gold	—	1800.00
☐ 1876–1880	25 Pesetas, Alfonso XII, 2nd Coinage, Gold	—	250.00
☐ 1881–1885	25 Pesetas, Alfonso XII, 3rd Coinage, Gold	—	408.00

Key to Grading: Bust

DATE	COIN TYPE/VARIETY/METAL	ABP FINE	AVERAGE FINE
☐ 1957–1984	25 Pesetas, Kingdom, Cupro-Nickel	.25	.42
☐ 1980	25 Pesetas, Kingdom, World Cup Soccer Games, Cupro-Nickel	.25	.42
☐ 1990–1991	25 Pesetas, Kingdom, 1992 Olympics—High Jumper, Nickel-Bronze	.25	.42
☐ 1990–1991	25 Pesetas, Kingdom, 1992 Olympics—Discus, Nickel-Bronze	.25	.42
☐ 1992	25 Pesetas, Kingdom, Sevilla Tower, Nickel-Bronze	.31	.52
☐ 1861–1863	40 Reales, Isabell II, 2nd Decimal Coinage, Gold	—	118.50

Key to Grading: Bust

DATE	COIN TYPE/VARIETY/METAL	ABP FINE	AVERAGE FINE
☐ 1957–1984	50 Pesetas, Kingdom, Cupro-Nickel	$.31	$ .52
☐ 1980	50 Pesetas, Kingdom, World Cup Soccer Games, Cupro-Nickel	.31	.52
☐ 1990	50 Pesetas, Kingdom, Expo 92— Juan Carlos, Cupro-Nickel	.31	.52
☐ 1990–1991	50 Pesetas, Kingdom, Expo 92— City View, Cupro-Nickel	.31	.52
☐ 1851–1855	100 Reales, Isabell II, Gold	—	535.00
☐ 1856–1862	100 Reales, Isabell II, 2nd Decimal Coinage, Gold	—	265.00
☐ 1897	100 Pesetas, Alfonso XIII, 3rd Coinage, Gold	—	950.00

Key to Grading: Bust

DATE	COIN TYPE/VARIETY/METAL	ABP FINE	AVERAGE FINE
☐ 1966	100 Pesetas, Kingdom, Silver	—	6.50
☐ 1976	100 Pesetas, Kingdom, Cupro-Nickel	1.40	2.35
☐ 1980	100 Pesetas, Kingdom, World Cup Soccer Games, Cupro-Nickel	.46	.77
☐ 1982–1990	100 Pesetas, Kingdom, Aluminum-Bronze	.78	1.30
☐ 1989	100 Pesetas, Kingdom, Discovery of America—Mayan Pyramid, Silver	—	8.00
☐ 1990	100 Pesetas, Kingdom, Brother Juniper Serra, Silver	—	13.50
☐ 1991	100 Pesetas, Kingdom, Celestino Mutis, Silver	—	18.50
☐ 1986–1988	200 Pesetas, Kingdom, Celestino Mutis, Cupro-Nickel	1.70	2.85
☐ 1987	200 Pesetas, Kingdom, Madrid Numismatic Exposition, Cupro-Nickel	25.00	46.35
☐ 1989	200 Pesetas, Kingdom, Discovery of America—Astrolabe, Silver	—	12.00
☐ 1990	200 Pesetas, Kingdom, Alonso de Frcilla, Silver	—	25.50
☐ 1990	200 Pesetas, Kingdom, Cupro-Nickel	2.65	4.40
☐ 1991	200 Pesetas, Kingdom, Las Casas, Silver	—	22.50
☐ 1992	200 Pesetas, Kingdom, Madrid— Capitol of European Culture, Copper-Nickel	4.10	6.85

Key to Grading: Bust

DATE	COIN TYPE/VARIETY/METAL	ABP FINE	AVERAGE FINE
☐ 1987–1990	500 Pesetas, Kingdom, Wedding Anniversary—Juan Carlos & Sofia, Copper-Aluminum-Nickel	$1.55	$2.60
☐ 1989	500 Pesetas, Kingdom, Discovery of America—Juego De Pelota Game, Silver	—	24.50
☐ 1990	500 Pesetas, Kingdom, Juan de la Costa, Silver	—	30.00
☐ 1991	500 Pesetas, Kingdom, Jorge Juan, Silver	—	42.50
☐ 1989	1000 Pesetas, Kingdom, Discovery of America—Capture of Granada, Silver	—	42.50
☐ 1990	1000 Pesetas, Kingdom, Magellanes and Elcano, Silver	—	42.50
☐ 1991	1000 Pesetas, Kingdom, Simon Bolivar & San Martin, Silver	—	42.50
☐ 1989	2000 Pesetas, Kingdom, Discovery of America—Columbus, Silver	—	60.50
☐ 1990	2000 Pesetas, Kingdom, 1992 Olympics—Archer, Silver	—	38.00
☐ 1990	2000 Pesetas, Kingdom, 1992 Olympics—Basketball Players, Silver	—	74.50
☐ 1990	2000 Pesetas, Kingdom, 1992 Olympics—Human Pyramid, Silver	—	36.50
☐ 1990	2000 Pesetas, Kingdom, Hidalgo, Morelos and Juarez, Silver	—	52.50
☐ 1990	2000 Pesetas, Kingdom, 1992 Olympics, Symbols, Silver	—	68.50
☐ 1990	2000 Pesetas, Kingdom, 1992 Olympics, Soccer Player, Silver	—	52.50
☐ 1990	2000 Pesetas, Kingdom, 1992 Olympics, Pelotal Player, Silver	—	75.50
☐ 1990	2000 Pesetas, Kingdom, 1992 Olympics, Greek Runner, Silver	—	75.50
☐ 1990	2000 Pesetas, Kingdom, 1992 Olympics, Ancient Boat, Silver	—	75.50

DATE	COIN TYPE/VARIETY/METAL	ABP FINE	AVERAGE FINE
☐ 1991	2000 Pesetas, Kingdom, Ibero American Series, Silver	—	$128.50
☐ 1991	2000 Pesetas, Kingdom, Olympics—Medieval Rider, Silver	—	125.50
☐ 1991	2000 Pesetas, Kingdom, Olympics—Torch & Flag, Silver	—	125.50
☐ 1991	2000 Pesetas, Kingdom, Olympics—Tennis Player, Silver	—	125.50
☐ 1991	2000 Pesetas, Kingdom, Olympics—Bowling, Silver	—	125.50
☐ 1991	2000 Pesetas, Kingdom, Federman, Quesada and Benalcazar, Silver	—	42.50
☐ 1992	2000 Pesetas, Kingdom, Olympics—Chariot Racing, Silver	—	100.00
☐ 1992	2000 Pesetas, Kingdom, Olympics—Sprinters, Silver	—	100.00
☐ 1992	2000 Pesetas, Kingdom, Olympics—Tug of War, Silver	—	100.00
☐ 1992	2000 Pesetas, Kingdom, Olympics—Wheelchair Basketball, Silver	—	82.50
☐ 1989	5000 Pesetas, Kingdom, Discovery of America—Compass Face, Gold	—	105.50
☐ 1989	5000 Pesetas, Kingdom, Discovery of America—Santa Maria, Silver	—	92.50
☐ 1990	5000 Pesetas, Kingdom, Philip V, Gold	—	114.00
☐ 1990	5000 Pesetas, Kingdom, Cortes, Montezuma, and Marina, Silver	—	100.00
☐ 1991	5000 Pesetas, Kingdom, Pizarro & Atahualpa, Silver	—	165.50
☐ 1991	5000 Pesetas, Kingdom, Fernando VI, Gold	—	250.00
☐ 1989	10,000 Pesetas, Kingdom, Discovery of America—Sphere, Gold	—	250.00
☐ 1990	10,000 Pesetas, Kingdom, Quauchtemoc, Gold	—	250.00
☐ 1990	10,000 Pesetas, Kingdom, Olympics—Field Hockey, Gold	—	250.00
☐ 1990	10,000 Pesetas, Kingdom, Olympics—Gymnast, Gold	—	250.00
☐ 1991	10,000 Pesetas, Kingdom, Regional Autonomy, Silver	—	250.00
☐ 1991	10,000 Pesetas, Kingdom, Discoverers & Liberators, Silver	—	308.00
☐ 1991	10,000 Pesetas, Kingdom, Tupac Amaru II, Gold	—	225.00
☐ 1991	10,000 Pesetas, Kingdom, Spanish Royal Family, Silver	—	308.00

DATE	COIN TYPE/VARIETY/METAL	ABP FINE	AVERAGE FINE
☐ 1991	10,000 Pesetas, Kingdom, Olympics—Karate, Gold	—	$420.00
☐ 1991	10,000 Pesetas, Kingdom, Olympics—Baseball, Gold	—	420.00
☐ 1989	20,000 Pesetas, Kingdom, Discovery of America—Pinzon Brother, Gold	—	260.00
☐ 1990	20,000 Pesetas, Kingdom, Tupac Amaru I, Gold		
☐ 1990	20,000 Pesetas, Kingdom, Huascar, Gold	—	485.00
☐ 1990	20,000 Pesetas, Kingdom, Olympics—Cathedral Tower, Gold	—	380.50
☐ 1990	20,000 Pesetas, Kingdom, Olympics—Dome Building, Gold	—	460.50
☐ 1990	20,000 Pesetas, Kingdom, Olympics—Ruins, Gold	—	338.00
☐ 1990	20,000 Pesetas, Kingdom, Olympics—Montjuic Stadium, Gold	—	458.00
☐ 1989	40,000 Pesetas, Kingdom, Discovery of America—Sea Monster Attacking Ship, Gold	—	765.00
☐ 1990	40,000 Pesetas, Kingdom, Juan Carlos, Gold	—	920.00
☐ 1991	40,000 Pesetas, Kingdom, Imperial Double Eagle, Gold	—	920.00
☐ 1989	80,000 Pesetas, Kingdom, Discovery of America—Ferdinand & Isabella, Gold	—	1200.00
☐ 1990	80,000 Pesetas, Kingdom, Carlos V, Gold	—	1200.00
☐ 1990	80,000 Pesetas, Kingdom, Olympics—Discus, Gold	—	1200.00
☐ 1990	80,000 Pesetas, Kingdom, Olympics—Prince Carlos on Horseback, Gold	—	1200.00
☐ 1991	80,000 Pesetas, Kindgom, Olympics—Women Tossing Man, Gold	—	1800.00
☐ 1991	80,000 Pesetas, Kingdom, Carlos III, Gold	—	1650.00
☐ 1992	80,000 Pesetas, Olympics—Children Playing, Gold	—	1800.00

SWITZERLAND

The first coins were Celtic issues of gold staters and fractions. The Swiss series began in the 3rd century B.C., and silver coins were issued in the 1st century B.C. In the 6th and 7th centuries, gold tremisses were produced, then silver deniers. In the 13th century, bracteate pfennigs were made. Gold coins were produced in the 1400s. The decimal system was developed in 1798. The currency in use today is the Swiss franc.

Switzerland—Type Coinage

Key to Grading: Bust

DATE	COIN TYPE/VARIETY/METAL	ABP FINE	AVERAGE FINE
☐ 1922–1954	5 Francs, William Tell, Rev: Shield, Silver	—	$18.00
☐ 1936	5 Francs, Commemorative, Armament Fund, Silver	—	24.50
☐ 1939	5 Francs, Commemorative, Zurich Exposition, Silver	—	100.00
☐ 1939	5 Francs, Commemorative, Laupen, Silver	—	375.50
☐ 1941	5 Francs, Commemorative, Confederation 650th Anniversary, Silver	—	38.50
☐ 1944	5 Francs, Commemorative, Battle of St. Jakob 500th Anniversary, Silver	—	38.50

DATE	COIN TYPE/VARIETY/METAL	ABP FINE	AVERAGE FINE
☐ 1948	5 Francs, Commemorative, Swiss Confederation Centenary, Silver	—	$10.50
☐ 1911–1922	10 Francs, Peasant Girl, Rev: Shield, Gold	—	50.00
☐ 1901–1935	20 Francs, Peasant Girl, Rev: Shield, Gold	—	BV

Switzerland—Shooting Festival Coinage

Key to Grading: Figures on Coin

DATE	COIN TYPE/VARIETY/METAL	ABP FINE	AVERAGE FINE
☐ 1855	5 Francs, Shooting Festival Solothurn, Silver	—	850.00
☐ 1857	5 Francs, Shooting Festival Berne, Silver	—	338.00
☐ 1859	5 Francs, Shooting Festival Zurich, Silver	—	126.50
☐ 1861	5 Francs, Shooting Festival Nidwalden, Silver	—	190.00
☐ 1863	5 Francs, Shooting Festival La Chaux-de-Fonds, Silver	—	190.00
☐ 1865	5 Francs, Shooting Festival Schaffhausen, Silver	—	120.00
☐ 1867	5 Francs, Shooting Festival Schwyz, Silver	—	92.50
☐ 1869	5 Francs, Shooting Festival Zug, Silver	—	122.50
☐ 1872	5 Francs, Shooting Festival Zurich, Silver	—	90.00
☐ 1874	5 Francs, Shooting Festival St. Gallen, Silver	—	75.50
☐ 1876	5 Francs, Shooting Festival Lausanne, Silver	—	75.50
☐ 1879	5 Francs, Shooting Festival Basle, Silver	—	
☐ 1881	5 Francs, Shooting Festival Fribourg, Silver	—	60.00
☐ 1883	5 Francs, Shooting Festival Lugano, Silver	—	44.50
☐ 1885	5 Francs, Shooting Festival Berne, Silver	—	44.50

Switzerland—Helvetian Confederation Coinage

Key to Grading: Bust

DATE	COIN TYPE/VARIETY/METAL	ABP FINE	AVERAGE FINE
☐ 1879–1954	5 Rappen, Helvetia Head. Rev: Wreath & Shield, Cupro-Nickel	$1.70	$2.85

Key to Grading: Bust

☐ 1879–1954	10 Rappen, Helvetia Head. Rev: Wreath & Shield, Cupro-Nickel	1.70	2.85

Key to Grading: Bust

☐ 1881–1954	20 Rappen, Helvetia Head. Rev: Wreath & Shield, Cupro-Nickel	.63	1.05
☐ 1850–1851	½ Franc, Helvetia, Silver	—	102.50

Key to Grading: Wreath

DATE	COIN TYPE/VARIETY/METAL	ABP FINE	AVERAGE FINE
☐ 1875–1953	½ Franc, Helvetia Standing. Rev: Wreath, Silver	—	$30.00
☐ 1850–1861	Franc, Helvetia, Silver	—	84.50

Key to Grading: Wreath

☐ 1875–1945	Franc, Helvetia Standing. Rev: Wreath, Silver	—	12.00
☐ 1850–1863	2 Francs, Helvetia, Silver	—	126.50

Key to Grading: Wreath

☐ 1874–1948	2 Francs, Helvetia Standing. Rev: Wreath, Silver	—	12.00
☐ 1850–1874	5 Francs, Helvetia, Silver	—	189.50
☐ 1888–1916	5 Francs, Helvetia Head. Rev: Wreath & Shield, Silver	—	175.50

SYRIA

The first coins were used in the 5th century B.C. and were Greek issues of silver coinage. The silver tetradrachm was in evidence in 200 B.C., followed by bronze coins in 200 A.D. The copper fals were used in the 600s, followed by the copper dinar, silver dirhem, and silver coins and dirhems in the 12th to 16th centuries. The nickel-brass, cupro-nickel, and aluminum-bronze piastre was used in the 1900s. Decimal coins were used in 1921. The currency today is the pound.

Syria—Syrian Arab Republic

Key to Grading: Eagle

DATE	COIN TYPE/VARIETY/METAL	ABP FINE	AVERAGE FINE
☐ 1962–1973	2½ Piastres, Aluminum-Bronze	$.28	$ .46
☐ 1962–1965	5 Piastres, Aluminum-Bronze	.32	.54

Key to Grading: Eagle

DATE	COIN TYPE/VARIETY/METAL	ABP FINE	AVERAGE FINE
☐ 1971–1979	5 Piastres, FAO Issue, Aluminum-Bronze	$.16	$ .26
☐ 1962–1974	10 Piastres, Aluminum-Bronze	.25	.41
☐ 1976–1979	10 Piastres, FAO Issue, Aluminum-Bronze	.25	.41
☐ 1968–1974	25 Piastres, Nickel	.31	.52
☐ 1976	25 Piastres, FAO Issue, Nickel	.31	.52
☐ 1979	25 Piastres, Cupro-Nickel	.31	.52
☐ 1968–1976	50 Piastres, Nickel	41.40	69.00
☐ 1979	50 Piastres, Cupro-Nickel	41.40	69.00
☐ 1968–1978	1 Pound, Nickel	.22	.36
☐ 1979	1 Pound, Cupro-Nickel	.22	.36
☐ 1991	1 Pound, Stainless Steel	.22	.36

Syria—United Arab Republic

DATE	COIN TYPE/VARIETY/METAL	ABP FINE	AVERAGE FINE
☐ 1960	2½ Piastres, Aluminum-Bronze	.16	.26
☐ 1960	5 Piastres, Aluminum-Bronze	.25	.41
☐ 1960	10 Piastres, Aluminum-Bronze	.31	.52
☐ 1958	25 Piastres, Silver	—	2.20
☐ 1958	50 Piastres, Silver	—	7.45
☐ 1959	50 Piastres, Anniversary of Founding of United Arab Republic, Silver	—	7.45

TURKEY

The first coins were used in the late 7th century B.C. and were made of electrum, an alloy of gold and silver. Pure gold and silver coins were produced in 500 B.C. Bronze and copper coins followed through several different periods in Turkey. The decimal system was set up in 1844. A new coinage was initiated in 1934. The currency today is the lira.

Turkey—Type Coinage

Key to Grading: Lettering

DATE	COIN TYPE/VARIETY/METAL	ABP FINE	AVERAGE FINE
☐ 1918–1919	2 Kurus, Mohammed VI, 1st Coinage, Silver	—	$250.00
☐ 1923–1924	100 Para, Republic, Aluminum-Bronze	1.70	2.85
☐ 1926	100 Para, Republic, Aluminum-Bronze	1.70	2.85
☐ 1918–1919	5 Kurus, Mohammed VI, 1st Coinage, Silver	—	250.00
☐ 1923–1924	5 Kurus, Republic, Aluminum-Bronze	1.55	2.60
☐ 1926	5 Kurus, Republic, Aluminum-Bronze	1.55	2.60
☐ 1918–1919	10 Kurus, Mohammed VI, 1st Coinage, Silver	—	385.00
☐ 1923–1924	10 Kurus, Republic, Aluminum-Bronze	2.95	4.90
☐ 1926	10 Kurus, Republic, Aluminum-Bronze	2.95	4.90
☐ 1918–1919	20 Kurus, Mohammed VI, 1st Coinage, Silver	—	152.50
☐ 1918–1919	25 Kurus, Mohammed VI, 1st Coinage, Gold	—	102.00
☐ 1924	25 Kurus, Republic, Nickel	2.65	4.40
☐ 1926–1928	25 Kurus, Republic, Nickel	2.65	4.40
☐ 1927–1928	25 Kurus, Republic, Monnaies de Luxe, Gold	—	152.50
☐ 1918–1922	50 Kurus, Mohammed VI, 1st Coinage, Gold	—	268.50
☐ 1926–1928	50 Kurus, Republic, Gold	—	91.70
☐ 1927–1928	50 Kurus, Republic, Monnaies de Luxe, Gold	—	135.00
☐ 1918–1919	100 Kurus, Mohammed VI, 1st Coinage, Gold	—	295.00
☐ 1926–1929	100 Kurus, Republic, Gold	—	295.00
☐ 1927–1928	100 Kurus, Republic, Monnaies de Luxe, Gold	—	228.00
☐ 1918	250 Kurus, Mohammed VI, 1st Coinage, Gold	—	3800.00
☐ 1926–1928	250 Kurus, Republic, Gold	—	52.00
☐ 1927–1928	250 Kurus, Republic, Monnaies de Luxe, Gold	—	BV
☐ 1918–1920	500 Kurus, Mohammed VI, 1st Coinage, Gold	—	1850.00
☐ 1926–1929	500 Kurus, Republic, Gold	—	BV
☐ 1927–1928	500 Kurus, Republic, Monnaies de Luxe, Gold	—	BV

Turkey—Western Date Coinage

DATE	COIN TYPE/VARIETY/METAL	ABP FINE	AVERAGE FINE
☐ 1940–1942	10 Para, Aluminum-Bronze	$1.55	$2.60
☐ 1948	½ Kurus, Brass	30.00	90.65

Key to Grading: Wheat

☐ 1935–1937	1 Kurus, President Ataturk, Cupro-Nickel	.72	2.10
☐ 1938–1944	1 Kurus, President Inonu, Cupro-Nickel	.34	.57
☐ 1947–1951	1 Kurus, Brass	.25	.44
☐ 1961–1963	1 Kurus, Bronze	.25	.44
☐ 1963–1974	1 Kurus, Bronze	.25	.44
☐ 1975–1977	1 Kurus, Aluminium	.25	.44
☐ 1948–1951	2½ Kurus, Brass	.34	.60

Key to Grading: Wreath

☐ 1935–1943	5 Kurus, President Ataturk, Cupro-Nickel	.46	.80
☐ 1949–1957	5 Kurus, Brass	.22	.36
☐ 1958–1968	5 Kurus, Bronze	.17	.32
☐ 1969–1974	5 Kurus, Bronze	.22	.36
☐ 1975–1977	5 Kurus, Aluminium	.19	.32

Key to Grading: Wreath

☐ 1935–1940	10 Kurus, President Ataturk, Cupro-Nickel	1.40	2.30
☐ 1949–1956	10 Kurus, Brass	.25	.44
☐ 1958–1968	10 Kurus, Bronze	.22	.36
☐ 1969–1974	10 Kurus, Bronze	.23	.40
☐ 1975–1980	10 Kurus, Aluminium	.22	.36

Key to Grading: Wreath

DATE	COIN TYPE/VARIETY/METAL	ABP FINE	AVERAGE FINE
☐ 1935–1937	25 Kurus, President Ataturk, Silver	—	$7.25
☐ 1943	25 Kurus, President Ataturk, Gold Bullion Issue	—	BV
☐ 1943–1949	25 Kurus, President Inonu, Gold	—	BV
☐ 1944–1946	25 Kurus Nickel-Brass	.40	.67
☐ 1948–1956	25 Kurus, Brass	.28	.46
☐ 1935–1937	50 Kurus, President Ataturk, Silver	—	10.00
☐ 1943–1951	50 Kurus, President Inonu, Gold	—	190.00
☐ 1943	50 Kurus, President Ataturk, Gold	—	248.00
☐ 1947–1948	50 Kurus, Silver	—	7.25
☐ 1934	100 Kurus, President Ataturk, Silver	—	62.50
☐ 1937–1939	1 Lira, President Ataturk, Silver	—	41.50
☐ 1940–1941	1 Lira, President Inonu, Silver	—	22.50
☐ 1947–1948	1 Lira, Silver	—	8.50
☐ 1943–1949	100 Kurus, President Inonu, Gold	—	285.00
☐ 1943–1980	100 Kurus, President Ataturk, Gold	—	252.50
☐ 1943–1980	250 Kurus, President Ataturk, Gold	—	410.00
☐ 1943–1947	250 Kurus, President Inonu, Gold	—	610.00
☐ 1943	500 Kurus, President Ataturk, Gold	—	1150.00
☐ 1943–1948	500 Kurus, President Inonu, Gold	—	1150.00

UNITED KINGDOM

Britain's first coins in the 1st century B.C. were potin pieces, a combination of tin and bronze, generally called staters. In 55–54 B.C. gold coins were being struck, followed by silver and bronze. In the late 6th century the gold thrymasas or shillings were reduced and replaced by silver pennies, or sceattas. By the 1200s, half pennies, farthings, and groats were produced, and in 1344 the florin, then the noble. The pound, angel, and sovereign existed in the 1500s, then the farthing and guinea in the 1600s. In 1971, the system of pounds, shillings, and pence was abandoned for the decimal system.

THE MODERN ROYAL MINT

Courtesy of the Royal Mint

Today the Royal Mint has become both a business and a Government Department. Since 1975 it has operated as a Government Trading Fund, giving it a degree of commercial freedom but at the same time requiring that income should not only balance expenditure but that there should be an additional return on the capital employed. The Deputy Master, who remains a civil servant like the one thousand or so other members of the staff, presides over a board of directors and acts as chief executive. After ten years under the new system, cumulative sales have exceeded £600 million and the Mint has operated profitably in each of the ten years, achieving an average return on capital which compares favourably with the private sector.

Acting under contract with the Treasury, the Mint continues to be responsible for the production and issue of the United Kingdom coinage. In recent years it has had to cope with the introduction of two new coins, the 20 pence and the pound; the $^1/_2$ penny, on the other hand, has been demonetised and withdrawn, and the Mint is constantly exploring with the help of outside experts the ways in which the coinage might develop in the future. Commemorative coins have become rather more frequent, with particularly successful crown pieces being issued in 1977 for the Queen's Silver Jubilee and in 1981 for the wedding of HRH The Prince of Wales. In 1986 a special two-pound piece was issued for the Commonwealth Games, the first time that a sporting occasion had been commemorated on the United Kingdom coinage. All new designs continue to be submitted to the Royal Mint Advisory Committee which, under the Presidency of HRH The Prince Philip since 1952, now normally meets at Buckingham Palace.

The striking of overseas coins has remained a large and successful feature of Mint output, reflecting a deservedly high reputation for quality and delivery in a business which has become more and more competitive. In most years well over half of total production is exported and in the financial year 1984–85, for instance, the Mint struck coins for no fewer than 67 countries, ranging from Ascension Island to Zambia. Sales staff based in the London office make regular trips overseas, and the Mint cooperates in a consortium with two private mints in Birmingham and the Currency Division of the De La

Rue Company to ensure that as many orders as possible are won for the United Kingdom. As part of its service to overseas customers, the Mint also operates with De La Rue a joint company, Royal Mint Services Limited, to provide advice and technical assistance to foreign mints. Results have been such that since the Mint moved to Llantrisant it has twice won the Queen's Award for Export Achievement, first in 1973 and then again in 1977.

An increasingly important aspect of Mint activity has been the sale of proof and uncirculated coins to collectors. Following the outstanding success of the sets of the last £sd coins of 1970 and of the first decimal coins of 1971, proof sets of United Kingdom coins have been struck every year. An expanding range of proof and uncirculated United Kingdom and overseas coins, in gold and silver as well as base metal, is now available by direct mail order from Llantrisant. The regular issue of colourful bulletins and brochures has been a new departure and the Mint has become a frequent exhibitor at shows and conventions, particularly in North America, which has proved a highly receptive market for collectors' coins.

More traditional activities, such as the making of medals and seals, have continued. As at Tower Hill, the production of medals still calls for the hand skills of craftsmen such as silversmiths, but like the rest of the Mint the Medal Department is not immune from pressure. In 1982, for instance, it responded with speed and success to the urgent requirement for medals to be awarded to those taking part in the campaign in the South Atlantic. As well as the normal range of military and civilian decorations, it produces a large variety of prize and commemorative medals for learned societies and private companies. Overseas orders are also received and the Medal Department accordingly makes a contribution to the Mint's export trade.

The modern Royal Mint at Llantrisant houses some of the most advanced coining machinery in the world and it has a larger capacity than any other mint in Western Europe. It is a mint in which the microprocessor and computer are increasingly prominent, yet at the same time there remains a vital role for the inherited skills and craftsmanship which have been built up during an unbroken history of more than 100 years. Clearly it is more than the thread of history which links the present Royal Mint to its Anglo-Saxon predecessor.

MINTING PROCESSES AT LLANTRISANT

The first stage in the coining process is the melting of the constituent metals, usually copper, nickel, zinc, or tin, in the appropriate proportions for the alloy required. At Tower Hill this was essentially a small-scale affair, with the molten metal being poured into vertical moulds, but the new mint has a continuous casting unit in operation twenty-four hours a day. By this system, virgin metals and process scrap are melted in primary electric furnaces and, when examination of a sample by X-ray fluorescence spectrometry has confirmed that the alloy is correct, the molten metal is transferred to holding furnaces. From the holding furnace it is drawn horizontally and continuously in the form of a strip about 200 millimetres wide and 15 millimetres thick, with cutting equipment built into the casting line dividing the strip into manageable 10 metre lengths weighing some 200 kilograms each.

A tandem rolling mill begins the process of reducing the metal to coin thickness. If, as with nickel-brass, intermediate annealing or softening is necessary, the strip is passed slowly through a furnace at a temperature of about 650°C. During the rolling process, for ease of handling, five of the cast lengths are welded together to create a large coil weighing about one tonne. A finishing mill then completes the task, its rolls reversible so that the coil of strip can pass backward and forward until it is reduced to the thickness required. From the finished coils blank discs are punched out in large presses at rates of up to 14,000 blanks a minute and collected in drums. The scrap metal, known for centuries as scissel, is passed back to the furnace for remelting.

The drums of blanks are then transferred from the Melting, Rolling, and Blanking Unit to the Annealing and Pickling Block. Here they are fed from large hoppers into gas-fired annealing furnaces where they are softened by being heated to high temperature, 850°C in the case of cupro-nickel and 750°C for bronze. After cooling they are passed to automatic pickling barrels where stains are removed by a solution of sulphuric acid and, after a final washing in tartaric acid, they are rinsed in water and dried by hot air. Most blanks then go to the marking machines, where they are rolled under pressure down a narrow groove to force the metal inwards in order to thicken the edge of the blank. This then makes it easier to give the coin a raised rim to protect it from wear and to enable coins to be stacked in piles.

The final process is the stamping on the blanks of the obverse and reverse designs and, when required, the milling on the edge. These operations are carried out simultaneously in a coining press, into which the blanks are fed by hopper. With most presses the blank is automatically placed on top of the lower die and is held in position by a restraining collar, which will be plain or milled depending on the type of edge required. The upper die is then squeezed down onto the blank with a force of up to 100 or more tonnes, so that the blank receives the impression of both dies while at the same time the metal is forced outward to take up the shape and pattern of the collar. The rate of striking depends on factors such as the size and design of the coins but with the sophisticated engineering of modern presses 400 coins can often be struck in a minute. A new generation of presses is likely to be faster still, achieving rates of up to 700 coins a minute.

After striking, the coins are automatically ejected from the press and fall into a container for inspection. A statistical sampling technique is used to ensure a rigorous quality control and after passing inspection the coins are counted into bags and check-weighed, the first task on which a robot has been used in the Mint. The bags are then conveyed to a secure area to await dispatch, either overseas or by the road to cash centers in the United Kingdom. Samples of all United Kingdom coins except bronze are taken for submission to the Trial of the Pyx which continues, as it has done for more than seven centuries, to provide an independent check on the accuracy of the coins struck by the Royal Mint.

A separate proof coin section is responsible for the special coins which are struck for sale to collectors. Since the seventeenth century proof coins have represented the perfection of the minter's art, and it is the combination of traditional skills and modern technology which has enabled Royal Mint proofs to reach their current level of excellence. The dies are given a matte finish and then a craftsman, using diamond paste, carefully polishes parts of the surface to produce a pleasing contrast between the frosted features of the design and the mirror background of the field. The blanks, too, are specially polished, either by burnishing or buffing, before being struck in a dust-free atmosphere.

Proofs are struck one at a time on a coining press and receive more than one blow from the dies to ensure that every detail of the designs is faithfully reproduced. The dies are kept clean and are replaced immediately if they show any sign of deterioration. After striking, each coin is carefully removed from the press to prevent damage and once it has satisfied trained inspectors it soon finds its way into the attractive packaging which is a feature of these special issues from the Mint.

DIE-MAKING AT LLANTRISANT

Modern die-making has been transformed by the introduction of the reducing machine. The traditional method whereby engravers cut a matrix or punch by hand, a painstaking process which might easily take three or four weeks, has now been largely superseded by the machine, which produces a master punch in relief from an electrotype copy of an artist's plaster model. The first of these machines to be used in the Mint was acquired by Benedetto Pistrucci in 1819 and a second was officially ordered for William Wyon in 1824; but it was probably not until the turn of the century, when machines were purchased from Janvier of Paris, that the Mint began to make full use of the reducing machine.

The plaster model, prepared either by a private artist or by a member of the Mint's small but highly skilled Engraving Department, is usually between six and ten inches in diameter.

Stages in die-making: the artist at work on his sketch; the preparation of a plaster model; the growing of the electrotype; and an engraver perfecting the steel matrix.

A silicon rubber mould is taken from the model and after one day's curing to make it pliable and flexible the mould is made electrically conductive to enable it to be plated with nickel. After about two hours it is transferred to a copper-plating bath, where it is left for three days to allow a sufficiently thick deposit of copper to back up the nickel on the mould. It is this nickel-faced copper electrotype which is then mounted on the reducing machine.

The machine is essentially a three-dimensional pantograph, so simple in its operation that the Mint craftsmen are still happiest with the old Janvier machines which were transferred from Tower Hill. The details of the electrotype, set firmly in wax and revolving slowly at one end of the machine, are scanned by a tracer at the free end of a rigid bar. The movements of the tracer as it follows the contours of the electrotype are communicated by the bar in reduced amplitude to a rotating cutter at the other end. The cutter, as it moves in and out, accordingly reproduces the details of the design at coin scale onto a block of steel to form a master punch with features in relief as on a coin. A first, or rough, cut takes a day, to be followed by a second cut which takes another day.

Above, left. An engraver ensures that there are no flaws or blemishes on the matrix.

Above, right. One of the Janvier reducing machines at work.

Minute blemishes and flaws are removed from the reduction punch by hand. It is then hardened so that it can be placed in a hydraulic press and its design transferred under pressure to a piece of soft steel. On this new tool, called a matrix, the design is incuse and it is at this stage that the engraver is able to add by hand the beads, the figures of the date, or any other feature not included on the original model. Once work on the matrix has been completed, it is hardened and then placed in a hydraulic press to produce the working punch. This, like the reduction punch, is in relief, and after turning and shaping it is returned to the engravers for final adjustment and cleaning. It is from this punch that working dies, all absolutely identical, are made for the coining presses.

To protect their surface and prolong their life the dies are chrome plated. Even so the life of an individual die remains a little unpredictable, though most now comfortably exceed 200,000 coins.

United Kingdom—Type Coinage

Key to Grading: Bust

DATE	COIN TYPE/VARIETY/METAL	ABP FINE	AVERAGE FINE
☐ 1839–1856	½ Farthing, Victoria, Young Portrait, Copper	$2.55	$9.20
☐ 1838–1860	1 Farthing, Victoria, Young Portrait, Copper	2.55	9.20

Key to Grading: Bust

☐ 1860–1895	1 Farthing, Victoria, Young Portrait, Bronze	1.20	4.15
☐ 1895–1901	1 Farthing, Victoria, Aged Portrait, Bronze	180.00	300.00
☐ 1902–1910	1 Farthing, Edward VII, Bronze	180.00	300.00
☐ 1911–1936	1 Farthing, George V, Bronze	1.25	2.10

DATE	COIN TYPE/VARIETY/METAL	ABP FINE	AVERAGE FINE
☐ 1937–1948	1 Farthing, George VI, Bronze	$.28	$ .50
☐ 1949–1952	1 Farthing, George VI, 2nd Coinage, Bronze	.28	.50
☐ 1953	1 Farthing, Elizabeth II, Bronze	.16	.26
☐ 1954–1956	1 Farthing, Elizabeth II, 2nd Coinage, Bronze	.28	.50
☐ 1838–1859	½ Penny, Victoria, Young Portrait, Copper	2.90	4.85

Key to Grading: Bust

DATE	COIN TYPE/VARIETY/METAL	ABP FINE	AVERAGE FINE
☐ 1860–1894	½ Penny, Victoria, Young Portrait, Bronze	2.50	4.15
☐ 1895–1901	½ Penny, Victoria, Aged Portrait, Bronze	1.70	2.85
☐ 1902–1910	½ Penny, Edward VII, Bronze	1.70	2.85
☐ 1911–1927	½ Penny, George V, Bronze	.37	.62
☐ 1928–1936	½ Penny, George V, Bronze	.28	.50
☐ 1937–1948	½ Penny, George VI, Bronze	.28	.50
☐ 1949–1952	½ Penny, George VI, 2nd Coinage, Bronze	.28	.50
☐ 1953	½ Penny, Elizabeth II, Bronze	.28	.50
☐ 1954–1967	½ Penny, Elizabeth II, 2nd Coinage, Bronze	.28	.50
☐ 1902–1910	1 Penny, Edward VII, Bronze	1.25	2.10

Key to Grading: Bust

DATE	COIN TYPE/VARIETY/METAL	ABP FINE	AVERAGE FINE
☐ 1911–1927	1 Penny, George V, Bronze	.63	1.05

DATE	COIN TYPE/VARIETY/METAL	ABP FINE	AVERAGE FINE
☐ 1928–1936	1 Penny, George V, Bronze	$.31	$ .52
☐ 1937–1948	1 Penny, George VI, Bronze	.31	.52
☐ 1949–1951	1 Penny, George VI, 2nd Coinage, Bronze	2.65	4.40
☐ 1953	1 Penny, Elizabeth II, Bronze	.49	.82
☐ 1954–1970	1 Penny, Elizabeth II, 2nd Coinage, Bronze	.34	.57
☐ 1841–1860	1 Penny, Victoria, Young Portrait, Copper	2.40	6.20
☐ 1860–1894	1 Penny, Victoria, Young Portrait, Bronze	3.40	5.70
☐ 1895–1901	1 Penny, Victoria, Aged Portrait, Bronze	2.50	4.15
☐ 1838–1887	3 Pence, Victoria, Young Portrait, Silver	—	8.95
☐ 1887–1893	3 Pence, Victoria, Golden Jubilee, Silver	—	8.95
☐ 1893–1901	3 Pence, Victoria, Aged Portrait, Silver	—	4.25

Key to Grading: Bust

☐ 1902–1910	3 Pence, Edward VII, Silver	—	4.25
☐ 1911–1926	3 Pence, George V, Silver	—	4.25
☐ 1927–1936	3 Pence, George V, Silver	—	4.25
☐ 1937–1945	3 Pence, George VI, Silver	—	4.25
☐ 1937–1948	3 Pence, George VI, Nickel-Brass	.46	.77
☐ 1949–1952	3 Pence, George VI, 2nd Coinage, Nickel-Brass	.49	.82
☐ 1953	3 Pence, Elizabeth II, Nickel-Brass	.34	.57
☐ 1954–1970	3 Pence, Elizabeth II, 2nd Coinage, Nickel-Brass	.34	.57

Key to Grading: Bust

☐ 1838–1862	4 Pence, Victoria, Young Portrait, Silver	—	9.00
☐ 1838–1887	6 Pence, Victoria, Young Portrait, Silver	—	12.00
☐ 1887	6 Pence, Victoria, Golden Jubilee, Silver	—	6.75

DATE	COIN TYPE/VARIETY/METAL	ABP FINE	AVERAGE FINE

Key to Grading: Bust

DATE	COIN TYPE/VARIETY/METAL	ABP FINE	AVERAGE FINE
☐ 1887–1893	6 Pence, Victoria, Golden Jubilee, Silver	—	$7.75
☐ 1893–1901	6 Pence, Victoria, Aged Portrait, Silver	—	7.75
☐ 1902–1910	6 Pence, Edward VII, Silver	—	7.75
☐ 1911–1927	6 Pence, George V, Silver	—	7.75
☐ 1927–1936	6 Pence, George V, Silver	—	7.75
☐ 1937–1946	6 Pence, George VI, Silver	—	7.75
☐ 1947–1948	6 Pence, George VI, Cupro-Nickel	.28	.46
☐ 1949–1952	6 Pence, George VI, 2nd Coinage, Cupro-Nickel	.28	.46
☐ 1953	6 Pence, Elizabeth II, Cupro-Nickel	.28	.46

Key to Grading: Bust

DATE	COIN TYPE/VARIETY/METAL	ABP FINE	AVERAGE FINE
☐ 1954–1970	6 Pence, Elizabeth II, 2nd Coinage, Cupro-Nickel	.25	.41
☐ 1838–1887	Shilling, Victoria, Young Portrait, Silver	—	9.45

Key to Grading: Bust

DATE	COIN TYPE/VARIETY/METAL	ABP FINE	AVERAGE FINE
☐ 1887–1892	Shilling, Victoria, Golden Jubilee, Silver	—	8.95
☐ 1893–1901	Shilling, Victoria, Aged Portrait, Silver	—	8.95
☐ 1902–1910	Shilling, Edward VII, Silver	—	10.25
☐ 1911–1927	Shilling, George V, Silver	—	6.65
☐ 1927–1936	Shilling, George V, Silver	—	3.50

DATE	COIN TYPE/VARIETY/METAL	ABP FINE	AVERAGE FINE
☐ 1937–1946	Shilling, George VI, Silver	—	$4.30
☐ 1947–1948	Shilling, George VI, Cupro-Nickel	.22	.36
☐ 1949–1951	Shilling, George VI, 2nd Coinage, Cupro-Nickel	.22	.36
☐ 1953	1 Shilling, Elizabeth II, Cupro-Nickel	.22	.36
☐ 1954–1970	1 Shilling, Elizabeth II, 2nd Coinage, Cupro-Nickel	.22	.36
☐ 1849	1 Florin, Victoria, Gothic, Silver	—	30.50
☐ 1851–1887	1 Florin, Victoria, Gothic, Silver	—	23.50
☐ 1887–1892	1 Florin, Victoria, Golden Jubilee, Silver	—	13.50

Key to Grading: Bust

DATE	COIN TYPE/VARIETY/METAL	ABP FINE	AVERAGE FINE
☐ 1893–1901	1 Florin, Victoria, Aged Portrait, Silver	—	9.25
☐ 1902–1910	1 Florin, Edward VII, Silver	—	20.75
☐ 1911–1926	1 Florin, George V, Silver	—	7.75
☐ 1927–1936	1 Florin, George V, Silver	—	4.00
☐ 1937–1946	2 Shillings, George VI, Silver	—	4.00
☐ 1947–1948	2 Shillings, George VI, Cupro-Nickel	.28	.46
☐ 1949–1951	2 Shillings, George VI, 2nd Coinage, Cupro-Nickel	.28	.46
☐ 1953	2 Shillings, Elizabeth II, Cupro-Nickel	.28	.46
☐ 1954–1970	2 Shillings, Elizabeth II, 2nd Coinage, Cupro-Nickel	.28	.46
☐ 1839–1887	1/2 Crown, Victoria, Young Portrait, Silver	—	24.00
☐ 1887–1892	1/2 Crown, Victoria, Golden Jubilee, Silver	—	24.00

Key to Grading: Bust

DATE	COIN TYPE/VARIETY/METAL	ABP FINE	AVERAGE FINE
☐ 1893–1901	1/2 Crown, Victoria, Aged Portrait, Silver	—	12.30
☐ 1902–1910	1/2 Crown, Edward VII, Silver	—	28.50
☐ 1911–1927	1/2 Crown, George V, Silver	—	9.65
☐ 1927–1936	1/2 Crown, George V, Silver	—	6.75

DATE	COIN TYPE/VARIETY/METAL	ABP FINE	AVERAGE FINE
☐ 1937–1946	½ Crown, George VI, Silver	—	$1.80
☐ 1947–1948	½ Crown, George VI, Cupro-Nickel	.31	.52
☐ 1949–1952	½ Crown, George VI, 2nd Coinage, Cupro-Nickel	.31	.52
☐ 1953	½ Crown, Elizabeth II, Cupro-Nickel	.45	.72
☐ 1954–1970	½ Crown, Elizabeth II, 2nd Coinage, Cupro-Nickel	.34	.57
☐ 1887–1890	2 Florins, Victoria, Golden Jubilee, Silver	—	15.25

Key to Grading: Bust

☐ 1935	1 Crown, George V, Silver Jubilee, Silver	—	10.85
☐ 1839–1847	1 Crown, Victoria, Young Portrait, Silver	—	62.00
☐ 1847–1853	1 Crown, Victoria, Gothic, Silver	—	495.00
☐ 1887–1892	1 Crown, Victoria, Golden Jubilee, Silver	—	22.75
☐ 1893–1901	1 Crown, Victoria, Aged Portrait, Silver	—	42.00
☐ 1902	1 Crown, Edward VII, Silver	—	48.50
☐ 1927–1936	1 Crown, George V, Silver	—	136.50
☐ 1937	1 Crown, George VI, Silver	—	21.50
☐ 1951	5 Shillings, George VI, 2nd Coinage, Cupro-Nickel Proof	21.65	36.05
☐ 1953	5 Shillings, Elizabeth II, Cupro-Nickel	1.25	2.10
☐ 1838–1885	½ Sovereign, Victoria, Young Portrait, Gold	—	142.50
☐ 1887–1893	½ Sovereign, Victoria, Golden Jubilee, Gold	—	128.50
☐ 1893–1901	½ Sovereign, Victoria, Aged Portrait, Gold	—	128.50
☐ 1902–1910	½ Sovereign, Edward VII, Gold	—	128.50
☐ 1911–1915	½ Sovereign, George V, Gold	—	128.50
☐ 1937	½ Sovereign, George VI, Gold Proof	—	—
☐ 1838–1874	1 Sovereign, Victoria, Young Portrait, Gold	—	285.00
☐ 1871–1885	1 Sovereign, Victoria, Young Portrait, Gold	—	285.00
☐ 1887–1892	1 Sovereign, Victoria, Golden Jubilee, Gold	—	285.00
☐ 1893–1901	1 Sovereign, Victoria, Aged Portrait, Gold	—	285.00
☐ 1902–1910	1 Sovereign, Edward VII, Gold	—	380.00
☐ 1911–1925	1 Sovereign, George V, Gold	—	380.00
☐ 1937	1 Sovereign, George VI, Gold Proof	—	—
☐ 1957–1968	1 Sovereign, Elizabeth II, 2nd Coinage, Gold	—	312.50

DATE	COIN TYPE/VARIETY/METAL	ABP FINE	AVERAGE FINE
☐ 1887	2 Pounds, Victoria, Golden Jubilee, Gold	—	$675.00
☐ 1893	2 Pounds, Victoria, Aged Portrait, Gold	—	738.00
☐ 1902	2 Pounds, Edward VII, Gold	—	675.00
☐ 1911	2 Pounds, George V, Gold Proof	—	—
☐ 1937	2 Pounds, George VI, Gold Proof	—	—
☐ 1887	5 Pounds, Victoria, Golden Jubilee, Gold	—	1250.00
☐ 1893	5 Pounds, Victoria, Aged Portrait, Gold	—	1475.00
☐ 1902	5 Pounds, Edward VII, Gold	—	1475.00
☐ 1911	5 Pounds, George V, Gold Proof	—	—
☐ 1937	5 Pounds, George VI, Gold Proof	—	—

United Kingdom—Decimal and Bullion Coinage

Key to Grading: Bust

☐ 1971–1981	½ New Penny, Elizabeth II, Bronze	.31	.52
☐ 1981–1984	½ Penny, Elizabeth II, Bronze	.16	.26

Key to Grading: Bust

☐ 1971–1981	1 New Penny, Elizabeth II, Bronze	.31	.52
☐ 1981–1992	1 Penny, Elizabeth II, Bronze	.19	.32

Key to Grading: Bust

☐ 1993 to Date	1 Penny, Elizabeth II, Copper-plated Steel	.31	.52

Key to Grading: Bust

DATE	COIN TYPE/VARIETY/METAL	ABP FINE	AVERAGE FINE
☐ 1971–1981	2 New Pence, Elizabeth II, Bronze	$.19	$ .31
☐ 1982–1984	2 Pence, Elizabeth II, Bronze	.28	.46

Key to Grading: Bust

☐ 1993 to Date	2 Pence, Elizabeth II, Copper-plated Steel	.28	.46

Key to Grading: Bust

☐ 1968–1981	5 New Pence, Elizabeth II, Cupro-Nickel	.28	.46
☐ 1990 to Date	5 Pence, Elizabeth II, Smaller Planchet, Cupro-Nickel	.28	.46
☐ 1982–1990	5 Pence, Elizabeth II, Cupro-Nickel	.16	.26
☐ 1990	5 Pence, Elizabeth II, Silver	—	2.00

Key to Grading: Bust

DATE	COIN TYPE/VARIETY/METAL	ABP FINE	AVERAGE FINE
□ 1968–1981	10 New Pence, Elizabeth II, Cupro-Nickel	$.31	$ .52
□ 1982–1992	10 New Pence, Elizabeth II, Cupro-Nickel	.19	.31
□ 1990–1993	10 Pence, Elizabeth II, Smaller Planchet, Cupro-Nickel	.31	.52
□ 1990	10 Pence, Elizabeth II, Smaller Planchet, Silver	.19	.31
□ 1992 to Date	10 Pence, Elizabeth II, Silver	—	2.00

Key to Grading: Bust

□ 1982 to Date	20 Pence, Elizabeth II, Cupro-Nickel	.37	.62
□ 1972	25 New Pence, Elizabeth II, Royal Silver Wedding Anniversary, Silver Proof	—	—
□ 1972	25 New Pence, Elizabeth II, Royal Silver Wedding Anniversary, Cupro-Nickel	.40	.67
□ 1977	25 New Pence, Elizabeth II, Silver Jubilee, Cupro-Nickel	.56	.93

Key to Grading: Bust

□ 1977	25 New Pence, Elizabeth II, Silver Jubilee, Silver Proof	—	—
□ 1980	25 New Pence, Elizabeth II, Queen Mother—80th Birthday, Cupro-Nickel	.46	.77
□ 1980	25 New Pence, Elizabeth II, Queen Mother—80th Birthday, Silver	—	3.50
□ 1981	1 Crown, Elizabeth II, Wedding of Prince Charles & Lady Diana, Silver	—	3.50
□ 1981	1 Crown, Elizabeth II, Wedding of Prince Charles & Lady Diana, Cupro-Nickel	1.00	1.70
□ 1981	50 New Pence, Elizabeth II, Cupro-Nickel	1.00	1.70
□ 1982 to Date	50 Pence, Elizabeth II, Cupro-Nickel	1.40	2.35

DATE	COIN TYPE/VARIETY/METAL	ABP FINE	AVERAGE FINE
☐ 1973	50 Pence, Elizabeth II, European Economic Community Entry, Cupro-Nickel	$1.70	$2.85
☐ 1992	50 Pence, Elizabeth II, European Council of Ministers—British Presidency, Cupro-Nickel	1.70	2.85
☐ 1992	50 Pence, Elizabeth II, European Council of Ministers—British Presidency, Silver Proof	—	—
☐ 1992	50 Pence, Elizabeth II, European Council of Ministers—British Presidency, Gold Proof	—	—
☐ 1983	1 Pound, Elizabeth II, Silver Proof	—	—

Key to Grading: Bust

DATE	COIN TYPE/VARIETY/METAL	ABP FINE	AVERAGE FINE
☐ 1983	1 Pound, Elizabeth II, Nickel-Brass	2.65	4.40
☐ 1984	1 Pound, Elizabeth II, Scottish Thistle, Silver	—	70.00
☐ 1984	1 Pound, Elizabeth II, Scottish Thistle, Nickel-Brass	2.65	4.40
☐ 1985	1 Pound, Elizabeth II, Welsh Leek, Nickel-Brass	2.65	4.40
☐ 1985	1 Pound, Elizabeth II, Welsh Leek, Silver	—	66.50
☐ 1985	1 Pound, Elizabeth II, Blooming Flax, Silver Proof	—	—
☐ 1986	1 Pound, Elizabeth II, Blooming Flax, Nickel-Brass	2.65	4.40
☐ 1987	1 Pound, Elizabeth II, Oak Tree, Nickel-Brass	2.65	4.40
☐ 1987	1 Pound, Elizabeth II, Oak Tree, Silver	—	61.50
☐ 1988	1 Pound, Elizabeth II, Silver	—	85.50
☐ 1988	1 Pound, Elizabeth II, Copper-Zinc-Nickel	2.65	4.40
☐ 1989	1 Pound, Elizabeth II, Scottish Flora, Silver	—	68.50
☐ 1989	1 Pound, Elizabeth II, Scottish Flora, Nickel-Brass	3.05	5.05
☐ 1990	1 Pound, Elizabeth II, Welsh Leek, Nickel-Brass	3.05	5.05

DATE	COIN TYPE/VARIETY/METAL	ABP FINE	AVERAGE FINE
☐ 1990	1 Pound, Elizabeth II, Welsh Leek, Silver	—	$68.50
☐ 1993	1 Pound, Elizabeth II, Scottish Flora, Nickel-Brass	2.90	4.85
☐ 1993	1 Pound, Elizabeth II, Scottish Flora, Silver Proof	—	—
☐ 1986	2 Pounds, Elizabeth II, Commonwealth Games, Silver Proof	—	—
☐ 1986	2 Pounds, Elizabeth II, Commonwealth Games, Gold Proof	—	—
☐ 1986	2 Pounds, Elizabeth II, Commonwealth Games, Nickel-Brass	2.40	7.70
☐ 1989	2 Pounds, Elizabeth II, Bill of Rights Tercentenary, Nickel-Brass	2.40	7.70
☐ 1989	2 Pounds, Elizabeth II, Bill of Rights Tercentenary, Silver	—	58.50
☐ 1989	2 Pounds, Elizabeth II, Claim of Right Tercentenary, Silver	—	58.50
☐ 1989	2 Pounds, Elizabeth II, Claim of Right Tercentenary, Nickel-Brass	2.40	7.95
☐ 1990	5 Pounds, Elizabeth II, Queen Mother—90th Birthday, Silver	—	82.50
☐ 1990	5 Pounds, Elizabeth II, Queen Mother—90th Birthday, Gold	—	1550.00
☐ 1990	5 Pounds, Elizabeth II, Queen Mother—90th Birthday, Cupro-Nickel	7.20	20.60
☐ 1993	5 Pounds, Elizabeth II, Reign—40th Anniversary, Cupro-Nickel	6.00	15.45
☐ 1987–1989	10 Pounds, Gold Proof	—	—
☐ 1990 to Date	10 Pounds, Gold-Silver Proof	—	—
☐ 1987–1989	25 Pounds, Gold Proof	—	—
☐ 1990 to Date	25 Pounds, Gold-Silver Proof	—	—
☐ 1987–1989	50 Pounds, Gold Proof	—	—
☐ 1990 to Date	50 Pounds, Gold-Silver Proof	—	—
☐ 1987–1989	100 Pounds, Gold Proof	—	—
☐ 1990 to Date	100 Pounds, Gold-Silver Proof	—	—

USSR

USSR—Type Coinage

Key to Grading: Wreath

DATE	COIN TYPE/VARIETY/METAL	ABP FINE	AVERAGE FINE
☐ 1921–1922	1 Ruble, 1st Coinage, Legend: PCOCP, Silver	—	$34.50
☐ 1924–1925	1 Kopek, 2nd Coinage, Legend: CCCP, Bronze	11.15	18.55

Key to Grading: Wreath

☐ 1924	1 Ruble, 2nd Coinage, Legend: CCCP, Silver	—	18.50
☐ 1925–1928	½ Kopek, 2nd Coinage, Legend: CCCP, Bronze	3.40	5.70
☐ 1926–1935	1 Kopek, 3rd Coinage, Legend: CCCP, Aluminum-Bronze	.63	1.05
☐ 1935–1936	1 Kopek, 4th Coinage, Legend: CCCP, Aluminum-Bronze	.63	1.05
☐ 1937–1946	1 Kopek, 5th Coinage, Legend: CCCP, Aluminum-Bronze	.34	.57
☐ 1948–1956	1 Kopek, 6th Coinage, Legend: CCCP, Aluminum-Bronze	.49	.82
☐ 1957	1 Kopek, 7th Coinage, Legend: CCCP, Aluminum-Bronze	1.40	2.30

Key to Grading: Wreath

DATE	COIN TYPE/VARIETY/METAL	ABP FINE	AVERAGE FINE
☐ 1961–1991	1 Kopek, 8th Coinage, Legend: CCCP, Brass	$.22	$ .36
☐ 1924–1925	2 Kopeks, 2nd Coinage, Legend: CCCP, Bronze	10.20	17.00
☐ 1926–1935	2 Kopeks, 3rd Coinage, Legend: CCCP, Aluminum-Bronze	.46	.80
☐ 1935–1936	2 Kopeks, 4th Coinage, Legend: CCCP, Aluminum-Bronze	.46	.80
☐ 1937–1946	2 Kopeks, 5th Coinage, Legend: CCCP, Aluminum-Bronze	.46	.80
☐ 1948–1956	2 Kopeks, 6th Coinage, Legend: CCCP, Aluminum-Bronze	.40	.67
☐ 1957	2 Kopeks, 7th Coinage, Legend: CCCP, Aluminum-Bronze	.46	.80

Key to Grading: Wreath

DATE	COIN TYPE/VARIETY/METAL	ABP FINE	AVERAGE FINE
☐ 1961–1991	2 Kopeks, 8th Coinage, Legend: CCCP, Brass	.34	.60
☐ 1924	3 Kopeks, 2nd Coinage, Legend: CCCP, Bronze	13.60	22.70
☐ 1926–1935	3 Kopeks, 3rd Coinage, Legend: CCCP, Aluminum-Bronze	.34	.60
☐ 1935–1936	3 Kopeks, 4th Coinage, Legend: CCCP, Aluminum-Bronze	.34	.60
☐ 1937–1946	3 Kopeks, 5th Coinage, Legend: CCCP, Aluminum-Bronze	.34	.60
☐ 1948–1957	3 Kopeks, 6th Coinage, Legend: CCCP, Aluminum-Bronze	.28	.46

DATE	COIN TYPE/VARIETY/METAL	ABP FINE	AVERAGE FINE
☐ 1957	3 Kopeks, 7th Coinage, Legend: CCCP, Aluminum-Bronze	$.46	$ .77

Key to Grading: Wreath

DATE	COIN TYPE/VARIETY/METAL	ABP FINE	AVERAGE FINE
☐ 1961–1990	3 Kopeks, 8th Coinage, Legend: CCCP, Brass	.34	.57
☐ 1924	5 Kopeks, 2nd Coinage, Legend: CCCP, Bronze	23.80	39.70
☐ 1926–1935	5 Kopeks, 3rd Coinage, Legend: CCCP, Aluminum-Bronze	1.25	2.10
☐ 1935–1936	5 Kopeks, 4th Coinage, Legend: CCCP, Aluminum-Bronze	2.50	4.15
☐ 1937–1946	5 Kopeks, 5th Coinage, Legend: CCCP, Aluminum-Bronze	.72	1.20
☐ 1948–1956	5 Kopeks, 6th Coinage, Legend: CCCP, Aluminum-Bronze	.72	1.20
☐ 1957	5 Kopeks, 7th Coinage, Legend: CCCP, Aluminum-Bronze	1.40	2.30

Key to Grading: Wreath

DATE	COIN TYPE/VARIETY/METAL	ABP FINE	AVERAGE FINE
☐ 1961–1990	5 Kopeks, 8th Coinage, Legend: CCCP, Aluminum-Bronze	.31	.52
☐ 1921–1923	10 Kopeks, 1st Coinage, Legend: PCOCP, Silver	—	8.50
☐ 1923	1 Chervonetz, 1st Coinage Legend: PCOCP, Gold	—	195.00
☐ 1924–1931	10 Kopeks, 2nd Coinage, Legend: CCCP, Silver	—	2.50
☐ 1931–1934	10 Kopeks, 3rd Coinage, Legend: CCCP, Cupro-Nickel	.43	.72

DATE	COIN TYPE/VARIETY/METAL	ABP FINE	AVERAGE FINE
☐ 1935–1936	10 Kopeks, 4th Coinage, Legend: CCCP, Cupro-Nickel	$.31	$ .60
☐ 1937–1946	10 Kopeks, 5th Coinage, Legend: CCCP, Cupro-Nickel	.63	1.05
☐ 1948–1956	10 Kopeks, 6th Coinage, Legend: CCCP, Cupro-Nickel	.63	1.05
☐ 1957	10 Kopeks, 7th Coinage, Legend: CCCP, Cupro-Nickel	.31	.60

Key to Grading: Wreath

DATE	COIN TYPE/VARIETY/METAL	ABP FINE	AVERAGE FINE
☐ 1961–1991	10 Kopeks, 8th Coinage, Legend: CCCP, Cupro-Nickel-Zinc	.28	.46
☐ 1975–1980	1 Chervonetz, 1st Coinage Legend: PCOCP, Gold	—	192.50
☐ 1921–1923	15 Kopeks, 1st Coinage, Legend: PCOCP, Silver	—	4.00
☐ 1924–1931	15 Kopeks, 2nd Coinage, Legend: CCCP, Silver	—	4.00
☐ 1931–1934	15 Kopeks, 3rd Coinage, Legend: CCCP, Cupro-Nickel	.63	1.05
☐ 1935–1936	15 Kopeks, 4th Coinage, Legend: CCCP, Cupro-Nickel	.63	1.05
☐ 1937–1946	15 Kopeks, 5th Coinage, Legend: CCCP, Cupro-Nickel	.46	.80
☐ 1948–1956	15 Kopeks, 6th Coinage, Legend: CCCP, Cupro-Nickel	.46	.80

DATE	COIN TYPE/VARIETY/METAL	ABP FINE	AVERAGE FINE
☐ 1957	15 Kopeks, 7th Coinage, Legend: CCCP, Cupro-Nickel	.28	.46

Key to Grading: Wreath

DATE	COIN TYPE/VARIETY/METAL	ABP FINE	AVERAGE FINE
☐ 1961–1991	15 Kopeks, 8th Coinage, Legend: CCCP, Cupro-Nickel	$.22	$ .36
☐ 1921–1923	20 Kopeks, 1st Coinage, Legend: PCOCP, Silver	—	7.75
☐ 1924–1931	20 Kopeks, 2nd Coinage, Legend: CCCP, Silver	—	4.25
☐ 1931–1934	20 Kopeks, 3rd Coinage, Legend: CCCP, Cupro-Nickel	.49	.85

Key to Grading: Wreath

DATE	COIN TYPE/VARIETY/METAL	ABP FINE	AVERAGE FINE
☐ 1935–1936	20 Kopeks, 4th Coinage, Legend: CCCP, Cupro-Nickel	.34	.57
☐ 1937–1946	20 Kopeks, 5th Coinage, Legend: CCCP, Cupro-Nickel	.49	.85
☐ 1948–1956	20 Kopeks, 6th Coinage, Legend: CCCP, Cupro-Nickel	.49	.85
☐ 1957	20 Kopeks, 7th Coinage, Legend: CCCP, Cupro-Nickel	.49	.85
☐ 1961–1991	20 Kopeks, 8th Coinage, Legend: CCCP, Cupro-Nickel-Zinc	.31	.52
☐ 1921–1922	50 Kopeks, 1st Coinage, Legend: PCOCP, Silver	—	10.25
☐ 1961–1991	50 Kopeks, 8th Coinage, Legend: CCCP, Cupro-Nickel-Zinc	.34	.57
☐ 1961–1991	Ruble, 8th Coinage, Legend: CCCP, Cupro-Nickel-Zinc	.43	.72

VATICAN CITY

The Kingdom of Italy took over the last remaining part of the Papal States in 1870, and the Papacy ceased issuing coinage until 1929. The centesimi and 1 and 2 lire were base metal. The 5 and 10 lire were silver until 1947, when they were changed to aluminum. The gold 100 lire was changed to stainless steel in 1959. Decimal coins were first used in 1929. The currency today is the euro.

Vatican City—Trade Coinage

Key to Grading: Bust

DATE	COIN TYPE/VARIETY/METAL	ABP FINE	AVERAGE FINE
☐ 1929–1938	5 Centesimi, Pius XI, Bronze	$1.70	$2.85
☐ 1933	5 Centesimi, Pius XI, Jubilee, Bronze	2.65	4.40
☐ 1939–1941	5 Centesimi, Pius XII, Bronze	1.70	2.85
☐ 1942–1946	5 Centesimi, Pius XII, Aluminum-Bronze	11.15	18.55

Key to Grading: Bust

☐ 1929–1938	10 Centesimi, Pius XI, Bronze	1.55	2.60
☐ 1933–1934	10 Centesimi, Pius XI, Jubilee, Bronze	2.95	4.95
☐ 1939–1941	10 Centesimi, Pius XII, Bronze	1.55	2.60
☐ 1942–1946	10 Centesimi, Pius XII, Aluminum-Bronze	20.40	34.00

Key to Grading: Crest or Bust

DATE	COIN TYPE/VARIETY/METAL	ABP FINE	AVERAGE FINE
☐ 1929–1937	20 Centesimi, Pius XI, Nickel	$1.10	$1.80
☐ 1933	20 Centesimi, Pius XI, Jubilee, Nickel	2.65	4.40
☐ 1939	20 Centesimi, Pius XII, Nickel	1.55	2.60
☐ 1940–1941	20 Centesimi, Pius XII, Stainless Steel	1.55	2.60
☐ 1942–1946	20 Centesimi, Pius XII, Stainless Steel	15.00	36.05

Key to Grading: Crest or Bust

☐ 1929–1937	50 Centesimi, Pius XI, Nickel	2.65	4.40
☐ 1933	50 Centesimi, Pius XI, Jubilee, Nickel	2.65	4.40
☐ 1939	50 Centesimi, Pius XII, Nickel	1.25	2.10
☐ 1940–1941	50 Centesimi, Pius XII, Stainless Steel	1.00	1.70
☐ 1942–1946	50 Centesimi, Pius XII, Stainless Steel	9.00	26.80
☐ 1929–1937	1 Lira, Pius XI, Nickel	.78	1.30
☐ 1933	1 Lira, Pius XI, Jubilee, Nickel	2.65	4.40
☐ 1939	1 Lira, Pius XII, Nickel	1.70	2.85
☐ 1940–1941	1 Lira, Pius XII, Stainless Steel	2.65	4.40

Key to Grading: Crest or Bust

☐ 1942–1946	1 Lira, Pius XII, Stainless Steel	7.20	28.35
☐ 1947–1949	1 Lira, Pius XII, Aluminum	1.55	2.60
☐ 1950	1 Lira, Pius XII, Holy Year— MCML, Aluminum	.63	1.05

DATE	COIN TYPE/VARIETY/METAL	ABP FINE	AVERAGE FINE
☐ 1951–1958	1 Lira, Pius XII, Aluminum	$.28	$ .46
☐ 1959–1962	1 Lira, John XXIII, Aluminum	.31	.52
☐ 1962	1 Lira, John XXIII, Ecumenical Council, Aluminum	.43	.72
☐ 1929–1937	2 Lire, Pius XI, Nickel	1.55	2.60
☐ 1933	2 Lire, Pius XI, Jubilee, Nickel	2.75	4.55
☐ 1939	2 Lire, Pius XII, Nickel	1.55	2.60

Key to Grading: Crest or Bust

DATE	COIN TYPE/VARIETY/METAL	ABP FINE	AVERAGE FINE
☐ 1940–1941	2 Lire, Pius XII, Stainless Steel	.46	.77
☐ 1942–1946	2 Lire, Pius XII, Stainless Steel	13.60	22.70
☐ 1947–1949	2 Lire, Pius XII, Aluminum	1.70	2.85
☐ 1950	2 Lire, Pius XII, Holy Year—MCML, Aluminum	.49	.82
☐ 1951–1958	2 Lire, Pius XII, Aluminum	.25	.41
☐ 1959–1962	2 Lire, John XXIII, Aluminum	.69	1.15
☐ 1962	2 Lire, John XXIII, Ecumenical Council, Aluminum	.63	1.05
☐ 1929–1937	5 Lire, Pius XI, Silver	—	4.30
☐ 1933	5 Lire, Pius XI, Jubilee, Silver	—	6.60
☐ 1939	5 Lire, Sede Vacante, Jubilee, Silver	—	75.50

Key to Grading: Crest or Bust

DATE	COIN TYPE/VARIETY/METAL	ABP FINE	AVERAGE FINE
☐ 1939–1941	5 Lire, Pius XII, Silver	—	9.25
☐ 1942–1946	5 Lire, Pius XII, Silver	—	52.50
☐ 1947–1949	5 Lire, Pius XII, Aluminum	1.55	2.60
☐ 1950	5 Lire, Pius XII, Holy Year—MCML, Aluminum	2.65	4.40
☐ 1951–1958	5 Lire, Pius XII, Aluminum	.31	.52
☐ 1959–1962	5 Lire, John XXIII, Aluminum	1.70	2.85

DATE	COIN TYPE/VARIETY/METAL	ABP FINE	AVERAGE FINE
☐ 1962	5 Lire, John XXIII, Ecumenical Council, Aluminum	$.28	$ .46
☐ 1929–1937	10 Lire, Pius XI, Silver	—	11.25
☐ 1933	10 Lire, Pius XI, Jubilee, Silver	—	11.25
☐ 1939	10 Lire, Sede Vacante, Jubilee, Silver	—	11.25
☐ 1939–1941	10 Lire, Pius XII, Silver	—	22.50
☐ 1942–1946	10 Lire, Pius XII, Silver	—	62.50
☐ 1947–1949	10 Lire, Pius XII, Aluminum	1.70	2.85
☐ 1950	10 Lire, Pius XII, Holy Year—MCML, Aluminum	1.55	2.60

Key to Grading: Crest or Bust

DATE	COIN TYPE/VARIETY/METAL	ABP FINE	AVERAGE FINE
☐ 1951–1958	10 Lire, Pius XII, Aluminum	.31	.52
☐ 1959–1962	10 Lire, John XXIII, Aluminum	.69	1.15
☐ 1962	10 Lire, John XXIII, Ecumenical Council, Aluminum	.69	1.15
☐ 1957–1958	20 Lire, Pius XII, Aluminum-Bronze	.22	.36
☐ 1959–1962	20 Lire, John XXIII, Aluminum-Bronze	.34	.57
☐ 1962	20 Lire, John XXIII, Ecumenical Council, Aluminum-Bronze	.34	.57
☐ 1955–1958	50 Lire, Pius XII, Stainless Steel	1.00	1.70
☐ 1959–1962	50 Lire, John XXIII, Stainless Steel	.46	.77
☐ 1929–1937	100 Lire, Pius XI, Gold	—	218.50
☐ 1933	100 Lire, Pius XI, Jubilee, Gold	—	218.50
☐ 1939–1941	100 Lire, Pius XII, Gold	—	218.50

Key to Grading: Crest or Bust

DATE	COIN TYPE/VARIETY/METAL	ABP FINE	AVERAGE FINE
☐ 1942–1949	100 Lire, Pius XII, Gold	—	214.00
☐ 1950	100 Lire, Pius XII, Holy Year—MCML, Gold	—	214.00

DATE	COIN TYPE/VARIETY/METAL	ABP FINE	AVERAGE FINE
☐ 1951–1958	100 Lire, Pius XII, Gold	—	$190.00
☐ 1955–1958	100 Lire, Pius XII, Stainless Steel	.31	.52
☐ 1959–1962	100 Lire, John XXIII, Stainless Steel	.31	.52
☐ 1959	100 Lire, John XXIII, Gold	—	210.00
☐ 1962	100 Lire, John XXIII, Ecumenical Council, Stainless Steel	.31	.52
☐ 1958	500 Lire, Sede Vacante, Silver	—	6.25

Key to Grading: Crest or Bust

DATE	COIN TYPE/VARIETY/METAL	ABP FINE	AVERAGE FINE
☐ 1958	500 Lire, Pius XII, Silver	—	7.00
☐ 1959–1962	500 Lire, John XXIII, Silver	—	7.00
☐ 1962	500 Lire, John XXIII, Ecumenical Council, Silver	—	7.75
☐ 1963	500 Lire, Sede Vacante, Silver	—	7.75

VENEZUELA

The first coins were used in 1802 and were mostly Spanish coins. Between 1808 and 1813, coins were issued in Maracaibo. In 1817, the copper real was issued, followed by the centavo, bolivares, and copper-clad steel centimos. The first decimal coins were used in 1843. The currency today is the bolivar.

Venezuela—Type Coinage

DATE	COIN TYPE/VARIETY/METAL	ABP FINE	AVERAGE FINE
☐ 1843–1852	¼ Centavo, Liberty Head, Copper	$8.00	$17.00

Key to Grading: Bust

☐ 1843–1852	½ Centavo, Liberty Head, Copper	8.00	17.00

Key to Grading: Bust

☐ 1843–1863	1 Centavo, Liberty Head, Copper	8.00	15.45
☐ 1858	1 Real, Liberty Head, Silver	—	238.00
☐ 1858	2 Reales, Liberty Head, Silver	—	425.00

Key to Grading: Bust

☐ 1858	5 Reales, Liberty Head, Silver	—	385.00

VIETNAM

The first coins were used in 970 and were cast, round, bronze coins with a square hole. Zinc coins were used in the 19th century, as were the silver ounce bar coin and the silver dollar. The first decimal coins were used circa 1830. The currency today is the dong.

Vietnam—Type Coinage

Key to Grading: Bust

DATE	COIN TYPE/VARIETY/METAL	ABP FINE	AVERAGE FINE
☐ 1958	1 Xu, Aluminum	$.69	$1.15
☐ 1958	2 Xu, Aluminum	.69	1.15
☐ 1958	5 Xu, Aluminum	.75	1.25
☐ 1953	10 Su, Aluminum	.31	.52
☐ 1945	20 Xu, Aluminum	30.60	51.00
☐ 1953	20 Su, Aluminum	.31	.52
☐ 1946	5 Hao, Aluminum	2.65	4.40
☐ 1953	50 Su, Aluminum	1.55	2.60
☐ 1960	50 Su, Aluminum	.34	.58
☐ 1963	50 Xu, Cupro-Nickel	.34	.58

Key to Grading: Bust			
☐ 1946	1 Dong, Aluminum	15.00	46.35
☐ 1960	1 Dong, Cupro-Nickel	.31	.52
☐ 1946	2 Dong, Bronze	4.80	13.60